T0271458

Finance

By providing a solid theoretical basis, this book introduces modern finance to readers, including students in science and technology, who already have a good foundation in quantitative skills. It combines the classical, decision-oriented approach and the traditional organization of corporate finance books with a quantitative approach that is particularly well suited to students with backgrounds in engineering and the natural sciences. This combination makes finance much more transparent and accessible than the definition-theorem-proof pattern that is common in mathematics and financial economics. The book's main emphasis is on investments in real assets and the real options attached to them, but it also includes extensive discussion of topics such as portfolio theory, market efficiency, capital structure and derivatives pricing. *Finance: A Quantitative Introduction* equips readers as future managers with the financial literacy necessary either to evaluate investment projects themselves or to engage critically with the analysis of financial managers.

A range of supplementary teaching and learning materials are available online at www. cambridge.org/wijst.

NICO VAN DER WIJST is Professor of Finance at the Department of Industrial Economics and Technology Management, Norwegian University of Science and Technology in Trondheim, where he has been teaching since 1997. He has published a book on financial structure in small business and a number of journal articles on different topics in finance.

Finance

A Quantitative Introduction

NICO VAN DER WIJST

Norwegian University of Science and Technology, Trondheim

CAMBRIDGE
UNIVERSITY PRESS

University Printing House, Cambridge CB2 8BS, United Kingdom

One Liberty Plaza, 20th Floor, New York, NY 10006, USA

477 Williamstown Road, Port Melbourne, VIC 3207, Australia

314-321, 3rd Floor, Plot 3, Splendor Forum, Jasola District Centre, New Delhi - 110025, India

79 Anson Road, #06-04/06, Singapore 079906

Cambridge University Press is part of the University of Cambridge.

It furthers the University's mission by disseminating knowledge in the pursuit of
education, learning and research at the highest international levels of excellence.

www.cambridge.org
Information on this title: www.cambridge.org/9781107029224

First published 2013
4th printing 2017

A catalogue record for this publication is available from the British Library

Library of Congress Cataloging in Publication data
Wijst, D. van der.
   Finance : a quantitative introduction / Nico van der Wijst.
      pages   cm
   Includes bibliographical references and index.
   ISBN 978-1-107-02922-4
1. Finance–Mathematical models.   2. Options (Finance)   3. Corporations–Finance.   4. Investments.   I. Title.
   HG106.W544 2013
   332–dc23

                                                                                2012038088

ISBN 978-1-107-02922-4 Hardback

Contents

Contents

Figures

Tables

Acronyms

APT	Arbitrage Pricing Theory
APV	adjusted present value
BIS	Bank for International Settlements
caar	cumulative average abnormal return
CAPM	Capital Asset Pricing Model
CEO	chief executive officer
CFO	chief financial officer
CML	capital market line
DCF	discounted cash flow
EMH	Efficient Market Hypothesis
FV	future value
IPO	initial public offering
IRR	internal rate of return
Nasdaq	National Association of Securities Dealers Automated Quotations
NPV	net present value
NYSE	New York Stock Exchange
OCC	opportunity cost of capital
OECD	Organisation for Economic Cooperation and Development
OTC	over the counter
PV	present value
S&P	Standard & Poor's
SDE	stochastic differential equation
SEC	Securities and Exchange Commission
SML	security market line
VaR	value at risk
WACC	weighted average cost of capital

Preface

Finance has undergone spectacular changes in the last four decades, both as a profession and as a scientific discipline. Before 1973 there were no option exchanges and there was no generally accepted model to price options. Today, the worldwide trade in derivative securities represents a much larger money amount than the global production of goods and services. The famous Black and Scholes option-pricing formula and its descendants are used in financial markets all over the world where an enormous number of derivative securities are traded every day. Professionals in sectors like engineering, telecommunications and manufacturing regularly find that their projects are evaluated with techniques such as real options analysis. Understanding the basic concepts of finance is increasingly becoming a prerequisite for the modern work place.

Many scientific developments in finance are fuelled by the use of quantitative methods; finance draws heavily on mathematics and statistics. This gives students and professionals who are familiar with quantitative techniques an advantage in mastering the principles of finance. As the title suggests, this book gives an introduction to finance in a manner and 'language' that are attuned to an audience with quantitative skills. It uses mathematical notations and derivations where appropriate and useful. But the book's main orientation is conceptual rather than mathematical; it explains core financial concepts without formally proving them. Avoiding the definition-theorem-proof pattern that is common in mathematical finance allows the book to use the more natural order of first presenting an insight from financial economics, then demonstrating its empirical relevance and practical applicability, and concluding with a discussion of the necessary assumptions. This 'reversed order' reduces the scientific rigour but it greatly enhances the readability for novice students of finance. It also allows the more demanding parts to be skipped or made non-mandatory without loss of coherence.

The need for a book like this arose during the many years that I have been teaching finance to science and technology students. Their introductory years give these students a good working knowledge of quantitative techniques, so they are particularly well placed to study modern finance. However, almost all introductory textbooks in finance are written for MBA students, who have a much less quantitative background. In my experience, teaching finance to numerate students using an MBA textbook is an unfortunate combination. It forces the teacher to supply much additional material to allow students to use their analytical skills and to highlight the quantitative aspects that are severely understated in MBA textbooks. Of course, there are many textbooks in finance that are analytically more advanced, but these are usually written for a second or third course. They assume familiarity with the terminology and basic concepts of finance, which first-time readers do not possess. This is also the case for introductory textbooks in financial economics, or the 'theory of finance'. In addition, many of these books are written in the definition-theorem-proof pattern, which makes them, in my opinion, less suitable for introductory courses. Students' first meeting with finance should be an appetizer that arouses their interest in finance as a science, shows them alternative uses for the quantitative techniques they have acquired, and welcomes them to the wonderful world of financial modelling. Formal proofs are not instrumental in that.

Readership

This book is primarily written for science and technology students who include a course in finance or project valuation in their study programmes. Most study programmes in mathematics, engineering, computer science and the natural sciences offer the opportunity to include such elective subjects; their typical place is late in the bachelor programme or early in the master programme. The book can be used as the only text for a course in finance or as one of several if other management aspects are included, such as project planning and organization. Given the limited room for these courses in most study programmes the book has to be concise, but it takes students from discounting to the Black and Scholes formula and its applications. To limit its size, the main emphasis is on investments in real assets and the real options attached to them. This is the area of finance that prospective natural scientists and engineers are most likely to meet later in their careers. Of course, a thorough analysis of such investments requires a theoretical basis in finance that includes portfolio theory and the pricing models based on it, market efficiency, capital structure, and derivatives pricing. Topics with a less direct connection with real assets are omitted, such as bond pricing, interest rate models, market microstructure, exotic options, cash and receivables management, etc.

I have also used the material in this book for intermediate courses in finance for business school students. The purpose of these courses is to deepen students' theoretical understanding of finance and to prepare them for more specialized subjects in, for example, continuous-time finance and derivatives pricing. The step from an introductory MBA book to a specialized text is often too large, and this book can fruitfully be used to bridge the gap. It introduces students to techniques that they will meet in later courses, but in a much more accessible and less formal way than is usual in the specialized literature. Greater accessibility is increasingly required because of the growing diversity in business school students' backgrounds. In my experience, students find the material in the book both interesting and demanding, but most students rise to the challenge and successfully complete the course.

A final use that I have made of the book's material is for a permanent education course aimed at professionals in science and technology and technical project leaders. After some years of work experience, many professionals feel the need for more knowledge about the way financial managers decide about projects, particularly how they value the flexibility in projects with real options analysis. The scope and depth of the book are sufficient to make such professionals competent discussion partners of financial managers in matters of project valuation, including the aspects of strategic value.

Acknowledgements

I would not have enjoyed writing this book as much as I did without the support of many more people than can be mentioned here. I am grateful to my present and former PhD students, especially John Marius Ørke and Tom E. S. Farmen, Ph.D., Senior Adviser and Senior Portfolio Manager at Norway's Central Bank. They were first in line to be asked to read and re-read the collection of lecture notes, exercises and manuscripts that grew into this book. I also want to thank Thomas Hartman and my other colleagues at the School of Business, Stockholm University. Teaching at the School of Business whetted my interest in the pedagogical features of the material in this book. I am indebted to Jaap Spronk at RSM/Rotterdam School of Management and to my other former colleagues at Erasmus University Rotterdam; this book owes much to discussions with them. A final word of thanks is due to my students who, over the years, have contributed in many ways to this book.

Nico van der Wijst
Kräftriket, Stockholm, 2013

1 Introduction

This opening chapter introduces finance as a scientific discipline and outlines its main research tools. We also take a brief look at the book's central theme, the calculation of value, and the main ways to account for risk in these calculations. To illustrate the differences between finance and the natural sciences we compare results of a Nobel prize-winning financial model with measurements of a NASA space probe.

1.1 Finance as a science

1.1.1 What is finance?

Finance studies how people choose between uncertain future values. Finance is part of economics, the social science that investigates how people allocate scarce resources, that have alternative uses, among competing goals. Both scarcity, i.e. insufficient resources to achieve all goals, and possible alternative uses are necessary ingredients of economic problems. Finance studies such problems for alternatives that involve money, risk and time. Financial problems can refer to businesses, in which case we speak of corporate finance, but also to individuals (personal finance), to governments (public finance) and other organizations. Financial choices can be made directly or through agents, such as business managers acting on behalf of stockholders or funds managers acting on behalf of investors. For the most part, we shall study choices made by businesses in financial markets, but the results have a wider validity. As we shall see, financial markets facilitate, simplify and increase the possibilities to choose. Some typical problems we will look at are:

- Should company X invest in project A or not?
- How should we combine stocks and risk-free borrowing or lending in our investment portfolio?
- What is the best way to finance project C?
- How can we price or eliminate (hedge) certain risks?
- What is the value of flexibility in investment projects?

Finance as a scientific discipline (also called the 'theory of finance' or 'financial economics') seeks to answer such questions in a way that generates knowledge of general validity. It evolved from the descriptive science it was about 100 years ago into the analytic science it is now. Modern finance draws heavily on mathematics, statistics and other disciplines, and many scientists working in finance today started their careers in the natural sciences. Table 1.1 lists some milestones in the development of finance over the past century as well as some of the people whose work we shall meet. The importance of their

Table 1.1 *Milestones in the development of finance*

Name	Period	Nobel prize	Topics
J. Fisher	1930s	–	Optimal investment/consumption
K. Arrow	1950s	1972	State-preference theory
G. Debreu	1950s	1983	State-preference theory
J. Nash	1950s	1994	Game theory
H. Markowitz	1950s	1990	Portfolio theory
F. Modigliani	1950–60s	1985	Capital structure, cost of capital
M. Miller	1950–60s	1990	Capital structure, cost of capital
P. Samuelson	1960s	1970	Market efficiency
W. Sharpe	1960s	1990	Capital Asset Pricing Model
R. Merton	1970s	1997	Option pricing
M. Scholes	1970s	1997	Option pricing
F. Black	1970s	–	Option pricing

contributions is reflected in the Nobel prizes awarded to them: we will be standing on the shoulders of these giants.

Finance is also a tool box for solving decision problems in practice; this part is usually referred to as managerial finance. There is not always a direct relation between practical decision making and scientific results. For a number of practical problems there is no scientifically satisfactory solution. Conversely, some scientific results are still far from practical applications. But generally the insights from the theory of finance are also applied in practice and usually well beyond the strictly defined context they were derived in. Modern portfolio theory, Black and Scholes' option-pricing formula, risk-adjusted discount rates and many more results all have found their way into practice and are now applied on a daily basis.

1.1.2 How does finance work?

As in many other sciences, the main tools in finance are the mathematical formulation (i.e. modelling) of theories and their empirical testing. What makes finance special among social sciences is that financial markets lend themselves very well to modelling and testing, as well as application of the results. The list of Nobel prizes in Table 1.1 is testimony to successful applications of these tools in finance.

Scientific research in finance usually has an actual problem as its starting point. The problem is first made manageable by making simplifying assumptions with regard to, for example, investor behaviour and the financial environment investors operate in. The stylized problem is then translated into mathematical terms (modelled) and the analytical power of mathematics is used to formulate predictions in terms of prices or hypotheses. The predictions are tested by confronting them with real-life data, such as prices in financial markets, or accounting and other data. If the tests do not reject the theories we can apply their results to practical decisions, such as buying or selling in a financial market, accepting or rejecting an investment proposal, or choosing a capital structure for a project or a company. Alternatively, we can use the test results to adapt the theory. This gives a full cycle of scientific research, from formal theories to tests and practical applications. Figure 1.1 illustrates the interlocking cycles of scientific and applied research.

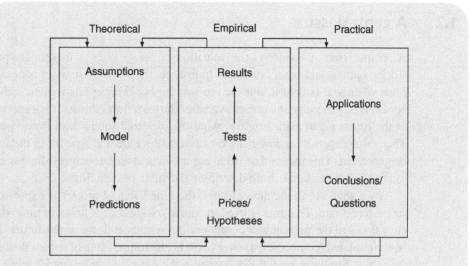

Figure 1.1 The interlocking cycles of scientific and applied research

Option pricing is a good example to illustrate the workings of finance. For many years, finding a good model to price options was an actual and very relevant problem in finance. Black and Scholes cracked this puzzle by making the simplifying assumptions of greedy[1] investors, a constant interest rate and stock price volatility and frictionless markets (we shall look at all these concepts later on). They then translated the problem in mathematical terms by formulating stock price changes as a stochastic differential equation and the option's payoff at maturity as a boundary condition. The analytical power of mathematics was used to solve this 'boundary value problem' and the result is the famous Black and Scholes option-pricing formula. Empirical tests have shown that this formula gives good predictions of actual market prices. So we can use the model to calculate the price of a new option that we want to create and sell ('write' an option) or to hedge (i.e. neutralize) the obligations from another contract, e.g. if we have to deliver a stock in three months' time. In fact, thousands of traders and investors use this formula every day to value stock options in markets throughout the world.

Scientific research does not necessarily begin with a problem and assumptions, it can also start in other parts of the cycles in Figure 1.1. For instance, in the 1950s statisticians analyzed stock prices in the expectation of finding regular cycles in them, comparable to the pig cycles in certain commodities.[2] All they could find were random changes. These empirical results later gave rise to the Efficient Market Hypothesis, which was accurately

---

1 This is not a moral judgement but the simple assumption that investors prefer more to less, mathematically expressed in the operator max[.].

2 Pig cycles are periodic fluctuations in price caused by delayed reactions in supply, named after cycles in pork prices corresponding to the time it takes to breed pigs.

and succinctly worded by Samuelson as 'properly anticipated prices fluctuate randomly'. Similarly, Myers' Pecking Order Theory of capital structure is based on the observation that managers prefer internal financing to external, and debt to equity.

1.2   A central issue

A central issue in finance is the valuation of *assets* such as investment projects, firms, stocks, options and other contracts. In finance, the value of an asset is not what you paid for it when you bought it, nor the amount the bookkeeper has written somewhere in the books. It is, generally, the present value of the cash flows the asset is expected to generate in the future or, in plain English, what the expected future cash flows are worth today. That value depends on how risky those cash flows are and how far in the future they will be generated. This means that value has a *time* and an *uncertainty* dimension; the pattern in time and the riskiness both determine the value of cash flows.

As we shall see in the next chapter, the time value of money is expressed in the risk-free interest rate. That rate is used to 'move' riskless cash flows in time: discount future cash flows to the present and compound present cash flows to the future. Since the rate is accumulated (compounded) over periods, the future value of a cash flow now increases with time. Similarly, cash flows further in the future are 'discounted' more and thus have a lower present value. We can express this a bit more formally in a general present-value formula (where t stands for time):

$$Value = \sum_t \frac{Exp\left[Cash\,flows_t\right]}{(1 + discount\,rate_t)^t} \tag{1.1}$$

The numerator of the right-hand side of (1.1) contains the expected cash flow in each period. If the cash flow is riskless, the future amount is always the same, no matter what happens. Such cash flows can be discounted at the risk-free interest rate. If the cash flow is risky, the future amount can be higher or lower, depending on the state of the economy, for example, or on how well a business is doing. The size of a risky cash flow has to be expressed in a probabilistic manner, for example 100 or 200 with equal probabilities. The expectation then is the probability weighted average of the possible amounts: $\sum_i p_i CFL_i$ where p_i is the probability and CFL_i the cash flow. In the example, the expected cash flow is $0.5 \times 100 + 0.5 \times 200 = 150$.

There are three different ways to account for risk in the valuation procedure. The first way is to adjust the discount rate to *a risk-adjusted discount rate* that reflects not only the time value of money but also the riskiness of the cash flows. For this adjustment we can use a beautiful theory of asset pricing, called the Capital Asset Pricing Model (CAPM) or, alternatively, the equally elegant and more general but less precise Arbitrage Pricing Theory (APT). The second way is to adjust the risky cash flows so that they become certain cash flows that have the same value as the risky ones. These *certainty equivalent cash flows* can be calculated with the CAPM or with derivative securities such as futures, and they are discounted to the present at the risk-free interest rate. The third way is to redefine the *probabilities*, that are incorporated in the expectations operator, in such a way that they contain pricing information. Risk is then 'embedded' in the probabilities and the expectation calculated with them can be discounted at the risk-free interest rate. Changing probabilities is the essence of the Black–Scholes–Merton Option Pricing Theory, and it accounts for risk in a fundamentally different way than the CAPM or APT. We shall look at all three methods in detail and use them to analyze questions and topics such as these:

- What risks are there? Are all risks equally bad? Is risk always bad?
  We will see that some risks don't count and that risk can even be beneficial to some investments and people.
- Portfolio theory and valuation models
  They demonstrate why investments should not be evaluated alone, but combined.
- Market efficiency
  that explains why you, and your pension fund, cannot quickly get rich if markets function properly.
- The variety of financial instruments
  and how they helped to create the credit crunch.
- Capital structure
  or why some projects are easy to finance and others are not.
- The wild beasts of finance: options and other derivatives
  and why most projects and firms are options.
- Real options analysis
  and how flexibility can make unprofitable projects profitable.
- Modern contracting and incentive theory
  which explains why good projects can be turned down and bad projects can be accepted.

1.3 Difference with the natural sciences

The natural sciences generally study phenomena that, at least in principle, can be very precisely measured. Moreover, the relations between different phenomena can often be accurately predicted from the laws of nature and/or established in experimental settings that control all conditions. As a result, observations in natural sciences such as physics and chemistry usually show little dispersion around their theoretically predicted values.

Finance, however, is a social science: it studies human behaviour. Controlled experiments are practically always impossible. Financial economists cannot keep firms in an isolated experiment, control all economic variables and then measure how firms react to changes in the interest rate that the experimenter introduces, for instance. They can only observe firms in some periods with low interest rates and other periods with high interest rates. But it is not only the interest rate that changes from period to period; everything else changes as well. Hence, financial data consist of noisy, real-life observations and not clean, experimental data. Furthermore, it is impossible to control for all other factors in the statistical analyses that are used to estimate financial relations. So these relations are necessarily incomplete. As a result, observations in finance usually are widely dispersed around their theoretically predicted values. Science and technology students may need some time to acquaint themselves with the nature of financial relations. An extreme example from both sciences will illustrate the differences.

Figure 1.2 plots data collected by NASA's Wilkinson Microwave Anisotropy Probe (WMAP), a satellite that has mapped the cosmic microwave background radiation. That is the oldest light in the universe, released approximately 380,000 years after the birth of the universe 13.73 billion years ago. WMAP produced a fine-resolution full-sky map of the microwave radiation using differences in temperature measured from opposite directions. These differences are minute: one spot of the sky may have a temperature of 2.7251° Kelvin, another spot 2.7249° Kelvin. It took a probe of $150 million to measure them. Figure 1.2 shows the relative brightness (temperature) of the spots in the map versus the size of the spots (angle). The shape of the curve contains a wealth of information about the history of the universe (see NASA's website at http://map.gsfc.nasa.gov/). The point here is that the observations, even of the oldest light in the universe, show very little dispersion.

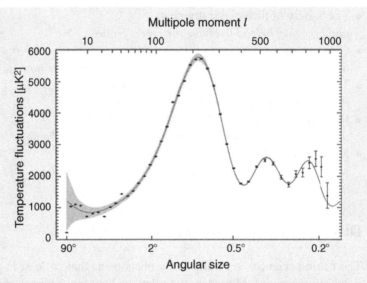

Figure 1.2 The angular spectrum of the fluctuations in the WMAP full-sky map. Credit: NASA/WMAP Science Team

Figure 1.3 plots the return versus the risk of companies in the Nasdaq-100 index in the period 4 October 2010 to 30 September 2011. As the name suggests, this index includes 100 of the largest US and international non-financial securities listed on Nasdaq, the world's first completely electronic stock market. Giants such as Apple, Adobe, Dell, Google, Intel and Microsoft are included in the data. Return is measured as the percentage price return (changes in stock price over the year, adjusted for dividends). Risk is the company's beta coefficient, which measures the contribution of the company's stock to the variance of a well-diversified portfolio.[3] The straight line is a theoretical model, the CAPM, for which Sharpe was awarded the Nobel prize in 1990. It gives the expected return of asset i, r_i, as a function of its beta coefficient β_i, the risk-free interest rate r_f

---

3 The beta coefficients are calculated relative to the Nasdaq-100 index using daily returns (adjusted for events such as dividends and splits) from 4 October 2010 to 30 September 2011.

1.3 Difference with the natural sciences

and the expected return on the market portfolio r_m:

$$E(r_i) = r_f + (E(r_m) - r_f)\beta_i$$

In the period October 2010 to September 2011 the risk-free interest rate in the USA was close to zero, say 0.5 per cent, and the return of the Nasdaq-100 index was 9.5 per cent, so the relation is:

$$r_i = 0.5 + (9.5 - 0.5)\beta$$

which is the formula of the plotted line. All these concepts are discussed in detail later on. The point here is that the observations, even of the largest US companies, show a very large dispersion, even around a Nobel prize-winning theoretical model.

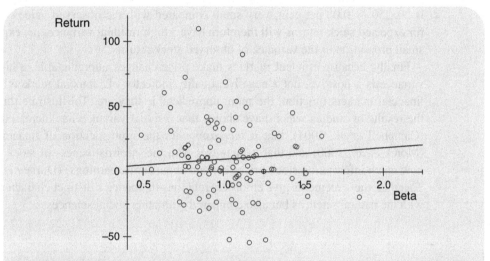

Figure 1.3 Risk–return relationship for Nasdaq-100 companies, October 2010 to September 2011

Of course, this extreme example does not imply that financial economics cannot predict at all, nor that empirical relations cannot explain more than a few per cent of variations in, for example, stock prices. On the contrary, the Fama–French three-factor model, which we shall meet in Chapter 3, explained more than 90 per cent of the variance in stock returns when it was first estimated. But it illustrates that empirical relations in finance have a different character compared with those in the natural sciences.

There is an additional reason why financial relations are less precise. Financial economics studies how people choose between uncertain future values. These future values are to a very large extent unpredictable, not because financial economists are not good at their jobs but because properly functioning financial markets make them unpredictable. In such markets, accurate predictions 'self-destruct'. For example, if news becomes available from which investors can reliably predict that the value of a stock will double over the next month, they will immediately buy the stock and keep on buying it until the doubling is included in the price. So the 'surprise' is instantly incorporated into the price and the price changes over the rest of the month depend on new news, which is unpredictable by definition. Unlike most other sciences, financial economics has developed a coherent theory, the Efficient Market Theory, that explains why some of its most important study-objects, such as stock price changes, should be unpredictable.

The same information effects that make future values unpredictable also make observed, historical data noisy, as Figure 1.3 shows. Returns (or stock price changes) can be regarded as the sum of an unobserved expected part, plus an unexpected part that is caused by the arrival of new information. There is a constant flow of economic news from all over the world and much of it is relevant for stock prices. As a result, the unexpected part is large relative to the expected part. For example, daily stock price changes are typically in the range from -2 per cent to $+2$ per cent. If a stock is expected to have an annual return of 20 per cent and a year has 250 trading days, the daily expected return is $20/250 \approx 0.08$ per cent, very small compared with the observed values. Any model for expected stock returns will therefore have a high residual variance, i.e. explain only a small proportion of the variance of observed stock returns.

Finally, because efficient markets make price changes unpredictable, a high residual variance is a positive, not a negative, quality indicator of financial markets. The better financial markets function, the more unpredictable they are. To illustrate this, consider the results of studies which have shown that residual variance has increased over time (Campbell *et al.*, 2001), that it *increases* with the sophistication of financial markets (Morck *et al.*, 2000) and that it *increases* with the informativeness of stock prices (i.e. how much information stock prices contain about future earnings) (Durnev *et al.*, 2003). Together, these elements give empirical relations in finance a distinct character compared with the natural sciences but also compared with other social sciences.

1.4 Contents

In the eleven chapters that follow this introduction, the book discusses selected financial topics in their approximate order of historical development. This is a natural way to acquaint students with the evolution of financial–economic thought and it ensures increasing sophistication of the analyses. The second chapter provides a basis for the later investigations by briefly recapitulating some fundamental concepts from financial calculus, accounting and micro economics. Most students will have met these concepts before, but the summary operationalizes their knowledge to the level necessary in later chapters. Chapter 2 also contains a short description of how financial markets work in practice. Modern portfolio theory is the subject of Chapter 3. It starts with Markowitz's classic portfolio selection model and continues with the equilibrium pricing models that are its natural descendants, the Capital Asset Pricing Model and Arbitrage Pricing Theory.

Chapter 4 covers market efficiency, a concept that is counter-intuitive to many students with a background in the natural sciences. A thorough discussion of the concept and the presentation of extensive empirical evidence aim to overcome their scepticism. The fifth chapter presents Modigliani and Miller's ground-breaking analyses of the capital structure and dividend decisions, along with Myers' pecking order theory and recent empirical tests. The main insights from capital structure theory are applied, in Chapter 6, to the problem of valuing projects that are partly financed with debt.

From Chapter 7 onwards, option pricing pervades the analyses. The characteristics of options as securities are described in Chapter 7, which also lays the foundations for option pricing in state-preference theory. The binomial option pricing model completes the chapter's analyses in discrete time. Chapter 8 surveys option pricing in continuous time. It introduces the technique of changing probability measure with an example from gambling and proceeds with an informal derivation of the celebrated Black and Scholes formula, followed by a discussion of some of its properties and applications. Option-pricing techniques are applied to a variety of real options in Chapter 9 and three other problems in corporate finance in Chapter 10.

Hedging financial risks is explored in Chapter 11, along with the pricing of the main derivative securities involved in the process. Hedging techniques are applied to cross hedging in commodity markets and foreign exchange rate risk. The final chapter examines two more general problems in corporate finance, the agency relations that exist between the firm and its stakeholders, and corporate governance, the way in which firms are directed and controlled.

2 Fundamental concepts and techniques

This chapter summarizes the basic concepts and techniques that are used throughout the other chapters. We first look at the time value of money and common interest rate calculations. We then recapitulate how a firm's accounting system records and reports financial data about the firm. An example illustrates how these techniques and data can be used for investment decisions. Subsequently, we introduce the economic concepts of utility and risk aversion, and their use in financial decision making. The chapter concludes with a brief look at the role of financial markets, both from a theoretical and practical perspective.

2.1 The time value of money

2.1.1 Sources of time value

The time value of money can be summarized in the simple statement that €1 now has a higher value than €1 later. The time value of money springs from two sources: time preference and productive investment opportunities. Time preference, or 'human impatience' as the economist Fisher (1930) calls it, is the preference for present rather than future consumption. This is more than just impatience. Some consumption cannot be postponed for very long, for example the necessities of life. For other goods, the time pattern of people's consumptive needs is almost inversely related to the time pattern of their incomes. People want to buy houses when they are young and starting families, but if they had to accumulate the necessary money by saving, only a few could afford to buy a house before retirement age. Moreover, postponing consumption involves risk. Even if the future money is certain, the beneficiary, or the consumptive opportunity, may no longer be around. As a result, people require a compensation for postponing consumption and are willing to pay a premium to advance it.

The alternative to consumption is using money for productive investments. Productive means that the investment generates more than the original amount. This is found in its simplest form in agriculture where grain and livestock can be consumed directly or cultivated to give a larger harvest after some time. But the same principle applies to investments in machinery, infrastructure or human capital: by giving up consumption today we can increase consumption later.

The time value of money is expressed in a positive risk-free interest rate.[1] In free markets, this rate is set by supply and demand which, in turn, are determined by factors such as the amounts of money people and businesses hold, the availability of productive

---

[1] Real-life interest rates often contain other elements as well, such as compensation for risk and inflation. We will deal with risk-adjusted rates later and assume no inflation.

investment opportunities and the aggregate time preference. Governments and central banks are big players on money markets.

A consequence of the time value is that money amounts on different points in time cannot be directly compared. We cannot say that €100 today is worth less or more than €110 next year. To make that comparison we have to 'move' amounts to the same point in time, adjusting for the time value. The process of moving money through time is called *compounding* or *discounting*, depending on whether we move forward or backward in time.

2.1.2 Compounding and discounting

Interest is compounded when it is added to the principal sum so that it starts earning interest (i.e. interest on interest). How much and when interest is compounded can be agreed upon in different ways. In its simplest form compounding takes place after the period for which the interest rate is set. For example, if you deposit €100 at a bank at a 10 per cent yearly interest rate compounded annually, then after one year 10 per cent or €10 is added to your account. Your new principal becomes €110 and in the second year you earn 10 per cent interest over €110, or €11, so that after two years the principal becomes €121, etc. In formula form, the future value after T years ($t = 1, 2, \ldots, T$), FV_T, is the present value, PV, times the compounded interest rate r:

$$FV_T = PV(1 + r)^T$$

The same principle applies to discounting, i.e. moving money in the opposite direction. A future value of €100 at time T has a value of €100/1.1 = €90.90 at T − 1. This, in turn, has a value of €90.90/1.1 = €82.60 at T − 2, etc. In the formula we simply move the interest rate factor to the other side of the equation:

$$PV = \frac{FV_T}{(1 + r)^T}$$

Of course, we can also re-write the formula to give an expression for the interest rate (or discretely compounded return):

$$r = \sqrt[T]{\frac{FV_T}{PV}} - 1$$

Note that this is the geometric average rate, which is lower than the arithmetic average if the interest rate fluctuates over time. The differences between the two averages are discussed in appendix 3A.

The period after which interest is compounded is not necessarily the same as the period for which the interest rate is set. For example, corporate bonds usually pay interest twice a year, even though the interest is set as an annual rate. An 8 per cent bond then pays 4 per cent every six months. It is easy to demonstrate what happens to the future value FV_T if a variable compounding frequency, n, is introduced: $FV_T = PV(1 + \frac{r}{n})^{Tn}$. So semi-annual compounding of 10 per cent per year gives $(1 + \frac{0.1}{2})^2 = 1.1025$ or an *effective annual rate* of 10.25 per cent. Table 2.1 gives the effective annual rates for some compounding frequencies of 10 per cent per year.

In the limit, as $n \to \infty$, the time spans over which compounding takes place become infinitesimal and compounding becomes continuous. Then, an expression for the effective

Table 2.1 *Effective annual rates*

Compounding frequency	n	Effective annual rate % (10% annual)
yearly	1	10.00
semi-annually	2	10.25
quarterly	4	10.38
monthly	12	10.47
weekly	52	10.51
continuously	∞	10.52

annual rate is found by multiplying Tn by r/r and splitting the term in n/r and rT :

$$FV_T = PV \left[\left(1 + \frac{r}{n} \right)^{n/r} \right]^{rT}$$

Defining $c = n/r$ this becomes:

$$FV_T = PV \left[\left(1 + \frac{1}{c} \right)^{c} \right]^{rT}$$

c increases with n and as both approach infinity, $(1 + \frac{1}{c})^c$ approaches the constant e, the base of natural logarithms:

$$\lim_{c \to \infty} \left(1 + \frac{1}{c} \right)^{c} = e = 2.71828....$$

so that the formula for the future value becomes:

$$FV_T = PVe^{rT} \quad or \quad PV = FV_Te^{-rT}$$

Re-writing this for the interest rate we get $FV_T/PV = e^{rT}$. Taking natural logarithms produces:

$$\ln \frac{FV_T}{PV} = \ln e^{rT} = rT$$

These logarithmic returns are easy to calculate from a series of daily or weekly closing prices on a stock exchange, say S_0, S_1, S_2, etc.: $\ln \frac{S_1}{S_0}$, $\ln \frac{S_2}{S_1}$, etc. They are additive over time, the compound return $\frac{S_1}{S_0} \times \frac{S_2}{S_1}$ can be calculated as $\ln \frac{S_1}{S_0} + \ln \frac{S_2}{S_1} = \ln e^{r_1} + \ln e^{r_2} = r_1 + r_2$. To obtain a weekly return we can simply add up the five daily returns. This makes log returns convenient to use in a times series context. On the other hand, log returns are non-additive across investments. The logarithmic transformation is non-linear, so that the log of a sum is not equal to the sum of the logs.

By contrast, the discretely compounded returns $\frac{S_1-S_0}{S_0}$, $\frac{S_2-S_1}{S_1}$, etc. are easily aggregated across investments because the 'weighted returns' (return × its weight) are additive. For two stocks A and B the weighted returns in period 1 are:

$$\frac{S_0^A}{S_0^A + S_0^B} \times \frac{S_1^A - S_0^A}{S_0^A} + \frac{S_0^B}{S_0^A + S_0^B} \times \frac{S_1^B - S_0^B}{S_0^B} = \frac{S_1^A - S_0^A}{S_0^A + S_0^B} + \frac{S_1^B - S_0^B}{S_0^A + S_0^B}$$

This property makes it attractive to use these returns in a portfolio context. But discrete compounding makes the returns non-additive over time: 5 per cent return over ten years gives 62.9 per cent (1.05^{10}) and not 50 per cent.

2.1.3 Annuities and perpetuities

Payments and receipts often come in series and their regularity can be exploited to make them more easy to handle.

The present value of annuities

An *annuity* is a series of equal payments at regular time intervals. Annuities derive their name from annual payments but the valuation principles apply to other time intervals as well, provided the interest rate is properly adjusted. Suppose we have a series of n payments[2] of amount A, starting at the end of the period. If the period interest rate is r the present value, PV, of this annuity can be written as:

$$PV = \frac{A}{1+r} + \frac{A}{(1+r)^2} + \cdots + \frac{A}{(1+r)^n}$$

Of course, we can discount the individual terms and sum the results. However, it is easy to recognize a geometric series in these payments, with A/1+r as the first term, n as the number of terms and 1/1+r as the common ratio. The sum[3] of this series is:

$$PV = \frac{A}{1+r} \frac{1 - \left(\frac{1}{1+r}\right)^n}{1 - \frac{1}{1+r}} \tag{2.1}$$

Note that n in (2.1) refers to the number of terms in the series and not to the number of discounting periods, although the two coincide in this case. Also note that the formula calls for the first term in the series, $A/(1 + r)$, which, in this case, does not coincide with

----

2 The symbols n and c are frequently re-used for counters and constants.

3 The sum S of a geometric series of n terms starting with s and with common ratio c ($c \neq 1$) is found by first writing out the sum, then multiplying both sides by the common ratio and then subtracting the latter from the former so that all but two terms drop from the right hand side of the equation:

$$S = s + sc + sc^2 + \cdots + sc^{n-1}$$

$$-(Sc = sc + sc^2 + \cdots + sc^{n-1} + sc^n)$$

$$S - Sc = s - sc^n$$

Solving for S then gives: $S = s\frac{1 - c^n}{1 - c}$

the size of the annuity A.[4] This becomes clear when we define the annuity such that it starts today:

$$PV = A + \frac{A}{1+r} + \frac{A}{(1+r)^2} + \cdots + \frac{A}{(1+r)^{n-1}}$$

In this case the first term is A while the number of terms still is n, one more than the number of discounting periods. The sum of this series is:

$$PV = A \frac{1 - \left(\frac{1}{1+r}\right)^n}{1 - \frac{1}{1+r}} \tag{2.2}$$

The following example illustrates the valuation of annuities. Suppose you just inherited €1 million from a distant relative. The accountancy firm that handles the estate suggests to make the money available over a longer period of time, so that you are not tempted to spend it all at once. They offer to pay out in fifteen amounts of €100, 000, one now and one after each of the following fourteen years. If the interest rate is 10 per cent, is this a fair offer? To answer that question we calculate the present value of the payments using equation (2.2) for the sum of a 15-year annuity of €100, 000 starting now:

$$PV = 100\,000 \frac{1 - \left(\frac{1}{1.1}\right)^{15}}{1 - \frac{1}{1.1}} = 836\,670$$

Of course, we get the same result if we use (2.1) to calculate the sum of the fourteen future end-of-period payments and add €100, 000 for the payment now:

$$PV = \frac{100\,000}{1.1} \frac{1 - \left(\frac{1}{1.1}\right)^{14}}{1 - \frac{1}{1.1}} + 100\,000 = 836\,670$$

So the offer is not fair; the value of the proposed payments is much less than the inheritance. The nominal value of the fifteen payments, €1.5 million, can be deceptive since it ignores the time value. For example, the last payment has a present value of only $100\,000/1.1^{14} = 26\,333$.

How large should the 15 annuities be to make their value equal to the €1 million inheritance? To answer that question we rewrite equation (2.2) into an expression for the annuity given the present value. This is simply a matter of moving A and PV to other sides of the equation:

$$A = PV \frac{1 - \frac{1}{1+r}}{1 - \left(\frac{1}{1+r}\right)^n}$$

Inserting the numbers gives:

$$A = 100\,000 \frac{1 - \frac{1}{1+0.1}}{1 - \left(\frac{1}{1+0.1}\right)^{15}} = 119\,520$$

---

4 The first term is somewhat obscured if (2.1) is simplified by multiplying the terms in the denominators $(1 + r)(1 - 1/(1 + r)) = r$, as is usually done in the literature.

2.1 The time value of money

For an end-of-period annuity we perform the same operation on (2.1):

$$\frac{A}{1+r} = PV\frac{1 - \frac{1}{1+r}}{1 - \left(\frac{1}{1+r}\right)^n}$$

Multiplying both sides by (1+r) we get:

$$A = PV\frac{r}{1 - \left(\frac{1}{1+r}\right)^n}$$

These calculations are often used in practice, when money is borrowed to buy business assets like machinery or private assets like cars. It is not unusual that the buyer borrows at least a part of the purchasing price and agrees to pay back the loan plus interest in a number of equal amounts, calculated as above. In such cases, end-of-period annuities are more logical, since it doesn't make sense to borrow money and immediately pay back some of it. Annuities to pay back a loan with interest are also known as *amortization factors*.

The future value of annuities

Annuities can also be saved so that they accumulate to some future value. The calculation of future annuity values rests on the same principle of geometric series summation, but since amounts are brought forward in time, the common ratio is the compounding factor. It is customary to calculate future values on the moment that the last payment is made, i.e. when the whole sum becomes available. This means that the last payment did not earn any interest, the last but one payment earned interest over one period, etc. The first payment earned interest over n-1 periods. The geometric series character is clearest when the payments are written out in the reverse order of time, the last payment first, etc. The future value, FV, of a series of n payments of amount A is then:

$$FV = A + A(1+r) + A(1+r)^2 + ... + A(1+r)^{n-1}$$

This is a geometric series of n terms with first term A and common ratio (1+r). The sum of that series is:

$$FV = A\frac{1 - (1+r)^n}{1 - (1+r)} = A\frac{(1+r)^n - 1}{r} \tag{2.3}$$

This formula can be used to calculate the future value of the fifteen payments of €119,520 that have the same value as the €1 million inheritance today:

$$FV = 119\,520\frac{1.1^{15} - 1}{0.1} = 3\,797\,447$$

It is easy to check this with the future value of the €1 million today: $1\,000\,000 \times 1.1^{14} = 3\,797\,498$. Note that the number of periods is fourteen, one less than the number of terms.

It is more common to calculate the annuity given the future value. This is done, for example, to calculate the yearly contributions to a so-called sinking fund, into which

Fundamental concepts and techniques

home-owners in an apartment block set aside money to pay for major work like replacing the roof. Rewriting (2.3) for the annuity given the future value is, again, simply a matter of moving A and PV to other sides of the equation:

$$A = FV \frac{r}{(1+r)^n - 1}$$

This formula can be used to calculate how much the home-owners should set aside each year if the roof on their apartment building needs to be replaced in 10 years at a cost of €75,000. If the interest rate is 10 per cent, the annual amount is:

$$75\,000 \frac{0.1}{(1+0.1)^{10} - 1} = 4\,706$$

Growing annuities

The valuation formulas for annuities can be extended to incorporate a constant growth factor. Growing annuities are usually defined as end-of-period payments, but they can also start immediately. Consider a series of n payments, starting today, of amount A that grows with g per cent each period. If the period interest rate is r, as before, the present value of this annuity can be written as:

$$PV = A + \frac{A(1+g)}{(1+r)} + \frac{A(1+g)^2}{(1+r)^2} + \cdots + \frac{A(1+g)^{n-1}}{(1+r)^{n-1}}$$

Using the sum formula for a geometric series with first term A and common ratio $\frac{(1+g)}{(1+r)}$ this equals:

$$PV = A \frac{1 - \left(\frac{(1+g)}{(1+r)}\right)^n}{1 - \left(\frac{(1+g)}{(1+r)}\right)} \tag{2.4}$$

When the annuity starts at the end of the period it is convenient to define the first term as $\frac{A(1+g)}{(1+r)}$ so that the growth and interest factor accumulate over the same number of periods. The present value then is:

$$PV = \frac{A(1+g)}{(1+r)} + \frac{A(1+g)^2}{(1+r)^2} + \cdots + \frac{A(1+g)^n}{(1+r)^n}$$

$$PV = \frac{A(1+g)}{(1+r)} \frac{1 - \left(\frac{(1+g)}{(1+r)}\right)^n}{1 - \left(\frac{(1+g)}{(1+r)}\right)}$$

Working out the terms in the denominators this becomes:

$$PV = A(1+g) \frac{1 - \left(\frac{(1+g)}{(1+r)}\right)^n}{r - g} \tag{2.5}$$

For example, if the interest rate is 10 per cent, the present value of a series of five payments that starts with €100 at the end of the period and grows with 5 per cent per period is:

$$PV = 100\frac{1 - \left(\frac{(1+0.05)}{(1+0.1)}\right)^5}{0.1 - 0.05} = 415.06$$

An expression for the future value of a growing annuity can be derived along the same lines as before, i.e. looking backwards on the moment that the last payment is made. That last payment is $A(1 + g)^n$ and has not earned any interest. The last but one payment is $A(1 + g)^{n-1}$ and earned one period interest, which can be written as $A(1 + g)^n\left(\frac{1+r}{1+g}\right)$. The last but two payment is $A(1 + g)^n\left(\frac{(1+r)^2}{(1+g)^2}\right)$, etc. So we have a geometric series with first term $A(1 + g)^n$ and common ratio $\frac{1+r}{1+g}$. The sum of this series is the future value:

$$FV = A(1 + g)^n\frac{1 - \left(\frac{1+r}{1+g}\right)^n}{1 - \left(\frac{1+r}{1+g}\right)}$$

Multiplying the growth factor from the first term, $(1 + g)^n$, with the numerator we get:

$$FV = A\frac{(1 + g)^n - (1 + r)^n}{1 - \left(\frac{1+r}{1+g}\right)}$$

Note that this formula calls for A, which is not the first term of the end-of-period annuity, that is A(1+g), but the first term divided by (1+g). With this formula we calculate the future value of the series of five payments above as:

$$FV = (100/1.05)\frac{(1 + 0.05)^5 - (1 + 0.1)^5}{1 - \left(\frac{1+0.1}{1+0.05}\right)} = 668.46$$

Checking this with the compounded present value we see that the result is the same: $415.06 \times (1 + 0.1)^5 = 668.46$. Expressions for an annuity given the present or future value are a matter of simple algebra.

Perpetuities

Perpetuities are annuities with an infinite number of payments. In technical terms this means that n becomes infinite, as does the future value. To see the effect on annuity present value, look at the formula for a growing end-of-period annuity in (2.5). The term affected by the number of periods is the ratio $((1 + g)/(1 + r))^n$. For all $r > g$, $\lim_{n \to \infty} \left(\frac{1+g}{1+r}\right)^n = 0$ so that the present value of the perpetuity becomes:

$$PV = \frac{A(1 + g)}{r - g} \tag{2.6}$$

Recall that $A(1 + g)$ is the first term. This formula is known as the *Gordon growth model* and is frequently used in practice. The simplification to an annuity without growth (g = 0) is straightforward:

$$PV = \frac{A}{r} \tag{2.7}$$

Because their present values are so easy to calculate, perpetuities are often included in exercises and exam questions. But they are not just theoretical constructs. Shares are permanent investments and their valuation is commonly based on an infinite stream of dividend payments that are assumed to grow over time. There are also perpetual bonds, called consols. The issuers of such bonds are not obliged to redeem them (although they sometimes have a right to do so). Their value is entirely based on the perpetual stream of interest payments.

2.2 The accounting representation of the firm

Finance is primarily concerned with market values, but accounting data (or *book values*) are often used in their place. This generally is the case when we look at non-traded parts of the firm, such as specific asset categories or bank loans, for which no market values are available. To produce these data, accounting uses its own set of rules (or *accounting principles*), that are framed by law and professional organizations such as the International Accounting Standards Board.[5] These rules have to cover exceptional situations as well as large, diversified companies, so they are both extensive and complex. Since we only look at simple, stylized situations, we can disregard most accounting issues. But even in those situations accounting values and concepts may differ from the corresponding market values and financial concepts, so it is important to know what the differences are and which accounting data to use.

2.2.1 Financial statements

In its very essence, a firm's accounting system records two things: the flows of goods and money through the firm and the effects these flows have on the firm's assets (its possessions) and the claims of various parties against these assets (liabilities and equity). The recorded data are reported in four financial statements that, together with the explanatory notes, make up the financial report. Firms have to publish a financial report at least yearly, but many stock exchanges also require a quarterly report from their listed firms. The four statements are the income statement, the balance sheet, the statement of cash flows and the statement of stockholders' equity. The latter can also be published in an abbreviated form, known as the statement of retained earnings. The purpose of these reports is to allow outsiders to evaluate the firm's performance and to assess its financial position and prospects.[6] We shall have a brief look at all of them and introduce some accounting concepts along the way.

The income statement

The income statement reports the firm's revenues, costs and profits over a particular period. It should give insight into the size and profitability of the firm's operations.

---

5 www.iasplus.com/index.htm

6 Financial reports can also play a role in determining the amount of taxes a firm has to pay, but large firms usually make a separate report for the tax authorities.

2.2 The accounting representation of the firm

Table 2.2 *Income statement ZX Co*

year ended 31 December:	2011	2012
Sales	250	300
− Cost of goods sold	175	200
Gross profit	75	100
− Personal cost	15	20
− Depreciation	15	20
− other cost	5	10
Operating income	40	50
+ Financial revenue (interest received)	3	4
− Interest paid and other financial cost	13	14
Profit before taxes	30	40
− Income taxes	9	12
± Income/loss from discontinued operations	–	–
Net profit	21	28

A considerable part of the accounting rules concerns the allocation of revenues and costs to particular periods but, as we shall see, this is much less relevant in finance. A simplified example of an income statement is presented in Table 2.2. The specification of costs and revenues can vary with the characteristics of the firm and the industry. For instance, the entry 'cost of goods sold' is common when the firm's activities include an element of trade, where goods are bought and re-sold after relocation and/or processing. The purchasing price of those goods is 'costs of goods sold' which is subtracted from sales to find gross profit. In manufacturing these two entries have little meaning and are usually replaced by the single entry 'cost of raw materials'. Similarly, costs can be broken down by their nature, as is done in Table 2.2, but also by their function (marketing, distribution, occupancy, administrative costs, etc.). The distinction between revenues and costs from normal operations and from financial transactions and incidental events (discontinued operations) is made to give investors a clearer picture of the firm's prospects. These are usually based on the firm's normal operations rather than financial transactions or incidental events as the sale of assets from discontinued operations.

Depreciation is the accounting way of spreading the costs of long-lived assets over time. When the purchasing price of these assets is paid, the payment is not recorded as a cost on the income statement but as an investment in assets on the balance sheet. This book value is gradually reduced (*depreciated*) over time by recording a predetermined amount of depreciation as a cost on the income statement in each period. As a result, costs and profits are more evenly distributed over time. It follows that depreciation is not a cash outflow in itself, i.e. no payment is made to parties outside the firm. But depreciation does influence the firm's cash flows because it is deductible from taxable income and, hence, reduces the amount of taxes the firm has to pay. This is illustrated in Section 2.3.

Table 2.3 *Balance sheet ZX Co*

at 31 December:	2011		2012	
Assets:				
Property, plant and equipment	225		250	
− accumulated depreciation	− 90		− 110	
Financial assets	35		40	
Intangible assets	20		25	
other non-current assets	10		10	
Total non-current assets		200		215
Cash, bank and marketable securities	35		40	
Accounts receivable	40		50	
Inventories	20		25	
other current assets	5		10	
Total current assets		100		125
Total assets		300		340
Liabilities and equity:				
Issued capital	50		50	
Retained earnings	130		150	
Total equity		180		200
Long-term bank loans	55		60	
other non-current borrowings	10		15	
Total non-current liabilities		65		75
Account payable	45		50	
other current borrowings	10		15	
Total current liabilities		55		65
Total equity and liabilities		300		340

The balance sheet

A typical balance sheet is presented in Table 2.3. It gives the firm's assets (its possessions, or what the firm's capital is invested in) and the claims against these assets (liabilities and equity, or from which sources the firm's capital was raised). In economic terms, the balance sheet is meant to give insight into the resources the firm has at its disposal and the firm's financial structure, i.e. the relative importance of the various sources of capital. Note that the balance sheet refers to a particular date, not a period. The combined value of the claims has to be the same as the combined value of the assets, so we have the balance sheet identity:

$$\text{total assets} = \text{equity} + \text{liabilities}$$

In bookkeeping terms, the value of equity is calculated as the difference between the values of assets and liabilities. This reflects the legal priority of the claims: debt comes before equity.

Non-current (or fixed) assets are the long-lived assets that the firm owns. They are not converted into cash within a short period, usually a year. In a similar way and for the same reasons as the revenues, they are divided in tangible assets (as property, plant and equipment), financial assets and intangible assets. Financial assets are the investments in other companies that are made for other reasons than the temporary use of excess cash. These temporary investments are included as 'marketable securities' under cash and bank balances. Intangible assets include items such as goodwill, patents, licences and leases. Most fixed assets are depreciated over their estimated productive life; land and financial assets are exceptions.

Current assets are cash at hand, bank accounts and securities that are very near cash, such as marketable securities. They also include assets that are owned by the firm for only a short time, usually less than a year, before they are converted into cash. Accounts receivable are the amounts owed to the company, mainly by its customers, that are expected to be paid within a short period. Finally, inventories comprise the stocks of raw materials, goods in processing and goods held for sale, all to be used or sold within the same short period of time.

The other half of the balance sheet specifies the claims against the assets by the parties that provided the funds to finance the firm. Equity is the capital supplied on a permanent basis by the owners. It consists of the deposits made by them (issued capital) and the profits that the firm made in the past and that were not paid out as dividends but retained within the firm (retained earnings).

The firm's creditors supplied the variety of debt listed under liabilities. Practically all debt is provided on a temporary basis, which means that it has to be paid back after an agreed period of time. That period may span decades for some bonds and long-term bank loans, or no more than a week or two for bills that have to be paid. The latter are recorded under accounts payable. The various forms of debt are discussed later.

In many investment calculations, current assets and current liabilities are summarized by the difference between the two, known as net working capital:

$$\text{net working capital} = \text{current assets} - \text{current liabilities}$$

For the balance sheets in Table 2.3 net working capital is $100 - 55 = 45$ in 2011 and $125 - 65 = 60$ in 2012.

The statements of cash flow and retained earnings

Accounting systems record transactions on an accrual basis, not on a cash basis. This means that a transaction is recognized (booked) when it is concluded, not when the payment is made. For instance, a sales transaction is recorded as 'sales' when the contract is signed, even if the payment is received later. The amount owed by the customer is booked as accounts receivable and when the customer later pays the bill, accounts receivable is reduced and cash is increased by the same amount.

In a steady state, i.e. when everything remains constant, sales equal cash receipts. To see this, suppose all sales occur evenly throughout the year and are promptly paid after one month. Then this year's January cash receipts refer to last year's December sales and this year's December sales are paid for in January next year. Since both December sales are of equal size, sales equal cash receipts. But when this year's December sales are larger than last year's, the difference does not appear as an increase in cash, but as an increase in accounts receivable. So to calculate how much money was actually received from sales in a period, the sales figure has to be adjusted for increases or decreases in the amount of money 'under way' in accounts receivable. In a similar way, money can be invested in, or become available from, the changes in the other items on the balance sheet. For example, inventories may increase, which means that more money is tied up in stocks of raw materials and finished products.[7] Conversely, if payments to creditors are delayed, the money that becomes available from that appears as an increase in accounts payable.

The cash flow statement summarizes all sources and uses of funds, i.e. how much money is invested in, or became available from, the changes in the non-cash items. Together, they add up to the change in cash on the balance sheet. These data are also contained in the income statement and balance sheet, but only in an implicit way, i.e. as the difference between two numbers.[8] The cash flow statement brings this information to the fore. The calculations are shown in Table 2.4. Note that depreciation is added to net profit because it is not a cash outflow. Also note that retained earnings are not included in the cash flow statement, but net profit and dividends are. Since retained earnings = net profits – dividends, including retained earnings would be double counting.

Some of the changes in the cash flow statement occur as a result of 'formal' investment or financing decisions, made by top-level management. This is typically the case with long-lived assets and long-term financing decisions. Other changes occur piecemeal as a result of the normal course of business: sales are made, customers pay their bills, raw materials are ordered and paid for, the bank overdraft is increased or decreased, etc. These decisions are usually made by low-level management, but that does not necessarily mean that they are less important. The current parts of both halves of the balance sheet often constitute 30 per cent–50 per cent of total asset/liabilities and equity, or even more.

A statement of retained earnings is shown in Table 2.5. This abbreviated form of the statement of equity is used when no changes in outstanding shares took place, i.e. when no shares were issued or repurchased. In our simple example it shows how net profit is divided, but in real-life situations this statement can be quite complex.

---

[7] That is why fast-growing companies have low cash flows, even when they are profitable: almost all items on the balance sheet increase. Mature companies, meanwhile, do not grow, they may even shrink. That means that money becomes available from decreasing accounts receivable, dwindling inventories, etc. Such companies have large cash flows and are often referred to as 'cash cows'.

[8] The distribution of net profit over dividends and retained earnings is usually mentioned in the explanatory notes.

2.2 The accounting representation of the firm

Table 2.4 *Statement of cash flows ZX Co*

year ended 31 December:		2012
Net profit after taxes	28	
+ Depreciation	20	
Movements in working capital:		
+ change in account receivable	−10	
+ change in inventories	−5	
+ change in other current assets	−5	
+ change in accounts payable	5	
+ change in other current borrowing	5	
Cash flow from operating activities		38
+ change in property, plant and equipment	−25	
+ change in other fixed assets (5 + 5 + 0)	−10	
Cash flow from investing activities		−35
+ change in long-term borrowing	+10	
− dividends paid	−8	
Cash flow from financing activities		+2
Net increase in cash and bank balances		+5

Table 2.5 *Statement of retained earnings ZX Co*

year ended 31 December:	2012
Retained earnings balance, year begin	130
+ Net profit	28
− Dividends paid	−8
Retained earnings balance, year end	150

2.2.2 Book versus market values

Most accounting data begin their lives as market values. When a firm buys its inputs, sells its outputs, raises or retires capital, the transactions are almost always concluded at market prices. But while market prices change continuously because economic news arrives continuously, the transactions that are recorded in an accounting system are 'frozen' to constant book values. This is not likely to produce large differences between book and market values if the items are only short-lived. Assets such as accounts receivable and inventories and liabilities such as accounts payable and short-term bank loans cease to exist before both values have had the opportunity to diverge substantially. Their book values are (almost) as good as market values.

For long-lived assets, on the other hand, market values can drift far away from the historical transaction prices, while the depreciated book values may approach zero. In practice, it is not unusual that assets such as land or buildings appear in the accounting system at the original purchasing prices minus the accumulated depreciation, even though they were bought many years ago. Obviously, such book values are almost devoid of economic meaning.

Additionally, there are assets whose values are not, or not fully, recorded in accounting systems. This can be the case for intangible assets such as patents, trade marks, brand names, reputations and knowledge that firms develop over time. When these intangibles are bought from outside the firm, then the transaction is, of course, recorded in the books. But when they have been developed gradually by years of research and development or sustained marketing efforts, then their values may not appear in the books at all. These assets can be very valuable because they enable the firm to generate larger cash flows than competitors that use the same physical assets to produce the same products, but without the brand name, reputation, etc. A comparable category of assets is the growth opportunities that firms create for themselves by being present in the right markets at the right time. Investors recognize the value of these intangible assets and they are willing to pay higher prices for the shares of companies that own them. The values of such companies in stock markets (price per share times number of shares) can be multiples of the recorded book values.

Finally, accounting systems sometimes use and produce information in a different way than does finance. An example is the allocation of profits to periods, through accrual accounting and depreciation, which is a primary goal of the income statement. For investment decisions net profits are not relevant, only the cash flows are. Another example are investments that were made in the past and that cannot be converted back into cash. These are known as 'irreversible investments' or 'sunk costs', and they appear in accounting statements as investments that are depreciated over time. These, too, are irrelevant for investment decisions because in economics bygones are forever bygones.

2.3   An example in investment analysis

This section elaborates a numerical example to demonstrate the use of accounting data for discounted cash flow calculations. To keep the example easy to follow, not all elements are fully expounded. The final sub-section provides a more general discussion of the details and some additions.

2.3.1   Background and problem

ZX Co is a construction company that designs, constructs and installs state of the art industrial installations in the petrochemical industry.[9] Over the past few years, its research staff designed an engineering solution for upgrading certain purification installations. The upgrade will increase the efficiency and extend the productive life of the installation. ZX Co has just concluded a successful large-scale test, which demonstrated the technical and economic viability of their engineering solution. The company is now considering a large-scale commercial launch of the technology. The commercial, technical and

---

[9] What do you call a fictitious firm in examples like this? At the time of writing, Google gave >240 million hits for ABC and >25 million for XYZ. ZX Co seems a safe choice, with <5,000 hits.

accounting staff produced the following estimated data, in €10 million, of the commercial project:

- The domestic market offers enough potential for three years of sales, the bulk of which will fall in the second year. After that, the purification installations will be phased out. Estimated sales figures for the years are 250, 500 and 250.
- About half of the construction work will be outsourced to subcontractors, who will supply the basic elements. The operating expenses to construct ZX Co's proprietary technology are 35, 65 and 30. There is hardly any learning effect, since ZX Co's personnel are very familiar with this type of construction.
- The project requires an immediate investment of 180, in addition to the 15 that was just paid for the test. The investment will be depreciated in three equal parts (*straight line depreciation*).
- The construction work also requires an immediate investment of 10 in net working capital (for instance, spare parts, raw materials and other inventories). Subsequent net working capital requirements are estimated at 20 and 35. The net working capital position will be liquidated in the final year of operation.
- The corporate tax rate is 30 per cent. For convenience, all cash flows can be assumed to occur at the end of each period.
- The discount rate for this project is set at 25 per cent by management. This rate includes the time value of money, expected inflation and a risk premium that was estimated from similar construction projects. Thus defined, it is the opportunity cost of capital, the return offered in the market for projects with the same risk.

The question is, of course, whether ZX Co should go ahead with the project or not.

2.3.2 Two representations of the project

In *accounting terms*, the project is represented by the estimated (pro forma) income statement and balance sheet for each year of the project's life. Table 2.6 gives the numbers of both statements in a condensed form. The total investment is 195, 180 for the commercial project and 15 for the test. With straight line depreciation this gives an annual amount of $195/3 = 65$ in depreciation. This, in turn, results in the estimated net profits for each of the years and the book values at the end of each year in Table 2.6.

In *financial terms*, the project is described by its relevant cash flows: financial decisions are made on the basis of cash flow values. The distribution of cash flows over time is relevant, since cash flows further away in the future are discounted more and, hence, have a lower present value. But for the investment decision it is not necessary to calculate a value for each year, it is the total value that counts. This means that the accounting rules that allocate costs and profits (evenly) to periods are superfluous. All cash inflows and outflows are included when they occur, they are not spread or delayed through depreciation or accounts receivable or payable.

To calculate the relevant cash flows we have to 'undo' the accounting actions that spread costs and profits. This is done by making three adjustments to the accounting representation of the project. The first is replacing depreciation by the cash outflow for the investment outlay. As we have seen, depreciation is not a cash outflow but an accounting entry to spread the costs of fixed assets over time. The second adjustment is to add the

Table 2.6 *Accounting representation of the project*

	year	0	1	2	3
	Income statement				
1	Sales	-	250	500	250
2	Cost of goods sold (outsourcing)	-	125	250	125
3	Gross profit (1–2)	-	125	250	125
4	Operating expenses	-	35	65	30
5	Depreciation	-	65	65	65
6	Profit before taxes (3–4–5)	-	25	120	30
7	Tax @ 30%	-	7.5	36	9
8	Net profit (6–7)	-	17.5	84	21
	Balance sheet				
9	Investment (gross)	195	195	195	195
10	Accumulated depreciation	-	65	130	195
11	Book value investment year end (9–10)	195	130	65	0
12	Net working capital	10	20	35	0
13	Book value project year end (11+12)	205	150	100	0
14	Book value project year begin	0	205	150	100
	Book return on investment (8/14)		.085	.560	.210

changes in net working capital caused by the project. Together, these two adjustments produce a cash flow statement along the lines we have seen in Table 2.4. The third adjustment is to remove the part of the investment that is not relevant for the decision to go ahead with the commercial project or not. That part is the investment of 15 in the test. Only the 'new' $180 + 10 = 190$ for the commercial project is relevant for the investment decision. The test is not relevant because it is already done and paid for; it cannot be undone or sold. It is an irreversible investment, or sunk cost, that should play no role in the investment decision.[10]

It can be argued that leaving out the cost of the test makes the project look better than it is. That is correct, and therefore the accounting representation of the project correctly includes the costs of the test. ZX Co's management is accountable to its shareholders and the authorities for how it spent the firm's money, including the 15 for the test, and the accounting system shows just that. However, the financial decision to be made now is whether to invest 190 in the commercial project or not. That decision depends not on how much was irreversibly spent in the past, but only on whether the value of the investment to be made now is smaller than the present value of the expected future cash inflows from the project. Table 2.7 summarizes the relevant data. Note that the project is fast growing in the first two years, which gives increases in working capital, while it becomes a cash cow in the final year, when the working capital position is liquidated.

---

10 It plays an indirect role because the depreciation of the test is tax deductible and, thus, increases the after-tax cash flow of the project.

2.3 An example in investment analysis

Table 2.7 *Financial representation of the project*

	year	0	1	2	3
	Cash flow statement				
1	Net profit	-	17.5	84	21
2	Depreciation	-	65	65	65
3	Change in net working capital	−10	−10	−15	35
4	Cash flow from operations (1 + 2 + 3)	−10	72.5	134	121
5	Cash flow from investment	−180			
6	Total cash flow (4 + 5)	−190	72.5	134	121
7	PV cash inflows @ 25%	205.7			
	Net present value NPV (6 + 7)	15.7			

The present value of the expected future cash flows is calculated by discounting the cash flows in Table 2.7 at the opportunity cost of capital of 25 per cent. Subtracting the investment gives the project's *net present value* (NPV):

$$\frac{72.5}{1.25} + \frac{134}{1.25^2} + \frac{121}{1.25^3} = 205.7 - 190 = 15.7 = NPV$$

ZX Co should go ahead with the project, it has a positive NPV and, hence, adds to the value of the company. Later on we will see a theoretical foundation for the use of NPV in investment decisions.

2.3.3 Some refinements and additions

Cash flow definition and value

The proper cash flows to be included in NPV calculations are the *incremental cash flows* caused by the project. These include the side-effects on other projects. A new project or product can partly replace (cannibalize) sales from existing projects or products. That reduction should be included in the calculations. The opposite is also possible; selling new installations can increase sales of the maintenance and repair department that services the installations. Similarly, if a project leads to additional overhead costs, the increment should be included in the project.

When an investment is made in stages, the investment outlay is spread over time as well, so that the cash outflows of the later stages have to be discounted to present. These outflows are usually known in advance; if that is the case, they can be discounted at the risk-free rate. Note that the changes in net working capital are tied to sales and, hence, just as risky as the project itself. They should be discounted at the same rate as the cash flows.

In addition to producing cash flows, a project can also generate intangible assets such as growth opportunities and reputation. The technology in the example may be exported to countries where this type of purification plant is still in operation. Or the technology can be adapted to next-generation purification plants. These follow-on investment opportunities can be very valuable and they should be part of the investment decision. They are known as real options and are analyzed in Chapter 9.

Finally, we analyzed the project as if it was all equity financed. No interest or other debt payments are mentioned in the example. Although almost all projects are partly financed with debt, it is common practice to analyze investment decisions in this way. It allows us to concentrate on the investment decisions and to postpone the financing decision to a later stage. As we shall see in Chapter 6, the effects of the way a project is financed are mainly accounted for in the discount rate, not in the cash flows.

Other investment criteria

The NPV is a theoretically correct criterion with which to evaluate investment proposals. This means that it leads to the correct decisions. The value of the firm will be maximized when all available proposals with a positive net present value are accepted. It rejects all proposals that do not 'earn' the opportunity cost of capital, for example the return on equal-risk investments available in the market.

In practice, some other investment criteria are used as well, but they do not live up to the same standard. One of these is the *book rate of return* in the bottom row of Table 2.6. The average book return of the project is $17.5 + 84 + 21/(205 + 150 + 100) = 0.269$ or 26.9 per cent. This criterion has three major deficiencies. First, it uses accounting returns instead of cash flows. Second, it ignores the fact that late returns are less valuable than early ones. Third, it contains no market-based required rate of return; the user has to set his or her own target rate.

A second criterion (apparently) used in practice is the *payback period*. This is defined as the time it takes to recover the investment outlay. The shorter that period is, the more attractive the investment is. For the example project the payback period is a little under two years, as the cumulative cash flow after two years is $72.5 + 134 = 206.5$. Obviously, this method does not discount cash flows and it completely ignores the cash flows after the payback period. Since these later cash flows can be extremely large or extremely negative, it is hard to see the rationale for this method.

A third criterion used in practice is the *internal rate of return (IRR)*. This is the discount rate that gives a net present value of zero. The IRR for the example project is found by solving:

$$-190 + \frac{72.5}{(1+r)} + \frac{134}{(1+r)^2} + \frac{121}{(1+r)^3} = 0$$

for r, which gives r = .3 or 30 per cent. The IRR is often used in combination with the decision rule to accept a project when the IRR is greater than the opportunity cost of capital. This will lead to correct decisions for normal cash flow patterns. Normal means that the investment cash outflow comes first and the inflows later. If that order is reversed, a negative IRR may result, or the decision rule may have to be reversed (accept a project when the IRR is *smaller* than the opportunity cost of capital). If the cash flow pattern changes sign more than once, there are multiple rates of return that give zero NPV.

Economic depreciation

Although not necessary for investment decisions, it is perfectly possible to calculate a cash flow present value for each year of the project's life. The year-to-year differences between these values are known as *economic depreciation*, the loss in project value as time progresses and more and more of the project value is realized. The calculations are straightforward and shown in Table 2.8. As we have just calculated, the discounted cash inflows have a present (i.e. end-of-year-0) value of 205.7. After one year, the first cash flow of 72.5 is realized and the two remaining cash flows of 134 and 121 are then one and two years away. They have an end-of-year-1 value of:

$$\frac{134}{1.25} + \frac{121}{1.25^2} = 184.6$$

The difference between both end-of-year values, $184.6 - 205.7 = -21.1$, is the economic depreciation of the project over the first year. Similarly, after two years there is only one remaining cash flow, which has an end-of-year-2 value of $121/1.25 = 96.8$. This gives an economic depreciation over the second year of $96.8 - 184.6 = -87.8$, etc. The profit from the project in any year is the cash flow plus the change in project value. Expressed as a fraction of the beginning-of-year project value this is the return on investment.

Table 2.8 *Economic depreciation of the project*

	year	0	1	2	3
1	Cash inflows from project		72.5	134	121
2	PV cash inflows, year end	205.7	184.6	96.8	0
3	PV cash inflows, year begin	0	205.7	184.6	96.8
4	Economic depreciation (2 − 3)	−	−21.1	−87.8	−96.8
5	Profit from project (1 + 4)	−	51.4	46.2	24.2
6	Return on investment (5/3)		0.25	0.25	0.25

The economic depreciation in Table 2.8 changes from year to year, but the economic profits change in proportion to the remaining value of the project. Hence, the return on investment is constant and equal to the opportunity cost of capital. In this representation, each of the three years of the project's life is as good as any other. In the accounting representation of the project in Table 2.6, depreciation is constant while the return on investment goes wildly up and down. This makes the second year stand out as an exceptionally good one (probably with bonuses all around).

2.4 Utility and risk aversion

Utility is a central concept in economics and although its role in finance is more modest, it is used to make certain financial decisions. Risk aversion is at the heart of finance and many models are formulated to find the proper price of risk. This section introduces both concepts in a simple economic setting.

2.4.1 The notion of utility

Finance studies the choices people make among uncertain future values. These choices express people's preferences; they make choices to reach preferred positions. A person can prefer good A to B, which is written as: $A \succ B$. Another person can prefer bundle 2 to bundle 1: $B2 \succ B1$. Preferences are based on what the alternatives 'mean' to people. The economic concept for that is *utility*: preferences are described by the notion of utility. When A is preferred to B this means that the utility of A, U(A), is greater than the utility of B:

$$A \succ B \iff U(A) > U(B)$$

This can also be said the other way around: if U(A) is greater than U(B) then A is preferred to B. Utility is individual and situation dependent. Old people usually have different preferences to young ones, and rich people to poor ones. To make a structured analysis of choice problems possible, we make three very simple and general assumptions:[11]

1. People are greedy: they always prefer more of a good to less
2. Each additional unit of a good gives less utility than its predecessor
3. People's preferences are well-behaved, meaning they are, among other things:
   (a) asymmetric: if $a \succ b$ then $b \not\succ a$
   (b) transitive: if $a \succ b$ and $b \succ c$ then $a \succ c$

These assumptions have important consequences. The third assumption means that preferences can be expressed in a *utility function*, that assigns numerical values to a set of choices. The first and second assumptions mean that utility functions are concave. They are strictly increasing, meaning that marginal utility is positive or, mathematically, that their first derivative is positive. But they are increasing at a decreasing rate, meaning that marginal utility is decreasing or, mathematically, that their second derivative is negative. Two well-known utility functions are the logarithmic utility function:

$$U(W) = \ln(W)$$

and the quadratic utility function:

$$U(W) = \alpha + \beta W - \gamma W^2$$

where α, β and γ are parameters. In financial analyses W typically stands for wealth, but it could also be apples, beer, bundle 32, etc. As a typical example, a quadratic utility function is depicted in Figure 2.1. Notice that these utility functions are not so well-behaved. The logarithmic function requires W to be positive, while wealth can be negative. The quadratic utility function is only increasing over a certain range of values of W, up to the 'bliss point' $W = \beta/2\gamma$ where utility is maximal. They are frequently used anyway.

Financial markets often facilitate choices independent of market participants' utility functions. This is an advantage because utility functions are individual and results that are independent of them are more general. But utility functions have their role to play, particularly through the two important concepts that can be derived from them: indifference curves and risk aversion.

---

[11] Formal utility theory requires more assumptions, but the discussion here is kept informal.

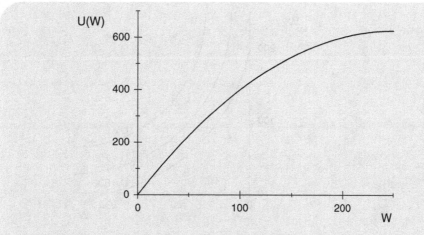

Figure 2.1 The utility function $U = 5W - 0.01W^2$

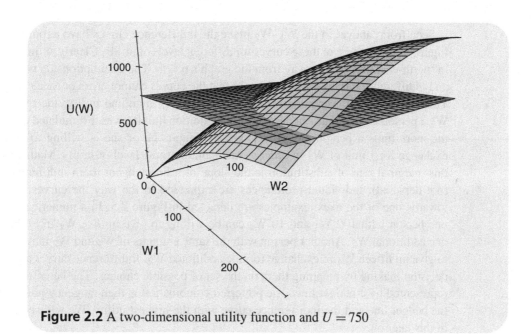

Figure 2.2 A two-dimensional utility function and $U = 750$

2.4.2 Indifference curves

Indifference curves depict combinations of choices that give the same utility. They are constructed by plotting a two-dimensional utility function, that gives utility as a function of combinations of two choices, for example saving and consuming, or apples and pears. Figure 2.2 plots the function $U = 5W_1 - 0.01W_1^2 + 5W_2 - 0.01W_2^2$. W_1 and W_2 can be thought of as wealth now and wealth next period. An indifference curve is a collection of points with the same value of $U(W)$. Graphically it is the intersection of the utility surface with a fixed value plane, such as 750 as in Figure 2.2.

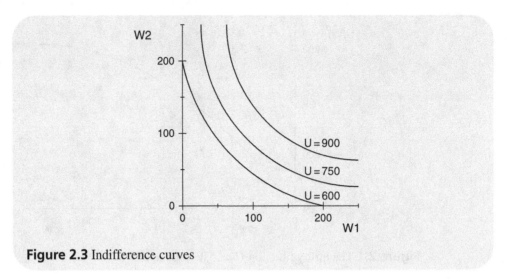

Figure 2.3 Indifference curves

Seen from 'above' in the W_1–W_2 plane the indifference curves have a rounded shape. Figure 2.3 plots three of these curves for different levels of utility. Clearly, utility increases in 'north-east' directions away from the graph's origin. The assumptions on which utility and indifference curves are based imply that the curves cannot cross or touch each other. The shape of indifference curves reflects decreasing marginal utility: the more W_1 or W_2 a person already has, the less utility an additional unit gives. Formulated conversely, the more units a person has of W_1, the more units he or she is willing to give up in exchange for 1 unit of W_2 in order to maintain the same level of utility. Mathematically, this marginal rate of substitution is the slope of a line tangent to an indifference curve (not depicted). Individual preferences are expressed in the way the curves are 'tilted' towards one of the axes; examples are depicted in Figure 2.5. In a numerical example: one person with 100 W_1 and 10 W_2 can be willing to give up five W_1 in exchange for one additional W_2. Another person with the same amounts of W_1 and W_2 may be willing to give up fifteen W_1 in exchange for one additional W_2. Indifference curves are used for decision making by mapping them on the set of possible choices. The latter are typically represented by a budget line. The preferred combination is then tangency point between the budget line and the indifference curve with the highest utility. We will see examples of this later on.

2.4.3   Risk aversion

Risk aversion implies that a safe €1 has a higher value than a risky €1. People require a reward (risk premium) if they are to accept risk and they are willing to pay (insurance premium) to eliminate risk. Risk aversion follows from concave utility functions and, thus, from positive but decreasing marginal utility. This can be illustrated with the simple quadratic utility function we used above: $U = 5W - .01W^2$, where W is now assumed to stand for wealth. With this function the utility of 100W is:

$$U(100) = 500 - 0.01 \times 100^2 = 400$$

2.4 Utility and risk aversion

What happens if this 100W is not certain, but the expectation of 50W and 150W, each with a probability of 50 per cent? We can calculate two different things. The first is $U(E[W])$, the utility of expected wealth. That equals the 400 we just calculated and that lies on the utility curve. The second thing is $E[U(W)]$, the expected utility of wealth:

$$U(50) = 250 - 0.01 \times 50^2 = 225$$

$$U(150) = 750 - 0.01 \times 150^2 = 525$$

so that $E[U(W)] = (225 + 525)/2 = 375$

$E[U(W)]$ is a probability weighted, straight line interpolation between the two points U(150) and U(50) on the utility curve. This is depicted in Figure 2.4. We see that $E[U(W)] < U(E[W])$; this expression is an application of Jensen's inequality that has a much wider validity. The difference between $E[U(W)]$ and $U(E[W])$ reflects risk aversion. We can calculate how much certain W corresponds to a utility of 375 by running the utility function in reverse: $375 = 5W - 0.01W^2 \rightarrow W = 91.89$. This is the *certainty equivalent* of the risky expectation of 100. The difference, $100 - 91.89 = 8.11$, is the risk premium that persons with this utility function require to accept the risk. It is depicted as the upper small horizontal line in Figure 2.4.

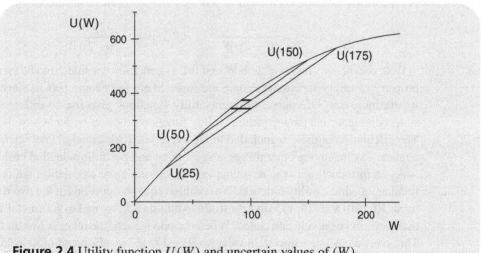

Figure 2.4 Utility function $U(W)$ and uncertain values of (W)

Figure 2.4 also illustrates that risk aversion follows from concave utility functions. Decreasing marginal utility means that the upside of a risky outcome (the 125 increase in utility if W goes from 100 to 150) is smaller than the corresponding downside (the 175 decrease in utility if W goes from 100 to 50). Next, we repeat the calculations with two different values that have the same expectation but more risk:

$$U(25) = 125 - 0.01 \times 25^2 = 118.75$$

$$U(175) = 875 - 0.01 \times 175^2 = 568.75$$

so that $E[U(W)] = (118.75 + 568.75)/2 = 343.75$

The straight-line interpolation between the points U(175) and U(25) is also depicted in Figure 2.4. The certainty equivalent corresponding to a utility of 343.75 is W = 82.3, so the risk premium is 17.7, the lower small horizontal line in Figure 2.4. Clearly, the risk premium increases with risk.

The risk premium also increases with the curvature of the utility function, i.e. how 'bent' the curve is. The curvature can be quantified by the second derivative of the utility function, that determines 'how fast the curve goes down'. This is used to formulate measures of risk aversion, or *risk aversion coefficients*. One of the oldest and best known is the Arrow–Pratt absolute risk aversion coefficient:

$$ARA(W) = -\frac{U''(W)}{U'(W)}$$

where $U'(W)$ and $U''(W)$ are the first and second derivative of the utility function, respectively. The corresponding relative risk aversion coefficient is obtained by multiplying by W:

$$RRA(W) = -W\frac{U''(W)}{U'(W)}$$

For the utility function $U(W) = \alpha + \beta W - \gamma W^2$ the coefficients are:

$$ARA(W) = \frac{2\gamma}{\beta - 2\gamma W} \qquad RRA(W) = \frac{2\gamma W}{\beta - 2\gamma W}$$

Both coefficients increase with W and this is generally considered to be an undesirable property of utility functions. People are more likely to become *less* risk averse as their wealth increases. Of course, different utility functions give rise to different risk aversion coefficients and the logarithmic utility function produces better behaved coefficients. The calculation of these is included in the exercises. Risk aversion coefficients find their applications in, among other things, asset pricing and portfolio selection problems.

As an introduction to the next chapters we do one more calculation with our, by now familiar, quadratic utility function. We combine equal proportions of the two risky alternatives (50, 150) and (25, 175) in a portfolio. Additionally, we make one crucial assumption: that they are negatively correlated. When the one is high, the other is low and vice versa. This gives us two new uncertain values: $(50 + 175)/2 = 112.5$ and $(150 + 25)/2 = 87.5$ with the utilities:

$$U(87.5) = 437.5 - 0.01 \times 87.5^2 = 361$$

$$U(112.5) = 562.5 - 0.01 \times 112.5^2 = 435.94$$

$$\text{so that } E[U(W)] = (361.19 + 435.94)/2 = 398.57$$

This combined portfolio has a certainty equivalent of 99.5. We see that risk can almost be made to disappear by combining risky choices. This risk reduction strategy is called diversification and its effect depends on the correlation characteristics of the choices. There is no diversification effect if the two risky choices are positively correlated, i.e. when the one is high (low), the other is also high (low). We will elaborate this in the next chapter.

2.5) The role of financial markets

Financial markets facilitate, simplify and increase the possibilities to choose. We will first illustrate their role in a simple theoretical setting, using Fisher's (1930) model. We will then have a brief look at how the complex system of financial markets and institutions works in practice.

2.5.1 Fisher's model

The effect of financial markets on decision making is very elegantly illustrated in Fisher's (1930) intertemporal analysis of optimal investment and consumption choices. It provides, in very simple terms, two major results. It shows why the decision by individuals to consume or save can be separated from the decision by firms to invest. It also demonstrates why net present value is the correct criterion for investment decisions. The following gives an informal presentation of the model; a formal treatment can be found in MacMinn (2005).

Financial markets

The setting of Fisher's analysis is very simple. It involves decisions regarding two periods without uncertainty, so that the problem can be graphically represented in two dimensions. The purpose of the analysis is to investigate how individuals allocate their budgets to consumption, saving and investments in the two periods. The analysis is built up gradually, first without, then with a financial market and finally with productive investment opportunities.

Assuming a world without financial markets looks absurdly restricted, but it is a real life situation for many employees in bureaucracies. At the time of writing, scientists at the institute where the author is employed receive a yearly budget of 10K, not enough to buy a good computer.[12] The budget cannot be saved (deposited at a bank), hoarded (put as cash in a drawer) or borrowed against. Without possibility to 'move' consumption of the budget over time, the scientists have no other option than to spend the whole budget every year. This situation is shown for two periods in the picture on the left hand side of Figure 2.5, where the entire budget space consists of the single point with coordinates (10, 10). Also depicted are the indifference curves of two persons with different time preferences. Both curves are tangent to the budget point, reflecting the choice that maximizes utility. Individual 2 can be thought of as a scientist in need of a computer and, hence, with a preference for spending in period 0: her indifference curve is tilted towards the x-axis. Individual 1 has less need of spending in period 0: his indifference curve is tilted towards the y-axis. However, without a financial market both spend 10K, not less.

The effect of a financial market is illustrated in the picture on the right hand side of Figure 2.5. A financial market gives the opportunity to borrow and lend and, hence, to move consumption back and forth in time. For simplicity we assume a perfect financial market. In *perfect markets* there are no transaction costs and all assets are infinitely and costlessly divisible. All investors have simultaneous access to the same information and they can unrestrictedly borrow and lend at the same rate. In short: all deals can be

---

12 I do not dare say in which currency.

done free of charge. Assuming an interest rate of 10 per cent, the single budget point is extended into the budget line between 21K and 19K. The slope of the budget line is -(1+r), where r is the interest rate. Borrowing against the entire next period budget, the maximum spending this period is the t_0 budget of 10 plus the present value of the t_1 budget: $10 + 10/1.1 = 19$. Of course, this means no spending next period. Depositing all of this period's budget at the bank, maximum spending next period is $10 \times 1.1 + 10 = 21$. The introduction of a financial market makes nobody worse off and most people better off. The two individuals in Figure 2.5 are better off: they can now attain an indifference curve that is farther from the origin and, thus, represents a higher utility. This is a classic example of economic decision making: people maximize their utility given the budget restriction. Individual 2 can now buy her computer by borrowing ±2.5K against next period's budget and spend 12.5K this period. Individual 1 can deposit the unused part of the period 1 budget at the bank. Only an individual who happens to prefer spending 10K in each period is not better off with a financial market.

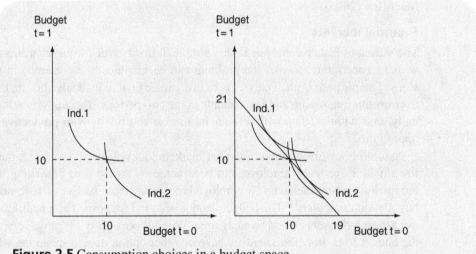

Figure 2.5 Consumption choices in a budget space

Productive investment opportunities

We now introduce the possibility to invest a part of this period's budget in productive projects, first without a financial market. Figure 2.6 depicts the available investment opportunities.

The picture on the left-hand side shows the opportunities as discrete projects, ordered left to right from bad to good. For each project, the horizontal distance along the x-axis shows how much budget must be invested in $t = 0$ and the vertical distance along the y-axis shows the payoff in $t = 1$. The bad projects on the left require a large investment and give a low payoff. The project on the extreme left, for example, may require an investment of 1 in $t = 0$ and pay off only 0.2 in $t = 1$, a loss of 80 per cent. The good projects on the right require a small investment and give a large payoff. The project on the extreme right may require an investment of 1 in $t = 0$ and pay off 2.5 in $t = 1$, a profit of 150 per cent. They are accumulated (stacked on top of each other) from right to left in the picture on

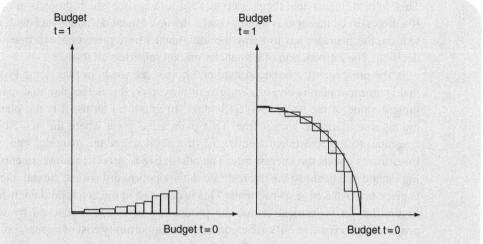

Figure 2.6 Investment opportunities and their continuous approximation

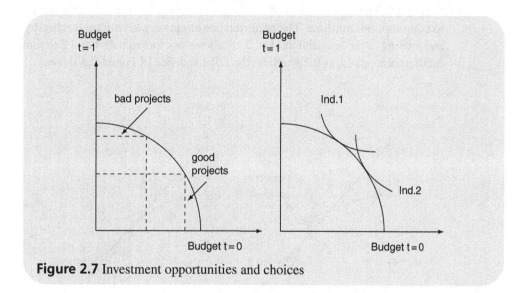

Figure 2.7 Investment opportunities and choices

the right-hand side. The picture also shows the cumulative, continuous approximation that corresponds to a large number of projects, each of which is small relative to the total.

Figure 2.7 summarizes the investment opportunities in the picture on the left-hand side. The continuous line connecting all investment opportunities is called the investment frontier along which choices are made. The picture on the right-hand side of Figure 2.7 shows how much our two individuals choose to invest in the absence of a financial market. Individual 2, who has a greater preference for consumption now (she needs money), wants to invest little. Individual 1, who has money to spare, wants to invest more. So different investors have different ideas about which projects should be taken into production. This looks trivial but it has important consequences. It means that the attractiveness of a project depends on who wants to carry it out, i.e. it matters 'where the money comes from'.

This, in turn, means that there is no general rule saying which projects are worthwhile. If a professional manager is hired to make the investment decisions on behalf of our individuals, the manager has to know the individual's time preferences to make an optimal decision. The introduction of a financial market remedies all this.

In the presence of a financial market, choices are made in two steps. First, the optimal investment plan is chosen. For greedy investors, this is the plan that maximizes the present value of the total ($t_0 + t_1$) budget. In graphical terms, it is the plan that gives the highest attainable budget line. That plan is the point where the new budget line is tangential to the investment frontier, i.e. the point where the marginal rate of return on investments equals the interest rate. The alternative to productive investments is depositing money at a bank, so the interest rate is the opportunity cost of capital, the return that is given up to make the investments. This is depicted in the graph on the left-hand side of Figure 2.8. In investment terms, the production optimum is reached by selecting all projects with a positive NPV (discounted at the opportunity cost of capital, i.e. the interest rate). Those are the projects to the right of the optimum, that earn more than the interest rate. Investments to the left of the optimal point earn less than the interest rate, so that they are unprofitable. In the second step, the optimal budget is spent by allocating it optimally to consumption over time. The preferred consumption patterns are reached by borrowing and lending in the financial market. This allows our individuals 1 and 2 to jump to higher indifference curves, as the graph on the left-hand side of Figure 2.8 shows.

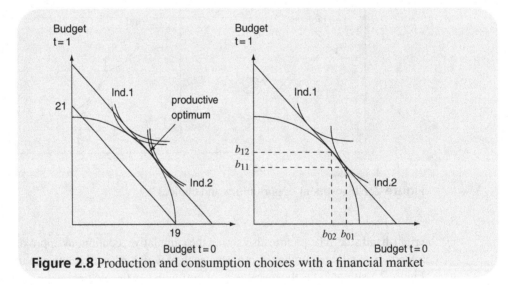

Figure 2.8 Production and consumption choices with a financial market

The introduction of a financial market has some far-reaching consequences. As before, nobody is made worse off by the introduction and most are better off. Further, everybody agrees on the optimal investment plan, because everybody prefers more budget to less and nobody needs productive investments to allocate consumption over time. This means that it does not matter 'where the money comes from', only 'where it goes to'. Consequently, the investment and consumption decisions can be separated; this is called *Fisher separation*. Under Fisher separation, professionals hired to manage investments do not have to know the individual preferences of their clients to make optimal decisions. Instead, they can use objective market data such as the returns on investment projects and the interest rate. Moreover, they can use a simple rule to manage investments: *maximize net present value*, which is equivalent to selecting all projects with a positive NPV. Note that the NPV rule is not imposed or assumed, it is a consequence of the assumption of greedy investors. But the NPV rule does ensure an optimal allocation of investments: it includes all projects that earn more than the opportunity cost of capital.

How does individual 2 reach her optimal consumption pattern of b_{01} in t_0 and b_{11} in t_1, as depicted in the graph on the right-hand side of Figure 2.8? This is done with the following steps:

- At t_0, borrow the maximum against the t_1 budget; this gives a total t_0 budget of 19 (where the investment frontier reaches the x-axis).
- Of this 19, invest $19 - b_{02}$ in productive assets, leaving $b_{02} - 0$ for spending in t_0.
- The productive investments pay off $b_{12} - 0$ in t_1; borrow against a part of this return, $b_{12} - b_{11}$. That part has a present value of $b_{01} - b_{02}$.
- This gives the optimal spending pattern:
  - in t_0: $(b_{02} - 0) + (b_{01} - b_{02}) = b_{01}$
  - in t_1: $(b_{12} - 0) - (b_{12} - b_{11}) = b_{11}$

2.5.2 The financial system in practice

Real world financial markets have many more functions than just allowing people to borrow and lend, as in the simple Fisher model. The modern financial system of markets and institutions facilitates trade in a wide range of financial assets, such as stocks, bonds, currencies, insurance, and derivatives like options and futures. That system is vast and complex and it has an immense infrastructure to carry out the enormous number of financial transactions that take place every day. In this section we will have a brief look at what the system does and how it does it; a more detailed description can be found in the specialized literature, e.g. Kohn (2004), Mishkin and Eakins (2009), Kidwell *et al.* (2008), and Saunders and Cornett (2011).

Functions of financial markets and institutions

Financial markets perform their functions in cooperation with a variety of financial institutions, intermediaries, service companies and regulators. For example, stock brokers and investment banks channel buyers and sellers to financial markets, clearing houses and regulators see to it that transactions are properly effectuated, and financial intermediaries such as commercial banks partly perform the same functions as financial markets. We will meet these institutions and companies later on; we begin by looking at the multitude of interrelated functions that the system of financial markets and institutions performs in modern economies. We summarize them in four main categories.

1. The system facilitates the flow of funds from units with a money surplus to units with a money deficit, and the flow of claims (securities) in the opposite direction.
2. It determines prices (facilitates price discovery).
3. It provides marketability and liquidity.
4. It maintains a system for settling payments and clearing.

A major function of the financial system is to facilitate the flow of funds from units with more money than investment opportunities (money surplus units) to units that have more investment opportunities than money (money deficit units). The surplus and deficit units can be people, companies and governments, both at home and abroad. In return for their money, the surplus units receive financial assets such as stocks, bonds, other securities or simply a bank account. An efficient flow of funds through the system has important benefits. It enables the allocation of capital to the most productive uses, e.g. by allowing companies to buy machines before they have sold the products made with them. Since most business investments are risky, this also involves an efficient allocation of risk (or *risk transfer*), particularly by spreading it among a large number of investors. An efficient flow of funds also gives people the opportunity to buy houses when they are young and to save money for retirement. More generally, it enables people, companies and governments to make their time patterns of consumption and investment independent of the time patterns of their incomes. The flow of funds can take many different routes; the most important distinction is between direct and indirect finance. Direct finance occurs when a money surplus unit buys securities straight from the issuer on a private or public market. A typical example is a so-called private placement, in which a company sells a large number of its shares to e.g. a pension fund. Direct financial markets are mostly wholesale markets where each transaction involves many securities and large sums of money. However, the main flow of funds follows the indirect route and does not pass through a financial market. Instead, it flows from surplus to deficit units through financial intermediaries. A common example is savings that people and companies deposit at commercial banks and that the banks use to make loans to other people and companies. The flows of funds through the financial system are schematically illustrated in Figure 2.9.

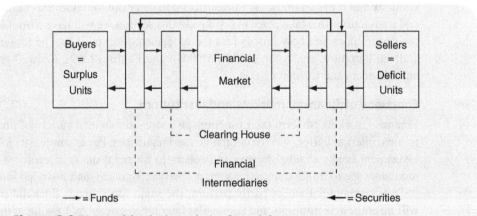

Figure 2.9 Flows of funds through the financial system

The second main function of the financial system is to determine prices of financial assets such as stocks, government and commercial bonds, derivatives, etc. In more general terms, financial markets determine the time value of money and the market price of risk. Market prices are found where demand meets supply and in financial markets this 'matchmaking' is organized as a continuous process in which buyers and sellers interact to determine the price of the specific quantity of financial assets at hand. The process by which buyers and sellers arrive at market prices is called *price discovery*. Financial markets facilitate this process by bringing many buyers and sellers together, setting rules to regulate the process and making it transparent. If the process is properly organized, the resulting market prices will reflect all the relevant information that buyers and sellers possess. Market participants reveal their private information through their bidding and asking in the market and by adjusting their bid and ask prices in reaction to other participants' actions. The price discovery process picks up all these private bits and pieces of information and expresses them in market prices. This phenomenon is called *information aggregation* and it is an important function of financial markets. It generates public information about the value of investments and resources such as oil or gold. Markets in which prices reflect all available information are called *efficient markets* and they have important consequences for financial decision making. We will look at market efficiency in a later chapter.

Financial assets such as shares can have ownership and voting rights attached to them, so financial markets are also markets for ownership and control. Trading in ownership allows investors to diversify, i.e. to spread their ownership over many different companies. It also creates the possibility of capital market intervention. By buying a majority of a company's shares, outsiders can take control and restructure companies e.g. through takeovers and mergers or, conversely, through spin-offs and split-offs. The threat of capital market intervention, which will cost them their jobs, gives corporate managers an important incentive to keep their companies profitable and efficient.

The third main function of the financial system is to provide marketability and liquidity. Marketability measures how easy it is to buy and sell a financial asset; liquidity measures how much value is lost in the transaction. Good marketability and liquidity make financial markets attractive because they give investors the flexibility to convert financial assets back to cash if and when they want to. It also gives them the possibility to make the length of their investment period independent of the maturity of financial assets. For example, they can buy a ten-year bond and sell it after two years, and they can buy a one-year bond and when it is paid back re-invest the money in another one-year bond, etc. Financial markets can increase their liquidity primarily by attracting large numbers of buyers and sellers, but also by keeping their transaction and information costs low.

The last but not the least main function of financial markets and institutions is to provide a system for settling payments and clearing. The origins of interbank payment systems go back more than two centuries, to the days when bank clerks in London started meeting in coffee houses to exchange cheques. Instead of one clerk walking from bank A to bank B to collect a £100 cheque and another clerk walking from bank B to bank A to collect an £80 cheque, they would meet half way, exchange cheques and settle only the £20 difference. Today, that job is done by the huge electronic infrastructure that banks and other financial institutions have created to deal with the enormous number of payments that take place every day.

When financial assets are traded, the transaction not only involves payment, but also the transfer of securities from the seller to the buyer. The tasks of settling payment and transferring securities can be outsourced to specialized financial service companies known as *clearing houses* (or clearing companies). When a securities deal is agreed upon, the clearing house takes over the clearing (or execution) of the deal by positioning itself between the buyer and the seller, as Figure 2.9 depicts. Buyers pay to the clearing house and sellers receive payment from it. The clearing house takes over the counterparty risk, i.e. the risk that the other party defaults its obligations. Buyers receive their securities and sellers get paid, even if their trading partner fails to deliver or pay. All exchanges have engaged clearing houses; they stimulate trade by making it safe.

Taxonomy of financial markets

There are many different financial markets; they can be classified according to the characteristics of the traded securities and the organization of the market and the price discovery process. Describing the various segments of financial markets gives a good impression of their workings and it introduces some terminology. The most common subdivisions of financial markets are by:

- maturity of the securities: money and capital markets
- newness of the securities: primary and secondary markets
- nature of the securities: stock, bond and derivative markets
- market organization: exchanges and over-the-counter markets
- price discovery process: quote-driven and order-driven markets.

In *money markets* short-term debt is traded, which has a maturity of less than a year. Frequently traded money market securities are treasury bills and commercial paper, i.e. short-term loans issued by a government and a company, respectively. Money markets are a form of direct finance and, hence, wholesale markets with large transaction sizes. They tend to be active markets with a high liquidity. *Capital markets* organize the trade in long-term securities, with a maturity of more than a year. These include stocks, which have an infinite maturity, and long-term government and commercial bonds. Capital markets are also active markets, but they are much more volatile than money markets so they have a lower liquidity.

New issues of stocks and bonds are sold by their issuers to initial buyers in *primary markets*. The process of introducing a new security into the market is called an *initial public offering* (IPO) if the issuing company sells its securities to the public for the first time. It is called a *seasoned public offering* if the issuing company already has securities that are traded in the market. Primary markets generate a flow of funds from investors to the issuing companies. In *secondary markets* investors buy and sell previously issued securities from and to each other. Secondary markets do not generate funds for companies, but they perform two of the four main functions discussed above: they provide marketability and liquidity, and they determine prices. The secondary markets for stocks and bonds are much larger than the primary ones.

Stocks, bonds and derivative securities are traded in separate segments of the financial market. The stock and the bond market are for immediate payment and delivery at the current price (although the clearing of a transaction may take a short period). Such markets are called *cash markets* or *spot markets*. Markets for derivatives, such as options and futures, determine prices today for a delivery that will (or can) take place in the future. The value of derivative securities depends on (is derived from) the value of the security to be delivered on some future date.

2.5 The role of financial markets

Financial markets can be organized as meeting places or networks of dealers. In traditional *exchanges* there is a physical place, the trading floor, where traders meet to buy and sell on behalf of their clients. Exchanges are rather strictly organized: only members have access to the facilities on the trading floor and are allowed to trade, and only in securities that are listed on the exchange. Modern exchanges conduct a large part of their trades through electronic networks, but traders on the floor still play a role. Exchanges have clearing houses attached to them, so there is no counterparty risk for buyers and sellers. The world's largest and probably best-known exchange is the New York Stock Exchange; its trading floor often appears in the media when there are large stock price movements. *Over-the-counter (OTC) markets* are more loosely organized than exchanges. They have no physical trading floor but consist of a large number of dealers that are connected through electronic networks. Because OTC markets are less strictly organized than exchanges, it is easier to become an OTC dealer than to acquire a, rather exclusive, place on an exchange. This means that OTC markets tend to be more competitive and to have lower transaction costs than exchanges. The classic example of an OTC market is the Nasdaq stock market, which started in 1971 as the world's first completely electronic stock market.[13] Although Nasdaq became officially registered as a stock exchange in 2006, it still is an OTC market without a trading floor.

The price discovery process can also be structured in two different ways. In *quote-driven markets* dealers act as market makers by quoting bid and ask prices. Dealers are willing to buy at their bid price and sell at their ask price. Technically, investors buy from and sell to dealers, not other investors. Dealers provide marketability by holding an inventory of the securities they trade in, so they can absorb imbalances between demand and supply. The difference between the bid and the ask price, the so-called *bid-ask spread*, is income for dealers. It is their reward for making the market, i.e. to stand ready to buy and sell at their quoted prices. The price discovery process rests with the dealers, who adjust their prices when new information becomes available. Quote-driven markets encourage competition by having at least two, but possibly many, dealers for each security. This should keep bid-ask spreads low and liquidity high. Quote-driven markets are also called dealer markets or price-driven markets. In *order-driven markets* buyers and sellers trade directly with each other, not with a dealer. Buyers and sellers often express their demand and supply in so-called *limit orders*, that specify how many securities they want to buy or sell and at what price or better. Through their brokers they send these limit orders to the market where they participate in the price discovery process: whenever a buy order matches a sell order, the trade is executed and a new price is determined. The price discovery process is very transparent when the outstanding limit orders are made public. Investors can see how much demand and supply there is at slightly lower and higher prices. In quote-driven markets only the bid and ask prices are public information. Because there is no market maker to provide marketability, order-driven markets function best when there are enough buyers and sellers to ensure a continuous stream of orders to the market. Order-driven markets are also called broker markets (as opposed to dealer markets).

---

[13] Nasdaq used to be the acronym for National Association of Securities Dealers Automated Quotations; it is now spelled as Nasdaq and used as a stock market name.

In practice, the various segments of financial markets overlap and exchanges and OTC markets use hybrid trading systems to avoid the disadvantages of each specific price discovery process. For example, the New York Stock Exchange also lists bonds, options and futures. It is mainly an order-driven market, but it also has designated market makers who have the obligation to quote bid and ask prices and to maintain a fair and orderly market in their stocks.[14] Similarly, the Nasdaq stock market also quotes commodities and options. It used to be a purely quote-driven market, but it increased its transparency by making public (some) information about outstanding limit orders. More generally, financial markets are developing in the direction of large-scale electronic networks that offer more or less continuous trading.

The role of financial intermediaries

The main flow of funds through the financial system takes the indirect route and is handled by financial intermediaries without passing through a financial market. Financial intermediaries are superfluous in the perfect markets that many theoretical models assume; in such markets investors can do all deals themselves, free of charge. In practice, however, most deals need some professional assistance because the funds that become available in surplus units do not automatically find a matching demand for funds by deficit units. For example, many savers set aside small amounts of money that they may want to spend after a short period, while many business investments require large sums of money that are committed for long periods. As a result, most buyers and sellers cannot do all deals themselves without incurring large transaction and information costs. The principal role of financial intermediaries is to provide services that facilitate financial transactions. There is a wide variety of such services; the finance industry is a large employer in modern economies. We shall group them, somewhat arbitrarily, as:

- transformation of the flow of funds
- reduction of transaction and information costs
- provision of investment services.

Financial intermediaries can transform the flow of funds by changing the denomination, currency, maturity and risk of financial assets. The activities of commercial banks are a good example of the process. Commercial banks are banks that offer a wide range of financial services to the public and the business community, including taking deposits, making loans and providing facilities for payment and foreign exchange. They mainly transform the flow of funds by pooling and repackaging. Pooling gives a diversification effect that makes the pool much more stable than the elements in it. Commercial banks pool the relatively small amounts that their many savers deposit for short periods of time. Although individual small deposits may be added to or withdrawn from the pool, the diversification effect will ensure that the total amount will only change within narrow bounds. This allows the bank to repackage a large proportion of the pool as other financial assets, including large, long-term loans to companies. The process transforms the denomination (from small deposits to large loans), the maturity (from short-term deposits

---

14 They are successors to the 'specialists' who had a somewhat different task package.

to long-term loans) and the risk (from safe deposits to risky loans). Pooling and diversification also work the other way round, for the risk of loans. Banks make many loans to companies so that each loan is small relative to the total portfolio. The diversification effect will make deviations from the expected loan default percentage small, so that they can be absorbed by banks' capital buffers without infringing depositors' claims. In the end, the risk that loans are defaulted is borne by (spread over) the bank's many shareholders. Pooling and repackaging services are also at the heart of the insurance industry. Insurance companies pool the risks of all their clients and repackage them in small amounts. Insurance transforms the risk of an improbable, but potentially catastrophic event, like a fire, into a certain but low insurance premium.

Financial intermediaries have acquired expertise and scale advantages that greatly reduce the transaction and information costs of financial contracting. For example, banks have developed standard contracts and procedures for most activities, including taking deposits and making loans, and they have years of experience in using them. They can collect information to assess the creditworthiness of their loan clients in a much more efficient way than outsiders can. Banks routinely require financial reports from their clients, they are experts in reading such reports, and clients are more willing to provide information to their banks than to private outside investors. Moreover, banks can monitor the cash flows going into and out of the clients' bank accounts. This leads to a substantial reduction in transaction and information costs, and a more efficient flow of funds. Consider, for instance, a situation in which a few households with small savings of, say, €30,000 each, want to make a direct loan of €300,000 to a small company at the other end of town. For ordinary households and small companies, the practical problems of such a deal would be virtually insurmountable. Modern financial intermediaries reduce this problem, for both the households and the small company, to choosing a bank.

Insurance companies, too, have acquired considerable expertise in writing policies that reduce transaction and information costs. Writing good policies is more difficult than it may appear to be at first sight because insurance changes the incentives that policy holders have regarding risk management. This phenomenon is called *moral hazard*. For example, buying a sprinkler installation may not be a good investment if it does not lead to a (large enough) reduction in insurance premia. Similarly, potential insurance clients that have already installed a sprinkler installation may find the insurance premium too high and seek coverage elsewhere. The result is *adverse selection*: only clients with an above average risk, given the conditions, will buy insurance. Moral hazard and adverse selection can lead to market failure, the inability of a market to allocate resources efficiently without regulatory intervention. This is described in the classic paper 'The market for "Lemons"' by Nobel prize laureate George Akerlof (1970). Insurance companies have to maintain a large apparatus to deal with the effects of moral hazard and adverse selection.

Financial intermediaries also facilitate transactions by providing numerous other investment services; we will look at a few of them. *Brokers* provide access to financial markets. Obviously, individual investors are not admitted to the trading floors of exchanges, nor do they have direct entry to the electronic networks of dealers. Financial markets have regulated access by authorizing a (large) number of brokers to route their clients' orders to the market and help them find the best possible price.

Brokers provide more services than giving access to markets. They safeguard the trading process by checking clients' accounts before they send their order to the market, some brokers give their clients advice regarding which securities to buy or sell, and they store securities that clients have deposited with them. Of course, brokers ask a fee for their services, called *commission*. Unlike dealers, brokers do not hold an inventory of securities, they do not trade on their own account.

At the other end of the flow funds are companies that issue securities. They are usually assisted by *investment banks,* i.e. banks that specialize in aiding large companies with issuing new securities and other large transactions such as mergers and takeovers.[15] Issuing new securities to the public is a complex process that involves many formalities and the disclosure of a large amount of financial information in a prospectus. Investment banks can manage this process for their clients; this activity is called *underwriting*. It involves giving advice about which securities to issue and at what price, and making the necessary preparations for an issue, including writing the prospectus. The underwriter's responsibility for selling the new securities can vary. For smaller issues the underwriter usually agrees to sell as many securities as possible, but does not guarantee that the entire issue will be sold. This leaves the risk of unsold securities with the issuer. For larger issues the underwriter often takes over the issue risk and buys all the securities at a discount. In both cases, the underwriter will use its contact network and try to sell large blocks of securities to pension funds and insurance companies. The remaining securities are sold in the market.

Still other financial intermediaries offer portfolio services. As we shall see in the chapter on portfolio theory, holding widely diversified portfolios is much less risky than investing in only a few different securities. Selecting and managing a well-diversified portfolio requires a certain scale of investment as well as some expertise. Many investors prefer to outsource portfolio management to professionals and mutual funds provide this service. In all developed financial markets there is a large variety of such funds and they are easily accessible to small and big investors. *Mutual funds* pool the money of a large number of investors and place it under professional management. The funds enable small investors to hold well-diversified portfolios and to increase and decrease their holdings with small amounts. Mutual funds can have different investment strategies; the most important distinction is between actively and passively managed funds. Actively managed funds aim to outperform the market as a whole by using the expertise of the fund's management. Passively managed funds seek to follow a market as closely as possible, without the purpose of performing better. The performance of actively managed funds is a hot topic in finance. The chapter on market efficiency summarizes the evidence, but there is little to suggest that actively managed funds systematically outperform the market. Pension funds are another form of pooled investment; they combine portfolio services with a life insurance element.

---

[15] The distinction between commercial banks, that take deposits, and investment banks, that do not, has its roots in US legislation from the 1930s, that was largely abolished in the late 1990s. Banking activities in Europe and Asia are traditionally less segregated, but the European *merchant banks* have a specialization roughly comparable with that of US investment banks. The financial crisis of 2008 may lead to a reintroduction of segregated banking activities.

Trading shares

Suppose you want to start investing in the stock market; what steps do you have to take? First, you will have to open an account at a brokerage firm, a *brokerage account*, and deposit some money. Brokers provide access to stock markets so you need a brokerage account to trade shares. You can choose a full service stock broker and personally discuss your plans with him or her, so that the broker can give you professional advice. When you have made up your mind you can give your order to the broker who will carry out the transaction on your behalf. The broker will store the securities for you and use your account to pay for the transaction and the brokerage fee. Alternatively, you can choose an online broker. They charge lower fees but do not give advice and simply provide secure access to the market. You can use the internet to send your order to the online broker, who will route the order to the market, store the securities for you and charge your account for the expenses.

Having established access to the market you will have to decide what position you want to take in stocks: a long or a short position. You take a *long position* by simply buying the shares you want. A long position corresponds with the expectation that the shares will rise in value, so that you profit from the increase. Most investors in stocks have long positions, particularly if they invest for the (very) long run. You take a *short position* by selling the shares short. *Short selling* (or *shorting*) is selling something that you do not own. To take a short position you borrow the shares from your stock broker for a period and sell them in the market. After the period you buy them back, hopefully at a lower market price than you sold them for. Short selling corresponds with the expectation that the shares will fall in value: it is a strategy to profit from price decreases. In practice, not all stockbrokers may be willing to lend you shares. If they do, they will require money from your brokerage account, a *margin* of e.g. 50 per cent of the shares' value, as insurance. They will also retain the proceeds from selling the shares. Of course, they will also charge a brokerage fee.

Suppose you have decided to take a long position in stocks. You then have to choose the type of buying order you will send to your broker. The main choice is between a market order and a limit order. We have already seen that a limit order specifies how many shares you want to buy at what price or better. A limit order guarantees the maximum price you will pay for the shares, but it does not guarantee that the order will be executed. If nobody wants to sell at the price you have specified then you have no deal. A *market order* only specifies to buy the shares at the best available price. Market orders are guaranteed to be executed, but there is no maximum price. Generally, brokers require a higher commission for limit orders than for market orders. If you are particular about what stock position you want, you can add more details to your order, e.g. for how long a limit order is valid, or that you want the precise number of shares you specified, not less (all-or-none order). When you have a long position in shares, you can give a *stop-loss order*. That is a market order to sell which is activated when a certain price level is reached. For example, if you have bought some shares for €15 each, you can give a stop-loss order on the shares at €10. Then nothing will happen as long as the price stays above €10 per share, but if it falls to or below €10, the stop-loss order will be activated into a market order and the shares will be sold.

When you have sent your order to your brokerage firm, the broker will first check if you have enough money in your brokerage account to pay for the transaction. Then the broker sends your order to the market, but that can mean different things. If the shares you want to buy are listed on an exchange to which your broker has direct access, then your order will be routed to the trading floor. If your broker has no direct access to the exchange, the order will be sent to another financial intermediary who has access, or who is willing to act as a dealer by quoting bid-ask prices. The latter intermediaries are called *third market makers* and they usually pay your broker a small fee as a reward for directing the order to them. If the shares you want to buy are quoted on an OTC market, your broker has to choose the dealer (market maker) to which the order will be sent. Dealers, too, pay your broker for directing orders to them. It is also possible that your broker sends your order to an electronic communications network. These are electronic trading systems in which buy and sell orders are automatically matched if they specify the same price. Hence, this route is best suited for limit orders, which are executed very quickly if matching prices are found. Finally, it is also possible that your broker internalizes your order. *Internalization* means that the order is filled from the inventory of shares that another part of the brokerage firm keeps, for example the dealer part of a broker-dealer firm. This gives the firm the additional benefit of the bid-ask spread.

If your order finds a match in the market, by whichever route, the clearing house will take care of the settlement and clearing and you will have established your long position in the stock market.

Exercises

1. People with a background in science and technology often complain that short-sighted economists reject visionary technology projects that will produce large benefits in the (far) future. Discuss this matter from a financial point of view using some numerical illustrations.

2. An oil company in the Middle East organized a competition for the best business plan for one of its obsolete refineries. Your student team participated with a plan for a chemistry theme park and won the first prize, which offers you the following choices:
   (a) An amount now of 300,000 AED (United Arab Emirates dirham, the currency of the United Arab Emirates, €1≈5.10 AED).
   (b) 425,000 AED under the festive opening of your project, four years from now.
   (c) A scholarship of 65,000 AED per year for six years; the first payment is now, to finish your study and get a PhD from a famous university.
   (d) A yearly payment of 30,000 AED for ever; the first payment is now.
   The interest in AED is 10 per cent per year and there is a well-functioning financial market. Which of the alternatives has the highest value? What is your answer if the interest rate is 12.5 per cent?

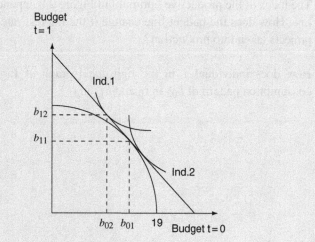

Figure 2.10 Production and consumption choices

3. Those who want to practise some calculus in a financial context can derive the formula for the future value of an annuity (2.3) by compounding the present value equation (2.2) to the end date.

4. When are book values close to market values and when are the differences large?

5. ZX Co is considering the development of a new product line. The project requires an investment now of €350 million and will generate income for four years, starting one year from now. The income amounts are €300 million, €400 million, €450 million and €350 million and the corresponding production cost will be €150 million, €175 million, €200 million and €150 million for these four years; operating costs will be €50 million, €75 million, €65 million and €60 million. The investment is linearly depreciated (in equal amounts every year) and it is worthless at the end of the fourth year. The project also requires working capital; the necessary amounts are €20 million now and €35 million, €50 million and €60 million in the following three years. The working capital will be liquidated in the final year of operation. The tax rate is 28 per cent and ZX Co calculated the cost of capital for the project at 10 per cent.
   (a) Should ZX Co accept the project or not? Support your answer with calculations and make additional assumptions if necessary.
   (b) What is the project's internal rate of return?

6. Calculate the Arrow–Pratt coefficients of absolute and relative risk aversion for the logarithmic utility function $U(W) = \ln(W)$. Discuss their properties.

7. Over the interval $W = 0$ to $W = 70$, person A has the utility function $U_A = 3W - .02W^2$ and person B has the utility function $U_B = 2W - .01W^2$. Which of the two is more risk averse, A or B?

8. The locus of the productive optimum in Figure 2.8 depends on the slope of the budget line. How does the budget line change if the interest rate is higher? Are more or less projects taken into production?

9. How does individual 1 in the right-hand graph of Figure 2.10 reach his optimal consumption pattern of b_{02} in t_0 and b_{12} in t_1?

3 Modern portfolio theory

In this chapter we elaborate the idea that the risks of investments may partly cancel out when they are held together in a portfolio. The strategy of diversification is, of course, common knowledge and many languages have a proverb for not putting all one's eggs in one basket or not staking everything on one card. Markowitz (1952) was the first to formalize this idea in a pioneering paper that became the basis of modern portfolio theory. In 1990 Markowitz was awarded the Nobel prize in economics. We look at his portfolio selection model and the pricing models that are based on it, the Capital Asset Pricing Model (CAPM) and Arbitrage Pricing Theory (APT).

3.1 Risk and return

3.1.1 Risk measures

Recall that finance studies how people choose between risky future values. Risk means that the future outcomes of choices can deviate from their expected values. Hence, risky future outcomes have to be expressed, or modelled, in a probabilistic manner. This can be done with discrete variables, that simply enumerate all possible future values and their associated discrete probabilities. It can also be done with continuous variables, that specify a probability distribution of possible values. Time can also be modelled in a discrete and continuous manner. Discretely modelled, time is a series of moments (points in time) at which the uncertainty over the previous period is resolved. In the periods between the moments 'nothing happens'. For example, a calendar year can be modelled as one period of a year, with two moments: beginning and end. But it can also be modelled as two periods of six months, with three moments, or as four quarters, twelve months or 365 days. The limiting case is continuous time, in which each period is infinitesimal and the number of periods is infinite. Table 3.1 places some well-known models and modelling techniques in the double dichotomy of discrete and continuous time and variables. We will meet most of them later on. Portfolio theory usually analyzes the continuous returns of investments over discrete holding periods. However, to keep the calculations easy to follow we will derive the main results using a small number of discrete possible outcomes.

The risk of investments is often depicted as in Figure 3.1, that shows the closing prices of the Nasdaq-100 stock index (ticker: NDX) over an arbitrary period of 253 trading days. As we have seen in Chapter 1, this index includes 100 of the largest US and international non-financial securities listed on the Nasdaq stock exchange. At the start of the period the index had a value of 1996.6 and at the end it was 2139.8, a gain of more than 7 per cent. However, in the beginning of the period the index rallied to almost 2400, a gain of 20 per cent, and later it plunged more than 10 per cent. Those were, with hindsight, the

Table 3.1 *Models and modelling techniques*

	Discrete time	Continuous time
Discrete variables	State preference theory	Bankruptcy
	Binomial Option Pricing	processes
Continuous var's	Portfolio theory, CAPM	Black and Scholes
	Capital structure models	Option pricing

risks faced by somebody who wanted to invest in this index for a couple of months during that period.

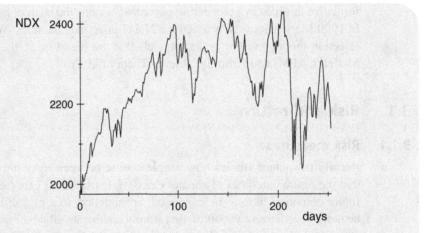

Figure 3.1 Nasdaq-100 index, daily closing prices, adjusted for dividends, for 253 trading days from 1 October 2010 to 30 September 2011

To analyze investments we usually transform the prices (p) into returns (r) by taking percentage first differences:[1]

$$r_t = 100 \times \frac{p_{t+1} - p_t}{p_t}$$

Recall from the previous chapter that such discretely compounded returns have the advantage over logarithmic returns that they are easily aggregated over investments in a portfolio. These daily returns are depicted in Figure 3.2 for the same period (minus one day). We see that most returns are between −2 per cent and +2 per cent, with (quite) a few spikes in both directions.

Although illustrative, Figure 3.2 is difficult to compare with similar graphs for other indices or periods. Comparability is provided by the statistical properties of the returns, particularly their distributional properties. Figure 3.3 plots the relative frequency of days with returns in each one-percentage interval. For instance, there were 101 days with a

1 Return also includes dividends; we use closing prices that are adjusted for dividends.

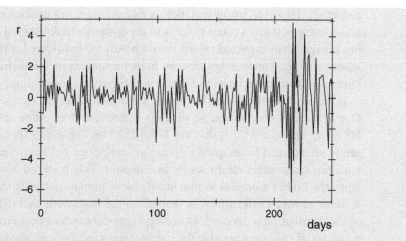

Figure 3.2 Daily returns Nasdaq-100 index for 252 days from 4 October 2010 to 30 September 2011

return between 0.5 per cent and 1.5 per cent; this is depicted as the peak diamond ($\Diamond$) with coordinates 1, 0.4 (101/252 = 0.4). The solid line connects these frequencies. The dashed line is a normal density function with the same mean and standard deviation as the returns ($\curvearrowright$N(0.036, 1.327)). When return data are used in this way it becomes natural to use a statistical measure of dispersion as risk measure. Indeed, the variance (or its square root, the standard deviation) is the most frequently used quantitative measure of risk.

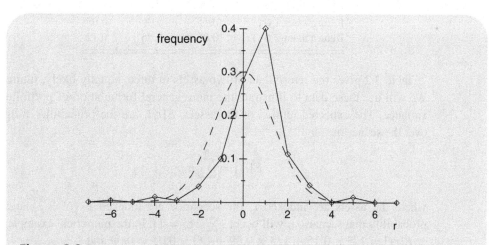

Figure 3.3 Frequency of daily returns Nasdaq-100 index over 252 days from 4 October 2010 to 30 September 2011

Variance can be used in a backward looking way (measuring the dispersion around an observed, historical mean) as well as in a forward looking way (measuring the dispersion around an expectation). It is easily calculated in both cases and has well-known statistical properties. However, using variance as risk measure in financial analyses also has clear disadvantages. It gives equal weights to the upward and downward deviations, but receiving a larger than expected return would hardly be considered a risk by most investors. Also, using the variance ignores the higher moments of the distribution (skewness and kurtosis). Most investors would prefer a distribution skewed towards higher returns.

In response to these disadvantages, some other risk measures have been suggested. One of these is *semi-variance*, which is calculated in the same way as normal variance, but using only the returns that are lower than the mean or expectation. The concept of semi-variance can be adapted to measure deviations not from the mean or expectation but from some target return set by the investor. This is called lower partial variance or, when the higher moments are included, lower partial moments. An alternative measure is *Value at Risk* (VaR) which is defined as the maximum loss if the x per cent left tail of the distribution is ignored. However, variance/standard deviation remain widely used measures of risk; they are also the risk measures in Markowitz's portfolio model, that we look at next.

3.1.2 Portfolio return and risk

The diversification effect that occurs when assets are held together in a portfolio is expressed in the portfolio's variance. We begin with a demonstration of this effect.

Calculating portfolio mean and variance

Table 3.2 *Asset returns in scenarios*

Scenario:	1	2	3
Probability (π)	1/3	1/3	1/3
Return asset 1 (r_1)	0.15	0.09	0.03
Return asset 2 (r_2)	0.06	0.06	0.12

Table 3.2 gives the return data of two assets in three, equally likely, future scenarios. We will use these data to illustrate the more general formulation of portfolio mean and variance. The expected returns of the assets, $E[r_i]$, are the probability weighted sums over the scenarios:

$$E[r_i] = \sum_{n=1}^{N} \pi_n r_{ni} \tag{3.1}$$

where the assets are indexed i, the scenarios are indexed n ($N = 3$) and π_n is the probability that scenario n will occur ($\sum_n \pi_n = 1$). In the numerical example:
$E[r_1] = 1/3 \times 0.15 + 1/3 \times 0.09 + 1/3 \times 0.03 = 0.09$ and
$E[r_2] = 1/3 \times 0.06 + 1/3 \times 0.06 + 1/3 \times 0.12 = 0.08$.

The assets' variances are the probability weighted sums of the squared deviations from the expected returns:

$$\sigma_i^2 = \sum_{n=1}^{N} \pi_n (r_{ni} - E[r_i])^2 \tag{3.2}$$

In the numerical example:
$$\sigma_1^2 = 1/3 \times (0.15 - 0.09)^2 + 1/3 \times (0.09 - 0.09)^2 + 1/3 \times (0.03 - 0.09)^2 = 0.0024$$
$$\sigma_2^2 = 1/3 \times (0.06 - 0.08)^2 + 1/3 \times (0.06 - 0.08)^2 + 1/3 \times (0.12 - 0.08)^2 = 0.0008.$$

If we combine equal parts of the assets in a portfolio, the expected portfolio return simply is the weighted average of the expected asset returns:

$$E[r_p] = \sum_{i=1}^{I} x_i E[r_i]$$

where x_i are the assets' weights $\left(\sum_i x_i = 1\right)$. In the numerical example:
$0.5 \times 0.09 + 0.5 \times 0.08 = 0.085$.

Of course, we get the same result if we first calculate the portfolio returns in the scenarios and then take the expectation over scenarios:
$1/3 \times 0.105 + 1/3 \times 0.075 + 1/3 \times 0.075 = 0.085$.

The variance of this portfolio return is:
$$\sigma_p^2 = 1/3 \times (0.105 - 0.085)^2 + 1/3 \times (0.075 - 0.085)^2 + 1/3 \times (0.075 - 0.085)^2 = 0.0002.$$

Obviously, portfolio variance is not the weighted average of the variances of the assets. Combining the two assets makes the portfolio variance lower than any of the asset variances. The variance reducing effect of diversification can be demonstrated by writing out the variance of the portfolio. This is easily done for a two-asset portfolio. By definition, the portfolio variance $var(x_1 r_1 + x_2 r_2) = \sigma_p^2$ is:

$$\sigma_p^2 = \sum_{n=1}^{N} \pi_n \left[x_1 r_{n1} + x_2 r_{n2} - (x_1 E[r_1] + x_2 E[r_2]) \right]^2$$

where the summation is over the N scenarios. Rearranging terms we get:

$$\sigma_p^2 = \sum_{n=1}^{N} \pi_n \left[x_1 (r_{n1} - E[r_1]) + x_2 (r_{n2} - E[r_2]) \right]^2$$

Working out the square produces:

$$\sigma_p^2 = \sum_{n=1}^{N} \pi_n [x_1^2 (r_{n1} - E[r_1])^2 + x_2^2 (r_{n2} - E[r_2])^2 + 2 x_1 x_2 (r_{n1} - E[r_1])(r_{n2} - E[r_2])]$$

and rewriting gives three recognizable terms:

$$\sigma_p^2 = x_1^2 \underbrace{\sum_{n=1}^{N} \pi_n (r_{n1} - E[r_1])^2}_{\sigma_1^2} + x_2^2 \underbrace{\sum_{n=1}^{N} \pi_n (r_{n2} - E[r_2])^2}_{\sigma_2^2} +$$

$$2 x_1 x_2 \underbrace{\sum_{n=1}^{N} \pi_n (r_{n1} - E[r_1])(r_{n2} - E[r_2])}_{\sigma_{1,2}}$$

Modern portfolio theory

So portfolio variance is the weighted sum of the asset variances plus two times their covariance:

$$\sigma_p^2 = x_1^2 \sigma_1^2 + x_2^2 \sigma_2^2 + 2x_1 x_2 \sigma_{1,2} \tag{3.3}$$

Covariance measures the degree in which assets move together through scenarios (or through time, if historical data are used). It is calculated as the probability weighted sum of the 'cross product' of deviations from the expected returns:

$$\sigma_{ij} = \sum_{n=1}^{N} \pi_n (r_{ni} - E[r_i])(r_{nj} - E[r_j]) \tag{3.4}$$

In our example the covariance between the two assets is

$\sigma_{1,2} = 1/3 \times (0.15 - 0.09)(0.06 - 0.08) + 1/3 \times (0.09 - 0.09)(0.06 - 0.08) + 1/3 \times (0.03 - 0.09)(0.12 - 0.08) = -0.0012$.

It is negative because asset 1 has its highest return in the first scenario, where the second asset has its lowest return, while it is the other way around in the third scenario. Hence, their deviations from the expected returns have opposite signs and this makes their cross products and covariance negative. Filling in the numbers reproduces the portfolio variance:

$$\sigma_p^2 = 0.5^2 \times 0.0024 + 0.5^2 \times 0.0008 + 2 \times 0.5 \times 0.5 \times -0.0012 = 0.0002$$

Portfolio variance can easily be represented in a *variance-covariance matrix*:

$$
\begin{array}{ccc}
x_1^2 \sigma_1^2 & x_1 x_2 \sigma_{1,2} & Asset1 \\
x_1 x_2 \sigma_{1,2} & x_2^2 \sigma_2^2 & Asset2 \\
Asset1 & Asset2 & \Sigma = \sigma_p^2
\end{array}
$$

Portfolio variance σ_p^2 is the sum of all cells in the variance-covariance matrix, which can be written in a general form as:

$$\sigma_p^2 = \sum_{i=1}^{I} \sum_{j=1}^{I} x_i x_j \sigma_{ij}$$

The double indexing and summation is because we sum over columns as well as rows. On the main diagonal of the variance-covariance matrix, where $i = j$, we find the covariances of asset returns with themselves, which are the variances σ_i^2. Off-diagonal are the covariances between different assets. As became evident in the numerical example, the covariances bring about the diversification effect: small or negative covariances reduce portfolio variance. The number of covariance terms and, hence, the diversification effect increases with the number of assets. For I assets, the variance-covariance matrix has I^2 cells, of which I are variances and $I(I - 1)$ are covariances. As I increases, the relative importance of the variances becomes smaller and that of the covariances becomes larger. So more assets mean proportionally more covariances which can be small or negative, hence the reduction in portfolio variance. The effect is depicted in Figure 3.4.

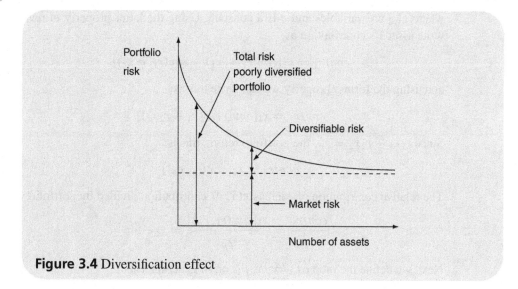

Figure 3.4 Diversification effect

The risk that disappears through diversification is called *unique* or *unsystematic* or diversifiable risk. It is the idiosyncratic risk of individual investments (that engineers are concerned with). The risk that remains is the *market risk*, or *systematic risk*, that cannot be diversified away because it affects the market as a whole. That is the risk that counts in finance. Financial markets allow easy and low-cost diversification; investors can choose from a very large number of financial instruments. Most European stock exchanges list hundreds of shares and bonds and many thousands of them are listed worldwide. Additionally, there is a plethora of investment funds so even small investors can hold well-diversified portfolios without much trouble or costs. Moreover, it takes only a very limited number of assets (some 20–30) to capture most of the diversification effect. Risk reduction through diversification is one of the very few 'free lunches' that finance has to offer: every investor can obtain it (almost) free of charge. If investors hold diversified portfolios, the inevitable consequence is that the relevant risk of an investment is not its stand-alone risk, but the risk in the context of a well-diversified portfolio.

Assets' contributions to portfolio risk

The contribution of each asset to portfolio variance is the sum of its row (or column) entries in the variance-covariance matrix. In our example, the contribution of asset 1 is: $x_1^2 \sigma_1^2 + x_1 x_2 \sigma_{1,2} = x_1 [x_1 \sigma_1^2 + x_2 \sigma_{1,2}]$.

Recall that a variable's variance is the covariance with itself, so we can write the contribution of asset 1 as:

$$contr_1 = x_1 [x_1 cov(r_1, r_1) + x_2 cov(r_1, r_2)]$$

We use the following two properties of covariance:

$$cov(z_1, y) + cov(z_2, y) = cov(z_1 + z_2, y)$$

$$cov(c \times z, y) = c \times cov(z, y)$$

where $z_{1,2}$ are variables and c is a constant. Using the latter property in reverse we can write asset 1's contribution as:

$$contr_1 = x_1[cov(r_1, r_1x_1) + cov(r_1, r_2x_2)]$$

and using the former property we can write this as:

$$contr_1 = x_1[cov(r_1, r_1x_1 + r_2x_2)]$$

Since $r_1x_1 + r_2x_2 = r_p$, the portfolio return, this is:

$$contr_1 = x_1[cov(r_1, r_p)]$$

The relative contribution of each asset is its contribution divided by portfolio variance:

$$\frac{contr_1}{\sigma_p^2} = \frac{x_1[cov(r_1, r_p)]}{\sigma_p^2} = x_1\frac{\sigma_{1p}}{\sigma_p^2}$$

Next, we define the ratio σ_{1p}/σ_p^2 as β_1, or, in general terms:

$$\beta_i = \frac{\sigma_{ip}}{\sigma_p^2} \tag{3.5}$$

The result is that the relative contribution of an asset to portfolio variance is its weight times its beta: $x_i\beta_i$.

The relation between an asset's β and the portfolio can also be interpreted the other way around: β measures the asset's sensitivity for changes in portfolio returns. If the portfolio represents the market as a whole, e.g. a stock index, then β measures the degree in which an asset's returns go up and down with the market as a whole. An asset with $\beta > 1$ changes more than proportionally with changes in the market, an asset with $\beta < 1$ less than proportionally.

Like variances, βs are objective measures of risk: people who use the same data set will calculate the same βs. Unlike variances, βs add linearly across investments in a portfolio: $\beta_p = \sum_i x_i\beta_i$. The additivity property also extends to other subdivisions. A company's β is the weighted average of the βs of its projects, or activities. Similarly, the company's β is also the weighted average of the βs of its debt and equity. We shall use this property in the analysis of capital structure in Chapter 5. Finally, using β as a measure of risk is a consequence of considering risk in the context of a portfolio, where the unsystematic risk is (partly) diversified away. It is not the result of a specific pricing model such as the CAPM that we will look at later on.

3.1.3 Correlation and diversification

We have seen that the diversification effect increases with the number of assets because their covariance terms can be low or negative. We will now analyze in more detail *when* they are low or negative. To make covariances more comparable they can be standardized into a *correlation coefficient* by dividing them by the product of the standard deviations of the variables:

$$\text{correlation coefficient } \rho_{ij} = \frac{\sigma_{ij}}{\sigma_i \times \sigma_j} \tag{3.6}$$

3.1 Risk and return

The correlation coefficient has the advantage of being independent of the units of measurements and is bounded by minus 1 and plus 1: $-1 \leq \rho \leq 1$. In the extreme cases we speak of perfectly negatively (-1) or perfectly positively ($+1$) correlated variables, while variables with a correlation coefficient of zero are statistically independent (or *orthogonal*). Investments are generally characterized by moderately positive correlations.

We can make the relation between correlation and diversification explicit by writing covariance in terms of correlation: $\sigma_{ij} = \rho_{ij}\sigma_i\sigma_j$ and substituting this, properly subscripted, into equation (3.3) for portfolio variance:

$$\sigma_p^2 = x_1^2\sigma_1^2 + x_2^2\sigma_2^2 + 2x_1x_2\rho_{1,2}\sigma_1\sigma_2 \tag{3.7}$$

As equation (3.7) shows, the diversification effect depends entirely on the correlation coefficient in the third term. If $\rho = 1$, the third term is included in portfolio variance with its full weight and there is no diversification effect. As ρ gets smaller, the third term gets smaller and the diversification effect increases. If $\rho = 0$, the third term will disappear altogether and negative values of ρ will make the third term contribute negatively to portfolio variance. The diversification effect reaches its maximum when ρ reaches its minimum at -1.

We will illustrate the diversification effect with a numerical example of four stocks in five different scenarios. Table 3.3 gives their returns, expected returns and standard deviations.

Table 3.3 *Stock returns in scenarios*

Scenario	Prob.	r_1	r_2	r_3	r_4
1	0.2	0.125	0.125	0.225	0.035
2	0.2	0.1	0.075	0.275	0.2
3	0.2	0.15	0.175	0.175	0.225
4	0.2	0.2	0.275	0.075	0.2
5	0.2	0.175	0.225	0.125	0.215
E[r]		0.15	0.175	0.175	0.175
$\sigma(r)$		0.0354	0.0707	0.0707	0.0706

The expected returns and standard deviations are calculated as in (3.1) and the square root of (3.2). Notice that the stocks 2, 3 and 4 all have the same expected return and standard deviation. So their risk-return characteristics are identical, they differ only with respect to their correlation with stock 1. The relevant covariances and correlations, calculated as in (3.4) and (3.6), are:

$$\sigma_{1,2} = 0.0025 \quad \rho_{1,2} = 1$$
$$\sigma_{1,3} = -0.0025 \quad \rho_{1,3} = -1$$
$$\sigma_{1,4} = 0.0009 \quad \rho_{1,4} = 0.36$$

The correlations between stocks 1 and 2, and 1 and 3 are extreme cases with perfectly positive and negative correlations. The combination of stocks 1 and 4 represents the normal cases with a moderately positive correlation coefficient.

Modern portfolio theory

We now combine stock 1 with, in turn, each of the three other stocks, so stock 1 and 2, 1 and 3, and 1 and 4. For each pair of stocks we make five different portfolios by combining them in different proportions. The composition of the portfolios, i.e. the weights of stock 1, x_1, and the other stock, $1 - x_1$, as well as their expected returns and standard deviations are given in Table 3.4. For example, the expected return of the portfolio with equal parts of stock 1 and 2 is $0.5 \times 0.15 + 0.5 \times 0.175 = 0.163$ and its variance is $0.5^2 \times 0.0354^2 + 0.5^2 \times 0.0707^2 + 2 \times 0.5 \times 0.5 \times 0.0025 = 0.0028129$ so that its standard deviation is $\sqrt{0.0028129} = 0.053$. Notice that the returns in the columns 3, 5 and 7 are the same. Since stocks 2, 3 and 4 have the same expected returns, it is irrelevant for portfolio return which one is included. Also notice that all the weights are ≥ 0, so the possibility of *short selling* is not included in this example.[2]

Table 3.4 *Portfolios of stock 1, and 2, 3 and 4*

x_1	$1-x_1$	Stock 1, 2		Stock 1, 3		Stock 1, 4	
		$E[r_p]$	σ_p	$E[r_p]$	σ_p	$E[r_p]$	σ_p
1	0	0.15	0.035	0.15	0.035	0.15	0.035
0.75	0.25	0.156	0.044	0.156	0.001	0.156	0.037
0.50	0.50	0.163	0.053	0.163	0.018	0.163	0.045
0.25	0.75	0.169	0.062	0.169	0.044	0.169	0.057
0	1	0.175	0.071	0.175	0.071	0.175	0.071

The return and risk data in Table 3.4 are plotted in Figure 3.5 in two different ways. On the left-hand side, $E[r_p]$ and σ_p are plotted as functions of portfolio composition (proportion of stock 1). The return line $E[r]$ is the same for all combinations of stocks: it is a straight line interpolation between the high return (0.175) of stock 2, 3 or 4 and the low return (0.15) of stock 1. Portfolio risk, on the other hand, is seen to depend on correlation. When the correlation coefficient is 1, there is no diversification effect and portfolio risk is a straight line interpolation between the standard deviations of the two stocks (of 0.071 and 0.035). This is depicted as the straight line connecting the boxes ($\square$). But as the correlation coefficient becomes lower, the diversification effect increases and the line becomes more curved downwards. In the normal case of moderately but positively correlated stocks, the diversification effect is present but not strong. For $\rho = 0.38$ this is depicted as the slightly curved line connecting the diamonds ($\Diamond$). The diversification effect is maximal when perfectly negatively correlated stocks are combined. This is depicted by the line connecting the dots (o), which almost reaches the x-axis.

On the right-hand side of Figure 3.5, the portfolios are plotted in a risk-return space, which visualizes the risk-return trade-off. The diversification effect is expressed in the curvature to the left, that reduces risk along the x-axis. Again, this effect is seen to increase

2 Recall from Chapter 2 that you short a share by borrowing it from your stock broker and selling it. After an agreed period you buy it back in the market, hopefully at a lower price than you sold it for: short selling is a strategy to profit from price decreases.

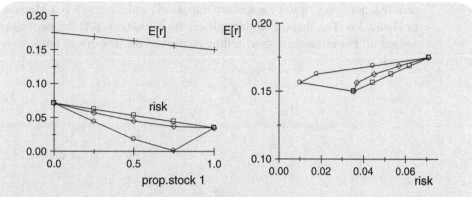

Figure 3.5 Portfolios' risk and return when correlation $= 1$ (boxes), 0.36 (diamonds) and -1 (dots)

from zero on the right (perfectly positively correlated stocks) to its maximum on the left (perfectly negatively correlated stocks). If $\rho = -1$, risk can even be completely eliminated by choosing the portfolio weights in inverse proportion to the standard deviations: $x_1 = \sigma_3/(\sigma_1 + \sigma_3) = 0.66$ (not depicted).[3]

Obviously, stocks that correlate negatively with other stocks would be very attractive to investors. Unfortunately, such stocks are not available in the market, although stocks do correlate negatively over short periods of time. The returns of most real-life assets depend on the economy as a whole, so most assets are positively correlated. However, correlation is already less than perfect if assets that go up and down together reach their peak returns in different scenarios or periods. This is very common in practice, and when it occurs, diversification lowers the risk of a portfolio. Thus, the behaviour of real-life investments resembles combinations of stock 1 and 4, which correlate positively and moderately.

3.2   Selecting and pricing portfolios

3.2.1   Markowitz efficient portfolios

As the number of assets increases, the number of risk-return combinations becomes very large. When depicted in a risk-return space, as in the picture on the right-hand side of Figure 3.5, the risk-return combinations become contiguous and form an egg- or cone-shaped area, or a 'Markowitz bullet' as it is sometimes called. Figure 3.6 depicts this, in a stylized way, as the area enclosed by the curve connecting the points A, B and C. That area represents all attainable risk-return combinations and is called the *investment opportunity set* or the *investment universe*. The precise shape of the investment universe depends on the means, variances and covariances of the assets in it. If most correlations between assets are moderately positive and (perfectly) negative correlations do not occur,

---

3 This follows directly from the expression for portfolio variance in (3.7): $\sigma_p^2 = x_1^2\sigma_1^2 + x_3^2\sigma_3^2 + 2x_1x_3\rho_{1,3}\sigma_1\sigma_3$. If $\rho_{1,3} = -1$ this becomes $\sigma_p^2 = x_1^2\sigma_1^2 + x_3^2\sigma_3^2 - 2x_1x_3\sigma_1\sigma_3 = (x_1\sigma_1 - x_3\sigma_3)^2$. This is only zero if $x_1\sigma_1 - x_3\sigma_3 = 0$. Since $x_1 + x_3 = 1$, this gives $x_1 = \sigma_3/(\sigma_1 + \sigma_3)$ and $x_3 = \sigma_1/(\sigma_1 + \sigma_3)$.

zero risk portfolios of risky assets are impossible and the result is a Markowitz bullet as in Figure 3.6. The shape also depends on the restrictions that the portfolio weights are subject to. For instance, if short selling is allowed the investment universe is larger than when it is not.

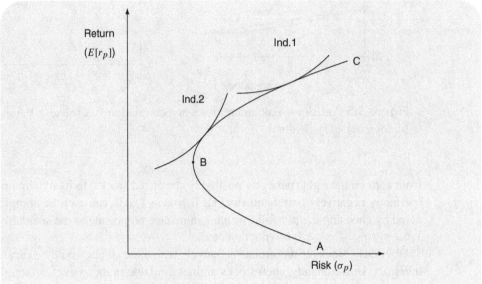

Figure 3.6 Investment universe and choices along the efficient frontier

Point C in Figure 3.6 is the maximum return portfolio. Without short selling it consists of a 100 per cent investment in the asset with the highest return. Diversification reduces the risk of a portfolio but it does not increase its return. So to obtain the highest possible expected return, diversification must be given up and the entire investment must be placed in the asset with the highest expected return. The minimum variance portfolio B, on the other hand, is likely to consist of a number of different assets so that the diversification effect is largest. The curve segment connecting the minimum variance and maximum return portfolios is called the *efficient frontier*. Rational, risk-averse investors will only choose combinations of investments that lie on this frontier. All other investment opportunities are inefficient, which means that they can be replaced by another investment that offers a higher return for the same risk or a lower risk for the same return. We will analyze how investors select their portfolios along the efficient frontier, first without and then with a financial market.

Without a financial market, investors choose their position on the efficient frontier according to their risk-return preferences. As we saw in the previous chapter, these preferences can be expressed in indifference curves that connect choices that give the same utility. In a risk-return space, indifference curves depict combinations of risk and return that give the same utility. Utility increases with return but decreases with risk. Hence, compared with Figure 2.3 in the previous chapter, the indifference curves are rotated around the vertical axis. Utility increases 'upwards' (more return is preferred to less) and to the left (less risk is preferred to more), so in north-west directions. Investors maximize their utility by choosing the point on the efficient frontier that is tangent to the highest attainable indifference curve. Figure 3.6 depicts the choices of two individuals. Individual 2 is more risk averse than individual 1: she requires a larger increase in expected return to accept an additional unit of risk (standard deviation). This marginal risk-return trade-off is measured by the slope of her indifference curve at the tangency point with the efficient frontier which, of course, has the same slope at the tangency point. Individual 1 finds his optimal point where the marginal risk-return trade-off of the efficient frontier equals his marginal risk preferences. Note that all investors will hold different portfolios, unless they have the same indifference curve.

In practice, the portfolio selection process is done in two steps. The first step is to choose the preferred risk-return combination. Notice that the individual preferences have to be known to make that decision. In the second step, the corresponding portfolio composition is calculated. This can be done by minimizing portfolio risk subject to the following restrictions:

1. The return is not less than the chosen return.
2. The portfolio weights sum to 1.
3. The weights are non-negative, if no short sales are allowed.

Alternatively, portfolio return can be maximized subject to the restriction that portfolio risk does not exceed the chosen level, with the same restrictions on the weights. The optimization can be done analytically, with Lagrange multipliers, or numerically. Banks used to provide such optimization routines as an (expensive) service to their customers. For a modest number of stocks (say, a few dozen) everybody can now do it at home with a spreadsheet program, as the next section illustrates.

3.2.2 Home-made portfolio optimization
Uncle Bob's portfolio

Late October 2011 your uncle Bob calculates the return of his stock portfolio over the previous year. He is very disappointed with the results. A former computer engineer, he used to invest all his money in Logitech International because, as he puts it, he understands the business of computer peripherals. However, following the advice of an investor magazine he diversified by allocating 10 per cent of his money to each of four other well-known companies on the Nasdaq stock exchange. His portfolio composition and returns over the period 21 October 2010 to 20 October 2011 are given in Table 3.5. To keep his management costs low, your uncle does not want to add stocks to his portfolio. However, he is willing to adjust the weights. He heard that you are taking a course in finance and asks your advice. What do you tell your uncle?

You begin by explaining that portfolio decisions are made on the basis of expected returns and risks. Historical data can give an impression of future possibilities but that requires long time series. There is no point in simply using last year's returns as estimates for next year, since three of the five stocks had zero or negative returns. Nobody invests in stocks that are expected to lose money. After much discussion and some gentle persuasion

Table 3.5 *Uncle Bob's portfolio October 2010 to October 2011*

Stock	ticker	weight	return	weight×return
Google	GOOG	0.1	0.000	0.0000
Cisco Systems	CSCO	0.1	−0.205	−0.0205
Logitech International	LOGI	0.6	−0.525	−0.3150
Amazon.com	AMZN	0.1	0.560	0.0560
Apple	AAPL	0.1	0.314	0.0314
Total		1		−0.2481

from your side, your uncle comes up with the return estimates for next year that are listed in Table 3.6.[4]

Table 3.6 *Uncle Bob's return estimates*

Stock	ticker	weight	return	weight×return
Google	GOOG	0.1	0.08	0.0080
Cisco Systems	CSCO	0.1	0.075	0.0075
Logitech International	LOGI	0.6	0.06	0.0360
Amazon.com	AMZN	0.1	0.125	0.0125
Apple	AAPL	0.1	0.10	0.0100
Total		1		0.0740

With the given portfolio weights, his estimates result in 7.4 per cent portfolio return. This still is disappointing to your uncle; he was hoping for at least 10 per cent. However, he hesitates to allocate more money to stocks with higher expected returns because he considers them riskier than his familiar Logitech. You point out that spreading the investments reduces risk and you ask him how much risk he is willing to accept to reach his target return. Since you don't get a clear answer, you decide to calculate the risk of his present portfolio first. You click to Yahoo.com and you download the daily closing prices, adjusted for dividends, of these five stocks over the past year.

Analyzing the portfolio

To analyze these data, the observed prices have to be transformed into returns and the first choice you are required to make is how to calculate returns. As we have seen, the alternatives are discretely compounded returns or continuously compounded, logarithmic returns. The former can easily be aggregated over stocks to give the portfolio return. The latter are easily aggregated over time to give the total, compound return over the entire investment period. You have time series of individual stocks in a portfolio, so you have to do both. This makes the choice rather arbitrary but since a major element in portfolio analysis is to determine how different stocks contribute to portfolio return and risk, you prefer discretely compounded returns. Ordinarily, the second choice you would have to

4 Make sure that it is clear to everybody involved that these are your uncle's, and not your, estimates.

3.2 Selecting and pricing portfolios

make is how to calculate historical averages: arithmetic or geometric ones. Geometric averages are based on multiplication and, hence, introduce compounding when applied to periods. The appendix to this chapter argues that arithmetic averages should be used to estimate future returns from historical time series. You do not base the expected returns on historical averages but on your uncle's estimates so you can skip the calculation of averages.

With 252 daily returns for each of the five stocks safely loaded in your spreadsheet you are ready to calculate risk. You use a built-in function in your spreadsheet program (such as STDEV(.:.) in Excel) to calculate standard deviations and you get the following (rounded) results: GOOG = 1.809, CSCO = 2.285, LOGI = 2.908, AMZN = 2.144, and AAPL = 1.577. The numbers are low because they are the standard deviations of the daily returns. They have to be 'scaled up' to an annual figure to match your uncle's estimates. You do that by assuming that the daily returns are independently, identically and normally distributed. You recall from statistics that the sum of two independently, normally distributed variables is again normally distributed, with a mean equal to the sum of the original two means and a variance equal to the sum of the original two variances. Applying this to your 252 daily returns you find the annual standard deviation by multiplying the daily standard deviation by $\sqrt{252} = 15.875$ (given the assumptions, variances increase with time, standard deviations with the square root of time). The results are in Table 3.7. Next, you calculate the correlations between the returns, using a built-in function (such as CORREL(.:.) in Excel) for each pair of stocks. The results are given in Table 3.7, together with the other relevant data.

Table 3.7 *Portfolio optimization inputs*

	Correlation matrix					Return	Ann. st.dev.	Weight
	GOOG	CSCO	LOGI	AMZN	AAPL			
GOOG	1					0.08	0.287	0.1
CSCO	0.43	1				0.075	0.363	0.1
LOGI	0.34	0.28	1			0.06	0.462	0.6
AMZN	0.55	0.34	0.35	1		0.125	0.340	0.1
AAPL	0.62	0.43	0.39	0.58	1	0.10	0.250	0.1

Optimizing the portfolio

Now you have all the ingredients for portfolio optimization. You set up a variance-covariance matrix by defining its cells as $x_i x_j \sigma_i \sigma_j \rho_{i,j}$, the product of the weight of the row entry, weight of the column entry, the row entry standard deviation, the column entry standard deviation and the correlation coefficient of the row and column entries. (After three cells and just as many typing errors you regret not having chosen a serious programming tool.) Portfolio variance is the sum of all cells in the variance-covariance matrix: $\sigma_p^2 = \sum_{i=1}^{I} \sum_{j=1}^{I} x_i x_j \sigma_i \sigma_j \rho_{i,j}$ and its square root the portfolio standard deviation. Portfolio return is the weighted sum of the stocks returns $\sum_i x_i r_i$. The optimization problem is formulated by defining the cell containing the portfolio standard deviation as the target cell to be minimized. The adjustable cells are the portfolio weights. You enter three restrictions. The first is that the weights have to be non-negative, since your uncle is not allowed to sell short. The second is that the weights have to sum to 1. The final restriction is that portfolio return should not be less than your uncle's target level of 10 per cent.

Before you press the button you pause a moment to reflect on the procedure. You have calculated the stocks' standard deviations and correlations from the daily returns over the last year and you have re-calculated the standard deviations to annual figures. By using them you assume that this covariance structure is constant and that it can be used for your uncle's return estimates. This implies that you consider uncle Bob's predictions unbiased estimates of the means of the distributions from which last year's results are a draw. You realize that it would be better to use longer time series and better estimation techniques but, then, Bob is (only) your uncle and you press the 'solve' button. The results are in column 3 (Min.var., $r_{p \geq 0.1}$) of Table 3.8.

Table 3.8 *Uncle Bob's optimal portfolio*

Portfolio:	Original	Min. var. $r_p \geq 0.1$	Min. var.
Google	0.1	0.12	0.22
Cisco Systems	0.1	0.10	0.14
Logitech International	0.6	0.0	0.05
Amazon.com	0.1	0.19	0.06
Apple	0.1	0.59	0.53
Total (sum weights)	1	1	1
Portf. return	0.074	0.10	0.092
Portf. stand. dev.	0.33	0.236	0.232

You are well pleased with the results and you point out to your uncle that both the expected return and the risk of the portfolio have improved: the return increases from 7.4 per cent to 10 per cent and the standard deviation drops from 33 per cent to 23.6 per cent. You also observe that the re-mixed portfolio has a lower standard deviation than any of the stocks in it. Uncle Bob agrees, but he is dissatisfied with the zero weight of his familiar Logitech. You explain that the restriction of at least 10 per cent portfolio return works against the inclusion of a stock with an expected return of 6 per cent. To demonstrate this, you calculate the minimum variance portfolio by removing the restriction on the portfolio return. The results are in column 4 (Min.var.) of Table 3.8. Logitech is now included with 5 per cent, but the reduction in portfolio standard deviation is very small and you suggest the alternative of putting a maximum of, say, 40 per cent on the weight that each stock can have. Uncle Bob gets more interested and takes your place behind the keyboard...

Short selling and the efficient frontier

When uncle Bob takes a break you decide to do some more experiments. First, you are curious about the shape of the efficient frontier in this small portfolio problem. To approximate the efficient frontier you calculate optimal (minimum variance) portfolios with

3.2 Selecting and pricing portfolios

successively higher minimal expected returns.[5] You have already calculated the optimal portfolio with uncle Bob's restriction of 10 per cent expected return, so you increase the return restriction in five steps of 0.5 percentage points until you reach the maximum return portfolio with 12.5 per cent return. The optimal risk-return combinations are plotted in Figure 3.7 and when you connect the dots the efficient frontier looks surprisingly like the pictures you remember from textbooks. You observe that, starting from the minimum variance portfolio, a small increase in risk leads to a relatively large increase in expected return. Uncle Bob's portfolio gives a 0.8 percentage points higher expected return than the minimum variance portfolio, but its standard deviation is only 0.4 percentage points higher. However, the 0.5 percentage points increase in expected return from 12 per cent to 12.5 per cent is accompanied by an increase in standard deviation of 3.6 percentage points (from 30.4 per cent to 34 per cent). You also observe that all five stocks are included in the minimum variance portfolio, four in uncle Bob's portfolio, and fewer and fewer stocks in the higher return portfolios until there is only one stock left in the maximum return portfolio. That is the diversification effect working in reverse!

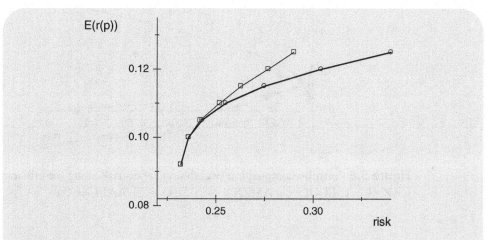

Figure 3.7 Efficient frontier with (lower) and without (upper) short selling restriction

Next, you investigate what the effects of short selling are. You remove the non-negativity restrictions on the portfolio weights and recalculate the minimum variance portfolio. You are disappointed to find that you get exactly the same portfolio as with the short selling restriction.[6] When you recalculate uncle Bob's portfolio without short selling restriction, the first negative weight appears (-0.01 for LOGI), but it is too small to have an appreciable effect on portfolio risk and return. As you further increase the minimum return restriction in the same five steps of 0.5 percentage points, more and larger

5 The efficient frontier can also be calculated analytically from any two points on it with a technique known as Black's result, after Black (1972).

6 This is not a general result, but it happens to be the case in this dataset.

negative weights appear. The portfolio weights are plotted in Figure 3.8 against portfolio standard deviation. Plotted in the risk-return space of Figure 3.7, short selling is seen to have a risk reducing effect. Portfolios with a higher expected return can be constructed more efficiently with short selling than without. Without short selling, an expected return restriction of 12.5 per cent means that all money has to be invested in the highest return stock, Amazon, which has a standard deviation of 34 per cent. With short selling, the optimal portfolio with at least 12.5 per cent return consists of -0.19 Google, -0.17 Logitech, 0.57 Amazon and 0.79 Apple. This portfolio[7] has a standard deviation of 29 per cent, which is 5 percentage points below the restricted maximum return portfolio. Removing the short selling restriction indeed expands the investment opportunity set and moves the efficient frontier upwards and to the left.

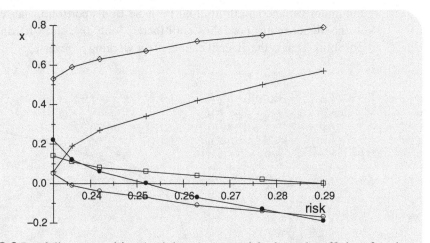

Figure 3.8 Portfolio composition (weights x) versus risk along the efficient frontier (GOOG = •, LOGI = ○, AMZN = +, CSCO = □, AAPL = ◇)

3.2.3 Pricing efficient portfolios in equilibrium

We now extend Markowitz's analysis with two additional elements: a financial (money) market and market equilibrium. In a portfolio context, the introduction of a financial market adds a new investment to the investment opportunity set: the risk-free asset. As usual we will assume a perfect financial market, where unlimited amounts of money can be borrowed or lent at the same rate and without transaction costs. As before, the introduction of a financial market may look trivial, but it has profound effects. It drastically changes the shape of the efficient frontier, so that all investors hold combinations of the risk-free asset and the so-called market portfolio, as we shall see.

Market equilibrium requires a set of *market clearing prices*, which ensure that investors' collective demand equals the supply for every asset. The process in which those

---

7 When short selling is allowed, there is no maximum return portfolio: return can always be increased by shorting more stocks with a low return and buying those with a high return.

3.2 Selecting and pricing portfolios

prices are established can be thought of as being directed by a market manager (the 'Walrasian auctioneer' from classical economics). This manager announces a set of prices and each investor informs the market manager how much of each asset they are willing to hold at those prices. If collective demand exceeds supply, the market manager raises the prices and if supply exceeds demand they are lowered. The new prices are announced and the process continues until demand equals supply. The result is that all assets are held; in equilibrium there is no excess demand (i.e. some investors want to invest more at current prices) or excess supply (i.e. some assets are not held at current prices). This includes the risk-free asset; the risk-free interest rate is set such that borrowing equals lending.

As Figure 3.9 illustrates, introducing the risk-free asset changes the efficient frontier from the curve BC to the straight line that runs from the risk-free interest rate r_f through the tangency point M with the risky investment opportunity set. This tangency point gives the line its steepest possible slope, which means the highest possible expected return per additional unit of risk. In all points except M, the new frontier offers a higher expected return for given levels of risk than the old frontier BC. In point M both offer the same expected return. The straight line is called the *capital market line* (CML) and all investors will choose their optimal positions along it. This means that all investors only hold combinations of two assets (or funds), the risk-free asset and the tangency portfolio M, regardless of the risk preferences that are expressed in their indifference curves. This remarkable result is called *two fund separation.*

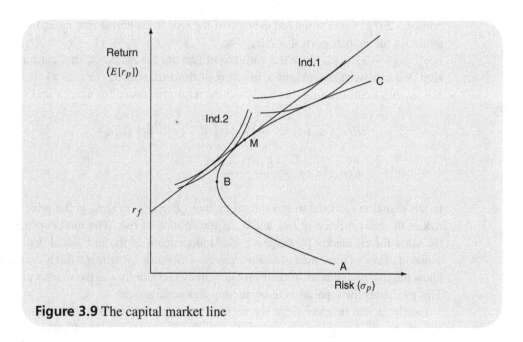

Figure 3.9 The capital market line

Note that portfolio M is chosen as the tangency point that gives the CML its maximum slope and M is therefore determined by the expected returns, variances and covariances of the risky investment universe plus the risk-free interest rate. It is *not* determined by the risk preferences of investors. But as it is the tangency point, two fund separation obtains and all investors will want to hold portfolio M. If all investors[8] want to hold portfolio M, market equilibrium requires that it contains all assets in the risky universe. Otherwise, there would be excess supply of the assets not in it. Hence, portfolio M is called the *market portfolio*. Equilibrium further requires that the prices are such that there is no excess demand or supply of the assets in the market portfolio. In equilibrium, with the equilibrium prices established, the price of each risky asset determines its weight in M. So each risky asset is held in the proportion of its market value relative to the total market value for all risky assets (i.e. each asset is held according to its market value weight). By consequence, all investors who hold risky assets, hold them in the same proportions, i.e. they hold a fraction of the market portfolio M.

The risk-return preferences of individual investors are expressed in the way they combine the riskless asset with the market portfolio M. Individual 2 in Figure 3.9, who is more risk averse than individual 1, lends some of her money risk-free and invests the rest in the risky market portfolio. Individual 1, who is less risk averse, borrows money risk-free and invests this together with his own money in the market portfolio. This increases his expected return, but also his risk, beyond those of the market portfolio. Notice that both are better off by the introduction of a financial market: they jump to higher indifference curves. No investor is worse off and only investors who (happened to) hold the market portfolio are not better off.

An expression for the CML can be derived as follows. If we invest a fraction x in the risk-free asset and a fraction $(1 - x)$ in the market portfolio, the expected return on this portfolio $E(r_p)$ is the weighted average of the risk-free interest rate r_f and the expected return on the market portfolio $E(r_m)$, so $E(r_p) = x \times r_f + (1 - x) \times E(r_m)$. Its risk is $\sigma_p = (1 - x) \times \sigma_m$ since the variance of and the covariance with a constant are both zero. We can write the weight x in terms of the variances: $\sigma_p/\sigma_m = (1 - x) \Rightarrow x = 1 - (\sigma_p/\sigma_m)$. Substituting this back into the return relation eliminates x and we get:

$$E(r_p) = \left(1 - \frac{\sigma_p}{\sigma_m}\right) r_f + \left(1 - 1 + \frac{\sigma_p}{\sigma_m}\right) E(r_m)$$

$$E(r_p) = r_f + \frac{(E(r_m) - r_f)}{\sigma_m} \sigma_p \tag{3.8}$$

In this equation r_f is the time value of money, $(E(r_m) - r_f)/\sigma_m$ is the price per unit of risk or the *market price of risk* and σ_p is the volume of risk. The market price of risk is the same for all market participants, it is independent of the individual degrees of risk aversion. This, in turn, means that managers of firms or investment funds do not have to know the risk preferences of their investors, they can simply use the market price of risk. This facilitates the separation of ownership and management.

Finally, it will be clear from the above that the capital market line is an equilibrium risk-return relation (or pricing relation) for efficient portfolios. In efficient portfolios, all risk comes from the fraction of the market portfolio M. The capital market line cannot be used for individual assets or other inefficient portfolios. To price these investments we need a different pricing relation, such as the Capital Asset Pricing Model.

---

[8] All but the most risk averse, who only invest in the risk-free asset.

3.3) The Capital Asset Pricing Model

The Capital Asset Pricing Model (CAPM) is a pricing relation for *all* assets, including individual assets and inefficient portfolios. We will first derive the model and then discuss some of its insights, underlying assumptions and empirical tests.

3.3.1 Derivation of the CAPM

Following the original approach by Sharpe (1964), the CAPM is usually derived by analyzing the risk-return properties of a two-asset portfolio, consisting of a fraction $(1 - x)$ of the market portfolio M and a fraction x of another asset i. The latter can be thought of as an individual stock. Notice that this is an inefficient portfolio. The analysis concerns the effect of varying the proportion x on the portfolio's risk and return. Graphically, the risk return values trace out the curve from I to I' in Figure 3.10.

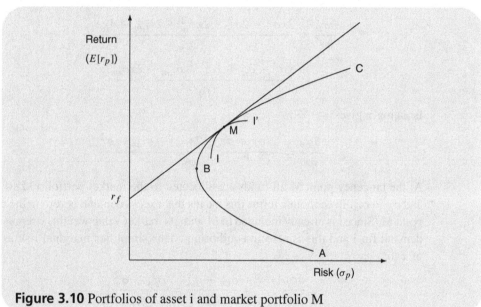

Figure 3.10 Portfolios of asset i and market portfolio M

At point I, all the funds of the portfolio are allocated to asset i, so $x = 1$. Along the curve the fraction x diminishes until it reaches zero at point M, where the curve I-I' is tangent to the capital market line. Of course, I-I' cannot cross the capital market line as this would invalidate the latter as the efficient frontier. At point M, $x = 0$ and the market portfolio is held, in which asset i is included with its market value weight. Between the points M and I' the weight x is negative, i.e. asset i has to be sold short to reduce its weight in M until it reaches zero at point I'. The risk and return of this portfolio along the trajectory I-I' are:

$$E(r_p) = xE(r_i) + (1 - x)E(r_m)$$

$$\sigma_p = \sqrt{[x^2\sigma_i^2 + (1 - x)^2\sigma_m^2 + 2x(1 - x)\sigma_{im}]}$$

where the subscript p stands for the portfolio, i for asset i and m for the market portfolio. The slope of the curve I-I' at any point is:

$$\frac{\partial E(r_p)}{\partial \sigma_p} = \frac{\partial E(r_p)/\partial x}{\partial \sigma_p/\partial x}$$

The numerator and denominator of this equation are calculated as follows:

$$\frac{\partial E(r_p)}{\partial x} = E(r_i) - E(r_m)$$

$$\frac{\partial \sigma_p}{\partial x} = \frac{1}{2} \left[x^2\sigma_i^2 + (1-x)^2\sigma_m^2 + 2x(1-x)\sigma_{im} \right]^{-\frac{1}{2}}$$
$$\times \left[2x\sigma_i^2 - 2\sigma_m^2 + 2x\sigma_m^2 + 2\sigma_{i,m} - 4x\sigma_{im} \right]$$

The first term of $\partial \sigma_p/\partial x$ is $\frac{1}{2}\sigma_p$, so:

$$\frac{\partial \sigma_p}{\partial x} = \frac{2x\sigma_i^2 - 2\sigma_m^2 + 2x\sigma_m^2 + 2\sigma_{i,m} - 4x\sigma_{im}}{2\sigma_p}$$

$$= \frac{x\sigma_i^2 - \sigma_m^2 + x\sigma_m^2 + \sigma_{i,m} - 2x\sigma_{im}}{\sigma_p}$$

Isolating x gives:

$$\frac{\partial \sigma_p}{\partial x} = \frac{x(\sigma_i^2 + \sigma_m^2 - 2\sigma_{im}) + \sigma_{i,m} - \sigma_m^2}{\sigma_p}$$

At the tangency point M all funds are allocated to the market portfolio M so that $x = 0$ and $\sigma_p = \sigma_m$. In economic terms this means that excess demand is zero in the equilibrium point M. Since i is already included in M with its market value weight, x represents excess demand for i and this is zero in equilibrium. This simplifies marginal risk as a function of x to:

$$\left. \frac{\partial \sigma_p}{\partial x} \right|_{x=0} = \frac{\sigma_{im} - \sigma_m^2}{\sigma_p} = \frac{\sigma_{im} - \sigma_m^2}{\sigma_m}$$

So the slope of the curve I-I' at the equilibrium point M is:

$$\left. \frac{\partial E(r_p)/\partial x}{\partial \sigma_p/\partial x} \right|_{x=0} = \frac{E(r_i) - E(r_m)}{\left(\sigma_{im} - \sigma_m^2\right)/\sigma_m}$$

But at point M the curve I-I' is also tangent to the CML, so its slope must be equal to the slope of the CML in (3.8), hence:

$$\frac{E(r_i) - E(r_m)}{\left(\sigma_{im} - \sigma_m^2\right)/\sigma_m} = \frac{E(r_m) - r_f}{\sigma_m}$$

Solving for $E(r_i)$ gives:

$$E(r_i) = r_f + (E(r_m) - r_f)\frac{\sigma_{im}}{\sigma_m^2}$$

3.3 The Capital Asset Pricing Model

Using the definition of β in (3.5) we get:

$$E(r_i) = r_f + (E(r_m) - r_f)\beta_i \tag{3.9}$$

This is the *Capital Asset Pricing Model* for which Sharpe was awarded the Nobel prize. Its graphical representation is known as the *Security Market Line*. It is a pricing relation for all risky assets, including inefficient portfolios and individual assets. It formalizes the intuition in financial markets that well-diversified investors value assets according to their contributions to the risk of the investor's portfolio: a higher risk contribution should be associated with higher returns. The model provides a clear measure of risk, β, and a clear price of risk, $E(r_m) - r_f$. It summarizes the risk return relationships for all assets in the investment universe in a simple and elegant linear relation.

3.3.2 Insights from the CAPM

The CAPM and the portfolio theory it is built on can be rewritten in various ways to highlight different insights. We shall analyze the differences between systematic and unsystematic risk a bit further, reformulate the CAPM for use as a discount rate or in certainty equivalent calculations, and look at some performances measures.

Systematic and unsystematic risk

The CML is a pricing relation for *efficient* portfolios:

$$E(r_p) = r_f + \frac{E(r_m) - r_f}{\sigma_m}\sigma_p$$

where $(E(r_m) - r_f)/\sigma_m$ is the price per unit of risk and σ_p is the volume of risk. The CML prices σ_p which includes *all risks* (systematic and unsystematic). It is therefore only valid when risk exclusively consists of systematic risk, i.e. for efficient portfolios in which all risk comes from the fraction of the market portfolio they contain. For other, inefficient portfolios, the CML uses the 'wrong' risk measure: for these portfolios σ_p comprises unsystematic risk that is not priced in the market.

The security market line (SML) only prices *systematic risk,* and it is therefore valid for all investments, including inefficient portfolios and individual stocks:

$$E(r_p) = r_f + (E(r_m) - r_f)\beta_p$$

where β_p is the volume of risk and $(E(r_m) - r_f)$ is the price per unit of risk. We can write β_p in terms of correlation (instead of covariance) as:

$$\beta_p = \frac{\sigma_{pm}}{\sigma_m^2} = \frac{\sigma_p \sigma_m \rho_{pm}}{\sigma_m^2} = \frac{\sigma_p \rho_{pm}}{\sigma_m}$$

so that the SML becomes:

$$E(r_p) = r_f + (E(r_m) - r_f)\frac{\sigma_p \rho_{pm}}{\sigma_m},$$

$$E(r_p) = r_f + \frac{E(r_m) - r_f}{\sigma_m}\sigma_p \rho_{pm}$$

Comparing this with the CML above we see that both relations use the same market price of risk $\left(E(r_m) - r_f\right)/\sigma_m$, but different measures for the volume of risk: σ_p in the CML and $\sigma_p\rho_{pm}$ in the SML. The difference is the correlation term, ρ_{pm}, that is ignored in the CML. It *can* be ignored in the CML because efficient portfolios only differ in the fraction of the market portfolio M they contain. This means that all efficient portfolios are perfectly positively correlated, because fractions of the market portfolio are perfectly positively correlated with each other and with the market portfolio. If a portfolio is perfectly positively correlated with the market portfolio $\rho_{pm} = 1$ so that $\sigma_p\rho_{pm} = \sigma_p$ and the CML is equivalent to the SML. For inefficient portfolios the volume of risk is adjusted in the SML by the correlation coefficient. Inefficient portfolios are less than perfectly positively correlated with the market portfolio: $\rho_{pm} < 1$. So the adjustment is downwards: risk is reduced because unsystematic risk is eliminated. Figure 3.11 illustrates this for some assets. The assets labelled B, G, F and C are inefficient: their standard deviations contain a part unsystematic risk. This means that their standard deviations overstate the risk that is relevant for pricing, that is why they plot to the right of the CML in the picture on the left-hand side of Figure 3.11. Only the market portfolio M is efficient, its standard deviation contains no unsystematic risk so it plots on the CML. When the standard deviations are 'corrected' for unsystematic risk through multiplication by the correlation coefficient, then all the remaining risk is priced and all assets plot on the SML, as the right-hand side of Figure 3.11 shows.

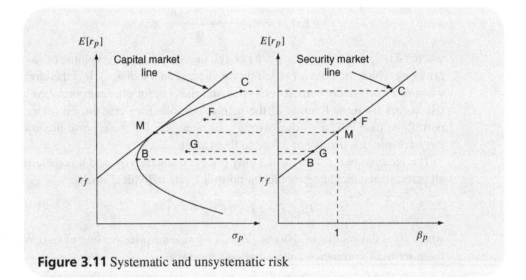

Figure 3.11 Systematic and unsystematic risk

Finally, for efficient portfolios $\beta_p = \sigma_p/\sigma_m$ or $\sigma_p = \beta_p\sigma_m$, so the risk (standard deviation) of efficient portfolios is proportional to the risk of the market portfolio and the proportionality is measured by β.

CAPM and discount rates

In the introduction we said that there are three different ways to account for risk in valuation procedures:

1. By adjusting the discount rate to a risk-adjusted discount rate.
2. By adjusting the cash flows to certainty equivalent cash flows.
3. By redefining the probabilities that are incorporated in the expectation operator.

The CAPM can be used in the first two ways. Writing the CAPM in terms of a discount rate is straightforward. The CAPM gives the expected (= required) return on portfolio p as:

$$E(r_p) = r_f + (E(r_m) - r_f)\beta_p$$

Return is also the expectation of the uncertain end-of-period value of portfolio p, V_{pT}, minus the value now, V_{p0}, as fraction of V_{p0}, similar to the discretely compounded returns we calculated before:

$$E(r_p) = \frac{E(V_{pT}) - V_{p0}}{V_{p0}}$$

in which the end-of-period value and, hence, the return are uncertain. The discount rate that links the expected end-of-period value, $E(V_{p,T})$, to the value now, $V_{p,0}$, is found by equating the two expressions:

$$\frac{E(V_{p,T}) - V_{p,0}}{V_{p,0}} = r_f + (E(r_m) - r_f)\beta_p$$

and then solving for $V_{p,0}$ which gives:

$$V_{p,0} = \frac{E(V_{p,T})}{1 + r_f + (E(r_m) - r_f)\beta_p}$$

where r_f represents the time value of money and $(E(r_m) - r_f)\beta_p$ is the adjustment for risk. Together they form the risk-adjusted discount rate.

Certainty equivalent formulation

The second way to account for risk is to adjust the uncertain end-of-period value of our portfolio into a certainty equivalent value, which can (and should) be discounted at the risk-free interest rate. This requires some calculations, and we start with the expression that equates the two formulas for expected portfolio return:

$$\frac{E(V_{p,T}) - V_{p,0}}{V_{p,0}} = r_f + (E(r_m) - r_f)\beta_p$$

We know that $\beta_p = covar(r_p, r_m)/\sigma_m^2$ and r_p can be written as $(V_{p,T} - V_{p,0})/V_{p,0} = (V_{p,T}/V_{p,0}) - 1$. Substituting both in the right-hand side expression of portfolio return above we get:

$$\frac{E(V_{p,T}) - V_{p,0}}{V_{p,0}} = r_f + (E(r_m) - r_f)\frac{cov\left(\frac{V_{p,T}}{V_{p,0}} - 1, r_m\right)}{\sigma_m^2}$$

Modern portfolio theory

We now redefine the *market price of risk* (λ) as the price per unit of variance, instead of the price per unit of standard deviation that we used before:

$$\lambda = \frac{E(r_m) - r_f}{\sigma_m^2}$$

Since σ_m is a constant in equilibrium this redefinition is trivial. Substituting this we get:

$$\frac{E(V_{p,T}) - V_{p,0}}{V_{p,0}} = r_f + \lambda cov\left(\frac{V_{p,T}}{V_{p,0}} - 1, r_m\right)$$

The multiplicative constant $1/V_{p,0}$ can be written before the *cov* operator and the additive constant -1 can be omitted from it:

$$\frac{E(V_{p,T}) - V_{p,0}}{V_{p,0}} = r_f + \lambda \frac{1}{V_{p,0}} cov\left(V_{p,T}, r_m\right)$$

Solving for $V_{p,0}$ gives:

$$E(V_{p,T}) - V_{p,0} = r_f V_{p,0} + \lambda cov\left(V_{p,T}, r_m\right)$$

$$V_{p,0} = \frac{E(V_{p,T}) - \lambda cov\left(V_{p,T}, r_m\right)}{1 + r_f}$$

This is the *certainty equivalent formulation* of the CAPM. We see that the uncertain end-of-period value is adjusted by the market price of risk, λ, times the volume of risk, which is the covariance of the uncertain end-of-period value with the return on the market portfolio. The resulting certainty equivalent value is discounted at the risk-free rate to find the present value.

Performance measures

The risk-return relationships in the CML and the SML can be reformulated to measure ex post, risk-adjusted performance. Such measures relate historical, realized returns to observed, historical risks. They are very useful to evaluate the performance of portfolios and portfolio managers because they integrate return and risk in one measure. Sharpe (1966) suggested to use the slope of the CML as performance measure. The CML in (3.8):

$$E(r_p) = r_f + \frac{(E(r_m) - r_f)}{\sigma_m} \sigma_p$$

can be rewritten as:

$$\frac{E(r_p) - r_f}{\sigma_p} = \frac{(E(r_m) - r_f)}{\sigma_m}$$

The ex post, empirical form of the left-hand side of this equation is known as the *reward-to-variability ratio* or the *Sharpe ratio*:

$$\text{Sharpe ratio:} \quad SR_p = \frac{\bar{r}_p - \bar{r}_f}{\hat{\sigma}_p} \tag{3.10}$$

in which SR_p stands for the Sharpe ratio of portfolio p, and $\bar{r}_p$ is the portfolio's historical average return over the observation period: $\bar{r}_p = \sum_t r_{pt}/T$. The average risk-free interest rate, $\bar{r}_f$, is calculated in a similar way, and $\widehat{\sigma}_p$ is the standard deviation of portfolio returns: $\widehat{\sigma}_p = \sqrt{\sum_t (r_{pt} - \bar{r}_p)^2 / T}$. The summations are over the T sub-periods (e.g. weekly returns over the past two years). A set of portfolios (or funds) can be ranked according to the Sharpe ratios. Where appropriate, the ranking can be used to identify portfolios that e.g. failed to diversify properly (too high $\widehat{\sigma}_p$) or charged too high fees ($\bar{r}_p$ too small). The Sharpe ratio can be adapted so that the risk premium is not measured relative to the risk-free rate, as in (3.10), but relative to some benchmark portfolio. This performance measure is known as the *information ratio*.

The Treynor ratio takes its risk measure from the SML and scales the risk premium by β:

$$\text{Treynor ratio:} \quad TR_p = \frac{\bar{r}_p - \bar{r}_f}{\widehat{\beta}_p} \tag{3.11}$$

where $\widehat{\beta}_p$ is estimated from the historical returns over the observation period (see equation (3.13) later on). The most obvious figure to compare the Treynor ratio with is the risk premium on the market portfolio $\bar{r}_m - \bar{r}_f$, which is the Treynor ratio for a portfolio with a β of 1. If the CAPM obtains, all assets and portfolios lie on the SML and have the same Treynor ratio.

A second performance measure that is directly based on the CAPM is Jensen's alpha. It measures the return of a portfolio in excess of what the CAPM specifies:

$$\text{Jensen's alpha:} \quad \widehat{\alpha}_p = \bar{r}_p - (\bar{r}_f + \widehat{B}_p(\bar{r}_m - \bar{r}_f)) \tag{3.12}$$

The alpha can be obtained by regressing the portfolio's risk premium on the risk premium of the market portfolio:

$$r_{pt} - r_{ft} = \widehat{\alpha}_p + \widehat{B}_p(r_{mt} - r_{ft}) + \widehat{\varepsilon}_{pt}$$

Taking averages over the observation period replaces the time-indexed variables with their averages and makes the error term disappear (its average is zero by the definition of a regression line): $\bar{r}_p - \bar{r}_f = \widehat{\alpha}_p + \widehat{B}_p(\bar{r}_m - \bar{r}_f)$. Rearranging terms gives Jensen's alpha as in (3.12). Regression analyses also provide the statistical significance of the estimated parameters $\widehat{\alpha}_p$ and $\widehat{B}_p$.

Comparing these performance measures we see that the Sharpe ratio uses total risk (σ), while the Treynor index and Jensen's alpha take only systematic risk (β) into account. This makes the Sharpe ratio better suited to evaluate an investor's total portfolio. When a portfolio is split into sub-portfolios by e.g. country, industry or portfolio manager, evaluating these sub-portfolios with the Sharpe ratio would ignore the correlations between them and overstate risk. The Treynor ratio is more appropriate for such sub-portfolios, particularly if they are well diversified. Jensen's alpha uses the CAPM as a benchmark. This makes alpha very easy to interpret: it is the return in excess of (or below) what the CAPM specifies. A major disadvantage is that alphas are difficult to compare between portfolios with different risk: 2 per cent excess return may be much when the expected return is 6 per cent, but not when it is 24 per cent. By contrast, the Sharpe and Treynor ratios can be used to compare, i.e. rank, portfolios with different levels of risk, but it is difficult to interpret their values as high or low. Finally, using systematic risk makes the risk measures in the Treynor index and Jensen's alpha dependent on the choice of market index or market portfolio. This makes them vulnerable to Roll's critique, as we shall see later on.

3.3.3   Underlying assumptions

The derivation of the CAPM is built on a number of assumptions that describe the functioning of financial markets and the behaviour of investors in them:

- Financial markets are perfect and competitive:
  - there are no taxes or transaction costs, the supply of assets is fixed and all assets are marketable and perfectly divisible, without limitations on short selling and risk-free borrowing and lending;
  - there are large numbers of buyers and sellers, none of which is large enough to individually influence prices, all information is simultaneously and costlessly available to all investors.
- Investors are risk averse and:
  - maximize the expected utility of their end wealth by choosing investments based on their mean-variance characteristics over a single holding period;
  - have homogeneous expectations w.r.t. returns (i.e. they observe the same efficient frontier).

These assumptions differ in background and importance. Some of them make modelling easy and the model does not break down if we include phenomena that are now assumed not to exist. It just becomes more complex. This is the case with assumptions such as the absence of taxes and transaction costs, the marketability and divisibility of all assets and even the existence of a risk-free asset. Adjusted versions of the CAPM, that include taxes or non-marketable assets, have been published. Another assumption points at an unresolved shortcoming of the model: a single holding period, albeit of undetermined length, is clearly unrealistic. There are multi-period versions of the model and a version in continuous time, but they have not been really successful. Still other assumptions have important consequences and relaxing them more or less undermines the CAPM. Two of them are depicted in Figure 3.12. If the borrowing rate differs from the lending rate, not all investors have the same risk-return trade-off. The efficient frontier is no longer a straight line but will plot from the risk-free lending rate r_{fl} to the tangency point M', follow the curved efficient frontier we had without a financial market to the tangency point M" and continue from there along the line that originates from the risk-free borrowing rate r_{fb}. Similarly, if investors have heterogeneous expectations w.r.t. returns they will observe different risky investment opportunity sets and, hence, different efficient frontiers. This is depicted on the right-hand side of Figure 3.12. Heterogeneous expectations do not necessarily invalidate the CAPM but expected returns, covariances and 'market' portfolios become the weighted averages of investors' expectations.

The picture on the right-hand side of Figure 3.12 also applies to restrictions on the risky investment universe or the portfolio weights. For example, the risky investment universe with market portfolio M could depict a universe without restrictions on short selling and the universe with M* one with such restrictions. Similarly, the universes could be constructed without and with ethical restrictions on the assets that can be held, as elaborated in Farmen and van der Wijst (2005).

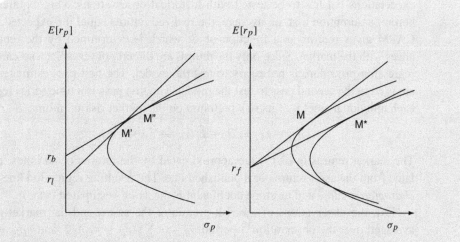

Figure 3.12 CML with different borrowing and lending rates (left) and heterogeneous expectations (right)

The key behavioural assertion is that investors maximize the expected utility of their end wealth by choosing investments based on their mean-variance characteristics. This assertion describes the behaviour (the force) that drives the model into equilibrium; mean variance optimization *must* take place for the model to work. This may appear to be a specific trait of modern portfolio theory, but that is not completely correct. Mean variance optimization is equivalent to the more general behavioural assertion of expected utility maximization if either asset returns are jointly normally distributed or investors have quadratic utility functions. Normal distributions are completely described by their first two moments, i.e. their means, variances and covariances, the higher moments are zero. If investors have utility function of the type $U(W) = \alpha + \beta W - \lambda W^2$ then choosing a portfolio to maximize utility only depends on $E[W]$ and $E[W^2]$, i.e. expected returns and (co-)variances. This means that investors only care about the first two moments.

Finally, the CAPM is an equilibrium pricing relation that describes the structure of asset prices as a function of systematic risk. If the model is valid, investors' mean variance optimization behaviour will drive prices into equilibrium and all investments will lie on the SML. If the model is not valid, the SML does not exist. This means that the model cannot be used to identify 'undervalued' or 'overvalued' assets by calculating their distance from an empirically estimated SML. In more general terms, there can be no disequilibrium in equilibrium models. That is true for all micro economic equilibrium models (even though you may not have been told so in micro economics).

3.3.4 Tests and testability

Testing the CAPM is not as straightforward as the model's simple linear structure suggests.[9] A first and formidable obstacle is that the theory is formulated in terms of

---

[9] Empirical tests of the CAPM are riddled with econometric problems, for which the reader is referred to specialized literature, e.g. Campbell *et al.* (1997).

expectations but has to be tested with historical observations. This requires the (rather heroic) assumption that, on average, the realized returns equal the expected returns. The CAPM gives returns as a function of β, which is determined by the returns' covariances with the market. Since only the returns are directly observable, a so-called two-pass regression procedure is necessary to test the model. The first pass estimates the βs that are used in the second pass to test the model. The first pass is a time series regression, for each individual asset i, of its risk premium on the market risk premium:

$$r_{it} - r_{ft} = \widehat{\alpha}_i + \widehat{\beta}_i(r_{mt} - r_{ft}) + \widehat{\varepsilon}_{it} \tag{3.13}$$

The market returns in (3.13) are approximated by the returns of an index, either calculated from the asset returns or a published one. The resulting regression line is called the *characteristic line* and its slope coefficient is the asset's estimated beta: $\widehat{\beta}$.

Next, the observations of the risk premia of the assets and the market portfolio are averaged over the observation[10] period: $\overline{rp}_i = \sum_t (r_{it} - r_{ft})/T$ and $\overline{rp}_m = \sum_t (r_{mt} - r_{ft})/T$, where rp stands for risk premium. The second pass regression is a cross section analysis of the assets' risk premia, which are regressed on the estimated betas from the first pass:

$$\overline{rp}_i = \gamma_0 + \gamma_1 \widehat{\beta}_i + \gamma_{2n}(testvar_n) + \widehat{u}_i \tag{3.14}$$

The CAPM predicts that, in the second pass regression, the intercept γ_0 is zero and the slope coefficient γ_1 equals the market risk premium $\overline{rp}_m$. Further predictions are that the relation is linear in β and that no other variables play a significant role in explaining $\overline{rp}_i$. To test the latter predictions the additional variables (testvar) are included in (3.14). Some of the variables that have been used are β^2, to test for linearity, σ_i^2, to test for effects of non-systematic risk, ln(market value) to test for size effects and various financial ratios.

Empirical tests of the CAPM following this and similar methodologies have been performed in large numbers over the past several decades. We shall exemplify this vast body of research by referring only to Fama and MacBeth (1973), Fama and French (1992) and Fama and French (1996). These are probably the best-known studies in this field, partly because they use very large data sets. The general picture that emerges from these three, and the multitude of other studies, is that the empirical SML is too horizontal (not steep enough): the intercept is too high (γ_0 significantly >0) and the slope is too low ($\gamma_1 < \overline{rp}_m$). Moreover, the SML is more horizontal in recent studies than in early ones, even to the degree that γ_1 is close to zero (popularly summarized as 'beta is dead'). Linearity is generally not rejected and, from a statistical point of view, variance is seldom a better risk measure than β.

A few other variables than β are frequently found to be related to asset returns. Of these, size is probably the most important. Smaller firms, as measured by (the ln of) their total market value (or *market capitalization*), are reported to earn higher returns than predicted by the CAPM and outperform large firms with the comparable β's. Additionally, high returns are found to be associated with factors such as low price-earnings ratios, high dividend yields and high book-to-market values. Stocks with these characteristics are called 'value stocks'. A common denominator of the three financial ratios

---

10 βs can be, and often are, estimated over a prior period.

seems to be the intangible assets we discussed in the previous chapter. As we have seen, assets such as patents, trade marks and growth opportunities are appreciated by investors because they indicate good future prospects. Firms that derive a large part of their value from future prospects, rather than current cash flows and assets in place, have high price-earnings ratios, low dividend yields and low book-to-market values. They are called 'growth stocks'. Apparently, the market requires lower rates of return from such growth companies than it does from mature, cash-generating 'value' firms. Of course, all these empirical results contradict the CAPM. The effects of size and 'value' are incorporated in a widely used empirical asset pricing model, the Fama–French three-factor model, that we shall look at in the next section. It should also be noted that the latest research in market efficiency, the next chapter's subject, seems to indicate that the size and value effects have diminished, or even disappeared, in more recent data sets.

Last but not least, Roll (1977) questions the testability of the CAPM in an article that has become known as Roll's critique. Recall that, in equilibrium, all investors hold the market portfolio that contains all risky assets. There is only one ex ante efficient market portfolio that uses the entire investment universe. This includes investments in human and venture capital, metals, vintage wines and collectors' items such as old masters' paintings and classic cars. Clearly, the true market portfolio is unobservable. In practice, samples from the investment universe are used, mainly stock market indices such as the Nasdaq-100 index or Standard & Poor's 500 index or local variants.[11] This leads to the so-called benchmark problem: the sample may be mean-variance efficient while the true market portfolio is not, or the other way around. However, if the sample is ex post mean variance efficient, then the mathematics of the model dictate that β's calculated relative to the sample will always satisfy the linear pricing relation in the CAPM, i.e. all assets will plot exactly on the SML. Hence, the only way to test the CAPM is to test whether the true market portfolio is mean variance efficient or not and that makes the CAPM untestable. In spite of its limitations, the CAPM still is a popular and widely used model, both in academia and in practice. It is predicted to remain a cornerstone in finance also in the 21th century (Levy, 2012).

3.4   Arbitrage pricing theory

Arbitrage pricing theory, or APT, was formulated by Ross (1976). It has certain similarities with the CAPM but it rests on different assumptions and on a different pricing mechanism.

3.4.1   A detour over index models

In the previous sections, portfolio risk is calculated using the whole variance-covariance matrix. For I assets, this requires the calculation of $\frac{1}{2}I(I-1)$ covariances and this gives practical problems for large I's. With ten assets the matrix contains forty five covariances but with 100 assets this is 4950. Moreover, the non-marked related covariances are often low or erratic. There is no strong reason to assume that an incidental good or bad return of

---

11 Standard & Poor's is a financial services company that, among other things, publishes stock indices; the S&P 500 includes 500 large companies on either the New York Stock Exchange or Nasdaq.

an oil company should affect the non-marked related return of e.g. a telecommunications company.

Single index models offer a practical way around the problem of large numbers of covariances by assuming that the *only* reason why assets covary is that they all respond to changes in the market as a whole. Different assets respond in different degrees, but assets do not respond to unsystematic (not marked related) changes in other assets' returns. This means that there are only two sources of return and variance: the market as a whole and asset-specific events. The market affects individual assets through their sensitivity coefficients β; an asset's sensitivity to its own asset-specific events is, of course, 1. Additionally, the single index model decomposes the asset-specific return in an expected part and an unexpected part or random disturbance term. The model can be formalized by writing the return on asset i as:

$$r_i = \alpha_i + \beta_i r_m + \varepsilon_i \qquad (3.15)$$

where r_i, r_m are the returns on asset i and the market, α is the expected value of the non-marked related return, β is the beta coefficient and ε is the random element of the non-marked related return. ε has an expectation of zero and a variance of σ_ε^2.

The single index model makes two assumptions about the covariance structure:

1. $cov(r_m, \varepsilon_i) = 0$: the random element of the non-marked related return of an asset is not correlated with the market return.
2. $cov(\varepsilon_i, \varepsilon_j) = 0$ for all $i \neq j$: the random elements of the non-marked related returns are uncorrelated.

The latter formalizes the assumption that assets only covary because they all respond to changes in the market as a whole. Since the disturbance term has zero expectation, the expected return on asset i is:

$$E(r_i) = \alpha_i + \beta_i E(r_m)$$

With these assumptions, a little algebra[12] shows that the variance and covariance of assets are:

$$\sigma_i^2 = \beta_i^2 \sigma_m^2 + \sigma_{\varepsilon i}^2 \qquad \sigma_{ij} = \beta_i \beta_j \sigma_m^2$$

which demonstrates that the covariances between assets are determined by their responses to changes in marked returns. To use the single index model we have to estimate, for each asset, the expected value of its non-marked related return α, its β and the variance of the unexpected part of its non-market related return σ_ε^2. We also have to estimate the market return and its variance, so for I assets in total 3I+2 estimates. With 100 assets, this makes 302, a substantial reduction from the 4950 for a full variance-covariance matrix. This drastically simplifies the analysis and management of large portfolios.

The single index model can also be looked upon as a *return generating process* that describes how the return on an asset is produced. In equation (3.15) the returns spring

---

12 By definition $\sigma_i^2 = E(r_i - E(r_i))^2$, substituting for r_i and $E(r_i)$ gives $\sigma_i^2 = E[(\alpha_i + \beta_i r_m + \varepsilon_i) - (\alpha_i + \beta_i E(r_m))]^2$. Rearranging and working out the square gives: $\sigma_i^2 = \beta_i^2 E(r_m - E(r_m))^2 + 2\beta_i E[\varepsilon_i(r_m - E(r_m))] + E(\varepsilon_i^2)$. The assumption of $cov(r_m, \varepsilon_i) = 0$ implies that the double cross terms are zero and since $E(\varepsilon_i) = 0$, $\sigma_{\varepsilon,i}^2 = E(\varepsilon_i^2)$. The covariance is derived in a similar way.

from one common factor, the market return, and an asset-specific factor. This return generating process is easily extended to more than one common index (or factor). For instance, we can split the market index into several industry indices: industrials, shipping, financial, etc. Alternatively, we can detail the developments in the market as a whole by distinguishing several general economic factors, such as the interest rate, inflation, the oil price, etc. With such a *multi-index model*, there are multiple common factors that determine the return of an asset so that the expression for asset returns becomes:

$$r_i = \alpha_i + b_{1i} F_1 + b_{2i} F_2 + ... + b_{Ki} F_K + \varepsilon_i \tag{3.16}$$

where b_{1i} is sensitivity of asset i for changes in factor F_1, comparable with the beta coefficient in the single index model. F_1 is the return on factor 1, etc. for K factors. As before, the disturbance term ε has an expectation of zero and a variance of σ_ε^2. The multi-index model's assumptions about the covariance structure are as follows:

- The factors are uncorrelated: $cov(F_m, F_k) = 0$ for all $m \neq k$.
- The residuals are uncorrelated with the factors: $cov(F_k, \varepsilon_i) = 0$.
- Residuals of different assets are uncorrelated: $cov(\varepsilon_i, \varepsilon_j) = 0$ for all $i \neq j$.

The first assumption is for convenience[13] rather than from necessity, the other two are as in the single index model. Arbitrage pricing theory builds on such a return generating process.

3.4.2   Arbitrage pricing theory

As the name suggests, Ross (1976) uses arbitrage arguments to derive a pricing relation from a multi-index return generating process as in (3.16). Arbitrage Pricing Theory (APT) does not rely on the assumption that investors maximize their utility by choosing investments based on their mean-variance characteristics. Instead, APT uses the absence of arbitrage opportunities as equilibrium condition. We shall first look at arbitrage strategies and then derive the theory.

Arbitrage strategies

Arbitrage is an investment strategy to profit from mispricing in markets. By buying what is too cheap or selling what is too expensive, an arbitrage strategy gives a profit without risk or investment. A simple example will illustrate the principle. Suppose gold costs $670 per ounce in New York and ¥80,000 per ounce in Tokyo. These prices imply an exchange rate of ¥119 for $1. If the exchange rate would be ¥115 per $1, this arbitrage opportunity would exist: buy gold in New York, which costs $670, sell gold in Tokyo, which gives ¥80,000, and then exchange ¥80,000 for $696, which gives $26 in riskless, instantaneous arbitrage profit. The strategy requires no investment because the same amount of gold is bought and sold and more dollars are received than paid. The strategy involves no risk because in modern markets all deals can be instantaneously and electronically executed at market prices. Obviously, such price inconsistencies cannot exist in well-functioning markets. Arbitrageurs would do the deals again and again with enormous amounts until the prices adjust and the arbitrage opportunity disappears.

---

[13] Correlated factors can always be converted into uncorrelated (orthogonal) factors by a linear transformation.

Modern portfolio theory

In a similar way, arbitrage can put certain restrictions on the pricing of future cash flows. Suppose security A pays off either €110 or €135 on some future date, depending on which state of the world occurs (say an interest rate increase or decrease). On the same date and in the same states, security B pays off €120 and €160 and security C €50 and €55. From this we can infer the following relation between the three security prices $P_{A,B,C}$: $P_A = \frac{1}{2}P_B + P_C$. We can replicate the cash flows from security A with a portfolio of $\frac{1}{2}$B+C, so the price of A *must* be the same as the price of the replicating portfolio. If the price of A is higher, the arbitrage strategy is to short sell A and use the proceeds to buy $\frac{1}{2}$B+C. The price difference is arbitrage profit. On the payoff date, $\frac{1}{2}$B+C produces exactly the same cash flow as A, so we can use the payoff from $\frac{1}{2}$B+C to meet the obligations from shorting A. Hence, the arbitrage strategy involves no net future payment. If the price of A is lower than $\frac{1}{2}$B+C, we reverse the positions: short sell $\frac{1}{2}$B+C and buy A. We can define an arbitrage strategy more formally and more precisely as a strategy that:

- either requires a non-positive net investment now (zero investment is possible), while all future payoffs are non-negative and at least one payoff is positive
- or requires a negative net investment now, while all future payoffs are non-negative (zero payoff is possible).

More popularly, and less precisely, an arbitrage strategy either costs nothing today and gives a payoff in the future, or it gives a payoff today without any obligations in the future. Either way, arbitrage opportunities are money machines that cannot exist in well-functioning markets. Arbitrage arguments are frequently used in finance, particularly in option pricing and, of course, in arbitrage pricing theory.

Derivation of APT

APT distinguishes between the *expected* part of an asset's return and the *unexpected* part. The unexpected part represents risk and consists of systematic (or market-related) risk and unsystematic (or idiosyncratic) risk. Given a multi-factor return generating process, market-related risk is expressed as a vector of sensitivities to a number of common factors. The derivation of the pricing relation starts with the multi-factor return generating process in (3.16):

$$r_i = \alpha_i + b_{1i}F_1 + b_{2i}F_2 + \ldots + b_{Ki}F_K + \varepsilon_i$$

Taking expectations we get:

$$E(r_i) = \alpha_i + b_{1i}E(F_1) + b_{2i}E(F_2) + \ldots + b_{Ki}E(F_K)$$

Subtracting the latter from the former gives:

$$r_i - E(r_i) = (\alpha_i + b_{1i}F_1 + . + b_{Ki}F_K + \varepsilon_i) - (\alpha_i + b_{1i}E(F_1) + . + b_{Ki}E(F_K))$$

Rewriting we get:

$$r_i = E(r_i) + \sum_{k=1}^{K} b_{ik}(F_k - E(F_k)) + \varepsilon_i \qquad (3.17)$$

where $E(r_i)$ is the expected return of asset i, b_{ik} is the sensitivity of asset i to factor k, F_k is the return of factor k and ε_i is the disturbance term as defined before. The two terms after $E(r_i)$ account for the 'error' part of the process that generates the deviations from the expected values. Note that the factor sensitivities refer to the unexpected part of the factor changes $F_k - E(F_k)$. The expected part of the factor change is included in the asset's expected return $E(r_i)$. The unexpected part has zero expectation: $E(F_k - E(F_k)) = 0$, as does the disturbance term ε_i. This gives the return generating process the character of a *fair game*, which means that in the long run the expectations are accurate.

If we make a portfolio of I assets, with weights x_i, the return on that portfolio is:

$$r_p = \sum_{i=1}^{I} x_i r_i$$

Substituting (3.17) gives:

$$r_p = \sum_{i=1}^{I} x_i E(r_i) + \sum_{i=1}^{I}\sum_{k=1}^{K} x_i b_{ik}(F_k - E(F_k)) + \sum_{i=1}^{I} x_i \varepsilon_i$$

In well-diversified portfolios the idiosyncratic risk in the last term will disappear.

The equilibrium condition in APT is the absence of arbitrage opportunities. The no-arbitrage condition can be formalized by stating that if a well-diversified portfolio is constructed:

1. That requires no net investment, i.e. the sum of the portfolio weights is zero: $\sum_i x_i = 0$.
2. That involves no risks, i.e. the weighted sum of all b_{ij} is zero: $\sum_i x_i b_{ik} = 0$ for all k; well diversified already implies that $\sum_i x_i \varepsilon_i$ is zero.
3. Then the expected return of that portfolio must be zero: $\sum_i x_i E(r_i) = 0$.

A positive or negative expected return would imply arbitrage opportunities. These no-arbitrage conditions can be interpreted as orthogonality conditions[14] from linear algebra:

1. $\sum_i x_i = 0$ means that the vector of weights is orthogonal to a vector of 1's (comparable to the intercept in linear regression).
2. $\sum_i x_i b_{ik} = 0$ means that the vector of weights is orthogonal to each of the vectors of sensitivities.
3. $\sum_i x_i E(r_i) = 0$ means that the vector of weights is orthogonal to the vector of expected returns.

This, in turn, means that the vector $E(r_i)$ can be written as a linear combination of the other two (i.e. a vector of 1's and the vector of sensitivities):

$$E(r_i) = \lambda_0 + \lambda_1 b_{1i} + \lambda_2 b_{2i} + \cdots + \lambda_k b_{ki}$$

The lambda's are simply coefficients in a linear equation, but they can be given economic meaning by constructing different portfolios that single out different lambda's. An obvious candidate is a risk free portfolio that, under the no-arbitrage condition, has an expected return equal to the risk-free interest rate and that has zero sensitivity to all factors, so all $b_k = 0$. This gives: $r_f = \lambda_0 + \lambda_1 0 + .. + \lambda_k 0$, which means $\lambda_0 = r_f$. In the

---

14 Two vectors are said to be orthogonal (perpendicular) to each other when their scalar product is zero.

same way, a *pure factor portfolio* can be constructed that has a sensitivity of 1 for factor 1 and zero value for all other b_k. Such a portfolio has an expected return equal to the expected return of factor 1: $E(F_1) = r_f + \lambda_1 1 + \lambda_1 0 + .. + \lambda_k 0 \Rightarrow \lambda_1 = E(F_1) - r_f$. Repeating this procedure for all factors gives the usual form of the APT as an equilibrium relation:

$$E(r_i) = r_f + \sum_{k=1}^{K} b_{ik}(E(F_k) - r_f) \tag{3.18}$$

As the structure of the arbitrage pricing relation suggests, the CAPM can be considered a special case of APT, where the only common factor is the expected return on the market portfolio. However, it should be clear by now that the two models come from very different backgrounds and rest on different assumptions.

3.4.3   An example

We will illustrate APT with an example of three well-diversified portfolios. The portfolios are priced to give the returns in Table 3.9, that also shows their sensitivities, $b_{1,2}$, to two factors. Portfolio returns are easily observable and the sensitivities could be obtained with a regression analysis, as will be explained in the next subsection.

Table 3.9 *Portfolios r and b*

	Portf.1	Portf.2	Portf.3
r_p	0.18	0.15	0.12
b_1	1.5	0.5	0.6
b_2	0.5	1.5	0.3

The portfolio returns are a function of the risk-free rate, the factor returns (risk premia) and the sensitivities. Given the portfolio returns and sensitivities, the risk-free rate and the factor returns are found by solving the three APT pricing relations $E(r_i) = \lambda_0 + \lambda_1 b_{i1} + \lambda_2 b_{i2}$ for the three unknowns lambda's:

$$.18 = \lambda_0 + \lambda_1 \times 1.5 + \lambda_2 \times 0.5$$
$$.15 = \lambda_0 + \lambda_1 \times 0.5 + \lambda_2 \times 1.5$$
$$.12 = \lambda_0 + \lambda_1 \times 0.6 + \lambda_2 \times 0.3$$

The solution is: $\lambda_0 = 0.075$, $\lambda_1 = 0.06$ and $\lambda_2 = 0.03$. So the equilibrium (i.e. arbitrage free) pricing relation is $E(r_i) = 0.075 + 0.06 b_{i1} + 0.03 b_{i2}$. This defines a return plane, or an arbitrage pricing plane, in two risk dimensions. All investments must lie on this plane, otherwise arbitrage opportunities exist. To illustrate this, suppose you make a portfolio with $b_1 = 0.75$ and $b_2 = 0.7$. Since the sensitivities are somewhere between P_1 and P_2, you decide to price it such that it offers a return of 0.16, because that is also somewhere between the returns of P_1 and P_2. The result will be that you quickly go bankrupt!

3.4 Arbitrage pricing theory

You offer the opportunity to construct[15] an arbitrage portfolio of $.2P_1 + .3P_2 + .5P_3$, which has:

- $b_1 = 0.2 \times 1.5 + 0.3 \times 0.5 + 0.5 \times 0.6 = 0.75$
- $b_2 = 0.2 \times 0.5 + 0.3 \times 1.5 + 0.5 \times 0.3 = 0.7$
- return of $0.2 \times 0.18 + 0.3 \times 0.15 + 0.5 \times 0.12 = 0.141$.

The arbitrage strategy is to buy what is cheap (your portfolio) and to sell what is expensive (arbitrage portfolio), as Table 3.10 shows.

Table 3.10 *Arbitrage strategy*

	Cfl. now	Cfl. later	b_1	b_2
buy your portfolio	−1	1.160	0.75	0.7
sell arbitrage portfolio	1	−1.141	−0.75	−0.7
net result	0	0.019	0.0	0.0

The 0.019 profit is risk free because the strategy has zero sensitivity to the risk factors.

3.4.4 Testing the APT

Tests of the APT are plagued by the same conceptual and econometric problems as tests of the CAPM. The model is formulated in expectations but has to be tested with observed realizations. An additional difficulty is that APT does not say which, or even how many, factors should be included. Within these limitations, tests of the APT can be performed with a two-pass regression procedure similar to the one used for the CAPM. Suppose we want to test a factor model that uses a number of industry indices, rather than one total market index. Then the first-pass regression is a time series analyses of each asset's risk premium on the industry indices' risk premia $I_{kt} - r_{ft}$:

$$r_{it} - r_{ft} = \widehat{\alpha}_i + \widehat{\beta}_{1i}(I_{1t} - r_{ft}) + \widehat{\beta}_{2i}(I_{2t} - r_{ft}) + .. + \widehat{\beta}_{Ki}(I_{Kt} - r_{ft}) + \widehat{\varepsilon}_{it}$$

The result could be called the 'characteristic hyperplane' analogous to the characteristic line in the CAPM. The estimated $\widehat{\beta}$ coefficients are the sensitivities. The $\widehat{\beta}$'s are used as explanatory variables in the second-pass, cross section regression in which the factor risk premia are estimated:

$$\overline{rp}_i = \gamma_0 + \gamma_1\widehat{\beta}_{1i} + \gamma_2\widehat{\beta}_{2i} + .. + \gamma_k\widehat{\beta}_{Ki} + \widehat{u}_i$$

where $\overline{rp}_i = \sum_T (r_{it} - r_{ft})/T$, asset i's average risk premium. APT predicts that the intercept γ_0 should be zero and the gammas should be equal to the averaged risk premia of the industry indices over the observation period: $\overline{I_1 - r_f}, \overline{I_2 - r_f}$, etc.

Industry indices are readily observable and they describe the market completely, i.e. the weighted industries' returns add up to the total market return. This makes the results easy to interpret: the estimated risk premia can be compared with the observed returns

---

15 The construction of this portfolio is included in the exercises.

of the indices. This is not the case if the factors are defined in terms of business characteristics, such as book-to-market value and price-earnings ratio, or general economic variables, such as inflation, productivity and the oil price. With these variables it is difficult (or impossible) to be complete, i.e. it is not clear how many factors should be used. Moreover, the results are less easy to interpret because there are no observed returns for these factors. In the absence of observed factor returns, directional predictions (i.e. returns will increase or decrease with a factor) are often resorted to. Another possibility is to construct factor portfolios and use their returns. That approach is followed in the well-known Fama–French three-factor model.

The empirical basis of Fama and French's (1993) three-factor model are long times series (1963–1991) of monthly returns of stocks on the three US stock exchanges.[16] These stocks are grouped into portfolios in various ways. The first way is according to size. In each year the stocks are ranked on size and split into two portfolios, one of small and one of big companies. For each month, the difference between the returns of the portfolios of small and big stocks (SMB, small minus big) is calculated. SMB is meant to mimic the risk premium of a size-related risk factor in returns. The second way of grouping is according to book-to-market value of equity. The stocks are assembled into three portfolios, one with high (top 30 per cent), one with medium (middle 40 per cent) and one with low (bottom 30 per cent) book-to-market values of equity. Again, for each month the difference between the returns of the portfolios of high and low book-to-market stocks (HML, high minus low) is calculated. HML is meant to mimic the risk premium of a book-to-market related risk factor in returns. Their construction makes these two portfolios almost pure factor portfolios, i.e. SMB is largely free of the influence of book-to-market equity and HML is largely free of the size factor in returns. The third factor represents the market as a whole and is measured as the return of a value weighted portfolio of all stocks minus the risk-free interest rate ($r_{mt} - r_{ft}$). The returns to be explained are those of 25 portfolios formed on size and book-to-market equity. The first-pass, time series regression estimates the portfolios' sensitivities (or factor loadings) for the three factor returns:

$$r_{it} - r_{ft} = \widehat{a}_i + \widehat{b}_i(r_{mt} - r_{ft}) + \widehat{s}_i SMB_t + \widehat{h}_i HML_t + \widehat{\varepsilon}_{it} \qquad (3.19)$$

where $\widehat{b}_i$, $\widehat{s}_i$ and $\widehat{h}_i$ are the sensitivities of portfolio i, $\widehat{\varepsilon}_{it}$ is the error term and $\widehat{a}_i$ is the intercept. Notice that SMB and HML already are risk premia (of small over large and high over low book-to-market) and, hence, are not taken in excess of the risk-free rate. The Fama–French three-factor model can then be formulated in expectations as:

$$E(r_i) - r_f = \widehat{a}_i + \widehat{b}_i[E(r_m) - r_f] + \widehat{s}_i E(SMB) + \widehat{h}_i E(HML) \qquad (3.20)$$

As we have just seen, APT predicts that the intercept in (3.20), $\widehat{a}_i$, should be zero and Fama and French (1993) find values close to zero in almost all cases. They also claim that the three-factor model in (3.20) explains much of the cross-sectional variation in average stock returns. The model is widely used to calculate expected returns of portfolios in situations where size and value effects can play a role. It should be noted, however, that later research (to be discussed in the next chapter) indicates that the model's relevance has diminished over time.

---

16 These are the New York Stock Exchange, American Stock Exchange and Nasdaq.

Instead of using characteristics of the business, industry or economy, factors can also be obtained with a statistical technique called factor analysis.[17] Consider a data matrix of T (t = 1, 2, ., T) returns for I (i = 1, 2, ., I) assets. It is always possible to completely describe the variance of the T returns with T new variables (the factors) which are linear combinations of the original variables (= returns):

$$F_1 = \alpha_{11}r_1 + \alpha_{12}r_2 + .. + \alpha_{1T}r_T$$
$$F_2 = \alpha_{21}r_1 + \alpha_{22}r_2 + .. + \alpha_{2T}r_T$$
$$.... \qquad .....$$
$$F_T = \alpha_{T1}r_1 + \alpha_{T2}r_2 + .. + \alpha_{TT}r_T$$

where F are the new factors, r are the returns and α are coefficients to be calculated. The rationale of the method lies in the way the factors are constructed (i.e. how the coefficients α are calculated). The most frequently used variant of factor analyses, called principal components analysis, constructs the first factor in such a way that it makes a maximal contribution to the sum of the variances of the T returns. The second factor is constructed such that it is orthogonal to the first and makes a maximal contribution to the remaining sum of the variances of the T returns, etc. In this way, the first few factors describe the bulk of the variance and the other factors can be omitted without much loss of information. Arguably, factors selected in this way are very close to the factor concept in APT.

A disadvantage of principal component analysis is that it is difficult to decide which factors should be included and which not. Nor does principal component analysis give any economic meaning to the factors; they are simply linear combinations of the original variables (i.e. returns). Factors can be interpreted by inspecting their correlations with characteristics of the business, industry or economy.

Like the CAPM, APT has been tested extensively; Roll and Ross (1980) and Chen *et al.* (1986) are among the most frequently cited publications. The former study uses factor analysis while the latter analyzes a number of macroeconomic factors. As we have seen, Fama and French's (1993) three-factor model defines factors by firm characteristics.

3.4.5 Underlying assumptions

APT is built on the assumption that asset returns are generated by a multi-factor process. The number of factors is not specified, but it has to be small relative to the number of assets, so that portfolios can be formed in which the idiosyncratic risk is completely diversified away.[18] APT relies on arbitrage to bring about equilibrium in the form of arbitrage-free prices. This requires markets to be perfect, for otherwise arbitrage would be hampered by market imperfections such as taxes or transaction costs. It also requires that market participants make use of arbitrage opportunities when they occur, which means that market participants have to be greedy (prefer more to less). It further requires that market participants 'see' the same opportunities, which implies that they

---

[17] Explanations of factor analysis can be found in most textbooks on financial econometrics, e.g. Tsay (2005). No longer modern but still very readable is Harman (1967).

[18] Strictly speaking, this implies that APT is only asymptotically valid as $\varepsilon \to 0$ and only for diversified portfolios. This reduces APT's testability, as has been pointed out in the literature.

have homogeneous expectations regarding asset returns and that they use the same factor model.

Clearly, the behavioural assumptions of APT are much weaker than those of the CAPM, which assumes that investors maximize their utility by choosing investments based on their mean-variance characteristics. Moreover, arbitrage concerns the prices of assets relative to each other and not relative to a market portfolio containing the entire investment universe. So APT 'works' on subsets of the investment universe, which makes the characteristics of the market portfolio irrelevant. All this underlines that APT is much more general than the CAPM. However, the price of this generality is paid in terms of precision. While the CAPM gives a clear measure and price of risk, APT gives neither. APT does not specify what or how many risk factors to use, nor what the risk premia on the factors are.

A) Calculating mean returns

A.1   The intuition: value and time weighted returns

Returns are often estimated from historical data and there is some controversy as to whether the arithmetic or the geometric average should be used for this. Both averages give different information on returns over time, except when the rate is constant. As we have seen, the geometric average, r_g, is the average compound return per period over the whole life of the investment: $r_g = \sqrt[T]{FV_T/PV} - 1$. This can also be written in terms of the rates per period r_t:

$$r_g = \sqrt[T]{\frac{FV_T}{FV_{T-1}} \times \frac{FV_{T-1}}{FV_{T-2}} \times .. \times \frac{FV_1}{PV}} - 1$$

$$= \sqrt[T]{(1 + r_T) \times (1 + r_{T-1}) \times .. \times (1 + r_1)} - 1$$

$$= \left(\prod_t (1 + r_t) \right)^{1/T} - 1$$

Because the geometric average is a compound return (it 'follows' an amount through time), it automatically becomes value weighted. The arithmetic average r_a, meanwhile, is time weighted. It gives the same weight to each period return, regardless of how much money was invested in that period. Hence, it can be interpreted as the return in an average period. It is calculated as the sum of the period returns divided by the number of periods:

$$r_a = \sum_t r_t/T$$

To illustrate the differences, consider a €100 investment that first doubles and then halves in value, so that the value after two periods is €100 again. The geometric average gives $\sqrt{(1 + 1)(1 - 0.5)} - 1 = 0$, which adequately describes the development from start to end value 'as if' the return was constant. The arithmetic average calculates a return of $(100 \text{ per cent} + (-50 \text{ per cent}))/2 = 25$ per cent, which obviously cannot be used to describe that development. The difference can be explained in two ways.

First, notice that the -50 per cent is realized over an amount twice as large as the amount that made $+100$ per cent. The same is true if the returns are made in the reverse order. This corresponds to a value weight of 2/3 (i.e. 200/(100+200)) for the -50 per cent return and a value weight of 1/3 for the $+100$ per cent return. The geometric average picks up these values weights, the arithmetic does not. In this example, calculating a weighted arithmetic average of the period returns gives the same result as the geometric average: $2/3 \times -50$ per cent $+ 1/3 \times 100$ per cent $= 0$, but generally that is not the case.

Second, we can write doubling and halving as an expected return of 25 per cent plus and minus a deviation of 75 per cent. In a more general notation this is $(1 + r) + \varepsilon$ and $(1+r) - \varepsilon$. The compound return over two periods is then $((1 + r) + \varepsilon) \times ((1 + r) - \varepsilon) = (1 + r)^2 - \varepsilon^2$ because the cross terms cancel out. In the example $1.25^2 - 0.75^2 = 1.5625 - 0.5625 = 1$. We see that return volatility reduces compound return. This idea is formalized in stochastic calculus, of which we shall see a glimpse later on in option pricing.

A.2   A forward looking example

A more elaborate numerical example is presented in Lattice 3A1. It gives a binomial tree of the possible values, V, over three periods of a €100 investment with a return rate of either $+50$ per cent or -25 per cent per period. Both returns are equally likely. The probabilities, p, geometric averages, r_g, and arithmetic averages, r_a, corresponding to the values are also included. The bottom line gives the expectations of the values and returns, calculated as the probability weighted sum of the possible values. For example, the expectation of the geometric average after two periods is $(0.25 \times 50) + (0.5 \times 6.1) + (0.25 \times -25) = 9.3$. The lattice illustrates a number of general characteristics of returns over time. First, when the return rates are constant, the geometric and arithmetic averages are the same. This is the case in all upper and lower nodes, including the nodes after one period.

Second, when the return rate fluctuates over time, the geometric average is always lower than the arithmetic.[19] This is the case in the three middle nodes (with V = 112.5, 168.75 and 84.38). Third, the expected geometric average decreases with time, even if the expected return is the same in each period and each node, as it is in Lattice 3A1. Since the expected arithmetic average is constant, the difference between the two expectations increases with time, as the bottom line of Lattice 3A1 shows. The difference also increases with the volatility of returns, but that is not shown.

Lattice 3A1 also shows what the proper discount rate is. That rate is usually referred to as the *opportunity cost of capital*, and it is the return that investors demand, and get, on investments with the same risk characteristics as the investment we are looking at. This rate includes a risk premium as well as the time value of money (and inflation, if any). Investors express their return demands in the price they are willing to pay for the investment. So if €100 is the proper market price now given the expected values in future periods, then the proper discount rate is the rate that connects present and expected

---

19 We can write the returns of $+50$ per cent or -25 per cent as an expected return of $+12.5$ per cent $\pm$ a deviation of 37.5 per cent. The first fluctuating compound return then becomes $1.125^2 - .375^2 = 1.125$. Repeating the procedure for the fluctuating compound returns in the other two middle nodes is possible, but there the cross terms do not cancel out and the process becomes messy.

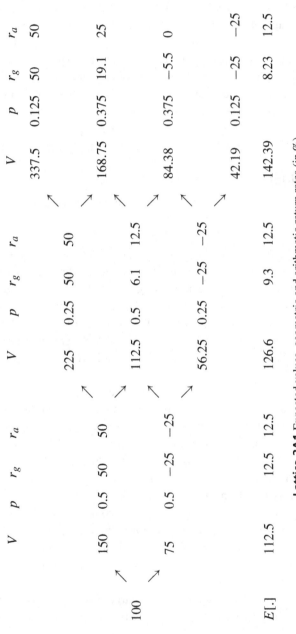

Lattice 3A1 Expected values, geometric and arithmetic return rates (in %)

future values: $PV = E[FV_T]/(1+r)^T$. Clearly, the rate that satisfies this equation for all periods is the arithmetic average rate of 12.5 per cent. The geometric average rate would understate the required return and overstate the value of the investment for all periods >1. So this answers the question which average should be used when return rates are calculated from time series of stock or index returns: the arithmetic average.

Conceptually, the opportunity costs of capital is a forward looking rate that reflects the required reward for risk. It is therefore independent of the 'history' of the investment. In the lattice example, the risk is expressed as a return of either $+50$ per cent or -25 per cent. That risk is the same in all nodes and periods, independent of the return that was realized in the previous period. So the opportunity cost of capital should also be the same in all nodes and periods. The rate that equates the expected value next period to the value now in all nodes is 12.5 per cent, the arithmetic average.

A more formal basis for using the arithmetic average is provided by probability theory. Suppose the continuously compounded, logarithmic returns per period on an asset are independently, identically and normally distributed with mean μ and variance σ^2. These are strong but not unusual assumptions. They mean that the expected return in each period $E[\ln(V_{t+1}/V_t)] = \mu$ where V is the asset's value. The iid assumption (independently and identically distributed) implies that cumulative return over T periods is also normally distributed with mean μT and variance $\sigma^2 T$. If the logreturns are normally distributed, then, by definition, the 'raw' returns (V_t/V_{t-1}) are lognormally distributed. By the properties of the lognormal distribution (see Aitchison and Brown, 1969) the expected return in each period $E[V_{t+1}/V_t] = e^{\mu+\frac{1}{2}\sigma^2}$ and the cumulative return over T periods is $E[V_{t+T}/V_t] = e^{(\mu+\frac{1}{2}\sigma^2)T}$. Since V_t is the known value today, we can write these as $E[V_{t+1}] = V_t e^{\mu+\frac{1}{2}\sigma^2}$ and $E[V_{t+T}] = V_t e^{(\mu+\frac{1}{2}\sigma^2)T}$. The return rate $\mu + \frac{1}{2}\sigma^2$ is the arithmetic average rate. So it can be concluded that an unbiased estimate of the asset's future value is found by compounding the present value forward at the arithmetic average rate of return.

However, the correctness of this conclusion depends on the assumptions that the returns are independently, identically and normally distributed (iid) and that the parameters of the distribution (expectation, variance) are known.[20] In practice, the iid assumption may not obtain. Moreover, the distribution's parameters usually are not known and have to be estimated, with error, from e.g. historical time series. If that is the case then the historical arithmetic average yields an upwardly biased estimate of the true return and more complex estimators have to be used. Such estimators, and a more thorough discussion of the matter, can be found in Blume (1974), Jacquier *et al.* (2003) and Cooper (1996).

Exercises

1. Mrs Pennymoney has invested 50 per cent of her money in a risk-free bank account and 50 per cent in an index fund that invests in all shares on the stock exchange. The risk-free interest rate is 5 per cent and the expected return on the market index is 15 per cent with a standard deviation of 20 per cent.

---

[20] For a large number of periods, normality may also follow from the central limit theorem.

(a) Is Mrs Pennymoney's portfolio mean-variance efficient?
(b) What is the expected return on the portfolio?
(c) What is the portfolio standard deviation?
(d) What is the portfolio β (relative to the market as a whole)?

2. Mr Poundmoney has invested 150 per cent of his money in an index fund that invests in all shares on the stock exchange. The risk-free interest rate is 5 per cent and all investors can borrow and lend unlimited amounts at this rate. The expected return on the market index is 15 per cent with a standard deviation of 20 per cent.
   (a) How can Mr Poundmoney invest more than 100 per cent of his money in the index fund?
   (b) Is Mr Poundmoney's portfolio mean-variance efficient?
   (c) What is the expected return on the portfolio?
   (d) What is the portfolio standard deviation?
   (e) What is the portfolio β (relative to the market as a whole)?

3. Ms Stonemoney has invested 50 per cent of her money in ADC (Aker Dissolution Company) and 50 per cent in NAC (Northern Aluminium Company). ADC has an expected return of 20 per cent and a standard deviation of 40 per cent and NAC has an expected return of 12.5 per cent and a standard deviation of 25 per cent. A statistical analysis of the returns in the dissolution and the aluminium industries over the period 2004–2007 (which was a period of stable growth) has shown that the two industries are statistically independent (i.e. uncorrelated – correlation coefficient is 0).
   (a) Is Ms Stonemoney's portfolio mean-variance efficient?
   (b) The correlation coefficient between the returns in the dissolution and the aluminium industries was measured over a period of stable growth. How does this correlation coefficient change in times of financial crises, such as the 2007–2008 credit crunch?
   (c) What is the expected return on the portfolio?
   (d) What is the portfolio standard deviation?

4. Suppose your financial newspaper of last Monday shows that the company with the highest β coefficient on your stock exchange was ZX Co. The company has a β of 2.1 and a market value of €4.25 billion (10^9). Assume that the company is financed only with equity, no debt, that the risk-free interest rate is 5 per cent and that the required rate of return of an appropriate index of all shares on the stock exchange is 15 per cent.
   (a) What is the required rate of return on ZX Co stocks?
   ZX Co's management proposes to raise €4.25 billion in additional equity capital and to invest this amount in risk-free government bonds. Ignoring taxes and transaction costs:
   (b) Calculate the required rate of return of ZX Co stocks after the proposed investment. What are the company's market value and its β coefficient?
   (c) What general phenomenon does this example illustrate?

5. Take another look at your uncle Bob's portfolio problem in Table 3.7.
   (a) Using the same setting as in the main text, where short sales are not allowed, what is the maximum return portfolio?
   (b) Do you see a practical way to find the efficient frontier?
   (c) The portfolio that maximizes return under the restriction that portfolio standard deviation is ≤ 0.25 consists of 0.02 Cisco, 0.36 Amazon and 0.62 Apple. Calculate, for each of these three stocks, its contribution to portfolio variance and its β relative to this three-stock portfolio. Check your results.

6. Download weekly closing prices over the last year of Microsoft (ticker: MSFT), Yahoo (YHOO) and the Nasdaq-100 index (NDX). Assuming an annual risk-free interest rate of 5.2 per cent and using the index as a proxy for the marked portfolio, calculate for each stock:
   (a) the characteristic line
   (b) the Sharpe ratio
   (c) the Treynor ratio
   (d) Jensen's alpha.

7. In the arbitrage example in the text (section 3.4.3) we had an arbitrage portfolio of $.2P_1 + .3P_2 + .5P_3$, but we did not say how the portfolio weights were obtained. The equilibrium (i.e. arbitrage-free) factor model (pricing relation) is $E(r_i) = .075 + .06b_{i1} + .03b_{i2}$ and the arbitrage portfolio's sensitivities to the two factors are .75 and .7.
   (a) Show how the portfolio weights are calculated.
   (b) A variation on the same theme: show the composition of the two pure factor portfolios.
   (c) Finally, just to make sure that you get the multi-factor concept, what are the risk and return of an equally weighted portfolio of the three portfolios P1–3 in Table 3.11? Check your return answer with an alternative calculation.

Table 3.11 *Portfolios r and b*

	Portf.1	Portf.2	Portf.3
r_p	.18	.15	.12
b_1	1.5	0.5	0.6
b_2	0.5	1.5	0.3

4 Market efficiency

In efficient markets prices change randomly. This is often misunderstood and can give rise to what Miller and Upton (2002) call the casino view of the stock market. In this view investors are gamblers whose buying and selling without apparent economic reason gives windfall profits to some and does random damage to others. The alleged casino nature of the stock market is often underlined by comparing graphs of stock price changes with graphs of random numbers, which are indistinguishable from each other. In this chapter we shall see that the opposite is true, that randomly changing prices are the hallmark of properly functioning markets. As we saw in Chapter 2, markets with properly organized price discovery processes aggregate all the information that buyers and sellers possess and that they reveal through their bidding and asking. As a result, prices in such markets will reflect all available information. By consequence, prices will only change if new information becomes available. But new information is random by nature, otherwise it would not be new. Hence, prices have to change randomly in efficient markets.

4.1　The concept of market efficiency

Market efficiency, or the *efficient market hypothesis*, is a deceptively simple concept. But its consequences are profound and not at all easy to understand or accept. We shall look at the concept from different angles and review some of the empirical evidence.

4.1.1　Why prices change randomly

We can introduce market efficiency by having another look at the calculation of economic depreciation in the second chapter. The relevant data of the example project are reproduced in Table 4.1. Recall from the description that the project's sales are highly cyclical, doubling from 125 in the first year to 250 in the second and then halving again to 125 in the third and last year. Also, a net working capital position is built up in the beginning and liquidated at the end of the project. As a result, the project's expected cash flows fluctuate strongly but, in spite of that, the expected return is constant. We can take the argument one step further and redo the analysis in terms of expected project values. To keep the scale of the project constant we assume that the cash flows that become available from the project can be reinvested at the same rate of 25 per cent, which is also the opportunity cost of capital. The calculations are as follows.

At the end of the first year the remaining project value is 184.6 and a cash flow of 72.5 becomes available. Together, this gives a project value of:

$$184.6 + 72.5 = 257.1$$

Table 4.1 *Economic depreciation of a project*

	year	0	1	2	3
1	Cash inflows from project		72.5	134	121
2	PV cash inflows, year end	205.7	184.6	96.8	0
3	PV cash inflows, year begin	0	205.7	184.6	96.8
4	Economic depreciation (2 − 3)	-	−21.1	−87.8	−96.8
5	Profit from project (1 + 4)	-	51.4	46.2	24.2
6	Return on investment (5/3)		.25	.25	.25

This is the same as the future value of the project's present value: $205.7 \times 1.25 = 257.1$. At the end of the second year the remaining project value is 96.8, a cash flow of 134 becomes available and the value of last year's reinvested cash flow is $72.5 \times 1.25 = 90.6$. Together, this is:

$$96.8 + 134 + 72.5 \times 1.25 = 321.4$$

the same as the future project value: $205.7 \times 1.25^2 = 321.4$. The same calculation applies to the final year where there is no remaining project value:

$$121 + (134 \times 1.25) + (72.5 \times 1.25^2) = 401.7$$

which equals $205.7 \times 1.25^3 = 401.7$. If we call the value of the project P we can summarize this 'present value in reverse' calculation as:

$$P_0 = \frac{E[P_t]}{(1+r)^t} \qquad (4.1)$$

for each of the three t's (t = 1, 2, 3) of the project's life. We see that the expected future values, with cash flows reinvested and properly discounted at the opportunity cost of capital, are constant and equal to the present value. The important point is that discounted future values are constant, even though the project's sales, cash flows and net working capital positions change drastically from year to year. However, all these changes are anticipated and properly accounted for, hence expected returns and future values are constants.

So what causes the project value and return to fluctuate randomly? That is the information *not* included in the calculation because it was unknown and could not be anticipated when we made the calculations. Sales figures can turn out higher or lower than our best estimates at t = 0 and so can costs, inflation, taxation, etc. If these developments are truly new information, which means that they could not be anticipated, then they are random by nature. Hence, as time passes, news arrives and prices and returns adjust to the new information, which means that they change randomly. This intuition had long been recognized in financial markets but it was first formulated in general terms in Samuelson's (1965) classic proof that properly anticipated prices fluctuate randomly.

4.1.2   Formalization and operationalization

The efficiency of markets refers to the way they incorporate information into prices, or *informational efficiency*, which is more general than mean-variance efficiency that we saw in portfolio theory. The most frequently used definition of market efficiency probably is Fama's (1970): a market in which prices always 'fully reflect' available information is called 'efficient'. This is a very general statement and it has to be made more precise to give it empirically testable content. Precision is obtained by defining what 'fully reflect' means and by specifying what the available information set contains.

Prices that fully reflect available information can be defined using the notion of excess return, which is the difference between the realized and the expected return:

$$\varepsilon_{i,t+1} = \frac{P_{i,t+1} - P_{i,t}}{P_{i,t}} - \frac{E[P_{i,t+1}|\Phi_t] - P_{i,t}}{P_{i,t}} = \frac{P_{i,t+1} - E[P_{i,t+1}|\Phi_t]}{P_{i,t}} \tag{4.2}$$

where ε is the excess return, P stands for price, Φ is the information set and i,t are subscripts for assets and time. Written in terms of returns the excess return is

$$\varepsilon_{i,t+1} = r_{i,t+1} - E[r_{i,t+1}|\Phi_t] \tag{4.3}$$

which corresponds to the two terms in the middle part of (4.2). The expected price or return can be the result of pricing models such as the CAPM or APT or any other model in which the information set Φ_t is fully utilized. However, if the latter is true, i.e. if the information set Φ_t is fully reflected in the expected price $E[P_{i,t+1}|\Phi_t]$, then it is impossible to use the same information set Φ_t to design trading systems or investment strategies that have expected excess returns larger than zero.

In practical terms this means that if Φ_t includes information about an extra return in t + 1, then that information will be reflected in P_t and not P_{t+1}. Using the project in the previous subsection as example again, suppose Φ_t contains the news that next year's project return will be 35 per cent instead of 25 per cent. Then the price now will immediately increase with the present value of the excess return, or $10/1.25 = 8$ per cent, so that the expected return over the next year remains the opportunity cost of capital of 25 per cent. Hence, $\varepsilon_t = .08$ and $E[\varepsilon_{t+1}|\Phi_t] = 0$. Reformulated as an old phrase: if one could be sure that a price will rise, it would have already risen.

With this definition of excess return, Fama (1970) formalizes (or models) market efficiency in three different ways:

1. Fair game model.
2. Martingale model.
3. Random walk model.

The *fair game* model directly specifies the expectation of the excess returns $\varepsilon_{i,t+1}$ regardless of the model that is used to produce expected prices or returns:

$$E[\varepsilon_{i,t+1}|\Phi_t] = 0 \tag{4.4}$$

This model says that in the long run the deviations from the expected returns are zero, which means that the information set Φ_t cannot be used to systematically generate positive excess returns. We have met the fair game model before in the 'error part' of the return generating process in APT. Note that a game can also be fair if the expected return is negative; fairness only requires the expectations to be unbiased. Gambling games such as roulette and lotteries have, in fact, negative expected returns.

The *martingale model* specifies the expectation of excess returns by modelling the time series properties of returns or prices. If all information regarding an asset is already reflected in its current price, as we have just seen, then the expected future price must be the present price times the expected return:

$$E[P_{i,t+1} | \Phi_t] = P_{i,t}(1 + E[r_{i,t+1} | \Phi_t]) \quad \text{or:}$$

$$E[P_{i,t+1} | \Phi_t]/(1 + E[r_{i,t+1} | \Phi_t]) = P_{i,t} \tag{4.5}$$

which is the same as (4.1) in expanded notation. It means that the expected future price, properly discounted, is equal to the current price, which makes it a *martingale*. Formally, a variable is said to follow a dynamic process called a martingale with respect to Φ if the conditional expected future value of that variable, given information sequence Φ, is equal to its current value. Note that the expected price is not a martingale, but the properly discounted expected price. The price itself is expected to increase with the expected return and is, thus, a submartingale.[1] By specifying the expected asset price or return, the martingale model indirectly specifies the expected excess return to be zero.

The fair game and martingale model of market efficiency only consider the expectation (first moment) of the excess profits. A more strict formalization of market efficiency is the *random walk* model, that specifies the entire distribution of excess returns. Successive price changes are said to follow a random walk if they are independently and identically distributed (iid), which includes all moments of the distribution. Random walks have the *Markov property* of memorylessness (so Alzheimer property could be a better name for it).[2] In economic terms, this means that past returns and patterns in past returns cannot be used to predict future returns. The random walk model requires the expected return to be constant and the excess return ε_{t+1} not only to have zero expectation but also to have identical variance and higher moments in each future period, i.e. the probability density function $f(\varepsilon_{t+1})$ must be the same for all t. The expected return is called the *drift* of the random walk.

Having defined what 'fully reflected' means, Fama (1970) then specifies the contents of the available information set in three overlapping categories. Together, they give the following, widely used taxonomy of market efficiency:

- *Weak form* market efficiency occurs when all past price histories are fully reflected in current prices.
- Under the *semi-strong form* of market efficiency current prices fully reflect all publicly available information; in addition to price histories this includes financial statements, articles in the (financial) press, product-, industry- and macroeconomic data, etc.
- A market is *strong form* efficient if all information is reflected in current prices, including private and inside information.

Obviously, strong form efficiency implies also semi-strong form efficiency which, in turn, implies weak form efficiency.

----

1 Martingales are usually defined with respect to their observation history. A variable follows a martingale if the conditional expected future value of that variable, given all past values, is equal to its current value. Formally: X is a martingale if $E(X_{t+1} | X_0, ...X_t) = X_t$. Similarly, X is a submartingale if $E(X_{t+1} | X_0, ...X_t) > X_t$ and X is a supermartingale if $E(X_{t+1} | X_0, ...X_t) < X_t$.

2 A dynamic process has the Markov property if the conditional probability distribution of future states of the process only depends upon the current state, i.e. it is independent of the past states (the path of the process to the present state).

4.1.3 Empirical implications

With these specifications, market efficiency yields a number of testable predictions. The common denominator of these predictions is that in efficient markets returns cannot be systematically increased without also systematically increasing risk. This means that it is impossible to systematically earn excess returns or, popularly summarized, efficient markets offer no 'free lunch'. The predictions can be grouped in the following four categories, which are based on Haugen (1990):

1. There should be no autocorrelation in excess returns.
2. Investment strategies that are based on historical information should not consistently give positive excess returns.
3. Differences in excess returns between investment funds and (groups of) investors should be caused by chance and, hence, not be persistent.
4. Security prices should adjust to new information in an efficient way, i.e. quickly and without bias.

Autocorrelation (or serial correlation) is the correlation of return with itself one or more periods back: $corr(r_t, r_{t-x})$ where $x = 1, 2,..$ etc. It is a formal expression of the idea that the excess return in this period says nothing about the return next period. As we have seen with the example project in the beginning of the chapter, all predictable cyclical movements in costs and revenues, etc. are already included in properly anticipated prices. What remains are the responses to new (random) information, which are uncorrelated by nature. Technically, the absence of autocorrelation in excess returns follows directly from the definition of a random walk: independently distributed means no autocorrelation. The fair game and martingale model imply the absence of autocorrelation in the deviations from expected returns (i.e. in excess returns) but the expected returns themselves can be autocorrelated.

Many investment strategies are based on the idea that future returns can be predicted using information from the past. These strategies assume some regularity or recognizable patterns in prices and returns. Some strategies predict that price movements will persist (have 'momentum'), others that they will reverse (contrarian) while still others base their predictions on patterns in prices plotted in graphs (chartists). The latter are printed on a daily basis in financial newspapers all around the world and are spread on an enormous scale. Yet if markets are efficient, all these strategies fail to consistently produce positive excess returns.

Selecting and managing a well-diversified portfolio requires some time and skills, and many investors prefer to outsource these activities to professionals. These services are provided by a large variety of mutual funds. Different types of funds operate under different restrictions and have different purposes, resulting in different investment strategies. Actively managed funds aim to outperform the market as a whole by using the expertise of the fund's management, while passively managed funds seek to follow a market as closely as possible without the purpose of performing better. Similarly, some mutual funds may focus on long-term value increase and choose a risky portfolio, while pension funds that have to pay pensions every month probably prefer a more conservative strategy. If markets are efficient, differences in risk-adjusted performance between such funds should be random, i.e. no fund should be able to systematically earn positive excess returns.

Finally, if new information becomes available, the response in prices should be quick and unbiased. There should be no predictable pattern after the news event that could be exploited by investors. Some possible patterns are schematically drawn in Figure 4.1. The solid line depicts an efficient response to bad news: the price drops instantaneously to its new level. The upper dashed line shows *underreaction*: a slow reaction that takes several periods to materialize. The lower dashed line depicts an *overreaction* that is followed by a correction. If prices would systematically under- or overreact, one of the dashed patterns would occur and the market would be inefficient. In efficient markets, however, investors would exploit such patterns and their trading would eliminate them. For instance, if investors would recognize a systematic slow reaction to bad news, they would short sell the security involved. This would drive the price down until it reaches the correct level. Similarly, if systematic overreaction could be recognized, investors would buy the security involved. This would drive the price up until the investment opportunity (free lunch) disappears.

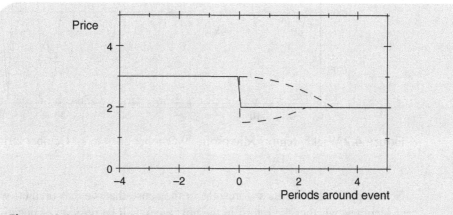

Figure 4.1 Efficient and inefficient price adjustments

4.2 Empirical evidence

In this section we will review some of the empirical evidence on market efficiency and the methods used to obtain it. Where feasible, the methods are illustrated with home-made tests using short time series of a few stocks. We will discuss the evidence using a less strict version of efficiency, by investigating whether information can be used to make excess profits that are adjusted for risk and net of all costs. This is necessary because, as Grossman and Stiglitz (1980) have argued, market efficiency in its strictest sense is impossible since it requires zero trading and information costs (i.e. the costs that have to be incurred to make prices reflect all information). In real life these costs exist so we have to use a version of market efficiency that takes them into account. Over the years, an enormous amount of research has been devoted to testing the efficient market hypothesis, so we can only cover some headlines of the evidence. However, we will first illustrate the possible rewards to the foresight that security analysis seeks to provide.

4.2.1 The value of foresight

Figure 4.2 shows the weekly returns of Microsoft stocks over an arbitrary period of fifty-one weeks (roughly the same period that we used in the previous chapter). The arithmetic average of these returns is 0.002358 or 0.2358 per cent per week, which makes $1.002358^{51} = 1.1276$ or 12.8 per cent over the whole period. These are good, but not exceptional returns of an ordinary stock in an ordinary period.

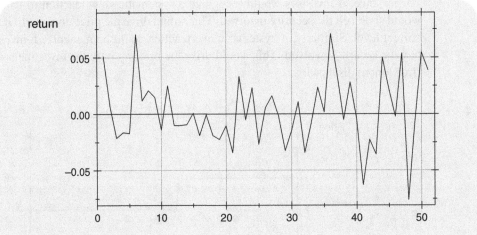

Figure 4.2 Weekly returns Microsoft, 29 October 2010 to 14 October 2011

Now suppose that we have foresight in the sense that we can predict, with 100 per cent accuracy, whether the return in the next week will be positive or negative. Suppose further that we can only use this information to avoid weeks with negative returns. If we own the stock, we sell it just before a week with a negative return and if we do not own the stock, we buy it just before a week with a positive return. If we sell the stock the money is kept in an account that pays no interest. The effect of this strategy is that weeks with negative returns are replaced by weeks with zero returns. However, given the returns pattern in Figure 4.2, we have to sell the stock and buy it back again around ten times during the period. The effect of this very simple strategy on return would be dramatic: the arithmetic average return of this strategy is 1.3049 per cent per week, which is $1.013049^{51} = 1.9371$ or 93.71 per cent over the whole period. Even with very high transaction costs this strategy would still be extremely profitable. The returns could be increased considerably by implementing a similar strategy for short selling during weeks with negative returns.

This example illustrates that the rewards of foresight are so large that even models or trading rules with far less than 100 per cent accuracy can still be profitable. An investment fund manager who can realize only a very small excess return over a number of years can quickly earn many millions for the fund. That is why financial markets around the world are researched and analyzed on such an enormous scale.[3] By consequence, it is to be expected that excess returns are hard to find, and an entire industry is looking for them.

4.2.2 Autocorrelation in returns

An easy way to visualize autocorrelation is to plot the returns in one period against those in the next. This is done in Figure 4.3 for the same five stocks that we used in the previous chapter, plus the Nasdaq-100 index (ticker: NDX). Daily returns over the period 21 October 2010 to 19 October 2011 are used. This makes it safe to assume that (changes in) expected returns can be ignored. If a stock is expected to generate e.g. 20 per cent return per year and a year has 250 trading days, then the expected return per day is $20/250 \approx 0.08$ per cent, negligibly small compared with the observed daily returns. Similarly, a firm can increase the expected return on its stock by increasing risk or leverage over time but that, too, will be negligible on a daily basis.[4] If the returns in Figure 4.3 were positively autocorrelated, positive returns would tend to be followed by positive ones and negative returns by negative ones. The observations would then be clustered in the upper right and lower left quadrants. With negative autocorrelation, positive returns would be followed by negative ones and vice versa, so that the observations would be clustered in the upper left and lower right quadrants. Since neither pattern is discernible, Figure 4.3 shows no autocorrelation. Graphs like these have been produced in large numbers, often using much longer time series than one year. Basically, they all look like Figure 4.3 and show no autocorrelation.

A more precise way to test for autocorrelation is to calculate the correlation coefficient between returns today and yesterday or, equivalently, run a regression analysis of the returns today against the returns yesterday. The autocorrelation coefficients of our example stocks and index are listed in Table 4.2. They are all low, and none of them is statistically significant. The square of the correlation coefficient measures the proportion of the variance of today's return that is explained by yesterday's return. Even for the highest coefficient this is less than 0.5 per cent: $-0.056^2 = 0.003136$.

Table 4.3 shows the estimated coefficients, γ, of a regression in which the return today is explained by the returns from one to five days back:

$$r_t = \gamma_0 + \gamma_1 r_{t-1} + \gamma_2 r_{t-2} + \gamma_3 r_{t-3} + \gamma_4 r_{t-4} + \gamma_5 r_{t-5} + u_t$$

The coefficients are low and only two of them are significantly different from zero (those for r_{t-5} of Cisco and r_{t-3} of NDX). These two contradict the efficient market hypothesis but it is doubtful whether this result persists in other periods and is large enough to be exploitable. The proportion of variance in today's return that is explained by the regression (measured by the R^2 statistic) is lower than 10 per cent.

Correlations and regressions such as the above have been estimated for a wide variety of stocks and indices and the results are comparable to those in Tables 4.2 and 4.3.

----

[3] For example, the CFA Institute, the professional organization of Certified Financial Analysts, has >100,000 members, almost 90,000 of which are charterholders (www.cfainstitute.org).

[4] We will look at the relation between stock returns and leverage (proportion of debt in total capital) later on.

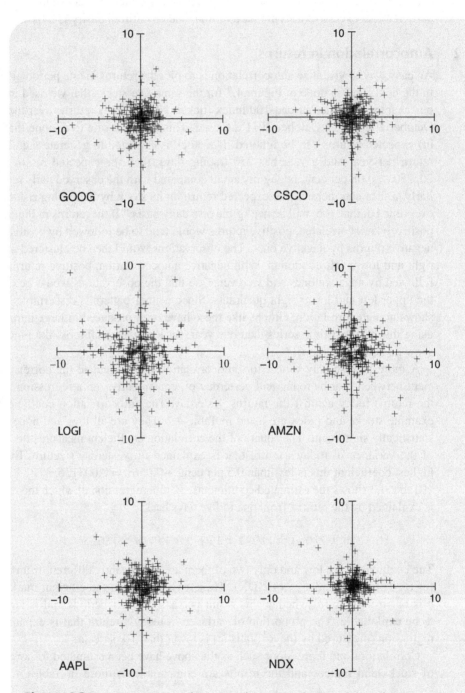

Figure 4.3 Percentage return day t (x-axis) versus day t + 1 (y-axis)

4.2 Empirical evidence

Table 4.2 *Autocorrelation coefficients*

Stock	ticker	$\rho_{r_t, r_{t-1}}$
Google	GOOG	−0.038
Cisco Systems	CSCO	0.019
Logitech International	LOGI	−0.032
Amazon.com	AMZN	−0.028
Apple	AAPL	0.026
NDX index	NDX	−0.056

Table 4.3 *Coefficients of time series regression, five lags*

Stock	γ_0 constant	γ_1 r_{t-1}	γ_2 r_{t-2}	γ_3 r_{t-3}	γ_4 r_{t-4}	γ_5 r_{t-5}	R^2
Google	−0.062	−0.018	0.082	−0.091	0.071	−0.089	0.037
Cisco Systems	−0.145	0.026	0.009	−0.074	−0.015	−0.20*	0.049
Logitech Int.	−0.290	−0.001	0.096	−0.090	0.011	0.032	0.018
Amazon.com	0.167	−0.013	0.064	−0.055	0.022	−0.075	0.015
Apple	0.101	0.032	0.100	−0.119	0.039	−0.100	0.043
NDX index	0.035	0.016	0.075	−0.20*	0.082	−0.118	0.084

*significantly $\neq 0$ (5% level, two-tailed test)

Granger (1972) compiled an overview of published correlations, which was later extended by Elton *et al.* (2007). The overview shows that the average coefficients are low and that positive and negative coefficients occur in roughly equal proportions. Although a number of the coefficients are statistically significant (both positive and negative ones), the past returns typically explain only a very small proportion of the variance in today's return. More international evidence of similar nature is presented in Poterba and Summers (1988), who analyze data from the United States and seventeen other countries. They find positive serial correlation in stock returns over short periods and negative correlation over longer intervals, but random walk price behaviour cannot be rejected at conventional statistical levels. Using a variance ratio test, Lee (1992) finds that the random walk model is the appropriate characterization of the weekly returns in eight of the ten industrial countries investigated. More recently, Narayan and Smyth (2005) used a sophisticated procedure to test the randomness of stock prices for a sample of twenty-two OECD countries and report strong support for the random walk hypothesis. These few examples may suffice to illustrate that the bulk of this evidence does not reject the efficient market hypothesis; if deviations from efficiency are found they are too small to be exploitable.

A third way to test for randomness in returns is to look at the order in which positive and negative returns occur over time. Suppose we toss a fair coin twenty times. Then it is highly unlikely that we first get ten times heads and then ten times tails. It is also highly unlikely that we get the sequence heads-tails ten times in a row. If we call a series of the same outcomes a *run*, then the first series of tosses has only two runs: HHH-HHHHHHHTTTTTTTTT, too few to be random. The second series has twenty runs: HTHTHTHTHTHTHTHTHTHT, too many to be random. The sampling distribution of the number of runs we can expect from random samples is known.[5] This allows us to test whether a given series has more or fewer runs than randomness predicts. That is what the so-called runs test does. Note that this test is based on the order in which observations occur, which is not reflected in their frequency. In the tossing examples heads and tails occur equally often, precisely what could be expected from a fair coin. Runs tests for our example stocks and index are reported in Table 4.4. Each test is based on 252 returns and no test shows a significant deviation from randomness. Since runs tests use the same data as autocorrelation analysis, they are often performed in combination with each other. The overview in Elton *et al.* (2007) mentions that the typical results show a small positive relationship between successive returns for one-day intervals. For longer intervals the deviations from randomness are barely perceptible.

Table 4.4 *Runs tests*

Stock	runs	Z	P(Z)
Google	118	−1.136	0.256
Cisco Systems	127	0.001	0.999
Logitech Int.	120	−0.884	0.377
Amazon.com	122	−0.631	0.528
Apple	121	−0.757	0.449
NDX index	120	−0.884	0.377

Taken as a whole, then, the vast majority of autocorrelations and runs tests do not reject randomness. Like the small-scale tests with our example stocks, they produce some evidence of relationships between returns over time, but these relationships are too weak to be exploitable in a trading strategy. Based on this evidence, we cannot reject the weak form of the efficient market hypothesis.

4.2.3   Tests of investment strategies

Many investment strategies try to reap some of the benefits of foresight by using historical price and other information in a more sophisticated way than correlations and runs. We shall have a brief look at some of them and summarize the empirical evidence.

Filter rules

Filter rules assume that there is a bandwidth of +x per cent and −x per cent around security prices within which price changes have no information value. As long as the price of a security changes with less than x per cent there is no reason to trade. However,

---

5 For small numbers of observations (≤ 20) the critical values of the distribution are tabled. For larger numbers the normal distribution can be used after transforming the number of runs r into a standard normal variable: $Z = (r - \mu_r)/\sigma_r$, where μ_r and σ_r are the mean and standard deviation of the number of runs. Formulas for μ_r and σ_r can be found in the literature (see Siegel, 1956).

when important new information arrives prices will have to find a 'new level'. The signal that this is about to happen is a price change of more than x per cent. Buying when the price goes up and selling when the price goes down should allow investors to participate in a security's major price trends without being misled by small fluctuations. Thus, filter rules are timing strategies that assume delayed reactions to new information. Technically, an x per cent filter rule prescribes that if the price of a security increases with at least x per cent the security should be bought and held until its price decreases with at least x per cent; then the security should be sold and sold short.

Filter rules are tested extensively in a pioneering paper by Fama and Blume (1966), who analyze long series of daily closing prices of each of the thirty stocks in the Dow-Jones Industrial Average.[6] They apply twenty-four different filter rules (i.e. sizes of x) ranging from 0.5 per cent to 50 per cent and calculate annual returns, adjusted for dividends but not for transaction costs, for both the filter rule and a buy-and-hold strategy. The latter consists of buying the stock and holding it for the entire period without any buying or selling. Comparing the results of these two strategies is the obvious way to test whether the trades suggested by filter rules produce additional returns. Averaged over the thirty stocks, the only filter rule that outperforms the buy-and-hold strategy is the smallest filter size of 0.5 per cent and the extra return is only 1.1 per cent (11.5 per cent versus 10.4 per cent). Even small transaction costs make this filter rule unprofitable. Averaged over the twenty-four filter sizes, only four of the thirty stocks show positive average returns when transaction costs are taken into account. These results are strong indications that filter rules cannot outperform a buy-and-hold strategy when dividends and transaction costs are taken into account.

Fama and Blume's (1966) results are reviewed by Sweeney (1988), who noticed that fifteen of the original thirty securities seem to offer potential profits for a 0.5 per cent filter rule. Using data of a later period he analyzes the remaining fourteen of those fifteen stocks. He concludes that a money manager, who can reduce transaction costs to one fifth of 1 per cent, can earn excess returns with this rule on an equally weighted portfolio of these fourteen stocks. However, the profits are a bit under 2 per cent per year, which is borderline significant. At commercial transaction costs rates, implementation of the filter rule would have been quite expensive. Using a much larger sample of 120 Dow-Jones and S&P 100 stocks, Corrado and Lee (1992) find that equally weighted portfolios of filter-rule-traded stocks consistently outperform a buy-and-hold portfolio of the same stocks before accounting for transaction costs. However, the difference in returns between filter rule and buy-and-hold portfolios is eliminated by one-way transaction costs of only 0.12 per cent. Similar results are obtained by Szakmary *et al.* (1999), who analyze 149 stocks listed on the Nasdaq stock exchange. Trading rules that are based on a stock's past price history perform poorly but those that use the overall Nasdaq market index appear to earn excess returns. But as in the other studies, the high transaction costs for the stock involved probably outweigh the excess returns.

Filter rules are sometimes extended to include not only changes in price, but also the volume of trade. However, while some predict that price changes that are accompanied by

---

6 The Dow-Jones Industrial Average is an often used stock market index; it measures the average price development of 30 large industrial corporations in the United States.

high trade volumes will tend to reverse (Campbell *et al.*, 1993), others predict that such changes will tend to continue (Wang, 1994). So in spite of the occasional contradictory results (e.g. Cooper, 1999), there is, in sum, little empirical evidence to suggest that filter rules can systematically earn excess profits.

Momentum and contrarian strategies

Momentum strategies are based on underreaction: they assume that once prices move in a certain direction (up or down), they will continue to move in that direction (or have 'momentum'). Trading strategies based on that assumption can be summarized as 'buying past winners and selling past losers'. Contrarian strategies, on the other hand, are based on overreaction: they assume that price movements will not continue but reverse. The corresponding trading strategy is 'buying past losers and selling past winners'. A common way to implement both strategies is to sort securities on their past performance in a sorting period and use the results to select (portfolios of) securities to be held or sold in the subsequent holding period. Contrarian strategies buy the losers, i.e. worst performing decile or quartile of the securities, and short the corresponding winners. Momentum strategies short the losers and buy the winners.

From this mere description it will be clear that both strategies cannot possibly be profitable in the same circumstances. The literature provides three reasons for the coexistence of these diametrically opposed strategies. The most controversial reason is suggested by authors such as Connolly and Stivers (2003) and Lee and Swaminathan (2000), who relate the price effect to the volume of trading. However, these two studies partly contradict each other regarding the nature of the relation (positive or negative), similar to what we just have seen in filter rules. Alternatively, Jegadeesh and Titman (1995) link the reaction to the nature of the information: stock prices underreact to common factors that affect all stocks but overreact to firm-specific information. So far, their results have not been corroborated on a wider scale. The third and most frequently mentioned reason is that both effects operate on different time scales, although there is disagreement on what those scales exactly are. Contrarian strategies are said to be profitable for very long sorting and holding periods of 3–5 years, while momentum strategies appear to work on shorter time scales. However, both momentum and contrarian effects are reported for sorting and holding periods that are measured in weeks and months, as the small sample of studies in Table 4.5 shows.

Additionally, there is a growing number of studies that explain momentum or contrarian profits by omitted or inadequately represented variables. Size is an obvious variable in this context, since empirical tests of the CAPM showed that smaller firms tend to generate higher returns. Zarowin (1990) re-examines de Bondt and Thaler's (1985) pioneering contrarian study and concludes that the size effect in performance accounts for losers' superior performance over winners. When past losers are smaller than past winners, losers outperform winners; when past winners are smaller than past losers, winners outperform losers. Ball and Kothari (1989) take a closer look at the risk of investment strategies. They use the CAPM and annual returns over five-year sorting and holding periods to distinguish between expected and excess returns, i.e. between $E[r_{i,t+1}|\Phi_t]$ and $\varepsilon_{i,t+1}$ in (4.3). If negative serial correlation in returns is due to mispricing, then both realized, total returns ($r_{i,t+1}$) and excess returns ($\varepsilon_{i,t+1}$) can be autocorrelated. If it is due

Table 4.5 *Return horizons of momentum and contrarian strategies*

	Contrarian	Momentum
de Bondt and Thaler (1985, 1987)	3–5 years	
Lo and MacKinlay (1988)		weekly
Zarowin (1990)	3 years	
Lehmann (1990)	weekly	
Jegadeesh (1990)	monthly	12 months
Chopra *et al.* (1992)	5 years	
Jegadeesh and Titman (1993)		3–12 months
Rouwenhorst (1998)		3–12 months
Chan *et al.* (2000)		1–26 weeks
Lee and Swaminathan (2000)	2–5 years*	3–12 months*
Connolly and Stivers (2003)	weekly*	weekly*

*= effect depends on trade volume

to relative risk changes, then $E[r_{i,t+1}| \Phi_t]$ will capture the time series variation so that the correctly risk-adjusted excess returns ($\varepsilon_{i,t+1}$) will not show time dependence. Their evidence suggests that the negative serial correlation in five-year returns is almost entirely caused by variations in relative risks and, therefore, expected relative returns, and not by stock market mispricing. Bulkley and Nawosah (2009) sidestep the problem of choosing a specific model to price risk and use the full sample mean return on each stock to measure unconditional expected returns. They then apply conventional momentum tests to the 'demeaned' returns, i.e. returns minus mean returns, and find that there is no evidence for momentum in the series of demeaned returns. This attributes momentum profits to the cross-sectional variation in expected stock returns, and not to momentum effects. However, Bhootra (2011) contests this conclusion. His analysis shows that the absence of momentum in unexpected returns is primarily attributable to the inclusion of so-called penny stocks in the sample. These stocks are priced at less than $5 and are very illiquid, which makes it difficult to short them. They represent only a small fraction of the sample by market capitalization but make up more than half of the loser portfolio. The exclusion of penny stocks results in a statistically significant and economically meaningful momentum payoff of 0.93 per cent per month. Finally, Chordia and Shivakumar (2002) identify a small set of lagged macroeconomic variables (mainly interest rates) that can explain the profits to momentum strategies. The momentum profits disappear once stock returns are adjusted for their predictability based on these macroeconomic variables.

Other studies analyze how the results of investment strategies are affected by practical aspects of trading stocks on an exchange. Bid-ask spreads and other transaction costs, such as brokers' commissions, are among these aspects. Recall from Chapter 2 that dealers quote ask prices, at which they are willing to sell securities, and (lower) bid prices, at which they are willing to buy. The difference between the two, the bid-ask spread, is income for the dealer and the size of the spread reflects the liquidity of the security. Conrad and Gultekin (1997) analyze the consequences of the bid-ask bounce, i.e. the fact that recorded closing prices may jump from bid to ask prices or vice versa. This creates spurious price changes when prices are, in fact, stable. They demonstrate that a predominant part of the profits from the investigated short-term price reversals is not due to market overreaction, but caused by negative serial covariance induced by bid-ask errors in transaction prices. Lesmond *et al.* (2004) draw a comparable conclusion in their review of momentum strategies. They find that previous studies underestimate trading costs because momentum returns are generated by frequent trading of stocks with disproportionally high trading costs. When transaction costs are properly accounted for, the returns of these strategies do not exceed trading costs.

What can we conclude about momentum and contrarian strategies from these few studies and the multitude of others that have been published? Based on the evidence we cannot confidently predict whether the next period will show contrarian or momentum returns, both appear to be equally likely over short to medium-term horizons. Fama (1998) reaches the same conclusion for long horizons: overreaction is about as common as underreaction and the continuation of returns is about as frequent as their reversal. All this underlines the random nature of price changes. Moreover, if we could identify either type of excess return, we could not be sure whether it is genuine excess return or the fair risk premium for some omitted effect such as size, varying risk or a higher transaction cost. It is hard to see how this contradictory evidence rejects market efficiency, although the enormous amount of empirical research documenting either momentum or contrarian effects, or both, remains puzzling.

Technical analysis

Technical analysis, or 'charting', goes back to the writings of Dow, which were published more than a century ago.[7] It primarily bases its predictions of future prices on perceived regularities or recognizable patterns in plotted past prices. Other data can be used in addition, such as trade volumes and surveys that measure consumer confidence or investor sentiment. The basic assumption of technical analysis is that the same patterns will recur because investors learn from experience. For example, if the price of a security increased more than once to some arbitrary level, say €17.60, then investors will conclude that it is unlikely to increase beyond that level. Hence, every investor who wants to sell the security will do so when the price once again is €17.60. This makes that price a 'resistance' level that will not be surpassed unless some significant 'break-out' event occurs. Similarly, if the price of a security bounced back from some low level more than once, this will become the 'support' level. Resistance and support levels can be functions of time; they are found by drawing lines that connect peaks and troughs in a chart of security prices. Figure 4.4 gives a home-made example using data of the Nasdaq-100 index, with the resistance line and support line drawn in. A common chartists' interpretation would be that the penetration (breaking out) of a resistance line is a buying signal and the penetration of a support line is a selling signal. In its most elaborate form, technical analysis distinguishes between a long-term primary trend, an intermediate term trend and short-term movements. In addition to trends, support and resistance lines, chartists also recognize specific patterns such as 'head and shoulders' (complete with 'neckline'), 'rounding bottoms' and 'flags' or 'pennants' etc.

---

7 Charles Dow was co-founder of Dow-Jones Company, which developed the Dow-Jones Industrial Average, one of the oldest stock indices in the world; he also founded *The Wall Street Journal*. A contemporary explanation of Dow's techniques can be found in Pring (2002).

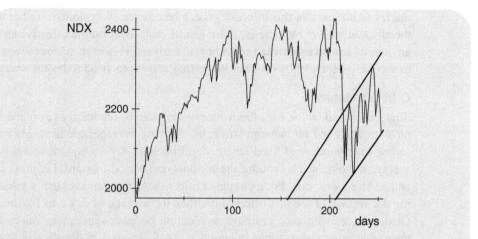

Figure 4.4 Nasdaq-100 index, daily closing prices from 1 October 2010 to 30 September 2011 with resistance line (upper) and support line (lower) in bold

As a practical tool based on subjective pattern recognition, technical analysis has no theoretical foundation that explains why security prices should move in head-and-shoulders or rounding-bottoms patterns. Moreover, the logic underlying some of its concepts is faulty. Consider the resistance level in security prices. If, in the above example, €17.60 really was a ceiling in the price, then nobody would buy the security for, say, €17 because the price can only increase with €0.60 but decrease all the way to the nearest support level. But that makes €17 the new resistance level and we can ask why anybody would want to buy the security at, say, €16.50. Continuing this procedure makes the concept of resistance levels lose its meaning. The fact that the security trades at €17.60 on a financial market *must* mean that some investors believe they earn a fair return on that price, which includes an upward potential. Finally, even if the patterns would exist, they would self-destruct once they become generally known, as we have seen in the discussion of Figure 4.1. Suppose that Figure 4.4 really implied that the NDX index would rise to its resistance level within a short period. Then investors would buy the stocks in the index and their trading would drive the index up until it reached the resistance level.

Perhaps because of the subjective nature of pattern recognition, technical analysis traditionally has a low standing in the academic finance community. Campbell *et al.* (1997, p. 43) describe its position as somewhere between astrology and voodoo. But technical analysis has also been tested scientifically, albeit on a smaller scale than momentum and contrarian strategies. For example, Allen and Karjalainen (1999) find that, out of sample, technical trading rules do not earn excess returns over a simple buy-and-hold strategy after transaction costs.[8] Ready (2002) presents comparable evidence. Authors such as Lo *et al.* (2000), meanwhile, find that several technical indicators do provide incremental information and may have some practical value. Treynor and Ferguson (1985) propagate technical analysis to determine whether private information has already been revealed to

8 A model's out of sample performance is measured in a later period than the one that was used to estimate the model.

market or not, so that this information can be efficiently exploited. Rather than rejecting the efficient market hypothesis, these results cast doubt on the effectiveness of the large amount of resources devoted to technical analysis. However, technical analysis appears to survive independently of scientific testing and is practised today on a very wide scale.

Other strategies

Strategies based on the use of *moving averages* can be regarded as a combination of technical analysis and momentum strategies. Moving averages are averages calculated in a rolling time window of fixed length, e.g. fifteen days. Subsequent values of the moving average are obtained by rolling the window one period forward, i.e. dropping the oldest and adding a new one. For example, a fifteen-days moving average is calculated by taking the average of the first fifteen days, then the average of day 2 to 16, then 3 to 17, etc. Obviously, moving averages have momentum because subsequent values have most of their underlying observations in common. They are used in statistics as smoothing techniques. Investment strategies generally use two moving averages, a long one and a short one, e.g. fifteen-days and twenty-five-days or thirteen-weeks and fifty-weeks. Figure 4.5 illustrates this for a ten-day and a twenty-day moving average, using roughly the same NDX data as in Figure 4.4. The strategy gives a selling signal when the short average crosses the long one from above, and a buying signal when the short average crosses the long one from below. Allen and Karjalainen (1999) simulate moving average rules using genetic algorithms and find that they produce no net excess returns, as was mentioned above. Brock *et al.* (1992), however, report results that are consistent with technical rules having predictive power, although they warn that transactions costs should be carefully considered before such strategies can be implemented.

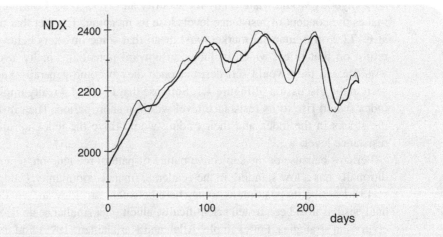

Figure 4.5 10-days (thin) and 20-days (thick) moving averages of daily closing prices, Nasdaq-100 index, 1 October 2010 to 30 September 2011

Pairs trading is a convergence strategy developed on Wall Street in the 1980s. It involves selecting two stocks whose prices moved together in the past but recently diverged. The strategy is a bet that the prices will converge again; it is implemented by shorting the winner and buying the loser. The implicit assumption is that markets overreact to firm specific news, along the lines suggested by Jegadeesh and Titman (1995). The selection of the pairs of stocks can be made purely on statistical grounds but it can also involve economic reasoning, e.g. by selecting companies that operate on the same markets, such as two oil companies or two telecom companies. If the long and short positions are properly matched, the strategy is market neutral, i.e. it is insensitive to movements of the market as a whole. But that does not make the strategy riskless, because there is no guarantee that the prices will converge. A large-scale test of pairs trading is performed by Gatev *et al.* (2006), who conclude that the strategy produces profits, which are robust to conservative estimates of transaction costs. The profits are not correlated with the market index (S&P 500), but they are lower in recent years, probably because the returns are competed away by increased hedge fund activity. These results contradict the efficient market hypothesis but it is too early to generalize these findings.

The concept of pairs trading can be extended to two portfolios, rather than two individual stocks. The portfolios are matched by industry and other characteristics to eliminate market risk and other factor risks. Strategies based on this principle are often called *statistical arbitrage*, but this term is misleading. Arbitrage suggests riskless profits while statistical arbitrage is a speculative strategy. The models used to select stocks and compose the portfolios can be wrong (there is *model risk*) and the convergence, on which the profitability relies, may not occur. Moreover, even if convergence does occur, it may take longer than the investor can maintain the strategy.[9] De Jong *et al.* (2009) illustrate this for the comparable case of arbitrage in dual-listed companies. Betting on convergence that fails to occur in time has led to some spectacular bankruptcies in the past. Pairs trading and statistical arbitrage are usually implemented in computer systems, that automatically collect the data, perform the analyses and place the orders. This way of trading is referred to as *algorithmic trading*.

Finally, when other news is scarce, newspapers occasionally report that some stock index was outperformed by a portfolio, that was selected by having monkeys throw darts at a list of stocks and including the ones that got hit. The accompanying comment usually is an indictment against financial markets and the finance profession. It should be clear by now that this result is to be expected in an efficient market: randomly selecting stocks will on average reproduce an index, with equal probabilities of over- and underperformance (assuming, of course, that the monkeys' darts produce a random sample). Groenendijk and Spronk (2000) take this *monkey strategy* one step further and propose the distribution of randomly selected portfolios as a benchmark for portfolio managers. The various restrictions that portfolio managers face (e.g. size restrictions or the prohibition to invest more than, say, 5 per cent in any stock) are not reflected in the index but can easily be incorporated in a simulation procedure that generates the distribution of possible portfolios.

Summarizing the tests of investment strategies we come to a similar conclusion as with autocorrelation. The majority of tests do not reject market efficiency and the ones that do are often contradictory or temporary.

---

9 This is illustrated by a quote attributed to Keynes: the market can stay irrational longer than you can stay solvent.

4.2.4   Performance persistence

As we have seen earlier, selecting and managing a well-diversified portfolio requires time and expertise, and many investors prefer to outsource these activities to professionals. The financial services industry caters for this preference by offering a large variety of mutual and other funds that are easily accessible to small and big investors. The performance of these funds has been the subject of scientific research – and controversy.

Types of funds

Funds can (1) provide different services to their investors, (2) be structured in three different ways and (3) have different investment policies. Most funds that are aimed at the general public provide some administrative services to their investors: they keep record of the amounts invested and the income earned. They also enable small investors to hold fully diversified portfolios and to increase or decrease their holdings with small amounts at low transaction costs. In addition, *actively managed funds* provide their management's professional expertise to make investment decisions on behalf of the investors. Actively managed funds aim to outperform the market by trying to select stocks with superior performance (*stock picking*) and/or by trying to buy stocks before a price increase and selling them before a price decrease (*timing*). By contrast, *index funds*, or passively managed funds, do not aim to beat the market but try to follow a market index as closely as possible. This is done either by buying all the stocks in the index or by buying a smaller number of carefully selected stocks that closely track the index. While actively managed funds compete on performance, index funds compete on cost level and deviation from the index (or *tracking error*).

A fund can be structured as an *open-end fund (or mutual fund)*, a *closed-end fund* or a *hedge fund*.[10] The most important type is the open-end fund. The shares of open-end funds are not traded on exchanges but sold and bought directly by the fund or indirectly through brokers. The fund issues new shares when investors want to buy them and redeems shares when investors want to sell them, so there is no fixed number of shares. Buying and selling takes place at the *net asset value*, which is the current market value of the assets held by the fund minus liabilities and divided by the number of outstanding shares. Mutual funds may charge an entry and/or exit fee, called *front-end load* and *back-end load*. Actively managed mutual funds also claim an annual management fee of 1–2 per cent. The management fees of index funds are much lower, typically 0.2 per cent per year. These are figures for the United States, to which most research refers; the fees in Europe are usually higher.

Closed-end funds issue a fixed number of shares, which are subsequently traded on exchanges. Investors cannot sell the shares back to the fund, they have to sell them to other investors on the exchange. Hence, the share price is determined by supply and demand and can differ from the net asset value. Both open-end and closed-end funds are regulated by the financial authorities because they offer their shares to the public at large. This limits, among other things, their possibilities to borrow, to use derivatives and to sell short.

---

10 In practice, the term 'mutual fund' is also used in a more general sense and may refer to both open-end and closed-end funds.

4.2 Empirical evidence

The third type of funds, *hedge funds*, are exempted from most regulations because they do not offer their services to the general public. Hedge funds have only a limited number of investors ($\leq$ 100) or only 'qualified' investors who meet certain income or net worth standards. Such investors are assumed to be able to look after themselves. Hedge funds also have a different fee structure. Like other actively managed funds, they charge an annual 1–2 per cent management fee but hedge funds managers also claim an incentive fee of, typically, 20 per cent of the investment gains above a certain threshold. Hedge funds can have lock-up periods, during which investors cannot withdraw money from the fund.

Each fund has its own investment policy: some only invest in fixed income securities (bond funds), others only in stocks (equity funds) or real estate, while still others spread their investments over two or more categories (balanced funds). Within each asset category, funds can specialize further. Equity funds can concentrate on income stocks, that pay out a large fraction of their earnings as dividends, or growth stocks that retain most earnings. Funds that specialize in geographical areas or industries are also very common. Many investment companies run a family of funds that includes actively and passively managed funds for several asset categories and specializations. The investment policies of hedge funds are even more diverse and may include the use of short positions and derivatives, as well as (heavy) borrowing.

In the context of market efficiency the important question is, of course, whether active, professional management can systematically generate excess returns. If markets are efficient, deviations from risk-adjusted expected returns are random, which means that neither funds-on-average nor (groups of) individual funds are able to systematically beat the market. These are very strong implications. After all, professional managers are in the best position to generate superior returns: they have access to the latest price information and the best databases and research tools, and it is their full-time job to search for and analyze information. Fund performance and its persistence is generally analyzed using data from actively managed, open-end mutual funds, since that is the dominant type of fund. In view of the importance of the mutual fund industry (its size in the United States alone is measured in trillions of dollars) it is not surprising that an enormous amount of research has been devoted to this question.

Evidence on fund performance and its persistence

Sharpe (1966) was among the first to examine the performance of mutual funds. Using the return-to-variability ratio, or Sharpe ratio (3.10) discussed in the previous chapter, he analyzes the performance of thirty-four mutual funds over the period 1954–1963. His findings are that the funds, on average, significantly underperformed the Dow-Jones Industrial Average. Twenty-three funds did worse, eleven did better than this index. Sharpe attributes this poor performance to the costs incurred by the funds, because their gross performance (before subtracting expenses) does not differ significantly from the index. He also finds a modest degree of persistence in the performance of these funds. Similar results are obtained by Jensen (1968), who analyzes the performance of 115 mutual funds in the period 1945–1964 with his own Jensen's alpha (3.12). He concludes that the funds, on average, were not able to outperform a buy-the-market-and-hold strategy. Moreover, only three of the funds performed significantly better than the market. Unlike

Sharpe's conclusions, Jensen's hold even when the funds' returns are measured gross of management expenses.

The stream of studies that followed Sharpe's and Jensen's seminal papers successively introduced more sophisticated statistical techniques, better and larger databases that are free from survivorship bias, and an international perspective.[11] Although the question of fund performance remains controversial, the majority of studies report that, on average, actively managed funds underperform the index and index funds. This gives strong support to the efficient market hypothesis. There is also agreement that some funds keep on performing poorly, mainly through excessive trading, and disappear. The remaining controversy is whether some funds can consistently outperform the market, i.e. whether some funds are managed by 'hot hands' that can generate excess returns.

Using a variety of databases, performance measures and analytical techniques, studies such as Grinblatt and Titman (1992), Hendricks *et al.* (1993), Brown and Goetzmann (1995), Elton *et al.* (1996), Droms and Walker (2001) and Bollen and Busse (2005) all report performance persistence, usually combined with average underperformance. The period over which the performance persists varies from a quarter to three years, but is usually short and the persistence decreases with time. Droms and Walker (2001) also analyze the persistence in other fund characteristics than returns and find no persistence in expenses ratios or turnover rates (trading activity). However, the persistence in performance is contested. Malkiel (1995), using a large database spanning two decades, finds that performance persistence is likely to be influenced by survivorship bias and may be limited to specific periods. He finds strong persistence in the 1970s but none in the 1980s and concludes that most investors would be considerably better off by buying a low-expense index fund than by trying to select an active fund manager with 'hot hands'. Carhart (1997) finds only very slight evidence consistent with skilled or informed fund managers and he attributes the 'hot hands' effect of Hendricks *et al.* (1993) to the one-year momentum in stock returns that was described by Jegadeesh and Titman (1993). Differences in expense ratios and transaction costs also contribute to persistence: the more actively a fund trades, the lower its net return to investors. Similar results are obtained more recently by Cuthbertson *et al.* (2008) who analyze a comprehensive data set on UK mutual funds. They find performance persistence among poorly performing funds but not among winners.

Wermers (2000) empirically decomposes mutual fund performance into its component parts. He finds that funds hold stocks that outperform a broad market index by 1.3 per cent per year. Of this, 0.6 per cent is due to the fact that mutual funds choose their stocks from a somewhat different universe than the whole market, and 0.7 per cent is due to the funds' stock picking ability within this universe. The funds show no timing ability. However, mutual funds do not always hold all their money in stocks, they also keep other securities and cash for transaction purposes. These non-stock holdings depress fund performance with 0.7 per cent per year relative to stocks. In addition, the funds incur 1.6 per cent costs per year, in almost equal parts management expenses and transaction costs. The net result

---

11 Taking a sample of existing funds and collecting their performance histories over a certain period overestimates average performance, because the funds that performed so poorly in the period that they ceased to exist are not included. The difference with the true average is called survivorship bias.

is an underperformance of 1 per cent per year. The ability of some mutual funds to pick stocks is confirmed by Kosowski *et al.* (2006), who conclude that a sizable minority of managers is able to persistently generate excess returns that more than cover their costs.

Table 4.6 summarizes the evidence on mutual fund performance. The reviewed studies almost unanimously report that funds, on average, underperform the market. The evidence on performance persistence is mixed. To the extent that persistence in overperformance is found, it appears to be limited to a (narrow) selection of funds and comparatively short periods. Moreover, the excess returns generated by persistence in overperformance are not always worthwhile. For example, both Hendricks *et al.* (1993) and Bollen and Busse (2005) notice that their results are statistically significant, but economically only marginally better than a naive buy-and-hold strategy. For some (e.g. Malkiel, 2003) these results are the most direct and most compelling evidence of market efficiency.

Table 4.6 *Overview of fund performance studies*

	Average underperformance	Persistence ('hot hands')
Sharpe (1966)	Yes	some (10 years)
Jensen (1968)	Yes	-
Grinblatt and Titman (1992)	-	5 years
Hendricks *et al.* (1993)	Yes	1 year
Malkiel (1995)	Yes	1 year (1970s) No (1980s)
Brown and Goetzmann (1995)	Yes	1 year
Elton *et al.* (1996)	Yes	1–3 years
Carhart (1997)	Yes	No (momentum)
Wermers (2000)	Yes	-
Droms and Walker (2001)	No (1970s) Yes (1980s)	1–3 years No (5+ years)
Bollen and Busse (2005)	Yes	3 months
Kosowski *et al.* (2006)	-	1 year
Cuthbertson *et al.* (2008)	-	only losers

4.2.5   Event studies

On 17 April 2008, after trading hours, Google announced its results over the first quarter. The company's profits were up 42 per cent compared with the same quarter last year, much more than analysts expected. The next day, Google's stock price opened almost 20 per cent higher and hovered on that level for some days. As we have seen, that is consistent with an efficient price reaction. However, by the end of the month the price had crept up another 6.5 per cent. Was that due to developments on the market? The Nasdaq Composite Index had gone up 4.1 per cent in the same period.[12] Or was it a correction after an initial underreaction to the announcement? The former does not

---

12 The Nasdaq Composite Index (ticker: IXIC) is a broader index than the Nasdaq-100 index. IXIC contains all domestic and international-based common type stocks listed on the Nasdaq stock exchange.

contradict the efficient market hypothesis, the latter does. *Event studies* are designed to answer such questions.

Methodology of event studies

Event studies measure the effect of a well-defined event on firm value. The event can be an announcement of earnings, dividends, a merger, a stock split, etc. but also a price jump on input or output markets, the introduction of regulation, etc. Measuring the effects of such events is complicated because information about an event never comes alone. There is a continuous stream of other, more general financial information about interest and exchange rates, prices of other stocks, bonds and commodities as well as macro-economic information. To assess the impact of the event, the effects of the other information have to be filtered out. The most common way to do this is to use the *market model* to calculate the *normal return* that could be expected given the reaction of the market as a whole to the other information. The difference between the realized return and the normal return is then the *abnormal return* which is attributed to the event. In efficient markets, abnormal returns only occur in the event period, without any predictable pattern afterwards.

The market model postulates a simple, empirical relation between the return of an individual security i, r_{it}, and the return on the market as a whole (approximated by a broad index), r_{mt}:

$$r_{it} = \widehat{\gamma}_{0i} + \widehat{\gamma}_{1i} r_{mt} + \varepsilon_{it} \tag{4.6}$$

where $\gamma_{0,1}$ are estimated coefficients, ε_{it} is an error term and t is a subscript for time. It is important to note that the market model is an empirical, not a theoretical, model. Its coefficients $\gamma_{0,1}$ are obtained by running a regression of the security returns r_{it} on the returns of the index r_{mt}. The estimates of a security's normal (or expected) return are generated by the market model's out-of-sample predictions, given the return on the market:

$$E(r_{it}) = \widehat{r}_{it} = \widehat{\gamma}_{0i} + \widehat{\gamma}_{1i} r_{mt} \tag{4.7}$$

where the coefficients $\widehat{\gamma}_0$ and $\widehat{\gamma}_1$ are estimated over a period prior to the predictions. The abnormal return, ar_{it}, is the difference between the realized and the expected return:

$$ar_{it} = r_{it} - E(r_{it}) = \varepsilon_{it} \tag{4.8}$$

Conclusions are usually based on the aggregated abnormal returns over the prediction period, the *cumulative abnormal return*, car_i:

$$car_i = \sum_t ar_{it} \tag{4.9}$$

The idea behind this methodology is straightforward. The market model measures how sensitive a stock is to changes in the market index. Given this sensitivity and the change in the index in the event period, it can be calculated what the stock's return in the event period would have been if only the general, market-related information would have become available. It can reasonably be assumed that the difference with the observed return springs from the event. This assumes that the event date can be observed accurately, which is not trivial since financial information has a tendency to leak out. A simpler version of the methodology takes the average return, $\overline{r}_i$, over a prior period as the normal return. More extended versions replace the market model with a multi-factor model, for example the Fama-French three-factor model (3.20) that includes size and book-to-market effects, or Carhart's (1997) four-factor model, that adds a momentum effect.

The market model is very similar to two other models that we have met in Chapter 3, the characteristic line (3.13) and the single index model (3.15). Although the differences are subtle, it is worthwhile to point them out. The characteristic line differs because it is an empirical expression of the equilibrium theory CAPM, which restricts its use and interpretation. For example, the interpretation of γ_0 would be the risk-free interest rate and that of γ_1 would be the CAPM β. The market model has no theoretical background so the interpretation follows from the statistical relationship between r_i and r_m: γ_0 is the change in r_i which is statistically independent from r_m and γ_1 is the statistical sensitivity of r_i for changes in r_m. The coefficients $\gamma_{0,1}$ are not required to have any specific values. The single index model differs in underlying assumptions. Recall from Chapter 3 that the single index model assumes that $cov(r_m, \varepsilon_i) = 0$ and $cov(\varepsilon_i, \varepsilon_j) = 0$, the error term is not correlated with the market return and the error terms of different securities are not correlated. The market model itself makes no assumptions about the error terms, but they may be implicit in the empirical technique used to estimate it (such as classical regression analysis).

A home-made example

A simple, home-made example, using Google's earnings announcement, may help to clarify the methodology of event studies. The first step in the study is choosing the *event window*, i.e. the period over which we want to analyze the impact of the announcement. As we shall see later on, earnings announcements are usually studied over comparatively long event windows, e.g. from twenty days before to ninety days after the announcement. However, to keep the calculations simple we shall use only ten trading days before and after Google's announcement. This gives an event window of 4 April to 1 May 2008. Next, we have to choose the *estimation window* over which we estimate the market model for Google. We use the three months preceding the event window, from 2 January to 31 March. That period comprises sixty trading days, enough to estimate the market model for this example. We download the daily closing prices of Google (ticker GOOG) and the Nasdaq Composite Index (ticker IXIC) over the period 2 January through 1 May from Yahoo.com. After transforming the closing prices into daily returns and using only the data in the estimation window, we estimate the market model for Google with regression analysis. The results are:

$$r_{goog} = -.005 + .922 r_{ixic} \quad R^2 = .278 \tag{4.10}$$

The standard errors of the coefficients are .003 and .189 respectively, so that the sensitivity coefficient is significantly $\neq 0$ but the intercept is not. We can now calculate Google's expected returns, using (4.7), and abnormal returns, using (4.8) in the event window. For example, on the first trading day after the announcement (day 1) the return on the index is .026. This gives an expected return for Google of $-.005 + .922 \times .026 = .019$. Google's actual return is .2, so the abnormal return is $.2 - .019 = 0.181$. Table 4.7 lists the various returns for a few days. The last column shows the cumulative abnormal returns over the event window; these are plotted in Figure 4.6.

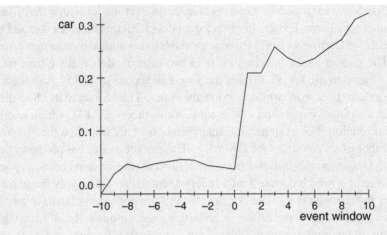

Figure 4.6 Cumulative abnormal returns of Google

Table 4.7 *Returns around event day*

Day	r_{ixic}	$E(r_{goog})$	r_{goog}	ar_{goog}	car_{goog}
10	0.028	0.021	0.033	0.012	0.321
5	0.010	0.004	−0.006	−0.010	0.226
1	0.026	0.019	0.200	0.181	0.209
−5	0.013	0.007	0.011	0.004	0.042
−10	0.001	−0.004	−0.023	−0.018	−0.018

A real event study would involve a sample of earnings announcing firms; the above calculations are then performed for each of them. The results are aggregated over firms, synchronized on the event date (day 0) because the announcements are made on different calendar dates. The result is a series of *cumulative average abnormal returns (caar)*, which can be tested on their statistical significance. The statistical properties of cumulative (average) abnormal returns are a bit complex, particularly for small or thinly traded samples, because they also involve the standard errors of the estimation of the market model. But they are well charted by, among others, Peterson (1989), MacKinlay (1997), Campbell *et al.* (1997) and Bartholdy *et al.* (2007). Tests that show a significant post-event drift in cumulative (average) abnormal returns reject the efficient market hypothesis. Drift in pre-event caar is a bit more difficult to interpret. It can be the result of information leaking out, which means that the event date is observed with error. But it is also possible that the market recognizes or anticipates information that is later formalized in the event. For example, dividend increases and stock splits (discussed below) are usually announced after a period of good performance. Hence, selecting companies that have split their stock implies selecting companies that have done well prior to the split, and that becomes manifest in the pre-event caar. This is usually referred to as *sample selection bias.*

4.2 Empirical evidence

The methodology outlined above was first used in the late 1960s in studies such as Ball and Brown (1968) and Fama *et al.* (1969). Since then, event studies have been used to analyze the effects of a wide variety of events, ranging from exchange offers, block trades and analysts' forecasts to the sudden death of chief executive officers. Kothari and Warner (2007) tallied the number of event studies published in five leading finance journals between 1974 and 2000 and report a grand total of 565. Obviously, we can only survey a few highlights of this vast literature.

Stock splits

A *stock split* is the exchange of a firm's outstanding shares for a larger number of new shares. A typical exchange ratio is 2:1 (or a 2-for-1 split), meaning that for every old share the owner receives two new shares, each of which is worth half the value of an old share. Other common exchange ratios are 3-for-2, 5-for-4 and 3-for-1, but 5-for-1 splits also occur. *Reverse stock splits* work the other way around and reduce the number of shares. Companies usually split their stocks after a period of price increases. The most frequently mentioned reason to split is the enhancement of tradability, for example by keeping the stock price in an affordable range for small investors or by letting the stock appear inexpensive compared with those of similar companies.[13] Stock splits neither add value nor dilute the claims of the existing shareholders, so in efficient markets their effects on stock prices should be zero (after adjusting for the split, of course). That is what Fama *et al.* (1969) found in their analysis of 940 splits in the period 1926–1960. Using an event window of twenty-nine months before and thirty months after the split, they report cumulative average abnormal returns (caar) that steadily increase before the event but are stable (around zero) after the event. They then split their sample in a large group (672 out of 940) of companies that increases and a smaller group that decreases its dividends after the split. The former group's cumulative average abnormal returns increase slightly after the split, but those of the dividend decreasers plummet in the few months after the event. This leads Fama *et al.* to the conclusion that investors use stock splits to re-evaluate the expected income from the stock. Anticipated or announced splits cause price adjustments only to the extent that splits are associated with changes in the expected dividends. If these expectations do not materialize after the event, prices revert to their normal level, consistent with market efficiency.

These results are both challenged and confirmed in later work. For example, Ikenberry and Ramnath (2002) examine a sample of more than 3,000 stock splits announced between 1988 and 1997 and estimate abnormal returns of 9 per cent in the year following the announcements of stock splits. Their result is robust to a variety of estimation techniques. It is also consistent with the positive drift that other studies observed following stock splits in the 1970s and 1980s. This pattern suggests that the abnormal return drift identified in these studies is not spurious. Their conclusion is that markets underreact to the news in splits, which is inconsistent with market efficiency. However, using an even larger sample of 12, 747 stock splits over the period 1927 through 1996, Byun and Rozeff (2003) come to the opposite conclusion. Although they isolate specific subperiods and

---

[13] Some companies have the opposite policy; for example, Warren Buffett's Berkshire Hathaway traded at less than $6,000 per share in the early 1990s and around $140,000 in 2008, but never split.

methods of estimation that yield significantly positive post-event returns, their overall results indicate that buyers and sellers of splitting stocks do not, on average, earn abnormal returns that are significantly different from zero. Their overall conclusion of market efficiency is based on a variety of subperiods and methodologies. Boehme and Danielsen (2007) emphasize the fact that stock split announcements are generally preceded by a period of strong performance. Taking the industry momentum effect into account, they find no consistent evidence of post-split positive abnormal returns, although abnormal returns do occur in some subperiods.

Earnings announcements

In a paper that pioneered event studies, Ball and Brown (1968) analyze the effects of *earnings announcements* in the annual reports of 261 firms. Using an event window of twelve months before to six months after the announcement, they observe that cumulative average abnormal returns (caar) already begin to drift in the direction of the announcement (upward for positive news, downwards for negative) twelve months before the announcement. This is not surprising since earnings information also becomes available from other sources, such as quarterly reports. They also observe that caar continue to drift in the same direction for as long as two months after the event date. By itself, this contradicts market efficiency. But the drift is so small that, unless transaction costs are within one per cent, it offers no opportunity for abnormal profit after the event date. Reinganum (1981) goes one step further and quantifies the surprise element in earnings announcements. He uses a simple time series regression model to forecast earnings per share ($\widehat{EPS}$) from historical data. The difference with the earnings per share in the announcement (EPS) is the surprise element, or unexpected earnings: $UE = \widehat{EPS} - EPS$. These unexpected earnings per share are standardized by scaling them with the standard error of estimate from the regression equation used in the prediction: $SUE = (\widehat{EPS} - EPS)/\widehat{\sigma}_{eps}$. With these standardized unexpected earnings, or SUEs, he constructs two equally risky portfolios, one containing firms with the highest SUEs and the other containing the lowest. The returns of these portfolios over the next 1–4 months are not significantly different from each other, and he concludes that no abnormal returns can be earned by using information in earnings announcements.

Reinganum's (1981) analyses are re-examined on a larger scale and using more advanced estimation techniques by Rendleman *et al.* (1982). Unlike Reinganum, they find a SUE effect, with significant differences of 3.4–6 per cent in return between the two extreme SUE portfolios over the next 1–5 months. In the second, frequently cited part of their study, they divide their sample in ten groups according to the size of the SUE, from strongly negative to strongly positive. Using an event window from 20 days before to 90 days after the announcement, they perform an event study for each group. Unsurprisingly, the abnormal return on the event day strongly depends on the size of the SUE. However, in the post-event period (day 1 to 90) the caar of all groups continue to drift in the direction of the earnings surprise and these post-event caar are statistically significant for all but one group. This clearly contradicts the efficient market hypothesis (even though the post-event caar are small, <2 per cent, for five middle groups). For example, the group with the highest SUE has a caar of 8 per cent over the entire event window. Of this, 2.4 per cent occurs in the pre-event period, 1.3 per cent on the event day and 4.3 per cent in the post-event period. The group with the lowest SUE has corresponding negative caar of −8.7 per cent over the entire window, −3.3 per cent before, −1.4 per cent on and −4 per cent after the event date. This is strong evidence against market efficiency.

Since then, the post-earnings-announcement drift has been confirmed in numerous other studies and various explanations for this phenomenon have been proposed. For example, Chordia and Shivakumar (2005) suggest that investors fail to account for the impact of inflation on their forecasts of future earnings growth. This causes firms with positive earnings sensitivities to inflation to be undervalued and stocks with negative earnings sensitivities to inflation to be overvalued. Alternatively, Battalio and Mendenhall (2005) argue that small investors (trading less than 500 shares) use an incomplete information set for their decisions. Compared with more sophisticated, large investors they ignore, or at least significantly underweight, the implications of the surprise in earnings announcements for future earnings levels. This leads to the underreaction that gives rise to the post-earnings-announcement drift. Mendenhall (2004) is among the researchers who ask why earnings announcements, which are easily observable, can have a predictable effect that has survived for several decades without being arbitraged away. His answer is that the practical possibilities to profit from arbitrage trades are limited. To exploit underreaction, specialized arbitrageurs would have to hold a few, relatively large positions and this would expose them to the stocks' unsystematic risk. He quantifies this arbitrage risk by the residual variance from a market model regression, i.e. the part of a stock's volatility that is not explained by movements of the market. Using this risk measure, he finds that the magnitude of post-earnings-announcement drift is significantly positively correlated to arbitrage risk. For example, firms in the highest arbitrage risk quintile experience drifts that are, ceteris paribus, 3–4 percentage points per quarter larger than those of firms in the lowest arbitrage risk quintile. These results are robust to a wide range of explanatory variables used in prior research. His conclusion is that arbitrage risk and transactions costs impede arbitrageurs who attempt to profit from the post-earnings-announcement drift.

Other event studies

Merger and acquisition announcements are generally analyzed to determine whether or not mergers create value, and if so, for whom: the bidder, the target or both. However, the pattern of abnormal returns over time may also allow conclusions regarding market efficiency. Early studies such as Keown and Pinkerton (1981) and Travlos (1987) show very little post-event drift, concurring with semi-strong market efficiency.[14] Later studies more often report significant post-acquisition caar, particularly for certain types of mergers. For example, Loughran and Vijh (1997) find insignificant caar for mergers that are paid for in cash, but significantly negative ones if the merger is paid for in stocks of the acquiring firm. This raises the question whether these returns are due to the merger or the associated stock issue.

---

14 Keown and Pinkerton (1981) report suspiciously large abnormal returns on days just before the event and conclude that merger announcements are poorly held secrets.

A long line of research investigates the effects of *stock issues*, both initial public offerings (IPOs), seasoned equity offerings (SEOs) and reverse issues, i.e. stock repurchases.[15] A representative example of these studies is the large-scale test by Pontiff and Woodgate (2008), who find a negative relation between net stock issues and average returns for the period after 1970, and no significant relation before 1970. Fama and French (2008) report similar results. Evidence to the contrary is provided in Brav *et al.* (2000), Eckbo *et al.* (2000) and Mitchell and Stafford (2000).

A final example of event studies is Liu *et al.* (2008), who investigate the effect of dividend-reductions and omissions. They report significantly negative post-announcement returns that last one year. However, when they control for the pre-event earnings performance of the dividend-reducing or omitting firms, the underperformance becomes insignificant. This leads them to the conclusion that the observed drift is a post-earnings-announcement drift, so that the price reaction to the dividend event is not necessarily inconsistent with market efficiency. The event studies discussed here are summarized in Table 4.8.

Table 4.8 *Overview of event studies*

Study	Event	Efficient?
Fama *et al.* (1969)	Stock splits	Yes
Ikenberry and Ramnath (2002)	Stock splits	No
Byun and Rozeff (2003)	Stock splits	Yes
Boehme and Danielsen (2007)	Stock splits	Yes
Ball and Brown (1968)	Earnings ann.	Yes
Reinganum (1981)	Earnings ann.	Yes
Rendleman *et al.* (1982)	Earnings ann.	No
Chordia and Shivakumar (2005)	Earnings ann.	No
Battalio and Mendenhall (2005)	Earnings ann.	No
Mendenhall (2004)	Earnings ann.	No
Keown and Pinkerton (1981)	Merger ann.	Yes
Travlos (1987)	Merger ann.	Yes
Loughran and Vijh (1997)	Merger ann.	Yes/No
Pontiff and Woodgate (2008)	Stock issue	No
Fama and French (2008)	Stock issue	No
Brav *et al.* (2000)	Stock issue	Yes
Eckbo *et al.* (2000)	Stock issue	Yes
Mitchell and Stafford (2000)	Stock issue	Yes
Liu *et al.* (2008)	Dividend ann.	Yes

Conclusions from event studies

What can we conclude from the very large number of event studies in the literature? It seems safe to say that a considerable part of these studies report at least some results that

---

15 Recall from Chapter 2 that an initial public offering occurs when a company sells stock to the public for the first time. Seasoned equity offerings are equity issues by companies that already have securities that are traded in the market.

contradict market efficiency. However, as Fama (1998) points out, there are two reasons why the impact of these apparent inefficiencies may be limited. First, reported over-reactions of stock prices to information in events are about as common as underreactions. This is consistent with the random nature of price changes that market efficiency predicts. Second, the reported abnormal returns are usually very sensitive to small and reasonable changes in the research design that produced them, which suggests model misspecification. For example, we just saw that the significant effect of dividend reductions and omission disappears when pre-event earnings are controlled for. Another frequently encountered example are abnormal returns that are found in equally weighted portfolios but not in value-weighted portfolios, which suggests that mispricing is limited to smaller, illiquid firms. Even though Fama (1998) admits that some abnormal returns seem to persist, he concludes that the evidence does not suggest that market efficiency should be abandoned.

4.2.6   Strong form tests

The distinguishing characteristic of strong form market efficiency is that also private or inside information (as opposed to public information) is fully reflected in security prices. We have already seen tests of one category of private information: the performance of mutual and other funds is generally considered a matter of strong form efficiency, since the funds' models and strategies are proprietary information. It is more difficult to test whether the use of inside information leads to excess returns, since it is illegal in most countries to trade on the basis of such information. However, not all trades by insiders are illegal and even illegal trades are sometimes accessible to research. Examples of the latter are the studies by Syed *et al.* (1989) and Meulbroek (1992), who use material collected by the financial authorities for the criminal investigation of insider trading.

Syed *et al.* (1989) analyze sixteen cases where information about a forthcoming investment column in *The Wall Street Journal* was leaked prior to publication (the persons involved were convicted). They report that the use of this inside information can yield a significant and substantial abnormal return of 6.25 per cent over a two-day period. This, of course, refutes strong form efficiency. In a later paper, the same authors report a more general analysis of the same column over a three-year period involving more than 1,000 buy or sell recommendations (Liu *et al.*, 1990). Publication of the column appears to have an impact on stock prices which begins two days before publication. The caar over the three-day period (day −2, −1 and 0) is 3 per cent, again refuting strong form market efficiency. The authors 'cannot exclude' the possibility that the pre-event caar are caused by insider trading. Meulbroek (1992) analyzes 183 episodes in which individuals were charged with insider trading by the SEC.[16] Almost 80 per cent of the episodes are associated with mergers and takeovers. She uses event study methodology to estimate abnormal returns on both insider trading days and the day the inside information becomes public. She reports significant and robust abnormal price movements on insider trading days which are 40–50 per cent of the subsequent price reaction to the public announcement of the inside information. These findings also contradict the efficient market hypothesis.

---

[16] Securities and Exchange Commission, a United States government agency which regulates the securities industry and financial markets, including stock and options exchanges.

The vast majority of strong form tests refers to legal insider trades. In the United States, insiders must report their open-market trades to the SEC on a monthly basis and summaries of these reports (the *Official Summary*) are made public soon after filing. Most European countries have similar regulations. The summary reports are the empirical basis of a large number of studies. An early example is Seyhun (1986), who analyzes daily returns around insider transactions in a sample of 790 firms. Using event study methodology and an event window from 200 days before to 300 days after insider trading days, the study demonstrates that insiders can predict abnormal future stock price changes. Insiders are shown to purchase stock prior to an abnormal rise in stock prices and sell stock prior to an abnormal decline in stock prices. The evidence also suggests that predictive success is related to how knowledgeable insiders are. Chairmen of the boards of directors or officer-directors are more successful predictors of future abnormal stock price changes than officers or shareholders. The evidence further suggests that insiders are aware of the value of their information and trade larger volumes of stock to exploit more valuable information. All these results contradict strong form market efficiency.

Givoly and Palmon (1985) analyze insider trading from a somewhat different perspective. They argue that insider trading is closely watched by many outside investors, who may imitate the behaviour of insiders. Hence, when an insider trade occurs it may trigger a wave of transactions in the same direction (buy or sell) by outsiders. This may generate subsequent abnormal returns to insiders, regardless of whether their trade was based on inside information or not. Givoly and Palmon's (1985) empirical results first of all confirm the abnormal returns of insider transactions that are found in almost all other studies. But the results also suggest that these returns are not associated with disclosure of company-specific news, because the abnormal return to insider transactions endures much longer than the typical market reaction to company-specific news. They conclude that outside investors appear to accept the superior knowledge of insiders and follow in their footsteps. This behaviour explains the profitability of insider trades in a larger degree than illegal exploitation of insider information.

Partly overlapping results are presented by Jeng *et al.* (2003), who use a very large database of insider transactions over approximately twenty-one years. They, too, report abnormal returns on insider trades. The returns are economically and statistically significant with a magnitude of ± 0.6 per cent per month for a value-weighted portfolio of all insiders' *purchases*. Approximately one quarter of the abnormal return is realized in the first five days after the purchase, which is consistent with outsiders following the trades of the insiders. However, none of the methods they use detects abnormal returns for their portfolio of insider *sales*. They further find that the trades of top executives do not earn higher abnormal returns than those of insiders with a lower position in the firm, but low-volume purchases have smaller abnormal returns than high-volume ones.

The study by Eckbo and Smith (1998) is an oddity among the strong form tests because it documents zero or negative abnormal performance by insiders. This result is based on an evaluation of all insider holdings and trades on Oslo Stock Exchange during the period January 1985 through December 1992, when regulation and enforcement of insider trading was relatively lax. Eckbo and Smith aggregate their data in a carefully constructed portfolio that tracks all movements of insiders in and out of firms on the Oslo exchange. Using three alternative performance estimators they find statistically insignificant or negative abnormal insider performance. As possible explanations they suggest that insiders in a market such as the Oslo Stock Exchange rarely possess inside information or, alternatively, that the value of maintaining corporate control offsets the value of trading on inside information.

Two recent papers look at the predictive capability of insiders on a longer time scale. Ke *et al.* (2003) investigate insider trading in connection with series of consecutive quarters with increasing earnings. When such series are broken by a quarter with a decreasing earnings (relative to the same quarter last year), stock prices are known to drop in an economically and statistically significant way. We saw this earlier as the surprise element in earnings announcements (cf. Rendleman *et al.*, 1982). Analyzing trading patterns in 16 quarters prior to the break in earnings, Ke *et al.* find little unusual insider trading in the two quarters immediately preceding the announcement of a break. However, they do find a robust increase in the frequency of net insider sales in the ninth through third quarter before the break. They interpret this result as evidence that insiders avoid the risks from regulatory actions by shareholders, the authorities or the press, but continue to profit from their private information by shifting their trades to an earlier time.

Marin and Olivier (2008) perform a similar analysis of insider trading around crashes, which they define as excess returns two standard deviations below their sixty months' moving average. Their empirical results show that the probability of a crash occurring in any given month is negatively related to insider sales in the previous month but positively related to insider sales two to twelve months earlier. They explain these results with a theoretical model in which rational uninformed investors react more strongly to the absence of insider sales than to their presence. Since they do not find a symmetric counterpart in the case of jumps (excess returns two standard deviations above their sixty months' moving average), they conclude that insider behaviour cannot be explained as avoiding regulatory actions. Together, these two studies underline that insider trading patterns may be more complicated than the early studies assumed.

The empirical evidence on strong form market efficiency is easy to summarize: the overwhelming majority of studies report inefficiencies in one way or another. There is contradictory evidence on whether insider sales give the same excess returns as insider purchases, and whether insider excess returns are related to knowledgeability and transaction size. But the overall conclusion must be that financial markets are not strong form efficient.

4.3 Conclusions

In this final section we will discuss some empirical problems that may have contributed to the disagreeing results we have seen. We will also look at some remaining anomalies and misconceptions, before we formulate a conclusion.

4.3.1 Problems and (un)solved puzzles

As any other empirical research, tests of market efficiency involve choices that can influence the results. Different research designs, data sets and sample periods can give different results. To illustrate this, some common problems are briefly discussed below.

Some empirical problems

The joint hypothesis problem arises when market efficiency is tested with a model that calculates expected normal returns, such as the market model in event studies or the CAPM in tests of fund performance. As Fama (1970, 1991) points out, the procedure is then a joint test of market efficiency and the validity of the normal return model. The implication is that if market efficiency is rejected, because significant abnormal returns are found, it is impossible to conclude from the test results alone whether the market is truly inefficient or the model for normal returns is wrong. Only an additional test with a different model can shed light on that. Suppose, for example, that we use the CAPM to calculate normal risk-adjusted returns. We have seen in the previous chapter that size is among the factors (other than the CAPM β) that are frequently found to be related to security returns. So if we have a portfolio or an investment rule that implicitly selects or overweights small firms, e.g. by looking at past performance, the result will be abnormal performance. If the test is repeated with a normal return model that incorporates size effects, such as the Fama-French three-factor model, the abnormal performance will disappear. Many apparently contradictory test results have been attributed to differences in the models of normal asset returns. It should be noted, however, that the argument only applies to studies with long event windows. As we have seen in the calculation of autocorrelations, (differences in) expected daily returns are negligibly small compared with the observed daily returns. If a stock is expected to generate a 10 per cent risk premium per year and a year has 250 trading days, the expected risk premium per day is $10/250 \approx 0.04$ per cent. Even if a different expected return model doubles (or halves) this premium, it takes very many days of compounding before such differences amount to a substantial influence on conclusions.

Data snooping occurs when a dataset is used more than once for selecting or testing a model (White, 2000). Given time, skilful researchers can usually construct a model that produces significant and 'interesting' results for any dataset, simply by trying many different combinations of variables. Results obtained in such a way are likely to be due to chance rather than to the qualities of the model. A similar situation arises when many hundreds or thousands of researchers all use the same dataset, for example data of the national stock market. Data snooping may be difficult to avoid, particularly in the analysis of time series data. The obvious solution, re-testing on an independent sample, may simply not be available: most countries have only one national stock market. Data snooping produces results that are specific to a certain dataset, i.e. results that cannot be reproduced using a different dataset. We have seen several examples of excess returns that were not found in a later re-test.

Biases can be introduced in many ways. We have already met survivorship bias (back-collecting data of existing firms omits the firms that went out of business), sample selection bias (firms announce dividend increases or stock splits after a period of good returns) and size bias (equally weighted portfolios show abnormal returns that are not found in value-weighted portfolios). An important bias probably is people's, and finance journals', preference for positive news which shows that excess returns can be earned. As a consequence, many thousands of tests that show no autocorrelation, unprofitable strategies or funds, and the efficient absorption of new information in security prices, remain unpublished.

4.3 Conclusions

Disappearing and persistent inefficiencies

The empirical problems may be among the reasons why some market inefficiencies seem to have disappeared over time. Another reason may be that investors became aware of the inefficiency and developed strategies that traded the inefficiency away. In recent surveys, Schwert (2003) and Malkiel (2003) discuss the evidence on inefficiencies that attracted much attention in the finance literature (Schwert re-tests many of them on a large database). Such inefficiencies are usually called 'puzzles' or 'anomalies'. Some of their results are briefly summarized below.

The small firm effect seems to have disappeared. The original research from the early 1980s (e.g. Reinganum, 1981) showed that during the period 1936–1975 small company stocks earned higher returns than large companies and higher returns than predicted by the CAPM.[17] Schwert (2003) estimates Jensen's alpha (equation 3.12) for a comprehensive small company portfolio over the period 1982–2002 and several sub-periods, and finds no significant values. In the 1980s several funds specializing in small firms became available for investors and this may have contributed to reducing the small firm effect by increasing demand for small firms' stocks.

Calendar effects is the generic term for excess returns over certain calendar periods. The January effect (or the turn-of-the-year effect) and the weekend effect (or day-of-the-week effect) are the best-known examples, but time-of-day and holiday effects have also been reported. Several researchers have found that returns in January are higher than in other months. Later research narrowed the effect down to the first two weeks of January and smaller stocks. Schwert's (2003) estimation results show significantly higher small firm returns in the first two weeks of January for data that span the period 1962–2001. This result is robust across several sub-periods and, thus, seems to persist. Several explanations of this effect have been suggested. The tax-loss selling hypothesis proposes that investors, at the end of the year, realize tax-deductible losses by selling stocks that have declined in price. Reinvestment of funds in the beginning of the following year creates an upward pressure on stock prices. This hypothesis is supported by the fact that the January effect is strongest in stocks that made losses in the previous year. It is contradicted by the absence of an equally strong opposite effect in December and by the presence of the January effect in countries with different fiscal years. An alternative explanation is offered by the window-dressing hypothesis, which argues that portfolio managers may be reluctant to report holdings of poorly performing small stocks in their year-end reports. This makes them sell these stocks in December, followed by a buy-back in January. This hypothesis, too, is contradicted by the absence of an equally strong opposite effect in December. Neither explanation is satisfactory because such a simple effect should be very easily traded away by observant investors. Thus, the January effect remains an unsolved puzzle.

The existence of the weekend effect, on the other hand, could no longer be confirmed by Schwert. Research in the 1980s reported that average returns tend to be negative over weekends (up on Fridays, down on Mondays). Using a very long time series, Schwert reproduces significantly negative weekend returns for the periods 1885–1927, 1928–1952 and 1953–1977, but not for the period 1978–2002.

---

[17] Small is usually defined as the smallest decile or quintile of companies listed on the American or New York Stock Exchange.

The value effect seems to have undergone a similar fate as the size and weekend effects. Recall from the discussion of the CAPM that 'value' firms, which have low price-earnings ratios, high dividend yields and high book-to-market values, are found to generate high returns. Firms with the opposite characteristics are called 'growth' firms and have lower returns. Schwert tests the value effect with the performance of a portfolio of value stocks that became available in 1993. Previous research shows that this portfolio would have earned significant abnormal returns (i.e. in excess of the CAPM) of about +0.5 per cent per month over the period 1963–1991. However, over the period 1994–2002 the estimated abnormal return is an insignificant −0.2 per cent per month.

Finally, *the momentum effect* is reported by Schwert to persist. Momentum effects are found for all tested sub-periods of 1926–2001 and the effects are robust across two different benchmarks, the CAPM and the three-factor Fama–French model.

What do we learn from these surveys and re-tests? The important point is that we cannot reliably predict which result will characterize the future. Will the momentum effect persist or will its contrarian counterpart re-emerge? Will value stocks outperform growth stocks over the next decade or will it be the other way around? Is the disappearance of the small firm effect permanent or will it come back, this time perhaps with the opposite sign? Somewhat rephrased, Fama's (1998) answer probably still is the best: about half of the strategies, funds, portfolios and effects will outperform the market but we cannot tell beforehand which half. That is what the efficient market hypothesis predicts.

4.3.2   Misconceptions and conclusions

In the beginning of this chapter we described market efficiency as a deceptively simple concept, with consequences that are not at all easy to understand or accept. It is therefore not surprising that a number of misconceptions about market efficiency and the way it is tested frequently (re-)appear.

Common misconceptions

Market efficiency means that the market is always right
Market efficiency requires that available information is fully reflected in prices, not that the information is sufficient or, with hindsight, correct. Suppose an oil company invested heavily in a new oil field and its stock price will jump to 100 if oil is found and plunge to 50 if the field is dry. The current price of 75 reflects the market's estimate of the probability that oil will be found, viz. 50–50. Obviously, this does not mean that the market was wrong and over- or undervalued the stock, when the uncertainty about the oil field is later resolved. Market efficiency does not imply perfect foresight. In the same way we can now, after the fact, say that the prices of internet (or dot com) stocks during the 1999–2000 bubble were too high, as were the prices of financials before the credit crunch of 2008. But that does not mean that markets were inefficient then.

People who made fortunes on the stock market disprove market efficiency
Market efficiency does not say that people cannot be lucky, nor that people cannot repeatedly be lucky. If excess returns are independently distributed with an expectation of zero, as market efficiency specifies, then (long) series of consecutive positive excess returns can still occur. They just have a low probability of occurring. Since there are very many investors, simple probability calculations will show that a fairly large number of investors

is expected to be lucky many times in a row. This is often illustrated with a coin-tossing analogy. Suppose we regard investing as a series of bets on the year-end stock prices. If you bet correctly you stay, if your bet is wrong you are out (this is not unlike the position of a junior portfolio manager). With equal probabilities of being right or wrong, this can be represented by coin tossing. We start with $100,000$ investors and make them flip a coin.[18] If heads comes up they stay, tails mean they go. After one year (toss) we have $50,000$ investors left, after two years $25,000$ etc. After ten years we have almost 100 investors left who were right ten years in a row ($0.5^{10} = 0.000977$). Investors who consistently bet correctly for that long a period probably made fortunes. Even though human nature makes it likely that most of them will ascribe their success to their extraordinary investing skills, and not to luck, this does not disprove market efficiency. Moreover, these statistics are easily misinterpreted, as the following example illustrates. Suppose you want to invest some money and you look at the track records of 250 mutual funds over the past ten years. You find that fund X has beaten the market in all ten years. We have just calculated that the probability of betting correctly ten years in a row is 0.000977 so you conclude that fund X must be managed by 'hot hands'. Your conclusion is not correct! The probability that fund X beat the market ten years in a row is indeed 0.000977 under the efficient market hypothesis. But you did not specifically analyze the performance of fund X, you looked at all 250 funds to see if *any of them* beat the market. The distinction is subtle, but both cases have very different probabilities. The latter probability, i.e. that any of the 250 funds beat the market in all ten years, is calculated as follows. For a specific fund, the probability that it does not beat the market is $(1 - 0.000977)$. If markets are efficient, excess returns are independent so the probability that *none of the funds* beat the market is $(1 - 0.000977)^{250} = 0.783$. Hence, the probability that at least one fund beat the market is $1 - 0.783 = 0.217$ or 21.7 per cent, no reason to assume 'hot hands'.

Large price fluctuations without apparent reason signal inefficiency

An enormous amount of information reaches the market every day, so large price fluctuations are to be expected. Rather, small or no price fluctuations would signal market inefficiency. The vast quantity of news makes it generally impossible to relate individual pieces of information to individual price movements (company-specific news is an exception, as we have seen in event studies). This may give the false impression that price movements without company-specific news are uncaused, particularly since these movements are random.

In efficient markets one stock is as good as another

Stocks can differ in many respects, also on efficient markets. Some are more risky than others, some pay more dividends or have more growth potential, etc. An investor who selects a well-diversified portfolio has to match all these aspects to their preferences. In that sense, no stock is as good as the next. But on efficient markets all these aspects are fairly priced, so that they cannot be used to select stocks that give excess returns. In that sense the statement is true.

---

[18] A survey conducted in 2005 by the Investment Company Institute and the Securities Industry Association estimates that 57 million US households (± 50 per cent) own stocks directly or through mutual funds.

Conclusions

So, are financial markets efficient? The answer depends a bit on who is asking. For corporate managers with inside information the answer is no. The empirical evidence almost unequivocally and convincingly shows that corporate insiders can earn excess returns and, in many cases, find ways to do so. But for the large majority of investors the answer has to be yes. Consider the evidence produced by the enormous amount of stock market studies:

- The vast majority of autocorrelations and runs tests do not reject randomness; they produce some evidence of relationships between returns over time, but these relationships are too weak to be exploitable in a trading strategy.
- The majority of tests of investment strategies do not reject market efficiency and the ones that do are often contradictory and restricted to certain periods. We cannot confidently predict whether the next period will show contrarian or momentum returns, overreaction is about as common as underreaction and the continuation of returns is about as frequent as their reversal. Moreover, if we could identify excess returns, we could not be sure whether they are genuine excess returns or the fair risk premia for omitted effects such as size, varying risk or higher transaction costs. Finally, the excess returns that are found are generally small and their exploitation is hampered by transaction costs and arbitrage risk.
- On average, mutual and other funds underperform the market and the evidence on performance persistence is, at best, mixed. To the extent that persistence in overperformance is found, it appears to be limited to a (narrow) selection of funds and comparatively short periods. Moreover, the excess returns generated by persistence in overperformance tend to be only marginally better than a naive buy-and-hold strategy.
- Event studies produced some of the cleanest evidence against market efficiency and some effects, such as the post-earnings-announcement drift and the January effect, seem to persist. But again, overreactions of stock prices to information in events are about as common as underreactions and the reported abnormal returns are usually very sensitive to the way they are measured.

The evidence is perhaps best summarized by Roll, who is also a portfolio manager (quoted by Malkiel, 2003, p. 72):

I have personally tried to invest money, my client's money and my own, in every single anomaly and predictive device that academics have dreamed up.... I have attempted to exploit the so-called year-end anomalies and a whole variety of strategies supposedly documented by academic research. And I have yet to make a nickel on any of these supposed market inefficiencies ... a true market inefficiency ought to be an exploitable opportunity. If there's nothing investors can exploit in a systematic way, time in and time out, then it's very hard to say that information is not being properly incorporated into stock prices.

Exercises

1. In September 1998 the investment banking and securities firm Goldman, Sachs & Company cancelled its plan to go public, i.e. to offer shares to the public. The decision was made after a sharp drop of 25 per cent in the results over the third quarter.

Goldman's co-chairman and chief executive Henry M. Paulson Jr. said to the *New York Times*: 'With the volatility we have, the falling valuations (of other investment banks) and uncertainty of earnings going forward, I can't imagine that we would advise a client that this is a good time to go public for a financial service company.' What does the Efficient Market Hypothesis (EMH) say about Goldman's decision to cancel the stock issue because of falling valuations?

2. Stocks are expected to earn (much) more than the risk-free interest rate. This means that stock prices are expected to increase over time which, in turn, means that stock prices will be positively autocorrelated and that they are not a fair game or a martingale as the EMH claims. Is this reasoning correct?

3. It is often reported that the price of a stock has increased over some period *before* the announcement of good news such as higher earnings, dividend increases, etc. Does this contradict the EMH?

4. There are cases in which the price of a stock *dropped* after the firm announced some good news, e.g. an increase in quarterly earnings. Does this contradict the EMH?

5. In almost all countries there are a few people who became very rich by speculating in the stock market. This proves that excess returns can be earned and that the stock market is not efficient. Is this reasoning correct?

6. What does the EMH imply about the net present value (NPV) of the purchase or sale of a security on an efficient market?

7. A local mutual fund says it has expertise in identifying stocks that are undervalued because they are underresearched or unpopular. To prove its point, the fund produces evidence that its return over the past four years was 3 per cent above the return on the market index.
   (a) What does the EMH say about undervalued stocks?
   (b) Does the fund's evidence contradict the EMH?

8. You are a student with good data skills and you decide to apply your talents to the stock market. After running a large number of regressions you find that the sign (+ or −) of the change in a company's stock price in one quarter is an accurate predictor of whether the company's earnings in the next quarter will increase or decrease.
   (a) Does this finding contradict the EMH?
   Next, you take daily return data of 100 stocks and test 10 different filter rules on each of them. You find that twenty-seven stock-rule combinations earn significantly higher returns than a buy-and-hold strategy.
   (b) Does this finding contradict the EMH?

You take a closer look at the stocks for which you found profitable filter rules and you see that they mainly belong to smaller, infrequently traded companies.

(c) Is this finding relevant for the application of filter rules?

Finally, you decide to apply an automatic function generator. You let your computer search through a very large number of functions that relate stock prices to variables in your dataset. You find that next month's stock prices are accurately predicted by the street number in the company's address plus the square root of the number of visitors to the company's website.

(d) Do these results contradict the EMH?

9. Many (financial) newspapers around the world regularly publish a ranking of mutual funds in their countries, based on the funds' performance, together with a relevant index as a benchmark. What would be the place of the benchmark index in the ranking in an efficient market? Distinguish between performance over short and long periods.

10. Suppose that the stock prices of a fertilizer producer move in the same cycles as the fertilizing seasons, high in spring and summer, low in autumn and winter. Explain how trading will eliminate the cyclical pattern.

11. It is sometimes said that market efficiency protects unknowledgeable investors, so that it does not matter what and how you buy and sell, you always pay and get a fair price. Comment on this statement.

12. It is sometimes argued that markets cannot be efficient because only a small proportion of investors follow the information on a stock and an even smaller proportion actively trade in a stock on a day or in a week. Is this argument correct?

13. Investors can disagree strongly about the implications of information for the price of a particular stock. Therefore, the information cannot be fully reflected in prices and markets are not efficient. Is this argument correct?

14. Szewczyk *et al.* analyzed a sample of companies announcing dividend omissions (announcements that no dividends will be paid). The caar (in per cent) on days relative to the announcement day (zero) are in the table below.[19]

Day:	−6	−4	−2	0	2	4	6
caar %	.108	.032	−.483	−5.012	−5.183	−4.563	−4.685

(a) Do the results of Szewczyk *et al.* contradict the EMH? If so, explain which form of the EMH they contradict. Make additional assumptions if necessary.

19 Szewczyk, S.H., G.P. Tsetsekos and Z.Z. Zantout, 1997, 'Do dividend omissions signal future earnings or past earnings?' *The Journal of Investing*, 6(1), 40–53.

(b) It is sometimes argued that management of firms announcing dividend omissions know beforehand what they are going to announce, so that they could have shorted (sold short) the stock a week before. This would give them, on average, 5 per cent return in a week $\rightarrow$ > 200 per cent a year. This would be insider trading, but that happens, it is not illegal in some cases and seldom discovered anyway. The conclusion is that the market is not strong form efficient. Is this argument correct?

5 Capital structure and dividends

The combination of capital categories that a firm uses to finance its operations is called its capital structure. It is expressed in ratios such as debt-to-equity or debt-to-total assets. Dividends are the payments that stockholders receive as return on their capital. An old issue in finance is whether the choice of dividend policy or capital structure can create value for investors. The traditional opinion was that dividends and capital structure decisions could increase firm value, even under idealized conditions. In their groundbreaking analyses, Modigliani and Miller (1958, 1961) conclude that both are irrelevant in perfect capital markets. The value of a firm is not affected by how it is divided over capital categories and the value of a share is unaffected by whether its income is in the form of dividends or capital gains. Their conclusions, often ridiculed at the time, are now generally accepted as a correct analysis, not an accurate description of the actual situation. Both were later awarded the Nobel prize in economics. We shall review their arguments and some later extensions. We begin, however, with a description of the categories that constitute capital structure.

5.1 Dimensions of securities

Securities are financial contracts that can be framed in infinitely many ways by varying the basic elements (or dimensions). In our analyses we concentrate on the general principles, so we only include the basic types of securities, such as common stock, ordinary debt and 'plain vanilla' options. This section sketches some of the wider variety of securities that exist today.

5.1.1 General dimensions

The most obvious characteristics of securities are their riskiness, maturity and the property rights attached to them. *Riskiness* primarily relates to the nature of the returns, which can be profit dependent (such as dividends or capital gains) or predetermined (such as interest payments). Profit-dependent returns are claims on the 'residual' income of the firm, i.e. the income that is left after all other claims with a higher priority are paid. On the other hand, profit-dependent returns have no upper limit, while the predetermined returns never exceed their predetermined level. Another dimension of risk is the probability that the counterparty defaults on the obligations from the financial contract (called counterparty, or default, or bankruptcy risk). *Maturity* is the time dimension of a security, i.e. the period for which the financial contract is valid. Maturities can be anything between a day and perpetuity. The usual distinction is between short- and long-term securities. Short-term securities have maturities of less than a year and are traded in money markets. Long-term securities have maturities of more than a year and are traded in capital markets. Shares have *property rights* (and usually voting rights) attached to them: a firm's shareholders are its owners and they have, at least in principle, the ultimate control over the firm. Debt is not associated with property rights, but, as creditors, debtholders have a more protected position. It is along these three dimensions that the most common securities are defined. Stocks are permanent investments that give property rights and low-priority, profit-dependent, open-end returns. Ordinary debt, such as a bond or a bank loan, is a temporary investment with a predetermined return without property rights.

The money involved in a security can be deposited or promised. Deposited money has a financing function: it is converted into the assets that generate the firm's income. Promised money generally has a guarantee function, investors only have to deposit the full amount in case of unusual events. Since the return is calculated over the full amount, this allows the investors to earn double income. The reverse side of this construction is that there may be no upper limit to the amount to be deposited. A famous (or notorious) example of this construction was the insurance company Lloyd's, whose policies traditionally were backed, with unlimited liability, by the capital of rich people (called 'names'). In the early 1990s hurricanes and other disasters were larger and more frequent than in previous decades and Lloyd's names were obliged to cover the damage (which put many of them into financial difficulties). Since then, Lloyd's gradually switched from personal to corporate backers with limited liability.

Financial contracts can be for immediate delivery and payment or for future delivery. The former are called spot (or cash) contracts, with spot (cash) prices, and the latter are called future, forward or option contracts, depending on their specifications. The contract prices are named correspondingly (future, forward and option prices). They are also called derivative contracts because they derive their value from the asset to be delivered in the future. We have seen in Chapter 2 that the markets for stocks and bonds are spot markets. However, we shall see later that there are circumstances under which common stocks and bonds can also be regarded, and priced, as derivatives. These derivatives are the subjects of later chapters.

Debt can be *secured*, i.e. made less risky, in different ways. The best-known example of secured debt is the mortgage loan, which is secured by the value of the real estate for which the loan was provided. If the borrower is unable to meet his or her obligations from the loan, the lender can repossess the real estate and sell it to recover the loan. There are also legal constructions to use other assets to secure loans, for example inventories and accounts receivable, and even private assets. Benmelech and Bergman (2009) give an empirical analysis of the value of collaterals in the airline industry. Debt can also be secured by clauses in the debt contract. One type of clause ('me first rules') gives priority to the lenders that included it. Debt with a higher priority in case of financial distress is called *senior* debt, debt with a lower priority is *junior* debt. Ratio clauses prohibit the borrowing firm from letting certain financial ratios grow higher or lower than predetermined values. An example is the clause prohibiting the ratio of current assets-to-current liabilities from being lower than 2. Action clauses are more common. They prohibit the borrowing firm from selling certain assets or paying out dividends before the debt obligations are met in full. Note that securing, i.e. to make safe, is not the same as securitization, which is converting 'internal' debt into publicly traded securities. We will see an example of securitization a bit later.

5.1.2 The variety of stocks, bonds and derivatives

Some examples will illustrate how the general dimensions can be combined in specific securities. Although the trend is towards more complex securities, the basic types are still among the most frequently used.

Stocks

If a company only issues common stock, then each stock has one vote and is entitled to an equal share of the profits. That is not an unusual situation, but companies can also issue other types of stock, e.g. with restricted voting rights and/or increased profit rights. Some companies issue *non-voting common stock*. Many stock exchanges allow non-voting stock to be listed (NYSE is an example, but only few companies have non-voting stock). A more usual way to restrict voting rights is issuing *dual-class stock*, one class with enhanced and one with reduced voting rights. For example, Google has class B shares which carry ten votes and which are owned by the company's founders and top managers. The general public can only buy class A shares which have one vote. This construction is designed to give companies access to the public capital market while the founders, or founding families, retain control of the company. Note that in the United States the designations class 'A' and 'B' are arbitrary: in companies such as Berkshire Hathaway, class A shares have enhanced and class B shares have reduced voting rights.

Golden shares were popular in Europe during the privatization wave in the 1980s. They gave the owner, usually a government, the right to overrule all other shareholders in certain decisions, such as mergers and takeovers. Many of these golden shares, particularly those that can prevent foreign takeovers, have since been ruled illegal in the EU. Golden shares are also used by companies to prevent competitors from taking over subsidiaries that have been split off as independent businesses.

Preferred shares have a priority claim on profits up to a certain percentage. For example, if a company has '8 per cent preferred stock' it has to pay 8 per cent dividends to the preferred stockholders before it can pay any dividends to the common stockholders. These preferred dividends may be cumulative; if they are skipped in a year the company has to pay them in later years before it can pay regular dividends. Preferred stock can also have priority over common stock in the distribution of the proceeds when the firm's assets are liquidated in a bankruptcy. Preferred stock usually has no voting rights. Among the more exotic shares are repayable shares and convertible shares, e.g. preferred shares that can be converted into common shares.

Bonds

Ordinary bonds, or coupon bonds, pay a fixed interest rate, or *coupon*, every year or half year.[1] The principal sum can be paid back gradually over the bond's life or in one lump sum at maturity; in the latter case we speak of a *bullet loan*. But there are many variations on this theme:

---

[1] The word 'coupon' (literally: piece cut off) stems from a detachable part that is attached to a printed security and that has to be presented to receive payment of interest (bonds) or dividends (shares).

Income bonds only pay interest if the earnings of the issuing company are large enough.

Index bonds pay interest that is dependent on something else, e.g. the inflation rate, the interest on government bonds or the price of a commodity or service.

Junk bonds are ordinary bonds with very high interest rates and very high default risks. Originally, junk bonds were ordinary bonds that had fallen drastically in value because their issuing companies had ended up in financial trouble. From the 1980s, junk bonds were purposely issued to finance highly speculative business ventures such as mergers, acquisitions and buyouts.

Zero-coupon bonds, or pure discount bonds, do not make periodic interest payments. Instead, they make one final payment at the end of the bond's lifetime that includes both repayment of the principal sum and interest over the entire period. Investors buy these bonds at a deep discount from their face value, i.e. the amount the bond will be worth when it matures. For example, if the market interest rate is 5 per cent, a €1,000 zero-coupon bond with an interest rate of 5 per cent and which matures in five years will sell for $1,000/1.05^5 = €783.53$. After five years the investors are paid the face value of €1,000.

Bull–bear bonds are issued in two parts, called tranches. In the bull tranche the repayment of the principal sum increases with the value of another security (e.g. a stock market index) and in the bear part it decreases with the value of that security.

Catastrophe bonds are usually issued by insurance companies to transfer specific risks to investors. They are an alternative to reinsurance. Catastrophe bonds are ordinary bonds except for one condition which states that investors may have to accept reduced, or zero, interest payments and/or principal repayments if a specific catastrophe, such as a hurricane or earthquake, occurs during the bond's life. An often quoted example is the catastrophe bond issued by the international football federation FIFA to cover the risk that the 2006 World Cup tournament would be postponed or cancelled. If that would have happened, investors would have lost 75 per cent of the money they invested in the bonds.

Convertible bonds can be converted into shares at a predetermined conversion ratio during a predetermined period in the bonds' life. There usually are many other clauses in the bond contracts, e.g. that, in a period prior to the conversion period, the company has the right to redeem the loan (which makes it a *callable bond*) and/or that the bondholders have the right to sell the bonds back to the company (which makes it a *putable bond*). A comparable package is an ordinary bond, issued together with a warrant, i.e. a long-term option to buy a share. The difference is that investors can sell the warrant independently from the bond, while the conversion right cannot be separated from the bond.

Profit sharing bonds and *consol bonds* (the perpetual bonds we met in Chapter 2) are more rarely used types.

Derivatives

Derivatives come in an even larger variety than stocks and bonds. As we have seen, derivatives derive their value from another asset, called the underlying. Almost all assets can be used as underlying: derivatives 'are written on' stocks, bonds, indices, currencies, many commodities such as wheat, metals and oil and there are even weather derivatives.

Forwards and *futures* have a long history of use in commodity markets. A forward contract involves the delivery of an asset on some future date at a predetermined price. Future contracts are standardized forward contracts, issued by an exchange. These contracts are frequently used to eliminate the price risk from a transaction that will be completed on some future date.

Options give the right, but not the obligation, to buy or sell the underlying on some future date at a predetermined price. So option contracts are not necessarily completed by a delivery at maturity, they may simply expire unused. The simplest standard options, usually referred to as 'plain vanilla' options, come in European and American styles. In addition, there is a great variety of more complex or 'exotic' options and new ones enter the market regularly. There are Asian, Bermuda, barrier, basket, chooser, compound, look-back, binary, rainbow options and many more. Haug (2007) contains a complete overview of their pricing formulas.

Swaps are financial contracts to exchange one set of obligations (or cash flows) against another. Common types of swaps are interest rate swaps, in which fixed-rate interest payments are exchanged against floating rate payments, and currency swaps, in which payments in one currency are exchanged against payments in another currency. Credit default swaps exchange a series of payments against one larger payment if the underlying security is defaulted. With these swaps investors can insure themselves against the default risk of e.g. a corporate bond by transferring this risk to other investors.

We will look at derivatives and their pricing later on.

5.1.3   An example of financial engineering

Financial engineering is the process of constructing new securities from other, existing securities. It is a form of financial asset transformation, one of the principal roles of financial intermediaries that we saw in Chapter 2. Like most other asset transformations, financial engineering is mainly done through pooling, restructuring and securitization. The new securities distribute risk and return in different ways than the original ones, which can make them accessible to, or customized for, groups of investors. We will illustrate the process with mortgage loans, but it is also used for car loans, credit card debt, companies' accounts receivable, etc. In the simplest case, the customers borrow money from e.g. a bank without involvement of other parties. The bank collects the interest and repayments and bears the risk that customers either default the loans or pay them back early (prepayment risk). The case becomes a bit more complex when large numbers of mortgages are pooled in a specially created legal entity (called special purpose entity or special purpose vehicle). The bank sells its mortgages to this entity, which issues bonds to finance its operations. Such bonds are called *asset-backed securities* because the interest and repayment of the bonds are backed by the loans in the pool. The entity collects interest and repayments of the mortgage loans and pays them out as interest and principal repayments on the bonds. This construction is an example of *securitization*: the mortgage loans, that were held by the bank, are transformed into bonds that can be bought by investors. The special entity, or the financial institution behind it, usually creates a secondary market for the bonds, so that investors can buy and sell them. The special entity charges a fee and pooling spreads the risks of the mortgages evenly over all bondholders, which makes them less sensitive to large losses on individual loans. But apart from that, risk and return are not transformed by this construction.

Risk and return are transformed if the special entity issues bonds that are structured in several tranches with different default or prepayment risk, the so-called structured products. For example, suppose a special purpose entity collects a pool of €80 million in mortgages that pay 8 per cent interest. The entity issues €80 million in bonds in three tranches. The first tranche of €20 million has a low interest rate of 6 per cent but it has priority over the other two tranches, so it has a low default risk. The second tranche of €40 million pays 8 per cent interest and has priority over the third tranche, so it has a medium default risk. The third tranche of €20 million has the lowest priority, so the highest default risk, but pays 10 per cent interest. In a year without defaults, the mortgage pool produces $80 \times 0.08 = 6.4$ million in interest, which is to be divided among the bondholders. The low-risk tranche receives $20 \times 0.06 = 1.2$ million, the medium-risk tranche gets $40 \times 0.08 = 3.2$ million and the high-risk tranche gets the remaining 2 million, which is 10 per cent. In a year when 15 per cent of the mortgages default on their interest payments, the pool produces $80 \times 0.85 = 68 \times 0.08 = 5.44$ million in interest. Of this, the low-risk tranche receives $20 \times 0.06 = 1.2$ million, the medium-risk tranche gets $40 \times 0.08 = 3.2$ million and the high-risk tranche gets the remaining 1.04 million, which is 5.2 per cent.

These constructions were used on a very large scale during the high tide of financial engineering, just before the credit crunch of 2007–2008. Their total amount was measured in hundreds of billions of dollars. It was even believed that top investment grade bonds (triple A rated) could be constructed from subprime mortgages, i.e. loans to borrowers with very poor credit ratings that had borrowed 100 per cent of the value of their houses.[2] That turned out not to be the case; several elements in the construction failed. Pooling mortgages in special purpose entities separates the investors who bear the default risk from the persons who sell the mortgages to customers. This gives the sellers an incentive to lower their standards, as they get commissions for new mortgages but are unaffected by defaults. Such an incentive structure calls for extensive risk management instruments, but not enough were put in place. As a consequence, the quality of the mortgages deteriorated. By comparison, in the simplest case sketched above, the bank both grants the loan and bears the risk of default, so it has a clear incentive not to lower standards. Moreover, the rating agencies were far too optimistic about the security of the best tranches that were created from subprime mortgages. Their estimates of price developments on the housing market were too rosy (allegedly, some computer programs used in the process did not allow negative price changes). Investors were too willing to buy the bonds, perhaps because they were sold too aggressively (some of the structured products from the United States even found their way to municipalities in arctic Norway). The result was the credit crunch.

5.2 Capital structure analyses

Our analyses of the firm's capital structure decisions start with the famous Modigliani and Miller (1958) irrelevance theorem. Together with Markowitz's portfolio theory, this is regarded by many as the beginnings of modern finance. The study of capital structure has a wider relevance than the name suggests. It includes the cost of capital and, hence,

---

2 Bonds can be graded according to their safety by rating agencies; the top rating is AAA or Aaa, and investment grade bonds have ratings of BBB or higher, or Baa or higher, depending on the agency.

capital budgeting issues. It also shows which projects are easy to finance because they can carry much debt. Capital structure is also a major factor in the evaluation of firms.

5.2.1 Capital structure in perfect markets

Modigliani and Miller base their analyses on the assumption of perfect markets. Recall that in perfect financial markets there are no taxes or transaction costs, all assets are marketable and perfectly divisible and there are no limitations on short selling and risk-free borrowing and lending by private investors or companies. There are large numbers of buyers and sellers, none of which is large enough to individually influence prices, and all information is simultaneously and costlessly available to all market participants. We now know that we also have to assume that firms cannot create unique investment opportunities by changing their capital structures, i.e. such changes should not expand the investment universe.[3] On such markets, the actions of investors are not hampered by transaction costs or higher interest rates than companies have to pay, etc. This means that investors can undo or redo many actions by companies. Modigliani and Miller were the first to formulate the insight that companies cannot create value through actions that can be costlessly undone or redone by investors. We shall restate their irrelevance theorem by comparing two firms with identical assets that produce identical profits. The firms only differ in capital structure (or leverage): one firm exclusively uses equity (is *unlevered*) and the other uses a mix of equity and debt (is *levered*). We analyze the risk and return of equity and total value of both firms. Their balance sheets are:

Unlevered firm U				Levered firm L		
Assets	A_u	Equity	E_u	Assets	A_l	Debt	D
						Equity	E_l
total	V_u	total	V_u	total	V_l	total	V_l

V stands for (total) value and u and l are subscripts for (un)levered. Both firms generate the same amount of net earnings (called *profits*). All values (A, V, E, D) can be regarded as market values, i.e. the present values of properly discounted cash flows. We compare two investment strategies:

1. Buy a fraction α of firm U's equity.
2. Buy a fraction α of firm L's debt and equity.

If we buy a fraction α of firm U's equity, we have to invest $\alpha E_u = \alpha V_u$ and the return is $\alpha(profits)$. If we buy a fraction α of firm L's debt and equity, we have to invest $\alpha D + \alpha E_l = \alpha V_l$. The return of that investment consists of two parts. The return on debt is $\alpha r_d D$, where r_d is interest rate on debt. For now, we assume that debt is riskless, so that r_d is the risk-free interest rate, but that assumption is not necessary. The return from the equity part of the investment is $\alpha(profits - r_d D)$. The total return on the investment is sum of both parts: $\alpha r_d D + \alpha(profits - r_d D) = \alpha(profits)$. We see that both strategies give the same return, so their values have to be the same as well:

$$\alpha V_u = \alpha V_l \quad so \quad V_u = V_l$$

---

[3] In technical terms, the market has to be *complete* in order to ensure the possibility of arbitrage. Market completeness is discussed in a later chapter.

This is *Modigliani–Miller Proposition 1*, their irrelevance theorem: in perfect capital markets, the market value of any firm is independent of its capital structure.

It follows from the argumentation that the 'mechanism' behind this proposition is arbitrage. In perfect capital markets, investors can undo or redo all capital structure decisions free of charge. This means that there are arbitrage opportunities if levered and unlevered firms have different prices. For instance, instead of buying a fraction of the levered firm's equity, we can buy a fraction of the unlevered firm's equity and borrow ourselves, i.e. use 'home-made' leverage. Compare the following two strategies:

1. Buy a fraction α of firm L's equity.
2. Buy a fraction α of firm U's equity and borrow αD ourselves.

If we buy a fraction α of firm L's equity, we have to invest $\alpha E_l = \alpha(V_l - D)$. The return on that investment is $\alpha(profits - r_d D)$. If we buy a fraction α of firm U's equity and borrow αD ourselves, the investment is $\alpha E_u - \alpha D = \alpha(V_u - D)$. The return on the debt is negative (we borrowed money, so we have to pay interest): $-\alpha r_d D$. The return on the unlevered equity is $\alpha(profits)$, so the total return is: $\alpha(profits - r_d D)$. Again, both strategies give the same return, so their values have to be the same:

$$\alpha(V_u - D) = \alpha(V_l - D) \quad so \quad V_u = V_l$$

In the same way, investors can undo a firm's leverage decision by private lending. Compare the following two strategies:

1. Buy a fraction α of firm U's equity.
2. Buy a fraction α of firm L's equity and put αD in the bank ourselves.

If we buy a fraction α of firm U's equity, we have to invest $\alpha E_u = \alpha V_u$ and we get a return of $\alpha(profits)$. If we buy a fraction α of firm L's equity and put αD in the bank, we have to invest $\alpha E_l + \alpha D$; since $E_l = V_l - D$ this equals αV_l. The return on that investment is $+\alpha r_d D$ from debt and $\alpha(profits - r_d D)$ from equity, which totals $\alpha(profits)$. Once again, both strategies give the same return, so their values have to be the same: $\alpha V_u = \alpha V_l$ so $V_u = V_l$. The inevitable conclusion is that in perfect capital markets, levered firms cannot sell at a premium or a discount compared with unlevered firms. If they did, there would be arbitrage possibilities through home-made levering or unlevering. Hence, managers cannot change the value of the firm by changing its capital structure: capital structure is irrelevant.

5.2.2   Risk, return and leverage

We will now analyze how the return and risk of equity change with leverage. We introduce the analyses with a simple numerical example of three scenarios for the return on assets, r_a: bust, with a return of 5 per cent, normal, with a return of 15 per cent and boom, with a return of 25 per cent. Again, we look at two firms: unlevered firm U and levered firm L, with 50 per cent debt and equity. Their balance sheets, this time with numerical values, are as follows:

Unlevered firm U				Levered firm L			
Assets	100	Equity	100	Assets	100	Debt	50
						Equity	50
total	100	total	100	total	100	total	100

The interest rate on debt, r_d, is 10 per cent. Given the priority rule that interest payments come before dividend payments, r_a and r_d together determine the return on levered equity, r_{el}, as Table 5.1 shows.

Table 5.1 *Returns in three scenarios*

scenario	bust	normal	boom
$r_a = r_{eu}$	5%	15%	25%
r_d	10%	10%	10%
profits	5	15	25
interest (firm L)	5	5	5
eq. income (firm L)	0	10	20
$r_{el} = eq.income/equity$	0%	20%	40%

We see that leverage makes equity riskier. If the return on assets, r_a, is higher than the interest rate on debt, the difference is added to the return on levered equity. But if the return on assets is lower than the interest rate, the difference lowers the return on levered equity. It is therefore to be expected that the return on equity also increases with leverage. This can be shown in more general terms with the concept of the *weighted average cost of capital*, or *WACC*. In the context of our analyses so far, the WACC simply is the weighted average of the cost of debt (r_d, the interest rate) and the cost of equity (r_e). The weights are, of course, the fractions of each capital category in total investment. The subscript for levered, l, is superfluous here. Since the value of debt (D) plus the value of equity (E) equals the value of total assets (V), the WACC must also equal r_a. This is expressed in the following formula for the WACC:

$$r_a = \frac{D}{V}r_d + \frac{E}{V}r_e \tag{5.1}$$

Multiplying both sides by V/E gives:

$$\frac{V}{E}r_a = \frac{D}{E}r_d + r_e$$

Since V = D + E this can be written as:

$$\frac{E+D}{E}r_a = \frac{D}{E}r_d + r_e$$

$$\frac{E}{E}r_a + \frac{D}{E}r_a = \frac{D}{E}r_d + r_e$$

$$r_e = r_a + \frac{D}{E}(r_a - r_d) \tag{5.2}$$

This is *Modigliani–Miller Proposition 2*: the return on equity is equal to the return on assets, r_a, plus a premium for financial risk, calculated as the debt-to-equity ratio times the spread between r_a and r_d. *Financial risk* is the additional risk that equity holders accept by giving debtholders a higher priority claim on the firm's cash flows. Reformulated, this proposition says that the cost of equity increases with leverage such that the

5.2 Capital structure analyses

WACC is constant. As the proportion of cheap debt increases, the required rate on equity also increases so that the WACC is constant. Figure 5.1 gives a graphical representation of the proposition.

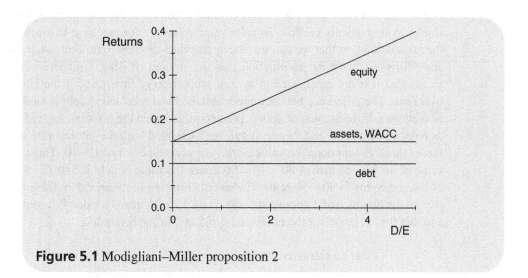

Figure 5.1 Modigliani–Miller proposition 2

5.2.3 The after-tax WACC

Modigliani and Miller's (1958) irrelevance theorem is only valid in perfect markets. In real markets, imperfections can make capital structure relevant. In a later publication, Modigliani and Miller (1963) themselves analyzed the effect of corporate income taxes on capital structure. The introduction of corporate taxes means that there is a third party, the tax collector, that claims a part of corporate value. This will reduce the value of the firm. However, interest payments are deductible from the firm's taxable income, while dividends are not. This means that the tax collector's part will decrease with debt, so that the sum of levered equity and debt will be larger than unlevered equity. The effect can be shown with our previous example; we will use the normal return scenario and a corporate income tax rate of 20 per cent. The numbers are in Table 5.2.

Table 5.2 *(Un)levered cash flows*

	unlevered	levered
profits (EBIT)	15	15
interest (10% of 50)	–	5
EBT	15	10
taxes (20%)	3	2
after-tax profits	12	8
total income investors	12	$8 + 5 = 13$

The total income for investors (debt and equity holders) is higher in the levered firm (13) than in the unlevered (12), because the tax collector's part is lower. If we assume that all cash flows are perpetuities, so that we can use (2.7), the value of the unlevered firm's assets and equity can be calculated as $12/0.15 = 80$. The value of the levered firm includes not only the assets but also the value of the tax reduction (or the value of its tax shield, as it is usually called). To calculate the latter value we have to know how risky the tax shield is, so that we can use the appropriate discount rate. Following Modigliani and Miller we make the assumption that the amount of debt is predetermined, which means that it is not rebalanced to a fixed proportion of firm value if the latter changes over time. The difference between predetermined and rebalanced debt is analyzed in the next chapter. If the amount of debt is predetermined, then the tax advantage of debt is just as risky as debt itself and, hence, it can be discounted with the interest rate on debt, r_d. Under these assumptions the value of the tax advantage is $1/0.1 = 10$. This gives a total value of the levered firm of $80 + 10 = 90$. Since the value of debt is $5/0.1 = 50$, the value of levered equity is $90 - 50 = 40$. The calculations are summarized in Table 5.3. We see that, in the presence of corporate income taxes, $V_u < V_l$: tax is a value flow out of the firm and that flow is larger for the unlevered firm than for the levered.

Table 5.3 *(Un)levered returns and values*

	unlevered	levered
r_a	0.15	0.15
Value assets (12/0.15)	80	80
Value tax shield (1/0.1)	–	10
Value of the firm V (V_u, V_l)	80	90
value debt D (5/0.1)	–	50
value equity (E_u, E_l)	80	$90 - 50 = 40$
r_e (r_{eu}, r_{el})	0.15	$8/40 = 0.2$

These calculations can be formulated in more general terms. If we use x for the firm's cash flow (earnings before interest and taxes, EBIT), and τ for the corporate income tax rate, then value of the *unlevered* firm, V_u, is:

$$V_u = \frac{(1 - \tau)x}{r_a}$$

The cash flows to the investors in the *levered* firm consist of two parts:

1. To shareholders: $(1 - \tau)(x - r_d D)$.
2. To debtholders: $r_d D$.

The first part should be discounted with r_{el}, second part with r_d. We sum the two cash flows and work out terms:

$$(1 - \tau)(x - r_d D) + r_d D$$
$$(1 - \tau)x - r_d D + \tau r_d D + r_d D$$
$$(1 - \tau)x + \tau r_d D$$

5.3 Models of optimal capital structure

The first part, $(1 - \tau)x$, is the cash flow to *unlevered* equity and the second part, $\tau r_d D$, is the tax advantage of debt. The first part should be discounted with r_a and the second part with r_d, as we just saw. This gives:

$$V_l = \frac{(1 - \tau)x}{r_a} + \frac{\tau r_d D}{r_d}$$

$$V_l = V_u + \tau D \tag{5.3}$$

This is *Modigliani–Miller proposition 1 with taxes*: the value of the levered firm is the value of the unlevered firm plus the value of the tax advantage of debt. The latter equals the present value of the tax shield under the assumptions we made (i.e. that debt is fixed and perpetual).

Using the same set of assumptions, we can also derive Modigliani–Miller's proposition 2 with taxes. As we did in the case without taxes, we can write the balance sheet identity assets = debt + equity in terms of returns. However, in the presence of taxes the levered firm has an additional asset: the value of its tax shields. The balance sheet then becomes:

Assets	A_l	Debt	D
Tax shields	τD	Equity	E_l
total	V	total	V

Writing this balance sheet in terms of returns, the weighted average cost of capital is (the subscript l is superfluous both for assets and equity and V_a is the value of assets):

$$r_a \frac{V_a}{V} + r_d \frac{\tau D}{V} = r_d \frac{D}{V} + r_e \frac{E}{V}$$

$$r_a \frac{V_a}{V} = r_d \frac{D}{V} - r_d \frac{\tau D}{V} + r_e \frac{E}{V}$$

$$r_a \frac{V_a}{V} = r_d (1 - \tau) \frac{D}{V} + r_e \frac{E}{V} = WACC$$

This formula for the after-tax WACC can be re-written to gives expressions for r_a and r_e:

$$r_a = r_d (1 - \tau) \frac{D}{V - \tau D} + r_e \frac{E}{V - \tau D}$$

Rewriting for r_e we get *Modigliani–Miller proposition 2 with taxes*:

$$r_e = r_a + (1 - \tau)(r_a - r_d) \frac{D}{E} \tag{5.4}$$

If corporate taxes are the only market imperfection, the value of the levered firm will increase and the WACC will decrease with the debt–equity ratio. The 'optimal' solution is then 100 per cent debt financing. Figure 5.2 depicts the decreasing WACC for the example we used.

5.3 Models of optimal capital structure

• •

Modigliani and Miller's conclusions of capital structure irrelevance and optimal capital structure at 100 per cent debt are clearly incompatible with observed capital structures. For an optimal capital structure with less than 100 per cent debt, other market imperfections have to be included that counterbalance the tax advantage of debt. We will look at some of these imperfections and two models that include them.

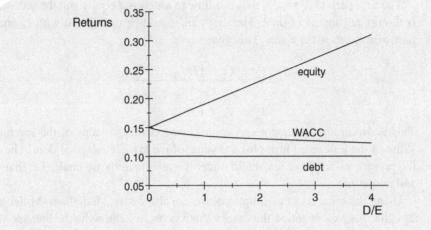

Figure 5.2 Modigliani–Miller proposition 2 with taxes

5.3.1 The trade-off theory

The trade-off theory can be regarded as a direct extension of Modigliani and Miller's propositions. It models the costs of financial distress as a broad, leverage-related cost category against which the tax advantage of debt is traded off. This produces an optimal capital structure which is not a corner solution.

Probability and costs of financial distress

Look again at the graphical illustration of Modigliani–Miller proposition 2 in Figure 5.1. The required return on debt is independent of the debt-equity ratio. This is a consequence of the fact that debt is risk free. But debt can only be risk free if the equity-holders are assumed to have unlimited liability and enough personal wealth to pay the debt obligations, no matter how low the profits (losses) are. If either assumption is relaxed, debt becomes subject to risk of default. If we assume limited liability, the probability of default will increase with leverage. The fixed debt obligations have to be paid from the firm's uncertain cash flow and the larger the debt obligations, the larger the probability that the cash flow will be insufficient. Suppose, for example, that there is only one future cash flow which is normally distributed with an expectation of 15 and a standard deviation of 3. If the debt obligations amount to 10, then it is easily verified that the probability of an insufficient cash flow is almost 5 per cent.[4] If the debt obligations are 15, the probability of an insufficient cash flow is, of course, 50 per cent. In general terms, as the debt–equity ratio increases, business risk is gradually transferred from the stockholders to the debtholders. This means that the cost of debt will increase with leverage and the expected return on equity will decrease correspondingly. This is depicted in Figure 5.3 for proposition 2 without taxes. In the extreme case of 100 per cent debt financing the position of debt

---

4 Transforming into a standard normal variable Z gives $Z = (10 - 15)/3 = -1.67$ and from a calculator or a table as in appendix 7B: $P(Z) = 0.047$.

5.3 Models of optimal capital structure

would be equal to that of unlevered equity and the required return on debt would equal r_a and r_{eu} (not depicted).

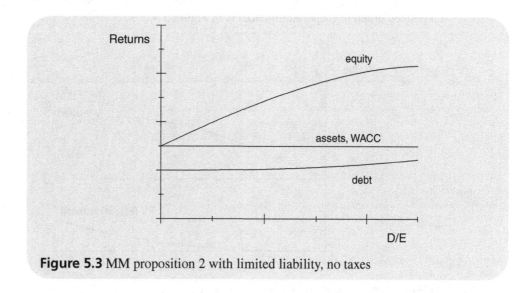

Figure 5.3 MM proposition 2 with limited liability, no taxes

The introduction of the risk of default alone does not alter Modigliani and Miller's conclusions in the case with taxes.[5] The debt payments become uncertain but the value of the levered firm will still increase and the WACC will still decrease with the debt-equity ratio, because the tax advantage of debt increases with the debt–equity ratio. An additional element is necessary to produce an optimal optical structure below 100 per cent debt. In the trade-off theory that element consists of the costs that have to be incurred if debt is too high. The collective terms for these costs are the *costs of bankruptcy* or, more generally, the *costs of financial distress*. As the probability of default increases, the firm is increasingly likely to get into increasing financial trouble, which makes costly measures necessary. The extreme case of financial trouble is bankruptcy, which involves costly bankruptcy procedures. But even if bankruptcy can be avoided, the costs of financial distress may be substantial:

- Income can decrease or even collapse because customers run away.
- Suppliers can stop delivering or require cash or advance payment.
- Key personnel may leave the company.
- Investors may require costly refinancing.
- Non-strategic assets, such as office buildings, may have to be sold at emergency prices.
- Risk-reducing financial instruments may no longer be available from banks.

These costs are a counterweight to the tax advantage of debt. As the debt ratio increases, the probability of default increases and, hence, also the probability that these costs will have to be incurred. That is the essence of the *trade-off theory of capital structure*: starting

5 A formal proof can be found in Rubinstein (1973).

with no leverage, debt will be increased as long as the marginal expected tax advantage outweighs the marginal expected costs of financial distress. Optimal capital structure is reached as both are equal. Its graphical representation (probably the most frequently reproduced graph in corporate finance) is in Figure 5.4.

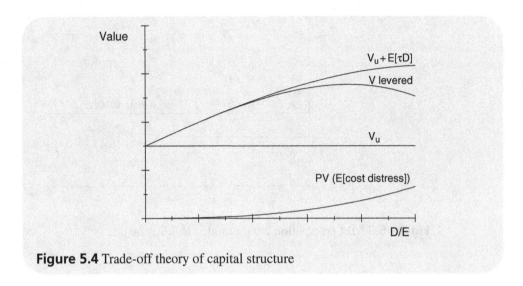

Figure 5.4 Trade-off theory of capital structure

In Figure 5.4, $V_u + E[\tau D]$ flattens off with increasing leverage. V_u is a constant, so the effect is caused by the expected tax advantage, $E[\tau D]$. This flattens off with increasing leverage, even though the interest rate increases, as we have seen in Figure 5.3. However, with increasing leverage, it becomes increasingly likely that the debt obligations are larger than the cash flow. If that is so, then there is no profit and, hence, no tax and no tax advantage. So with increasing leverage it becomes increasingly likely that the tax advantage will not be realized, which is another way of saying that the expected tax advantage $E[\tau D]$ will level off at high D/E ratios. Notice, however, that marginal increases in $E[\tau D]$ cannot become negative,[6] so that $V_u + E[\tau D]$ cannot become decreasing. That is why risky debt alone does not give an optimal capital structure below 100 per cent debt; the expected costs of financial distress are necessary to counterbalance the tax advantage. It can be shown that the trade-off theory produces a well-behaved optimal capital structure with less than 100 per cent debt. The optimum is attainable, which means that the debtholders are willing to provide the debt that corresponds to the optimum (popularly summarized as 'the debtholders will not chicken out before the stockholders'). A more complete description of these models can found in, e.g. Scott (1976), Kim (1978) and Van der Wijst (1989). A survey of related theoretical models is presented in Harris and Raviv (1991).

The importance of taxes and distress costs

Like the Modigliani–Miller propositions, the trade-off model is hardly contentious as a theoretical analysis. But the relevance of both elements of the trade-off theory, taxes

---

6 Probabilities and the tax rate cannot be negative and D increases with D/E.

and default costs, has been questioned. As regards taxes, Miller (1977) argues that the corporate tax advantage of debt may be reduced or even undone by a tax disadvantage at the personal level. In many countries, capital gains are not taxed until they are realized and dividend income may be taxed at a lower rate than interest payments. This could make capital structure irrelevant, even in the presence of corporate taxes. In several early empirical papers, taxes appear to have a weak (Fischer *et al.*, 1989) or erroneous (Bradley *et al.*, 1984) influence. However, in major, more recent studies such as MacKie-Mason (1990), Graham (2000) and Kemsley and Nissim (2002), taxes are firmly established as a major determinant of capital structure.

The relevance of the costs of financial distress has been debated in a similar way. The first estimates of direct bankruptcy costs were very low, some 2–4 per cent of firm value prior to bankruptcy (Warner, 1977). Such low costs make the expected bankruptcy costs negligible and, thus, the trade-off model empirically indistinguishable from the Modigliani–Miller proposition. However, later studies produced considerably higher estimates, in the order of magnitude of 20 per cent (Altman, 1984) to 35 per cent (Alderson and Betker, 1995) of the pre-bankruptcy value. Andrade and Kaplan (1998) present quantitative and qualitative estimates of the (direct and indirect) costs of financial distress and their determinants. They estimate financial distress costs to be 10 to 20 per cent of firm value. More recently, Bris *et al.* (2006) show that the costs of bankruptcy are sensitive to the variant of the legal bankruptcy procedure that was followed, to the denominator (i.e. how assets are measured), and to the statistical procedure used. Their estimates vary widely (and predictably) from 2 per cent to 20 per cent; apparently, bankruptcy costs are modest in some firms, and large in others.

A very illustrative demonstration of distress costs emerged from Texaco's filing for bankruptcy after a dispute with Pennzoil over a takeover (of Getty Oil). The case is documented and analyzed by Cutler and Summers (1988). Using event study methodology, they report that Texaco's value fell $4.1 *billion* over the entire conflict. That is the stock market's estimate of the bankruptcy costs. Pennzoil's value rose only $682 million. The total costs for both parties amounted to more than 32 per cent of the total pre-conflict value. When the conflict was resolved without any bankruptcies, this led to a $2.3 billion increase in value, so that 65 per cent of losses were recovered. Texaco's legal fees were estimated at $165 million after tax; Pennzoil's fees were probably in the same order of magnitude. The rest of the losses in value are indirect bankruptcy costs or costs of financial distress. For Texaco these costs were documented as follows:

- Difficulty in obtaining credit.
- Distraction of management attention.
- Suppliers demanded cash payment before performance or secured forms of payment, such as prepayment.
- Suppliers halted or cancelled shipments of crude oil to Texaco, fearing they would not be paid.
- Banks refused or limited Texaco's use of exchange rate future contracts (to hedge foreign currency risk).

Such quantitative estimates of the costs of financial distress are very illustrative, but difficult to obtain. In empirical research is it more usual to work with qualitative indicators, that often have a long history of use in banking. For example, the costs of bankruptcy and financial distress are related to the nature and the 'specificity' of assets. General purpose (i.e. non-specific) assets such as buildings and trucks can easily be re-deployed by other companies and lose little value in a bankruptcy. Business sectors such as retailing and restaurants mainly use general purpose assets; they can carry much debt and have high default rates. On the other hand, specialized (specific) assets such as employees' expertise, the results of advertising campaigns or firm-specific growth opportunities, have limited or no value to other firms. Many companies in the service sectors own such assets; their debt ratios and default rates are low.

The nature of the products that a firm supplies is also relevant for its capital structure. For instance, Titman (1984) points out that durables, which require future maintenance and service, decrease in value (or even stop selling) as the firm's default probability increases. The implication is that firms supplying durables have lower optimal debt ratios than firms supplying non-durables. Similarly, perishable and fashion-sensitive goods may lose all their value in a bankruptcy; firms supplying such goods cannot carry much debt.

Bankruptcy costs are also related to the transparency of the firm. Complex legal constructions are difficult (expensive) to dismantle and can obscure ownership relations. Secure assets may be owned by a holding company while risky operations are located in independent working companies that have very little value in a bankruptcy. Finally, size is also a factor; there are economies of scale even in going bankrupt.

5.3.2   The pecking order theory

Myers and Majluf (1984) provide an alternative explanation of capital structures, based on the observation that managers seem to prefer internal financing to external, and debt to equity. Their pecking order theory, as they call it, is based on the market imperfection of information asymmetry and the conflicts of interest that follow from it.[7] Recall that in perfect markets all information is simultaneously and costlessly available to all market participants. If this assumption is relaxed, differences in information level (asymmetries) will arise. Generally, managers are more knowledgeable about firms' prospects than outside investors. But it may be costly (or impossible) for them to reveal this information to outsiders, for instance because that would undermine their negotiating position with suppliers and customers, or because it may allow competitors to appropriate key features of the firm's projects. If managers have information that is not fully reflected in security prices, conflicts of interest are almost inevitable. Managers are hired by the existing shareholders to manage the firm in their, i.e. the shareholders', best interest.[8] This means that managers should use their inside information to issue the type of security that benefits the existing shareholders: debt will be issued when good news is coming up (and equity is underpriced) and equity when bad news is coming up (equity is overpriced).

---

7 These conflicts of interest are discussed in a more general context in a later chapter.

8 Managers can be regarded as agents that are hired by principals, in this case the stockholders; these *agency relations* are discussed later on.

This behaviour is recognized and anticipated in the market. For example, firms sometimes exchange one type of security for another, e.g. debt for equity. These transactions do not involve any payments. Studies of such exchange offers (e.g. Masulis, 1980) show that the stock price falls if stock is exchanged for debt (so that stock increases). But when debt is exchanged for stock (so that stock decreases), the stock price rises. The trade-off theory predicts stock price increases for both these capital structure changes, because they should move the firm closer to its optimal capital structure. If the market expects that new equity is only issued when it is overvalued, potential new stockholders will require a discount.[9] In this situation, managers who need funds face the dilemma of either issuing equity at a price they know is too low, or forgoing positive NPV investment opportunities. Debt is in principle troubled with the same problems, but to a much lesser extent: debt has a higher priority claim, it can be secured and it can have shorter maturities. Managers will try to avoid the dilemma by building up 'financial slack' in the form of cash and marketable securities or reserve borrowing power. This argumentation leads to the following pecking order in financing alternatives:

1. Internal equity.
2. (External) debt (first short then long term).
3. External equity.

The pecking order theory has some other implications as well. To avoid a shortage of funds, firms will adapt their long-term payout ratios (the fraction of profits that is paid out as dividends) to their investments and level out fluctuations in both dividends and investments through financial slack. This means that firms will have no optimal or target debt ratio, as in the trade-off theory. The debt ratio will depend on the firm's financing needs and its cumulative profitability in past periods. Modelled in this way, financial slack is a rational and valuable instrument to abate the consequences of information asymmetry. The pecking order does not imply that equity will never be issued. When the firm reaches its debt capacity, i.e. when its borrowing possibilities are exhausted because the expected bankruptcy costs have become prohibitive, then equity issues are no longer considered 'bad news' by the market. Similarly, firms with very limited borrowing opportunities, because their assets mainly consist of intangible assets, such as R&D-based firms, are expected to issue equity.

5.3.3 Some empirical tests

Like most other theories in finance, capital structure theory has been empirically tested on a vast scale. We will have a brief look at some of the best known papers.

Shared and opposite predictions

The trade-off and pecking order theory share some of their empirical implications: both predict that leverage decreases with earnings volatility and with the value of growth opportunities. In the pecking order theory, volatile earnings increase the probability that the internally generated funds are insufficient to cover the investment needs. So firms

---

9 This situation is equivalent to the old Groucho Marx joke: 'I don't want to belong to any club that will accept me as a member.'

with more volatile earnings have lower leverage to reduce the risk that new equity has to be issued or that profitable investment opportunities have to be forgone. Similarly, financial slack is particularly valuable to firms with large expected investments in growth opportunities, so these firms maintain reserve borrowing power by keeping their current debt ratios low. In the trade-off theory, volatile earnings increase the probability that debt obligations cannot be paid so that default costs have to be incurred. This lowers optimal leverage for firms with more volatile earnings. In a trade-off context, growth opportunities are assets that do not produce current income, which gives a low value of interest tax shields, and that have limited value to other firms, which gives high bankruptcy costs. So the trade-off theory also predicts low debt ratios for firms that derive a considerable part of their value from growth opportunities.

But in other cases the predictions of the pecking order theory are the opposite of those of the trade-off theory. The pecking order theory predicts a negative relationship between leverage and profitability. The trade-off theory predicts the reverse because the value of tax shields increases with profitability. Also, the pecking order theory does not lead to an optimal or target level of leverage. This means that debt ratios should not be mean reverting, i.e. have no tendency to return to their long-term average value after a period above or below that value. In the trade-off theory, firms adjust their capital structures 'back' to the optimum, which is mean reverting by nature.

Trade-off theory tests

The predictions of the trade-off theory are generally tested by regressing observed debt ratios on proxy variables for the tax advantage of debt and for the costs of financial distress.[10] The qualitative indicators of distress costs, that were mentioned above, are examples of such proxy variables. In their survey of nine major empirical contributions from the 1980s, Harris and Raviv (1991) report on variables such as stock price volatility (as proxy for business risk), fixed-to-total assets (proxy for the tangibility or liquidation value of assets), advertising and R&D expenditure (specificity of assets), market-to-book value (growth opportunities), profitability and size. Fixed-to-total assets is the only variable that consistently has a positive effect on leverage in all studies where it is included. In most, but not all, studies where they are included, high levels of volatility and profitability are associated with low leverage. The latter supports the pecking order theory and contradicts the trade-off theory. The influence of the other variables is less consistent across studies, but Harris and Raviv conclude that the empirical evidence thus far accumulated is broadly consistent with the theory.

Rajan and Zingales (1995) test the influence of a subset of these variables on leverage in seven large, industrialized countries. They, too, find that the tangibility of assets (fixed-to-total assets) consistently has a positive influence on leverage in all analyses in all countries. Growth opportunities (proxied by the market-to-book ratio) are consistently negatively related to leverage in all countries and analyses, and significantly so in most cases. Size is positively correlated with leverage in all but one country (Germany) and

---

10 In statistical tests, unobserved variables are often approximated by other, observed variables that are expected to be highly correlated with them; the observed variables are called *proxy variables* or *proxies*.

profitability is negatively correlated with leverage in all countries with the same exception (Germany). Again, this last result supports the pecking order theory and contradicts the trade-off theory. Frank and Goyal (2003) provide similar empirical evidence for a large sample of US firms, while Hol and Van der Wijst (2008) do so for a sample of small, European firms.

Hovakimian *et al.* (2001) analyze firms' financing behaviour with a two-stage procedure. In the first stage they regress the leverage ratio (debt/assets) on a vector of explanatory variables like the ones discussed above. This provides an estimate of each firm's optimal or target leverage ratio. In the second stage they perform a logit regression that predicts a firm's financing choice in a given year (debt or equity).[11] The difference between a firm's observed leverage and estimated target leverage is a key variable in this stage. Their main conclusion is that when firms raise or retire significant amounts of new capital, their choices move them towards the target capital structures suggested by the trade-off theory. Interestingly, this effect is stronger for equity repurchases and debt retirements than for the issuance of new capital.

Welch (2004) analyzes a different adjustment process, viz. whether firms allow their market-based debt ratios to fluctuate with stock prices or readjust them to their previous values. He estimates a simple regression model on a very large data set of US firms and concludes that these firms do little to readjust debt ratios in reaction to stock price changes. Hence, debt ratios covary closely with stock prices and this makes stock returns a first-order determinant of debt ratios, explaining about 40 per cent of debt ratio dynamics. The remaining 60 per cent is explained by issuing activities, but the motivation for these activities is far less understood. This study underlines the importance of stock returns in explaining capital structure.

Fama and French (2002) use a large database and solid statistical techniques to perform a comprehensive test of the predictions of the trade-off and pecking order theories. Their analyses tend to confirm the predictions shared by both theories. They report strong evidence that leverage in market value terms is negatively related to growth opportunities (market-to-book value). The evidence for book value leverage is less convincing. They also report consistently positive relations between leverage and firm size. As in the studies mentioned above, Fama and French find a strong negative relation between profitability and leverage. Their analyses also produce statistically reliable evidence that leverage is mean reverting, albeit at a 'suspiciously' slow rate. So their support and rejection of both theories are along the by now familiar lines.

Pecking order theory tests

The pecking order theory can also be tested in a more direct way. A central element in the theory is that firms issue new external securities only when there is a cash deficit, i.e. when the internally generated funds are insufficient to finance all investments. This makes the probability that debt or equity will be issued a direct function of the cash deficit. Helwege and Liang (1996) test this by estimating the probability of external issues with logit analysis using the cash deficit (measured as cash flow minus investments) as

---

11 Logit analysis is a form of regression that allows for a binary (0,1) dependent variable; it is discussed in more detail later on.

one of the explanatory variables. Their results provide meagre support for the pecking order theory: the probability of obtaining external capital appears to be unrelated to the shortfall in internally generated funds. Cash surpluses, however, are negatively related to the probability of obtaining external capital. Helwege and Liang interpret their results as evidence against the pecking order theory and consistent with the trade-off theory.

Shyam-Sunder and Myers (1999) perform a similar direct test by regressing the change in debt on the cash deficit. They report strong support for the pecking order theory, but their approach has been questioned from a statistical point of view (Chirinko and Singha, 2000). Frank and Goyal (2003) repeat Shyam-Sunder and Myers' test on a much larger cross-section of US firms and place the results in the context of general developments in corporate financial statistics. Over the period 1971–1998, net equity issues track the cash deficit quite closely, while net debt does not, contrary to the pecking order theory's predictions. Frank and Goyal further examine the relative importance of the pecking order and trade-off theories by using specifications that combine the two approaches. If the pecking order is the key driver of financing behaviour, adding the cash deficit to a trade-off regression should wipe out the effects of variables like fixed-to-total assets, market-to-book, size, etc. However, adding the cash deficit does not have much effect on the sign and significance of the trade-off variables. The coefficient of the cash deficit is significant, though. They also find fairly large and significant mean reversion effects. Frank and Goyal's (2003) conclusion is that the evidence poses serious problems for the pecking order theory, but that the cash deficit is not irrelevant. When firms adjust their leverage, the cash deficit appears to be factored in along with the determinants from the trade-off theory.

Conclusions

As the short review of the empirical evidence above shows, there is fairly general support for the trade-off theory. Its main elements are found to be empirically relevant and their proxy variables, such as business risk (volatility), tangibility of assets (fixed-to-total assets), specificity of assets (advertising and R&D expenditure) and growth opportunities (market-to-book value), show reasonably consistent empirical results in a large number of tests. However, the exception is the consistently negative relation between leverage and profitability, which strongly contradicts the trade-off theory. This negative relation is the strong point of the pecking order theory. Its other major empirical implication, a dominant role for the cash deficit, is not or only partially supported. Net equity issues appear to track the cash deficit more closely than net debt issues. Mean reversion is less frequently tested, but where it is, it tends to support the trade-off theory.

5.4 Dividends

Dividend policy attracted much less attention in the finance literature than investment or capital structure analyses. This may be in part because the room for making dividend decisions is restricted by both investment and capital structure decisions, which makes it hard to isolate dividend decisions.

5.4.1 Value in perfect markets

We follow the classic line of analysis by first demonstrating the irrelevance of dividends in perfect markets and subsequently introducing market imperfections. Some empirical studies round off the discussion.

Some technicalities

Dividends are paid in various forms. The most common way is to pay them in cash as ordinary, or regular, dividends. Such dividends have the implicit expectation of a certain continuity in them, i.e. a change in dividend payments is an event that conveys information to the market. Companies can also pay special, or incidental, dividends without the expectation of continuity, for example after the sale of a subsidiary or another unusual event. The largest special dividend in history was announced in July 2004 by Microsoft. It would pay its shareholders more than $60 billion, beginning with a one-time, special dividend worth $32 billion, or $3 per share, in December of that year.[12] The rest of the plan was to buy back up to $30 billion in Microsoft common stock over the next four years. The reason announced for the cash return was the reduction in legal uncertainties facing the company and for which it had been stockpiling an enormous sum of cash. This example shows that dividends can also be paid as stock repurchases, when the company buys back a number of its outstanding shares. Finally, dividends can be paid in stock, as stock dividends; shareholders then receive, for example, one new stock for every ten stocks they hold.

Dividends are announced before they are paid. After the announcement, stocks are traded with the right to receive the dividend payment ('cum dividend') until a preset date. After that, stocks are traded 'ex dividend'. Dividend payments are limited by law in certain cases, e.g. in a bankruptcy. They can be limited by contractual obligations: as we have seen, loan contracts may specify that no dividends can be paid before the debt obligations are met in full. Dividends used to be paid against a 'coupon' attached to the printed share, in the same way that we saw with bonds. In some countries 'coupon cutter' is still used as a derogatory term for investors. Nowadays most dividends are paid electronically.

Irrelevance in perfect markets

As was the case with capital structure, the common opinion before Miller and Modigliani (1961) was that dividends increase shareholder wealth, even under idealized conditions. Miller and Modigliani analyze dividends along the same lines, and draw the same conclusion, as with capital structure: dividends are irrelevant in a perfect capital market. The value of a share is not affected by whether its income is in the form of dividends or capital gains, in the same way that the value of a firm is unaffected by how it is divided over bond- and stockholders. The 'mechanism' to bring about irrelevance is again arbitrage. In a perfect capital market, investors can undo or redo management's dividend decisions free of charge, so any price effects of dividends would give arbitrage opportunities. Since these decisions cannot create value for the company, they are irrelevant.

---

12 www.microsoft.com/msft/reports/ar04/downloads/MSAR_10K_091404.doc

Much of the confusion before Miller and Modigliani was due to an improper analysis, that mixed the effects of dividends with those of investment policy and capital structure decisions. The following example illustrates this. Below is the balance sheet of a company before dividends are paid:

Balance sheet before dividends

Cash	250	Debt	375
Other assets	500	Equity (100 shares)	375
total	750	total	750

If the company uses 125 of its cash to pay a dividend, the balance sheet becomes:

Balance sheet after dividends

Cash	125	Debt	375
Other assets	500	Equity (100 shares)	250
total	625	total	625

We see that, in addition to the dividend payment, the company:

- changed its investment policy: total assets are reduced with 125 or 16.7 per cent
- changed its financial policy: the debt/equity ratio goes from 1 to 1.5.

This makes it impossible to separate the effect of the dividend payment from the effects of changes in investment and financial policy. If investment and financial policy are to be kept constant, dividends can be financed only by issuing shares. If dividends are financed this way, the example becomes as follows. After 125 is paid in dividends, equity is worth 250, 100 shares at 2.5. The company then has to issue $125/2.5 = 50$ new shares to refinance, so the new balance sheet becomes:

Balance sheet after dividends and refinancing

Cash	250	Debt	375
Other assets	500	Equity (150 shares)	375
total	750	total	750

The result of these transactions is that the old shares drop 1.25 in value, but the loss is exactly offset by the cash dividend of 1.25 per share. For every 'old' share of 3.75, the investors now hold a share of 2.5 and 1.25 in cash. If capital markets are perfect, shareholders can obtain the same effect without dividends by selling one-third of their shares. Conversely, shareholders can undo the dividend decision by using the 125 to buy the new shares: they then hold 150 shares of 2.5 instead of 100 shares of 3.75. In perfect capital markets all 'undo' and 'redo' decisions are free of charge: investors can convert shares to cash and cash to shares independently of the company's dividend-policy. This means that dividend-paying stocks cannot sell at a premium or a discount compared with non-dividend-paying stocks. So management cannot change the value of the firm by changing its dividend policy, hence dividend policy is irrelevant (in perfect capital markets).

Stock repurchases

Instead of paying dividends, firms can buy back shares. The result is roughly the same for the firm's investors: the value of their shareholdings is reduced in exchange for cash.

Stock repurchases became increasingly popular during the 1990s and they were larger than cash dividends by the end of that decade. Stock repurchases have to be analyzed a bit differently than cash dividends, because simultaneously issuing and retiring stock is nonsense. The easiest way is to assume disinvestment. If we apply that to our example, it means that 125 of the firm's cash is used to buy $125/3.75 = 33\frac{1}{3}$ shares, so both cash and equity are reduced by 125. The balance sheet after the stock repurchase, with changed investment policy and capital structure, then becomes:

Balance sheet after stock repurchase

Cash	125	Debt	375
Other assets	500	Equity ($66\frac{2}{3}$ shares)	250
total	625	total	625

Collectively, the shareholders now hold $66\frac{2}{3}$ shares at $3.75 = 250$ plus 125 in cash from the repurchase, which is 375, the same as before. The difference with cash dividends is that the reduction in share holdings is realized by a volume reduction (lower the number of shares at the same price) and not by a price reduction (same number of shares at a lower price). In perfect markets, investors can easily undo or redo such repurchases.

Why would it be important that the stock price remains the same? We have seen that stock splits have no effects in efficient markets, so the reverse should have no effect either. However, the value of some securities depends on the stock price, not on the total value of equity. A prime example are the stock options that go into managements' compensation plans. Kahle (2002) analyzes the conditions under which stocks are repurchased and concludes that firms announce repurchases when executives have large numbers of options outstanding and when employees have large numbers of options currently exercisable. Another reason may be that stock option plans increase the number shares and, hence, dilute the claims of the existing shareholders. To compensate for this, the firm can buy back shares instead of paying dividends.

5.4.2   Imperfections and empirical analyses

The market imperfections that can make dividend policy relevant are largely the same as the ones we saw in capital structure analysis. We illustrate the principle with a few examples.

Market imperfections

Taxes and transaction costs can induce a preference among categories of investors for certain dividend policies. The tax rate can differ for dividends and capital gains; unrealized capital gains may not be taxed at all. This creates a preference for capital gains over dividends. Transaction costs, meanwhile, can make dividends a cheaper way of obtaining cash than selling shares, particularly for investors in low tax brackets. Combined, this can create clientele effects, e.g. pensioners with a low tax rate who need cash for their cost of living will hold a certain proportion of their portfolio in dividend-paying shares. Investors in high tax brackets without need for cash may prefer non-dividend-paying stocks. But if there is a large supply of both dividend-paying and non-dividend-paying stocks, this clientele effect does not necessarily increase firm value. However, *changing* dividend-policy can decrease firm value if it forces investors to make costly adjustments in their portfolios.

Information asymmetry can be reduced by using dividend policy to signal information to the market. However, the information conveyed by dividends can be ambiguous. No dividends can mean that the firm has so many growth opportunities that it needs every penny for its investments. It can also mean that the firm has no penny. Similarly, paying dividends can signal ample cash flows, but also a lack of investment opportunities. For example, one stock analyst commented on Microsoft's 2004 dividend announcement by remarking that the business had matured and was potentially running out of investment ideas.[13] Generally, however, dividend *increases* are considered a good signal (which is very hard to mimic in the long run), while dividend *decreases* are considered a bad signal.

Notice that risk is not a valid argument for paying dividends. It is true that dividend money, once the payment is received, is safe, while capital gains remain in the firm and, hence, are risky. But this is true for all money, not just dividend money. The example shows that dividends are equivalent to selling a part of the shareholders' investment in the firm to the new shareholders in exchange for cash. This does not change the riskiness of the firm's cash flows and, hence, not its value either, it just divides it differently over old and new stockholders (Miller and Modigliani call this the 'bird-in-the-hand' fallacy).

Empirical studies

Firms are reluctant to increase or decrease their dividend payments because such changes would signal information about their long-term prospects to the capital market. As a result, dividends tend to remain stable over time or, as it is often called, they are 'sticky'. Obviously, sticky dividends are largely independent of short-term fluctuations in cash in- and outflows. This, in turn, makes empirical analyses of dividends not only difficult but also particularly exposed to spurious correlations. For example, if earnings vary strongly, the stable dividend amounts will be a low fraction of average earnings (low dividend rate or payout ratio). But if earnings vary strongly, their value is likely to be low, which may lead to the spurious conclusion that low payout ratios give low firm values. Incidental earnings may lead to a similarly spurious interaction between dividends and the price–earnings ratio. Suppose that earnings double because of a one-time event, e.g. the sale of a subsidiary. Dividends are kept stable, so the payout ratio drops. The stock price will go up, but does not double because the market recognizes the earnings increase as a one-time event. This means that the price–earnings ratio drops. The spurious conclusion would be that lower payout ratios give lower price–earnings ratios. The reversed effect would occur in case of an incidental drop in earnings. Finally, we have seen that both very good and very bad prospects may reduce a firm's payout ratio. This means that there is a curved relation between the payout ratio and performance. The turning point is likely to be in the neighbourhood of average performance, where most observations are. If this curvilinear relation is approximated by a linear function, e.g. in ordinary regression, the

13 http://news.bbc.co.uk/2/hi/business/3912159.stm

function may be increasing or decreasing, depending on whether most observations are below or above the turning point. There may be no relation if the observations on both sides of the turning point are of equal weight.

Fama and French (2001) describe and analyze US firms' propensity to pay dividends. They document that, over the period 1978–1999, the percentage of firms paying cash dividends declined from over 66 per cent to around 20 per cent. They attribute this fall mainly to the changing characteristics of newly listed firms: there has been a large inflow of smaller, less profitable firms with strong growth opportunities. These are exactly the characteristics of firms that have never paid dividends. They also show that, regardless of their characteristics, firms have become less likely to pay dividends. Their conclusion is that the benefits (or perceived benefits) of dividends have declined through time, possibly because of lower transaction costs of selling stocks, or larger holdings of stock options by managers who prefer capital gains to dividends. Von Eije and Megginson (2008) come to largely the same conclusions for firms in the European Union. They report that, in the fifteen member states included in their analyses, the fraction of firms paying dividends declines, while total amount of dividends paid increases and share repurchases surge. They also find that the propensity to pay dividends increases with company age. Worldwide evidence is provided by Fatemi and Bildik (2012), who analyze a large sample (>17,000 companies) from thirty-three different countries. They, too, find evidence of a significant and worldwide decline in the propensity to pay dividends. Like Fama and French (2001), they find that most of the decline is due to the payout policies of smaller and less profitable firms with comparatively more investment opportunities. They also find that larger firms, those with higher profitability, and firms with low growth opportunities have a greater propensity to pay dividends. But, again like Fama and French (2001), they find that the proportion of firms paying dividends has declined over time, even after firms' characteristics have been controlled for.

In their confrontation of the pecking order and trade-off theories, Fama and French (2002) also include the predictions regarding dividends. Both theories predict that more profitable firms pay more, and firms with more investment opportunities pay fewer dividends. The statistical evidence they present, although somewhat weak, is consistent with these predictions.

Graham and Kumar (2006) is a recent addition to a long series of papers that investigates the clientele effect. They study stock holdings and trading behaviour of a large number (>60,000) of households, and report a preference for dividend yield that increases with age and decreases with income, consistent with age and tax clienteles, respectively. Trading patterns reinforce this evidence: older, low-income investors disproportionally purchase stocks before the ex-dividend day. On average, though, retail investors prefer non-dividend-paying stocks while institutions prefer to hold dividend-paying stocks.

Exercises

1. Below is a list of characteristics that a stock can have or not have. State for each characteristic whether this will increase or decrease the value of the stock, other things being equal:

(a) voting rights
(b) priority claim on profits
(c) priority voting rights in merger and takeover decisions
(d) a clause that gives the issuer of the stock the right to repay the amount received for the stock and to redeem the share
(e) a clause that gives the investor the right to convert a priority share to a common share
(f) a clause that gives the issuer the right to convert a priority share to a common share.

2. Below is a list of characteristics that a bond can have or not have. State for each characteristic whether this will increase or decrease the value of the bond, other things being equal:
(a) a clause that makes the interest payments dependent on the income earned by the issuer
(b) a *call provision*, i.e. a clause that gives the issuer the right to buy back the bond before maturity at a pre-specified price (callable bond)
(c) a clause that gives the investor the right to sell the bond back to the issuer before maturity at a pre-specified price (putable bond)
(d) a clause that gives the investor the right to convert the bond into a common share
(e) a seniority ('me first') clause.

3. A tricky question: suppose you have lent money to a company. You are the only party from which the company has borrowed money, i.e. there are no other creditors. The company wants to negotiate a lower interest rate and offers to secure the loan with its buildings. Is that a good deal?

4. Explain briefly the advantages and dangers of securitization. (Securitization is transforming internally held capital categories into securities that can be traded.)

5. Abacus Corp. and Calculator Inc. have identical assets that produce an identical, perpetual cash flow of €20 million per year. Both companies have 20 million shares outstanding. However, Calculator Inc. has issued €100 million in perpetual risk-free debt, while Abacus Corp. has no debt. The risk-free interest rate is 5 per cent and the price of Calculator's shares is €5. Given the assumptions of Modigliani and Miller's analyses without taxes:
(a) Calculate the price of Abacus' shares.
(b) Show how the payoff of an investment in shares of Abacus can be replicated by an investment in Calculator plus risk-free borrowing or lending.
(c) Show how the payoff of an investment in shares of Calculator can be replicated by an investment in Abacus plus risk-free borrowing or lending.
(d) Use Modigliani–Miller proposition 2 to calculate the required return on Calculator's shares. Check your results with an alternative calculation.

6. ZX Co is financed with 80 per cent equity and the β of its equity is 1.2. The risk-free rate is 4 per cent and the market risk premium, i.e. $r_m - r_f$, is 6 per cent. All debt can be considered risk free and there are no taxes.
(a) Calculate ZX Co's WACC.

ZX Co decides to change its capital structure and increase debt to 60 per cent. Assuming that debt remains risk free:
(b) calculate ZX Co's equity β, the required return on its equity and its WACC after the refinancing.

7. AG Goldmünzen & Verschuldung has plans to open a new mine. The plan is to finance the mine with 80 per cent debt. Other mining companies are more conservative and finance their operations with, on average, 40 per cent debt. The shares of these companies are priced such that they generate an expected return of, on average, 11.4 per cent. Since the mining industry is very safe (at least, for investors), all debt can be considered risk free. The risk-free interest rate is 7 per cent. All mining firms use the same technology and generate the same return on assets. The tax rate is 30 per cent and all the assumptions of the Modigliani–Miller tax case apply.
(a) What is the required return on AG Goldmünzen & Verschuldung's equity investment in the planned mine?

8. TechCon is a technical construction company run by engineers. It is financed entirely with equity because, as the leading engineers put it, construction is a risky business. A newly employed engineer, who followed a course in finance for science and technology students, suggests financing the company partly with debt because that would increase its value. TechCon has earnings before interest and taxes (EBIT) of 100 per year. Its equity is priced to give an expected return of 10 per cent and the corporate tax rate is 20 per cent. The company can borrow at the risk-free rate of 4 per cent. Its earnings can be treated as a perpetuity and all the assumptions of the Modigliani–Miller tax case apply.
(a) By how much will the value of TechCon change if it refinances 50 per cent of its current value with a perpetual loan?

9. A consequence of the so-called clientele effect is that dividends are 'sticky', i.e. that dividend payments tend to be stable over time.
(a) Explain what the clientele effect is and why it leads to sticky dividends.
(b) What is the effect of sticky dividends on the payout ratio (fraction of earnings paid out as dividends) of firms with very volatile earnings?
(c) To what erroneous conclusion can that lead?
(d) What is the effect of sticky dividends on the payout ratio of firms that were hit by a strike and had an occasional year of low earnings?
(e) To what erroneous conclusion can that lead?

10. MacroHard is a successful software company that has been generating cash at a phenomenal rate over the past few years. Now it has decided to pay out $250 million of it as cash dividends to its shareholders. The total market value of MacroHard is

$1,250 million, including $550 million of debt. The company has 2.5 million shares outstanding.

(a) Calculate the change in MacroHard's stock price due to the dividend payment. Assume perfect markets.

(b) State the changes in investment policy and financial policy due to the dividend payment.

(c) How can MacroHard pay out the same amount in dividends without changing its investment and financial policy? Be precise in number of shares and price per share.

(d) Now suppose that MacroHard uses the money to buy back shares instead of paying dividends. Calculate the effects of the buyback on the firm's total market value, the share price and the number of shares outstanding.

11. Exodus Biofuel converts agricultural waste into diesel fuel. The market value of its equity is €200 million and since investors regard the biofuel business (or its managers) as very risky, it is priced to give a return of 16.5 per cent. To strengthen investor confidence, Biofuel pays out all its earnings as dividends to its shareholders; no earnings are retained for new investments. For next year, Biofuel has announced a dividend of €2.50 per share and the expectation is that earnings and dividends will grow at the inflation rate of 4 per cent.

(a) Explain why paying out all earnings as dividends may strengthen confidence in a firm (or a firm's management).

(b) Calculate the price per share based on the expected return and growth rate.

6 Valuing levered projects

Modigliani and Miller's proposition 2 provides a basic relation for the distribution of risk and return over debt and equity holders. In this chapter we will elaborate that relation in more detail. This gives a good illustration of how the interaction between financing and investment decisions can be analyzed. However, the analysis is restricted by the fact that only one market imperfection, taxes, can be incorporated in return rates. The limiting effect of default costs is treated as an exogenous factor.

6.1 Basic elements

6.1.1 Risks and discount rates

In the Modigliani and Miller analyses we compared two companies with the same assets that produce the same cash flows. Such companies have the same business risk. *Business risk* is the uncertainty of the cash flows that are generated by the firm's assets. It is the risk of, for example, operating a fleet of trucks, or a chemical plant, or a software company. The market price for this risk is the *opportunity cost of capital*, which is the return that the market offers on investments with the same risk characteristics as the investment we are looking at. If shareholders provide the whole investment sum, so that they bear all the risks and receive the entire cash flow, they will require the opportunity cost of capital as return. Shareholders express their requirements in the price they are willing to pay for the shares – they will set the price such that the expected return on the shares equals the opportunity cost of capital. If there are more categories of investors, financial contracts specify how risk and return are divided over them. The simple, stylized situation we will analyse involves a division of cash flows in a low-risk, low-return part for the debtholders, and a high-risk, high-return part for the equity holders. As we saw in the previous chapter, the additional risk that equity holders accept by giving debtholders a higher priority claim on the firm's cash flows is called *financial risk*. Assuming no personal taxes and a fixed corporate tax rate, τ, we have the following return rates:

- $r = r_a = OCC$ – the opportunity cost of capital, the expected rate of return of equivalent risk, all equity-financed assets; the subscript a is for assets
- $r' = WACC$ – the after-tax weighted average cost of capital:

$$WACC = r_e \frac{E}{V} + r_d(1 - \tau)\frac{D}{V} \tag{6.1}$$

where $V = E + D$, the value of the firm is the sum of equity and debt
- r_d = cost of debt
- r_e = cost of equity, the subscript u, l is for (un)levered.

The different rates and their relations with leverage are depicted in Figure 6.1. Recall that, as leverage increases, the return of debt slopes upwards and the return of equity levels off, because business risk is gradually transferred from the stockholders to the debtholders. As we have seen, this is an effect of limited liability and risk of default. In the extreme case of 100 per cent debt financing, the position of debt would be equal to that of unlevered equity and the required return on debt would equal r_a (not depicted in Figure 6.1). Also recall that, if taxes are the only market imperfection, optimal capital structure will contain 100 per cent debt. This is depicted in Figure 6.1 by the WACC, which monotonically decreases with leverage. In the following analyses, we assume that leverage is limited by an exogenously given optimal value (i.e. we do not model that value). Finally, notice that the WACC incorporates the tax advantage of debt because it includes the after-tax cost of debt, $r_d(1-\tau)$. This means that the WACC is the appropriate rate to discount the *unlevered* after-tax cash flows, i.e. the cash flows calculated as if the investment is all equity financed. The tax advantage would be included twice if the WACC is used to discount *levered* after-tax cash flows, i.e. cash flows from which a lower amount of taxes is deducted because of the interest tax shield.

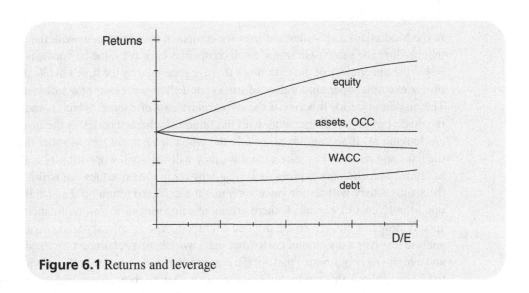

Figure 6.1 Returns and leverage

The return rates in Figure 6.1 are primarily used to evaluate levered projects within an existing company. This is a trivial problem if the project has the same business and financial risk as the company as a whole. This is the case with an across-the-board expansion of the existing activities, financed with the same debt ratio. Examples are a trucking company buying new trucks or a chemical company expanding its plant, both financed in the same way as the existing assets. In such cases we can simply use the company's WACC, which is known from previous investment decisions. But finding the proper discount rate for projects with different business and/or financial risk is far from trivial; the rest of this chapter is devoted to that problem.

When the project has a different business risk, we have to estimate this risk first. A common way of doing this is measuring the asset β of a number of existing companies that are engaged in the same activities. Since only equity βs are observable, we have to adjust the observations for financial risk ('unlever' the βs). By taking the average of a number of companies, the measurement errors are likely to cancel out. Given the asset β, the CAPM can be used to calculate the OCC. An example is elaborated later on.

When the opportunity cost of capital is known, the next step is to include the effects of financial leverage. These effects are the division of the cash flows over debt and equity and the resulting effect on taxes, i.e. the value of the tax shields. This can be done in two different ways:

1. Adjust the discount rate, from the OCC downwards to the WACC, so that the value of the interest tax shields is included.
2. Adjust the present value by separately calculating the value of all side-effects; this is called *adjusted present value* (APV), a phrase coined by Myers (1974).

We begin with the latter way because the problem of discounting tax shields presents itself in a very clear way in adjusted present values. To calculate a project's adjusted present value, we first calculate its *base case* value. This is the value of the project as if it is all equity financed and without side-effects. This step consists of the calculation of the present value of the project's cash flows, discounted at the OCC. We then separately calculate the value of the side-effects and sum the results. The power of the adjusted present value method is that the side-effects can be anything: tax shields, issue costs, effects on other projects, agency costs, fees to the stock exchange or lawyers, etc. Generally, the most important side-effect of leverage is the reduction in taxes. The value of the interest tax shields depends on how certain they are in the future and this, in turn, depends on how leverage ratios are chosen in the future. Again, there are two possibilities:

1. The money amounts of debt are *predetermined* – they follow a fixed schedule that is agreed beforehand and that is independent of the future project values.
2. Debt is *rebalanced* to a constant fraction of the future project values, which means that the money amounts of debt go up and down with the future project values.

Under the first financing rule, the interest tax shields are as safe as debt itself; both follow the predetermined schedule.[1] This means that the market price of debt, r_d, is the appropriate discount rate for the interest tax shields. Under the second financing rule, the tax shields go up and down with the future project values, so the value of the tax shields is tied to the fortunes of the project. This means that the tax shields incorporate business risk, so that the opportunity cost of capital is the appropriate discount rate.

6.1.2 Adjusted present value: some examples

Some examples will illustrate how APV is used and what the effects of the financing rules are. We begin with a base case. Suppose we have a project that generates a perpetual risky

---

1 Actually, tax shields are not as safe because their value depends on the firm making profits. Even though losses can be carried forwards and backwards, i.e. deducted from past and future profits, it is possible that the tax advantage is lost. We tacitly assume that this possibility is included in the expected corporate tax rate τ.

cash flow (EBIT) of 1562.5 per year. The project requires an investment of 8000. The tax rate is 20 per cent and the opportunity cost of capital for assets with the same risk is 15 per cent. This means that

$$r = r_a = r_{eu} = 0.15$$

The value of the 'unlevered' cash flows is:

$$\frac{(1 - 0.2) \times 1562.5 = 1250}{0.15} = 8333$$

so that the base case NPV is $8333 - 8000 = 333$.

Now we add issue costs. Suppose that the firm issues equity to finance the project and that the issue costs are 7.5 per cent. That means that the firm has to issue:

$$\frac{100}{92.5} \times 8000 = 8649$$

to collect 8000. The issue costs are $8649 - 8000 = 649$, so that the APV is $333 - 649 = -316$.

The effect of tax shields is calculated as follows. Assume that the project has an optimal capital structure with 50 per cent debt and equity. To finance the project, the firm takes up a perpetual loan of 4000; this is a predetermined money amount, independent of the future project value. The interest rate of the loan is 10 per cent, so that the yearly interest charge is 400. This gives a tax advantage of $0.2 \times 400 = 80$. Since debt is fixed, the appropriate discount rate for the tax advantage is the cost of debt, r_d. The value of the tax shields is then $80/0.1 = 800$. The other half of the investment is raised by issuing equity. To raise 4000:

$$4000 \times \frac{100}{92.5} = 4324$$

has to be issued, so the issue costs are 324. This gives an APV of $333 - 324 + 800 = 809$.

How does the value of the tax shields change if debt is not predetermined but rebalanced every year? Rebalancing once a year means that debt is fixed for the coming year, so we know the first year's tax shield $= 80$. Since this amount is fixed, we have to discount it to present (t_0) at the cost of debt, $r_d = 0.1$:

$$\frac{80}{1 + r_d}$$

At the end of the first year, debt is rebalanced to 50 per cent of the project value, which is unknown today. But then, at $t = 1$, debt is fixed for the coming ($=$ second) year, so then the second year's tax shield is known. This tax shield has to be discounted over year 2 to the end of year 1 ($t = 1$) with r_d, just as we did above. But it is uncertain how the project value will develop in year 1, so we have to discount the second year's tax advantage from $t = 1$ to $t = 0$ at the OCC:

$$\frac{80}{\underbrace{(1 + r_a)}_{yr.1-rebal.} \times \underbrace{(1 + r_d)}_{yr.2-fixed}}$$

or in numbers $80/(1.15 \times 1.1)$. Note that we use the long-term expectation of the project cash flow and the corresponding value of the tax shield of 80. In some years it will be higher, in others lower – that is why we have to discount the 'uncertain' years at the OCC. Similarly, at the end of the second year, debt is rebalanced to 50 per cent of the project value, which is unknown today. Then, at t = 2, the third year's tax shield is known and it has to be discounted over year 3 to the end of year 2 (t = 2) with r_d. But the project value developments in year 1 and 2 are uncertain, so we have to discount over these years to the present (t = 0) at r_a; in numbers: $80/(1.15^2 \times 1.1)$. The timeline for rebalancing and discounting the third year's tax shield is depicted in Figure 6.2.

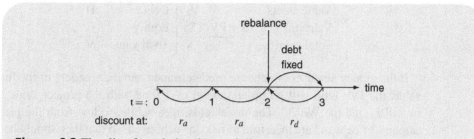

Figure 6.2 Timeline for rebalancing and discounting

The values of the tax shields further in the future are calculated in a similar way. Summing all tax shields gives the series:

$$\frac{80}{1 + r_d} + \frac{80}{(1 + r_a)(1 + r_d)} + \frac{80}{(1 + r_a)^2(1 + r_d)} + \dots$$

The value of this series can be calculated with the following simple two-step procedure, which is easily derived from (2.7):

1. Discount all values at r_a, the opportunity cost of capital.
2. Multiply the result by: $(1 + r_a)/(1 + r_d)$.

For our example project this procedure gives:

$$\frac{80}{0.15} = 533 \times \frac{1.15}{1.1} = 557$$

so that the APV is $333 + (-324) + 557 = 566$. Notice that rebalancing reduces the value of the tax shields because they become riskier and, hence, are discounted at the higher OCC over the uncertain years. Also notice that if debt is rebalanced continuously, and not fixed on a year-to-year basis, the tax shields are exactly as risky as the assets and they should be discounted at r_a without the correction term $(1 + r_a)/(1 + r_d)$. In the example, that would reduce their value even further to 533.

6.2 Financing rules and discount rates

• •

In this section we analyse the second way to express the effect of leverage, viz. by adjusting the discount rate. As we have seen, the rate needs to be adjusted downwards, from the OCC to the WACC, to include the value of the interest tax shields. We have also seen that the two different financing policies, predetermined or rebalanced debt, have different implications for the riskiness of the tax shields. Hence, different discount rates must be used to calculate their values. This may seem a bit complicated at first sight, but the analysis involves no more than rewriting the balance sheet identity with the two different discount rates for the tax shields.

6.2.1 Predetermined amounts of debt

Starting point of the analyses is the following balance sheet for the project:

Value assets	V_a	Debt	D
Value tax shields	PV(TS)	Equity	E
Total value	V	Total value	V

If the money amounts of debt are predetermined and independent of the future project value, the D/E ratio will go up and down over time with the project value and, hence, so will r_e and the WACC. The tax shields, meanwhile, follow from the predetermined amounts of debt and are therefore as risky as debt itself, so that they should be discounted at the cost of debt, r_d. This means that we can write the balance sheet identity total assets = debt + equity in terms of the costs of capital as follows:

$$r_a V_a + r_d PV(TS) = r_e E + r_d D \tag{6.2}$$

Rearranging terms gives expressions for r_a and r_e:

$$r_a = r_e \frac{E}{V_a} + r_d \frac{D - PV(TS)}{V_a} \quad \text{or} \quad r_a \frac{V_a}{V} = r_e \frac{E}{V} + r_d \frac{D - PV(TS)}{V} \tag{6.3}$$

and

$$r_e = r_a + (r_a - r_d)\frac{D - PV(TS)}{E} \tag{6.4}$$

These are general expressions that can also be used for projects with limited lives. They are not, however, very useful since they call for the present value of the tax shields which is usually unknown before the project value is calculated. If we make the Modigliani–Miller assumption that all cash flows are perpetuities, so that debt is permanent (as well as predetermined), then the present value of the tax shields is:

$$PV(TS) = \frac{\tau(r_d D)}{r_d} = \tau D \tag{6.5}$$

Substituting (6.5) in (6.4) and (6.3) gives the Modigliani–Miller expressions for r_e and r_a that we derived in the previous chapter:

$$r_e = r_a + (r_a - r_d)\frac{D - \tau D}{E}$$

$$r_e = r_a + (r_a - r_d)(1 - \tau)\frac{D}{E} \tag{6.6}$$

i.e. MM proposition 2 with taxes, and for r_a:

$$r_a \frac{V_a}{V} = r_e \frac{E}{V} + r_d \frac{D - \tau D}{V}$$

$$r_a \frac{V_a}{V} = r_e \frac{E}{V} + r_d (1 - \tau) \frac{D}{V} = WACC = r' \qquad (6.7)$$

The WACC formula in (6.7) can be rewritten in two ways. The first gives an explicit relation between r_a and r' (which is exact for predetermined, permanent values):

$$r_a \frac{V_a}{V} = WACC = r'$$

$$r_a \frac{V - \tau D}{V} = r'$$

$$r_a \left(1 - \tau \frac{D}{V}\right) = r'$$

Defining $L = D/V$, i.e. the debt–value ratio, we get the Modigliani–Miller formula:

$$WACC = r' = r_a (1 - \tau L) \qquad (6.8)$$

The MM formula can be used to 'unlever' and 'relever'. Given the WACC, the formula can be used to unlever, i.e. to calculate r_a, the required return of unlevered cash flows. This is very useful because in most situations, r_e, r_d and τ are (at least in principle) observable, but r_a is not. The obtained value of r_a can then be used to calculate the WACC for a different debt ratio, i.e. to relever the return. This is elaborated in the next section. The Modigliani–Miller formula can also be derived by substituting (6.6) into the WACC formula (6.7).

The second way to rewrite the WACC formula (6.7) under the MM assumptions gives an alternative expression for r_a, as we saw in the previous chapter:

$$r_a = r_d (1 - \tau) \frac{D}{V - \tau D} + r_e \frac{E}{V - \tau D}$$

Finally, since βs are additive across investments, just as returns are, we can do the same analysis in terms of β:

$$\beta_e = \beta_a + (1 - \tau)(\beta_a - \beta_d) \frac{D}{E}$$

$$\beta_a = \beta_d (1 - \tau) \frac{D}{V - \tau D} + \beta_e \frac{E}{V - \tau D}$$

6.2.2 Rebalanced debt

Debt can be rebalanced continuously, so that the D/E ratio always has the same value, but also periodically, e.g. from year to year. In the latter case, we have to account for the periods in which debt is predetermined.

Continuous rebalancing

We start with the same project balance sheet as before:

Value assets	V_A	Debt	D
Value tax shields	PV(TS)	Equity	E
Total value	V	Total value	V

Continuous rebalancing means that the D/E ratio is constant over time. If we assume that the cost of debt, r_d, is fixed, then r_e and the WACC will also be constant over time. Meanwhile, the tax shields will go up and down with the value of the project. This makes them as risky as the assets, so that they should be discounted at the same rate as the assets, i.e. $r_a = r$. This means that both items on the left-hand side of the balance sheet, assets and tax shields, have the same return. Hence, their relative sizes (V_A/V and PV(TS)/V) are irrelevant for the total return of the project. This, in turn, must then also apply to the right-hand side of the balance sheet: the total return required by debt and equity holders must equal $r_a = r$, regardless of the relative sizes of V_A and PV(TS).[2] The result is that taxes disappear from the equation and the opportunity cost of capital simply is the weighted average of the costs of debt and equity:

$$r_a \frac{V_a}{V} + r_a \frac{PV(TS)}{V} = r_a = r = r_d \frac{D}{V} + r_e \frac{E}{V}$$

This can also be rewritten in terms of r_e or β, which gives Modigliani–Miller proposition 2 without taxes:

$$r_e = r + (r - r_d)\frac{D}{E}$$

and:

$$\beta_e = \beta_a + (\beta_a - \beta_d)\frac{D}{E}$$

Periodical rebalancing

If debt is rebalanced periodically, we have to use a combination of discounting at r_d and r_a. More specifically,[3] the tax shield over the next period is predetermined and should be discounted at r_d. That tax shield is $\tau r_d D$ and its discounted value is $(\tau r_d D)/(1+r_d)$. The tax shields further in future depend on the value of the project; they are more uncertain and should be discounted at r_a. Their value is the total PV(TS) minus the first period's value: $PV(TS) - (\tau r_d D)/(1 + r_d)$. If we include these two terms in the balance sheet identity in return terms the result is:

$$V_a r_a + \frac{\tau r_d D}{1 + r_d} r_d + \left(PV(TS) - \frac{\tau r_d D}{1 + r_d} \right) r_a = r_e E + r_d D$$

---

2 In comparison: with predetermined debt the total return in (6.2) decreases with the relative size of the tax shields, since $r_d < r_a$.

3 The following elegant derivation is suggested by Inselbag and Kaufold (1997).

This can be rewritten (using $V_a = E + D - PV(TS)$) to give an expression for r_e:

$$r_e = r_a + (r_a - r_d)\frac{D}{E}\left(1 - \frac{\tau r_d}{1 + r_d}\right) \tag{6.9}$$

The expression in (6.9) is the equivalent of Modigliani–Miller proposition 2, under the assumption that debt is periodically rebalanced. Substituting (6.9) into the formula for the WACC (6.1) gives (after extensive rewriting):

$$r' = WACC = r_a - \frac{D}{V}r_d\tau\left(\frac{1 + r_a}{1 + r_d}\right) \tag{6.10}$$

This formula is known as the Miles–Ezzell formula. It is the equivalent of the Modigliani–Miller formula (6.8) under the assumption that debt is periodically rebalanced. The Miles–Ezzell formula is used in the same way as the Modigliani–Miller formula for unlevering and relevering:

- For a given WACC, the formula gives r_a, the opportunity cost of capital.
- When r_a is known, the formula can be used to calculate the WACC for a different debt ratio (and different cost of debt).

The Miles–Ezzell formula can also be derived with a backward iteration procedure, that starts with the last period and works its way to the beginning (as was originally done by Miles and Ezzell (1980)).

6.3 Project values with different debt ratios

The variety of formulas we have developed so far may look confusing at first sight, but their application is fairly straightforward. In this section we demonstrate how they are used by going through the different methods step by step.

6.3.1 Outline

Recall that our problem is to find the value of a project with the same business risk but a different debt ratio, compared with the existing operations. We find that value either by adjusting the base case present value or by adjusting the WACC. The WACC can be adjusted stepwise, by calculating it from new values for r_e and r_d, or directly with a formula. The choice of the method and formulas to be used depends on the characteristics of the project, mainly whether its debt is rebalanced or predetermined.

The formulas enable us to calculate a complete set of returns for the project from the returns of the existing operations plus one new rate. The new rate usually is the project's cost of debt, given its level of leverage. In practice, this rate is easily obtained by asking the bank for an offer. In addition, we use the opportunity cost of capital, which can be calculated from the existing operations. The OCC and the project's cost of debt are used in the formulas that give the project's cost of equity or WACC. We then have all the information to calculate the project's value, either with the WACC or APV. Figure 6.3 places the methods in a decision tree that shows when the methods are appropriate.

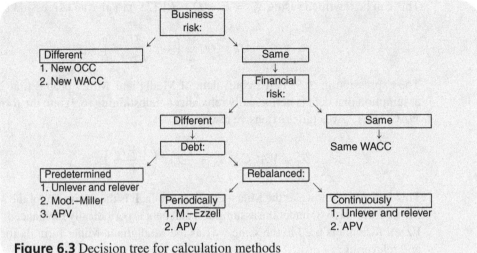

Figure 6.3 Decision tree for calculation methods

From the discussion so far it should be clear that the main distinction is between predetermined or rebalanced debt. As we have seen, the value of tax shields can be considerably lower if they vary with the project's value. The distinction between continuous and periodical rebalancing is seldom made, and the formulas are used interchangeably. Similarly, formulas for perpetuities are often used for shorter-lived projects. The errors introduced by this are probably small compared with the estimation errors of the future cash flows.

6.3.2   Debt rebalanced

Our starting position is that we know the returns ($\mathbf{r_e}$ and $\mathbf{r_d}$) and relative sizes ($\mathbf{V_e/V}$ and $\mathbf{V_d/V}$) of debt and equity in the existing operations. We use **bold** symbols to denote data of the existing operations. We also know the firm's financial policy (rebalanced debt, in this case) and we have obtained the interest rate against which the new project can borrow its chosen amount of debt. We can then calculate the project value by adjusting the WACC (stepwise or with a formula) or by using APV. We will go through the different methods step by step.

First way: stepwise adjust the WACC

This method requires continuous rebalancing and involves the following three steps:

1. Unlever: calculate the opportunity cost of capital from the existing operations, i.e. using the returns and capital structure of the existing operations:

$$r = \mathbf{r_d}\frac{\mathbf{D}}{\mathbf{V}} + \mathbf{r_e}\frac{\mathbf{E}}{\mathbf{V}}$$

2. Use this OCC plus the project's cost of debt and debt–equity ratio to calculate the project's cost of equity:

$$r_e = r + (r - r_d)\frac{D}{E}$$

These steps can also be done in terms of βs, after which the CAPM can be used to calculate the returns.

3. Relever: calculate the after-tax WACC using the project's costs and weights:

$$WACC = r_e \frac{E}{V} + r_d(1 - \tau)\frac{D}{V}$$

Second way: adjust the WACC using Miles–Ezzell's formula

This method requires periodical rebalancing and is done in two steps.

1. Unlever: we use Miles–Ezzell and the returns and capital structure of the existing operations to calculate the opportunity cost of capital by solving:

$$\mathbf{r'} = r - \tau\mathbf{r_d}\frac{\mathbf{D}}{\mathbf{V}}\left(\frac{(1+r)}{(1+\mathbf{r_d})}\right)$$

for r, i.e. we use Miles–Ezzell 'in reverse'.

2. Relever: we use Miles–Ezzell again, this time with OCC and the project's cost of debt and debt-to-value ratio to calculate the project's WACC:

$$r' = r - \tau r_d\frac{D}{V}\left(\frac{(1+r)}{(1+r_d)}\right)$$

Third way: use APV

To calculate the APV, we first have to calculate the OCC using either the first or the second way above, depending on whether debt is continuously or periodically rebalanced. We can then discount the project's (unlevered) cash flows to calculate its base case NPV. The value of the tax shields is found by discounting them at opportunity cost of capital and, if debt is rebalanced periodically, by multiplying the result with $(1 + r)/(1 + r_d)$. The sum of the base-case NPV and the value of the tax shields is the APV.

6.3.3 Debt amounts predetermined

If debt is predetermined, we can use the same three ways to calculate project values, we just have to use different formulas. Our starting position is also the same, i.e. we know the returns ($\mathbf{r_e}$ and $\mathbf{r_d}$) and relative sizes ($\mathbf{V_e}/\mathbf{V}$ and $\mathbf{V_d}/\mathbf{V}$) of debt and equity in the existing operations. We also know the firm's financial policy (predetermined debt, in this case) and we have obtained the interest rate against which the new project can borrow its chosen amount of debt. We can then, as before, calculate the project value by adjusting the WACC (stepwise or with a formula) or by using APV.

First way: stepwise adjust the WACC

1. Unlever: calculate the opportunity cost of capital $r = r_a$ from the existing operations, i.e. using the returns and capital structure of the existing operations:

$$r_a = \mathbf{r_e}\frac{\mathbf{E}}{\mathbf{V_a}} + \mathbf{r_d}\frac{\mathbf{D - PV(TS)}}{\mathbf{V_a}} \quad \text{or } r_a\frac{\mathbf{V_a}}{\mathbf{V}} = \mathbf{r_e}\frac{\mathbf{E}}{\mathbf{V}} + \mathbf{r_d}\frac{\mathbf{D - PV(TS)}}{\mathbf{V}}$$

As we have seen, this is not a very practical way because we have to calculate the present value of the tax shields first. But under the Modigliani–Miller assumption that all cash flows are perpetuities, this method is more practical:

$$r = r_a = \mathbf{r_d}(1 - \tau)\frac{\mathbf{D}}{\mathbf{V} - \tau\mathbf{D}} + \mathbf{r_e}\frac{\mathbf{E}}{\mathbf{V} - \tau\mathbf{D}}$$

2. Use the project's cost of debt and the project's debt–equity ratio to calculate the project's cost of equity using:

$$r_e = r_a + (r_a - r_d)\frac{D - PV(TS)}{E}$$

or under the Modigliani–Miller assumptions:

$$r_e = r + (1 - \tau)(r - r_d)\frac{D}{E}$$

3. Relever: calculate the after-tax WACC using the project's costs and weights:

$$WACC = r_e\frac{E}{V} + r_d(1 - \tau)\frac{D}{V}$$

Second way: adjust the WACC using Modigliani–Miller's formula

This, of course, requires the Modigliani–Miller assumptions and is done in two steps:

1. Unlever: use the Modigliani–Miller formula and the WACC and capital structure of the existing operations to calculate the opportunity cost of capital by solving:

$$\mathbf{r'} = r_a(1 - \tau\mathbf{L})$$

for r_a (run MM in reverse).

2. Relever: use Modigliani–Miller again, with the OCC (r_a) and the project's debt-to-value ratio to calculate the project's WACC:

$$r' = r_a(1 - \tau L)$$

Although the Modigliani–Miller formula assumes that debt is predetermined and permanent, it gives a good approximation for projects with limited lives if debt is predetermined.

Third way: APV

Also in the case of predetermined debt we first have to calculate the OCC to calculate the base-case NPV. We can then add the value of the tax shields by using the predetermined schedule for interest payments and discount the tax shield at the cost of debt.

6.4 Some examples

6.4.1 Unlevering βs

If the project is in a different line of business, it is likely to have a different business risk and we cannot use the returns of the existing operations to calculate the appropriate OCC. The most common way to estimate business risk is to measure the asset β of a number of existing companies that are active in the line of business. This method is often called the *pure play method* because it works best if the existing companies are pure plays, i.e. stand-alone companies that are engaged in a single business activity. There are two practical problems with this approach. The first is that pure plays may be hard to find because most companies are not engaged in only one activity, but rather in a portfolio of different activities. The second is that only equity βs are observable, not asset βs. The first problem is solved by taking the average of a number of companies so that the errors caused by other activities will (hopefully) cancel out. For instance, a sample of trucking companies will contain some firms that also offer warehousing facilities, others will operate a truck repair shop or are engaged in trading activities, etc. Some of these activities will be more risky than trucking, others less so, so that the sample average probably is a good estimate of the risk of trucking.

The second problem is solved by unlevering the observed equity βs so that financial risk is removed from them. In principle, this requires knowledge of the financial structure (D/E ratios), financial policy (predetermined or rebalanced) and the riskiness of the debt of the companies involved. However, the latter two are usually approximated by assuming that the prevalent financial policy in the industry is used by all firms and that low proportions of debt are risk free. An example will illustrate the procedure. Suppose the three firms in Table 6.1 are representative of the business risk (asset beta) in an industry. All debt is rebalanced and can be considered risk free. The problem is how to calculate the asset β from these data.

Table 6.1 *Equity betas*

Firm	Stock β	D/V
1	1.35	0.40
2	1.25	0.50
3	1.30	0.55

If debt is rebalanced continuously, the relation between the asset β_a and the equity β_e is the same as the relation between the returns:

$$\beta_a = \beta_d \frac{D}{V} + \beta_e \frac{E}{V}$$

If debt is risk free, this reduces to:

$$\beta_a = \beta_e \frac{E}{V}$$

so that the calculations become as in Table 6.2. The result is an average asset β of $2.02/3 = 0.67$, which, together with the CAPM ($E(r_i) = r_f + (E(r_m) - r_f)\beta_i$), produces the OCC in the industry.

Table 6.2 *Equity and asset betas*

Firm	Stock β	E/V	Asset β
1	1.35	0.60	0.810
2	1.25	0.50	0.625
3	1.30	0.45	0.585
sum/av.			$2.020/3 = 0.67$

6.4.2   A worked-out example

To illustrate the valuation of levered projects we elaborate a somewhat larger example below.

The problem

The condensed balance sheet (in book values, $€10^6$) of ZX Co company is:

Balance sheet ZX Co

Property, plant and equipment	40	Equity		40
Other fixed assets	20	Long-term debt		20
Total fixed assets	60	Accounts payable	10	
Cash	10	Short-term debt	20	
Account receivable	10	*Current liabilities*		30
Inventories	10			
Current assets	30			
Total assets	90	Total liabilities and equity		90

The company frequently renegotiates and adjusts its debt, so that its capital structure remains constant and the book values of €20 million short-term debt and €20 million long-term debt are equal to the market values. The interest rate is 11 per cent on its long-term debt and 9 per cent on its short-term debt. ZX Co has 10 million shares outstanding, which are priced at €6 to give a 20 per cent return. The corporate tax rate is 35 per cent.

ZX Co is considering expanding its operations into an adjacent geographical area within Euroland. The expansion requires an investment of €50 million and is expected to generate a perpetual, after-tax cash flow of €7 million per year. The newest version of the required assets is more generally deployable than the earlier version and has an optimal debt-value ratio of 60 per cent. ZX Co's bank has extended an offer to supply this debt against an interest rate of 12 per cent. The company will apply its financial policy of frequently renegotiation and adjustment and constant capital structure also to the project.

The question is, of course, whether ZX Co should accept the project or not.

Analysis

The project should be accepted if it has a positive net present value. To calculate the NPV we need the proper discount rate; alternatively, we can use adjusted present value. The first question is whether the project has a different business risk than ZX Co's existing operations. Since it involves an expansion of the same activities in a different geographical area with the same currency, business risk will be the same. This means that we can calculate the opportunity cost of capital from the existing operations. But we cannot use the company cost of capital (WACC) because the project has a higher optimal debt ratio than the company as a whole. So we can adjust the WACC, either stepwise or with the Miles–Ezzell formula, or calculate the APV. We shall go through the calculations of all three methods.

Beforehand, however, we have to adjust the balance sheet. The first adjustment is to replace book values by market values. ZX Co's debt is frequently renegotiated so that the book values equal the market values. But the market value of equity is the number of shares times the price per share, so 10 million times €6 is €60 million. The second adjustment is to 'net out' accounts payable against current assets, i.e. we include net working capital on the left-hand side as the difference between current assets and accounts payable. We keep the interest-bearing short-term debt on the right-hand side. The balance sheet's right-hand side then contains:

Equity	60
Long-term debt	20
Short-term debt	20
total	100

We can now calculate ZX Co's WACC as:

$$WACC = (1 - 0.35) \times 0.11 \times 0.2 + (1 - 0.35) \times 0.09 \times 0.2 + 0.2 \times 0.6 = 0.146$$

We use different interest rates for short- and long-term debt, which is no problem in calculating the WACC. However, in formulas such as Miles–Ezzell it is more convenient to work with a single interest rate. We then use the weighted average of the long- and short-term rates, $\frac{1}{2} \times 0.11 + \frac{1}{2} \times 0.09 = 0.1$. We can now calculate the project's value with the three methods. We start with the stepwise adjustment of the WACC. Recall that this requires continuous rebalancing. To stepwise adjust the WACC:

1. Unlever: to calculate the opportunity cost of capital from ZX Co's existing operations, i.e. using the company returns and capital structure, we use the average of the two debt rates this time:

$$r = r_d \frac{D}{V} + r_e \frac{E}{V}$$

$$= 0.1 \frac{40}{100} + 0.2 \frac{60}{100} = 0.16$$

2. Use this OCC plus the project's cost of debt and debt–equity ratio to calculate the project's cost of equity:

$$r_e = r + (r - r_d)\frac{D}{E}$$

$$= 0.16 + (0.16 - 0.12)\frac{30}{20} = 0.22$$

3. Relever: calculate after-tax WACC using the project's costs and weights:

$$WACC = r_e\frac{E}{V} + r_d(1 - \tau)\frac{D}{V}$$

$$= 0.22\frac{20}{50} + 0.12(1 - 0.35)\frac{30}{50} = 0.1348$$

The second way is to adjust the WACC with the Miles–Ezzell formula (this assumes discrete rebalancing):

1. Unlever: using the returns and capital structure of ZX Co, we solve the Miles–Ezzell formula for r, the opportunity cost of capital:

$$\mathbf{r'} = r - \tau\mathbf{r_d}\frac{\mathbf{D}}{\mathbf{V}}\left(\frac{(1 + r)}{(1 + \mathbf{r_d})}\right)$$

$$0.146 = r - 0.35 \times 0.1 \times 0.4 \times \left(\frac{(1 + r)}{(1 + 0.1)}\right) \Rightarrow r = 0.16$$

2. Relever: we use Miles–Ezzell again, this time with the OCC and the project's cost of debt and debt-to-value ratio to calculate the project's WACC:

$$r' = r - \tau r_d\frac{D}{V}\left(\frac{(1 + r)}{(1 + r_d)}\right)$$

$$r' = 0.16 - 0.35 \times 0.12 \times 0.6 \times \left(\frac{1.16}{1.12}\right) = 0.134$$

The value of a perpetual cash flow of €7 million with a discount rate of 0.134 is $7/0.134 = 52.25$. Since the investment is €50 million, the NPV $= 2.25 > 0$, so that the project should be accepted.

The third method uses APV:

1. First calculate the base-case NPV as if all equity financed, i.e. using the OCC: $7/0.16 = 43.75$.
2. Then calculate the tax shield: $\tau r_d D = 0.35 \times 0.12 \times 30 = 1.26$. ($D = 0.6 \times 50$).
3. Since debt is rebalanced, the tax shields should be discounted at the opportunity cost of capital, OCC: $1.26/0.16 = 7.875$.
4. If debt is rebalanced periodically, the result should be multiplied by $(1 + r)/(1 + r_d)$: $((1 + 0.16)/(1 + 0.12)) \times 7.875 = 8.16$.
5. The total APV is $43.75 + 8.16 = 51.91$, so that the NPV is 1.91, which leads to the same conclusion: accept the project.

Different methods give (slightly) different project values because they are based on different assumptions.

6.4.3   Flow to equity method

So far, we have looked at the whole cash flow and expressed the effects of financial leverage in the discount rate or in the adjustments to the present value. Another method, that is sometimes used in practice, is to split the cash flow into a part for the equity holders and a part for the debtholders and value them separately. If we apply this method to our example, we have to start with the *before tax* cash flow. The cash flow calculation then becomes:

Before tax cash flow (EBIT): $7/(1 - .35)$	10.77
− interest: 30 @ 12%	3.60
earnings before taxes	7.17
− taxes @ 35%	2.51
flow to equity	4.66

The cost of equity is calculated above as 0.22, so the value of the perpetual flow to equity is $4.66/0.22 = 21.18$. The value of the flow to debt is $3.60/0.12 = 30$, which gives a total value of the project's cash flows of $21.18 + 30 = 51.18$. The conclusion about the project is the same (accept).

Although it is legitimate to calculate the flows to and the value of equity in this way, it is also important to note that the necessary elements for this calculation come from the methods discussed above. For instance, if we assume a different project debt ratio of 50 per cent, it would be wrong to use the same interest rate and required equity return to calculate the value of the flow to equity. To apply the flow to equity method with this debt ratio, we first have to obtain a new cost of debt and then calculate the required return of equity using one of the methods above. But having done that we are already very close to obtaining the value of the project. Similarly, when debt is predetermined we have to calculate the present value of the tax savings before we apply the flow to equity method. But with the PV(TS) available, it is only a small step to calculate the project value.

6.5   Concluding remarks

At this point, it is only natural to ask which of the many methods discussed above are used in practice. Again, the main distinction is between predetermined and rebalanced debt. A first answer is already provided by the empirical tests of capital structure theories in the previous chapter. The mean reversion effects reported by Hovakimian *et al.* (2001), Fama and French (2002) and Frank and Goyal (2003) document that firms adjust their capital structures towards some target and, hence, rebalance their debt ratios. Other studies address the question more directly. Graham and Harvey (2001) collected the answers of 392 chief financial officers (CFOs) in the USA to questions about the cost of capital, capital budgeting and capital structure. One of the questions is whether firms have an optimal or target debt–equity ratio. Only 19 per cent of the firms do not have a target debt ratio or target range, 37 per cent have a flexible target and 34 per cent have a somewhat tight target or range. The remaining 10 per cent have a strict target debt ratio. This evidence, too, points in the direction of rebalancing. They also report that the CAPM is by far the most popular method of estimating the cost of equity capital, used by almost 75 per cent of the CFOs. However, the CAPM or NPV rule are not always applied correctly, since more than half of the respondents would use their firm's overall discount rate to evaluate a project in an overseas market, even though the project is likely to have different risk attributes than the firm as a whole. This lack of financial sophistication appears to decrease with firm size. Brounen *et al.* (2004) report that the CAPM is similarly popular among European CFOs, although the preference for the simple payback period criterion is stronger in Europe. They also find that financial flexibility, i.e. pecking order behaviour, is a more important determinant of capital structure decisions than trade-off theory arguments, for which they also find evidence.

Leary and Roberts (2005) empirically analyse whether firms rebalance their capital structures, taking into account that adjustment is costly. They show that firms tend to make capital structure adjustments relatively infrequently (on average once a year), which is largely consistent with the direct evidence describing adjustment costs. Their results are strongly supportive of rebalancing: firms respond to equity issuances and equity price shocks by rebalancing their leverage over the next two to four years.

Similar evidence is provided by Flannery and Rangan (2006), who find strong evidence that firms pursue target capital structure ratios. Their evidence is equally strong across size classes and time periods. Firms that are under- or overlevered soon adjust their debt ratios to offset the observed gap. This targeting behaviour is evident in both market-valued and book-valued leverage measures. Like the Leary and Roberts (2005) study, they find that firms return relatively quickly to their target leverage ratios. The leverage gap is closed at a rate of more than 30 per cent per year, so that the transitory effects of share price fluctuations are offset within a few years. Harford *et al.* (2009) analyse capital structure adjustments in the context of large acquisitions, that can markedly alter a firm's capital structure. They find that managers actively move the firm back to its target leverage after debt-financed acquisitions. More than 75 per cent of the acquisition's leverage effect is reversed within five years. Also their results are consistent with a model of capital structure that includes a target level and adjustment costs.

These few studies illustrate that rebalancing debt is the dominant financial policy in practice. As we have seen, the WACC is a very practical approach to calculating project values when debt is rebalanced, so this method is extensively used in practice. The differences between continuous and periodical rebalancing are so small that the formulas are used interchangeably: the WACC is also adjusted stepwise when debt is rebalanced periodically and the Miles–Ezzell formula is also used when debt is frequently rebalanced. In the more incidental cases that debt is predetermined, APV is more practical to apply.

Exercises

1. TeleSouth considers investing in a new mobile broadband network in Westmark. The company wants to finance the project with 25 per cent debt, which it can borrow at 5 per cent interest. The rest would be financed with equity, on which TeleSouth expects a 15 per cent return. Together with the corporate tax rate of 28 per cent this gives the

project a WACC of 12.15 per cent ($WACC = (1 - \tau)r_d\frac{D}{V} + r_e\frac{E}{V} = (1 - .28) \times .05 \times .25 + .15 \times .75 = .1215$). However, calculations show that the project is unprofitable if the discount rate is higher than 10 per cent. The project's chief engineer suggests financing the project with 50 per cent debt because that would bring the WACC below 10 per cent: $(1 - .28) \times .05 \times .5 + .15 \times .5 = 0.093$.

(a) Is the chief engineer's argument correct? Explain.

2. A firm is considering investing in a new line of business. As preparation for the decision, a junior financial manager collected the following data on the four main competitors in the business:

Firm	r_e	r_d	D/V
1	16.0%	5.2%	.6
2	14.5%	4.9%	.5
3	13.6%	4.6%	.5
4	12.4%	4.3%	.4

All debt is continuously rebalanced.
(a) Use the data of the four firms to calculate the opportunity cost of capital (r_a) in the industry.

3. A company obtained a €400,000 loan from its bank. The loan has to be paid back in amounts of €100,000 after each of the following four years. The interest on the loan is 10 per cent and the company has a tax rate of 30 per cent.
(a) Calculate the value of the tax savings on the loan, assuming that the interest and taxes are paid at the end of each year.
Suppose the company knows it will have to settle an old conflict with the tax authorities. It therefore agreed with the bank to double the loan in year 2 on the same conditions. The extra money will be paid back in year 3. This will make the tax advantage go up and down strongly.
(b) Is this volatility in the tax savings a reason to adjust the discount rate? Explain.

4. The following is known about a company and a financial market:
company: $\beta_e = 1.5$, $r_d = .08$, $D/E = 1$, tax rate $\tau = .3$
financial market: $r_f = .07$, $r_m = .13$.
(a) Assuming that the MM assumptions obtain, i.e. that debt is predetermined and permanent, calculate r_e, r_a, β_a, β_d, $WACC$.
(b) Assuming that debt is rebalanced, calculate r_e, r_a, β_a, β_d, $WACC$.
(c) Explain the differences between (a) and (b).

5. E-razor Corp. is considering the introduction of a new product. The introduction requires an immediate investment of €1,000 and the product is expected to generate an after-tax cash flow of €333 per year for four years starting one year from now. E-razor estimates the risk of the project to be such that the company would require

a return of 12.5 per cent if it financed the projects exclusively with equity. For this project, E-razor plans to raise 50 per cent of the investment by issuing new shares. The issue costs are 5 per cent. The remaining 50 per cent of the investment is financed with a loan. E-razor agreed with its bank to pay 8 per cent interest at the end of each of the following four years. The loan will be redeemed in one payment together with the last interest payment. E-razor has a tax rate of 30 per cent.

(a) Should E-razor go ahead with the project or not? Use APV calculations to support your answer.

(b) Explain why APV is the preferred method in this case.

6. Korkla is a large conglomerate active in, among other things, soft drinks, heavy metals and financial services. As a well-diversified firm that has excellent relations with its banks, it has a low company average costs of capital. Although 60 per cent of its total value is financed with debt, its cost of debt is only 7 per cent, or 1 per cent over the risk-free rate of 6 per cent. It is now considering a project to enter the NO-WITS (Novel wireless internet telephone service) business, the latest development in telecommunications. This will require an immediate investment of 750 million and is expected to produce a perpetual after-tax cash flow of 100 million per year starting one year from now. Korkla plans to finance the investment with 25 per cent debt, for which the bank has made an offer at 8 per cent interest. At present there is only one firm active in the NO-WITS industry, the Checkers company. Checkers is financed with equal parts of debt and equity, its debt has a 9 per cent interest rate and its equity has a β of 1.4. The market risk premium is 8 per cent and the corporate tax rate for all firms is 40 per cent. All debt is rebalanced.

(a) Should Korkla accept the NO-WITS project or not? Use calculations to support your answer and make additional assumptions if necessary.

Option pricing in discrete time

Options are financial contracts that give their holders the right, but not the obligation, to buy or sell something on a future date at a price determined today. The distinction between right and obligation, which gives the holder a choice, is an essential characteristic. Options are derivative securities, they derive their values from the assets to be bought or sold in the future. The use of option-like contracts is very old. The oldest examples go back to Greek antiquity and in the 1600s options on rice were traded in Japan and options on tulips in the Netherlands. However, the world's first options exchange did not open until 1973 in Chicago (Chicago Board of Options Exchange). In the same year Black and Scholes published their famous option-pricing formula. The trade in standardized options in Europe started in 1978 on the European Options Exchange in Amsterdam and has grown tremendously since then.

In this chapter we will model option prices in discrete time. After discussing the basic characteristics of options, we will lay the foundations of option pricing in state-preference theory. We then look at binomial option pricing with the wonderful Cox–Ross–Rubinstein model.

7.1 Options as securities

This introductory section describes the most important characteristics of options and introduces some terminology, option positions and bounds on option prices.

7.1.1 Characteristics of options

The majority of options traded today are standard options that are created by exchanges. Standard options are easily traded because they refer to a fixed quantity of the underlying asset (e.g. options on 100 shares, bonds, ounces of gold) and to a limited number of maturity dates and exercise prices. This concentrates trade in the available standard options and, thus, enhances the liquidity of the market. In addition to standardization, option exchanges make trading easy by operating clearing houses. As we have seen, a clearing house sees to it that transactions are properly effectuated, and it takes over counterparty risk. Today, standard options are available on a wide range of financial instruments and commodities, such as stocks, bonds, gold, silver, foreign currencies and stock indices. Standard options are also available on future contracts in these instruments and commodities. For special, large deals, tailor-made options can be negotiated with banks; they are traded in over the counter markets, not on exchanges.

Option terminology

A *call option* is a contract that gives its holder the right, but not the obligation, to buy 'something' (the underlying) at a specified price (= the exercise price or strike price) on (in the case of a European option) or at any time before (in the case of an American option) a specified date (= the exercise date or maturity).

A *put option* is a contract that gives its holder the right, but not the obligation, to sell 'something' (the underlying) at a specified price (= the exercise price or strike price) on (in the case of a European option) or at any time before (in the case of an American option) a specified date (= the exercise date or maturity).

The exercise possibilities on or before maturity are sometimes referred to as the *style* of the option: *American-style* and *European-style* options. This is not a geographical distinction – most traded options, also in Europe, are American options. In addition to the plain vanilla (i.e. simplest variant of) European and American options, there is a wide range of exotic options: Asian, Bermudan, barrier, forward start, binary, lookback and chooser options are examples. An extensive overview of option contracts and their pricing formulas can be found in the renowned collection of Haug (2007).

The price that you pay when you buy an option, or that you receive when you sell an option, is called the *option premium*.

For example, if you have bought a European call option on a share of Apple with a strike price of $425 and maturity on 18 February, you have the right, but not the obligation, to buy that share on that date at that price. If the share price of Apple on 18 February is higher than $425, you will *exercise* the option (you have to *do* something) and will have earned the difference between the share price and the exercise price. If the share price of Apple on 18 February is lower than $425, you will not exercise the option (do nothing) and let the option expire worthlessly. If you have bought a European put option on a share of Apple with a strike price of $425 and maturity on 18 February, you have the right to sell that share on that date at that price. You will exercise the put option if the share price at maturity is lower than $425. If you have bought American options you can do the same things, but on any date before maturity.

For every option buyer there is a counterparty who has sold the option. To sell an option is also called to *write* an option. The position of the seller of an option is the opposite of that of the buyer: the writer of a call option is obliged to sell at the buyer's request, but the writer cannot force the call option owner to buy. This implies that the writer cannot expect to earn money when the option is exercised and has to be compensated for the expected loss in the option premium. The rights and obligations attached to options are summarized in Table 7.1.

Table 7.1 *Rights and obligations attached to options*

	Buyer (long position)	Seller (short position)
Call	right to buy	obligation to sell
Put	right to sell	obligation to buy

7.1 Options as securities

An option is said to be *at the money* if the price of the underlying is equal to the exercise price. It is *in the money* if the price of the underlying is such that it would be profitable to exercise the option if it expired immediately. In the opposite case the option is *out of the money*. The different possibilities are listed in Table 7.2.

Table 7.2 *Moneyness of options*

Moneyness	Call	Put
in the money	underlying > strike	underlying < strike
at the money	underlying = strike	underlying = strike
out of the money	underlying < strike	underlying > strike

The total value of an option is sometimes broken down into two parts: the *intrinsic value* (also called parity value) and the *time value* (also called premium over parity). The intrinsic value is the amount that the option is in the money, so an out-of-the-money option has no intrinsic value. The time value is the difference between the option price and the intrinsic value.

Economic characteristics

The word option implies a free choice. In an economic context, freedom of choice is often labelled *flexibility* and this is indeed the most prominent characteristic of options. The economic flexibility of a long option position is the possibility to choose the best alternative and to walk away when bad outcomes appear. In the context of share trading this means exercising the option when this is profitable and trading at market prices when that is better. In the context of real investments, flexibility means changing cash flows along the way, profiting from good opportunities and cutting off losses. This characteristic makes options difficult to price, but with the famous Black and Scholes option-pricing formula and its descendants we now have the instruments to value flexibility. As we shall see later on, discounted cash flow (DCF) calculation assumes a passive, not a flexible, position: it accepts cash flows as they come. Therefore, DCF cannot handle flexibility very well; this is elaborated in the discussion of real options later on.

A long option is a *limited liability* investment: if it is not profitable to exercise the option, it can expire worthlessly and all the option-holder will have lost is the option premium. However, a short position in options is not necessarily a limited-liability investment (as Figure 7.2 on page 189 shows).

Options are a *zero sum game*: one's losses are someone else's profits. If you buy and sell the same option, your net position is always zero (except for transaction costs, of course). Notice that this is not the same as buying (or selling) a put and a call. With these characteristics, options enable a redistribution of risk at market prices. For instance, if an investor does not want to run the risk that the price of a stock will fall below a certain level, she can buy a put from another investor who is willing to accept that risk in return for the option premium (the protective put is depicted in Figure 7.5). The former investor wants to insure her investment, the latter may want to buy the stock against the exercise price or speculate that the stock price will not fall.

Options are almost always riskier than the underlying values they are written on. This property can be used to speculate, as the following example illustrates. Suppose that, early January, call options on Apple shares[1] (ticker: AAPL) with a strike price of \$425 and maturity on 18 February cost \$15.65. The price of Apple shares early January is \$422.40. So for \$422.40 you can buy 1 share or 27 options. If on 18 February the price of Apple shares is \$450, an investment in the share has a net payoff of $450 - 422.4 = 27.6$ or $27.6/422.4 = 0.0653$, i.e. 6.5 per cent. An investment in the options has a net payoff of $27 \times (450 - 425) - (27 \times 15.65) = 252.45$ or $252.45/422.4 = 0.5977$, i.e. 60 per cent. If, however, on 18 February the price of Apple shares is \$420, an investment in the share has a net payoff of -2.40 or -0.6 per cent – you have 99.4 per cent of your investment left. An investment in the option has a net payoff of zero, so -100 per cent – you have lost your entire investment.

7.1.2   Some option positions

The payoff or profit of an option position is often depicted graphically as a function of the value of the underlying. *Payoff diagrams* (also called position diagrams) show the payoff at maturity, ignoring the premium that was paid to acquire the option.[2] *Profit diagrams* incorporate the option premium. Since payoff diagrams can give a misleading impression we will look mainly at profit diagrams, first of positions in a single option, then of positions in combinations of options or other securities.

Simple option positions

Figure 7.1 gives a detailed profit diagram for a call option that has a value of 4.50 and a strike price of 150. The option will be exercised if, at maturity, the price of the underlying share is higher than 150. But the owner of the option will have earned money only if the share price is higher than the exercise price plus the future value of the option premium. We use the future value because the premium and the payoff occur at different points in time so that an adjustment for the time value of money is necessary. Normally, profit diagrams are less detailed but they show the option premium.

A position in only one option is called a naked option position. These positions can be (very) risky and they are not used often – it is more usual to combine an option with other options and/or other securities. Figure 7.2 summarizes the naked option positions, using a share as the underlying asset. This figure also illustrates the zero sum character of options: the long and short positions in the same option cancel out. Figure 7.2 further shows that writing options is much riskier than buying options.[3] The possible loss of a long option is limited to the option premium. The possible loss from a short call is in principle unlimited, because there is no upper limit on the value of the underlying. This makes a short call not very suitable as a single investment, even for an investor who very strongly expects a price decrease. A short call can be used as an instrument to earn the option premium as part of a strategy in which the loss is limited by another security, e.g. a long position in the stock on which the call is written, or a long call with a higher exercise price.

---

1 Actual prices can be found at www.nasdaq.com

2 Figure 7.5 on page 192 contains the payoff diagrams for two option positions.

3 That is why, in practice, brokers demand deposits of cash or other assets as security for naked short positions in options, the so-called margin requirements we saw earlier. We will ignore them here.

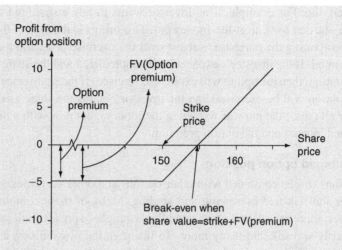

Figure 7.1 Profit diagram for a call option with a value of 4.50 and a strike price of 150

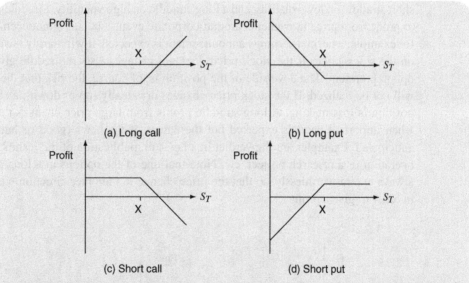

Figure 7.2 Profit from simple option positions as a function of the share price at maturity, S_T, and the strike price, X

For a short put the maximum loss is equal to the exercise price and that maximum is reached when the value of the underlying is zero. This loss can be much larger than the price for which the put was sold. Most investors buy puts as insurance against a price fall (the protective put mentioned above and depicted in Figure 7.5). So selling puts can be regarded as collecting insurance premiums and that should be done only if sufficient coverage is available. Short puts can be used by an investor who really wants to buy the underlying. For example, if an investor wants to buy a share but thinks the price is too high, she can write an at-the-money put. This brings in the cash of the option premium and by postponing the purchase, interest over the exercise price and the option premium can be earned. If the investor's expectation is not realized and the share price has increased at expiration, then the option will expire unexercised. If the share price is lower at expiration, the option will be exercised and the investor obtains the share against the exercise price after all (since the put was written at the money), but now with a discount because of the earned interest and the option premium.

Combined option positions

Options can be combined with other options and other securities, such as the underlying asset and risk-free borrowing and lending. Many of these combinations have colourful names: there are strips, straps, straddles, strangles, spreads (bull spread, bear spread and butterfly spread), and many more. To illustrate the possibilities, a few combined option positions are depicted and briefly discussed.

Figure 7.3 shows combinations of puts and calls that are called straddles. The separate options are drawn as dashed lines, the total position as a solid line. A short put combined with a short call with the same exercise price is called a short straddle and a long straddle is a similar combination of a long call and a long put. Straddles are bets on volatility: a short straddle on low volatility and a long straddle on high volatility. Straddles can be used to profit from price movements around corporate events such as announcements. When, for example, a normal earnings announcement is expected, it will hardly have any impact on the stock price. If the stock price does not change, a short straddle gives a double option premium. The downside of the position is, of course, the risk that the expectation will not be realized. If the stock price changes drastically (up or down), a short straddle position is loss-making. A long straddle profits from large price changes that can occur when important news is expected but the nature of the news (good or bad) cannot be anticipated. Examples are the verdict in a law suit, publication of the results of a drilling operation or a research project, etc. Note that one of the options in a long straddle will always expire worthlessly, so that the price change in the other direction has to be large in order to give a profit.

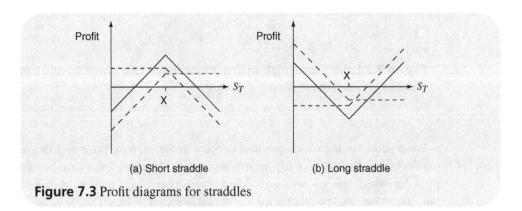

(a) Short straddle   (b) Long straddle

Figure 7.3 Profit diagrams for straddles

Figure 7.4 shows two other option combinations that are known as spreads. Spreads consist of two or more options of the same type (puts or calls). Different payoff patterns are created by buying and selling options with different exercise prices or maturities. A bull spread reflects the expectation of an increasing stock price. This position can be created by buying a call option on a stock and selling a call option on the same stock with a higher exercise price. The price of a call decreases with the exercise price so that the sold option brings in less than the bought option costs. Hence, the initial balance is negative (i.e. a cash outflow). In a bear spread the bought and sold positions are reversed: the call with the lower exercise price is sold and the call with the higher exercise price is bought. This means that the initial balance of the two option premiums is positive (a cash inflow, so a negative investment) since the higher priced option is sold. A bear spread is consistent with the expectation of a price decrease. The possible payoffs of spread positions are limited both on the upside and the downside. On the upside, possible high payoffs are replaced by the certain but lower premium of the sold option. This is consistent with the expectation that a large increase (bull spread) or decrease (bear spread) in the stock price is unlikely. The speculative nature of spreads can be varied by choosing exercise prices in relation to the stock price when the position is opened. For example, a bull spread set up with both options out of the money is very cheap and offers a high payoff with a low probability. With one, or both, options in the money the bull spread becomes less speculative.

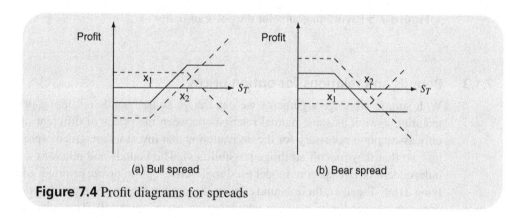

Figure 7.4 Profit diagrams for spreads

The put–call parity

Figure 7.5 shows the payoffs at maturity of two other combined option positions (note that the option premiums are not depicted in this payoff diagram). The left-hand side of Figure 7.5 illustrates the use of a protective put to hedge the risk of a price decrease in a long share. Hedging is a financial strategy to offset the risk of a security (here: the share) with another security (here: the put). Hedging is discussed in a later chapter. As Figure 7.5 shows, the value of the combined position cannot be less than the put's exercise price. The right-hand side of Figure 7.5 shows that exactly the same value at maturity is obtained by a combination of a long call and a risk-free bank deposit of the present value of the exercise price. If the values at maturity are the same, then the prices of the combinations now have to be the same as well, otherwise there are arbitrage possibilities. This gives rise to the following relation between put and call prices that is known as *the put–call parity*:

$$share + long\ put = long\ call + PV(X) \tag{7.1}$$

Note that the put–call parity is only valid for European options on non-dividend-paying stocks. Both early exercise and dividends invalidate the relation. The put–call parity can be rearranged to give an expression for the price of a put:

$$long\ put = long\ call + PV(X) - share \tag{7.2}$$

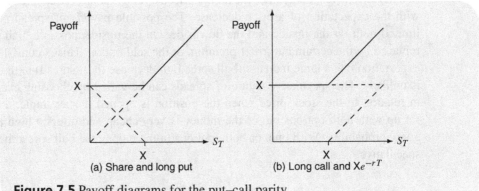

Figure 7.5 Payoff diagrams for the put–call parity

7.1.3 Bounds and relations for option prices

With simple arbitrage arguments we can derive some bounds on option prices before maturity, as well as some mutual relations between the prices of different options. The only assumption necessary for the derivation is that investors are greedy (prefer more to less, so that they exploit arbitrage possibilities). The bounds and relations are therefore independent of any specific model used to describe option prices or prices of the underlying asset. Together, these bounds define the acceptable range in option prices, i.e. the upper and lower limits between which option prices must fall. They also define some mutual price relations between options of different style, strike or maturity that must obtain in order to have arbitrage-free prices. With all this they also provide good intuition of the structure of option prices and the difficulty of constructing a good option-pricing model that does not violate any of the bounds.

Not all possible bounds are discussed here and to keep the discussion simple they are formulated for stock options, although most of them have a wider validity. A more rigorous and complete overview of option-price bounds can be found in the literature, e.g. Merton (1973) or Smith (1976). In the following, S is used to denote the stock price now and S_T the stock price at time T, X is the strike price and $O_{c,p}^{A,E}$ means option-price with superscripts for American and European and subscripts for call and put. We discuss the bounds assuming that there are no short sales restrictions or margin requirements and no transaction costs such as commissions, bid–ask spreads or taxes.

Upper and lower bounds

There is one lower limit that applies to all options.

Bound 1 The price of an option cannot be negative.

A negative price means that a buyer receives money when they purchase the option. Since options give future rights but no future obligations, the owner can simply let the option expire so that negative prices would mean a money machine.

An option cannot be worth more than what you 'get' when the option is exercised, so there is a general upper bound on option prices.

Bound 2 A call option cannot be worth more than the stock it is written on and a put option cannot be worth more than the exercise price.

A call option gives the right to buy the stock so this right cannot be worth more than the stock itself. More formally, if the price of the call would be higher than the price of the stock it is written on, writing a covered call (i.e. writing the call and buying the stock as cover) would be an arbitrage opportunity. Writing the call brings in O_c and buying the stock costs S. If $O_c > S$ then $O_c - S > 0$, so the portfolio would generate a positive cash flow today. But it would also generate a positive or non-negative cash flow in the future. If the option is exercised before or on maturity, the stock is given up in return for the exercise price, which gives a positive cash flow. If the option is not exercised, the value of the stock remains, which cannot be negative. Such arbitrage opportunities cannot exist in properly functioning markets and, hence, O_c cannot be larger than S. Similarly, a put option gives the right to sell a stock for the exercise price so the value can never be larger than the exercise price. This maximum is reached when the stock price is zero.

These general bounds can be narrowed down by arbitrage arguments that apply to more specific situations, particularly non-dividend-paying stocks.

Bound 3 The minimum value of a call option on a stock that pays no dividends is $\max[0, S - PV(X)]$.

We have already seen that option prices must be positive. If a call would sell for less than the (positive) difference between the stock price and the present value of the exercise price, the following arbitrage opportunity would exist. If $O_c < S - PV(X)$, then $-O_c + S - PV(X) > 0$, so constructing a portfolio consisting of a long call, a short stock and risk-free lending of the present value of the exercise price would generate a positive cash flow now. But that portfolio would also generate a non-negative cash flow at maturity, as Table 7.3 shows.

American calls have a lower (weaker) lower bound that can be enforced immediately by taking instantaneous arbitrage profits. That minimum value is $\max[0, S - X]$. If $O_c^A < S - X$, then buying the call, exercising it immediately and selling the stock obtained through the exercise will produce $-O_c^A + S - X > 0$. This is a weaker restriction since $PV(X) < X$. Note, however, that this weaker restriction is also valid if the stock pays dividends before the expiration date.

Similar lower bounds can be derived for put options, but with a difference between the styles.

Table 7.3 *Lower arbitrage bound on call options*

| | Now | At expiration | |
		$S_T > X$	$S_T < X$
Buy call	$-O_c$	$+(S_T - X)$	0
Short stock	$+S$	$-S_T$	$-S_T$
Lend $PV(X)$	$-PV(X)$	X	X
Total position	> 0	0	$-S_T + X > 0$

Bound 4 An American put option on a non-dividend-paying stock cannot be worth less than its intrinsic value $O_p^A \geq \max[0, X - S]$.

American puts can be exercised immediately, so if a put sells for less than the (positive) difference between the exercise price and the stock price, buying the stock and buying the put and then exercising it immediately produces an instantaneous profit $(-O_p^A + X - S > 0)$.

European puts on a non-dividend-paying stock have a lower (weaker) lower bound.

Bound 5 A European put option on a non-dividend-paying stock cannot be worth less than $\max[0, PV(X) - S]$.

If a European put sells for less than the (positive) difference between the present value of the exercise price and the stock price, the following arbitrage opportunity exists: if $O_p^E < PV(X) - S$ then $-O_p^E + PV(X) - S > 0$. So buying the put, borrowing PV(X) and buying the stock generates a positive cash flow today. But that portfolio also generates a non-negative payoff at maturity, as Table 7.4 shows.

Table 7.4 *Lower arbitrage bound on European put options*

| | Now | At expiration | |
		$S_T > X$	$S_T < X$
Buy put	$-O_p^E$	0	$+(X - S_T)$
Buy stock	$-S$	$+S_T$	$+S_T$
Borrow $PV(X)$	$+PV(X)$	$-X$	$-X$
Total position	> 0	$S_T - X > 0$	0

Finally, a more stringent upper bound than the exercise price can be derived for European puts.

Bound 6 A European put option cannot be worth more than the present value of the exercise price.

7.1 Options as securities

Violation of this bound opens the arbitrage opportunity of selling the put and lending the present value of the exercise price: if $O_p^E > PV(X)$ then $O_p^E - PV(X) > 0$. This gives a positive payoff now and a positive payoff later, as Table 7.5 shows.

Table 7.5 *Upper arbitrage bound on European put options*

		At expiration	
	Now	$S_T > X$	$S_T < X$
Sell put	$+O_p^E$	0	$-(X - S_T)$
Lend $PV(X)$	$-PV(X)$	X	X
Total position	> 0	$X > 0$	$S_T > 0$

Together these bounds define the acceptable ranges in option prices that are depicted in Figure 7.6. The upper bound on the calls on the left-hand side of the figure is the stock price, represented by the 45-degree line from the graph's origin. The lower bound on calls is $max[0, S - PV(X)]$, which is the parallel line from PV(X). The right-hand side of Figure 7.6 shows that American puts have both a higher upper bound (X versus PV(X)) and a higher lower bound than European puts (from X to X versus from PV(X) to PV(X)).

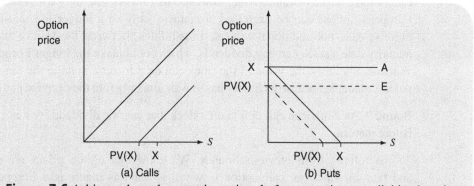

Figure 7.6 Arbitrage bounds on option prices before maturity, non-dividend paying stocks; A = American, E = European

The right of early exercise is valuable for put options, even if the underlying stock does not pay dividends. As we shall see in the next sub-section (bound 9), the right of early exercise has no value for call options on non-dividend-paying stocks. This is different for puts for two reasons. First, puts have a limited upward potential: the payoff cannot be larger than the exercise price. If the stock price falls to a level close to zero, the value of the put will be close to its maximum value of X. Keeping the option alive and waiting for the stock price to fall even further can only marginally increase the value of the put while the risk of a (large) decrease in value is not excluded. Second, the exercise price of a put is received and can be invested to earn the risk-free rate. So if the stock price drops to a sufficiently low level, the possible increase in intrinsic value will not outweigh the interest that can be earned on the exercise price. Therefore, in-the-money American puts are often exercised in practice.

Relations between option prices

The difference between European and American options can be expressed in a very general relation.

Bound 7 American options are worth at least as much as otherwise identical European options.

It follows from the definition that American options offer all the possibilities of European options plus the added flexibility of early exercise. This flexibility may have no value (as we shall see later on), but it cannot have negative value. Hence, an American option cannot be worth less than an otherwise identical European option.

Following the same reasoning we can say:

Bound 8 An American option is worth at least as much as an otherwise identical American option that has a shorter time to maturity.

The option with the longer time to maturity offers all the possibilities of the option with the shorter maturity plus the extra flexibility of a longer life. Again, this flexibility cannot have negative value. Note, however, that this is true only for American options. European options can be exercised at maturity only so a longer life means a different exercise date, not additional exercise possibilities. Between the shorter and the longer maturity date a stock can pay dividends, which could make the longer European call less valuable. Similarly, the value of the stock can drop to zero, making the longer European put less valuable because its holder has to wait longer before the exercise price is received.

Bound 9 An American call option on a stock that pays no dividends will not be exercised before maturity.

This follows from previous bounds. We know that option prices are non-negative and that an American call option is worth at least as much as a European call. We also know that the minimum value of a call option on a stock that pays no dividends is $\max[0, S - PV(X)]$. So $O_c^A \geq O_c^E \geq \max[0, S - PV(X)]$, which means that $O_c^A \geq [S - PV(X)]$. If the option is exercised, its value is $[S - X]$. Since $X > PV(X)$, early exercise is not optimal. To put it differently, since the minimum value 'alive' of $\max[0, S - PV(X)]$ is larger than the value 'dead' of $\max[0, S - X]$, selling the call is always better than exercising it. An implication of this is that an American call on a non-dividend-paying stock will have the same price as an otherwise equal European call; for all practical purposes they are the same. This relation does not hold for put options because, as we have seen, American puts can be exercised early even if the stock does not pay dividends.

Finally, the relations between otherwise identical options with different strike prices, that are expressed in Bound 10, will be intuitively clear. The value of a call option is based on the right to buy 'cheaply' so the lower the (exercise) price, the more valuable the call will be, other things being equal. Similarly, the value of a put springs from the right to sell 'expensively', so the higher the (exercise) price, the more valuable the put will be, other things being equal. Hence, the value of a call decreases with the exercise price and the value of a put increases with the exercise price.

Bound 10 A call option is worth at least as much as an otherwise identical call option but with a higher strike price, and a put option is worth at least as much as an otherwise identical put option but with a lower strike price.

The bounds are summarized in Table 7.6.

Table 7.6 *Arbitrage bounds on and relations between option prices*

	Calls		Puts	
	European	American	European	American
Upper	S	S		X
			$PV(X)$	
Style	$O_c^E \leq O_c^A$		$O_p^E \leq O_p^A$	
Time	$O_{c,T}^E \lesseqgtr O_{c,T+h}^E$	$O_{c,T}^A \leq O_{c,T+h}^A$	$O_{p,T}^E \lesseqgtr O_{p,T+h}^E$	$O_{p,T}^A \leq O_{p,T+h}^A$
Strike	value decreases with strike		value increases with strike	
Lower	$\max[0, S - PV(X)]$	$\max[0, S - PV(X)]$		$\max[0, X - S]$
		$\max[0, S - X]$	$\max[0, PV(X) - S]$	
	0	0	0	0

7.2 Foundations in state-preference theory

● ●

We now introduce option pricing in a setting of discrete variables and discrete time. This setting facilitates a transparent derivation of the major features of option pricing with hardly any loss of generality. Before discussing the Binomial Option Pricing model, we look at some of the concepts underlying option pricing in the more general framework of state-preference theory.

7.2.1 The setting: time and states

State-preference theory was developed in the 1950s and 1960s by the later Nobel prize laureates Arrow and Debreu. It now has a minor place in finance, but it has been a fruitful and above all transparent modelling technique, with which many important results have been obtained. In state-preference theory, time is modelled as a series of discrete points in time at which the uncertainty over the previous period is resolved and new decisions are made. In the periods between the points, 'nothing happens'.[4] This can be thought of as making investments at the first point in time, wait until the results become known at

---

4 This reflects Albert Einstein's view that 'the only reason for time is so that everything does not happen at once'.

the next and then adjust the investments, etc. A more popular view is placing bets, wait until the ball comes to rest on the roulette wheel and then make new bets, etc.

Uncertainty in variables is modelled by distinguishing a number of discrete 'states of the world' or 'states of nature', that can occur on the future points in time. Each state is associated with a numerical value of the variables under consideration. The states of the world can relate to general circumstances such as 'recession' and 'expansion', with a return on a stock portfolio of −5 per cent and +16 per cent respectively. But they can also refer to the result of a specific action, such as drilling for oil, with 'states of the world' as 'large well', 'medium-sized well' and 'dry well', each with a different cash flow attached to it. We shall elaborate a simple example with one period and two points in time and the following three future states of the world:

$$W = \begin{bmatrix} w_1 \\ w_2 \\ w_3 \end{bmatrix} = \begin{bmatrix} bust \\ normal \\ boom \end{bmatrix}$$

The states have a given probability of occurring (which can be based on, for example, long-term frequency of occurrence or the estimates of experts):

$$prob(w_i) = \begin{bmatrix} 0.3 \\ 0.45 \\ 0.25 \end{bmatrix}$$

There are three investment opportunities or securities, Y_1, Y_2 and Y_3. Investment Y_1, for example, has a payoff of 4 in state 1, 5 in state 2 and 6 in state 3, or:

$$Y_1(W) = \begin{bmatrix} 4 \\ 5 \\ 6 \end{bmatrix}$$

For simplicity, the addition (W) will be omitted from the notation. The payoffs of all securities in the different states are given in the payoff matrix Ψ:

$$\Psi = \begin{bmatrix} 4 & 1 & 2 \\ 5 & 7 & 4 \\ 6 & 10 & 16 \end{bmatrix}$$

Notice that the risk of the securities is expressed in the distribution of their payoffs over the states. Compared with the other two, the first security is rather safe: the difference between its highest and lowest payoff is only 2 $(6 - 4)$. The present value of the securities Y can be found by taking the expectation of their payoffs and discounting them with an appropriate rate. Assume that the present values of Y_1, Y_2, Y_3 are $v = \begin{bmatrix} 4.5 & 5.25 & 5.5 \end{bmatrix}$. Given the expected payoffs of, in matrix notation, $prob^T \Psi = \begin{bmatrix} 4.95 & 5.95 & 6.40 \end{bmatrix}$, this means that the returns on the investment opportunities are 10 per cent, 13 per cent and 16 per cent. However, it is not the prices themselves that are of primary interest here but the mutual relations between investments and what these relations mean for the capital market.

7.2.2   Complete markets

One of the concepts on which option-pricing models are built is market completeness. We briefly met the concept in Chapter 5 and it is elaborated in more detail here.

Risk-free and state securities

On the perfect capital markets we assume here, all securities are costlessly and infinitely divisible. This means we can combine securities in all possible ways in order to create the payoff pattern we want. An obvious candidate for a desirable pattern is one that gives the same payoff in all states of the world, i.e. creating a *riskless security*. This is done by combining the investments Y_{1-3} in a portfolio and choosing the weights x_n such that the payoffs are equal in all states:

$$4x_1 + 1x_2 + 2x_3 = 1$$

$$5x_1 + 7x_2 + 4x_3 = 1$$

$$6x_1 + 10x_2 + 16x_3 = 1$$

Since we have three equations with three unknowns, the system can be solved: $x_1 = 33/124$, $x_2 = -5/124$, and $x_3 = -3/248$. For example, $(4 \times 33/124) + (1 \times -5/124) + (2 \times -3/248) = 1$. So with these weights we can construct a portfolio that gives a riskless payoff, i.e. we can construct a riskless security. This portfolio also determines the *risk-free interest rate*. By multiplying the weights with the present values of the three original investment opportunities we get the present value of the riskless security: $(4.5 \times 33/124) + (5.25 \times -5/124) + (5.5 \times -3/248) = 0.9194$. Since an investment with this present value pays off 1 at the end of the period and in all states, the risk-free interest rate can be calculated as $1/0.9194 = 1.088$ or 8.8 per cent.

In the same way, we can create a portfolio that pays off 1 if state of the world 1 occurs and zero in all other states:

$$4x_{1'} + 1x_{2'} + 2x_{3'} = 1$$

$$5x_{1'} + 7x_{2'} + 4x_{3'} = 0$$

$$6x_{1'} + 10x_{2'} + 16x_{3'} = 0$$

This system is solvable too: $x_{1'} = 9/31$, $x_{2'} = -7/31$ and $x_{3'} = 1/31$. Again, by multiplying the weights with the present values of the original investment opportunities we can calculate the present value of an investment that pays off 1 in the first state of the world and zero in all other states: $(4.5 \times 9/31) + (5.25 \times -7/31) + (5.5 \times 1/31) = 0.298$. We can repeat the operation to find a portfolio that pays off 1 if the second state of the world occurs and zero in all other states, etc. However, rather than solving three systems we use a bit of matrix algebra to find the same solution. We want to find the matrix of weights X that satisfies:

$$\Psi X = I$$

where Ψ is the payoff matrix, X is a 3×3 matrix of the three weights in the three equations and I is the identity matrix:

$$\begin{bmatrix} 4 & 1 & 2 \\ 5 & 7 & 4 \\ 6 & 10 & 16 \end{bmatrix} \begin{bmatrix} x_{1,1} & x_{2,1} & x_{3,1} \\ x_{1,2} & x_{2,2} & x_{3,2} \\ x_{1,3} & x_{2,3} & x_{3,3} \end{bmatrix} = \begin{bmatrix} 1 & 0 & 0 \\ 0 & 1 & 0 \\ 0 & 0 & 1 \end{bmatrix}$$

This system is solved by:

$$X = \Psi^{-1} I = \Psi^{-1}$$

i.e. by taking the inverse of the payoff matrix:

$$\Psi^{-1} = \begin{bmatrix} \frac{9}{31} & \frac{1}{62} & -\frac{5}{124} \\ -\frac{7}{31} & \frac{13}{62} & -\frac{3}{124} \\ \frac{1}{31} & -\frac{17}{124} & \frac{23}{248} \end{bmatrix}$$

With these weights we can construct three portfolios, each of which pays off 1 in only one state of the world and zero in all states. Such securities are called *state securities* or *pure securities*, *primitive securities* or *Arrow–Debreu securities*. Multiplying the weights matrix with the vector of present values of the existing securities gives the price of the state securities, also known under the name *state prices*:

$$v\Psi^{-1} = \begin{bmatrix} 0.298 & 0.419 & 0.202 \end{bmatrix}$$

State prices reflect the probability that a particular state occurs: the higher this probability, the higher the state price will be. State prices also reflect the marginal utility of money that the market assigns to payoffs in a particular state, or the *market price of risk*. An investment that pays off in a bust is likely to have a higher present value than an investment that pays off in a boom, other things being equal. We will analyse this in more detail later on. Of course, a portfolio of the three state securities reproduces the risk-free security, so their values are the same: $0.298 + 0.419 + 0.202 = 0.919$.

Market completeness defined

The state securities allow the construction and pricing of *any payoff pattern across states*, simply as a combination of the state securities and their prices. We were able to construct state securities because the existing securities *span* all states, i.e. there are no states without a payoff. A market where that is the case is said to be *complete*. It is complete because no 'new' securities can be constructed, new in the sense that their payoff patterns cannot be duplicated by a portfolio of existing securities. We can also say this the other way around: if state securities can be constructed for all states, the market has to be complete. On such a market, all additional securities must be linear combinations of the original ones. The additional securities are called *redundant* securities. In the example above, the risk-free and state securities are also redundant: they are formed as combinations of the existing securities. Note that a market can be complete only if the number of different (i.e. not redundant) securities is equal to the number of states. In mathematical terms this means that the payoff matrix must be square and non-singular (or, in terms of the above example, we must have three non-trivial equations with three unknowns). The state prices offer an easy way of pricing redundant securities. We can simply multiply a security's payoff in each state with the state price and sum over the states to find the security's price. This follows directly from the definition of state prices.

Market completeness can also be represented in a geometric way. Suppose there are only two securities, A and B, and only two future states. A pays off 5 in state 1 and 2 in state 2, and B 2.5 in state 1 and 4 in state 2. The pay-offs are plotted as (radius) vectors in Figure 7.7. The securities themselves are represented by the bold lines from the origin into the upper right-hand quadrant. The line in between them, from (0, 0) to (7.5, 6), represents the sum of A and B. So in order to reach the point with coordinates (7.5, 6) we take the sum of the two vectors representing A and B. We could extend the line twice as far by taking 2A+2B, etc. In a similar way the lines representing (A–B), (B–A) and –A are drawn in the other quadrants. From this it will be clear that any point in the two-dimensional space in Figure 7.7 can be reached by combinations of A and B, simply by extending A and B either upwards or downwards. For instance, the point (−2.5, 6) can be reached by a combination of $-1\frac{2}{3}$A and $2\frac{1}{3}$B. So two linearly independent vectors can completely *span* a two-dimensional space. However, if the payoff of B would be 10 in state 1 and 4 in state 2, the second vector would be an extension of the first, and a single vector cannot span a two-dimensional space (only a one-dimensional line). In the same way, two linearly independent securities can be used to create any payoff pattern across two states.

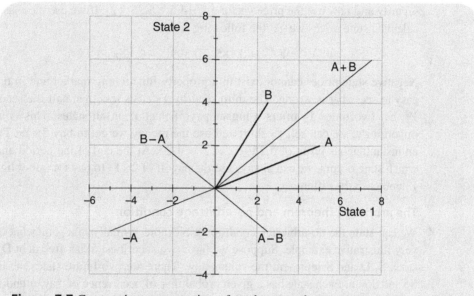

Figure 7.7 Geometric representation of market completeness

7.2.3 Arbitrage-free markets

A second concept that is essential to option-pricing models is arbitrage. We have seen several times before that arbitrage enforces certain pricing relations in well-functioning markets. We will have a closer look at arbitrage in the context of state-preference theory.

Arbitrage opportunities

In the discussion of Arbitrage Pricing Theory we saw that arbitrage opportunities exist if a self-financing investment strategy can be designed that:

- either requires a non-positive net investment now (zero investment is possible), while all future payoffs are non-negative and at least one payoff is positive,
- or requires a negative net investment now, while all future payoffs are non-negative (zero payoff is possible).

Self-financing means that no extra cash is required along the way, i.e. all additional outlays must be part of the strategy. From the above definition of arbitrage we can immediately infer a characteristic of the state prices: they have to be positive. A negative state price would mean that if we buy the state security, we pay a negative price (= receive money) and possibly (if the corresponding state occurs) get a payoff of 1 later. This means a negative net investment now and a non-negative expected profit later, so a money machine. Let us modify the previous example slightly to illustrate arbitrage possibilities. We still have the same assets Y_1, Y_2 and Y_3 with the same payoff matrix Ψ:

$$\Psi = \begin{bmatrix} 4 & 1 & 2 \\ 5 & 7 & 4 \\ 6 & 10 & 16 \end{bmatrix}$$

But instead of the old prices $v = \begin{bmatrix} 4.5 & 5.25 & 5.5 \end{bmatrix}$ we change the price of the third security and now use the price vector $z = \begin{bmatrix} 4.5 & 5.25 & 2 \end{bmatrix}$. If we use these asset prices to calculate state prices we get the following result:

$$z\Psi^{-1} = 0.185 \quad 0.899 \quad -0.123$$

Negative state prices cannot exist in a properly functioning market and in this case it is easy to see what is wrong. The third security Y_3 costs less than half the second security Y_2, but two times Y_3 offers a higher payoff than Y_2 in all states. This is an arbitrage opportunity: we can sell Y_2 short and use the money we get to buy $2 \times Y_3$. This gives us an instantaneous profit of $5.25 - 2 \times 2 = 1.25$. At the end of the period and no matter which state occurs, we can always use the payoff of $2 \times Y_3$ to pay for our obligations from Y_2 and cash the difference.

The arbitrage theorem and no-arbitrage condition

We can state the no-arbitrage condition a bit more formally in a somewhat different but very illustrative example. Suppose we have two securities, a risk-free debt D and a risky stock S. D and S represent the values now. There are two future states, let us call them up and down. Each state has a given probability of occurrence of, say, q and $(1 - q)$ and each state is associated with a different stock return. This makes the payoff matrix Ψ (we re-use the same symbols):

$$\Psi = \begin{bmatrix} (1 + r_f)D & (1 + u)S \\ (1 + r_f)D & (1 + d)S \end{bmatrix}$$

in which u represents the return rate for the stock if the up state occurs and d the down return rate. For normal stocks we assume $d < u$ (for anti-cyclical stocks it could be the other way around). We can represent this market as follows:

$$\begin{bmatrix} D & S \end{bmatrix} = \begin{bmatrix} \psi_1 & \psi_2 \end{bmatrix} \begin{bmatrix} (1 + r_f)D & (1 + u)S \\ (1 + r_f)D & (1 + d)S \end{bmatrix} \tag{7.3}$$

in which $\psi_{1,2}$ represent the state prices. As we have seen, we can find the value of a security now by multiplying its payoffs in future states with the state prices and summing over the states. That is what equation (7.3) says in matrix algebra. The *arbitrage theorem* can now be stated as follows: given the payoff matrix Ψ there are no arbitrage opportunities if and only if there is a strictly positive state price vector $\psi_{1,2}$ such that the security price vector $\begin{bmatrix} D & S \end{bmatrix}$ satisfies (7.3). We can also formulate this the other way round: if there are no arbitrage opportunities, then there is a positive state price vector $\psi_{1,2}$ such that the security price vector $\begin{bmatrix} D & S \end{bmatrix}$ satisfies (7.3). We can analyse in more detail under which conditions this is the case. We do this by first writing out the values of D and S:

$$D = \psi_1(1 + r_f)D + \psi_2(1 + r_f)D$$
$$S = \psi_1(1 + u)S + \psi_2(1 + d)S \tag{7.4}$$

Then we divide both equations by the values of the securities now (D and S respectively):

$$1 = \psi_1(1 + r_f) + \psi_2(1 + r_f)$$
$$1 = \psi_1(1 + u) + \psi_2(1 + d) \tag{7.5}$$

If we subtract the second row of (7.5) from the first and rearrange terms we get the result:

$$0 = \psi_1[(1 + r_f) - (1 + u)] + \psi_2[(1 + r_f) - (1 + d)] \tag{7.6}$$

If the state prices are to be positive, equation (7.6) can be zero in a non-trivial way only if one of the terms in square brackets is positive and the other one negative. Since $d < u$ for normal stocks, this will be the case if and only if:

$$(1 + d) < (1 + r_f) < (1 + u) \tag{7.7}$$

This is the *no-arbitrage condition* for this market: the risk-free rate of return has to be between the low and the high return of the stock. So the arbitrage theorem, that requires positive state prices, is translated into a return relation that has to be valid if the market is to be arbitrage free. In this simple market we can see immediately why this is so. If $(1 + r_f) < (1 + d)$, we could borrow risk free and invest in the stock to make a sure profit in any state of the world. If $(1 + u) < (1 + r_f)$ the stock would always pay off less than the risk-free asset, then we could short sell the stock and invest risk free to make a sure profit. These arbitrage deals would drive the price of the undervalued security up and the price of the overvalued security down until the arbitrage opportunity ceases to exist.

7.2.4 Risk-neutral valuation

The analyses can be extended to produce an important pricing relation, called risk-neutral valuation, which is at the heart of option pricing.

Pricing with risk-neutral probabilities

Look again at the first row of (7.5):

$$1 = \psi_1(1 + r_f) + \psi_2(1 + r_f)$$

We can define:

$$p_1 = \psi_1(1 + r_f) \text{ and } p_2 = \psi_2(1 + r_f). \tag{7.8}$$

With this definition, $p_{1,2}$ behave as probabilities in the sense that $0 \leq p_{1,2} \leq 1$ and $p_1 + p_2 = 1$. Hence, they can be used as probabilities associated with the two states of nature. They are different from the true probabilities *prob* and q that we used earlier.

$p_{1,2}$ are (somewhat confusingly) called *risk-neutral* probabilities or *risk-adjusted* or *equivalent martingale* probabilities (later we will see why). Notice that we use the state prices and the risk-free interest rate to define them. As we have seen, the state prices reflect the market price of risk, so the risk-neutral probabilities contain the pricing information in this market. Now look again at the second row of (7.4):

$$S = \psi_1(1+u)S + \psi_2(1+d)S$$

If we multiply the right-hand side with $(1+r_f)/(1+r_f)$ we get:

$$S = \frac{(1+r_f)\psi_1(1+u)S + (1+r_f)\psi_2(1+d)S}{1+r_f}$$

Using the definition of $p_{1,2}$ in (7.8) we get:

$$S = \frac{p_1(1+u)S + p_2(1+d)S}{1+r_f} \tag{7.9}$$

This very important result says that the expected payoff of the *risky* asset S can be discounted with the *risk-free* rate to find the true value of the asset *if the expected payoff is calculated with the risk-neutral probabilities*. This remarkable conclusion represents the essence of Black and Scholes' Nobel prize-winning breakthrough. In this approach risk is priced in a fundamentally different way than in equilibrium models such as the CAPM. In the latter, risk is expressed in the discount rate by adjusting it with a risk premium. In the *risk-neutral valuation* or *arbitrage-pricing* approach, as it is also called, we do not adjust the discount rate, but we adjust the probabilities. The market price of risk is contained, or embedded, in the probability terms so that discounting can be done with the risk-free rate, which is easily observable. This enables us to price assets for which it is difficult to calculate risk-adjusted discount rates, such as options.

Recall that we said in the introduction that uncertainty in valuation procedures can be accounted for in three different ways: (1) by adjusting the discount rate to a risk-adjusted discount rate, (2) by adjusting the cash flows to certainty equivalent cash flows, and (3) by adjusting the probabilities from normal to risk-neutral or equivalent martingale probabilities. The risk-neutral valuation in (7.9) is the third way. Some of its characteristics deserve further attention and are discussed below.

Conditional nature

A striking characteristic of the risk-neutral valuation formula in (7.9) is what is *not* in it. The original or real probabilities q and $(1-q)$ of an upward or downward movement do not appear in the formula, nor is there anything about the investors' attitudes towards risk, nor is there any reference to other securities or portfolios, such as the market portfolio. This is because risk-neutral valuation rests only on the absence of arbitrage opportunities and not on a matching of demand and supply as in equilibrium models such as the CAPM. In equilibrium models, investors express their preferences and expectations about stock prices in their demand for securities. Together with the supply characteristics this ultimately results in a set of market-clearing equilibrium prices as a function of ('explained' by) those preferences, expectations, etc. We saw how this market mechanism works in the discussion of portfolio theory. Risk-neutral valuation does not 'explain' the prices of existing securities on a complete and arbitrage-free market, it takes them as given. It does no more than 'translate' the prices of the existing securities in that market into prices for additional redundant securities, with arbitrage as the mechanism that brings about proper prices. So it is a relative, or conditional, pricing approach in the sense that it provides prices for additional securities *given* the prices for existing securities. Without the prices of existing securities, risk-neutral valuation cannot produce prices.

Return equalization

The risk-neutral probabilities are defined in such a way that they contain pricing information. If we calculate expectations with these probabilities, the market price of risk (i.e. the state prices) is already included in the expectation. By consequence, under the risk-neutral probabilities all securities 'earn' the same expected riskless return, so the returns are equalized. This can be shown by dividing both equations in (7.4) by the values of the securities now (D and S respectively):

$$1 = \psi_1 \frac{(1+r_f)D}{D} + \psi_2 \frac{(1+r_f)D}{D}$$

$$1 = \psi_1 \frac{(1+u)S}{S} + \psi_2 \frac{(1+d)S}{S}$$

Multiplying both sides of both equations with $(1 + r_f)$ and using the definition of $p_{1,2}$ we get:

$$(1+r_f) = p_1 \frac{(1+r_f)D}{D} + p_2 \frac{(1+r_f)D}{D}$$

$$(1+r_f) = p_1 \frac{(1+u)S}{S} + p_2 \frac{(1+d)S}{S} \tag{7.10}$$

The expected rate of return of both securities is the same and equal to the riskless rate, again provided that the expected rates are calculated with the risk-neutral probabilities. In the case of risk-free debt this result is trivial, but for the stock it is not.

Martingale property

If all assets are expected to earn the risk-free rate of return, this must mean that the expectation of the future asset price, discounted at the risk-free rate, is the same as its price now. This follows straight from the risk-neutral valuation formula (7.9). The expectation of the future stock price S_{t+1} is $E^p[S_{t+1}] = p_1(1+u)S_t + p_2(1+d)S_t$, i.e. the numerator of (7.9) with time subscripts added and where E^p stands for the expectation operator with respect to the probabilities p. This means that $S_t = E^p[S_{t+1}]/(1+r_f)$. As we have seen in Chapter 4, a dynamic process is called *a martingale* if the conditional expected future value of a variable, given all past values, is equal to its current value.[5] Under the risk-neutral probabilities, the expected future prices of *all* assets, discounted at the risk-free rate, are martingales. Hence the word martingale in the term 'equivalent martingale probabilities'. Note that the asset prices themselves are not martingales but the asset prices divided (or normalized) by the risk-free discount factor. Asset prices are expected to increase with the risk-free rate under the equivalent martingale probability measure.

---

5 Recall that a variable X is a martingale, defined with respect to its own observation history, if $E(X_{t+1} \mid X_0, ...X_t) = X_t$.

A *probability measure* is a set of probabilities, one for each possible outcome. The real probability measures in our examples could be estimated from, for example, the long-term frequency of occurrence of the states of nature. The risk-neutral probabilities are based on the state prices, as we have seen. Two probability measures are said to be *equivalent* if they assign positive probability to the same set of outcomes, i.e. they agree on which outcomes have zero probability. Hence the term *equivalent martingale probabilities*.

An alternative look at state prices

Look again at the definition of the risk-neutral probabilities in (7.8):

$$p_1 = \psi_1(1 + r_f) \text{ and } p_2 = \psi_2(1 + r_f).$$

We can rewrite this in term of state prices:

$$\psi_1 = \frac{p_1}{(1 + r_f)} \text{ and } \psi_2 = \frac{p_2}{(1 + r_f)} \tag{7.11}$$

and then divide both sides of the equations by the sum of the two:

$$\frac{\psi_1}{\psi_1 + \psi_2} = \frac{p_1/(1 + r_f)}{\frac{p_1 + p_2}{(1 + r_f)}} \text{ and } \frac{\psi_2}{\psi_1 + \psi_2} = \frac{p_2/(1 + r_f)}{\frac{p_1 + p_2}{(1 + r_f)}}$$

$$\frac{\psi_1}{\psi_1 + \psi_2} = \frac{p_1}{p_1 + p_2} = p_1 \text{ and } \frac{\psi_2}{\psi_1 + \psi_2} = \frac{p_2}{p_1 + p_2} = p_2 \tag{7.12}$$

So the risk-neutral probabilities can also be calculated by standardizing the state prices into a variable with a sum of 1. This makes the relation between state prices and risk-neutral probabilities even more explicit than in (7.8) and clearly demonstrates why risk-neutral probabilities can be used for pricing purposes.

From the derivation of (7.12) it will also be clear that the existence of a positive state price vector is really the same thing as the existence of positive risk-neutral probabilities or, in terms of probability theory, the existence of an equivalent martingale measure. This means that we can reformulate the no-arbitrage condition in probabilistic terms, as is done often in the literature: *There are no arbitrage possibilities if and only if there exists an equivalent martingale measure*.

State prices and the pricing kernel

In the initial sections on state preference theory we found the state price vector as $v\Psi^{-1} = [0.298 \quad 0.419 \quad 0.202]$. So far we have taken these state prices as given, without investigating why the price of one money unit differs across states. Clearly, the probability that the state occurs is of importance: the higher this probability, the higher the state price will be. But even if we calculate the price per unit of probability, differences remain, as Table 7.7 shows. We use the real probabilities for this, not the equivalent martingale probabilities. The resulting vector of probability deflated state prices is called the *pricing kernel*. The pricing kernel reflects the marginal utility of money that the market assigns to the different states which, in turn, expresses the risk aversion in the market. In our example, the marginal utility of an extra money unit is apparently higher in a bust than in a boom. In a bust, good results are scarce so investments that pay off just then are valuable. In a boom, almost every investment pays off so an extra money unit in that state contributes comparatively little to total wealth.

Table 7.7 *Calculation of the pricing kernel*

State	Price	Real prob.	Pricing kernel
bust	0.298	0.3	0.9933
normal	0.419	0.45	0.9311
boom	0.202	0.25	0.808

Since both the state prices and probabilities are required to be positive, the pricing kernel allows us to reformulate the no-arbitrage condition in yet another way: the existence of a positive pricing kernel excludes arbitrage possibilities. So now we have three equivalent ways of formulating the no-arbitrage condition. There are no arbitrage possibilities if and only if:

1. there exists a positive state price vector
2. there exists an equivalent martingale measure
3. there exists a positive pricing kernel.

7.3   Binomial option pricing

Binomial option pricing was introduced in a paper by Cox, Ross and Rubinstein (Cox *et al.*, 1979). Their binomial model provides an elegant and easy way of demonstrating the economic intuition behind option pricing and its principal techniques. But the model should not be regarded as a simple approximation of a complex problem. On the contrary, it is a powerful tool for valuing quite general derivative securities and it can be used when no analytical closed-form solution of the continuous time models exists. Moreover, in the limit, when the discrete steps converge to a continuum, the model converges to an exact formula in continuous time.

7.3.1   The setting

The binomial method, like state-preference theory, uses discrete time and discrete variables. Time is modelled as a series of points in time at which the uncertainty over the previous period is resolved. Uncertainty in variables is modelled by distinguishing only two different states of the world, usually called an 'up' state and a 'down' state. Both states have a return factor for the underlying variable, for which we re-use u and d as symbols. The probability that state 'up' occurs is, again, called q, so for 'down' it is $(1-q)$. Since $u \times d = d \times u$ the result is a recombining binomial tree (or lattice) and the underlying variable follows a multiplicative binomial process. An example of such a tree for a security priced A is given in Lattice 1.

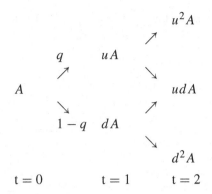

Lattice 1 Price process of security priced A

The riskiness of a security is expressed in the size of the up and down factors, in combination with the size of the time steps. For example, a security with an up factor of 1.22 and a down factor of 0.82 is riskier than a security with u = 1.11 and d = 0.9 over the same time interval. If the number of time steps increases for a given period of 'calendar time', the difference between the up and down factors has to decrease in order to express the same riskiness. For instance, an up factor of 1.22 per year corresponds to an up factor of 1.105 per half year ($1.105^2 = 1.221$). In the next chapter we will elaborate a formula that relates the up and down factors to the size of the time steps.

Other trees are possible, e.g. non-recombining trees with additive instead of multiplicative returns (increase or decrease in amounts rather than factors), or trinomial trees, but the binomial model uses binomial lattices. It is customary to use return factors and interest rate factors, rather than rates, in the binomial model. So an interest rate of 8 per cent is expressed as $r = 1.08$. Similarly, the up and down factors are expressed as 1 + the rate.

At first sight, it may look excessively restrictive to model uncertainty in variables by allowing only two discrete changes, one up and one down. However, many variables that we think of as being continuous actually move in discrete, albeit small, steps. The prices of stocks and most other securities change with *ticks*, i.e. a minimum allowed amount. Changes in interest rates are expressed in discrete basis points of one hundredth of a per cent. Moreover, as we can see from Lattice 1, the number of states increases with the number of time steps, so by increasing the number of points in time within a given (calendar-) time interval we can increase the number of possible end states. This makes binomial modelling of stock prices not as unrealistic as it may seem: over a short period of time, many stock prices indeed change only with one or two ticks.

7.3.2 A simple one-period model

To introduce the binomial method we begin with a very simple example in a one-period–two-moment setting. We assume a perfect financial market without taxes, transaction costs, margin requirements, etc. A stock with a current price of S is traded in the market. The stock price follows a multiplicative binomial process with an up factor u and a downward factor d. The probability of an upward movement is q so the probability of a downward movement is $1 - q$. There is also trade in a European call option on the stock with an exercise price of X. The unknown current price of the option is O. The option matures at the end of the period and pays off the maximum of zero and the stock price minus the exercise price. Riskless debt is also available in the market with an interest rate factor of r (remember that r, u, and d are defined as $1 +$ the rate). The payoffs of the stock and the option are depicted in Lattice 2.

$$q \qquad uS \qquad\qquad q \qquad O_u = \max[0, uS - X]$$
$$\nearrow \qquad\qquad\qquad \nearrow$$
$$S \qquad\qquad\qquad\qquad O$$
$$\searrow \qquad\qquad\qquad \searrow$$
$$1-q \quad dS \qquad\qquad 1-q \quad O_d = \max[0, dS - X]$$

Lattice 2 Price processes of stock S and option O

From the previous section we know that this market is complete if the stock and the risk-free debt are linearly independent, which is the case here unless $r = u = d$. Assuming completeness we can create any payoff pattern over the two states. We also know that the no-arbitrage condition on this market is $d < r < u$. The problem is, of course, to find the current price of the option O.

The general approach to the problem is to construct a *replicating* portfolio of existing and, thus, priced securities that gives the same payoffs as the option. The price of the option then has to be the same as the price of the replicating portfolio, otherwise there will be arbitrage opportunities. Note that we need a complete market to be able to create any payoff structure, including that of the option. The existing securities are the stock and risk-free debt. So we form a portfolio with some fraction Δ of the stock and a risk-free loan of D. The portfolio has a payoff tree as in Lattice 3.

$$q \qquad uS\Delta + rD$$
$$\nearrow$$
$$\Delta S + D$$
$$\searrow$$
$$1-q \quad dS\Delta + rD$$

Lattice 3 The replicating portfolio

Δ and D can be positive or negative, so both positions (in the stock and risk-free debt) can be long or short. In a perfect market Δ and D can be chosen freely and we choose them such that they make the end-of-period value of the portfolio equal to the end-of-period value of the option:

$$uS\Delta + rD = O_u$$
$$dS\Delta + rD = O_d \qquad\qquad (7.13)$$

The two equations in (7.13) can be solved for Δ and D which gives:

$$\Delta = \frac{O_u - O_d}{(u - d)S} \qquad\qquad (7.14)$$

and:

$$D = \frac{uO_d - dO_u}{(u - d)r} \tag{7.15}$$

Δ, the number of shares needed to replicate the option, is called the 'hedge ratio' or the 'option delta'. Δ is measured as the spread in option values divided by the spread in stock values. The portfolio with these Δ and D is called the *hedging portfolio* or the *option-equivalent portfolio*. It is equivalent to the option because, at maturity, it generates the same payoffs as the option. This means that they must have the same current price, otherwise there will be arbitrage opportunities. So:

$$O = \Delta S + D \tag{7.16}$$

Substituting (7.14) and (7.15) into (7.16) gives:

$$O = \frac{O_u - O_d}{(u - d)} + \frac{uO_d - dO_u}{(u - d)r} = \frac{\left[\frac{r-d}{u-d}\right]O_u + \left[\frac{u-r}{u-d}\right]O_d}{r} \tag{7.17}$$

To simplify equation (7.17) we recall the return equalization expressed in (7.10), which states that the expected rates of return of all securities are the same and equal to the riskless rate, provided that the expected rates are calculated with the risk-neutral probabilities. If we apply this to the stock (which is the same as rewriting the lower row of (7.10) in terms of return factors) we get:

$$r = p_1 u + (1 - p_1)d$$

This determines the risk-neutral probability of an upward movement p_1 uniquely as:

$$p_1 = \frac{r - d}{u - d} \rightarrow p_2 = (1 - p_1) = \frac{u - r}{u - d} \tag{7.18}$$

Substituting (7.18) into (7.17) we get:

$$O = \frac{pO_u + (1 - p)O_d}{r} \tag{7.19}$$

This is an exact formula to price the option. Of course, we immediately recognize the risk-neutral valuation formula (7.9) – they are, in fact, the same.

In an option context, some elements are easier to explain – the conditional nature of the pricing approach, for example. It will be clear that the price of an option on a stock depends on the price of the stock. This means that the real probabilities q and $1 - q$ are not needed to price the option: even if investors have different subjective expectations regarding q, they still agree on the value of the option relative to the share. Again, the investors' attitudes towards risk are not expressed, but one characteristic is modelled more explicitly: investors have to be greedy. At maturity, they have to choose the largest (max.) of the two possible option values. But greedy investors are implicit in all arbitrage arguments, otherwise arbitrage opportunities will not be used.

The binomial option-pricing formula (7.19) and the risk-neutral valuation formula (7.9) can be rewritten in terms of state prices. Recall that risk-neutral probabilities were defined in (7.8) as the state prices times the risk-free interest rate: $p_1 = \psi_1 r$ and $p_2 = \psi_2 r$

and that, consequently, the state prices could be written as the discounted risk-neutral probabilities in (7.11). In the present notation this becomes:

$$\psi_1 = \frac{p_1}{r} \quad \text{and} \quad \psi_2 = \frac{p_2}{r} \tag{7.20}$$

Alternatively, the state prices can be derived by writing the values of the two securities on this market, the stock and the riskless security, in terms of state prices:

$$D = \psi_1 r D + \psi_2 r D$$

$$S = \psi_1 u S + \psi_2 d S$$

Solving this for ψ_1 and ψ_2 gives:

$$\psi_1 = \frac{1}{r}\left[\frac{r-d}{u-d}\right] \quad \text{and} \quad \psi_2 = \frac{1}{r}\left[\frac{u-r}{u-d}\right]$$

which reproduces the state prices as the discounted risk-neutral probabilities.

7.3.3   A two-period example

The further characteristics and the use of binomial option pricing can best be illustrated with some examples. We start by extending the time period to two periods and three moments.

The example

As before, we assume a perfect financial market. In that market a stock is traded at a current price of 400. The stock price follows a multiplicative binomial process and can go up with a factor 1.25 or go down with 0.8. The stock pays no dividends. Risk-free debt is available at 7 per cent interest. A European call option on the stock with an exercise price of 375 is also traded. The option matures at the end of the second period.

The parameters of the binomial process are u = 1.25, d = 0.8 and r = 1.07, so $p = (r-d)/(u-d) = (1.07-0.8)/(1.25-0.8) = 0.6$ and $(1-p) = 0.4$. The development of the stock prices is depicted in Lattice 4.

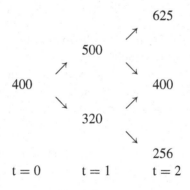

$t = 0 \qquad t = 1 \qquad t = 2$

Lattice 4 Price process of a stock

We know the value of the option at maturity in each end state: $max[0, S - X]$. Given those, we can apply the binomial option-pricing formula (7.19) and work our way to t_0.

So the tree is solved from the end backwards, as illustrated in Lattice 5. First O_u and O_d are calculated using (7.19) and then O can be found by repeating the procedure:

$O_u = ((0.6 \times 250) + (0.4 \times 25))/1.07 = 149.53$ and

$O_d = ((0.6 \times 25) + (0.4 \times 0))/1.07 = 14.02$ so that

$O = ((0.6 \times 149.53) + (0.4 \times 14.02))/1.07 = 89.09$.

$$O_{uu} = \max[0, 625 - 375] = 250$$

$$O_u = 149.53$$

$$O = 89.09$$

$$O_{ud} = \max[0, 400 - 375] = 25$$

$$O_d = 14.02$$

$$O_{dd} = \max[0, 256 - 375] = 0$$

$t = 0 \qquad\qquad t = 1 \qquad\qquad t = 2$

Lattice 5 A European call option on the stock in Lattice 4

Of course, we can substitute the binomial option-pricing formula for O_u and O_d in the formula for O to get a two-period formula:

$$O = \frac{p^2 O_{uu} + 2p(1-p)O_{ud} + (1-p)^2 O_{dd}}{r^2}$$

However, it is more usual to write out the recursive procedure to allow for events in the nodes O_u and O_d, such as dividend payments and early exercise of American options.

The hedging portfolio

The binomial option-pricing formula is developed using arbitrage arguments, based on the possibility of making a hedging portfolio with exactly the same payoffs as the option. This allowed us to use the price of the portfolio to price the option. We will now check whether the hedging portfolio indeed exactly replicates the option. We do this by assuming that we sell the option and hedge (i.e. neutralize) the obligations arising from selling the option with a hedging portfolio of the stock and debt. Look back at the binomial trees for the stock and the option in Lattices 4 and 5. We calculated the t_0 value of the option at 89.09. The t_0 option delta is:

$$\Delta = \frac{O_u - O_d}{uS - dS} = \frac{149.53 - 14.02}{500 - 320} = \frac{135.51}{180} = 0.753$$

So the t_0 hedging portfolio contains 0.753 shares at a price of 400, which costs 301.2. We receive 89.09 for the option, so we have to borrow $301.2 - 89.09 = 212.11$. We could have calculated the same amount using the formula for D in (7.15). The hedging portfolio is thus a levered long position in the stock.

Suppose the stock price rises to 500 at t_1. The new hedge ratio becomes:

$$\Delta = \frac{O_u - O_d}{uS - dS} = \frac{250 - 25}{625 - 400} = \frac{225}{225} = 1$$

So we have to buy $1 - 0.753 = 0.247$ stock extra at a cost of $0.247 \times 500 = 123.50$. We borrow the extra 123.50 so that our total debt now is $123.50 + 212.11 \times 1.07 = 350.46$. From 500 at t_1, the stock price can rise to 625 or fall to 400 at t_2. In either case, the option ends in the money and we are required to give up the stock we have in the portfolio for the exercise price of 375. This 375 is exactly enough to pay off the debt, which now amounts to $1.07 \times 350.46 = 375$. So our net position is zero, a perfect hedge.

Now look at the lower half of the tree and suppose the stock price falls to 320 at t_1. In that case the hedge ratio becomes:

$$\Delta = \frac{O_u - O_d}{uS - dS} = \frac{25 - 0}{400 - 256} = \frac{25}{144} = .174$$

We have to sell $0.753 - 0.174 = 0.579$ stock at 320, which brings in 185.28. We use the 185.28 to pay back debt, so that the new amount of debt becomes $(1.07 \times 212.11) - 185.28 = 41.68$. From the lower node at t_1 the stock price can increase to 400 or fall to 256 at t_2. If the stock price increases to 400, the option ends in the money and we have to deliver a stock against a price of 375. We have only 0.174 stock in portfolio, so we have to buy $1 - 0.174 = 0.826$ stock at a price of 400, which costs 330.40. The net amount we get from the stock is $375 - 330.40 = 44.60$. This is just enough to pay off the debt, which is now $41.68 \times 1.07 = 44.60$. So we have a perfect hedge.

If the stock price falls to 256 at t_2, the option ends out of the money and expires worthlessly. What we have left in our portfolio is 0.174 stock with a value of $0.174 \times 256 = 44.54$. Allowing for some rounding error, this is again just enough to pay off the debt of 44.60, so we have a perfect hedge.

Notice that when we adjust the portfolio at t_1, we do not know what is going to happen at t_2. We make our adjustment on the basis of the current stock price. We do know, however, that there is no risk: we always have a perfect hedge with a self-financing strategy.

7.3.4 Dividends

We now relax the assumption of no dividends and assume that the stock pays out 25 per cent of its value at t_1. In a perfect capital market, dividends are not relevant for the stockholders because they can undo or redo all dividend decisions by buying or selling stock. But dividends are relevant to European call option holders, who only have the right to buy the stock at maturity and do not receive any dividends. If a part of the stock value is transformed into cash, the remaining stock loses value. In the extreme case, the firm could sell all its assets and pay out the proceeds as dividends to the stockholders. This would leave the option-holders with the right to buy worthless stock. For the option-holders, dividends are a stream of value out of the stock. If we make the assumption that the value of the stock drops with the amount of dividend right after the payment, the binomial tree for the stock becomes as in Lattice 6.

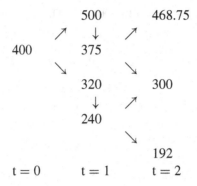

```
                      500          468.75
                 ↗     ↓      ↗
          400          375
                 ↘            ↘
                      320          300
                       ↓      ↗
                      240
                              ↘
                                   192
          t = 0      t = 1    t = 2
```

Lattice 6 Price process of a dividend-paying stock

The loss in value of the stock is represented by the ex-dividend value below the cum-dividend value. Note that the parameters of the binomial process refer to all values so that *u, d* and *p* do not change. The binomial tree continues from the ex-dividend value. We can calculate the price of the option in the same way as before by starting with the values at maturity and then solve the tree backwards, as in Lattice 7.

$$O_{uu} = \max[0, 468.75 - 375] = 93.75$$

$$O_u = 52.57$$

$$O = 29.48$$

$$O_{ud} = \max[0, 300 - 375] = 0$$

$$O_d = 0$$

$$O_{dd} = \max[0, 192 - 375] = 0$$

t = 0   t = 1   t = 2

Lattice 7 A European call option on the stock in Lattice 6

$O_u = ((0.6 \times 93.75) + (0.4 \times 0))/1.07 = 52.57$ and $O_d = 0$ so that $O = ((0.6 \times 52.57) + (0.4 \times 0))/1.07 = 29.48$.

7.3.5   An American option

An American call option on a non-dividend-paying stock will not be exercised early, so it is for all practical purposes the same as a European call. But when the stock pays dividends it may be optimal to exercise early. In order to test whether the option should be exercised or not, we include the condition max[exercising, keeping] (or popularly: max[dead, alive]) in the relevant nodes of the valuation procedure. So let us assume that the option in the previous subsection is an American call option and calculate its value.

The values at maturity remain unchanged because the option cannot be kept at maturity: it either expires or is exercised. So the end nodes in the tree remain the same. Calculating the t_1 values of the payoffs at maturity gives the option values 'alive'. They are the same as the values we just calculated for the European option. We have to compare these values with the t_1 values 'dead', which are the differences between *cum-dividend values* and the exercise price. The whole point of exercising early is to receive the dividends, so we have to exercise before the dividends are paid. The values are depicted in Lattice 8. In the case of O_u at t_1, early exercise is profitable: the value dead is 125, which is higher than the value alive of 52.57. The higher value is reflected in the higher t_0 value of $(0.6 \times 125)/1.07 = 70.09$. This latter value should also be checked against the value dead at t_0, which is $400 - 375 = 25$. Comparing the value of the American option with its European counterpart shows that the right of early exercise is valuable if the payout ratio of the stock is high.

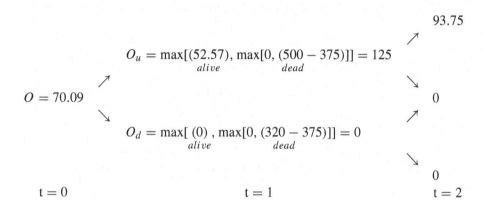

Lattice 8 An American call option on the stock in Lattice 6

7.3.6   A put option

Binomial option-pricing works just as well for put options as it does for calls. In the derivation of the option-pricing formula, we did not explicitly model the nature of the option. We defined the option's payoff as $O_{u,d} = \max[0, S_{u,d} - X]$, but changing this definition to $O_{u,d} = \max[0, X - S_{u,d}]$ does not change the derivation. To illustrate this we go back to the original two-period example and redefine the call as a European put option with the same exercise price of 375. The stock price development remains as in Lattice 4 and the option values are depicted in Lattice 9.

$O_d = ((0.6 \times 0) + (0.4 \times 119))/1.07 = 44.49$ and $O_u = 0$ so that $O = ((0.6 \times 0) + (0.4 \times 44.486))/1.07 = 16.63$.

Of course, we could have obtained the same result using the put–call parity: *call* + $PV(X) = S + put$ or $put = call + PV(X) - S$. The price of the call was calculated at 89.09. The present value of the exercise price is $375/1.07^2 = 327.54$ and the stock price is 400. So the price of the put is: $89.09 + 327.54 - 400 = 16.63$.

$$O_{uu} = \max[0, 375 - 625] = 0$$

$$O_u = 0$$

$$O = 16.63$$

$$O_{ud} = \max[0, 375 - 400] = 0$$

$$O_d = 44.49$$

$$O_{dd} = \max[0, 375 - 256] = 119$$

t = 0   t = 1   t = 2

Lattice 9 A European put option on the stock in Lattice 4

If we calculate the option's Δ and D at t_0 we get:

$$\Delta = \frac{O_u - O_d}{(u - d)S} = \frac{0 - 44.49}{500 - 320} = -0.247 \text{ and}$$

$$D = \frac{uO_d - dO_u}{(u - d)r} = \frac{1.25 \times 44.49 - .8 \times 0}{1.25 \times 1.07 - .8 \times 1.07} = 115.50$$

So the hedging portfolio for a put is a short position in the stock and a long position in risk-free debt, the reverse of what we calculated for the call.

7.3.7 Convergence to Black and Scholes

In the examples and models discussed so far, we have used only a few time steps, resulting in two or three end nodes. Our basic example in Lattice 4 has three points in time, $t_{0,1,2}$, two periods and three end nodes. It will be clear that we can choose different numbers of time steps for any given period of calendar time. For example, we can model a year as one period of a year, giving two end nodes, as two periods of six months, giving three end nodes, as four quarters, giving five end nodes, and as 12 months or 52 weeks with 13 and 53 end nodes. The limiting case is when the number of time steps becomes infinite, so that the time steps become infinitesimal. We then have continuous time and an infinite number of end nodes, which means a continuous distribution of end values. Cox *et al.* (1979) show in their paper that, under certain assumptions regarding the binomial parameters, the binomial option-pricing formula converges to the Black and Scholes formula if the number of time steps becomes infinite. Figure 7.8 illustrates the process of convergence with a binomial lattice containing many time steps.

Figure 7.8 also contains a sample path, that a stock price, for example, could have followed through the binomial lattice. With small enough time steps, this path becomes a continuous line graph of a stock price, like the graphs that are routinely printed in newspapers. The mathematical tools to model such continuous dynamic processes are discussed in the next chapter.

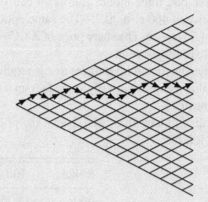

Figure 7.8 Binomial lattice and sample path

Exercises

1. You have done some option trading and you now hold the following option contracts: you have written (sold) a put with an exercise price of 75, you have bought a put with an exercise price of 100, you have bought a call with an exercise price of 75 and you have written a call with an exercise price of 100. All options are on the same underlying share and have the same maturity.
   (a) Construct the payoff diagram (not the profit diagram) for your total position over the share price interval from 0 to 150.

2. It is sometimes said that the prices of at-the-money puts and calls on the same underlying and with the same maturity have to be the same, since simultaneously buying and selling cancels out. Is this reasoning correct? Assume European options on non-dividend-paying stocks.

3. The option position depicted in the figure below is known as a butterfly spread.

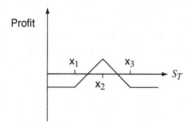

   (a) Work out a combination of call options that produces the butterfly spread in the figure.
   (b) Work out a combination of put options that produces the butterfly spread in the figure.

4. On 1 November, three-month European call options on a share in ZX Co with an exercise price of 460 cost 20.75. The same options with an exercise price of 480 resp. 500 cost 11.75 resp. 6. The share price of ZX Co is 462.5 and the three-months risk-free interest rate is 1.5 per cent.
   (a) Calculate the initial investment that is required to set up a butterfly spread.
   (b) Show that the same butterfly spread set up with put options requires the same initial investment.
   (c) According to a business newspaper, the prices of three-month put options ZX Co are as follows:

Strike	Bid	Ask
460	15.25	17.50
480	26.00	29.00
500	40.00	43.25

   Explain why these prices are the same as, or different from, the prices you used in question b.

5. The figure below repeats the profit diagrams for option positions known as spreads that were used in the main text.

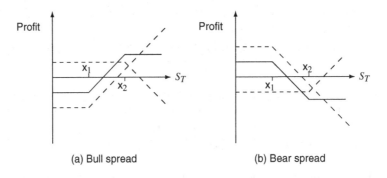

(a) Bull spread   (b) Bear spread

   (a) Construct the spreads in this figure using put options.
   (b) What happens to the initial investment (initial balance of the option premiums) required to set up the position, compared with the same position in calls? Hint: look at the prices of options in relation to the exercise prices.

6. In Bound 6 the following maximum value for European put options is formulated: a European put option cannot be worth more than the present value of the exercise price. Explain why this bound is or is not valid for American options.

7. In a financial market a stock is traded at a price of 100. At the end of the period, the stock price can either increase with 20 to 120 or decrease with 20 to 80. Risk-free debt is available at 5 per cent per period. Using state prices, calculate the value of an at-the-money call option on the stock which matures at the end of the period.

8. A financial market can have two possible future states. Both states are equally likely. In the market two securities, A and B, are traded. The securities' payoffs in the future states are as follows:

	A	B
State 1	6	4
State 2	12	14

The required rates of return on the securities are 8 per cent for A and 12 per cent for B.

(a) Calculate the value of the securities A and B using the risk-adjusted discount rates.

(b) Calculate the state prices and the risk-free interest rate on the market. Check your results.

(c) Recalculate the values of the securities A and B:
   i. using the state prices
   ii. using the risk-neutral valuation formula.

(d) Calculate the values of call options on the two securities A and B with an exercise price of 10 and that mature in the future state (of course).

9. In a financial market a stock is traded with a current price of 100. The price of the stock can either go up with 50 per cent next period or go down with 50 per cent next period. Risk-free debt is available with an interest rate of 25 per cent. Also traded is a European call option on the stock with an exercise price of 110 and a time to maturity of 2 (i.e. the option matures at end of the second period on the third moment).

(a) Discuss the completeness and the arbitrage properties of this market.

(b) Calculate the value of the option assuming that:
   i. The stock pays no dividend.
   ii. The stock pays out 25 per cent of its value in dividends on the second moment (end of the first period).
   iii. Repeat step b(i) for an American call option.
   iv. Repeat step b(ii) for an American call option.
   v. Repeat step b(i) for a European put option.
   vi. Repeat step b(ii) for a European put option.

10. In a financial market a stock is traded with a current price of 50. Next period the price of the stock can either go up with 30 per cent or go down with 25 per cent. Risk-free debt is available with an interest rate of 8 per cent. Also traded are European options on the stock with an exercise price of 45 and a time to maturity of 1, i.e. they mature next period.

(a) Calculate the price of a call option by constructing and pricing a replicating portfolio.

(b) Calculate the price of a put option by constructing and pricing a replicating portfolio.

8 Option pricing in continuous time

After the groundbreaking contributions by Black, Scholes and Merton in the early 1970s, continuous time finance quickly grew into a large branch of financial economics. The area was strongly invigorated by the enormous proliferation of option trading and it received scientific recognition with the Nobel prize for Merton and Scholes in 1997. Sundaresan (2000) gives an overview of its developments and applications in various areas. Continuous time finance is an area where the mathematical approach can be fully exploited. Given securities prices on complete and arbitrage-free markets, the full force of mathematics can be brought to bear on the problem of how to price new securities. We have already developed the conceptual framework in discrete time, so we can introduce the continuous time techniques with minimal effort. We begin by having another look at the properties of stock returns. We then illustrate how probabilities can be transformed with the simple example of loading a die. Transformation is applied to stock returns, which results, in an equivalent martingale probability measure for stock returns. Pricing can then be done in the by now familiar way of discounting the risk-neutral expectation using the risk-free discount rate. The result is the celebrated Black and Scholes formula.

8.1 Preliminaries: stock returns and a die

So far we have mainly used simple, discretely compounded returns. In Black and Scholes' option pricing we follow individual stocks in continuous time and this makes it necessary to use continuously compounded returns and to detail their properties.

8.1.1 Properties of log returns

Recall from the second chapter that continuous compounding means that the time spans over which compounding takes place are infinitesimal and the return is instantaneous (i.e. per instant). We calculated continuously compounded returns as $S_T = S_0 e^{\mu T}$ or $S_T / S_0 = e^{\mu T}$, where $S_{T,0}$ is the stock price at time T and 0 (= now) respectively and μ is the instantaneous return. Also recall that these returns are easily calculated from series of successive stock prices by taking natural logarithms: $\ln(S_T / S_0) = \ln e^{rT} = rT$, hence the name log returns, and that they are additive over time but not over investments.

In Chapter 2 we used these log returns as if they were constant, but future stock returns are uncertain (stochastic). They contain a random element, so they have a variance as well as an expectation. This means that we have to describe their stochastic behaviour over time by making some assumptions. Our most important assumption is that successive log returns are independently and identically distributed (iid). Although the iid assumption

8.1 Preliminaries: stock returns and a die

looks like a rather innocent way of making life easy from a statistical point of view, it has far-reaching consequences, both technically and economically.

Technically, the iid assumption means that we can invoke the Central Limit Theorem, which states that the standardized sum of n iid random variables is approximately standard normally distributed. The theorem holds under very general conditions with respect to the distributions of the original variables, and the approximation becomes better as n becomes larger. Since we analyse stock returns over very short (in principle: infinitesimal) time intervals, the approximation should hold well. So we can assume that the log returns are normally distributed and this, in turn, has three consequences.

First, we calculated the returns as logarithms of stock prices, so if the returns are normally distributed then the stock prices themselves have to be lognormally distributed. This follows straight from the definition of a lognormally distributed variable, i.e. a variable the logarithm of which is normally distributed. Second, the sum of two independent, normally distributed variables is again a normally distributed variable with a mean equal to the sum of the original means and a variance equal to the sum of the original variances (see, for example, Grimmeth and Stirzaker (2001, p. 114)). If we extend the argument to a large number of successive short time periods, we can say that the mean and variance of the returns grow linearly with the time horizon. It will be intuitively clear that returns grow over time. Likewise, the possibilities to grow farther and farther away from the starting point will also increase with time. So if the instantaneous return is μ, then under the iid assumption the expected continuously compounded return over the time horizon $[0, T]$, R_T, is normally distributed with expectation $E[R_T] = \mu T$ and variance $var[R_T] = \sigma^2 T$. Technically, this property ensures that the process behaves well if the time horizon is increased or decreased, i.e. it does not explode or collapse into a fixed point without variance. Finally, iid returns mean that they follow a random walk. The combination of independent and identical distributions produces the random walk model, as we have seen in Chapter 4. Recall that random walks have the *Markov property* of memorylessness. In economic terms, this means that past returns and patterns in past returns cannot be used to predict future returns. This is another way of saying that the market is weak form efficient.

How well do these assumptions and their consequences fit stock returns in the real world? As we have seen, the majority of empirical studies shows that stock markets are weak form efficient. So the random walk assumption[1] is probably pretty accurate, and research supports this (e.g. Narayan and Smyth (2005)). The implicitly assumed shape of the normal distribution reflects the nature of stock returns: normally distributed returns can take positive and negative values and are not bounded upwards or downwards. Similarly, the lognormal distribution can take positive values only and this is in agreement with the limited liability of investments in stocks. Real-life stock returns, meanwhile, usually have fatter tails and more skewness and kurtosis than the normal distribution allows for (see e.g. Aparicio and Estrada (2001)). Fatter tails lead to an underpricing of financial risks. So we have to be aware of the possibility that pricing models built on these assumptions may not be accurate.

....

[1] Recall that the random walk assumption is stronger than weak form market efficiency.

8.1.2   Transforming probabilities: loading a die

In binomial option pricing, the concept of risk-neutral probabilities emerged almost naturally from the analyses. In continuous time analyses, changing probability measure is a more explicit step that may seem counter-intuitive at first sight. To clarify this important concept, we introduce it with a simple gambling example. Imagine a gambling game with a die. You have to pay to get into the game and your payoff is equal to the number of spots that turns up: $1, 2, \ldots, 6$. What would be a reasonable price to enter the game? Given a fair die, all outcomes have an equal probability of 1/6. Calling the payoffs R and the probabilities p, the expected payoff from the game is $\Sigma p_i R_i = 3.5$ and its variance is $\Sigma p_i (R_i - (\Sigma p_i R_i))^2 = 2.917$. So 3.5 seems a fair price for the game since it gives both players an equal expected gain or loss (of zero). In the long run they break even.

But organizers of gambling games don't want to break even, they want to make money. An obvious way to do this is raising the entrance price. A price of 4.5 gives a net expected payoff of 1 for the organizer and an equally large expected loss for the other player. The same effect can be obtained by adjusting the spots on the die. Blotting out the 6 (replacing it with 0) reduces the expected payoff with 1 to 2.5 but leaves the variance at 2.917. Both ways are rather obvious and may not lure many players to the game. (However, both ways are used with considerable success in practice, the former in lotteries and the latter in roulette.)

There is a third way to change the expected payoff and that is by changing the probabilities. Crooked gamblers have come up with several methods to do this. One method is making dice that are not perfect cubes (called 'shapes') that tend to land on the largest face. Another method is putting a sticky substance (possibly activated by blowing on it) on the side you want the die to land on. A third method is 'loading' a die by putting a weight inside it that favours landing on the side with the weight. The organizer of the game in our example will want the die to land on the side with six spots, so that the side with one spot comes on top.

If we move the problem from crooked gambling to honest science, the question becomes whether we can transform the *probability measure* for a die in such a way that the expected payoff is lowered to 2.5 while the variance is left unchanged. The restrictions we put on the problem are that the measures are equivalent (i.e. assign positive probability to the same set of events) and that the probabilities are between 0 and 1, and sum to 1. For convenience, we can introduce the additional 'smoothness' restriction that the probability of 1 spot $\geq$ prob. 2 spots $\geq$ prob. 3 spots, etc.

The probabilities for the outcomes of a fair die are: $p_{fair} = 1/6 = .1667$. We want to load the die in such a way that the sides with few spots have a higher probability of turning up, and the sides with many spots a lower probability. So the function that relates the probabilities to the number of spots has to look somewhat like a hyperbola. Since we have only six data points, we increase the curvature by adding a power:

$$p_{X,loaded} = \left(\frac{\alpha}{X}\right)^{\beta} + \gamma \tag{8.1}$$

where α, β and γ are coefficients to be estimated and X is the number of spots $1, 2, \ldots, 6$. Values for the coefficients are easily found by the solver of a spreadsheet program if it is fed with the proper data and restrictions[2]: $\alpha = .6$, $\beta = 2$ and $\gamma = .077$. The resulting probabilities and (contributions to) expectation and variance are given in Table 8.1.

Table 8.1 *Transformed probabilities for a die*

spots	prob.	expectation	variance
1	.437	.437	.9833
2	.167	.334	.0418
3	.117	.351	.0293
4	.100	.400	.2250
5	.091	.455	.5688
6	.087	.522	1.0658
sum:	.999	2.499	2.914

Within a small rounding error, the alternative probability measure[3] gives the specified lower expectation and the same variance as the original one. We can now express one measure as a function of the other:

$$\frac{p_{X,loaded}}{p_{X,fair}} = \frac{\left(\frac{.6}{X}\right)^2 + .077}{.1667} = \frac{2.16}{X^2} + .462$$

and write this as the following two 'measure transformation functions':

$$p_{X,loaded} = \left(\frac{2.16}{X^2} + .462\right) p_{X,fair} \quad \text{and} \quad p_{X,fair} = \frac{p_{X,loaded}}{\left(\frac{2.16}{X^2} + .462\right)}$$

Note that the transformation ensures that both measures are equivalent. A zero p_{fair} cannot be transformed into a positive p_{loaded} and vice versa. So we can use the functions to transform one probability measure into another and back again.

It may be useful to restate what the simple die example demonstrates. By changing the probability measure (loading the die) we have left the 'probability process' intact (we still roll the die) but the process now produces another expectation (2.5 instead of 3.5) while the variance remains 2.9. In a manner of speaking, the process changes gear: it increases with an average of 2.5 per roll of the die instead of 3.5. In the next section we apply the same idea to a model of stock price behaviour.

8.2 Pricing options

We now apply the properties of stock returns and the technique of changing probability measure to the problem of option pricing. Although the elaboration is a bit more complex, the ideas behind them are the same as in the previous section.

---

2 The set-up for the spreadsheet is straightforward: define the probabilities p_i as in (8.1) and the expectation and variance of the number of spots as $\Sigma p_i X_i$ and $\Sigma p_i (X_i - (\Sigma p_i X_i))^2$. The restrictions are $\Sigma p_i = 1$ and $0 \leq p_i \leq 1$ plus either the expection = 2.5 or the variance = 2.917; the other one is then the target cell. The coefficients α, β and γ are the adjustable cells.

3 It is likely that other probability measures can give the same results, so the measure is probably not unique.

8.2.1   Stock returns in continuous time

In order to be usable in pricing models, the behaviour of stock returns has to be modelled in a forward-looking way. The first step in the modelling process is the introduction of Brownian motion, a standard tool in dynamic modelling.

Brownian motion

In the models with discrete time and variables we modelled returns by specifying all possible ways in which stock values can develop over time. These possibilities were enumerated as states of the world or values in a binomial tree. In models with continuous time and variables we have an infinite number of possible values and paths through time, so they cannot be enumerated. We have to express the development in a probabilistic way. The standard equipment for that is a *continuous time stochastic process* and the most frequently used process in finance is *Brownian motion*, which is also called a Wiener process. The motion was discovered by the biologist Robert Brown around 1825 and formally described by Norbert Wiener in 1923. To honour both, we shall use the name Brownian motion and the symbol W. Standard Brownian motion is the continuous time analogue of a random walk. It can be thought of as a series of very small (infinitesimal) steps whereby each step is drawn randomly from the standard normal distribution. More formally, a process $\widetilde{W}$ is a standard Brownian motion if:

- $\widetilde{W}_t$ is continuous and $\widetilde{W}_0 = 0$,
- it has independent increments and
- the increments $\widetilde{W}_{s+t} - \widetilde{W}_s$ are normally distributed with zero mean and standard deviation $\sqrt{t}$, which implies that
- the increments are stationary, i.e. their distribution is only a function of the length of the time interval t and not of the location s.

From the definition it follows that standard Brownian motion is a martingale and that it has the Markov property. In discrete terms, the increments in a standard Brownian motion over a short period of time δt can be represented as $\epsilon \sqrt{\delta t}$ where ϵ is a random drawing from the standard normal distribution. We will elaborate an example later on.

Brownian motion has some remarkable properties. Since its increments are drawn from a normal distribution, it has no upper or lower bounds. Its behaviour is 'wild' in the sense that it will eventually hit any barrier, no matter how large or small. And although Brownian motion is continuous everywhere, it is differentiable nowhere, a truly remarkable combination. It never smooths out: no matter how much the scale of the motion is compressed or stretched, the picture always remains jagged, as in Figure 8.1 on page 227. It is, in fact, a fractal. Odd as it may be, Brownian motion is the stochastic element in the model of stock price behaviour that is commonly used for option pricing and that is elaborated in the next subsection.

Modelling stock price behaviour

Standard Brownian motion by itself is a poor model of stock price behaviour, as it catches only the random element of it. This can be thought of as the stock price's reaction to new information which, by definition, is random. Since some stocks react more strongly to new information than others, the random element has to be scaled by an individual parameter representing the stock's volatility. But stocks do not only vary randomly, they are also expected to earn a positive return. Hence, stock prices are expected to move upwards (or have a positive *drift*). This element is usually expressed by adding a deterministic (i.e. non-stochastic) drift term to the equation, representing the stock's expected return. A final element is proportionality: both the expected return and the random movements (or volatility) should be measured in proportion to the stock's value. We expect a stock to earn, for example, 15 per cent return, no matter whether the stock price is €50 or €500. Similarly, we measure volatility in percentages, not money amounts.

The standard way of modelling all these elements of stock price behaviour is by expressing the stock price as a *geometric Brownian motion* in a stochastic differential equation:

$$dS_t = \mu S_t dt + \sigma S_t d\widetilde{W}_t \qquad (8.2)$$

$$S_0 > 0$$

where:

d = next instant's incremental change
S_t = stock price at time t
μ = drift coefficient, representing the stock's return
σ = diffusion coefficient, representing the stock's volatility
$\widetilde{W}$ = standard Brownian motion
S_0 = initial condition (a process has to start somewhere).

In equation (8.2) μ is the expected instantaneous rate of return (that we met in the previous subsection). The first term of the right-hand side of the expression, $\mu S_t dt$, is called the drift term. σ is the standard deviation of the instantaneous return, also known as the volatility of the stock price. This parameter scales the random movements in the standard Brownian motion $\widetilde{W}$, which is the stochastic disturbance term, or 'white noise', representing unpredictable events. Together, they form the diffusion term of the equation: $\sigma S_t d\widetilde{W}_t$. Both μ and σ are assumed to be constants.

Both the drift and the disturbance term in (8.2) are multiplied by the stock price (hence the term *geometric* Brownian motion). This multiplicative specification ensures proportionality and, together with the positive initial condition, limits the stock price to positive values. As a consequence, the iid property refers to the percentage stock returns – $dS_t / S_t = \mu dt + \sigma d\widetilde{W}_t$ – not the money amounts dS_t in (8.2). The increments dS_t do not have the martingale property: stock prices are expected to grow over time. They do have the Markov property, however: all the information in the history of stock prices is reflected in the present stock price. dS_t / S_t is also normally distributed, since it is a linear transformation of the normally distributed variable $d\widetilde{W}_t$. Its expectation over short periods of time is μdt and its variance is $\sigma^2 dt$. So the process has all the properties we set out to model: the returns are normally distributed and their expectation and variance increase with time.

Equation (8.2) is a stochastic differential equation (SDE), i.e. a differential equation with a stochastic process in it. We need a specialized mathematical tool box, stochastic calculus, to manipulate these SDEs. They are notoriously difficult to solve, but there are a few exceptions. However, since we have the conceptual framework already in place from our analyses in discrete time, we need only minimal mathematics to replicate the results in continuous time.

The financial market in which the stock is traded also contains risk-free debt, D, that is defined in a similar, but simpler manner:

$$dD_t = rD_t dt \tag{8.3}$$

where r is short for r_f, the risk-free interest rate. Risk-free debt is also referred to as money market account or simply a bond. Since the debt is risk free, (8.3) contains no stochastic disturbance term and we can treat it as an ordinary differential equation. The natural interpretation for r is the short rate of interest, which is variable over time. However, for convenience we assume that r is a constant.

Using the model

Since the stochastic differential equation (8.2) is central in continuous-time option pricing, it is useful to become familiar with its properties. First, note that (8.2) has a deterministic drift and a stochastic disturbance term. The latter is the source of the underlying randomness. It is easy to see what would happen if a 'stock' would have zero volatility. Then $\sigma = 0$ and the second term drops from the equation:

$$dS_t = \mu S_t dt \quad or \quad \frac{dS_t}{S_t} = \mu dt$$

and we have a process similar to that of debt D. Note that in this special case we also could have written $dS_t/dt = \mu S_t$ since the non-differentiable stochastic term drops from the equation. If we integrate this over the time interval $[0, T]$ we get $S_T = S_0 e^{\mu T}$, the return we saw in the previous subsection.

Equation (8.2) can also be regarded as an instruction for generating a time series of stock prices or stock returns, e.g. for a Monte Carlo simulation. Suppose we want a series of daily returns for a stock with a current price of 100, an expected annual return of 15 per cent and an annual volatility of 30 per cent. Assuming 250 trading days per year, the daily time steps are 1/250. The drift part is then $.15/250 = .0006$. For the stochastic part we need to draw from a normal distribution with mean zero and variance 1/250 (or, equivalently, draw from a standard normal distribution and multiply the outcome by $\sqrt{1/250}$). Let the first draw be $-.00664065$. Then:

$$\delta S = .0006 \times 100 + .3 \times 100 \times -.00664065 = -0.13922$$

The new stock price becomes $100 - 0.13922 = 99.861$ and we can repeat the calculations for the next day. Note that we use δ instead of d in the discrete time version of the model. Two sample paths for this Brownian motion over 250 days are depicted in Figure 8.1.

8.2.2   Transforming probabilities: changing measure

We now turn to the second part of our modelling operation, changing the probability measure. We first restate why this step is necessary and then apply it to our model of stock returns.

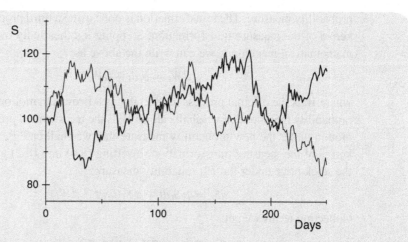

Figure 8.1 Sample paths of geometric Brownian motion with $\mu = 0.15$, $\sigma = 0.3$ and T $= 250$

Why changing measure is necessary

Look again at our model of stock price behaviour in (8.2):

$$dS_t = \mu S_t dt + \sigma S_t d\widetilde{W}_t$$

It describes the development of a stock price over time using the risk-adjusted expected return μ and the real uncertainty (real probabilities) in the stochastic term. It is the continuous-time equivalent of a binomial value tree for a stock. We know from the analyses in discrete time that the approach to pricing derivatives is to adjust the probabilities in such a way that they embed the market's pricing information (market price of risk). If that is the case then all securities are expected to 'earn' the risk-free rate (return equalization) so that their values, discounted at the risk-free rate, become martingales (martingale property). We also know that this risk-neutral valuation approach is necessary because the discounted cash flow approach cannot effectively handle options' intrinsic flexibility. So we have to adjust the drift of the process by adjusting the probabilities expressed in the disturbance term.

As an outline of what follows, it may be useful to invoke the loaded die example one last time, but in more precise terms. We want to change the probability measure (to load the die) in such a way that the stochastic process remains a Brownian motion (we still roll the die) but with a drift of r instead of μ (the expectation of the number of spots becomes 2.5 instead of 3.5) while leaving the variance of the process unaltered (the die variance remains 2.9). To repeat the manner of speaking, we want the process to change gear from an instantaneous increase of μ to r and leave the rest as before.

Technique of changing measure

The mathematical instrument to change measure is Girsanov's theorem. It says that a stochastic process, that is Brownian motion under one probability measure, can be transformed into another stochastic process, that is a Brownian motion under another probability measure. The transformation is done using a third process, called the Girsanov kernel of the measure transformation. Stepping lightheartedly over the intricacies of the mathematical machinery, we can write the above as:

$$d\widetilde{W}_t = \theta_t dt + dW_t \tag{8.4}$$

where $\widetilde{W}$ is the original process in (8.2) that is a Brownian motion under the original, real probability measure that we shall call Q, W is the transformed process, that is a Brownian motion under the new probability measure that we shall call P, while θ is the Girsanov kernel of the measure transformation. Inserting (8.4) into (8.2) gives us the dynamics of the stock price under the P probability measure:

$$dS_t = \mu S_t dt + \sigma S_t (\theta_t dt + dW_t)$$

Collecting terms we get:

$$dS_t = (\mu + \sigma\theta_t) S_t dt + \sigma S_t dW_t \tag{8.5}$$

The original process $\widetilde{W}$ has been replaced with the new process W. We have changed the probability measure! At first sight it looks as if we did not get very far by transforming the dynamic process. We switched from a Q-Brownian motion with drift μ to a P-Brownian motion with drift $(\mu + \sigma\theta_t)$. But the latter contains a process, θ, that we have not yet defined. We know the result we want to obtain with the definition. The new probability measure should contain information to price risk, comparable to the state prices in discrete time. If the price of risk is embedded in the Girsanov kernel, the remaining drift for all securities becomes equal to the risk-free interest rate, i.e. the return equalization we saw in the previous chapter. This is accomplished by defining θ as minus the market price of risk:

$$\theta_t = -\frac{\mu - r}{\sigma} \tag{8.6}$$

We have seen the market price of risk before in portfolio theory, where it was used in the CML and the SML, as well as in the Sharpe ratio (3.10). Substituting this θ in the drift term of (8.5) gives a drift equal to the risk-free rate r:

$$\mu + \sigma\left(-\frac{\mu - r}{\sigma}\right) = r \tag{8.7}$$

With the definition in (8.6) the Girsanov kernel process is deterministic, because it contains no stochastic term, and it is constant, because μ, r and σ are assumed to be constant. Substituting (8.6) into (8.5) we have a dynamic process with a drift equal to the risk-free rate and, under measure P, a Brownian motion as disturbance term:

$$dS_t = r S_t dt + \sigma S_t dW_t \tag{8.8}$$

Note that we can also run the process in reverse and go from P-dynamics to Q-dynamics. The transformation can be shown to produce an equivalent measure.

Solving the SDE

We have already pointed out that SDEs are difficult to solve,[4] but since the deterministic equivalent of (8.8) is simplified by taking logarithms, we can try the same

---

4 Even worse, solving an SDE can mean different things; we will ignore this matter here.

transformation here. We have to use stochastic calculus to manipulate SDEs. As a little sample of this technique, the logarithmic transformation is elaborated in the appendices to this chapter and the result is that:

$$d(\ln S_t) = \left(r - \frac{1}{2}\sigma^2\right) dt + \sigma dW_t \tag{8.9}$$

So the changes in the logarithm of the stock price also follow a Brownian motion, with a drift of $\left(r - \frac{1}{2}\sigma^2\right)$ and a diffusion coefficient of σ. Since both the drift and the diffusion are constants, the changes in $\ln(S_t)$ over the time horizon $[0, T]$ will be normally distributed with mean $\left(r - \frac{1}{2}\sigma^2\right)T$ and variance $\sigma^2 T$, i.e. $\ln S_T - \ln S_0 \sim N\left(\left(r - \frac{1}{2}\sigma^2\right)T, \sigma^2 T\right)$ or $\ln S_T \sim N\left(\ln S_0 + \left(r - \frac{1}{2}\sigma^2\right)T, \sigma^2 T\right)$. We will use this property later on.

Equation (8.9) is a very simple SDE. The right-hand side does not contain $d(\ln S_t)$ and r and σ are constants. This means that we can find the solution to the SDE by integrating it directly (as in normal calculus) over the time interval $[0, T]$:

$$\int_0^T d(\ln S_t) = \left(r - \frac{1}{2}\sigma^2\right) \int_0^T dt + \sigma \int_0^T dW_t$$

$$\ln S_T - \ln S_0 = \left(r - \frac{1}{2}\sigma^2\right) T + \sigma(W_T - W_0)$$

Taking exponentials and recalling from the definition of Brownian motion that $W_0 = 0$, we get an expression for S_T as a function of S_0 under a geometric Brownian motion:

$$S_T = S_0 e^{(r - \frac{1}{2}\sigma^2)T + \sigma W_T} \tag{8.10}$$

If $\ln S_T$ is normally distributed, S_T must be lognormally distributed. The expectation of a lognormally distributed variable is $e^{m + 0.5s^2}$, where m and s^2 are the mean and variance of the corresponding normal distribution (Aitchison and Brown, 1969). We just saw that $\ln S_T \sim N\left(\ln S_0 + \left(r - \frac{1}{2}\sigma^2\right)T, \sigma^2 T\right)$ and since the expectation of a Brownian motion is zero, the expectation of S_T is:

$$E[S_T] = e^{\ln S_0 + (r - \frac{1}{2}\sigma^2)T + \frac{1}{2}\sigma^2 T}$$

$$E[S_T] = S_0 e^{rT}$$

This means that:

$$e^{-rT} E[S_T] = S_0$$

i.e. that the discounted future expected stock price is equal to the current stock price, provided that the expectation is with respect to probability measure P and that the discounting is done with the risk-free rate. This is another way of saying that the discounted stock price has the martingale property under measure P. So we have our equivalent martingale measure.

8.2.3   The Black and Scholes option-pricing formula

We now have all the necessary elements to derive the option-pricing formula. But that requires complete and arbitrage-free markets, so we have to check these market conditions first.

Market conditions

The application of the results of the previous subsection in a pricing relation is possible only if the financial market that we have modelled with stock S and risk-free debt D is free of arbitrage and complete.[5] Recall from our analyses in discrete time that a market is arbitrage free if the existing (non-redundant) securities are priced in such a way that they offer no riskless arbitrage profits. That was the case if we had a positive state price vector. We also saw that the state price vector can be standardized into a vector of risk-neutral probabilities and we concluded that there is no arbitrage if and only if there exists an equivalent martingale measure. This conclusion also applies to our analyses in continuous time. The no-arbitrage condition can be shown to hold for the market modelled in the Black and Scholes analysis.

Market completeness could be defined easily in discrete time by a square and non-singular payoff matrix. This concept is less easily translated to continuous time, but the idea remains the same. The existing securities should allow all other claims (such as options) to be replicated by a combination of existing securities. To say it the other way around: all other claims should be reachable by a replicating portfolio. In continuous time and assuming the absence of arbitrage, the market is complete if and only if the equivalent martingale measure is unique. This condition also holds for the market modelled in the Black and Scholes analysis.

Deriving the formula

Having laid the groundwork we can now proceed with the Black and Scholes analysis. Their famous formula can be obtained in several ways; they are all a little complex and involve lengthy expressions. The original work of Black and Scholes (1973) uses the partial differential equation (PDE) approach, in which a PDE for the option price is constructed. With an appropriate boundary condition the PDE can be solved analytically. An outline of this approach is included in the appendices. Alternatively, Cox *et al.* (1979) show that, in the limit, their binomial approach converges to the Black and Scholes formula. The third way is the martingale method, that prices by directly calculating the expectation under the equivalent martingale measure and discounting the result using the risk-free rate. This approach was pioneered by Cox and Ross (1976) and Harrison and Kreps (1979). It is generally considered to be the simplest method. We will also use the martingale method in a short and elegant derivation based on Cerný (2004).

We want to find the price now (t = 0) of a European call option $O^E_{c,0}$ with exercise price X that matures at time T. The option is written on a stock that pays no dividends. Using the martingale method we take the option's expected value at maturity, $E^P[O^E_{c,T}]$, where the expectation is under probability measure P, and discount this value to the present at the risk-free interest rate:

$$O^E_{c,0} = e^{-rT} E^P[O^E_{c,T}]$$

Dropping the superscripts for European and the probability measure we get:

$$O_{c,0} = e^{-rT} E[O_{c,T}] \tag{8.11}$$

---

5 Other formal requirements are a frictionless, competitive market without counterparty risk or short sale restrictions and with continuous trading. As usual, we tacitly assume these conditions to be fulfilled.

where r is the risk-free rate as before. We know the option's payoff at maturity:

$$O_{c,T} = \begin{cases} S_T - X & \text{if} \quad S_T > X \\ 0 & \text{if} \quad S_T \leq X \end{cases}$$

We can write this payoff as:

$$O_{c,T} = (S_T - X)1_{S_T > X} \tag{8.12}$$

where $1_{S_T > X}$ is a so-called step function that has the value 1 if the inequality in the subscript obtains and the value zero otherwise:

$$1_{S_T > X} = \begin{cases} 1 & \text{if} \quad S_T > X \\ 0 & \text{if} \quad S_T \leq X \end{cases}$$

Substituting the step function (8.12) into (8.11) the option value becomes:

$$O_{c,0} = e^{-rT} E\left[(S_T - X)1_{S_T > X}\right] \tag{8.13}$$

To prepare for the rest of the derivation we write (8.13) as:

$$O_{c,0} = e^{-rT} E\left[(e^{\ln S_T} - e^{\ln X})1_{\ln S_T > \ln X}\right] \tag{8.14}$$

In the rest of the derivation we use two key elements. The first is the fact that $\ln S_T$ is normally distributed with mean $(\ln S_0 + (r - \frac{1}{2}\sigma^2)T)$ and variance $\sigma^2 T$. We know this from the discussion of the SDE for $\ln S_T$ in (8.9). The second element is that we can regard the step function in (8.12) as a truncation of the distribution of S_T on left: all values smaller than X are replaced by zero. Truncated normal distributions are comparatively well researched[6] and we can use the following step function that was derived for normally distributed variables. If a variable Y is normally distributed with mean M and variance v^2 and is truncated at A then:

$$E\left[\left(e^Y - e^A\right)1_{Y > A}\right] = e^{M + \frac{1}{2}v^2} N\left(\frac{M + v^2 - A}{v}\right) - e^A N\left(\frac{M - A}{v}\right) \tag{8.15}$$

where $N(.)$ is the cumulative distribution function of a standard normal variable. If we apply this step function to our option-pricing problem in (8.14) we have:

$$M = \ln S_0 + \left(r - \frac{1}{2}\sigma^2\right)T$$

$$v^2 = \sigma^2 T \rightarrow v = \sigma\sqrt{T}$$

$$Y = \ln S_T$$

$$A = \ln X$$

---

6 For example, Winkler *et al.* (1972) discuss the computation of partial moments for several probability distributions.

Substituting this into (8.15) gives:

$$
E\left[\left(e^{\ln S_T} - e^{\ln X}\right)1_{\ln S_T > \ln X}\right] = e^{\ln S_0 + \left(r - \frac{1}{2}\sigma^2\right)T + \frac{1}{2}\sigma^2 T} N
$$
$$
\times \left(\frac{\ln S_0 + \left(r - \frac{1}{2}\sigma^2\right)T + \sigma^2 T - \ln X}{\sigma\sqrt{T}}\right)
$$
$$
- e^{\ln X} N\left(\frac{\ln S_0 + \left(r - \frac{1}{2}\sigma^2\right)T - \ln X}{\sigma\sqrt{T}}\right)
$$

Collecting terms we get:

$$
E\left[\left(e^{\ln S_T} - e^{\ln X}\right)1_{\ln S_T > \ln X}\right] = S_0 e^{rT} N\left(\frac{\ln(S_0/X) + \left(r + \frac{1}{2}\sigma^2\right)T}{\sigma\sqrt{T}}\right)
$$
$$
- XN\left(\frac{\ln(S_0/X) + \left(r - \frac{1}{2}\sigma^2\right)T}{\sigma\sqrt{T}}\right) \tag{8.16}
$$

Substituting (8.16) into (8.14) and netting out the discounting factor e^{-rT} we get the famous Black and Scholes formula:

$$
O_{c,0} = S_0 N\left(\frac{\ln(S_0/X) + \left(r + \frac{1}{2}\sigma^2\right)T}{\sigma\sqrt{T}}\right) - Xe^{-rT} N\left(\frac{\ln(S_0/X) + \left(r - \frac{1}{2}\sigma^2\right)T}{\sigma\sqrt{T}}\right) \tag{8.17}
$$

Defining, as is commonly done:

$$
d_1 = \frac{\ln(S_0/X) + \left(r + \frac{1}{2}\sigma^2\right)T}{\sigma\sqrt{T}} \tag{8.18}
$$

$$
d_2 = \frac{\ln(S_0/X) + \left(r - \frac{1}{2}\sigma^2\right)T}{\sigma\sqrt{T}} = d_1 - \sigma\sqrt{T} \tag{8.19}
$$

we get the usual form of the formula:

$$
O_{c,0} = S_0 N(d_1) - Xe^{-rT} N(d_2) \tag{8.20}
$$

with the corresponding value of a European put:

$$
O_{p,0} = Xe^{-rT} N(-d_2) - S_0 N(-d_1) \tag{8.21}
$$

8.3 Working with Black and Scholes

Although the derivation of the Black and Scholes formula looks a little complex, the result is easy to use. We shall look at its interpretation, work out some examples and introduce some additional elements.

8.3.1   Interpretation

We derived the Black and Scholes formula by calculating the option's expected value at maturity under the equivalent martingale measure and discounting the result using the risk-free rate. It is therefore tempting to interpret its content as the present value of the expected payoffs at maturity minus the present value of the expected costs of exercising. But this is true only for the latter part of the equation: Xe^{-rT} is the present value of the exercise price and $N(d_2)$ is the risk-neutral probability that the option will finish in the money and will be exercised. Since $N(d_1) \neq N(d_2)$ the first term has a different interpretation. $N(d_1)$ is the option delta, which can be interpreted in different ways. We have met the first interpretation before as equation (7.14) in binomial option-pricing: it is the the hedge ratio, i.e. the number of shares needed to replicate the option with a hedging portfolio. The second interpretation is that of a sensitivity: the option delta expresses how much the option price will change as a result of a single-unit change in the stock price. Technically, delta is the partial derivative of the option-pricing function with respect to the stock price; this derivative is calculated in the appendices to this chapter as $\partial O_{c,0}/\partial S_0 = N(d_1)$. This is the slope of the curve that describes the option price as a function of the stock price which, in turn, can be represented as a line tangent to the option value curve. This is illustrated in Figure 8.4 on page 237 for two different values of the underlying value and, hence, two different values of delta.

In both interpretations it will be clear that the option delta is more than just the probability that the option will be exercised, it also encompasses the option's moneyness. The content of the Black and Scholes formula can be summarized as follows:

$$O_{c,0} = \underbrace{(S_0)}_{\substack{\text{stock}\\\text{price}}} \underbrace{N(d_1)}_{\substack{\text{option}\\\text{delta}}} - \underbrace{(Xe^{-rT})}_{\substack{\text{PV}\\\text{(exerc.p.)}}} \underbrace{N(d_2)}_{\substack{\text{prob.of}\\\text{exercise}}}$$

As with the binomial model, it is worth noticing what is *not* in the Black and Scholes formula. It requires knowledge of neither the real drift parameter μ nor the investors' attitudes towards risk nor other securities or portfolios, such as the market portfolio. Greediness, to ensure the proper choice in $max[.]$ expressions, is the only assumption implicit in the analysis. This reflects the conditional nature of option pricing that we saw in the binomial model and that also applies to the Black and Scholes formula: it translates security prices on complete and arbitrage-free markets into prices for additional redundant securities.

8.3.2   Determinants of option prices

In addition to the stock price there are four other variables in the Black and Scholes formula, as equation (8.17) shows. The sensitivities of the option price for single-unit changes in these variables can be derived in a similar way as for changes in the stock price, i.e. by taking partial derivatives. The calculations are included in the appendices to this chapter. Like the option's delta, most of these sensitivities are represented by a Greek letter, so they are collectively known as 'the Greeks'. Table 8.2 summarizes the determinants of Black and Scholes option prices and their Greeks.

As Table 8.2 shows, there is one determinant without a Greek, the exercise price, and one Greek without a determinant, viz. gamma. Moreover, 'vega' is not a Greek letter so

Table 8.2 *Option price determinants and their Greeks*

Determinant	Greek	Effect on call option	Effect on put option
Exercise price		<0	>0
Stock price	Delta	$0 < \Delta_c < 1$	$-1 < \Delta_p < 0$
Volatility	Vega	$\nu_c > 0$	$\nu_p > 0$
Time to maturity	Theta	$-\Theta_c < 0$	$-\Theta_p <> 0$
Interest rate	Rho	$\rho_c > 0$	$\rho_p < 0$
	Gamma	$\Gamma_c > 0$	$\Gamma_p > 0$

the collective term 'Greeks' is slightly sloppy. (The Greek letter nu (ν) is used to represent vega.) Table 8.2 also shows that the price of a call option decreases with the exercise price while the price of a put option increases, other things being equal. Since a call option gives the right to buy, it will be intuitively clear that its value is inversely related to the price against which the underlying can be bought. Similarly, a put gives the right to sell, so one would expect a positive relation between the put's value and its exercise price, and the calculations in the appendices confirm this.

A call option's delta, $\Delta_c = N(d_1)$, is a probability so its values are limited to the range between zero and 1. When the option is very far out of the money, the option is likely to expire worthlessly and small changes in the stock price will have hardly any effect on the option price. The option delta is then close to zero. Conversely, if the option is very far in the money then, for most practical purposes, holding the option is equivalent to holding the share (only without having paid for it yet). What happens to the share also happens to the option[7] and, hence, delta is close to 1. Figure 8.4 illustrates this. The delta of a put option is $\Delta_p = N(d_1) - 1$, so its value becomes more negative as the option becomes more in-the-money with lower values of the underlying.

Both calls and puts increase in value with the volatility of the underlying: the calculations in the appendices show that $\nu_c = \nu_p > 0$. As limited liability investments, options profit from the upward potential but are protected against the downside risk. This positive sensitivity to risk has important consequences, as we shall see in later chapters. The value of call options increases with time to maturity, so it decreases with the passage of calendar time, given a fixed maturity date. Theta is used in the latter way; it is also called the time decay of option value. For put options the sign of the partial derivative cannot be unequivocally determined; Θ_p can be positive or negative. Generally options increase in value with time to maturity, and this is also true for puts. But deep in-the-money European puts can decrease in value with time to maturity. In the extreme case, when the underlying value falls to zero, a longer time to maturity only means a longer waiting time before the money from the exercise is received. Early exercise would then be beneficial but that is prohibited by the European style of the option.

Call options increase in value with the risk-free interest rate. As we have just seen, holding an in-the-money call is equivalent to holding the underlying share, but without

---

7 Except for dividends, which the shareholder receives but the option-holder does not. Dividends are discussed later.

having paid for it yet. The advantage of delayed payment increases with the interest rate. Conversely, holding an in-the-money put means having a right to delayed payment of the exercise price and the value of future payments decreases with the interest rate. Finally, gamma measures the effect of a marginal increase in the stock price on delta, so it is the second derivative of the option-pricing function with respect to the stock price. Gamma is positive, both for calls and puts.

8.3.3   Numerical examples

A call option

Using the Black and Scholes formula is simply a matter of filling in the values of the variables and calculating the result. A simple example will illustrate this. We calculate the value of an at-the-money European call option that matures in one year and has a strike price of €100. The underlying stock pays no dividends and has an annual volatility of 20 per cent. The risk-free interest rate is 10 per cent per year. With this we have our five determinants: $S_0 = 100$, $X = 100$, $r = 0.1$, $\sigma = 0.2$ and $T = 1$.

$$d_1 = \frac{\ln(S_0/X) + \left(r + \frac{1}{2}\sigma^2\right)T}{\sigma\sqrt{T}} = \frac{\ln(100/100) + \left(0.1 + \frac{1}{2} \times 0.2^2\right)1}{0.2\sqrt{1}} = 0.6$$

$$d_2 = d_1 - \sigma\sqrt{T} = 0.6 - 0.2\sqrt{1} = 0.4$$

The areas under the normal curve for the values of d_1 and d_2 can easily be found in a table (a home-made table is included in the appendices to this chapter) or with a pre-programmed function in a calculator, spreadsheet or, as here, with a scientific word processor: NormalDist(0.6) = 0.72575, which is the option delta, and NormalDist(0.4) = 0.65542, which is the risk-neutral probability that the option will end in the money and will be exercised. So the option price becomes:

$$O_{c,0} = 100 \times (0.72575) - 100e^{-0.1}(0.65542) = 13.27$$

The call option price is depicted as a function of the price of the underlying stock in Figure 8.2. The dashed lines show the coordinates of the option price that is calculated above (13.27, 100). The three curves represent option prices for three different stock volatilities, holding X, r and T constant. The lower curve, closest to the straight line representing the value at maturity $\max[S - X, 0]$, shows the value of the option when the stock has a volatility of 0.2. The other two curves show the option values for stock volatilities of 0.4 and 0.5. This illustrates that option values increase with volatility.

Figure 8.3 repeats this procedure for three different times to maturity (one, two and three years), holding X, r and σ constant. In the absence of dividends, the European call option prices are seen to increase with maturity. As time and uncertainty diminish, the option value curves will approach the minimum of $\max[S - X, 0]$ more and more closely until, at maturity, they coincide.

A put option

The value of a put option with the same specifications can be calculated with equation (8.21):

$$O_{p,0} = Xe^{-rT}N(-d_2) - S_0N(-d_1)$$

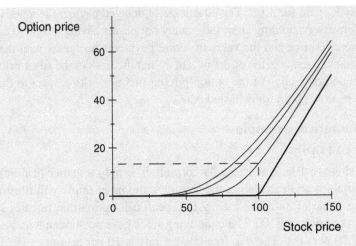

Figure 8.2 Call option prices for $\sigma = 0.5$ (top), 0.4 and 0.2 (bottom)

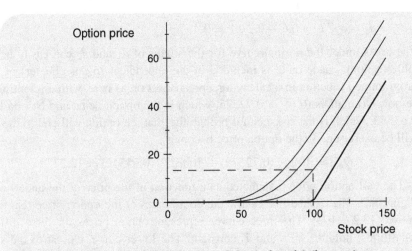

Figure 8.3 Call option prices for $T = 3$ (top), 2 and 1 (bottom)

We have calculated above that $d_1 = 0.6$ and $d_2 = 0.4$, so that the probability terms become: NormalDist(-0.6) = 0.27425 and NormalDist(-0.4) = 0.34458. Filling in the numbers produces:

$$O_{p,0} = 100 \times e^{-0.1}\,(0.34458) - 100 \times (0.27425) = 3.75$$

Using the put–call parity gives the same result:

$$O_{p,0} = O_{c,0} + Xe^{-rT} - S_0 = 13.27 + 100e^{-0.1} - 100 = 3.75$$

Delta and delta hedging

Figure 8.4 shows the call option for which we have just calculated the at-the-money value as €13.27. The two straight tangent lines depict the option's deltas for two different values of the underlying stock, €80 and €110. If the stock price is 80, d_1 is:

$$d_1 = \big(\ln(80/100) + (0.1 + 0.5 \times 0.2^2) \times 1\big)/0.2\sqrt{1} = -0.51572$$

so the option delta is $N(d_1) = \text{NormalDist}(-0.51572) = 0.3$. This is the slope of the line tangent to the option-price curve at the point where the stock price is 80.

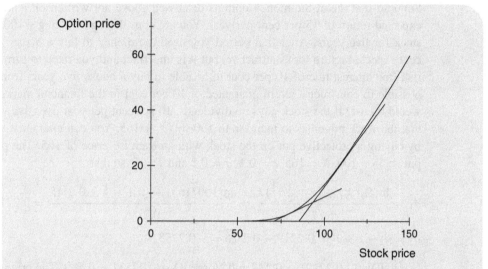

Figure 8.4 Black and Scholes option prices and option delta at S = 80 and S = 110; T = 1, r = 0.1, σ = 0.2, X = 100

Now suppose that a bank has sold 50 contracts of the at-the-money options, each on 100 shares. This gives the option-holders the right to buy 5,000 shares from the bank when the options mature. How does the bank hedge its obligations from these contracts? We have calculated that the at-the-money option delta, $N(d_1)$, is 0.73, so to 'delta-hedge' its position the bank has to buy $0.73 \times 5000 = 3650$ shares. If the stock price goes up with one euro, the options increase in value with $5000 \times 0.73 = 3650$ euro. The bank has a short position in the options, so it loses €3650. But this loss is exactly compensated by the bank's share position, which gains $3650 \times 1 = 3650$ euro. The bank has a perfect hedge; its portfolio of short calls and long shares is 'delta neutral'. We have seen this delta hedging before, in the context of the binomial model in Section 7.3.3. Delta hedging is dynamic, both in the binomial and in the Black and Scholes model. The option delta increases with the stock price (gamma is positive, as Table 8.2 shows). So when the stock price increases, the bank has to adjust its hedge and buy more shares to remain delta neutral. Suppose the stock price increases to €110. Then d_1 becomes:

$$d_1 = \big(\ln(110/100) + (0.1 + 0.5 \times 0.2^2) \times 1\big)/0.2\sqrt{1} = 1.077$$

and the option delta becomes NormalDist(1.077) = 0.8593. This is the slope of the line tangent to the option price curve in Figure 8.4 at the point where the stock price is 110. The bank then needs $0.8593 \times 5000 = 4297$ shares to hedge its position, so it has to rebalance its hedge by buying $4297 - 3650 = 647$ additional shares. The Black and Scholes model assumes continuous rebalancing but that is, of course, impossible. In practice, traders frequently rebalance their portfolios so that they are delta neutral once a day or once every few days.

Cost of a return guarantee

Suppose that the at-the-money options discussed above are written on a stock with an expected return of 15 per cent per year. You are considering investing €100,000 in this stock for five years. After that period you need the money to buy a house. The 15 per cent expected return looks attractive, but it is uncertain and you need to earn at least the risk-free interest rate of 10 per cent to be able to buy a house five years from now. Is it possible to construct a return guarantee of 10 per cent in the financial market and what would it cost? If the stock pays no dividends, 10 per cent per year over five years means that the stock price has to increase to $100e^{0.1 \times 5} \approx 165$. You can guarantee that amount by buying a protective put on the stock with an exercise price of 165. The price of that put is: $S_0 = 100$, $X = 165$, $r = 0.1$, $\sigma = 0.2$ and $T = 5$, so that:

$$d_1 = \frac{\ln(S_0/X) + \left(r + \frac{1}{2}\sigma^2\right)T}{\sigma\sqrt{T}} = \frac{\ln(100/165) + \left(0.1 + \frac{1}{2} \times 0.2^2\right)5}{0.2\sqrt{5}} = 0.2219$$

$$d_2 = d_1 - \sigma\sqrt{T} = 0.2219 - 0.2\sqrt{5} = -0.2253$$

NormalDist(-0.2219) = 0.412 and NormalDist(0.2253) = 0.589. The price then is:

$$O_{p,0} = 165 \times e^{-0.1 \times 5}(0.589) - 100 \times (0.412) = 17.75$$

So it is possible to get a minimum guaranteed return on a risky stock, but the insurance premium is high: more than 17 per cent of the amount you want to invest.

8.3.4   Dividends

The Black and Scholes formula was developed under the assumption that the underlying stock doesn't pay dividends. However, the formula can be adapted to allow for dividends that can be predicted with certainty, i.e. deterministic (non-stochastic) dividends. Recall from the analyses in discrete time that dividends are a stream of value out of the stock. This stream accrues to the stockholders but not to the holders of a European option. Hence, the stock price for the stockholders can be regarded as the sum of a stochastic part (the value of the stock apart from the dividends) and a deterministic part (the present value of the dividends paid before the option's maturity).

For European option-holders, only the stochastic part of the stock is relevant. By definition, they receive the stochastic part of the stock only if the option is exercised at maturity. So an obvious way of adapting the Black and Scholes formula is by redefining the inputs in terms of the stochastic part as well. In practice, the only adaptation that needs to be done is subtracting the present value of the dividends from the stock price now (S_0), since the dividends are certain they can be discounted with the risk-free rate. Note that this implicitly redefines the volatility parameter σ as referring to the stochastic part only. The other determinants (X, T and r) remain unaffected by dividends. We will illustrate the procedure with an example.

Suppose the stock we used in the previous sub-section pays semi-annual dividends of 2.625, the first after three months and the second after nine months. If the stock price now is 100, what is the value of a European call option that matures in one year and has a strike price of 100? The underlying stock's annual volatility remains at 20 per cent and the risk-free interest rate at 10 per cent per year. So $S_0 = 100$, $X = 100$, $r = 0.1$, $\sigma = 0.2$ and $T = 1$.

We start by calculating the present value of the dividends: $2.625e^{-0.25 \times 0.1} + 2.625e^{-0.75 \times 0.1} = 5$. This makes the adjusted stock price $S_0 = 100 - 5 = 95$ and we can proceed as before:

$$d_1 = \frac{\ln(S_0/X) + \left(r + \frac{1}{2}\sigma^2\right)T}{\sigma\sqrt{T}} = \frac{\ln(95/100) + \left(0.1 + \frac{1}{2} \times 0.2^2\right)1}{0.2\sqrt{1}} = 0.34353$$

$$d_2 = d_1 - \sigma\sqrt{T} = 0.34353 - 0.2\sqrt{1} = 0.14353$$

The areas under the normal curve for the values of d_1 and d_2 are:
NormalDist(0.34353) = 0.6344 and NormalDist(0.14353) = 0.5571. So the option price becomes:

$$O_{c,0} = 95 \times (0.6344) - 100e^{-0.1}(0.5571) = 9.86$$

The value of a put option with the same specifications is, again, calculated with equation (8.21):

$$O_{p,0} = Xe^{-rT}N(-d_2) - S_0N(-d_1)$$

We have calculated above that $d_1 = 0.34353$ and $d_2 = 0.14353$, so that the probability terms become:
NormalDist(−0.34353) = 0.3656 and NormalDist(−0.14353) = 0.44294. With these numbers the value of the put is:

$$O_{p,0} = 100 \times e^{-0.1}(0.44294) - 95 \times (0.3656) = 5.35$$

We see that the value of the call is indeed lowered by the dividends (from 13.27 to 9.86) while the value of the put has increased (from 3.75 to 5.35).

8.3.5   Matching discrete and continuous time-parameters

We have modelled the volatility and expected return of the underlying stock in two different ways, one in discrete time and one in continuous time. In discrete time, volatility is expressed as the difference between the upward and downward movement of the stock prices in the binomial tree. The continuous-time equivalent is the volatility parameter that is used to scale the random movements of the Brownian motion. In both models, the expected return under the equivalent martingale measure is the risk-free rate.

Since we may have to switch from one model to the other, it would be useful to have a way to match the parameters of both models. In practice this means choosing the parameters of the binomial model in such a way that it has the same mean and variance as the continuous-time model. These parameters are obtained by equating the expressions for mean and variance in discrete time to the continuous time 'values'. If we take a (small) time interval δt, the expected continuous time return per unit[8] is $e^{r\delta t}$ and equating this to the expectation of a one-step binomial tree we get:

$$e^{r\delta t} = pu + (1 - p)d$$

where r is the risk-free rate and p, u and d are the binomial parameters. Following the same procedure for the variance we get:

$$\sigma^2 \delta t = pu^2 + (1 - p)d^2 - [pu + (1 - p)d]^2$$

where $\sigma^2 \delta t$ is the continuous time variance and the discrete time variance is expressed using the definition that the variance of a variable A is $E(A^2) - [E(A)]^2$.

This gives us two equations for three unknown parameters (p, u and d) so that at least one additional assumption is necessary. The most common extra assumption is:

$$u = \frac{1}{d}$$

Together, these three equations imply[9] that:

$$u = e^{\sigma\sqrt{\delta t}}, \quad d = e^{-\sigma\sqrt{\delta t}} \quad \text{and} \quad p = \frac{e^{r\delta t} - d}{u - d}$$

i.e. the definition of p we already derived in discrete time. Cox et al. (1979) show that, with this parametrization, the Black and Scholes formula can be derived as the limit of their binomial model. Since $ud = 1$, the resulting binomial tree is symmetric around the starting price (in number of nodes, not in values), and the starting price reoccurs every other step. The positive drift in the stock price, r, is expressed in the different probabilities and size of the upward and downward movement: $p \neq (1 - p)$ and $|u - 1| \neq |d - 1|$.

An alternative choice is to set $p = (1 - p) = \frac{1}{2}$. This results in u and d such that $ud > 1$ and the whole tree grows in the direction of the drift (see Wilmott et al. (1995) for an elaboration of this case). In both cases $ud = du$ so that the trees recombine. A third possibility is to add a drift term to u and d such that $u = e^{r\delta t + \sigma\sqrt{\delta t}}$ and $d = e^{r\delta t - \sigma\sqrt{\delta t}}$. To be in line with most of the literature we will use the first choice $u = 1/d$.

8.3.6   Implied volatility

Four of the five determinants of option prices in the Black and Scholes formula are, at least in principle, directly observable. The exercise price X and time to maturity T are specified in the option contract and the stock price S and risk-free rate r are quoted on public markets. Their numerical values are readily available in the financial press. The unobservable

---

8 The stock price S appears in all elements of the equation and can be dropped.
9 Derivation of this requires a series expansion and is omitted here.

determinant is σ, the volatility of the stock price over the option's life span. There are two ways of obtaining a numerical value for σ. The first is to estimate it from historical stock prices and extrapolate this value into future life span of the option. This assumes, as the Black and Scholes formula does, that volatility is constant over time. This may give a good approximation in many cases, but volatility is also known to peak around certain events, such as quarterly reports.

The second way is to estimate σ from the prices of other options. Given X, T, S and r, each value for σ corresponds to a Black and Scholes price and vice versa. This allows us to run the Black and Scholes formula in reverse[10] and find the σ that equates the Black and Scholes price to a given market price. That volatility is called the *implied volatility*. This quantity is commonly used in practice: option traders quote option prices in volatilities, not in US dollar or euro amounts.

Implied volatility can also be used to test the validity of the Black and Scholes model. If the model is correct and all its underlying assumptions obtain in the market, then otherwise identical options with different exercise prices or maturities should give the same implied volatility. This is typically not the case: far in- and out-of-the-money options tend to give higher implied volatilities than at-the-money options. This phenomenon is called *volatility smile* after its graphical representation. Figure 8.5 illustrates the volatility smile in a stylized way.

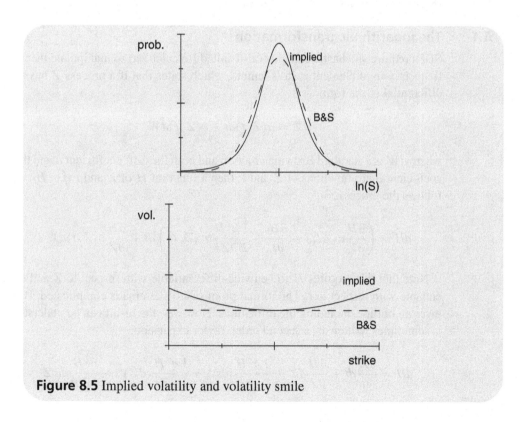

Figure 8.5 Implied volatility and volatility smile

---

10 This is done numerically; most option price calculators offer this possibility.

The upper graph depicts distributions of stock prices S. In the Black and Scholes model, this distribution is assumed to be lognormal, as depicted by the dashed line. The distribution implied by option prices deviates from lognormality, as the solid line shows. The lower graph shows the relation with the volatilities that are implied by options with different strike prices. Calls plot from left to right from (far) in the money to (far) out of the money. Puts plot the other way around, from out of the money on the left to in the money on the right. Both are at the money in the middle of the x-axis, where the implied volatility is equal to the Black and Scholes volatility.[11] Implied volatility is seen to increase at both ends of the scale, which corresponds to the implied distribution in the upper graph. Figure 8.5 is illustrative for the general results of empirical volatility studies. Implied distributions of stock prices tend to have more kurtosis (peakedness) and fatter tails, so that intermediate prices are less likely. Stock options are also known to imply volatility skewness: far out-of-the-money calls are priced lower than far out-of-the-money puts (or far in-the-money calls). This implies a skewed distribution of stock prices, where the left tail is fatter than the right one. Finally, implied volatility may also increase with time to maturity. Empirical examples of volatility smiles can be found in Ederington and Guan (2002).

A   A pinch of stochastic calculus

A.1   The logarithmic transformation

SDEs require stochastic calculus (also called Itô calculus) to manipulate them. The most frequently used element is Itô's lemma, which states that if a process Z has a stochastic differential of the form

$$dZ = a(Z, t)dt + b(Z, t)dW \tag{8.22}$$

where dW is a standard Brownian motion and both the drift coefficient a and the diffusion coefficient b are functions of Z and t, then a function H of Z and t (i.e. $H_t = f(t, Z_t)$) follows the process:

$$dH = \left(\frac{\partial H}{\partial Z} a(Z, t) + \frac{\partial H}{\partial t} + \frac{1}{2} \frac{\partial^2 H}{\partial Z^2} b^2(Z, t) \right) dt + \frac{\partial H}{\partial Z} b(Z, t) dW \tag{8.23}$$

Note that this requires H to be twice differentiable with respect to Z and once differentiable with respect to t. The formal proof of Itô's lemma is complicated; Björk (2004) gives an outline, including the difficulties. However, the result can be understood as, and is sometimes written as, a second order Taylor expansion:

$$dH = \frac{\partial H}{\partial t} dt + \frac{\partial H}{\partial Z} dZ + \frac{1}{2} \frac{\partial^2 H}{\partial t^2} (dt)^2 + \frac{1}{2} \frac{\partial^2 H}{\partial Z^2} (dZ)^2 + \frac{\partial^2 H}{\partial Z \partial t} dt dZ$$

11 The graph shows the structure of volatilities relative to the volatility of at-the-money options; this does not necessarily mean that for at-the-money options all distributional assumptions of Black and Scholes obtain.

With the following multiplication rules:

$$(dt)^2 = 0$$

$$dt \times dW = 0$$

$$(dW)^2 = dt$$

and since we have, in simplified notation, $dZ = adt + bdW$ so that $dtdZ = a(dt)^2 + bdWdt = 0$, this simplifies to

$$dH = \frac{\partial H}{\partial t}dt + \frac{\partial H}{\partial Z}dZ + \frac{1}{2}\frac{\partial^2 H}{\partial Z^2}(dZ)^2 \tag{8.24}$$

which is the Taylor expansion form of Itô's lemma. Substituting (8.22) into (8.24) and calculating $(dZ)^2 = a^2(dt)^2 + b^2(dW)^2 + 2ab(dt)(dW) = 0 + b^2dt + 0$ reproduces the lemma in (8.23).

In the main text we have the process:

$$dS_t = rS_tdt + \sigma S_tdW_t$$

and we want to apply a logarithmic transformation to it. Then $H = \ln S_t$ so that:

$$\frac{\partial H}{\partial S_t} = \frac{1}{S_t}, \quad \frac{\partial^2 H}{\partial S_t^2} = -\frac{1}{S_t^2} \quad \text{and} \quad \frac{\partial H}{\partial t} = 0$$

with $a(Z, t) = rS_t$ and $b(Z, t) = \sigma S_t$. Substituting all this into (8.23) we get:

$$d \ln S_t = \left(\frac{1}{S_t}rS_t + \frac{1}{2}\left(-\frac{1}{S_t^2} \right)\sigma^2 S_t^2 \right) dt + \frac{1}{S_t}\sigma S_tdW_t$$

which simplifies to:

$$d(\ln S_t) = \left(r - \frac{1}{2}\sigma^2 \right) dt + \sigma dW_t$$

The term $-\frac{1}{2}\sigma^2$ follows from the stochastic nature of the returns. It would not have appeared if we (wrongly!) had used ordinary instead of Itô calculus. Recall the simple example that was used earlier to illustrate why volatility lowers compound returns. Suppose a security has return of $(1 + r)$ over 2 periods, with an error of $+\varepsilon$ in one period and $-\varepsilon$ in the other. The combined return is $((1 + r) + \varepsilon)((1 + r) - \varepsilon) = (1 + r)^2 - \varepsilon^2$. The cross-terms $(1 + r)\varepsilon$ cancel out, but not the square, so volatility reduces compound return and end value. We reached a similar conclusion in the discussion of arithmetic vs. geometric averages in the appendix to Chapter 3.

A.2   Black and Scholes in the PDE approach

There are several ways to derive the Black and Scholes option-pricing formula using the partial differential equations (PDE) approach. One possibility is to explicitly model the pricing kernel. Another way is to model different hedging portfolios consisting of e.g. bonds and stocks or options and stocks. Here we choose the latter way and model a hedging portfolio of the option and the underlying stock. Alternative models can be found in Baz and Chacko (2004). Our analysis starts with the by now familiar process for the price of a stock under the objective probability measure:

$$dS_t = \mu S_t dt + \sigma S_t d\widetilde{W}_t \tag{8.25}$$

If a derivative is written on the stock such that its price is a function of both the price of the stock and time, then we can use Itô's lemma to find the stochastic process of the derivative. If we call the derivative H, its price at time t is H_t and its stochastic price process is by Itô's lemma:

$$dH_t = \left(\frac{\partial H_t}{\partial S_t} \mu S_t + \frac{\partial H_t}{\partial t} + \frac{1}{2} \frac{\partial^2 H_t}{\partial S_t^2} \sigma^2 S_t^2 \right) dt + \frac{\partial H_t}{\partial S_t} \sigma S_t d\widetilde{W}_t \tag{8.26}$$

There are two elements worth noticing about this equation. First, we did not say anything about the nature of the derivative (put, call, European or American), so (8.26) is a very general relation. Second, the Brownian motions in (8.25) and (8.26) are the same. This means that it is possible to make a portfolio of the stock and the derivative from which the Brownian motion disappears. We call that portfolio V and guess (or recall from our analyses in discrete time) that it consists of a short position in the derivative and a long position in a fraction Δ of the stock: $V = -H + \Delta S$. The dynamics of this portfolio are:

$$dV_t = -dH_t + \Delta dS_t \tag{8.27}$$

Δ is held fixed during the time step, otherwise a $d\Delta$ term would have to be included in (8.27). Substituting (8.26) and (8.25) into (8.27) we get:

$$dV_t = -\left(\frac{\partial H_t}{\partial S_t} \mu S_t + \frac{\partial H_t}{\partial t} + \frac{1}{2} \frac{\partial^2 H_t}{\partial S_t^2} \sigma^2 S_t^2 \right) dt - \frac{\partial H_t}{\partial S_t} \sigma S_t d\widetilde{W}_t + \Delta \mu S_t dt + \Delta \sigma S_t d\widetilde{W}_t$$

It is clear from this equation that the Brownian motion terms cancel out if we choose the fraction of the stock as $\Delta = \partial H_t / \partial S_t$ (in which we recognize our old friend the option delta). With this Δ the $\mu S_t dt$ terms also cancel out, so that the portfolio dynamics reduce to:

$$dV_t = -\left(\frac{\partial H_t}{\partial t} + \frac{1}{2} \frac{\partial^2 H_t}{\partial S_t^2} \sigma^2 S_t^2 \right) dt \tag{8.28}$$

The dynamic process in (8.28) contains only a drift term, no diffusion. Hence, the portfolio is riskless and in an arbitrage-free market its return is the risk-free interest rate r. So:

$$dV_t = r V_t dt \tag{8.29}$$

Substituting (8.28) into the left-hand side of (8.29) and the portfolio definition $V_t = -H_t + (\partial H_t / \partial S_t) S_t$ into the right-hand side we get:

$$-\left(\frac{\partial H_t}{\partial t} + \frac{1}{2} \frac{\partial^2 H_t}{\partial S_t^2} \sigma^2 S_t^2 \right) dt = r \left(-H_t + \frac{\partial H_t}{\partial S_t} S_t \right) dt$$

Dropping dt and rearranging terms gives:

$$\frac{\partial H_t}{\partial t} + \frac{1}{2}\frac{\partial^2 H_t}{\partial S_t^2}\sigma^2 S_t^2 + \frac{\partial H_t}{\partial S_t}S_t r - rH_t = 0 \qquad (8.30)$$

This is the famous Black and Scholes partial differential equation[12] that derivative prices must satisfy if they are to be arbitrage free. Since we did not say anything about the nature of the derivative, the PDE describes the value dynamics for any derivative that meets the underlying assumptions. Among the assumptions we implicitly or explicitly made are that the stock follows a geometric Brownian motion with constant drift and volatility and that the derivative's payoff depends on the stock price. The latter rules out Asian options, whose payoff depends on the average stock price. But the PDE holds for, among others, European and American puts and calls. Also notice that the expected return of the stock, μ, is not included in the PDE, only its volatility σ. So the price of the derivative is independent of the stock return.

Solutions to Black and Scholes' PDE are functions, whose partial derivatives satisfy (8.30). There are many such functions, which is another way of saying that the PDE is valid for a broad range of derivatives. To find a solution for a particular derivative we have to use the additional information in the derivative's payoff structure and other characteristics. These can be formulated as *boundary conditions* that apply on the edges of the region where the PDE is valid. The solution must satisfy both the PDE and the boundary conditions. The boundaries of derivatives are typically along the possible values of the underlying, between 0 and S_T, and the time until the derivative expires, $0 \le t \le T$. For instance, we know that if the stock price ever becomes zero, it will remain zero. This follows directly from the multiplicative specification in (8.25). So a European call option written on the stock will also have zero value. This is a boundary condition: $H_t = 0$ for all t where $S_t = 0$. Similarly, we know that a European call option has a value at maturity of $\max[0, S_T - X]$, where X is the exercise price. This gives us another boundary[13] condition for a European call option:

$$H_T = \max[0, S_T - X] \qquad (8.31)$$

Together, the two equations in (8.30) and (8.31) constitute one of the many variants of the *boundary value problem*. The problem is well posed, meaning that a unique solution exists. It is solved by a change of variable transformation, i.e. using temporary variables for complex expressions. In this way the equations are reduced until a recognizable form appears, such as the heat equation in Black and Scholes' original derivation. This equation is solved, after which the steps have to be retraced by substituting back the original variables. This is an operation that stretches over several pages and that, more importantly, is devoid of economic reasoning. So we will follow Black and Scholes' good example and refer to the literature for proof that this boundary value problem is solved by the celebrated Black and Scholes formula in (8.20). Derivations can be found in Baz and Chacko (2004), Björk (2004), Kallianpur and Karandikar (2000), Nielsen (1999) and Wilmott *et al.* (1995).

----

[12] Or in short *Black and Scholes equation*, not to be confused with the Black and Scholes *formula* for pricing European call options.

[13] The boundary condition applying at the final time $t = T$ is also called *final condition*; similarly, the *initial condition* applies at $t = 0$.

The Greeks of Black and Scholes' model

Option Greeks measure the sensitivities of option prices for single-unit changes in their determinants. Hence, they measure the risk and reward potential of options. Greeks are calculated by taking the partial derivatives of an option-pricing formula with respect to its determinants. This appendix shows the calculations for the five determinants in Black and Scholes' formula for pricing European options on a non-dividend-paying stock, plus gamma. For options on dividend-paying stocks, an additional Greek, psi (Ψ), can be calculated to measure the sensitivity for changes in the dividend rate.

B.1   Preparatory calculations

We start with the option-pricing formulas for a European call:

$$O_{c,0} = S_0 N(d_1) - X e^{-rT} N(d_2) \tag{8.32}$$

and a European put:

$$O_{p,0} = X e^{-rT} N(-d_2) - S_0 N(-d_1) \tag{8.33}$$

where:

$$d_1 = \frac{\ln(S_0/X) + \left(r + \frac{1}{2}\sigma^2\right)T}{\sigma\sqrt{T}} \tag{8.34}$$

$$d_2 = \frac{\ln(S_0/X) + \left(r - \frac{1}{2}\sigma^2\right)T}{\sigma\sqrt{T}} = d_1 - \sigma\sqrt{T} \tag{8.35}$$

and $N(.)$ is the cumulative distribution function of the standard normal distribution:

$$N(z) = \int_{-\infty}^{z} \frac{1}{\sqrt{2\pi}} e^{-z^2/2} dz$$

and:

$$\frac{\partial N(z)}{\partial z} = \frac{1}{\sqrt{2\pi}} e^{-z^2/2} = n(z) \tag{8.36}$$

where $n(z)$ is the probability density function of the standard normal distribution evaluated at z. We first calculate some results that are used later. To calculate $\partial d_1 / \partial S_0$ we start by differentiating the numerator of (8.34):

$$\frac{\partial \ln(S_0/X) + \left(r + \frac{1}{2}\sigma^2\right)T}{\partial S_0} = \frac{\partial \ln(S_0/X)}{\partial S_0} + \frac{\partial \left(r + \frac{1}{2}\sigma^2\right)T}{\partial S_0} = \frac{1}{S_0} + 0 = \frac{1}{S_0}$$

and then the denominator:

$$\frac{\partial \sigma\sqrt{T}}{\partial S_0} = 0$$

so that:

$$\frac{\partial d_1}{\partial S_0} = \frac{\sigma\sqrt{T}\frac{1}{S_0}}{(\sigma\sqrt{T})^2} = \frac{1}{S_0 \sigma\sqrt{T}} = \frac{\partial d_2}{\partial S_0} \tag{8.37}$$

B The Greeks of Black and Scholes' model

It is easy to see that $\partial d_2/\partial S_0 = \partial d_1/\partial S_0$, since the derivatives of the second terms in the numerators of (8.34) and (8.35) are both zero. Similarly, $\partial d_1/\partial r$ is calculated in parts as:

$$\frac{\partial \ln(S_0/X) + \left(r + \frac{1}{2}\sigma^2\right)T}{\partial r} = \frac{\partial \ln(S_0/X)}{\partial r} + \frac{\partial\left(r + \frac{1}{2}\sigma^2\right)T}{\partial r} = 0 + T = T$$

and:

$$\frac{\partial \sigma\sqrt{T}}{\partial r} = 0$$

so that:

$$\frac{\partial d_1}{\partial r} = \frac{T\sigma\sqrt{T} - 0}{(\sigma\sqrt{T})^2} = \frac{T\sigma\sqrt{T}}{\sigma^2 T} = \frac{\sqrt{T}}{\sigma} = \frac{\partial d_2}{\partial r} \tag{8.38}$$

Again, it is easy to see that $\partial d_1/\partial r = \partial d_2/\partial r$ because the only terms they do not have in common, $+$ and $-\frac{1}{2}\sigma^2$, drop from the derivation. Finally, $\partial d_1/\partial X$ and $\partial d_2/\partial X$ are calculated in parts as:

$$\frac{\partial \ln(S_0/X) + \left(r + \frac{1}{2}\sigma^2\right)T}{\partial X} = -\frac{1}{X}$$

while the derivative of $d_{1,2}$'s denominator w.r.t. X is zero, so that:

$$\frac{\partial d_1}{\partial X} = \frac{\sigma\sqrt{T}\frac{-1}{X}}{(\sigma\sqrt{T})^2} = \frac{-\sqrt{T}}{\sigma T X} = \frac{\partial d_2}{\partial X} \tag{8.39}$$

It is also very useful to express $n(d_2)$ in terms of $n(d_1)$; since $d_2 = d_1 - \sigma\sqrt{T}$:

$$n(d_2) = \frac{1}{\sqrt{2\pi}}e^{-d_2^2/2} = \frac{1}{\sqrt{2\pi}}e^{-(d_1 - \sigma\sqrt{T})^2/2}$$

working out the square in the exponent gives:

$$n(d_2) = \frac{1}{\sqrt{2\pi}}e^{-(d_1^2 - 2d_1\sigma\sqrt{T} + (\sigma\sqrt{T})^2)/2}$$

rewriting the exponent:

$$n(d_2) = \frac{1}{\sqrt{2\pi}}e^{-d_1^2/2}e^{d_1\sigma\sqrt{T} - (\sigma\sqrt{T})^2/2}$$

The first part of the term on the left-hand side is the normal density function in (8.36) evaluated at d_1; substituting from (8.36) and the definition of d_1 from (8.35) in the second exponent we get, after some rewriting:

$$n(d_2) = n(d_1)e^{\ln(S_0/X) + (r + \frac{1}{2}\sigma^2)T - (\sigma\sqrt{T})^2/2}$$

Working out the last two terms in the exponent gives:

$$n(d_2) = n(d_1)e^{\ln(S_0/X) + rT + \frac{1}{2}\sigma^2 T - \frac{1}{2}\sigma^2 T}$$

which reduces to:

$$n(d_2) = n(d_1)\frac{S_0}{X}e^{rT} \tag{8.40}$$

B.2   Delta

Delta measures the sensitivity of option prices for single-unit changes in the underlying value S_0. The underlying value is usually expressed in money units as euros or dollars, so Δ gives the change in option price resulting from a €1 or \$1 change in the underlying value. The delta of a call option is found by differentiating (8.32) w.r.t. S_0. It is tempting to simply equate this derivative to $N(d_1)$, particularly since it happens to give the correct result, but this would ignore the fact that S_0 appears in the arguments of $N(.)$. The correct derivation is:

$$\Delta_c = \frac{\partial\left(S_0 N(d_1) - Xe^{-rT}N(d_2)\right)}{\partial S_0}$$

$$\frac{\partial S_0 N(d_1)}{\partial S_0} = N(d_1) + \frac{\partial N(d_1)}{\partial S_0}S_0 \quad \text{and} \quad \frac{\partial Xe^{-rT}N(d_2)}{\partial S_0} = \frac{\partial N(d_2)}{\partial S_0}Xe^{-rT}$$

Adding both terms and using the chain rule for the probability terms we get:

$$\Delta_c = N(d_1) + \frac{\partial N(d_1)}{\partial d_1}\frac{\partial d_1}{\partial S_0}S_0 - \frac{\partial N(d_2)}{\partial d_2}\frac{\partial d_2}{\partial S_0}Xe^{-rT}$$

Substituting from (8.36) and (8.37) produces:

$$\Delta_c = N(d_1) + n(d_1)\frac{1}{S_0\sigma\sqrt{T}}S_0 - n(d_2)\frac{1}{S_0\sigma\sqrt{T}}Xe^{-rT}$$

Eliminating S_0 from the second term on the right-hand side and substituting (8.40) for $n(d_2)$ in the third term gives:

$$\Delta_c = N(d_1) + n(d_1)\frac{1}{\sigma\sqrt{T}} - n(d_1)\frac{S_0}{X}e^{rT}\frac{1}{S_0\sigma\sqrt{T}}Xe^{-rT}$$

which simplifies to:

$$\Delta_c = N(d_1) \tag{8.41}$$

This, obviously, limits the values of Δ_c to the range from zero to one:

$$0 \le \Delta_c \le 1$$

Following the same procedure for a put:

$$\Delta_p = \frac{\partial\left(Xe^{-rT}N(-d_2) - S_0 N(-d_1)\right)}{\partial S_0}$$

using the symmetry of the standard normal distribution around its mean of zero:

$$\Delta_p = \frac{\partial\left(Xe^{-rT}(1 - N(d_2)) - S_0(1 - N(d_1))\right)}{\partial S_0}$$

$$\frac{\partial Xe^{-rT}(1 - N(d_2))}{\partial S_0} = Xe^{-rT}\left(-\frac{\partial N(d_2)}{\partial d_2}\frac{\partial d_2}{\partial S_0}\right)$$

and:

$$\frac{\partial S_0(1 - N(d_1))}{\partial S_0} = (1 - N(d_1)) - S_0\frac{\partial N(d_1)}{\partial d_1}\frac{\partial d_1}{\partial S_0}$$

Adding both terms and substituting from (8.36) and (8.37) produces:

$$\Delta_p = -Xe^{-rT}n(d_2)\frac{1}{S_0\sigma\sqrt{T}} - (1 - N(d_1)) + S_0n(d_1)\frac{1}{S_0\sigma\sqrt{T}}$$

Simplifying and substituting (8.40) for $n(d_2)$:

$$\Delta_p = -Xe^{-rT}n(d_1)\frac{S_0}{X}e^{rT}\frac{1}{S_0\sigma\sqrt{T}} - (1 - N(d_1)) + n(d_1)\frac{1}{\sigma\sqrt{T}}$$

So that:

$$\Delta_p = -(1 - N(d_1)) = N(d_1) - 1 \tag{8.42}$$

This limits the values of Δ_c to the range minus one to zero:

$$-1 \leq \Delta_p \leq 0$$

A simpler way to derive Δ_p using the put–call parity is included in the exercises.

B.3   Vega

Vega is the sensitivity of option prices for single-unit changes in volatility σ. Volatility is usually measured in decimal fractions; 20 per cent volatility is entered into the calculations as 0.2. Dividing vega by 100 transforms the single-unit change into a change in option price per percentage point change in volatility. The derivation of vega is made much simpler by noticing that $d_2 = d_1 - \sigma\sqrt{T}$, so that:

$$\frac{\partial d_2}{\partial \sigma} = \frac{\partial d_1}{\partial \sigma} - \frac{\partial\sigma\sqrt{T}}{\partial\sigma} \quad \text{or} \quad \frac{\partial d_1}{\partial\sigma} - \frac{\partial d_2}{\partial\sigma} = \sqrt{T} \tag{8.43}$$

The vega of a call option is derived along the same lines as delta:[14]

$$\nu_c = \frac{\partial\left(S_0 N(d_1) - Xe^{-rT}N(d_2)\right)}{\partial\sigma}$$

$$\nu_c = S_0\frac{\partial N(d_1)}{\partial\sigma} - Xe^{-rT}\frac{\partial N(d_2)}{\partial\sigma} = S_0\frac{\partial N(d_1)}{\partial d_1}\frac{\partial d_1}{\partial\sigma} - Xe^{-rT}\frac{\partial N(d_2)}{\partial d_2}\frac{\partial d_2}{\partial\sigma}$$

Substituting first (8.36) in both terms and then (8.40) for $n(d_2)$ in the last term gives:

$$\nu_c = S_0 n(d_1)\frac{\partial d_1}{\partial\sigma} - Xe^{-rT}n(d_1)\frac{S_0}{X}e^{rT}\frac{\partial d_2}{\partial\sigma}$$

which simplifies to:

$$\nu_c = S_0 n(d_1)\frac{\partial d_1}{\partial\sigma} - n(d_1)S_0\frac{\partial d_2}{\partial\sigma} = S_0 n(d_1)\left(\frac{\partial d_1}{\partial\sigma} - \frac{\partial d_2}{\partial\sigma}\right)$$

Substituting the result in (8.43) produces the solution:

$$\nu_c = S_0 n(d_1)\sqrt{T} > 0 \tag{8.44}$$

ν_c is always positive because neither S_0 nor $n(d_1)$ nor $\sqrt{T}$ can be negative.

---

14 As we have noticed in the main text, vega is not a Greek letter; instead the Greek letter ν (nu) is used.

Similarly, the vega of a put is:

$$v_p = \frac{\partial \left(Xe^{-rT} N\left(-d_2\right) - S_0 N\left(-d_1\right)\right)}{\partial \sigma} = \frac{\partial \left(Xe^{-rT} \left(1 - N\left(d_2\right)\right) - S_0 \left(1 - N\left(d_1\right)\right)\right)}{\partial \sigma}$$

$$v_p = Xe^{-rT}\frac{-\partial N\left(d_2\right)}{\partial \sigma} - S_0\frac{-\partial N\left(d_1\right)}{\partial \sigma} = Xe^{-rT}\frac{-\partial N\left(d_2\right)}{\partial d_2}\frac{\partial d_2}{\partial \sigma} - S_0\frac{-\partial N\left(d_1\right)}{\partial d_1}\frac{\partial d_1}{\partial \sigma}$$

Substituting from (8.36) in both terms and then from (8.40) in the first term gives:

$$v_p = Xe^{-rT}\left(-n(d_1)\right)\frac{S_0}{X}e^{rT}\frac{\partial d_2}{\partial \sigma} - S_0\left(-n(d_1)\right)\frac{\partial d_1}{\partial \sigma}$$

which simplifies to:

$$v_p = S_0 n(d_1)\left(\frac{\partial d_1}{\partial \sigma} - \frac{\partial d_2}{\partial \sigma}\right) = S_0 n(d_1)\sqrt{T} = v_c > 0 \tag{8.45}$$

B.4   Theta

Theta is the sensitivity of option prices for single-unit changes in time T. It can be interpreted in different ways. We will first calculate the partial derivative and this is, again, made simpler by noticing that $d_2 = d_1 - \sigma\sqrt{T}$, so that:

$$\frac{\partial d_2}{\partial T} = \frac{\partial d_1}{\partial T} - \frac{\partial \sigma\sqrt{T}}{\partial T} \quad\text{or}\quad \frac{\partial d_1}{\partial \sigma} - \frac{\partial d_2}{\partial \sigma} = \sigma\frac{1}{2}T^{-\frac{1}{2}} = \frac{\sigma}{2\sqrt{T}} \tag{8.46}$$

The derivation is along the by now familiar lines:

$$\Theta_c = \frac{\partial \left(S_0 N\left(d_1\right) - Xe^{-rT} N\left(d_2\right)\right)}{\partial T}$$

$$\Theta_c = S_0\frac{\partial N\left(d_1\right)}{\partial T} - \left(\frac{\partial Xe^{-rT}}{\partial T}N\left(d_2\right) + Xe^{-rT}\frac{\partial N\left(d_2\right)}{\partial T}\right)$$

$$\Theta_c = S_0\frac{\partial N\left(d_1\right)}{\partial T} - \left(-rXe^{-rT} N\left(d_2\right) + Xe^{-rT}\frac{\partial N\left(d_2\right)}{\partial T}\right)$$

$$\Theta_c = S_0\frac{\partial N\left(d_1\right)}{\partial d_1}\frac{\partial d_1}{\partial T} - \left(-rXe^{-rT} N\left(d_2\right) + Xe^{-rT}\frac{\partial N\left(d_2\right)}{\partial d_2}\frac{\partial d_2}{\partial T}\right)$$

Substituting first from (8.36) and then from (8.40) produces:

$$\Theta_c = S_0 n(d_1)\frac{\partial d_1}{\partial T} - \left(-rXe^{-rT} N\left(d_2\right) + Xe^{-rT} n(d_1)\frac{S_0}{X}e^{rT}\frac{\partial d_2}{\partial T}\right)$$

which simplifies to:

$$\Theta_c = S_0 n(d_1)\frac{\partial d_1}{\partial T} + rXe^{-rT} N\left(d_2\right) - n(d_1)S_0\frac{\partial d_2}{\partial T}$$

Rearranging terms yields:

$$\Theta_c = S_0 n(d_1)\left(\frac{\partial d_1}{\partial T} - \frac{\partial d_2}{\partial T}\right) + rXe^{-rT} N\left(d_2\right)$$

Using the result in (8.46) gives the final result:

$$\Theta_c = S_0 n(d_1)\frac{\sigma}{2\sqrt{T}} + rXe^{-rT} N\left(d_2\right) > 0 \tag{8.47}$$

Both terms on the right-hand side of (8.47) are strictly positive, so $\Theta_c > 0$. The interpretation of this result is that the price of a European call option (on a non-dividend-paying stock) increases with the time to maturity, other things being equal. Dividends can invalidate this result. In practice, however, theta is used to measure the sensitivity of option prices for the passage of calendar time, given a fixed maturity date; theta is also called the time decay of option value. Used in this way, the time to maturity decreases with calendar time so that $-\Theta_c$ must be used. In option-price calculations the time to maturity is usually measured in years; the time decay is then an annual rate. The time decay per day is the annual rate divided by 365. Of course, the passage of calendar time is certain, so theta does not measure a risk factor, but it shows how much value is gained or lost with each unit of time decay.

The theta of a put is calculated in the same way:

$$\Theta_p = \frac{\partial \left(Xe^{-rT} N(-d_2) - S_0 N(-d_1) \right)}{\partial T}$$

$$\Theta_p = \frac{\partial Xe^{-rT}}{\partial T} N(-d_2) + Xe^{-rT} \frac{\partial (1 - N(d_2))}{\partial T} - S_0 \frac{\partial (1 - N(d_1))}{\partial T}$$

$$\Theta_p = -rXe^{-rT} N(-d_2) + Xe^{-rT} \left(-\frac{\partial (N(d_2))}{\partial d_2} \frac{\partial d_2}{\partial T} \right) - S_0 \left(-\frac{\partial N(d_1)}{\partial d_1} \frac{\partial d_1}{\partial T} \right)$$

Substituting from (8.36) and (8.40) gives:

$$\Theta_p = -rXe^{-rT} N(-d_2) + Xe^{-rT} \left(-n(d_1) \frac{S_0}{X} e^{rT} \frac{\partial d_2}{\partial T} \right) - S_0 \left(-n(d_1) \frac{\partial d_1}{\partial T} \right)$$

Simplifying and rearranging terms yields:

$$\Theta_p = -rXe^{-rT} N(-d_2) + S_0 n(d_1) \left(\frac{\partial d_1}{\partial T} - \frac{\partial d_2}{\partial T} \right)$$

so that substitution from (8.46) produces the final result:

$$\Theta_p = -rXe^{-rT} N(-d_2) + S_0 n(d_1) \frac{\sigma}{2\sqrt{T}} <> 0 \tag{8.48}$$

The sign of Θ_p cannot be determined – it depends on the relative magnitudes of the positive and negative terms on the right-hand side of (8.48).

B.5   Rho

Rho is the sensitivity of option prices for single-unit changes in the interest rate r. Dividing rho by 100 transforms the single-unit change into a change in option price per percentage point change in the interest rate. Rho is calculated for a call as:

$$\rho_c = \frac{\partial \left(S_0 N(d_1) - Xe^{-rT} N(d_2) \right)}{\partial r}$$

$$\rho_c = S_0 \frac{\partial N(d_1)}{\partial d_1} \frac{\partial d_1}{\partial r} - \left(\frac{\partial Xe^{-rT}}{\partial r} N(d_2) + Xe^{-rT} \frac{\partial (N(d_2))}{\partial d_2} \frac{\partial d_2}{\partial r} \right)$$

Differentiating the first term in the parenthesis and substituting from (8.36) we get:

$$\rho_c = S_0 n(d_1) \frac{\partial d_1}{\partial r} - \left(-XTe^{-rT} N(d_2) + Xe^{-rT} n(d_2) \frac{\partial d_2}{\partial r} \right)$$

Substituting from (8.38) and (8.40) gives:

$$\rho_c = S_0 n(d_1) \frac{\sqrt{T}}{\sigma} - \left(-XTe^{-rT} N(d_2) + Xe^{-rT} n(d_1) \frac{S_0}{X} e^{rT} \frac{\sqrt{T}}{\sigma} \right)$$

which reduces to:

$$\rho_c = S_0 n(d_1) \frac{\sqrt{T}}{\sigma} + XTe^{-rT} N(d_2) - n(d_1) S_0 \frac{\sqrt{T}}{\sigma}$$

$$\rho_c = XTe^{-rT} N(d_2) > 0 \tag{8.49}$$

The rho of a put is:

$$\rho_p = \frac{\partial \left(Xe^{-rT} N(-d_2) - S_0 N(-d_1) \right)}{\partial r}$$

$$\rho_p = \frac{\partial Xe^{-rT}}{\partial r} N(-d_2) + Xe^{-rT} \left(-\frac{\partial (N(d_2))}{\partial d_2} \frac{\partial d_2}{\partial r} \right) - S_0 \left(-\frac{\partial N(d_1)}{\partial d_1} \frac{\partial d_1}{\partial r} \right)$$

Differentiating the first term and substituting from (8.36) and (8.40) we get:

$$\rho_p = -XTe^{-rT} N(-d_2) + Xe^{-rT} \left(-n(d_1) \frac{S_0}{X} e^{rT} \frac{\partial d_2}{\partial r} \right) - S_0 \left(-n(d_1) \frac{\partial d_1}{\partial r} \right)$$

Working out the last two terms on the right-hand side yields:

$$\rho_p = -XTe^{-rT} N(-d_2) - n(d_1) S_0 \frac{\partial d_2}{\partial r} + S_0 n(d_1) \frac{\partial d_1}{\partial r}$$

$$\rho_p = -XTe^{-rT} N(-d_2) < 0 \tag{8.50}$$

B.6 Gamma

Gamma is a measure of the sensitivity of delta, Δ, for changes in the underlying value S_0, so it is the second derivative of the option-pricing formula with respect to S_0. Its derivation is a simple extension of the foregoing:

$$\Gamma_c = \frac{\partial \Delta_c}{\partial S_0} = \frac{\partial^2 O_c}{\partial S_0^2} = \frac{\partial N d_1}{\partial S_0} = \frac{\partial N(d_1)}{\partial d_1} \frac{\partial d_1}{\partial S_0}$$

Substituting from (8.36) and (8.37) gives the result:

$$\Gamma_c = n(d_1) \frac{1}{S_0 \sigma \sqrt{T}} = \frac{n(d_1)}{S_0 \sigma \sqrt{T}} = \Gamma_P > 0 \tag{8.51}$$

Since Δ_c and Δ_p differ only by the constant -1, their derivatives are the same.

B.7 Exercise price

The sensitivity of option prices for single-unit changes in the exercise price is not represented by a Greek letter, but X is a determinant of option prices nonetheless. However, the exercise price cannot change during the option's lifetime, unlike the underlying value, its volatility, the remaining calendar time, and the interest rate. So, like theta, the partial derivative w.r.t. X does not measure a risk factor of an option. The calculations are:

$$\frac{\partial O_c}{\partial X} = \frac{\partial \left(S_0 N\,(d_1) - Xe^{-rT} N\,(d_2) \right)}{\partial X}$$

$$\frac{\partial O_c}{\partial X} = S_0 \frac{\partial N\,(d_1)}{\partial d_1} \frac{\partial d_1}{\partial X} - \left(\frac{\partial X e^{-rT}}{\partial X} N\,(d_2) + Xe^{-rT} \frac{\partial N\,(d_2)}{\partial d_2} \frac{\partial d_2}{\partial X} \right)$$

Differentiating and substituting from (8.36), (8.40) and (8.39) yields:

$$\frac{\partial O_c}{\partial X} = S_0 n(d_1) \frac{-\sqrt{T}}{\sigma T X} - \left(e^{-rT} N\,(d_2) + Xe^{-rT} n(d_1) \frac{S_0}{X} e^{rT} \frac{-\sqrt{T}}{\sigma T X} \right)$$

Simplifying gives:

$$\frac{\partial O_c}{\partial X} = -S_0 n(d_1) \frac{\sqrt{T}}{\sigma T X} - e^{-rT} N\,(d_2) + n(d_1) S_0 \frac{\sqrt{T}}{\sigma T X}$$

so that:

$$\frac{\partial O_c}{\partial X} = -e^{-rT} N\,(d_2) < 0 \qquad (8.52)$$

Finally, for a put:

$$\frac{\partial O_p}{\partial X} = \frac{\partial \left(Xe^{-rT} N\,(-d_2) - S_0 N\,(-d_1) \right)}{\partial X}$$

$$\frac{\partial O_p}{\partial X} = \frac{\partial X e^{-rT}}{\partial X} N\,(-d_2) + Xe^{-rT} \frac{\partial \left(1 - N(d_2) \right)}{\partial X} - S_0 \frac{\partial \left(1 - N(d_1) \right)}{\partial X}$$

$$\frac{\partial O_p}{\partial X} = e^{-rT} N\,(-d_2) + Xe^{-rT} \left(-\frac{\partial \left(N\,(d_2) \right)}{\partial d_2} \frac{\partial d_2}{\partial X} \right) - S_0 \left(-\frac{\partial N\,(d_1)}{\partial d_1} \frac{\partial d_1}{\partial X} \right)$$

Performing the usual substitutions yields:

$$\frac{\partial O_p}{\partial X} = e^{-rT} N\,(-d_2) + Xe^{-rT} \left(-n(d_1) \frac{S_0}{X} e^{rT} \frac{-\sqrt{T}}{\sigma T X} \right) - S_0 \left(-n(d_1) \frac{-\sqrt{T}}{\sigma T X} \right)$$

which reduces to:

$$\frac{\partial O_p}{\partial X} = e^{-rT} N\,(-d_2) + n(d_1) S_0 \frac{\sqrt{T}}{\sigma T X} - S_0 n(d_1) \frac{\sqrt{T}}{\sigma T X}$$

$$\frac{\partial O_p}{\partial X} = e^{-rT} N\,(-d_2) > 0 \qquad (8.53)$$

C Cumulative standard normal distribution

The body of Table 8.3 gives the area to the left of d under the standard normal density function, i.e. the one-tailed probability of a random variable not being more than d standard deviations above its mean. For example, if $d = 1.16$, $N(1.16) = 0.877$. For negative values of d, use the symmetric property of the normal distribution: $N(-d) = 1 - N(d)$.

Table 8.3 *Area in the left tail of the standard normal density function*

$d =$	0	0.01	0.02	0.03	0.04	0.05	0.06	0.07	0.08	0.09
0	0.500	0.504	0.508	0.512	0.516	0.520	0.524	0.528	0.532	0.536
0.1	0.540	0.544	0.548	0.552	0.556	0.560	0.564	0.567	0.571	0.575
0.2	0.579	0.583	0.587	0.591	0.595	0.599	0.603	0.606	0.610	0.614
0.3	0.618	0.622	0.626	0.629	0.633	0.637	0.641	0.644	0.648	0.652
0.4	0.655	0.659	0.663	0.666	0.670	0.674	0.677	0.681	0.684	0.688
0.5	0.691	0.695	0.698	0.702	0.705	0.709	0.712	0.716	0.719	0.722
0.6	0.726	0.729	0.732	0.736	0.739	0.742	0.745	0.749	0.752	0.755
0.7	0.758	0.761	0.764	0.767	0.770	0.773	0.776	0.779	0.782	0.785
0.8	0.788	0.791	0.794	0.797	0.800	0.802	0.805	0.808	0.811	0.813
0.9	0.816	0.819	0.821	0.824	0.826	0.829	0.831	0.834	0.836	0.839
1	0.841	0.844	0.846	0.848	0.851	0.853	0.855	0.858	0.860	0.862
1.1	0.864	0.867	0.869	0.871	0.873	0.875	0.877	0.879	0.881	0.883
1.2	0.885	0.887	0.889	0.891	0.893	0.894	0.896	0.898	0.900	0.901
1.3	0.903	0.905	0.907	0.908	0.910	0.911	0.913	0.915	0.916	0.918
1.4	0.919	0.921	0.922	0.924	0.925	0.926	0.928	0.929	0.931	0.932
1.5	0.933	0.934	0.936	0.937	0.938	0.939	0.941	0.942	0.943	0.944
1.6	0.945	0.946	0.947	0.948	0.949	0.951	0.952	0.953	0.954	0.954
1.7	0.955	0.956	0.957	0.958	0.959	0.960	0.961	0.962	0.962	0.963
1.8	0.964	0.965	0.966	0.966	0.967	0.968	0.969	0.969	0.970	0.971
1.9	0.971	0.972	0.973	0.973	0.974	0.974	0.975	0.976	0.976	0.977
2	0.977	0.978	0.978	0.979	0.979	0.980	0.980	0.981	0.981	0.982
2.1	0.982	0.983	0.983	0.983	0.984	0.984	0.985	0.985	0.985	0.986
2.2	0.986	0.986	0.987	0.987	0.987	0.988	0.988	0.988	0.989	0.989
2.3	0.989	0.990	0.990	0.990	0.990	0.991	0.991	0.991	0.991	0.992
2.4	0.992	0.992	0.992	0.992	0.993	0.993	0.993	0.993	0.993	0.994
2.5	0.994	0.994	0.994	0.994	0.994	0.995	0.995	0.995	0.995	0.995

Exercises

1. In the discussion of the properties of log returns we made the assumption that these returns are independently and identically distributed, which means that they follow a random walk. Does this mean that stock prices also follow a random walk?

2. The iid assumption means that the distribution of stock returns is stable over time. Does this stability mean that past stock returns can be used to predict future ones?

3. Explain why the value of options increases with the volatility of the underlying.

4. Explain why the value of a call increases with the risk-free interest rate while the value of a put decreases.

5. Use the put–call parity to work out a relation between the Greek 'delta' of puts and calls.

6. Look again at the graphs in Figures 8.2 and 8.3 in the main text. All options have an exercise price of 100, a risk-free interest rate of 10 per cent and are written on a stock that pays no dividends. Figure 8.2 plots options with a time to maturity of one year and three different volatilities: $\sigma = 0.5$ (top), 0.4 and 0.2 (bottom). Figure 8.3 plots options with a volatility of 0.2 and three different maturities: $T = 3$ (top), 2 and 1 (bottom). Explain briefly why the options with different volatilities converge to a common value as the stock price increases and why the options with different maturities do not converge to a common value as the stock price increases.

7. In a financial market a stock is traded at a price of €240. The stock has an annual volatility of 25 per cent. Call options on the stock with an exercise price of €250 and a time to maturity of one year are also traded. The risk-free interest rate is 6 per cent. Calculate the price of the option.

8. Suppose the price of a share Nordic Timber at some point in the future is NOK 100. Over each of the next two periods of half a year, the price can either increase with 7.5 per cent or decrease with 7 per cent, corresponding to a yearly standard deviation of 10.228 per cent. After the first half year, Nordic Timber pays out a dividend of NOK 10. The six months risk-free rate is 2.5 per cent, so slightly more than 5 per cent per year.
   (a) Calculate the value of an American call option on the stock, that matures in one year and has an exercise price of 102.5.
   (b) Calculate the hedge portfolio of the option for the first half-year period and show that it gives a perfect hedge.
   (c) Explain in general terms how the call option delta changes as the stock prices changes.

9. Assume that the following information on option prices, stock prices and interest rates was published in a financial newspaper on 5 September.

Option price quotes

Ticker	T	X	call option bid	call option ask	put option bid	put option ask
NHY	nov.5	620	68.00	70.00	9.25	10.00
NHY	"	680	28.75	30.25	29.00	31.25
NHY	feb.6	620	82.00	83.75	19.00	20.75
NHY	"	680	44.00	47.00	41.50	44.25
ORK	jan.6	240	25.50	26.75	5.00	5.50
NSG	dec.5	100	10.00	11.00	2.85	3.35

Stock price quotes

Ticker	stock price	
	bid	ask
NHY	677.00	678.50
ORK	259.00	259.50
NSG	108.75	109.50

IBOR rates

1 month	2.180
2 month	2.235
3 month	2.290
4 month	2.313
5 month	2.337

IBOR is the InterBank Offer Rate that can be used as the yearly risk-free interest rate for the different maturities. (IBOR rates have a prefix for the market, e.g. LIBOR, the London Interbank Offer Rate.) Ask prices are prices at which a dealer is willing to sell, bid prices are prices at which a dealer is willing to buy.

(a) Is there any sign of mispricing on the market? If so, how would you profit from it?

(b) Is there an alternative explanation for price differences, if you find any?

9 Real options analysis

As the name suggests, real options have investments in real assets, not financial securities such as stocks and bonds, as their underlying values. Real options analysis is aimed at the valuation of such investments using the option pricing techniques discussed in the previous chapters. Real options analysis is a comparatively new area in finance: the term real options was coined in 1977 by Stewart Myers. But publications on the topic did not appear in significant numbers until the mid 1980s, ten years after the publication of the Black and Scholes model. Real options analysis is rapidly gaining importance and some even predict that it will replace NPV as the central paradigm for investment decisions (Copeland and Antikarov, 2001, p. VI). As we shall see, real options analysis overcomes the weakness of NPV in valuing flexible projects. The Black and Scholes formula and its descendants allow us to calculate the value of flexibility, that is difficult to price with traditional discounted cash flow methods.

9.1 Investment opportunities as options

Before we turn to the valuation of real options, we shall first explore the similarities and differences between real and financial options and investigate what the sources of real option value are.

9.1.1 The option analogy

The flexibility to exercise or not is the essential characteristic that distinguishes options from passively held securities such as stocks and bonds. A similar flexibility is also attached to many investment projects in real (i.e. non-financial) assets. Most projects can be delayed or speeded up, made bigger or smaller, extended beyond their originally planned life-time or abandoned earlier. Each of those possibilities reflects managerial flexibility that, at least in principle, can be analyzed and valued like an option. That is the subject of real options analysis.

The option character of managerial flexibility can easily be illustrated with an example. Suppose a company has an exclusive one-year licence to run a project, say to develop a natural resource. The investment required for the project can be estimated accurately, but the revenue is subject to price uncertainty. The licence gives the company the flexibility to wait and see, i.e. to defer development until some of the price uncertainty is resolved and then make a better decision. This situation is analogous to holding a call option: the company has the right, but not the obligation, to 'buy' the revenue from the project by paying the required investment. Thus, the project's revenue can be regarded as the option's underlying value and the investment amount as the exercise price. The volatility is that of the price on which the revenue is based and the option expires with the licence, so in one year. Given a risk-free interest rate we have the five determinants of option prices: underlying value, exercise price, volatility, time to expiration and the risk-free interest rate. The analogy between the determinants of real and financial options is summarized in Table 9.1.

Table 9.1 *Stock–real option analogy*

Determinant	Stock option	Real option
underlying	stock	project revenue
strike	exercise price	investment
time to maturity	maturity	licence validity
volatility	stock σ	price volatility
interest rate	r_f	r_f

In the same way, the possibilities to expand a project to a larger size, or to extend it in time, can be regarded as call options on the cash flows generated by the expansion or extension. Alternatively, the possibility to reduce a project to a smaller size, to temporarily shut it down or to abandon it and sell its assets in a second-hand market, is equivalent to holding a put option. Table 9.2 lists some common real options, broken down by their character: calls, puts and compound options. Compound options are options on options.

Table 9.2 *Some common real options*

Call options	Put options	Compound options
defer	default	phase investment
expand	contract	switch inputs
extend	abandon	switch outputs
re-open	shut down	switch technology

9.1.2 Sources of real option value

For a financial option the source of value is obvious: a financial option is a written contract giving its holder the right to buy or sell at a fixed (exercise) price, while the market price is uncertain. This is also the case for some real options, such as the option to extend a service contract or a rent contract at a predetermined price; we will see an example of that later on. However, it is more usual that real options are not written contracts but investment opportunities with a varying degree of exclusiveness. For such real options the source of value is less simple than the difference between a fixed contractual price and a volatile market price. They rather derive their value from the advantages that a firm has over its competitors, enabling it to realize projects at lower costs. Major sources of this real option value are:

- patents and copyrights
- mineral (extraction) or surface (development) rights

- other property rights
- the firm's technical, commercial or managerial know-how
- the firm's market position, reputation or size
- market opportunities.

Patents, copyrights and mineral rights are probably the most obvious sources of real option value. Like financial options, they can be licensed or traded independently of any projects based on them. Ownership, too, is a straightforward source of option value: the owner of an asset has the right to sell it, thus exercising the abandonment option. In principle these rights are exclusive, so the real options based on them are *proprietary* (as opposed to *shared* options that are jointly held by a number of market parties). In practice, however, the proprietary nature of such real options tends to be eroded over time because competitors develop close substitutes.

A firm's expertise, in a broad sense, may put it in a better position to develop projects than competitors without this expertise. This is particularly true for follow-up projects that build on the technology, production facilities, distribution channels and/or customer base of established products. These follow-up projects can be realized at substantially lower costs than comparable projects by competitors who have to begin from scratch. In option terms, the established firm has an exercise price below the market price that competitors have to pay. Many options to expand or extend derive their values from this. These real options are also likely to lose their proprietary nature over time as competitors acquire the same know-how.

Although follow-up projects have become a classic case of real options (and we shall elaborate an example in a later section), they are not *necessarily* real options. The option nature can be absent in mature, established markets where large numbers of competitors face the same conditions on their input and output markets. On such markets, a firm's expertise, market position, reputation or size are not likely to make a difference when, e.g. capacity can be expanded with another production unit. All competitors can realize such an expansion against the same costs and generate the same revenue from it. In these circumstances the opportunity to expand has no option value. Expressed in option terminology: the option to buy or sell at market prices on some future date is worthless.

Market opportunities are a typical example of shared options. All competitors on a market have the possibility to introduce new products, technologies or distribution channels. These possibilities may have an option character if, for example, the first company to come with such a novelty has an advantage over latecomers.

9.1.3   Limitations of the option analogy

The analogy between managerial flexibility and financial options can be limited by several practical aspects, but also by the functioning of financial markets, or rather the lack thereof. Obvious practical differences are that real options are more complex and less clearly defined than financial options and that their determinants are less easy to measure. For example, the price today of a traded stock is readily observable and its volatility can be measured from historical data or implied from other option prices. The underlying value of a real option may be a project that is still in the planning stage; its value and volatility can be very difficult to ascertain.

Because financial options are written contracts, the provisions of the contract give a full specification of the option characteristics in terms of style, put or call, time to maturity and exercise price. Using these characteristics as inputs for option pricing models is no problem at all. Real options are not so well defined: they can have no determined time to maturity and the exercise price can be uncertain. This uncertainty does not necessarily decrease as time goes to maturity, so that the exercise decision may have to be made under uncertainty. At maturity, the payoffs of financial options are certain since both the exercise price and the value of the underlying are known. Table 9.3 summarizes some of the differences in input parameters.

Table 9.3 *Stock versus real option input parameters*

Determinant	Stock option	Real option
underlying	stock price today, known	PV (project revenue), estimated using asset pricing model
strike	fixed, specified in contract	investment amount, estimated, can vary over time
time to maturity	fixed, specified in contract	may be undetermined or dependent on actions competition
volatility	historical or implied	estimated or simulated
interest rate	r_f known, assumed constant	r_f known, assumed constant

Other practical differences are that most real options have much longer lives than financial ones and that real assets usually have a package of options attached to them. So unlike their financial counterparts, most real options are compound by nature. Compound options can interact, as we shall see later on. Moreover, exercising a financial option has no effect on the value of other financial options. When a real option is shared in some degree, its value to a company will depend on the exercise decisions of other companies that hold the same option. This means that the exercise decision not only depends on the difference between the underlying value and the exercise price, but also on the anticipation of decisions by other companies. All sorts of strategic or game theoretic arguments may play a role in such decisions. We will see a glimpse of that later on. As a rule, these arguments point to an early exercise of the option. This effect comes in addition to the erosion of the sources of real option value over time that we saw before. These arguments for early exercise do not apply to financial options.

As regards the functioning of financial markets, both the binomial and the Black and Scholes model rely on arbitrage and a replicating portfolio of existing assets to price options. To ensure that a replicating portfolio can be constructed in all cases, financial markets have to be perfect, complete and arbitrage free. If these assumptions are substantially violated, arbitrage can be hampered so that the application of option pricing techniques can be unwarranted. This argument applies to financial and real options alike. In practice, however, it is much easier to construct a replicating portfolio with a traded security than with an untraded project in the planning stage.

Several solutions to this problem have been suggested in the literature. Brennan and Schwartz (2001) evaluate investments in natural resource extraction, such as copper and gold mining, and use replicating portfolios consisting of future contracts in the relevant commodity. Where such contracts are available, this can be a theoretically and practically satisfactory solution. Notice, however, that future contracts only cover the price risk and not the risk of volume and quality that is inherent to mining operations. To handle this problem, Dixit and Pindyck (1994) suggest a dual approach in which the price risk is modelled by option valuation techniques and dynamic programming is used to model the volume and quality risks. Trigeorgis and Mason (2001) value a number of real options attached to the opportunity to build a plant; their replicating portfolio uses the stock of an 'identical' plant. Where feasible, this variant of the pure play method can be equally satisfactory as the previous one, but most stocks represent more than just one plant. Copeland and Antikarov (2001) take another approach and suggest to use the present value of the project itself, but without flexibility, to construct replicating portfolios for the real options attached to the project. They argue that this present value is the best unbiased estimate of the project's market value were it a traded asset. Their procedure allows the valuation of real options on any real asset for which a traditional, inflexible NPV can be calculated. However, the arbitrage that enforces the equality between the replicating portfolio and the real option, is not part of the argument.

We shall disregard these practical aspects and their possible solutions. Instead, we use a common practical short cut and assume that, for all underlying projects, a perfectly correlated 'twin security' is traded, or can be constructed, in financial markets. This means that we assume that the market is, at least locally, complete. Since most investment projects do not generate payoff patterns that expand the investment universe, this is not an unrealistic assumption. The analysis of various real options in the following sections is confined to this kind of project and, as usual, we will tacitly assume that the assumptions, that warrant the use of real options analysis, obtain.

9.2   The option to defer

To highlight the characteristics of real options pricing, the simple real option to defer an investment with one period is discussed in detail in this section, including a comparison with discounted cash flow techniques in decision trees.

9.2.1   Background and setting

To introduce the option to defer, we redefine our familiar binomial example as the problem of developing a natural resource, say an oil well that can be taken into production. The size of the reserve and the quality of the oil in it are accurately measured so that its value only depends on the oil price. This value develops over time as a binomial tree and is given as Lattice 10 below. The numbers in Lattice 10 represent the value of future production from the well, properly discounted, not cash flows. After two periods all uncertainty is assumed to be resolved and the values become stable. The risk-free interest rate is 7 per cent as before.

The real probability of upward movement is 80 per cent, and the risk-adjusted discount rate for oil production from wells such as this is 16 per cent. This is consistent with the tree in Lattice 10. The investment that is necessary to bring the well into production is 375 and the investment is irreversible, i.e. the firm cannot get the 375 back by closing the well. The investment amount increases with the risk-free rate over time.[1] Production is profitable from the start: $400 - 375 = 25$, a positive NPV.

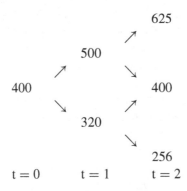

Lattice 10 The value of an oil well

To create a simple setting, we assume that a firm has an exclusive one-period licence to develop the well, so the source of real option value is clear. The licence gives the firm the flexibility to defer the decision to develop with one period and then make a better decision as some of the oil price uncertainty will be resolved. This flexibility is a real option because the firm has the right, but not the obligation, to develop the well. The project has the ingredients that make an option valuable: time and uncertainty. Without time, i.e. if the decision has to be made now or never, real options analysis offers no advantage over a traditional discounted cash flow approach. Similarly, without uncertainty the basis for a decision will be exactly the same one period later. But the combination of oil price uncertainty and one period to wait and see makes this real option valuable.

9.2.2 Valuing the real option

To value the option to defer, we have to reformulate the project as an option. The licence gives the firm the right to buy the value of production from the well by incurring the development costs of the 375. This makes it a call option with the value of the production as the underlying and the investment of 375 as the exercise price. The licence, and thus the option, has a time to maturity of one period. Together with the binomial process in Lattice 10 and the risk-free interest rate, that is all we need to value the option. The parameters of the binomial process are as before: $u = 1.25$, $d = 0.8$ and $r = 1.07$, so $p = (r - d)/(u - d) = (1.07 - .8)/(1.25 - .8) = 0.6$ and $(1 - p) = 0.4$.

As usual, we begin with the values at maturity, that is at $t = 1$ for this option, where the value is $max[0, project\ value - investment]$. Lattice 11 summarizes the calculations.

---

1 The choice of the risk-free rate here is arbitrary; the only purpose is to avoid that fixed investment costs become relatively cheaper over time.

The investment has become $375 \times 1.07 = 401.25$ because we calculate as if the project started one period later. In the upper node at t $= 1$ this is max$[0, 500 - 401.25] = 98.75$ and in the lower node max$[0, 320 - 401.25] = 0$. This makes the value of the option to defer $(0.6 \times 98.75)/1.07 = 55.37$.

$$\text{max}[0, 500 - 401.25] = 98.75$$

$$\nearrow$$

$$55.37$$

$$\searrow$$

$$\text{max}[0, 320 - 401.25] = 0$$

$$t = 0 \qquad\qquad\qquad t = 1$$

Lattice 11 The value of the option to defer

In the calculation we used the values of the whole project, so 55.37 is the project value plus the option to defer. Since the static (inflexible) project has a value of 25, the option is worth 30.37 and is more valuable than the project itself. In this simple setting it is easy to see why. The project is very profitable in the up node, but loss making in the down node. Both possibilities are included in the static t_0 value of 25. But the real option gives the firm the possibility to wait one period and see what the value becomes. If the oil price goes up, the well is developed and the firm profits from the opportunity. If the oil price goes down, the well is not developed and the firm avoids a loss. Moreover, not much is lost by waiting one period. The oil still is in the well, the licence still is valid. This is the essence of real option valuation. Note that after one period the licence is about to expire, so that the decision gets the now-or-never character that is inherent to the discounted cash flow approach. Also notice the difference in decision rules between NPV and real options analysis. The NPV method would accept the project right from the start (t $= 0$), since its NPV>0. Real options analysis recognizes the additional value of the flexibility embedded in the project (30.37), and this value would be given up if the real option is exercised by taking the well into production.

9.2.3 Comparison with discounted cash flow valuation in decision trees

It can be argued that it is also possible to capture the value of flexibility in a traditional discounted cash flow approach. We could calculate the NPV as if we start the project one period later and decide to abandon the project if the NPV is negative. This would give us the same 98.75 in the upper node and 0 in the lower node. The graphical representation is a decision tree with the same branches as in Lattice 11. A common way to calculate the value today in decision trees is to weight the branches with the real probabilities and discount the expected value with the risk-adjusted discount rate of, in this case, 16 per cent. The result is $((0.8 \times 98.75) + (0.2 \times 0))/1.16 = 68.10$. This differs from the 55.37 we got from the risk neutral valuation.

How can we ascertain which value is correct? The answer in modern finance is: by making a replicating portfolio. At this point we need the assumption of a locally complete financial market, so that a 'twin' security with the same payoff structure as in Lattice 10 can be constructed. Then we can replicate the payoffs and use the prices of the existing securities to price our investment opportunity. To replicate our option to invest we start with the option's delta and D, which are:

$$\Delta = \frac{O_u - O_d}{(u - d)S} = \frac{98.75 - 0}{500 - 320} = 0.5486 \text{ and}$$

$$D = \frac{uO_d - dO_u}{(u - d)r} = \frac{1.25 \times 0 - 0.8 \times 98.75}{1.25 \times 1.07 - 0.8 \times 1.07} = -164.07$$

At time t_1 this portfolio pays off either:

$$(0.5486 \times 500) - 164.07 \times 1.07 = 98.745 \text{ or}$$

$$(0.5486 \times 320) - 164.07 \times 1.07 = 0$$

so that the payoffs are replicated. The value now of the replicating portfolio is $(0.5486 \times 400) - 164.07 = 55.37$. This shows that the real option value is correct: no rational investor would pay 68.10 for a payoff pattern that can be replicated for 55.37 in the market.

So where does the decision tree approach go wrong? The error we made was applying the risk-adjusted discount rate for oil production from the well to the opportunity to develop the well. The *opportunity to do a project* seldom has the same risk characteristics as the project itself, precisely because the flexibility embedded in the opportunity is used to change the risk characteristics: the upward potential is enhanced and the downside risk is reduced. Once the well is taken into production, then its fortunes are tied to the oil price and the proper discount rate for cash flows and values from the well is 16 per cent. These values move through time with an uncertainty expressed in up factor of 1.25 and a down factor of 0.8. The opportunity to do the project, on the other hand, has a much larger uncertainty. It moves through time from 25 at t_0 to either 98.75 or 0 at t_1, an up factor of 3.95 and a down factor of 0. This corresponds to a much higher risk-adjusted discount rate.

In principle, it is possible to calculate the correct option value in a decision tree using the real probabilities and a risk-adjusted discount rate. The real probabilities are given as 0.8 and 0.2; they correspond to the risk-adjusted rate of 16 per cent for the project: $0.8 \times 0.25 + 0.2 \times -0.2 = 0.16$. But the risk-adjusted rate for the option has to be calculated from the replicating portfolio. That portfolio consists of $\Delta S = 0.5486 \times 400 = 219.44$ in the twin security S and a risk-free loan of -164.07. The weighted average return of this portfolio is:

$$\frac{219.44}{219.44 - 164.07} \times 0.16 + \frac{-164.07}{219.44 - 164.07} \times 0.07 = 0.427$$

This is more than twice the discount rate for the project. Discounting the expectation of the option's payoff with this rate gives the correct option value: $(0.8 \times 98.75 + 0.2 \times 0)/1.427 = 55.36$. However, once we have calculated ΔS and D, we already know the option value: $O = \Delta S + D = 219.44 - 164.07 = 55.37$. So this boils down to calculating the risk-adjusted discount rate *given* the option value: $55.37 = (0.8 \times 98.75)/r_{adj} \Rightarrow r_{adj} = 1.427$. Moreover, Δ and D can differ from node to node, so for each node in a tree a different risk-adjusted discount rate for the option has to be calculated. This makes the correct use of decision trees to calculate option values highly impractical: real options analysis is the preferred approach to valuing flexibility.

9.3 More real options

. . . .

9.3.1 A classic: follow-up investments

Many projects generate opportunities for follow-up investments that capitalize on the technology, production facilities, distribution channels and customer base that were developed in the first project. These follow-up projects have a real option nature if the original project, once completed successfully, gives the company an advantage over its competitors. This is obviously the case if the original project develops technology that can be protected by patents or copyrights. The probably best-known examples of this are found in the information technology sector. The pentium microprocessor, that powers most personal computers today, is the seventh or eighth generation of the x86 series of microprocessors that started in 1978 with the Intel 8086. Similarly, the Vista and Windows operating systems can be seen as follow-up projects of the original MS-DOS that was launched in 1979 to run on the 8086 processor. Clearly, the values of these follow-up projects are multiples of the original ones. But proprietary technology is not the only source of real option value. Another example is product-specific investments, that customers can have made, e.g. by learning how to use the product, and that would be lost if they switch to competitors' follow-up projects. Still other sources of real option value are the technical or commercial know-how and the reputation for reliability and good service that a firm can build up in the original project and that give it an advantage over inexperienced or unknown competitors in following projects.

To illustrate the option to do follow-up investments we reformulate our example in Lattice 10 in three ways. First, since an oil well is not a good example for follow-up projects, we re-interpret the data in more general terms, say a technology development project. The numbers in Lattice 10 still represent the properly discounted values of future revenues from the project; the uncertainty springs from the market's reaction to the project. Second, we now assume that the investment required for the original project is 450. This gives the project a negative NPV of $400 - 450 = -50$. Third, we assume that the project generates the opportunity to be repeated on a double scale after two periods. The first project is a prerequisite for the second; it can be thought of as an extension of the initial technology that doubles its application area. In financial terms this means that, at $t = 2$, the company can invest twice the exercise price in order to get twice the value of the future revenues in the end nodes of Lattice 10. As before, we assume that the exercise price increases with the risk-free interest rate of 7 per cent, that the real probability of an upward movement is 80 per cent and that the risk-adjusted discount rate is 16 per cent.

Since the follow-up project is twice the original project, its NPV is simply $2 \times -50 = -100$. The calculations are as follows. At $t = 2$, the value of the future revenues of the follow-up project are either $2 \times 625 = 1250$ or $2 \times 400 = 800$ or $2 \times 256 = 512$. The associated real probabilities are, in the same order: $0.8 \times 0.8 = .64$, $0.8 \times 0.2 + 0.2 \times 0.8 = 0.32$ and $0.2 \times 0.2 = 0.04$. So the expected value of the revenues is

$$0.64 \times 1250 + 0.32 \times 800 + 0.04 \times 512 = 1076.48$$

The present value of the expected revenues is $1076.48/1.16^2 = 800$, twice that of the original project. The NPV is $800 - (2 \times 450) = -100$. So with the information available today, the follow-up project is loss making, just as the first project. If the firm commits itself now to take it on, it is expected to lose money on it.

Real options analysis gives a different picture. It models the flexibility to take on the follow-up project if the market's reaction to the first project is favourable and to walk away when it is not. In options terms, the opportunity to do the follow-up project is a call option on the value of the project's future revenues with an exercise price of $2 \times 450 \times 1.07^2 = 1030.41$. The option will only be exercised at maturity when that is profitable, i.e. in the upper node at $t = 2$ where its payoff is $max[0, 1250 - 1030.41] = 219.59$. The option expires worthlessly in the other two nodes. This makes the $t = 1$ value $(0.6 \times 219.59)/1.07 = 123.13$ so that the value now is $(0.6 \times 123.13)/1.07 = 69.05$. The calculations are summarized in Lattice 12.

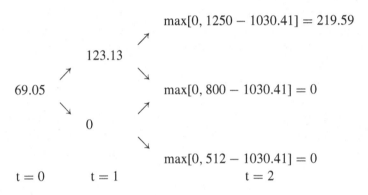

Lattice 12 The value of a follow-up project

Even though the option to do the follow-up project is (far) out of the money, it still has considerable value. It is so valuable that it makes it profitable to take on the first project: $-50 + 69.05 = 19.05$. The possibility to profit from market potential by doubling or tripling an unprofitable project makes this case a classic among real options and it is included in many textbooks on the subject. Of course, the value of follow-up investments was also recognized before real options analysis became available. It was usually estimated roughly as the 'strategic' value of a project. Modern option pricing techniques allow us to calculate that value more precisely. Again, it is easy to see that we cannot use the project's risk-adjusted return to discount the option's expected payoff, calculated with the real probabilities. The calculation would be $(0.64 \times 219.59)/1.16^2 = 104.44$. This overestimates the value because the flexibility embedded in the follow-up project makes it more risky than the project itself. Finally, notice that the future expansion opportunity, that makes the whole project profitable, is uncertain. It is possible that the market develops unfavourably, so that the follow-up option expires out of the money at $t = 2$. With hindsight, this may give the false impression that too much was paid for the first project or that investors were 'irrationally exuberant'.

9.3.2 The abandonment option

In the chapter on capital structure we saw that general-purpose assets such as buildings and trucks are easy to finance. They can readily be re-deployed by other companies and, hence, have a high second-hand value. From a real options perspective, a high second-hand value means a valuable opportunity to abandon a project and sell its assets in the second-hand market if that is more profitable than continuing its operations. That flexibility is more general and includes the opportunity to re-deploy assets in another project if that is more profitable. For example, a shipyard situated on an attractive riverside location may have the option to abandon shipbuilding and re-develop its site as a residential area.

A typical way to model second-hand value (or alternative use) is to assume a dynamic process with a lower volatility (smaller up and down steps) for the second-hand value than for the original project. Combined with the lower second-hand value at $t = 0$, this means that the project value will fall below the second-hand value after a number of down steps. A simpler way, that we shall use, is to assume no volatility, i.e. a constant second-hand value.

To illustrate the abandonment option we return to our example in Lattice 10 and extend it with the possibility to sell the project's assets in the second-hand market for a fixed price of 325. Thus formulated, the abandonment option is an American put. We can value this option by including the condition max[*continue, abandon*] in all nodes of the value tree for the project, as Lattice 13 shows. The 'continue' value in the lower node at $t = 1$ is calculated as $((0.6 \times 400) + (0.4 \times 325))/1.07 = 345.79$, which is larger than the abandonment value of 325. The $t = 0$ value is calculated as $((0.6 \times 500) + (0.4 \times 345.79))/1.07 = 409.64$, which again is larger than the abandonment value of 325. Since the corresponding value without the option is 400, the abandonment option has a value of 9.64. Notice that we can also include the condition max[*continue, abandon*] in the final ($t = 2$) nodes of Lattice 13 because the numbers are the values of future cash flows from the project. Lattice 13 summarizes the calculations.

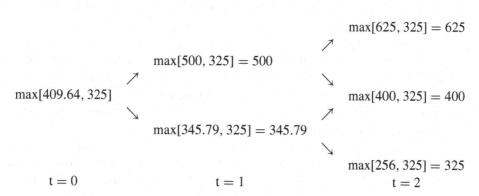

Lattice 13 Project value with abandonment option

We can also value the option separately. The abandonment option is an American put, so we have to check the exercise condition max[*dead, alive*] in all nodes. When the option is exercised we sell the project in the second-hand market for 325 so the option value is max[0, 325 − *project value*]. At $t = 2$, the option is only in the money in the lower node, where its value is max[0, 325 − 256] = 69. The value of this option alive in the lower node at $t = 1$ is $(0.4 \times 69)/1.07 = 25.79$. The corresponding value dead is max[0, 325 − 320] = 5. This gives a value alive now of $(0.4 \times 25.79)/1.07 = 9.64$, which is higher than the value dead of $\max[0, 325 - 400] = 0$. Lattice 14 summarizes the calculations.

Lattice 14 The abandonment option

9.3.3 The option to phase investments

Many projects are completed in a number of more or less separate stages. A construction project, for example, can involve a preparation stage to obtain the necessary licences and do the groundwork, a construction stage for the building proper and a finishing stage. With such a project structure, the required investment is not made in one large outlay, but in a series of smaller successive amounts. From a real options perspective, this situation offers the flexibility, at each stage, to continue the project or to abandon it. Each stage can be regarded as a call option on the next. In this option analogy, the investment required for the first stage is the option premium that has to be paid to buy a call option on the second stage, etc. As every other call, the option on the next stage will only be exercised if the underlying value is larger than the exercise price. The underlying is the option on the next stage, including the value of the options on all subsequent stages, which is equal to the properly calculated project value.

To illustrate the option to phase investments, we extend our binomial example with the assumption that the project's investment of 375 can be made in two stages, 50 now and the rest next period. As usual, we assume that investment amounts grow at risk-free rate over time so that the t = 1 investment is $(375 - 50) \times 1.07 = 347.75$. In the nodes at t = 1 we include the condition that the project value is $\max[0, project\ value - investment]$. If the required investment is larger than the remaining project value, the project is abandoned and its value drops to zero. The t = 0 value is calculated as $(0.6 \times 152.25)/1.07 = 85.37$, which gives a net present project value of $85.37 - 50 = 35.37$. So the value of the option to phase the investment is $35.37 - 25 = 10.37$. The calculations are summarized in Lattice 15. Of course, we can also calculate the option value separately. The exercise condition is then that we keep the investment amount (i.e. we do not invest) by giving up the project value: $\max[0, investment - project\ value]$. The option is only in the money in the lower node of t = 1, where its exercise value is $\max[0, 347.75 - 320] = 27.75$. This gives a t = 0 value of $(0.4 \times 27.75)/1.07 = 10.37$.

$$625$$

$$\max[0, 500 - 347.75] = 152.25$$

$$400$$

$$\max[0, 85.37 - 50] = 35.37$$

$$\max[0, 320 - 347.75] = 0$$

$$I = -50 \qquad\qquad I = -347.75$$
$$t = 0 \qquad\qquad t = 1 \qquad\qquad t = 2$$

Lattice 15 Project value with phased investments

This option has some counter-intuitive elements, that often lead to confusion. The first of these elements is that, at $t = 0$, we only consider the investment for the present stage, while we know that another investment is required next period to complete the project. Would not it be better to include the present value of all future investments? That is what the discounted cash flow approach would do. In real options analysis, the future investments are not ignored, they are included as the exercise prices of the later options that are part of the project's value. The decision whether or not to exercise these options is made later, based on the information that will be available then. Another element that may be confusing is that we ignore the value of investments in earlier stages. Would not those investments be wasted if we decide to abandon the project, as in the lower node of $t = 1$? To the extent that the earlier investments are irreversible (and they usually are), they are 'wasted' already. Including them would be the 'sunk cost fallacy' we saw in the second chapter.[2] But if much is already invested, would not a comparatively small investment produce a large project? Exactly, and that is what we model in real options analysis, but the project should be large in terms of future cash flows, not past investments.

9.3.4 The option to default a loan

Options attached to a loan are financial, not real options. But since most projects are partly financed with debt, the option to default a loan is often discussed in the context of real options. Financial leverage can be included in our binomial example by assuming that the initial investment of 375 is partly financed with a loan of 300. The remaining 75 is provided by the owners. We further assume that the debt consists of a zero coupon loan with a nominal interest rate of 9.5 per cent and a maturity of two periods. This means that the lenders provide 300 today against the promise to be paid back 359.71 $(= 300 \times 1.095^2)$ after two periods, with no interest payments in between. If the owners have limited liability, they have the option to default the loan. When the project value is less than the amount due to the lenders, the owners will default and be declared bankrupt, so that the remaining project value goes to the lenders. It is easy to see that this will only happen in the lower node at $t = 2$, where the project value is 256.

---

2 Also called 'Concorde fallacy' after the British-French supersonic airliner; the United States has its own striking example with the Lockheed TriStar, described by Reinhardt (1973).

In the perfect markets we model here, the transfer of the project from the owners to the lenders is costless, i.e. there are no bankruptcy costs. Moreover, there are no taxes that favour debt, nor is there any information asymmetry that may lead to under- or over-pricing. We know from our earlier analyses that capital structure is irrelevant under such circumstances: the division over debt and equity does not change the total project value. Each capital category gets the market price for the risk it bears. We can calculate the value of equity as in Lattice 16.

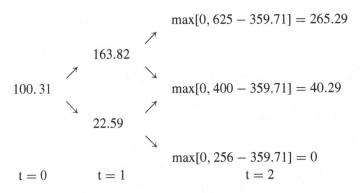

Lattice 16 The value of levered equity

The equity values at $t = 1$ are calculated as $((0.6 \times 265.29) + (0.4 \times 40.29))/1.07 = 163.82$ and $((0.6 \times 40.29) + (0.4 \times 0))/1.07 = 22.59$ so that the value of equity is $((0.6 \times 163.82) + (0.4 \times 22.59))/1.07 = 100.31$. This gives an NPV of $100.31 - 75 = 25.31$ practically equal to the 25 we had before. The value of debt can be calculated in the same way, as Lattice 17 shows.

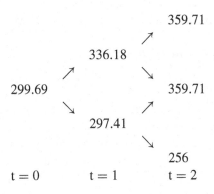

Lattice 17 The value of debt

The $t = 1$ values are $359.71/1.07 = 336.18$ and $((0.6 \times 359.71) + (0.4 \times 256))/1.07 = 297.41$, so that the value of debt is $((0.6 \times 336.18) + (0.4 \times 297.41))/1.07 = 299.69$. The total project value is $100.31 + 299.69 = 400$ as before, the change in capital structure doesn't add value, it just divides it differently. From this we can also infer that the market interest rate for loans as risky as the one in our project is 8.9 per cent. This is calculated by taking the loan's expected payoff using the real probabilities:

$$0.8^2 \times 359.71 + 2 \times 0.8 \times 0.2 \times 359.71 + 0.2^2 \times 256 = 355.56$$

and then solving $355.56/r^2 = 300$ for r, which gives 1.0887.

The fact that total project value does not change does *not* mean that the option to default a loan has no value. Rather, the option transfers value from one capital category to other. To demonstrate this, we first calculate the value of the option separately. The option to default gives the owners the flexibility to:

- either keep the project by paying the debtholders the amount due to them
- or keep the amount due the debtholders by giving them the project.

The former part formulates the flexibility as the owners' right to 'buy back' the project from the debtholders by paying them off. Hence, it models limited liability equity as a call option on the project's assets with the amount due to debtholders as the exercise price. We valued this option in Lattice 16 (without saying that it is an option). It gives the value of the project to the shareholders including the option to walk away if the project value is lower than what they have to pay the debtholders.

The latter part formulates the same flexibility as the owners' right to 'sell' the project to the debtholders by keeping the amount due to them. So it models the flexibility as a put option, with the exercise condition max[0, *amount due − project value*]. This option is only in the money in the lower node of t = 2, where its exercise value is max[0, 359.71 − 256] = 103. 71. This gives a t = 0 value of $(0.4^2 \times 103.71)/1.07^2 = 14.49$.

By giving the loan, the lenders have effectively written the put as part of the deal. But the put is included at its proper price. If the payment to the debtholders would have been risk-free, its value would have been $359.71/1.07^2 = 314.18$. Since the debtholders only supplied 300, they correctly subtracted the value of the written put. Without the put, equity would have unlimited liability, which means that it can have negative value. Its value would be as is calculated in Lattice 18. The t = 1 values are $((0.6 \times 265.29) + (0.4 \times 40.29))/1.07 = 163.82$ and $((0.6 \times 40.29) + (0.4 \times (-103.71)))/1.07 = -16.18$ so that the t = 0 value is $((0.6 \times 163.82) + (0.4 \times (-16.18)))/1.07 = 85.81$.

Lattice 18 The value of unlimited liability equity

We see that the value of limited liability equity (100.31) is the value of unlimited liability equity (85.81) plus the value of the put (14.49). Finally, notice that the value of unlimited liability equity is the difference between the value of the underlying project (400) and the present value of the risk-free payment to the debtholders ($359.71/1.07^2 = 314.18$). If we combine these two equalities we get that the value of limited liability equity (100.31) equals the value of the underlying project (400) minus the present value of the risk-free payment to the debtholders (314.18) plus the value of the put (14.49). This is the put–call parity: call = share − PV(X) + put, but now in a very different corporate context.

The option to default a loan has some other, far-reaching consequences that we will discuss in the next chapter.

9.4   Interacting real options

Most projects have several real options attached to them and the options can interact. This occurs when their values meet somewhere in the value tree. Option interaction is discussed with a longer example from the dredging industry.

9.4.1   Background and problem

ZX Co is an international dredging contractor with projects around the world. Its main activities are the construction of waterways and harbours, coastal defences and waterway protection. It operates a fleet of dredging and support vessels ranging from modern cutter suction dredgers to traditional bucket dredgers.

The company is negotiating a harbour renovation project with a port authority in the Middle East. The project will involve one of the largest bucket dredgers in the fleet with a capacity of over $30,000 \text{m}^3$. ZX Co's project engineers have calculated that it will take the dredger one and a half years (three periods of six months, a frequently used time unit in dredging) to complete the project. The state of the negotiations is that the port authority is willing to pay the current world market rate of €30 million per half year for the entire one-and-a-half-year period. ZX Co is inclined to accept that price, since it can operate the dredger and its support vessels for considerably less money per half year. However, the port authority wants to include one or both of the following two clauses in the contract:

- The clause that it can extend the contract with one half-year period at the same rate; the extra half year will be used to construct a small marina adjacent to the harbour.
- The clause that it can terminate the contract at the beginning of the second and third half-year period by paying a penalty of €2.5 million per remaining period; reduction of the project may be necessary because of budget cuts.

To help the negotiating team, that mainly consists of engineers, we are asked to calculate how the clauses affect the value of the project, both separately and in combination.

We can use the following background information. The world market rate for this type of dredging project is very volatile, corresponding to a yearly standard deviation of 25 per cent. For practical purposes, it can be assumed that the rates are only adjusted at the beginning of each half-year period and then stay constant until the beginning of the next period. The risk-free interest rate is 6 per cent per year. The market for dredging projects is such that the vessels can be redeployed immediately at market prices, so we can ignore the cost of idle capacity.

9.4.2 Analysis

The clause to extend the contract gives the port authority the right, but not the obligation, to buy dredging services 18 months from now at a price fixed today. So it is a real option equivalent to a long position in a European call. Note that the addition 'at a price fixed today' is essential for the option character. The right to buy or sell something at market prices is not a valuable option. Similarly, the clause to terminate the contract after six and twelve months is equivalent to a long position in an American put option. It gives the port authority the right, but not the obligation, to 'sell back' the obligation to pay €30 million per half year in return for paying €2.5 million plus the market price for dredging services that have to be bought elsewhere if the contract is terminated. The port authority's request to include the clauses means that it asks ZX Co to write the two options. The value of the project changes therefore with the values of the options. We analyze these values from an economic perspective, i.e. we assume that the options will be exercised if that is beneficial to their holder, without regard for the apparent motives to include them in the contract.

The underlying values of the options are (elements of) the contract and the source of volatility is the world market rate for this type of dredging project. Since the rates are only adjusted at the beginning of each half year, we can calculate the value of these options with the binomial method. The parameters of the binomial process can be calculated as follows:

$$u = e^{0.25\sqrt{0.5}} = 1.193 \qquad d = 1/u = .838 \qquad r = \sqrt{1.06} = 1.03$$

$$p = \frac{1.03 - 0.838}{1.193 - 0.838} = 0.541 \qquad 1 - p = 0.459$$

Note that the volatility and the interest rate are re-scaled to half-year values. With these parameters we can construct the binomial tree for dredging rates. Since both options refer to half-year periods, it is convenient to use half-year rates. The tree is presented in Lattice 19.

9.4.3 The option to extend

The value of this option is found with the familiar procedure of calculating the pay-offs at maturity and then working our way back through the lattice. The option will be exercised if the market rate is higher than the contract rate and it will expire worth-lessly otherwise: max[0, *market rate − contract rate*]. The value tree for the option is given in Lattice 20, which shows that the option ends in the money in the upper two end nodes. Discounting these two end node values back through the tree using the risk-neutral probabilities and the risk-free rate we get the values in Lattice 20 and the option value now of 5.17.

9.4.4 The option to terminate

To value this option we use the procedure for American options that can be exercised early, i.e. we compare the values 'dead' and 'alive'. We start at the end of the tree, which, for this option, is at t = 2, the beginning of the third period (the option

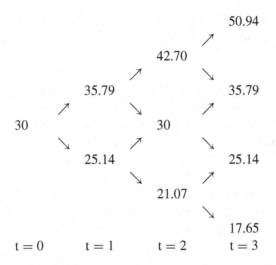

Lattice 19 Tree for half-year dredging rates

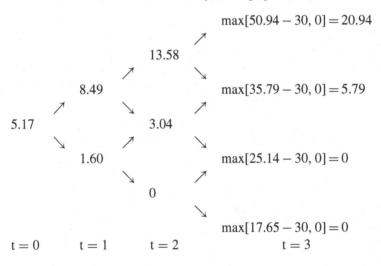

Lattice 20 Value tree for the option to extend

can only be exercised after six and twelve months). After the third period the contract ends (unless it is extended). The inputs for this real option require some extra attention. Consider the lower node at $t=2$ where the dredging rate is 21.07. If the option to terminate is exercised, the port authority reverses the obligation to pay €30 million for half a year's dredging. So it does not have to pay €30 million, but instead it has to pay €2.5 million penalty plus the market rate for dredging for the third period. This makes the payoff at maturity $max[(30 - (21.07 + 2.5)), 0] = 6.43$. Applying the same calculation to the two upper $t=2$ nodes gives zero values for both. Discounting these values back one period gives $(0.459 \times 6.643)/1.03 = 2.87$ in the lower node at $t=1$ and 0 in the other. These are the $t=1$ values 'alive', as depicted in Lattice 21.

$$max[(30 - (42.70 + 2.5)), 0] = 0$$

(0)
dead or alive

1.71

$$max[(30 - (30 + 2.5)), 0] = 0$$

max[(3.84), (2.87)]
dead   alive

$$max[(30 - (21.07 + 2.5)), 0] = 6.43$$

t = 0   t = 1   t = 2

Lattice 21 Value tree for the option to terminate

The payoff of exercising the option in the lower node at t = 1 consists of three parts. The first part is the price advantage over the second period of $30 - 25.14 = 4.86$. The second part is the present value of the expected price advantage over the third period, that is $(0.459 \times (30 - 21.07))/1.03 = 3.98$. In the middle node of t = 2 there is no price advantage. The third part is the penalty of $2 \times 2.5 = 5$ million. So the total value 'dead' is $4.86 + 3.98 - 5 = 3.84$. The value dead is larger than the value alive, so the option should be exercised. This gives a value now of $(0.459 \times 3.84)/1.03 = 1.71$.

9.4.5 Combined option value

It is tempting to calculate the value now (t = 0) of both options combined as simply the sum of the two: $1.71 + 5.17 = 6.88$. But this would be wrong because the options interact, making their combined value *less* than the sum of the separate values. In this simple example it is easy to see why. Analyzing the options separately we concluded that the optimal decision is to exercise the option to terminate in the lower node at t = 1. However, comparing the value trees for the options in Lattices 20 and 21 we see that the option to extend the contract also has value in this node. Exercising the option to terminate will eliminate this value; it is impossible to extend a contract that was cancelled two periods ago.

To calculate the combined option value we have to adjust the 'dead' value of the option to terminate at t = 1 with the lost value of the option to extend: $3.84 - 1.60 = 2.24$. This makes the value 'dead' lower than the value 'alive', which is 2.87, so the optimal decision is *not* to exercise the option. The t = 0 value thus becomes $(0.459 \times 2.87)/1.03 = 1.28$ and the total value of the options combined is $1.28 + 5.17 = 6.45$, or 0.43 less than the sum of the separate values. The combined option values are depicted in Lattice 22. Notice that the payoff of exercising the option to terminate at t = 2 does not have to be corrected for any lost value of the option to extend. It will only be exercised in the lower node at t = 2 where the option to extend has no value. The two options do interact, however, because the option to extend influences the value of the option to terminate as well as the optimal exercise decision.

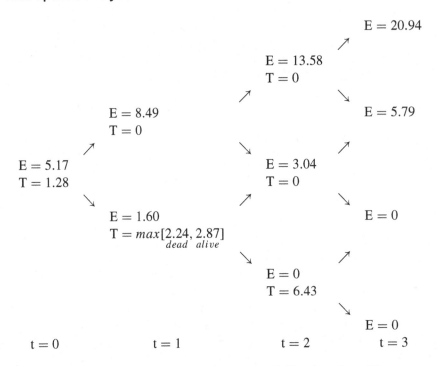

Lattice 22 Value tree for the options to extend (E) and terminate (T)

The example also illustrates more general aspects of real options in contracting. In the case elaborated here, the port authority skilfully uses clauses in the contract to create real options that enhance its upward potential and reduce its downside risk. If the market rate for dredging goes up, it has the option to extend the agreement at the lower contract rate. If the market rate goes down, it has the option to terminate the contract and buy dredging services at the lower market rate. These real options constitute a considerable value: the combined option value of €6.45 million is likely to be the lion's share of the project's profits. ZX Co should not include them in the contract without proper compensation. Also notice that the option to extend may look favourable from a salesperson's point of view. The present rate is profitable and extending a profitable contract appears to be profitable as well. This ignores the drivers of real option value: flexibility, time and uncertainty. Flexibility means that the contract will only be extended if the uncertain market rate becomes higher over time, so that extension is unprofitable for ZX Co.

9.5 Two extensions

9.5.1 More on option interaction

Financial options seldom interact. They are traded independently of the asset they are written on and exercising a financial option usually affects neither other options nor the underlying value. Among the rare examples of interacting financial options are the options embedded in complex securities, such as callable convertible bonds and putable callable bonds.

Most real options interact because exercising a real option affects its underlying value and, hence, the value of subsequent real options. To analyze the interaction a bit further we first look at the theoretical interaction effects, holding everything else equal. This procedure is comparable to the calculation of Greeks for a financial option, but we only look at the qualitative effect (plus or minus). Then we investigate how well the ceteris paribus condition fits the nature of real options. For the theoretical analysis we assume a project with two real options whose exercise dates are separated in time.

Since options cannot have negative values, the presence of the second option increases the underlying value of the first option.[3] This means that the value of the first option will increase if it is a call and decrease if it is a put. Moreover, if the first option is a call it will, if exercised, increase the value of the underlying. This will, in turn, increase the value of the second option if the second option is a call, and decrease the value of the second option if the second option is a put. Similarly, if the first option is a put it will, if exercised, decrease the value of the underlying. This will increase the value of the second option if the second option is a put, and decrease the value of the second option if the second option is a call. This pattern of interactions is depicted in Figure 9.1, where ⇑ means increased value and ⇓ means decreased value.

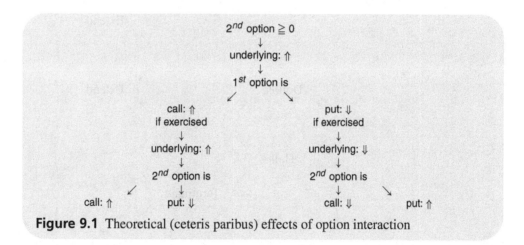

Figure 9.1 Theoretical (ceteris paribus) effects of option interaction

Obviously, the total interaction effect is strongest if all the value arrows (⇑ or ⇓) point in the same direction. Options combinations of the same type (two puts or two calls) tend to increase the total interaction effect, combinations of different types (a put and a call) tend to decrease it. Further, the options have to 'meet' somewhere in the value tree, i.e. there must be nodes in which one option can be exercised and the other one has value, i.e. a non-zero probability of ending in the money. This will generally be the

---

3 We ignore the trivial case of options with zero value.

case with two options of the same type, because they are exercised in the same sort of scenarios of value development (typically calls in the upper part of the tree, puts in the lower part). But options of opposite type must have different times to maturity and/or exercise prices in order to interact. For example, a put and call on the same underlying with the same exercise price and maturity will not interact because they are exercised in mutually exclusive scenarios. If one is exercised, the other has zero value. The probability of interaction increases as the possible exercise dates are more spread in time and as the exercise prices are closer or overlap more.

The theoretical effects also apply to real options, but without the ceteris paribus condition. Exercising a real option not only changes the value of the underlying, but also the specifications of later options, particularly the exercise price. To illustrate this, we reformulate the dredging example from the previous section and analyze it qualitatively (i.e. without calculating values). Assume that there are three options attached to the project. The first is the option to reduce the project by 50 per cent (e.g. by switching to a dredger with half the capacity at half the rate) or double the project (by hiring a second dredger at the same rate). This option matures at $t = 1$. The second is the option to terminate the project at $t = 2$, with a penalty of €2.5 million per remaining period as specified in the previous section. The third is the option to extend the project at $t = 3$ at the same rate, also as specified before. These options are depicted in Lattice 23 in the nodes where they will be exercised.

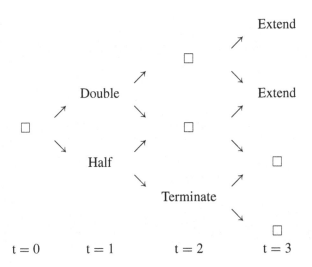

Lattice 23 Real options attached to dredging project

If the dredging rate increases from 30 to 35.79 at $t = 1$, the option to double the project will be exercised. If the dredging rate subsequently reaches one of the two upper nodes at $t = 3$, the double-sized project will be extended. This makes the option to extend almost twice as valuable, because the port authority now holds two options to hire a dredger at the rate of 30 for one additional period.[4] Notice that this is not the same as holding one option on twice as valuable an underlying, as the theoretical analysis above would suggest. The difference is the exercise price, that also doubles to two times 30. Similarly, if the project is halved in the lower node of t = 1, the specifications of the option to terminate the project will also be changed. Only half of the obligation to pay €30 million for six months' dredging will be reversed, and only half of the capacity will have to be bought at market prices. The provisions of the contract are also likely to stipulate that the €2.5 million penalty will be halved, or at least reduced. So here, too, 'other things' are not likely to be equal.

It is also possible that exercising a real option changes the time to maturity of a later option. This would be the case in the dredging example if the project had some terminal value, e.g. temporary equipment that can be sold. The time to maturity of this abandonment option would be lengthened by exercising the option to extend the project.

9.5.2 A game-theoretic extension

The main source of uncertainty in the real options we have analyzed so far is the market, more precisely the price the market is willing to pay for (the products of) our underlying project. That price may depend on the actions of competitors but we did not explicitly model that dependence, i.e. we assumed that competition is exogenous. However, when a real option is shared in some degree, the exercise decision of one of the firms that holds the option is likely to influence the value of the option for the other firms. In such a situation, option pricing techniques are no longer sufficient and we have to extend them with elements from game theory.

Game theory studies decision making behaviour in situations where the results of participants' choices depend on the choices of other participants. Game theory is a comparatively new branch of (economic) science; its seminal text is 'Theory of Games and Economic Behavior' by von Neumann and Morgenstern (1944). The basic theory was developed in the 1950s and 1960s, it expanded into many other sciences in later decades and is now a blossoming academic discipline.[5] A pioneering publication, that links game theory and real options analysis, is Smit and Trigeorgis (2004). We shall illustrate the use of game theory with an example based on one of its most widely known topics, the prisoners' dilemma.

In the prisoners' dilemma, two suspects of a crime, A and B, are interrogated separately by the police. Each is offered the deal that when he or she confesses, the sentence will be reduced to ten years. If he or she is willing to provide evidence against the other, while the other denies, the sentence of the confessor will be further reduced to two and a half years, while the denier gets the full sentence of twenty years. However, the evidence against the suspects is so weak that both will be sentenced to five years if they both deny. The choices and their consequences are summarized in Table 9.4.

---

[4] The lower of the two upper nodes at $t = 3$ can also be reached through the 'half' node at $t = 1$, which reduces the value of the option to extend.

[5] Among the game theorists that were awarded the Nobel prize in economics are J.C. Harsanyi, J.F. Nash and R. Selten, who shared the prize in 1994, and R.J. Aumann and T.J. Schelling, who shared the prize in 2005.

Table 9.4 *Prisoners' dilemma*

		B	
		confess	**deny**
A	confess	10, **10**	2.5, **20**
	deny	20, **2.5**	5, **5**

Data for B are **in bold**

The dilemma for each suspect is what to do, confess or deny. In this case they both have a *dominant strategy*, i.e. a strategy that gives better results than all other strategies, no matter what the other suspect chooses. If suspect B confesses, A is better off when she confesses than when she denies (ten versus twenty years). But if suspect B denies, suspect A is also better off when she confesses than when she denies (two and a half versus five years). The same is true for suspect B: he is better off if he confesses, no matter whether A confesses or denies. The equilibrium situation that arises is known as *Nash equilibrium*, after the Nobel prize-winning mathematician and economist John Nash. In such an equilibrium, no participant wants to change his or her strategy, once the strategies of the other participants become known.

Strategic choices with a payoff structure as in Table 9.4 are found in many different situations in economics and finance. Shared real options, for example, can have such a payoff structure. To illustrate that, we return to the option to defer in our binomial example (Lattices 10 and 11) and make the following adjustments. First, we assume that the investment amount of 375 increases over time with the risk-adjusted rate of 16 per cent per period. This makes the t = 1 investment $375 \times 1.16 = 435$. The value of the option to defer then becomes as in Lattice 24.

$$\max[0, 500 - 435] = 65$$

$$36.45 \nearrow$$
$$\searrow$$

$$\max[0, 320 - 435] = 0$$

t = 0   t = 1

Lattice 24 The value of the option to defer

The t = 0 value is calculated as $(0.6 \times 65)/1.07 = 36.45$. The NPV of investing now (t = 0) remains $400 - 375 = 25$, as before. Deferring is still more profitable than investing immediately. The second adjustment is that we now assume that the option does not refer to a proprietary option such as developing an oil well, but to a market opportunity that is shared by two competitors, A and B. The opportunity can be thought of as the introduction of a new product, or an existing product in a new market. Each firm has the option to invest immediately or to defer investment with one period. We further assume that if both competitors choose the same action simultaneously, they equally share the market value.

Hence, if both invest now, each gets $25/2 = 12.5$ and if both defer investment with one period, each gets $36.45/2 = 18.22$. Finally, we assume that the market is characterized by a first mover advantage: the first firm to enter the market acquires a decisive advantage over its competitors. The sources of first mover advantage include technological leadership, the monopolization of distribution channels with limited capacity and product switching costs for customers. In our example, first mover advantage means that if one firm invests before the other, the investment becomes pre-emptive and prevents the competitor from entering the market. Hence, the investing firm appropriates the whole market value. This gives the payoff structure in Table 9.5.

The market situation in Table 9.5 is equivalent to the prisoners' dilemma. Both firms have a dominant strategy. If firm B invests, it is more profitable for firm A to invest than to defer (NPV of 12.5 versus 0). But if firm B defers, it is also more profitable for firm A to invest than to defer (NPV of 25 versus 18.22). The same is true for firm B: it is more profitable for B to invest, regardless of A's timing decision. The resulting Nash equilibrium is that both firms invest immediately. Of course, the irony of this equilibrium, both in the original prisoners' dilemma and in the application in strategic investment timing, is that both participants would be better off if they could cooperate. The example also illustrates the more general result that, in a real options context, the strategic anticipation of competitors' actions tends to lead to an early exercise of real options.

Table 9.5 *Strategic investment timing*

		B	
		invest	**defer**
A	invest	12.5, **12.5**	25, **0**
	defer	0, **25**	18.22, **18.22**

Data for B are **in bold**

Summarizing, we have now seen three influences on the timing of investment decisions. The first springs from the analogy between investment decisions and financial options. This influence tends to favour late investment: it is profitable to maintain flexibility because uncertainty resolves over time. The second follows from the nature of real options, particularly the sources of real options value. This influence generally leads to early investment, because the sources of real options value erode over time. The third influence stems from game-theoretic considerations, that also contribute to early investment.

Exercises

1. Discuss the following cases from a (real) options point of view:
   (a) Norsk Hydro, a global supplier of aluminium with activities throughout the value chain, considers expanding its aluminium production by installing an aluminium

smelter. Smelter installations use standard technology that is available in the market in any quantity. The produced aluminium is a bulk product that is sold in commodity markets by large numbers of producers.

(b) The presence of vacant plots of land in city centres.

(c) Hewlett-Packard decided to adapt its inkjet printers to local languages in local depositories. Although adaptation in central production facilities is much cheaper, HP's decision proved to be very profitable.

2. In the section about bounds on option prices we saw that American call options on non-dividend-paying stocks are never exercised before maturity (bound 9). Explain why real options with a call nature are often exercised early.

3. State Drilling has a concession that gives it the right to develop a small natural gas field. The concession expires in one year. The field will produce 100 million m^3 gas per year for four years. The investment required to develop the field is $30 million, to be paid immediately. If development is postponed the investment amount will increase over time with the risk-free interest rate. Production and cash flows from selling the gas will start one year after the investment. The current gas price is $0.08 per m^3 but that price develops over time according to a binomial process: after each period the price can go up with 25 per cent or down with 20 per cent. The probability of an upward movement in price is 80 per cent. The risk-adjusted discount rate for cash flows from gas production from the field is 16 per cent and the risk-free interest rate is 7 per cent.

(a) What is the value of the gas reserve in the field?

(b) What is the value of the opportunity to develop the field and when should it be developed?

4. The well-known investor Peter Smalldale owns a chain of hotels. He plans to expand his activities into a city that has announced its candidacy to host the European football championship two years from now. If the city gets the championship, the new hotel's (and the city's) reputation will be made and it will generate a perpetual cash flow of €20 million per year. However, if the city does not get the championship, the hotel will fall into oblivion and the perpetual cash flow will only be €10 million per year. The football association will decide one year from now where the championship is to be held. There is general agreement among insiders that the probability that the city in question will get the championship is 37.5 per cent. Peter Smalldale has an offer from CCI, Construction Consortium Inc., to build the hotel for a price of €120 million, to be paid when the offer is accepted. Construction will start immediately and the hotel will be ready two years from now, in time for the championship. However, the offer is only valid if accepted immediately.

(a) If the proper discount rate for cash flows and values from the hotel is 10 per cent, what is the NPV of the project if it is accepted immediately?

Smalldale wants to postpone his investment decision until it becomes known where the championship will be held. CCI can build the hotel in one year for the same price of €120 million by allocating a double workforce to the project. However, CCI's director followed a course in finance for science and technology students and anticipates that

Smalldale will cancel the project if the championship goes to another city. To compensate for the profit that CCI misses if the project is cancelled, it asks an immediate payment of €12 million. When that payment is made, CCI is willing to build the centre in one year, starting one year from now, for €120 million (to be paid at the start).

(b) If the risk-free rate is 5 per cent, is postponement profitable for Smalldale with this offer from CCI? Calculate the increase or decrease in project value compared with the now-or-never project under (a).

(c) What is the risk-adjusted discount rate for the project opportunity under (b)?

5. In June 2007 the Norwegian company Aker ASA signed a cooperation agreement with the Norwegian Ministry of Trade and Industry and the Swedish Wallenberg group. The cooperation was organized in a new company, Aker Holding, in which Aker ASA held 60 per cent of the shares, the Norwegian state 30 per cent and the Wallenberg group 10 per cent. When the agreement was signed, the total value of the shares was 16 billion (10^9) Norwegian kroner. The agreement stipulated that Aker ASA and the Norwegian state would hold their position in Aker Holding for at least ten years, but the Wallenberg group had the right to sell its shares to Aker ASA after four years at their original price plus a return of 10 per cent. In addition, Aker ASA had the right to buy the Wallenberg group's shares after four years at their original price plus a return of 40 per cent. (Data are based on a press release from Aker ASA dated 22 June 2007.)

(a) Describe the position of the Wallenberg group when the deal was signed in terms of option positions. Be precise in style, moneyness and maturity.

(b) Assuming no dividends, a risk-free interest rate of 5 per cent per year, and an annual volatility of Aker Holding returns of 20 per cent, what was the value of the Wallenberg group's right to sell its shares in Aker Holding when the deal was signed?

(c) Using the same assumptions, what was the value of Aker ASA's right to buy the Wallenberg group's shares when the deal was signed?

(d) On 1 January 2011 the value of Aker Holding had dropped to 12.5 billion. What was the value of the Wallenberg group's re-sell right then? Assume six months to maturity and that the interest rate and volatility remain the same.

6. ShortSight Ltd. is the investment vehicle of three optometrists. It specializes in short-term optometry projects of the now or never type. It came across the following project: by investing 10 now (t_0) in the design of spectacles, it can let subcontractors produce a party of spectacles which will be ready one period later at t_1. The spectacles will be sold immediately after delivery. The production costs are 67, to be paid upon delivery at t_1. The price of the spectacles now (at t_0) is 75, but that price will increase over the next period with $\frac{2}{3}$ if the design is well received in the market. On the other hand, if the design is not well received, the price will decrease with $\frac{1}{3}$ over the next period. Both possibilities have equal probabilities. The risk-free interest rate is 10 per cent.

(a) What is the value of the project if accepted completely on a now or never basis?

A newcomer at ShortSight wants to introduce long-term thinking by postponing the production decision to next period.

(b) What is the value of the project if the production decision is postponed with one period? Assume that the t_1 prices remain the same in t_2 and that the production costs remain constant at 67.

7. Your government wants to stimulate economic development in the remote coastal regions of your country and has handed out (free) licences to start fish farms. Your grandfather obtained a licence because he used to be a fisherman, and now you hold the licence, which is valid for two more years. However, in order to stimulate early development of fish farms, the government requires a fee of €0.5 million for every year that the licence is not used. The equipment to start a fish farm is readily available in the market, costs €8 million and can be installed immediately. The investment amount increases over time with the risk-free interest rate. The expected cash flows over the lifetime of the fish farm have a present value of €10 million, but that value is very uncertain. It can go up with 25 per cent or down with 20 per cent per year; both possibilities are equally likely.

(a) If the annual risk-free interest rate is 7 per cent, what is the value of the licence and when should it be exercised? Use the binomial option pricing model.

(b) What would the option value be and when would it be exercised if there was no licence fee?

8. Smart Inc. runs a production process that converts fish offal into food for fish farms. The company presently produces 16,000 tons of fish food per period which, at the current price of €1,000 per ton, give a cash flow of €16 million per period. The risk-adjusted discount rate for cash flows from this process is 20 per cent per period and the risk-free interest rate is 10 per cent per period. Assuming perpetual cash flows, the present value of the expected cash flows from the process is $16/0.2 =$ €80 million. However, the food safety authorities fear that feeding fish offal to fish may lead to PSE (Piscine Spongiform Encephalopathy, or mad fish disease). The stricter demands on the production process will lead to a decrease in production volume of 20 per cent per period over the next two periods. Apart from this volume decrease, the value of the process will go up and down with the price of fish food, which depends on the fortunes of the fish farming industry. Over the next two periods, the price will move according to a binomial process with parameters $u = 1.5$ and $d = 0.5$. After two periods, the uncertainty is resolved and the values become fixed. Smart owns an old machine that it can use to instantaneously increase production capacity with 100 per cent in only one period by investing €5 million in repairs and replacement of worn-out parts. After that one period the machine becomes defective and can no longer be used. Smart's facilities are located on an attractive plot of land, for which it holds a flexible lease contract. The contract gives Smart the possibility to sell its lease to real estate developers at any time during the next two periods for €50 million. After two periods the contract becomes fixed without possibility to sell. In combination with the process above, this means that all decisions take place in a three moment two period context.

(a) Identify all options available to Smart Inc.

(b) Calculate the value of each option separately.

(c) Calculate the combined option value.

10 Selected option applications

Flexibility and option-like payoff structures are found in many decision problems in finance and an increasing number of them are analysed with option-pricing techniques. The results sometimes offer a new perspective on phenomena that are difficult to explain in the traditional DCF framework. In this chapter, we look at three such problems: the option nature of corporate securities, credit risk and mergers.

10.1 Corporate securities as options

Valuing debt and equity as options on the firm's assets, as we did in the previous chapter, is one of the earliest applications of option pricing. Black and Scholes (1973) had already demonstrated the principle in their seminal paper and it was later analytically elaborated by Merton (1974). Analysing corporate securities as options profoundly changed our understanding of corporate decision making. We will present the application in simple examples, first with discrete, later with continuous time and variables. Along the way we will introduce another important concept in finance.

10.1.1 An example

Consider a wealthy investor who has found two related but alternative project possibilities. They can be thought of as the technical development of a product idea in two alternative directions, each with its own market risk. Both projects require an investment of €36 million and will give an uncertain payoff with an expectation of €48.4 million two periods from now. The payoff of project 1 is estimated to have a present value of €40 million, but depending on market developments this value can either increase by 22 per cent or decrease by 18 per cent in each period. The real probability of an increase is 70 per cent. The payoff of project 2 is estimated to have a present value of €38 million, which is equally likely to either increase with 65 per cent or decrease with 39 per cent in each period. Lattice 25 gives the value dynamics for both projects. These data correspond to an expected payoff of $0.7^2 \times 59.5 + 2 \times 0.7 \times 0.3 \times 40 + 0.3^2 \times 26.9 = 48.38$ for project 1 and a risk-adjusted discount rate of $\sqrt{48.38/40} = 1.10$ or 10 per cent. The corresponding numbers for project 2 are $0.5^2 \times 103.5 + 2 \times 0.5^2 \times 38 + 0.5^2 \times 14.1 = 48.40$ and a risk-adjusted discount rate of $\sqrt{48.4/38} = 1.129$ or 12.9 per cent.

Any rational investor would prefer project 1 to project 2, since the former offers both a higher present value of the payoffs and a lower risk than the latter. Armed with the details of project 1, our investor approaches her bank with the request for a zero-coupon loan with a face value of €26 million to finance the project. The bank has quoted an interest rate of 5 per cent for loans like this, which would give the loan a present value of

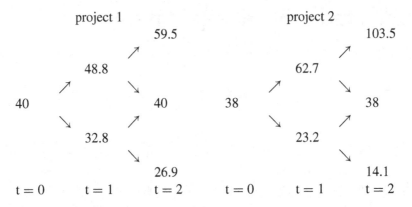

Lattice 25 The values (in €10^6) of two alternative projects

€23.58 million (26/1.05^2). The remaining €12.42 million will be financed from the investor's private means by taking a share interest in the project. This looks like a very safe deal for the bank. No matter how the value of project 1 develops, its payoff is always large enough to pay back the loan. To our investor's surprise, the bank refuses the €26 million loan and offers a loan with a much lower face value.

To understand why this decision can be made by rational economic parties, we have to look at both projects' payoffs to the shareholder in the presence of the €26 million loan. Lattice 26 shows project 1's equity.

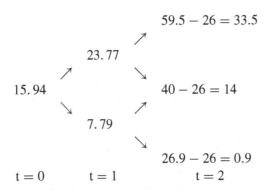

Lattice 26 Equity value (in €10^6) of project 1

Given the project's value dynamics, we can use the binomial model to calculate the value of its equity investment. The parameters are $u = 1.22$ and $d = .82$ and, assuming a risk-free interest rate of 4 per cent, the risk-neutral probability of an upward movement is $(1.04 - 0.82)/(1.22 - 0.82) = 0.55$. With these parameters, we find $t = 1$ values of $((0.55 \times 33.5) + (0.45 \times 14))/1.04 = 23.77$ and $((0.55 \times 14) + (0.45 \times 0.9))/1.04 = 7.79$. These $t = 1$ values produce the present value of $((0.55 \times 23.77) + (0.45 \times 7.79))/1.04 = 15.94$ in Lattice 26. Together with the value of debt of $26/1.04^2 = 24.03$ this gives a (rounded) total project value of 40. Notice that debt has an NPV of $24.03 - 23.58 = 0.45$ because the bank charges 5 per cent for a risk-free loan.

The calculations for project 2 are summarized in Lattice 27. The numbers are based on the assumptions that the loan is used for project 2 and that the shareholder has limited liability. The latter is necessary because the project's payoff is not always large enough to meet the debt obligations. As we have seen in the previous chapter, this gives equity an option character, formalized by the max[.] expression.

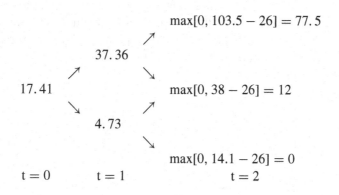

$$\text{max}[0, 103.5 - 26] = 77.5$$

$$37.36$$

$$17.41$$

$$\text{max}[0, 38 - 26] = 12$$

$$4.73$$

$$\text{max}[0, 14.1 - 26] = 0$$

$$t = 0 \qquad t = 1 \qquad t = 2$$

Lattice 27 Equity value (in €10^6) of project 2

The binomial parameters for project 2 are $u = 1.65$ and $d = 0.61$, so that $p = (1.04 - 0.61)/(1.65 - 0.61) = 0.41$. This gives t = 1 values of $((0.41 \times 77.5) + (0.59 \times 12))/1.04 = 37.36$ and $((0.41 \times 12) + (0.59 \times 0))/1.04 = 4.73$, and a t = 0 value of $((0.41 \times 37.36) + (0.59 \times 4.73))/1.04 = 17.41$. The value of debt, if the loan is used for project 2, is $(((0.41^2 + 2 \times 0.41 \times 0.59) \times 26) + (0.59^2 \times 14.1))/1.04^2 = 20.21$, so that the (rounded) project value of $20.21 + 17.41 \approx 38$ is reproduced.

We see that the equity value of project 2 is larger than that of project 1. This gives our wealthy investor an incentive to choose the more risky project 2 *once the loan is granted*. If the incentive is strong enough, she will probably find a legitimate reason to do so, particularly if the two projects are closely related. This phenomenon, which was first pointed out by Jensen and Meckling (1976), is known as *shareholders' risk incentive*. Given the opportunity, 'levered' shareholders will use the financing, that was obtained for a safe project, to invest in a more risky project. Since most assets have limited lifetimes, safe assets can be gradually replaced with risky ones. This gave rise to an alternative term for this phenomenon: *asset substitution*, the replacement of safe assets by risky ones if that is beneficial to the decision maker. The shareholder's value increase is at the bank's expense: the value of debt is $24.03 - 20.21 = 3.82$ lower in project 2. However, the bank has probably handled hundreds of similar loan applications before and knows, or suspects, about project 2. Hence the bank's decision to offer a loan with a much lower face value.

Two important conclusions can be drawn from this example. The first is that the loan induces a divergence between the bank's interests and the investor's interests. Since it is beneficial to the investor to choose project 2, the bank cannot take for granted that the investor will act in the bank's interests, that are best served by project 1. Such conflicts of interest are analysed in *agency theory*, which is discussed in a later chapter. The second conclusion is that the investor, who was risk averse before the loan, apparently develops a preference for risky projects once the loan is in place. Option valuation explains why.

10.1.2 Option characteristics of corporate securities

If the project is all equity financed, the value of equity is, of course, the same as the value of the project. Assuming continuous variables instead of the discrete outcomes we used in the previous subsection, this can be depicted as in the graph on the right-hand side of Figure 10.1. With the €26 million loan, the payoff to equity is the project value *in excess* of €26 million, or nothing if the project value at maturity is lower than the face value of debt. In the latter case, the shareholder is protected by limited liability and can walk away. This gives a payoff structure equal to that of a long call option, as the right-hand side of Figure 10.1 shows.

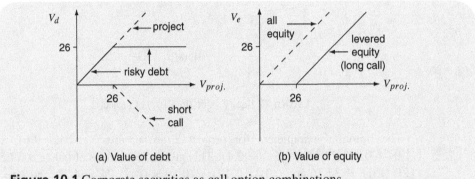

Figure 10.1 Corporate securities as call option combinations

The bank has the opposite position. If the project value at maturity is higher than the face value of debt, the shareholder will pay back her debt to the bank and keep the rest of the project's value. So the bank receives its €26 million. If the project value at maturity is below the face value of debt, the shareholder will default the loan and be declared bankrupt. Ownership of the project will then be transferred to the bank, so that it receives the residual value between €0 and €26 million. This position is equivalent to ownership of the project combined with a written call option with an exercise price of €26 million, as depicted in the graph on the left-hand side of Figure 10.1.

Notice that it is the opportunity to default, rather than the loan itself, that introduces the option characteristics. Without the possibility to default, i.e. with unlimited liability equity, the value of equity would simply be *project value-debt obligations*, as we saw in the previous chapter. Equity holders would be exposed to the downside risk of project 2 and have to accept its negative equity value in the lower node at t = 2. The flexibility of the default option changes the expression for the payoff into max[0, *project value-debt obligations*], which gives the higher expected payoff to project 2. That is why limited liability equity holders prefer risky projects if debt is present. Limited liability protects them from the projects' downside risk, while they fully profit from their upward potential. It is a corporate application of the option Greek vega: the value of an option increases with the volatility of its underlying value.

Also notice the alternative formulations of the option to default a loan. Here, the value of debt is depicted as the value of the project's assets minus a written call option on them. By taking up the loan the owners have, in effect, sold the firm's assets to the debtholders while retaining a call option to buy them back when the loan matures. In the previous chapter we modelled that flexibility in an alternative way, viz. as the put option to sell the project's assets to the debtholders by not paying the amount due to them.

In practice, firms have much more complex debt structures than a single, zero-coupon loan and although valuing equity as a series of compound options (options on options) can be difficult, the same principle applies. Moreover, the option analogy is not limited to loans. Firms can default on any payment they have to make and by paying they buy the next option to default.

10.1.3 Example in continuous time

Corporate securities can, of course, also be valued as options with the Black and Scholes formula. Since the result can be depicted in a very illustrative way, we will restate the example in the previous subsection in terms of continuous time and variables. This boils down to translating the up and down movements in Lattice 25 into a continuous standard deviation, σ. The binomial models that we used are parametrized such that $u = 1/d$, so we can use the formula from Chapter 8 that matches discrete and continuous time parameters: $u = e^{\sigma\sqrt{\delta t}}$. For project 1, we want to translate an up movement of 1.22 into a one-period standard deviation: $1.22 = e^{\sigma\sqrt{1}}$, so $1.22 = e^{\sigma} \Rightarrow \sigma = \ln 1.22 = 0.2$ or 20 per cent. Similarly, for project 2: $1.65 = e^{\sigma\sqrt{1}} \Rightarrow \sigma = 0.5$ or 50 per cent. The inputs for the Black and Scholes formula are summarized in Table 10.1.

Table 10.1 *Two projects*

Project	1	2
Present value	40	38
Strike	26	26
Volatility (σ)	20%	50%
r_f	4%	4%
Time	2	2

As in the binomial case, we calculate equity values as call options on the projects' revenues. The data for project 1 in Table 10.1 are in terms of the Black and Scholes formula: $S_0 = 40$, $X = 26$, $r = 0.04$, $\sigma = 0.2$ and $T = 2$. Filling in the numbers:

$$d_1 = \frac{\ln(S_0/X) + (r + \frac{1}{2}\sigma^2)T}{\sigma\sqrt{T}}$$

$$d_1 = \frac{\ln(40/26) + (0.04 + 0.5 \times 0.2^2)2}{0.2\sqrt{2}} = 1.9473$$

$$d_2 = d_1 - \sigma\sqrt{T} = 1.9473 - 0.2\sqrt{2} = 1.6645$$

The areas under the normal curve for d_1 and d_2 are NormalDist(1.9473) = 0.97425 and NormalDist(1.6645) = 0.95199, so that the option price becomes:

$$O_{c,0} = 40 \times 0.97425 - 26e^{-0.04 \times 2} \times 0.95199 = 16.12$$

For project 2 we have: $S_0 = 38$, $X = 26$, $r = 0.04$, $\sigma = 0.5$ and $T = 2$.

$$d_1 = \frac{\ln(S_0/X) + (r + \frac{1}{2}\sigma^2)T}{\sigma\sqrt{T}}$$

$$d_1 = \frac{\ln(38/26) + (0.04 + 0.5 \times 0.5^2)2}{0.5\sqrt{2}} = 1.0034$$

$$d_2 = d_1 - \sigma\sqrt{T} = 1.0034 - 0.5\sqrt{2} = 0.29629$$

The areas under the normal curve for d_1 and d_2 are NormalDist(1.0034) = 0.84217 and NormalDist(0.29629) = 0.6165. The option price then is:

$$O_{c,0} = 38 \times 0.84217 - 26e^{-0.04 \times 2} \times 0.6165 = 17.21$$

These are approximately the same option values as the ones we found with the two-period binomial model in the beginning of this chapter. They are depicted as functions of the underlying project value in Figure 10.2. The horizontal straight lines represent the option values of 16.12 and 17.21. They divide the vertical straight lines, that represent the total project values, in an equity part, which is equal to the option value, and the remaining debt part. We see that project 2 has a lower present value, but the higher uncertainty makes it more valuable to the shareholder: she gets a larger share of a less valuable project. This is at the expense of the bank, which gets a smaller part of a less valuable project. That is why bad projects can be preferred to good projects.

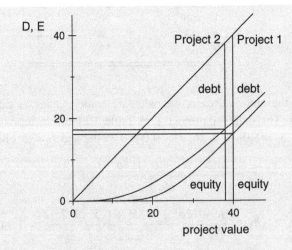

Figure 10.2 Option values of corporate claims on two projects

10.1.4 Insights from option valuation

Black and Scholes' observation that corporate securities can be valued as options on the firm's assets offers new insight into several phenomena that are difficult to explain in a discounted cash flow context. The first of these is equity holders' preference for risky projects if debt is present. The combination of limited liability and debt financing produces an option-like payoff structure for equity, as Figure 10.1 shows. Since option values increase with volatility, equity holders have an incentive to choose risky investments. This is not restricted to equity holders. Managers who are paid in bonuses or stock options have the same incentive. For example, hedge fund managers are paid a fee of typically 20 per cent of the fund's profits above a certain threshold. This gives a strong incentive to make very risky investments. Excessive risk taking in financial institutions, fuelled by a bonus culture, is widely regarded as a major contributor to the credit crisis of 2007–2008.

The risk incentive of limited liability equity holders also increases our understanding of why banks and other lenders sometimes seem over-cautious. When asset substitution is possible, projects should not only be evaluated on their own merits, but also in the context of alternative courses projects could take. A simple way to ensure that a project takes the 'right' course, in which the interests of banks and equity holders are aligned, is to use a low maximum amount of debt (a low credit limit or, in the example, a low face value of debt). This reduces the equity holders' risk incentive by exposing them to the downside risks of their projects. In technical terms, lowering the face value of debt means lowering the exercise price of the written call option. This increases the probability that the option will be exercised so that the loan will be paid back in full.

Another phenomenon that is easy to explain in an options context is the positive equity value of firms or projects that are technically insolvent. Suppose the value of project 2 in the previous subsection suddenly drops to 22, e.g. because a competitor unexpectedly launches a very similar product. This means that the project is technically insolvent: the present value of its debt obligations $(26/1.05^2 = 23.58)$ is larger than the value of its assets (this condition is known as balance sheet insolvency). In discounted cash flow terms, equity is worthless under such conditions. In option pricing terms, the equity value of project 2 would be calculated as: $S_0 = 22$, $X = 26$, $r = 0.04$, $\sigma = 0.5$ and $T = 2$, so that:

$$d_1 = \frac{\ln(S_0/X) + (r + \frac{1}{2}\sigma^2)T}{\sigma\sqrt{T}}$$

$$d_1 = \frac{\ln(22/26) + (0.04 + 0.5 \times 0.5^2)2}{0.5\sqrt{2}} = 0.23044$$

$$d_2 = d_1 - \sigma\sqrt{T} = 0.23044 - 0.5\sqrt{2} = -0.47667$$

The areas under the normal curve for d_1 and d_2 are NormalDist$(0.23044) = 0.59113$ and NormalDist$(-0.47667) = 0.3168$. The option price then is:

$$O_{c,0} = 22 \times 0.59113 - 26e^{-0.04 \times 2} \times 0.3168 = 5.40$$

Equity still has considerable value, even if the current value of assets falls below the value of debt. Equity is then an out of the money option that has value just as any other out of the money option.

10.2 Credit risk

Credit risk, or counterparty risk, is the risk that a financial contract loses value because the counterparty defaults on its obligations (default risk), or because the risk of future default increases. For example, a corporate bond can lose most of its market value when the company that issued the bond fails to make a scheduled coupon payment. The bond can also lose value if the company's prospects deteriorate, so that the risk of future default increases. Credit risk plays a role in most financial contracts and many techniques have been employed to analyse and manage this risk. An application of option pricing, known as Merton's model, is among the more recent additions. After sketching some background of credit risk, we shall have a brief look at a few of these techniques.

10.2.1 Insuring and measuring credit risk

In some markets, counterparty risk is automatically taken care of. This is generally the case for securities that are traded on exchanges, where the risk is taken over by the exchange's clearing house. As we have seen, clearing houses guarantee payment and delivery of securities by positioning themselves between the trading parties. By operating clearing houses, exchanges make it easy and safe to trade, which may expand their market. The credit (default) risk of most other transactions, both with domestic and foreign partners, can be insured on a commercial basis. In many countries the state offers a guarantee for insuring the credit risk of export transactions to 'risky' countries that insurers are not willing to cover themselves. Such guarantees are meant to stimulate exports as part of economic policy. Accounts receivable management, and credit risk with it, can also be 'outsourced' to specialized companies, called factoring companies. A factoring company buys the accounts receivable of its clients at a discount and then collects the outstanding amounts for its own account and risk.

Credit risk is particularly important for bank lending and other commercial activities that operate with small margins. Traditionally, the income of a bank consists of the interest margin, the difference between its borrowing and lending rate. If the interest margin is 2 per cent, it takes the profits of fifty equally large loans to compensate for a completely lost loan. This gives banks a strong incentive to minimize risk in various ways, including conservative lending policies, careful risk analysis and the securitization of loans. It also gives an incentive to minimize losses in case of default by asking for collateral and guarantees and by charging fees and commissions for an increasing number of bank services. The latter replace uncertain, future interest income with non-interest income that is received immediately.[1]

Credit risk can be measured in two ways:

1. *Direct measurement*: for a minority of firms, rating agencies publish an assessment of the credit quality of the firm's outstanding debt. For the other firms and private persons, that information has to be based on official or commercial registrations of bankruptcies

---

[1] According to the European Central Bank, the non-interest income of banks increased from about 25 per cent in the early 1990s to more than 40 per cent a decade later.

and loan defaults. These data can be analysed in combination with accounting data for business loans, or personal background data for consumer credit.

2. *Indirect measurement through market prices*: on well-functioning markets, a firm's probability to default is reflected in the price of its securities. Different techniques can be used to 'extract' that probability from prices.

We shall have a brief look at both ways.

10.2.2 Direct measurement

The creditworthiness of corporate bonds is assessed by companies called *rating agencies*.[2] They express their professional opinion in ratings varying from triple A (best) to D (default) with various categories in between, depending on the agency. Figure 10.3 gives a condensed example of the kind of data rating agencies report (historical default rates of corporate bonds by aggregated rating category and year).[3]

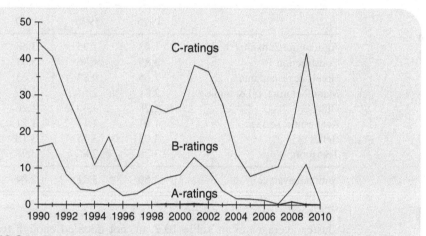

Figure 10.3 Default rates in percentages by rating category and year (compiled from various sources on the internet)

The agencies also issue reports on cumulative default rates over a number of years, recovery rates (percentage of value recovered from defaulted bonds) and rating migrations, i.e. the frequency of transitions from one rating category to another. Clearly, such information can give a good picture of the credit risk of the rated bonds. High credit ratings are valuable to a firm: the interest rate required by the market decreases with better ratings. However, it should also be noted that the predictive power of ratings is debated: some claim that market prices adjust to new information before ratings are changed.[4] Moreover, the rating agencies' reputations were damaged by the 2007–2008

---

2 The main rating agencies in the USA are Moody's-KMV, Standard & Poor's and Fitch.

3 Moody's rating scale consists of twenty-one categories, from Aaa to C; S&P uses twenty-two categories, from AAA to D, and Fitch uses twenty from AAA to D.

4 *The Journal of Banking and Finance* published a special issue on 'Recent research on credit ratings' in November 2004; see Cantor (2004) for the introduction to this issue.

credit crunch, when triple A-rated mortgage bundles (the special-purpose entities we saw in Chapter 5) deteriorated rapidly and shortly afterwards experienced high default rates.

In the USA the majority of traded bonds are rated; in Europe rating is much less common. But on both continents the vast majority of firms (in numbers, not value) are neither listed on a stock exchange nor rated by an agency. For those firms, the assessment of credit risk has to be based on bankruptcy or default registrations combined with financial background information. A typical example of registered corporate bankruptcy rates is given in Table 10.2 (taken from Westgaard and Van der Wijst, 2001). Similar data are available in most countries. Notice that the pattern across industries is roughly in line with the discussion of bankruptcy costs in Chapter 5: industries that mainly use general-purpose assets, such as hotels, restaurants and transportation companies, have relatively high bankruptcy rates.

Table 10.2 *Bankruptcy rates (%) in Norwegian industries*

	1995	1996	1997	1998
Agriculture & fishing	1.43	1.95	3.68	2.10
Construction	3.85	4.36	5.07	5.32
Hotels & restaurants	7.65	9.84	9.63	7.75
Manufacturing, oil & mining	2.81	2.61	2.69	2.40
Other	2.78	1.90	1.26	1.39
Real estate, service	1.61	1.11	1.21	1.08
Retail	3.03	3.55	3.18	3.03
Transport	3.26	2.86	3.98	3.58
National average	3.50	3.21	2.84	2.57

Industry averages as in Table 10.2 are not detailed enough to be directly usable in credit decisions. More detailed rates can be obtained by estimating a statistical relationship between defaults and accounting data. If the estimation is successful, such a relation will differentiate the average default rate into individualized default probabilities that depend on a firm's accounting data. Given the ubiquity of credit risk, it is not surprising that an enormous amount of research has been devoted to estimating such relations. Over the years, very many (perhaps all) statistical techniques have been applied to this area. We shall illustrate the approach with just one example.

Westgaard and Van der Wijst (2001) use logistic regression analysis (or logit analysis) to estimate a relation between the incidence of bankruptcy and accounting data of $35,287$ Norwegian companies, 954 of which (2.7 per cent) are bankrupt. Logistic regression is designed to analyse dichotomous dependent variables, i.e. variables that can take only two alternative values (here: 'bankrupt' or 'not bankrupt'). In essence, logit analysis estimates the probability that a firm is classified as bankrupt as a function of the explanatory variables x_j and their coefficients β_j. This makes certain demands on the form of the function that relates bankruptcy probability to the variables x_j. A linear function as in ordinary regression analysis, for example, is not very suitable because it could give estimated probabilities that are negative or larger than 1. Since the function values have to be limited to the range (0,1), it is more logical to choose some cumulative distribution function. Logit analysis uses the logistic distribution function: $F(x) = e^x/(1 + e^x)$.[5] Using this function can be thought of as transforming probabilities into *log-odds ratios*, $\ln(p_i/(1 - p_i))$, which are not bounded by 0 and 1. Using odds $p_i/(1 - p_i)$ instead of probabilities p_i removes the upper limit of 1 and taking logarithms $\ln(p_i/(1 - p_i))$ removes the lower limit of 0. In the logit model the log-odds ratio is a linear function of the explanatory variables x_j:

$$\ln\left(\frac{p_i}{1 - p_i}\right) = \beta_0 + \sum_{j=1}^{k} \beta_j x_{ij}$$

Taking exponentials gives the odds ratio as:

$$\frac{p_i}{1 - p_i} = e^{\left(\beta_0 + \sum_{j=1}^{k} \beta_j x_{ij}\right)}$$

and solving for p_i returns the probability as:

$$p_i = \frac{e^{\left(\beta_0 + \sum_{j=1}^{k} \beta_j x_{ij}\right)}}{1 + e^{\left(\beta_0 + \sum_{j=1}^{k} \beta_j x_{ij}\right)}} = \frac{1}{1 + e^{-\left(\beta_0 + \sum_{j=1}^{k} \beta_j x_{ij}\right)}}$$

i.e. the probability is a logistic function of the explanatory variables x_j and their coefficients β_j. The logistic function gives output values between 0 and 1 for all input values between $-\infty$ and ∞. The coefficients of logit models are estimated with a maximum likelihood procedure that is available in most statistical packages.

Westgaard and Van der Wijst (2001) include five financial variables and age (plus a number of dummy variables, which are omitted here) in their estimation procedure. The results are reported in Table 10.3. All variables are defined such that higher values are associated with lower default risk. To illustrate how these results can be used, Table 10.3 also lists the values of the explanatory variables for two example companies, a bad and a good one. The bad company is only nine months old, it has a negative cash flow and operating income, a small size (1 million total assets, which gives $\log_{10}(1000) = 3$) and it is financed with 90 per cent debt. Substituting these data and the estimated coefficients in the logistic function gives an estimated default probability of:

$$p_{bad} = 1/\left(1 + e^{1.77 \times -0.2 + 0.12 \times 3 + 0.28 \times 0.25 + 0.01 \times -0.1 + 0.58 \times 0.1 + 0.32 \times 0.75}\right)$$

which is 0.4078 or 40.8 per cent. The good company is seven years old, has a positive cash flow and operating income, a larger size (10 million total assets, which gives $\log_{10}(10\,000) = 4$) and it is financed with 50 per cent debt. This makes the estimated default probability:

$$p_{good} = 1/\left(1 + e^{1.77 \times 0.3 + 0.12 \times 4 + 0.28 \times 2 + 0.01 \times 2 + 0.58 \times 0.5 + 0.32 \times 7}\right)$$

which is 0.0160 or 1.6 per cent. Individualized default probabilities, that are estimated with models such as this, can be a substantial improvement upon industry average

---

5 An alternative formulation, that uses the normal distribution function, is known as *probit analysis*; the formulation that uses a linear function (despite its obvious disadvantages) is called *the linear probability model*.

default rates. However, it is also clear that these models have a considerable margin of error. When applied out of sample, some fraction of the bankrupt companies will have very low estimated default probabilities and a fraction of the non-bankrupt companies will have very high estimated default probabilities. The size of these fractions determines the quality of the model.

Table 10.3 *Logit estimates and example companies*

Variable	Coefficient	Example company	
		Bad	Good
Cash flow/total debt	−1.77	−0.2	0.3
Log (total assets)	−0.12	3	4
Curr. assets/curr. liabilities	−0.28	0.25	2
Operating income/financial cost	−0.01	−0.1	2
Equity/total assets	−0.58	0.1	0.5
Age (years)	−0.32	0.75	7

all coefficients are significantly $\neq 0$ at a 1% confidence level

10.2.3 Indirect measurement

Default probabilities can also be measured indirectly by inferring them from observed market prices. The principle is easily demonstrated with a stylized example that compares the prices of two bonds. Both are zero-coupon bonds with a face value of 100 and a maturity of one year, but one is a risk-free government bond and the other a risky corporate bond. The government bond sells for 95.92 and the corporate bond for 95.47. This means that the risk-free interest rate on the government bond is $100/(1 + r_f) = 95.92 \Rightarrow r_f = 4.25$ per cent and the interest rate on the corporate bond is $100/(1 + r_c) = 95.47 \Rightarrow r_c = 4.75$ per cent, where the subscript c is for corporate. The corporate bond sells at a discount of $(95.92–95.47)/95.92 = .0047$ or 0.47 per cent compared with the government bond.[6] Since the promised payment at maturity is the same for both bonds, the corporate bondholders apparently expect to lose 0.47 per cent. The possibility of default is the main difference between corporate and government bonds and the main source of loss. If we assume that the corporate bond is completely lost upon default, then 0.47 per cent is also the expected default probability. This means that about one in every 200 corporate bonds is lost completely to default.

However, most defaulted bonds are not completely lost. Usually, a part of the bond value is recovered from the resolution of the default in the form of cash, other securities or even physical assets. Default resolutions often contain a combination of these assets. The long-term average recovery rate across bonds of different seniority and security is between 40 per cent and 50 per cent. If we assume a recovery rate of 40 per cent, then the implied default probability is $0.47/(1 − 0.4) = 0.783$ per cent. That probability can be calculated in an alternative way that more clearly shows its nature. At maturity the

---

6 The discount is usually calculated from the interest rates: $1 − (1.0425/1.0475) = 0.0047$.

corporate bond can be in two possible states, default or not. The price now is the present value of the expectation of these states:

$$95.47 = \frac{(1 - p) \times 100 + p \times 100 \times .4}{1.0425} \Rightarrow p = .00783$$

It is easy to recognize the risk-neutral valuation formula (7.9) from Chapter 7. Hence, the implied probabilities are the risk-neutral (equivalent martingale) probabilities. The real (historical) probabilities are much lower. The lower price of the corporate bond is not only a compensation for the loss if default occurs, investors also require a premium for accepting the risk.

In a similar way, default probabilities can be inferred from equity prices in an application that has become known as the Merton model (after Merton, 1974). It models the value of equity as a call option on the assets of a levered firm, as shown at the beginning of this chapter. We use the simple situation where the firm pays no dividends and its debt consists of a single zero-coupon bond. The Black and Scholes formula for the value of equity is then:

$$E_0 = V_0 N (d_1) - D e^{-rT} N (d_2) \tag{10.1}$$

with:

$$d_1 = \frac{\ln(V_0/D) + (r + \frac{1}{2}\sigma_V^2)T}{\sigma_V \sqrt{T}}$$

and:

$$d_2 = d_1 - \sigma_V \sqrt{T} = \frac{\ln(V_0/D) + (r - \frac{1}{2}\sigma_V^2)T}{\sigma_V \sqrt{T}} \tag{10.2}$$

where E_0 is the value of equity now, V_0 is the value of the firm's assets now, σ_V is the volatility of the firm's assets value, D is the face value of the bond, which matures at time T, and r is the risk-free interest rate.

Recall from the discussion of the Black and Scholes formula that $N (d_1)$ is the option delta and $N (d_2)$ is the probability that the option will be exercised. In the context of Merton's model, exercising means 'buying back' the firm's assets from the debtholders by paying them the face value of the zero-coupon bond at maturity. Hence, $1 - N (d_2)$, or $N (-d_2)$, is the probability that the option will *not* be exercised, which means that the loan will be defaulted. Merton's model provides an elegant way to derive that probability from equity prices, which are continuously available. This insight quickly found its way into practice and it is now applied in several commercial credit quality assessment services that are used worldwide.

Although the Merton model is theoretically elegant, its practical implementation is not without problems. A first problem is that (10.1) and (10.2) call for the value of the firm's assets, V_0, and its volatility, σ_V, which are unobservable in financial markets. If the firm's stock is traded on an exchange, we can observe the dynamic process of equity values but not the asset value process. Numerical values for V_0 and σ_V can be obtained in several ways, for example by computing proxy values from the market value of the firm's equity and the book value of its debt (as done by Brockman and Turtle (2003), for example). However, the most common way is to calculate the values for V_0 and σ_V that are implied by the model itself. In the option-pricing formula in (10.1), the observable equity value is related to the two unknowns, asset value and volatility. A second equation for this relation can be obtained by writing out (and manipulating) the stochastic process for equity. This gives two equations for two unknowns and the system can be solved numerically (e.g. with the solver of a spreadsheet program). A description of the procedure can be found in e.g. Cossin and Pirotte (2001).

A second problem is that the Merton model, like the procedure with bond prices above, gives the risk-neutral probability of default. This problem can also be solved in different ways. Since the Merton model appears to produce a good ranking of default probabilities, the risk-neutral probabilities can be mapped on a known distribution of real probabilities. The results of such a mapping are provided on a commercial basis by the financial services industry; the details of the mapping procedure are proprietary information. An alternative way to obtain real probabilities is to derive the Merton model without changing the probability measure. The resulting formula cannot be used for pricing purposes but it contains probabilities under the real probability measure. The formula for d_2 then becomes:

$$d_2^* = \frac{\ln(V_0/D) + (\mu - \frac{1}{2}\sigma_V^2)T}{\sigma_V\sqrt{T}}$$

where the * signifies the difference with the Black and Scholes d_2, and μ is the continuously compounded expected return on assets. The real probability of default is $N(-d_2^*)$. This procedure calls for the real drift parameter in the asset value process, μ, which is not observable on financial markets. But also here stochastic calculus can be used to rewrite the model so that it uses the drift in equity value, which is easier obtained from stock market data. Alternatively, the expected growth rate in asset values can approximated with an empirical ad hoc procedure, as done by Hillegeist *et al.* (2004).

Despite these and other practical problems, the Merton model remains popular because it combines a solid theoretical foundation with relative simplicity. It is the basis of a number of commercial applications for credit risk analysis that are widely used in the financial industry.[7] Moreover, the Merton model appears to perform well compared with other approaches, probably because it uses equity prices which, unlike accounting data, are continually updated. Hillegeist *et al.* (2004) compare predictions of the Merton model with those of models that are based on accounting data, like the logit analysis discussed above. Their conclusion is that the Merton probabilities provide significantly more information than any of the accounting-based measures and that this finding is robust to various modifications of the accounting models. Brockman and Turtle (2003) use a similar procedure, but with a different option-pricing model, and conclude that in most cases the failure probabilities implied by the option framework dominate those estimated with accounting data.

---

[7] The best known applications are the KMV model (from Moody's-KMV), CreditMetrics (from RiskMetrics Group), CreditRisk+ (from Credit Suisse Financial Products) and Credit Portfolio View (from McKinsey).

10.3 Conglomerate mergers

Mergers are a comparatively poorly understood phenomenon in finance. In some textbooks, merger waves are included in the list of unsolved financial problems. A telling sign of the lack of understanding is the multitude of different merger theories in circulation, ranging from various efficiency increase and wealth redistribution theories to managerial hubris (Roll, 1986). We shall have a brief look at only one type, the conglomerate merger, because it offers a nice illustration of the evolution of financial thought.

10.3.1 Financial effects of conglomerate mergers

A merger is called conglomerate when it is neither horizontal (i.e. between two companies in the same line of business, e.g. two banks) nor vertical (between companies in different stages of the production process, e.g. an oil company and a petrochemical company). Put differently, conglomerate mergers involve two companies that are unrelated, for example because they are in different industries. Unrelated companies have no economic relationships, so the merger of two such companies is unlikely to generate economies of scale or scope in production, distribution, marketing and management. These synergetic effects are the most common (stated) motivation for both horizontal and vertical mergers. In the absence of operational economies, financial economies have been suggested as a reason for conglomerate mergers. More specifically, the diversification effect of pooling two unrelated cash flows was suggested to produce value in the context of a Markowitz portfolio optimization. However, it was demonstrated by, among others, Levy and Sarnat (1970) that a purely conglomerate merger cannot produce economic gain in a perfect capital market. The two firms will be included in the market portfolio with the same value proportions, regardless of whether they merge or not.

As an alternative explanation, Levy and Sarnat (1970) suggest size-related transaction and information costs that could give larger firms easier access to capital markets. Moreover, the costs of debt would be lower for the larger, merged firm because the joint probability of default of two merged firms is lower than the sum of the separate probabilities of each firm. This argument is elaborated by Lewellen (1971) as a pure financial rationale for the conglomerate merger. He illustrates his argument with the following example. Suppose there are two firms whose cash flows are identically but independently distributed over three possible outcomes. The distribution is given in Table 10.4.

Table 10.4 *Cash flow distribution*

Outcome	1	2	3
Cash flow	100	250	500
Probability	0.1	0.2	0.7

Both firms are partly financed with debt and both have the contractual obligation to pay 240 to the debtholders. The probability that one of the firms, or both, default on their debt obligation is (using the sum rule of probability theory):

$$0.1 + 0.1 - 0.1 \times 0.1 = 0.19$$

Now suppose that the two firms merge. Then the distribution of their combined cash flows becomes as in Table 10.5.

The combined debt obligation is 480, so the probability of default becomes:

$$0.01 + 0.04 = 0.05$$

Table 10.5 *Joint cash flow distribution*

Outcome	(1,1)	(1,2)(2,1)	(2,2)	(1,3)(3,1)	(2,3)(3,2)	(3,3)
Cash flow	200	350	500	600	750	1000
Probability	0.01	0.04	0.04	0.14	0.28	0.49

This is much lower than the 0.19 of unmerged firms. Lewellen concludes from this that conglomerate mergers create additional borrowing power. Since additional borrowing gives a larger tax advantage, this will lead to positive share price increments for the owners. Hence, valuation gains are obtainable merely from joining unrelated companies, i.e. pure financial synergy can be released by mergers.

This conclusion is contested by, among others, Higgins and Schall (1975). They argue that if a merger is purely conglomerate, it generates no additional cash flow. Hence, the cash flow of the merged firm is simply the sum of the cash flows of the unmerged firms and this implies that the value of the merged firm has to be the sum of the values of the unmerged firms. Any other value would give arbitrage opportunities, since investors can undo or redo the merger decision by dividing or combining the cash flows on financial markets. For example, if the merged firm would trade at a discount, investors could make arbitrage profits by buying the merged firm's stock, dividing its cash flow into the original cash flows and selling them at the original prices. Notice that this argument refers to the cash flow generated by the firms' assets, i.e. to the left-hand side of the balance sheet. It is therefore independent of any reduction in default probability on the right-hand side. However, this does not mean that the division of firm values over debt and equity remains the same. On the contrary, if there are outcomes in which one of the pre-merger firms has a positive cash flow while the other firm is insolvent, Lewellen's diversification effect will obtain for the merged firm. This is the case for the outcomes (1,3) and (3,1) in Table 10.5, where one of the unmerged firms would default but the merged firm uses the cash flow of one firm to pay the other's debt. So the cash flows of both firms co-insure each other's debt obligations if they merge. Hence, the value of debt is increased by the merger and since the total firm value remains the same, the value of equity is decreased.

Galai and Masulis (1976) were among the first to make the same point from an option-pricing perspective. They observe that the conglomerate merger of firms with less than perfectly correlated cash flows will reduce the variance of the merged firm's cash flow. This will reduce the value of equity as a call option on the merged firm's assets.

10.3 Conglomerate mergers

Since no value is created in a conglomerate merger, the result is a redistribution of value from equity to debt. An alternative formulation is modelling the opportunity to default as a put option to sell the firm's assets to debtholders by defaulting the debt obligations, as we did in Chapter 9. That option is valuable to equity holders and its value is reduced by the reduction in variance that results from a conglomerate merger. Galai and Masulis (1976) suggest that equity holders can be compensated for their loss in value if the merged firm issues more debt with the same seniority and retires a part of its equity. If the proper amounts are chosen, this will reduce the value of the pre-merger debt to its original level.

Kim and McConnell (1977) empirically investigate the effects of mergers. Using both paired comparisons and event study methodology they find no statistical evidence that the bondholders of merged firms earn abnormal positive returns around the time of merger. They also find that the merged firms increase their use of financial leverage after the merger. Normally, bondholders would be expected to suffer abnormal negative returns if leverage is increased. Since no abnormal returns are found, Kim and McConnell conclude that a co-insurance effect does occur, but that its value redistribution effect is negated by the increased use of debt financing.

10.3.2 A numerical example

The financial effects of conglomerate mergers can best be illustrated with a numerical example. We shall first present the two firms and then value the effects in two different ways.

The merger case

Consider two firms, Construct and Questor, whose activities are unrelated. They can be thought of as a construction company that manufactures offshore platforms for the oil industry and a factoring company that collects the outstanding debts of its clients. To evaluate the effect of a merger between the two companies, consider the data listed in Table 10.6.

Table 10.6 *Merger candidates' data*

	Construct	Questor
Market value of the firm ($€10^6$)	45	55
Face value of debt ($€10^6$)	30	40
Debt maturity (years)	4	4
Standard deviation in firm value (%)	30	40

Both firms have only one zero-coupon bond and both bonds mature on the same date four years from now. If the merger is effectuated the bondholders maintain an identical claim (same face value, maturity and seniority) which is guaranteed by the new firm. Stockholders receive new shares in proportion to the pre-merger equity values. Since the activities of both firms are unrelated, no synergy effects as a result of the merger are anticipated and the correlation between the companies' cash flows is 0. The risk-free

Selected option applications

interest rate is 8 per cent. We are asked to calculate the value of equity and debt in both firms before the merger and to calculate the benefits of the merger for the equity holders.

Valuation as call options

In both firms debt is already in place, so equity can be valued as a call option on assets. The zero-coupon bond gives the call a European style. The firm-related input values are as in Table 10.6. For Construct the inputs are: $S_0 = 45$, $X = 30$, $r = 0.08$, $\sigma = 0.3$ and $T = 4$, so that:

$$d_1 = \frac{\ln(S_0/X) + (r + \frac{1}{2}\sigma^2)T}{\sigma\sqrt{T}}$$

$$d_1 = \frac{\ln(45/30) + (0.08 + 0.5 \times 0.3^2) \times 4}{0.3\sqrt{4}} = 1.5091$$

$$d_2 = d_1 - \sigma\sqrt{T} = 1.5091 - 0.3\sqrt{4} = 0.9091$$

The areas under normal curve for values of d_1 and d_2 are: NormalDist(1.5091) = 0.934 and NormalDist(0.9091) = 0.818. The option price then becomes:

$$O_{c,0} = 45 \times 0.934 - 30e^{-0.08 \times 4} \times 0.818 = 24.21$$

The corresponding data and calculations for Questor are: $S_0 = 55$, $X = 40$, $r = 0.08$, $\sigma = .4$ and $T = 4$, so that:

$$d_1 = \frac{\ln(S_0/X) + (r + \frac{1}{2}\sigma^2)T}{\sigma\sqrt{T}}$$

$$d_1 = \frac{\ln(55/40) + (0.08 + 0.5 \times 0.4^2) \times 4}{0.4\sqrt{4}} = 1.1981$$

$$d_2 = d_1 - \sigma\sqrt{T} = 1.1981 - 0.4\sqrt{4} = 0.3981$$

The areas under normal curve for values of d_1 and d_2 are: NormalDist(1.1981) = 0.885 and NormalDist(0.3981) = 0.655, so that the option price is:

$$O_{c,0} = 55 \times 0.885 - 40e^{-0.08 \times 4} \times 0.655 = 29.65$$

The values of debt can be calculated as the difference between firm and equity values. Table 10.7 shows the results.

Table 10.7 *Merger candidates' values*

	Construct	Questor
Value of equity	24.21	29.65
Value of debt	20.79	25.35
Value of firm	45.00	55.00

The next step is the calculation of the values of debt and equity in the merged firm. The total firm value is easy: since no synergy effects are anticipated, the value of the merged firm is the sum of the pre-merger firm values, $45 + 55 = 100$. The variance of the merged firm's value is also easy to calculate once we realise that the merged firm can be regarded as a portfolio of the pre-merger firms. We have seen in Chapter 3, equation (3.7), how the variance of a two-stock portfolio is calculated: $\sigma_p^2 = x_1^2 \sigma_1^2 + x_2^2 \sigma_2^2 + 2x_1 x_2 \rho_{1,2} \sigma_1 \sigma_2$. The weights $x_{1,2}$ of the firms are $45/100 = 0.45$ and 0.55. Applying this to our case we get: $(0.45)^2 (0.3)^2 + (0.55)^2 (0.4)^2 + 2 \times (0.45)(0.55)(0)(0.3)(0.4) = 0.066625$ or a standard deviation of $\sqrt{0.066625} = 0.258$. The diversification effect is strong because the firms' cash flows are uncorrelated ($\rho = 0$). This makes the double covariance term equal to 0. Under the merger conditions stipulated above, the face value of debt is the sum of the pre-merger face values while the maturity remains four years. The inputs for the option valuation are then: $S_0 = 100$, $X = 70$, $r = 0.08$, $\sigma = 0.258$ and $T = 4$, so that

$$d_1 = \frac{\ln(S_0/X) + (r + \frac{1}{2}\sigma^2)T}{\sigma \sqrt{T}}$$

$$d_1 = \frac{\ln(100/70) + (0.08 + 0.5 \times 0.258^2) \times 4}{0.258\sqrt{4}} = 1.5694$$

$$d_2 = d_1 - \sigma\sqrt{T} = 1.5694 - 0.258\sqrt{4} = 1.0534$$

The areas under normal curve for values of d_1 and d_2 are: NormalDist(1.5694) = 0.942 and NormalDist(1.0534) = 0.854. The option price then becomes:

$$O_{c,0} = 100 \times 0.942 - 70e^{-0.08 \times 4} \times 0.854 = 50.79$$

Adding these results to Table 10.7 produces Table 10.8, which demonstrates the financial effects of the merger.

Table 10.8 *Merger candidates' values and benefits*

	Construct	Questor	Merged	Benefit
Value of equity	24.21	29.65	50.79	−3.07
Value of debt	20.79	25.35	49.21	3.07
Value of firm	45.00	55.00	100.00	0

We see that the bondholders benefit from the co-insurance effect of the merger, at the expense of the equity holders.

Valuation as put options

It is also possible to value the opportunity to default more explicitly by modelling it as a put option. When a bond matures, the firm's owners have the possibility to default the loan and, thus, 'sell' the firm to the bondholders in exchange for the face value of the bond. Of course, the owners will do so only if the face of the bond is larger than the firm value. The value of the put can be found with the Black and Scholes formula for puts in equation (8.21):

$$O_{p,0} = Xe^{-rT} N(-d_2) - S_0 N(-d_1)$$

We have already calculated the ingredients in the previous subsection. Filling in the numbers for Construct we get $N(-d_1)$ is NormalDist$(-1.5091) = 0.066$ and $N(-d_2)$ is NormalDist$(-0.9091) = 0.182$ so that the value of the put is:

$$30e^{-0.08 \times 4} \times 0.182 - 45 \times 0.066 = 0.995$$

Using the put–call parity in equation (7.2) put $=$ call $+$ PV(X) $-$ share gives the same result: $24.21 + 30e^{-0.08 \times 4} - 45 = 0.995$.

For Questor the calculations are $N(-d_1)$ is NormalDist$(-1.1981) = 0.115$ and $N(-d_2)$ is NormalDist$(-0.3981) = 0.345$ so that the value of the put is:

$$40e^{-0.08 \times 4} \times 0.345 - 55 \times 0.115 = 3.70$$

The put–call parity gives $29.65 + 40e^{-0.08 \times 4} - 55 = 3.70$. For the post-merger firm the numbers are: NormalDist$(-1.5694) = 0.0583$ and NormalDist$(-1.0534) = 0.146$ so that the put value is:

$$70e^{-0.08 \times 4} \times 0.146 - 100 \times 0.0583 = 1.59$$

We see that the value of the put for the merged firm is about 3 lower than the sum of the put values for the unmerged firms: $1.59 - (0.995 + 3.70) = -3.11$.

Finally, notice that we can write the put–call parity as:

call value = share value − PV(X) + put value

Recall from the previous chapter that we can interpret this as:

equity value = firm value − value of risk free debt + default option value

The present value of the exercise price is calculated with the risk-free rate, so it represents the value that the single payment to the bondholders would have if the payment would be certain. This value is higher than the market value of risky debt (so we subtract too much from the firm value). The difference between risky and risk-free debt is the default option value, which is added to find the market value of equity. The default option value is also the difference between limited and unlimited liability equity, as we saw in the previous chapter.

With this relation we can explicate the effects of the merger as follows. Since the merger is conglomerate, no value is added so the value of the merged firm is the sum of the pre-merger firm values. The face values of the bonds remain the same so the value of risk-free debt is also the sum of the pre-merger values. But the default option value for the merged firm is *less* than the sum of the pre-merger values. Hence, the equity value of the merged is also less than the sum of the pre-merger values.

Exercises

1. The figure below, copied from the main text, depicts corporate debt and equity as call options. Construct the payoffs to corporate debt and equity in this figure with put options. Be sure to describe the securities involved in a precise manner.

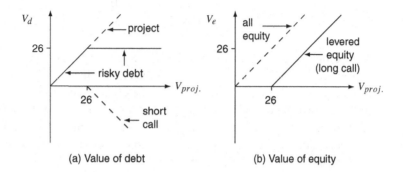

(a) Value of debt   (b) Value of equity

2. NettIT is a young and fast-growing company in the telecoms industry. Its assets, which mainly consist of patents and service contracts, have a present value of €65 million. The telecoms industry is dynamic and NettIT's present value has an annual volatility of 30 per cent. The company is financed with equity capital and a single zero-coupon loan with a face value of €50 million that matures one year from now. The risk-free interest rate is 7 per cent per year.
   (a) Calculate the value of NettIT's equity as a call option.
   (b) Calculate the value of NettIT's equity as a put option.
   (c) What is the value of NettIT's debt, i.e. the zero-coupon loan?
   (d) What is the interest rate on the zero-coupon loan?
   (e) What is the risk-neutral probability that the zero-coupon loan will be defaulted?
   NettIT's management proposes to sell some of the company's patents for €20 million and use the money to buy a company that specializes in systems for tablet computers. The company has a market value of €19 million but the present owner will not sell for less than €20 million. NettIT's bank advised against the takeover, saying that it is a negative NPV investment with −1 million NPV and that it will increase NettIT's volatility by 20 per cent from 30 per cent to 50 per cent. The bank announced that it will increase the risk premium NettIT has to pay on any new loans. NettIT's management agrees with these figures but wants to go ahead with the takeover anyway because it has strategic value.
   (f) What is the effect of the proposed takeover on the total value of NettIT?
   (g) What is the effect of the proposed takeover on the value of NettIT's equity?
   (h) What is the effect of the proposed takeover on the value of NettIT's debt, i.e. the zero-coupon loan?
   (i) What is the risk-neutral probability that the zero-coupon loan will be defaulted after the takeover?

3. AfterStudy is a financing company that specializes in loans to people who have just left university. To control its risk, it estimated a logistic regression equation for the

probability that a client defaults their loan. The variables in the equation and their estimated coefficients are in the table below.

Variable	Coefficient
NM	0.35
INC	−0.30
DFST	−0.80

All coefficients are significantly $\neq 0$. The variable NM is the number of times a client moved during the past four years, INC is the client's income (in 100,000), and $DFST$ is a dummy variable that has the value 1 if the client successfully completed the course 'Finance for Science and Technology students' and the value 0 otherwise.

(a) Calculate the default probability for a client who moved five times during the past four years, who earns 250,000 and who did not successfully complete the course 'Finance for Science and Technology students'.

(b) Calculate the default probability for a client who moved once during the past four years, who earns 600,000 and who successfully completed the course 'Finance for Science and Technology students'.

4. Reid Ottan, a local millionaire, has acquired an exclusive licence to develop the heart of the inner city. The project, appropriately called Heartbreak Project, requires an immediate investment of €50 million. The project will generate cash flows with a present value of also €50 million, but this value is uncertain. Over the next two years, the present value of the cash flows can either increase by 40 per cent or decrease by 29 per cent per year. The probability of an increase is 60 per cent, that of a decrease is 40 per cent. The city council wants Ottan to start the project immediately, but Ottan is negotiating a one-year delay. Assume discrete time with steps of one year and a risk-free interest rate of 8 per cent.

(a) By how much will the value of Ottan's licence change if the city council allows the one-year delay? Use calculations to support your answer and make additional assumptions if necessary.

The city council refuses the one-year delay, but gives Ottan the possibility of developing the plan in two phases: a demolition phase starting immediately and a construction phase starting next year. The demolition phase costs €15 million and the construction phase €35 million, but the delayed costs increase with the risk-free rate over time.

(b) Explain, with some keywords, under which conditions the possibility to develop the project in two phases has value.

(c) Assuming that these conditions obtain, calculate the value of the possibility to develop the project in two phases. Use calculations to support your answer and make additional assumptions if necessary.

Ottan approaches BB (Business Bank) with a request for a loan to finance the first phase of the project. He proposes a zero-coupon loan with a face value of €17.5 million to be paid after two years and a value now (to be received) of €15 million. Ottan argues that the value of the project after two years is always large enough to pay the loan so that the loan is risk-free and should bear the risk-free rate. BB refuses Ottan's proposal. Assume that the conditions, under which the possibility to develop the project in two phases has value, obtain.

(d) Explain with some keywords why BB refuses the loan as requested by Ottan.

(e) Assuming that BB's analysis under d) is correct, calculate how much BB is willing to loan now in return for Ottan's promise to pay back €17.5 million in two years' time.

(f) What is the effective interest rate on the loan?

After BB's refusal, Ottan approaches Marvin Blisett of Savings Bank1 with the same proposal he made to BB. After a copious meal, Blisett accepts Ottan's proposal without any changes.

(g) Calculate the value of this deal for Ottan.

(h) Calculate the value of this deal for Savings Bank1.

5. As the name suggests, Conglomerate Inc. is a conglomerate company. It consists of two divisions, one produces soft drinks and the other ferrous metals. The activities of both divisions are in different markets and unrelated, their returns are uncorrelated and there are no economies of scale or scope. Both divisions have about the same value and the same volatility. The combined assets of Conglomerate Inc. have a market value of £100 million and an annual volatility (standard deviation) of 25 per cent. The company is financed with equity capital and, in addition, each division has taken up a zero-coupon loan with a face value of £40 million and a time to maturity of two years. A corporate raider (of the Carl Icahn type) considers taking over all Conglomerate Inc. shares, splitting up the company so that the two divisions become separate companies and then floating them on the stock exchange.

(a) What are the benefits to a corporate raider of splitting up the company? Assume that all transactions take place at market prices, that there are no transaction costs, and that the risk-free interest rate is 8 per cent.

11 Hedging

The general meaning of the word hedging is to protect oneself from losing or failing by a counterbalancing action. The specific meaning in finance is risk reduction with offsetting transactions that usually involve derivative securities. Hedge funds got their name because they originally hedged themselves against the downside risk of a bear market. Today, many hedge funds use strategies that are much riskier than the overall market, the exact opposite of hedging. We have already met hedging when we analysed the hedging portfolio in the binomial option-pricing model. In this chapter we take a more detailed look at some of the contracts involved in hedging and the way they are priced.

11.1 The basics of hedging

Hedging with futures and forwards has a long tradition, particularly in markets for agricultural commodities. This section elaborates a classic example from such markets. It also sketches some other ways to hedge risks, and the principles and motives behind the hedging decision.

11.1.1 Some background

The simplest way of hedging a risk is buying insurance against it. That is what most people and businesses do for rare and potentially catastrophic events such as fires and natural disasters. Other risks can be insured on the capital market. For example, investors can protect themselves against a price fall of certain securities by buying put options written on them, the 'protective put' we saw in Chapter 7. Conversely, investors can provide insurance to others, e.g. by buying catastrophe bonds that give reduced repayments if a specific catastrophe occurs.

Corporations can structure their businesses in such a way that some risks are automatically hedged. By carefully planning and controlling incoming and outgoing cash flows, a company can avoid or reduce the risk of cash shortages. Exchange rate risk can be mitigated by locating a part of the production process in major foreign markets, so that costs and revenues are in the same currency. That is why most non-US car producers have some production or assembly facilities in the USA: paying a part of their costs in dollars makes them less sensitive to the dollar exchange rate. EADS, the owner of Europe's leading aircraft producer Airbus, does not have this flexibility. It pays most of its costs in euros but most of its aircraft are paid for in dollars, so a weak dollar against the euro reduces its profits.

11.1 The basics of hedging

Hedging as a financial strategy refers to transactions that offset the price risk of one asset by taking an opposite position in another asset. The other asset often is a derivative written on (or related to) the original asset. The principle is the same as that of pricing by a replicating portfolio, but the positions are reversed. For pricing we take the same position in the other asset, for hedging we take the opposite position. For example, consider a European company that has to pay an amount in US dollars three months from now. The company can hedge the €/$ exchange rate risk by opening a so-called forward contract (discussed below) to buy the necessary dollars three months from now at a price agreed upon today. The short position in dollars, induced by the obligation to pay, is then offset by a long position in the forward contract so that currency risk is eliminated. All major banks offer such forward currency contracts.

In perfect capital markets hedging is a zero NPV deal. It transfers certain risks from one party to another at market prices. In practice, markets are imperfect and all sorts of transaction and information costs play a role. Hence, hedging costs money in good times but makes money in bad times. For example, buying an insurance policy against fire involves a costly contracting process which, in the long run, makes the sum of the premia larger than the total damage that is covered. Contracting is costly not only because of administrative costs but also because insurance induces moral hazard and adverse selection, as we have seen in Chapter 2.

11.1.2 Contracts

A *spot contract* is for immediate delivery and payment; the price of such a contract is called the *spot price*. Most of the prices that we have discussed so far are spot prices, including the stock prices that are published in newspapers and on the internet. The 'cash' prices on the London Metal Exchange in Table 11.1 on page 310 are also spot prices.

Forward contracts, or forwards, give the obligation to buy or sell something on some future date at a price agreed upon today, the *forward price*. Forward contracts can be long or short, i.e. give the obligation to buy or to sell something. At maturity (or the *settlement date*), the short investor delivers the asset to the long investor and receives the forward price from the long investor. Forward contracts are usually tailor-made for a specific client or transaction. In the currency example above, the forward contract is for a specific dollar amount on a specific day. Because of their non-general nature, forward contracts are seldom resold and there is no organized market for them. As we shall see, forward contracts involve no payments before maturity so they are easy to price. Notice the difference with option contracts: options give the right, but not the obligation, to buy or sell something on some future date at a price agreed upon today.

Future contracts, or futures, are standardized forward contracts that are traded in a special, organised way. Futures are standardized with respect to maturity dates, quantity and, where relevant, quality. This enhances their tradability. Futures are created by an exchange that also organizes a secondary market for them, with traders and speculators to provide liquidity. In much the same way as we saw with option exchanges, futures exchanges also operate clearing houses that see to it that transactions are properly effectuated. They also guarantee all trades by taking over counterparty risk. To limit its risk, the exchange administers the investors' accounts in a special way, called *marking to market*.

When an investor opens a futures contract, they must deposit a margin with the exchange, usually 5 per cent–15 per cent of the underlying value. After every day, the price changes are added to or subtracted from this margin account. For example, when the price of the underlying goes down, a long futures position loses value and a short position increases in value. That price difference is added to the margin account of the short investor and subtracted from the margin account of the long investor. When the margin account falls below some threshold value, investors are notified that they are required to make an additional deposit (these 'margin calls' are feared by speculators). By keeping the margin account marked to market, future contracts are, in effect, settled on a daily basis and not only at maturity. It is possible to hold futures contracts open until delivery, but most contracts are closed before delivery by taking an offsetting position. Long investors take a short position, and short investors take a long position, so that their obligations to the clearing house cancel out. Futures are traded for a wide variety of securities and commodities, ranging from stock indices, currencies and interest rates to commodities such as metals and milling wheat. Table 11.1 lists some spot and future prices of non-ferrous metals on the London Metal Exchange on an arbitrary day in December 2009. Notice the bid–ask spread.

Table 11.1 *LME official prices, US$ per tonne for 16 December 2009*

	Aluminium	Copper	Lead	Nickel	Tin	Zinc
Cash buyer	2241	6945	2365	17205	15300	2370.5
Cash seller	2241.5	6946	2368	17210	15325	2371
3-month buyer	2279	6994.5	2390	17205	15350	2400
3-month seller	2279.5	6995.5	2395	17210	15385	2400.5
15-month buyer	2378	7050	2445	17265	15400	2460
15-month seller	2383	7060	2450	17365	15450	2465
27-month buyer	2457	7055	2458	17200	–	2478
27-month seller	2462	7065	2463	17300	–	2483

11.1.3 A classic example

It is March, the spot price of wheat is €70 per tonne and the price of October futures in wheat is €73.50. Farmer has sown wheat, and he expects to harvest 500 tonnes in October. If he can sell his wheat at the current price range of €70 to €75 per tonne, he can pay all his bills and make a living. If the wheat price in October is €80 he has a very good year. However, if the October wheat price is €60 he cannot pay all his bills and his agribusiness will end up in financial distress.

At the same time, Baker has made her production plans for Christmas cakes. She will need 500 tonnes of wheat in October. If she can buy the wheat at the current price range of €70 to €75 per tonne, she can sell her whole production of cakes, pay all her bills and make a living. If the price of wheat in October is €80 she cannot cover all costs and her baking business will end up in financial distress. However, if the October wheat price is €60 she will have a very good year.

Both Farmer and Baker can eliminate the price risk of wheat through offsetting transactions in the futures market. To hedge himself, Farmer sells 500 October future contracts of 1 tonne at €73.50 per tonne:

- he has a long position in wheat, since he expects to own 500 tonnes in October;
- so he offsets the price risk by selling (shorting) the same quantity in futures market.

Baker's hedge, meanwhile, involves buying 500 October future contracts of 1 tonne at €73.50 per tonne:

- she has a short position in wheat: she needs 500 tonnes in October that she does not yet own;
- she offsets the price risk by buying the same quantity (i.e. by taking a long position) in the futures market.

In October, Farmer sells his wheat on the spot market. He also closes his futures position with an offsetting trade: he sold futures in March, so he closes the position by buying spot in October. His closing position is summarized in Table 11.2 for two different prices. No matter what the wheat price is in October, Farmer's position is always the same: his hedge eliminated all price risk.

Table 11.2 *Farmer's closing position*

Wheat price:		€60		€80
Sell spot:		30,000		40,000
Close future position:				
future (short)	73.50		73.50	
buy spot	−60.00		−80.00	
500×	13.50	6,750	−6.50	−3,250
Total position:		36,750		36,750

Baker's transactions are exactly the opposite. In October, she buys her wheat on the spot market and closes her futures position with an offsetting trade. She bought futures in March, so she closes the position by selling spot in October. Her closing position is summarized in Table 11.3 for the same two closing prices. Again, no matter what the wheat price is in October, Baker's position is always the same: her hedge also eliminated all price risk.

If Farmer and Baker would have closed a deal with each other in March for 500 tonnes of wheat in October at a price of €73.50 the effect would have been the same: no price risk. However, using the futures exchange makes it much easier for market participants to find the quantity and dates they need. It also gives the opportunity to hedge price risk independent of physical delivery. Moreover, the futures exchange provides insurance against counterparty risk as well as liquidity and, thus, flexibility: if Baker changes her production plans she can simply buy or sell futures contracts. Notice that, by hedging all price risk, Baker and Farmer have also hedged the opportunity to have a very good year.

Table 11.3 *Baker's closing position*

Wheat price:		€60		€80
Buy spot:		−30,000		−40,000
Close future position:				
future (long)	−73.50		−73.50	
sell spot	60.00		80.00	
500×	−13.50	−6,750	6.50	3,250
Total position:		−36,750		−36,750

Also notice that hedging covers price risk, not the risk of, for example, a different volume (good or bad harvest).

In the classic example above, the hedge is perfect, i.e. all price risk is eliminated. In practice that is usually not the case: most hedges leave some basis risk uncovered. *Basis risk* is the risk that the prices of the two sides of a hedge develop differently over time, i.e. that the spot price and the futures price do not move exactly together. This can occur because spot and future prices may refer to different products or product qualities, different locations or different points in time. The wheat futures in the above example may refer to soft red winter wheat (a specific type of wheat), to be delivered in October at a specific place. Farmer may have sown a different type of wheat, may harvest it in September and deliver it to a local market to be sold spot.

The oil market provides other examples of basis risk. Most crude oil contracts have as underlying either West Texas Intermediate oil (WTI), which is traded on the New York Mercantile Exchange, or Brent oil, which is traded on London's International Petroleum Exchange. Both WTI and Brent are light, sweet oil that contains little sulphur. The Middle East accounts for one third of the world's oil production. Its oil is predominantly heavy, sour crude, which can have a different price development than WTI or Brent. This reduces the suitability of WTI or Brent contracts to hedge the price risk of Middle East oil contracts: such hedging can give a considerable basis risk. Airlines that want to hedge the price risk of jet fuel with WTI or Brent contracts face a similar basis risk. Setting up a hedge with basis risk is discussed in a later section.

11.1.4 Reasons for hedging

Since most people are risk averse, the rationale for hedging seems obvious at first sight. But on closer examination the matter is less straightforward. We have already seen that hedging does not add value in perfect markets (it has zero NPV). Because it is costly in imperfect markets, hedging may not be in the interest of well-diversified investors, who hold shares in both parties involved in the hedge (Farmer and Baker in the above example). For such investors it is irrelevant which of the two has a good or a bad year and the double costs of hedging reduce their returns. Hedging can also hamper investors who use their (real or supposed) special insight into the market for the underlying asset to take a speculative position. In the example, an investor can believe that the price of wheat will be high in October and buy shares of Farmer. The investor will be disappointed to find that a high wheat price has no effect on Farmer's share price because its wheat position is fully hedged.

Theoretical arguments

The economic reasons for hedging rest mainly on the smoother, less volatile performance that hedging brings about. This can increase firm value by alleviating the effects of a number of market imperfections.

One of these imperfections is costly financial distress and hedging can affect distress costs in three different ways. First, a less volatile performance reduces the probability that financial distress occurs and, thus, the expected costs of financial distress. Second, a less volatile performance will also reduce the volume part of expected distress costs. Many of the firm's stakeholders, such as customers, suppliers and employees, are likely to be poorly diversified. These business partners will demand compensation by adjusting their terms of trade according to the risk that the firm defaults its obligations.[1] Hence, reducing volatility with hedging can give more favourable terms of trade. Third and last (but not least), reducing the expected costs of financial distress will increase the optimal degree of leverage which, in turn, increases firm value through a larger tax advantage. This partly negates the other two effects because increased leverage gives a higher default probability. These three effects are difficult to quantify, but authors such as Leland (1998) argue that the tax advantage constitutes the largest contribution to firm value.

Hedging can also diminish the agency costs (to be discussed later) that are associated with very good and very bad performance. Corporate decision makers whose incomes depend on peak performance can have an incentive to make sub-optimal decisions for the firm as whole. Such income structures are typical for limited liability equity holders in a levered firm and for managers who receive bonuses in good years without being punished in bad years. Their incomes are sensitive only to the upward potential of risky investments, not the downside risk. This gives them a risk incentive which can induce them to choose sub-optimal strategies such as asset substitution. We saw an example of that in the previous chapter. By removing or reducing peak performance, hedging makes risky investments less attractive to decision makers with such income structures. Avoiding excessive risk taking will increase firm value.

Conversely, if the firm performs very poorly, corporate decision makers may rationally decide not to increase firm value by rejecting positive NPV projects. This can occur if the project requires an equity investment while the firm has default-risky debt outstanding. Under such circumstances the project will increase the value of debt and this increase can be so large that the residual benefits to equity holders are less than the required investment. A simple example is a firm whose outstanding debt obligations are larger than the value of its assets. Any project that increases asset value without making it larger than the debt obligations will only benefit the debtholders. Hence, management acting in the shareholders' best interest will reject such projects. Hedging can be thought of as transferring funds from good times to bad times and this obviously abates the *underinvestment problem*.

[1] A more extensive discussion of these effects is included in Chapter 5 on optimal capital structure.

Hedging also allows a firm to structure its risk profile. An oil company, for example, may decide that oil price risk is part of its profile and should be reflected in its stock price, while foreign exchange risks are outsourced to its bank. An airline, meanwhile, may decide to hedge its oil price risk and expose itself to the risk of uncertain demand for air transportation.

Finally, hedging can also be used to separate performance from (uncontrollable) price changes. An often used example in this context is the vertically integrated firm, say an oil company that also operates a petrochemical division. If internal deliveries are at market prices, a high oil price means that the oil division will perform well and the petrochemical division will perform less well, while a low oil price will have the opposite effect. Since neither division has any control over the oil price, evaluation of their performance should be net of oil price effects and hedging techniques can be used for that. In this example it is also clear that hedging by both divisions is not likely to benefit the firm as a whole.

Empirical findings

A number of empirical studies address the difficult task of estimating the effect of hedging on firm value. An important problem of such studies is measuring and controlling for differences in risk exposure between firms. Another major problem is the possible endogeny of value and hedging, i.e. determining the cause and effect relation between hedging and value. Allayannis and Weston (2001) use a sample of 720 large non-financial firms between 1990 and 1995 to examine whether the use of foreign currency derivatives leads to a higher market value. They find significant evidence that using such derivatives has a positive relation with market value. On average, firms that are exposed to currency risk and use currency derivatives have a 4.87 per cent higher value than firms that do not use currency derivatives. Their results are robust to numerous control variables, to the use of alternative measures of firm value and to alternative estimation techniques. They also test for reversed causality. If firms with above-average market values also have an above-average number of profitable investment opportunities, then these firms have a more than average incentive to hedge as well. The higher market values of firms that use derivatives may then reflect their incentive to hedge, and not that hedging causes higher values. However, Allayannis and Weston find no evidence that the correlation between the use of foreign currency derivatives and firm value stems from reversed causality.

Other studies focus on hedging activities in specific industries. For example, Carter *et al.* (2006) analyse the effect of jet fuel hedging on firm value in the airline industry and they, too, find a positive relation. They attribute the value increase to the interaction of hedging with investment, consistent with a reduction of underinvestment costs. Adam and Fernando (2006) document that gold-mining firms have consistently realized economically significant cash flow gains from their derivatives transactions. These cash flows have increased shareholder value since there is no evidence of an offsetting adjustment in firms' systematic risk.

Methodological criticism, as well as contradictory evidence, is provided by Guay and Kothari (2003), who base their analysis on detailed information from 234 large non-financial corporations that use derivatives. They analyse the magnitudes of the firms' risk exposures that are hedged by financial derivatives and their main conclusion is that firms appear to maintain derivatives programmes that have a relatively small effect on total risk exposure. Even extreme, simultaneous changes of three standard deviations in the underlying risk factors (interest rates, currency exchange rates and commodity prices) would generate only modest changes in firms' cash flows and values. They conclude that the use of derivatives is only a small piece of the firms' overall risk profile.

Some studies look more directly at the apparent reasons behind the use of hedging instruments. For example, Graham and Rogers (2002) test whether tax incentives affect the extent of corporate hedging with derivatives. Their analysis indicates that firms hedge to increase debt capacity, although the increased tax benefits average no more than 1.1 per cent of firm value. Their results also indicate that firms hedge because of expected financial distress costs. Supanvanij and Strauss (2006) investigate the relation between corporate hedging and the structure of managerial compensation. They find that firms use fewer derivatives to hedge interest rate and currency risk when their management is compensated with options, while compensation of management with shares increases firms' hedging activity. These results underline the importance of agency costs in the firm's use of hedging instruments.

11.2 Pricing futures and forwards

Futures are easy to use because they are standardized and traded in an organized way. Forwards involve only one payment and are therefore easy to price. Future prices may differ from forward prices because of the marking to market procedure in combination with uncertain interest rates. When the interest rate is non-stochastic, the prices of forwards and otherwise identical futures are the same. In practice, the differences between short-lived forwards and futures are so small that they can be ignored. Some currency futures, however, can have maturities of many years and their prices can be substantially different from forward prices. We concentrate on forwards but use constant interest rates, so the results have a wider validity. As usual, we also assume perfect markets with no transaction costs and without restrictions on borrowing, lending and short-selling. The basic pricing relation is developed first and some more aspects are added later.

11.2.1 Cash-and-carry forward prices

A general procedure to price an asset is to take the expectation of its payoff at maturity and discount it to the present. As we have seen, this can be done with real probabilities and a risk-adjusted discount rate or with risk-neutral probabilities and the risk-free interest rate. Forward prices, however, are traditionally derived in a different way, that is based on alternative strategies to obtain the underlying at maturity. This pricing relation is introduced with a simple example.

The cash-and-carry relation

Suppose the price of a share of ZX Co is €500 today and that you are offered a forward contract on the share with a maturity of three months and a forward price of €510.

Suppose further that the stock pays no dividends and that the three-month risk-free interest rate is 2.5 per cent. At what price would you be willing to buy the forward? To answer that question, compare the following two strategies to obtain the share by paying €510 three months from now:

1. Buy the forward contract.
2. Buy one share of ZX Co today and borrow the present value of €510 at the risk-free interest rate $(510/1.025 = 497.6)$.

Table 11.4 *ZX Co forward 1*

Strategy	Costs today	Value at maturity
1	?	$S_T - 510$
2	share-PV(510) = 500–497.6	$S_T - 510$

Using S_T for the share price at maturity T, we can summarize both strategies as in Table 11.4. Since both strategies have the same payoff at maturity, it will be clear from Table 11.4 that any price other than €2.40 for the forward contract will give arbitrage opportunities. So €2.40 has to be the price of the forward in a well-functioning market. In practice, forward prices are set such that the initial value of the contract is zero. This means that no initial payment is required, only one final payment at maturity. If we call that forward price F, the example becomes as in Table 11.5. From Table 11.5 follows a forward price of €512.50; any other price will give arbitrage opportunities.

Table 11.5 *ZX Co. forward 2*

Strategy	Costs today	Value at maturity
1	0	$S_T - F$
2	share-PV(F) = 500-F/1.025	$S_T - F$

This example demonstrates the construction of a *synthetic forward* using a *cash-and-carry strategy*. As the name suggests, a cash-and-carry strategy consists of two parts:

- Buy the underlying asset by borrowing its price risk free, using the asset as collateral – this is the cash part.
- Store and insure the asset until the expiration of the derivative contract written on the asset – this is the carry part.

On the settlement date, the initial borrowing is paid back. This exactly replicates the forward's cash flow at maturity, so the cash-and-carry price has to be the forward price in arbitrage-free markets. The cash-and-carry relation between spot and forward prices can be derived more formally in a general notation as follows. Suppose we construct a portfolio by buying one non-dividend-paying share at a price S_0, borrowing the purchasing price S_0 risk free and writing (selling) a forward contract on the share with maturity T and a forward price of F. The net costs of that portfolio are zero since the share price and the borrowing cancel out, and the initial value of the forward contract is zero. At maturity the share has a value of S_T, the amount borrowed has to be repaid with interest and the forward has a payoff of $F - S_T$. The initial and final positions are summarized in Table 11.6. Note that the initial position is in terms of costs and the final position in terms of payoffs, so the signs of individual entries are the same.

Table 11.6 *Cash-and-carry portfolio*

Portfolio	Costs today	Value at maturity
1 share	S_0	S_T
borrowing	$-S_0$	$-S_0(1 + r_f)^T$
1 short forward	0	$F - S_T$
Total	0	$F - S_0(1 + r_f)^T$

Table 11.6 shows the two essential characteristics of a cash-and-carry strategy. First, it requires no net investment. Second, the final position contains only values that are known today. The uncertain future value of the share, S_T, drops from the equation because the obligation to deliver the share, that follows from the short forward, is hedged by the stock in the portfolio. This means that the strategy involves no risk. In well-functioning markets, any strategy that requires no investment and has no risk must have zero payoff. More precisely, to avoid arbitrage possibilities the forward price F *must* be set such that the final position has zero value. This gives the following relation for the forward price F:

$$F - S_0(1 + r_f)^T = 0 \quad \Rightarrow \quad F = S_0(1 + r_f)^T \tag{11.1}$$

Equation (11.1) is known as the cash-and-carry relation between spot and forwards prices.

A closer look at the cash-and-carry relation

A notable aspect of the forward-pricing relation in (11.1) is its simplicity compared with option-pricing formulas. This is brought about by the absence of flexibility: the buyer of a forward contract on a share is *certain* to end up with the share. Hence, the forward contract can be priced by alternative ways of ending up with the share. The buyer of a call option on a share is *not certain* to end up with the share: the option can be exercised or not. Consequently, option-pricing formulas have to include the probability that the option will be exercised as well as a reward for the risk involved. As we have seen, this is accomplished by the risk-neutral probabilities that capture both the market price of risk and the exercise probability. If a call option must be exercised it becomes equivalent to a forward.[2] To see this, look again at the Black and Scholes option-pricing formula in (8.20): $O_{c,0} = S_0 N(d_1) - X e^{-rT} N(d_2)$. If exercise is certain, the probability terms $N(d_1)$ and $N(d_2)$ both become 1: $O_{c,0} = S_0 - X e^{-rT}$. If, in addition, the exercise price

---

2 Of course, an option that must be exercised is not an option but it illustrates the point.

is chosen such that the initial value is zero, the result is $S_0 - Xe^{-rT} = 0 \Rightarrow X = S_0 e^{rT}$, the continuous time equivalent of (11.1).

In view of the way equation (11.1) is derived, it will be intuitively clear that the forward price is not a prediction of the expected price of the underlying at maturity. This is easy to demonstrate with a one-period forward, which has a forward price of $F = S_0(1 + r_f)$. The value of the underlying share, meanwhile, is expected to grow at a higher, risk-adjusted rate that includes a risk premium of, say, rp: $E(S_T) = S_0(1 + r_f + rp)$. The forward price F equals $E(S_T)$ only if the risk premium is zero, i.e. if the underlying has no systematic risk. For forwards written on risky assets, the forward price will systematically underestimate the expected price of the underlying at maturity. Formulated differently, if the cash-and-carry strategy is available, the forward price contains no information on S_T beyond the information already contained in S_0. However, if the cash-and-carry strategy is *not* available, then the arbitrage relation is broken so that the forward price can convey information that is not reflected in S_0. This may be the case for assets that cannot be stored, such as electricity.

The expected return on a forward can be calculated from the same, one-period example. At maturity, the holder of a forward contract has to pay the forward price F and receives the underlying $E(S_T)$. So the expected payoff is $E(S_T) - F = S_0(1 + r_f + rp) - S_0(1 + r_f) = S_0(rp)$. Since there is no initial investment, the holder of a long forward does not earn the time value of money r_f, but can expect to earn the risk premium on the underlying. Of course, this is the market price for bearing the price risk of the underlying.

An example

Suppose the price of a share of ZX Co is €500. Forward contracts with a 90-day maturity cost €507.50 and the risk-free interest rate is 5 per cent per year. Are the forwards correctly priced and, if not, how can we profit from it? The arbitrage-free forward price can be calculated with the cash-and-carry relation: $F = S_0(1 + r_f)^T = 500 \times (1 + 0.05)^{90/365} = 506.05$. So the forwards are priced too high. To profit from the mispricing we have to sell what is overvalued: Table 11.7 gives the arbitrage portfolio.

Table 11.7 *Arbitrage portfolio 1*

Portfolio	Costs today	Value at maturity
1 share	500	S_T
borrowing	−500	−506.05
1 short forward	0	$-(S_T - 507.50)$
Total	0	1.45

Notice that simply selling forwards would give an exposure to the risk of share price changes, which would result in a loss if the share price increases. To hedge that risk, we have to include the share in the portfolio. Selling forwards gives a short position, which is hedged by taking a long position in the shares. Borrowing is included to finance the share purchase. As Table 11.7 shows, the portfolio gives a risk-free arbitrage profit of €1.45 at maturity.

It is also possible to take out the arbitrage profit today, instead of at maturity. This is done by borrowing the present value of 507.50: $507.50/(1 + 0.05)^{90/365} = 501.43$. The portfolio then becomes as in Table 11.8, with a negative cost (= profit) of $1.45/(1 + 0.05)^{90/365} = 1.43$ today.

Table 11.8 *Arbitrage portfolio 2*

Portfolio	Costs today	Value at maturity
1 share	500	S_T
borrowing	−501.43	−507.50
1 short forward	0	−(S_T − 507.50)
Total	−1.43	0

11.2.2 Cost-of-carry forward prices

The cash-and-carry relationship in the previous section is derived for financial assets that do not generate (cash) income, such as non-dividend paying stocks. In this section we introduce some more elements, such as dividends and storage costs.

Dividends

For financial assets without (cash) income, the 'carry' part of the cash-and-carry relationship involves only the interest on the borrowing. The storage and insurance costs of financial assets such as stocks and bonds are practically zero. For other assets, the cost of carry can comprise more elements. One such element is known (i.e. not uncertain) income, such as dividends for stocks and coupon payments for bonds. Holders of long forward contracts on stocks do not receive dividends that are paid during the forward's lifetime. At maturity, holders of short forwards are required only to deliver the stock, not the cash dividends that were paid. Dividends can be handled in the same way that we used for call options: their present value can be subtracted from the stock price. More formally, we can regard the stock price today as the sum of the present value of the stock price at maturity T and the present value of the dividends:

$$S_0 = PV(S_T) + PV(dividends)$$

Since the forward contract refers only to the stock part, not the dividends, the pricing relation becomes:

$$F = [S_0 - PV(dividends)](1 + r_f)^T \tag{11.2}$$

Suppose that, in the previous example, the price of a share of ZX Co is still €500 but that the company pays a cash dividend of €10 after forty-five days. The risk-free interest rate is 5 per cent per year. To calculate the ninety-day forward price, we first calculate the present value of the dividend: $10/(1+0.05)^{45/365} = 9.94$. Using (11.2) the forward price becomes: $F = (500 - 9.94) \times (1 + 0.05)^{90/365} = 495.99$. The same procedure can be used for interest that underlying assets such as bonds earn during the life of the forward; we shall meet some examples later on.

Commodities

Commodities can have negative income in the form of storage and insurance costs. These costs are (practically) zero for financial assets, but they cannot be ignored for commodities such as wheat, copper or frozen pork bellies. Just like dividends are income that forward holders do not receive, storage costs are expenses that forward holders do not have to pay. Storage costs can be treated as negative dividends: their present value is added to the value of the underlying. Besides storage costs, holders of forward contracts on commodities miss out on something else: the benefit of having the real thing instead of derivative securities written on them. In the classic example, Baker cannot bake Christmas cakes of wheat futures, she needs real wheat for that. Production companies face large costs if they run out of essential raw materials, so they keep sizeable stores of them. The benefit of having the real thing is called the *convenience yield* provided by the commodity. It is expressed as a present value. Including both storage costs and convenience yield, the forward-pricing relation for commodities becomes:

$$F = [S_0 + PV(sc) - PV(cy)](1 + r_f)^T \tag{11.3}$$

where $PV(sc)$ is the present value of storage costs, $PV(cy)$ is the present value of the convenience yield and S_0 now represents the spot price of the underlying commodity. Equation (11.3) is known as the *cost-of-carry* relation.

It should be noted that including the convenience yield in (11.3) gives the cost-of-carry relation a different nature than the cash-and-carry relation in (11.1) and (11.2). The cash-and-carry relation is developed for assets that are held for investment purposes, such as stocks and bonds. Investment assets are characterized, and priced, by their risk-return properties. Popularly summarized, one risky euro at time T is as good as any other euro with the same risk at the same point in time. All arbitrage arguments are based on that. For example, in Table 11.7 the financial forward is overpriced, so the arbitrage strategy is selling the forward and buying the share on the spot market. Continued transactions will drive the price of the forward down and the spot price of the share up until the arbitrage opportunity disappears and the cash-and-carry relation is restored.

The cost-of-carry relation refers to commodities that are held for production (or consumption) purposes. They are held not only for their risk–return properties but mainly for their role in the production process. Hence, companies that hold an inventory of a commodity may not be willing to sell in the spot market, even if there is apparent mispricing between spot and forward markets. Using the classic example again, Baker will not sell her supply of wheat to profit from mispricing if that jeopardizes her production of Christmas cakes. That effect is captured by the convenience yield. In a manner of speaking, the convenience yield is an expression for the degree in which the arbitrage relation between spot and forward prices does *not* work. Its addition makes the left-hand side of (11.3) equal to the right-hand side. A more positive interpretation is that the convenience yield expresses the market's expectation of the future supply of the commodity.

Net convenience yield

By its very nature, the convenience yield is difficult to measure directly. In practice, the *net convenience yield* is often used, the difference between the present value of the convenience yield and the present value of the storage costs:

$$ncy = PV(cy) - PV(sc)$$

so that the cost-of-carry relation becomes:

$$F = [S_0 - ncy](1 + r_f)^T \tag{11.4}$$

The net convenience yield can be positive or negative. It is typically positive for metals, that can be stored very cheaply. Copper, for example, can be stored for less than US$1 per tonne per month. The net convenience yield of agricultural commodities can vary with the harvest cycle. When crops are harvested in the autumn supply is plentiful and the net convenience yield is low. It rises slowly over the year until the next harvest. Similarly, just before winter sets in, storage tanks of domestic heating oil are likely to be filled to the brim and net convenience yield is low. After a particularly cold winter, stores of heating oil are running low and the net convenience yield will be high.

Empirically, the net convenience yield is inferred from the spot price and the discounted forward price. For example, on an arbitrary date the London Metal Exchange (www.lme.com) gave the following copper prices in US$ per tonne: cash buyer $4109 and three-month buyer $3943. The annual interest rate was 2.5 per cent. Using equation (11.4) we get:

$$3943 = [4109 - ncy](1 + 0.025)^{0.25}$$

or $-190.3 = -ncy$ so that the net convenience yield is 190.3 per tonne or $190.3/3943 \approx 4.8$ per cent.

11.3 Some applications of hedging

Hedging is applied in many areas in finance. Delta, gamma and vega hedging are important topics in option trading, as is hedging the risk of index futures in equity trading. On commodity markets, hedging with derivatives has a long history as well as a large volume. To illustrate this wide area, we look at two common applications: cross hedging a commodity and hedging exchange rate risk.

11.3.1 Cross hedging

When the price risk of an asset is hedged with a derivative written on another asset we speak of a *cross hedge*. An example of cross hedging we saw earlier in this chapter is hedging the price risk of jet fuel with crude oil futures. Since futures are highly standardized, most commodity hedges are cross hedges. But also financial assets may have to be cross hedged, for instance because there are no financial futures with the exact same maturity as the 'spot' security. Cross hedges generally involve basis risk. Recall that basis risk means that the prices of the two sides of a hedge can develop differently over time. This is likely to be the case if spot and future prices refer to different products or product qualities. For a cross hedge it is necessary to decide how many future contracts should be used to cover a given position in the spot market, i.e. to select the appropriate *hedge ratio*. We will look at a commonly used procedure to set up a cross hedge with basis risk, again using our classic example. A practical case study in agricultural commodity markets can be found in Rahman *et al.* (2001).

Suppose Farmer plans to sell his 500 tonnes of wheat in a local spot market and wants to hedge the price risk with Milling Wheat Futures in Euronext.[3] Variations in local circumstances and product quality can easily lead to different price movements in those two markets. Hence, Farmer has to determine how the price changes in his local market relate to price changes in Euronext. They have to be correlated, otherwise Euronext futures are useless to hedge local price risk. Further, if the price changes in Euronext are larger than in the local market, Farmer needs futures on less than 500 tonnes. If the local price changes are larger he needs futures on more than 500 tonnes. The ratio of the positions in the futures and spot market is the *hedge ratio*. We have met the hedge ratio before in equation (7.14) in binomial option-pricing, where it represents the number of shares necessary to replicate or hedge an option. In the present context, the hedge ratio is the number of future contracts necessary to hedge a position in the spot market. A common way to estimate the hedge ratio is running a regression on historical price data from both markets:

$$\Delta P_{local} = \alpha + \beta \Delta P_{Euronext} + \varepsilon \qquad (11.5)$$

where P stands for price and Δ is the first difference operator (i.e. $\Delta P_t = P_t - P_{t-1}$). The slope coefficient β is the hedge ratio.[4] It measures the sensitivity of local prices to changes in the Euronext futures prices. Ignoring the intercept α and error term ε, we can write the hedge ratio as $\beta = \Delta P_{local}/\Delta P_{Euronext}$ which is comparable to (7.14) in the binomial model. Of course, the strength of the statistical relation in (11.5) determines how reliable the hedge is. If the historical prices are scattered widely around the regression line, the statistical relation is weak and the hedge will have a large basis risk. If the historical prices are very close to the regression line, the hedge will be nearly perfect. We will illustrate both possibilities numerically.

Assume that Farmer performs a regression analysis as in (11.5) and finds a hedge ratio of 1.2, which means that the local price changes are larger than on Euronext. With a hedge ratio of 1.2, Farmer has to short $1.2 \times 500 = 600$ tonnes in the futures markets. If the regression has a very good fit, the error terms are very close to zero and Farmer's closing position can be summarized as in Table 11.9. The two closing prices are the same ones we used before.

Assuming that the March spot price was €70 on both markets, a Euronext price of €60 gives a price change of $\Delta P = -10$. If the error term is zero, $\Delta P_{Euronext} = -10$ means that $\Delta P_{local} = 1.2 \times -10 = -12$, so a local spot price of €58. The prices corresponding to $\Delta P = 10$ are €80 and €82. Without error term, the local and Euronext

3 The underlying asset of no. 2 Milling Wheat Futures on Euronext is wheat of European Union origin and of sound, fair and merchantable quality (www.euronext.com/).

4 By the properties of least squares regression, this estimation procedure gives the hedge ratio that minimizes the variance of the hedged position, provided certain statistical conditions are met.

11.3 Some applications of hedging

Table 11.9 *Farmer's closing position with perfect cross hedging*

Wheat price Euronext:		€60		€80
Wheat price local:		€58		€82
Sell spot:	500 × 58	29,000	500 × 82	41,000
Close future position:				
future (short)	73.50		73.50	
buy spot	−60.00		−80.00	
600×	13.50	8,100	−6.50	−3,900
Total position:		37,100		37,100

prices are perfectly correlated, so they move exactly together. Such a cross hedge has no basis risk, as Table 11.9 shows. Farmer's closing position is independent of the wheat price. However, perfect correlation is highly unlikely to occur in practice.

In the more realistic situation of imperfect correlation between the two prices, the local prices will deviate from the regression relation. This is illustrated in Table 11.10 for the case where the local market 'overshoots' the Euronext price changes with €3. For a Euronext price change of −10 this gives a local price of $\Delta P_{local} = (1.2 \times -10) - 3 = -15$ and for an equally large price increase $\Delta P_{local} = (1.2 \times 10) + 3 = 15$. The closing positions change with unexpected price deviations of €3 per tonne, so with €1,500. It is impossible to eliminate all price risk with imperfect cross hedges: basis risk remains.

Table 11.10 *Farmer's closing position with imperfect cross hedging*

Wheat price Euronext:		€60		€80
Wheat price local:		€55		€85
Sell spot:	500 × 55	27,500	500 × 85	42,500
Close future position:				
future (short)	73.50		73.50	
buy spot	−60.00		−80.00	
600×	13.50	8,100	−6.50	−3,900
Total position:		35,600		38,600

11.3.2 Hedging exchange rate risk

The size of the foreign exchange market is gigantic. The Bank for International Settlements (BIS) in Basel, Switzerland, publishes an often quoted triennial survey that includes data on foreign exchange market activity.[5] The 2010 edition reports that in April of that year the average daily global foreign exchange market turnover was $4.0 trillion. The total includes spot transactions, outright forwards, swaps and currency options.

5 Triennial Central Bank Survey 2010, www.bis.org/publ/rpfxf10t.pdf

Spot transactions account for $1.5 trillion, or 37 per cent, of total turnover. The total *daily* turnover exceeds the spending of the US government in that *year*. We shall look at foreign exchange spot and forward transactions on a much smaller scale.

Some terminology

An exchange rate is the price of one currency in terms of another. We follow the convention of denoting an exchange rate as the number of domestic currency units per unit of foreign currency. We use the euro as domestic currency. So, for example, the euro/dollar exchange rate is the number of euros it takes to buy one dollar, in the same way as the price of a share is the number of euros it takes to buy a share. We use the notation €0.714/$ to express that it costs €0.714 to buy a dollar, or $S_{€\$} = 0.714$ where S stands for the spot rate. Of course, this implies that it takes $0.714^{-1} = 1.4$ dollars to buy one euro, so the dollar/euro exchange rate is 1.4 or $1.4/€.

Regrettably, these conventions are not universally followed. For example, the financial press may refer to the above euro/dollar rate as EUR/USD = 1.4, meaning that the value of €1, expressed in US$, is 1.4. Some currencies are quoted in 100s, e.g. the Norwegian, Swedish and Danish kroner. A Norwegian newspaper may write SEK/NOK = 80.33, meaning that it takes 80.33 Norwegian kroner to buy 100 Swedish kronor. In a Swedish newspaper the same exchange rate will be written as NOK/SEK = 124.49. Professionals also use nicknames for currencies (e.g. kiwi for the New Zealand dollar) and for pairs of currencies (EUR/USD = Fiber and EUR/GBP = Chunnel). All these conventions and traditions make foreign exchange a tricky subject for outsiders. It is very easy to confuse the EUR/USD rate with the USD/EUR rate, particularly if both are around 1. To illustrate this, Table 11.11 shows the different ways in which exchange rates are presented in two popular media on the same day (25 January 2010).

Table 11.11 *Currency rates*

Country/ Currency	BBC website		Financial Times Currency cross rates			
	£1 buys		GPB £	EUR €	USD $	JPY ¥
CA, Dollar	1.7058	CAD	0.5862	0.6680	0.9473	85.480
EU, Euro	1.1392	EUR	0.8775	N/A	1.4177	127.94
JP, Yen	145.82	JPY	0.0069	0.0078	0.0111	N/A
CH, Franc	1.6771	CHF	0.5959	0.6789	0.9627	86.890
GB, Pound	–	GBP	N/A	1.1392	1.6157	145.78
US, Dollar	1.6149	USD	0.6189	0.7051	N/A	90.210

CA = Canada, EU = European Union, JP = Japan, CH = Switzerland, GB = United Kingdom, US = United States

A numerical derivation of the forward rate

Forward currency contracts are traded and priced in the same way as the forwards we have discussed so far. However, interest and exchange rates are also studied in international finance, which sometimes uses a somewhat different approach and terminology. We shall first derive the forward rate as it is commonly done in international finance and then demonstrate the equivalence with the cash-and-carry relation.

Suppose a European company, with the euro as domestic currency, has to pay $100,000 one year from now. The spot exchange rate is €0.714/$ or $S_{€\$} = 0.714$, the euro interest rate is 8 per cent and the dollar interest rate is 4 per cent. The company can hedge the exchange rate risk in two ways:

1. Buy the present value of $100,000 in the spot market and place the money in a US bank to earn the dollar interest rate.
2. Open a forward contract to buy $100,000 one year from now at the forward rate $F_{€\$}$.

Following the first strategy, the firm has to buy $100,000/1.04 = \$96,154$ in the spot market. This costs $96,154 \times 0.714 = €68,654$ today and will produce $100,000 in one year.

Following the second strategy involves no payment today. Just like forward prices of stocks and commodities, the forward exchange rate $F_{€\$}$ is set such that the forward contract has zero value today. The second strategy also produces $100,000 in one year, against the payment of $100,000 \times$ the forward rate. Since both strategies produce $100,000 at the same time, the present values of their costs must also be the same, otherwise there are arbitrage opportunities. This means that $€68,654 = PV(100,000F_{€\$})$ or $€68,654 = 100,000F_{€\$}/1.08$, which gives a forward rate of $F_{€\$} = 0.741$.

Any other forward rate opens the possibility for a strategy that is called *covered interest arbitrage* in international finance. To illustrate the strategy, assume the forward rate is too high, say $F = 0.775$. We will see later how to determine whether the forward rate is too high or too low. As in any arbitrage strategy, we sell what is expensive (forwards) and buy what is cheap ($). A covered interest arbitrage involves the following steps:

1. Borrow an amount, say €100,000, for one year.
2. Exchange the €100,000 for dollars at the spot rate; this gives $100,000/0.714 = \$140,056$.
3. Deposit these dollars in a US account to earn the dollar interest rate; this gives $140,056 \times 1.04 = \$145,658$ after one year.
4. Sell these $145,658 forward for euros; this gives $145,658 \times 0.775 = €112,885$ after one year.
5. Use these euros to pay back the loan and interest of $1.08 \times 100,0000 = €108,000$.
6. The difference of $112,885 - 108,000 = €4,885$ is arbitrage profit.
7. Repeat the above steps until the arbitrage opportunity has disappeared.

The position is 'covered' because the long position in dollars is hedged by a short position in forwards. With a small adjustment it is possible to take out the arbitrage profit today, instead of after one year. The strategy produces €112,885 after one year and this amount can pay back a loan plus interest of $112,885/1.08 = €104,523$. Borrowing this amount and continuing as in step 2 gives an instantaneous arbitrage profit of €4,523 (i.e. 4,885/1.08).

It should be obvious that covered interest arbitrage and the cash-and-carry relation differ in name only. Both strategies consist of borrowing money to buy an asset and storing it to obtain the same position that is provided by the forward contract. In the cash-and-carry relation we used a stock that may pay known dividends as underlying asset. In interest arbitrage the underlying is a money amount in a foreign currency that will generate interest. We can demonstrate the equivalence between the two by using relation (11.2) to calculate the forward exchange rate:

$$F = [S_0 - PV(dividends)](1 + r_f)^T$$

Writing the relation in currency symbols and for a maturity of 1 period ($T = 1$), it becomes:

$$F_{€\$} = [S_{€\$} - PV(interest)](1 + r_€)$$

where $F_{€\$}$ is the one-year forward euro/dollar rate, $S_{€\$}$ is spot euro/dollar rate and $r_€$ is the risk-free euro interest rate. The interest earned is the dollar amount times the risk-free dollar interest rate $r_\$$, so $S_{€\$} \times r_\$$. Its present value is $(S_{€\$} \times r_\$)/(1 + r_\$)$. Substituting this we get:

$$F_{€\$} = \left[S_{€\$} - \frac{r_\$ S_{€\$}}{(1 + r_\$)}\right](1 + r_€) = \left[\frac{S_{€\$}}{(1 + r_\$)}\right](1 + r_€)$$

Filling in the numbers from the example above we get the same forward rate as before:

$$F_{€\$} = \left[\frac{S_{€\$}}{(1 + r_\$)}\right](1 + r_€) = \left[\frac{0.714}{1.04}\right](1.08) = 0.741$$

Parity relations

International finance has developed a set of equilibrium relations that describes how the spot and forward exchange rates of countries are linked to their interest and inflation rates. They are called *parity relations* that obtain when international financial markets are in equilibrium. There are five parity relations; we shall look at the two that have most relevance for currency hedging: the interest rate parity and the Fisher effect. The interest rate parity is equivalent to the forward-pricing relations that we derived above. The forward-pricing relation:

$$F_{€\$} = \left[\frac{S_{€\$}}{(1 + r_\$)}\right](1 + r_€)$$

can be written as:

$$\frac{F_{€\$}}{S_{€\$}} = \frac{1 + r_€}{1 + r_\$} \tag{11.6}$$

Equation (11.6) is known in international finance as the *interest rate parity*, which links foreign exchange markets to international money markets. It states the equilibrium condition that the ratio of domestic to foreign interest rates of two countries equals the ratio of their forward to spot exchange rates. As we have seen, this parity relation is 'enforced' by covered interest arbitrage; it holds very well in practice. From an empirical point of view, it is one of the best documented relations in international finance. In many cases the relation is so strong that dealers set the forward rate by calculating the interest rate difference between two countries.

The second parity relation is the *Fisher effect*,[6] which explains where the interest rate differences come from: it links them to differences in expected inflation:

$$\frac{1+r_{€}}{1+r_{\$}} = \frac{E(1+i_{€})}{E(1+i_{\$})} \tag{11.7}$$

where i stands for inflation rate. The Fisher effect says that *real* interest rates, i.e. corrected for inflation, are the same in both countries. On open markets, differences in risk-free interest rates must be small and short-lived: in equilibrium the parity relation holds. Because the Fisher effect contains expectations, it is difficult to verify empirically. However, on an ex-post basis (i.e. using historical interest and inflation rates) the relation holds well for short-term debt. It is weaker for long-term debt.

Together, these parity relations make clear why it is not advantageous to invest in foreign countries with a higher interest rate than at home. The higher foreign interest rate generates a larger amount of foreign currency, but this advantage is lost in a lower exchange rate when the foreign investment is brought home again. In the same way, it is not profitable to take up a loan in a foreign currency that has a lower interest than at home. The interest is lower but more domestic currency must be used to buy the foreign currency necessary to service the loan. In both cases the parity relations imply that what the investor wins on the interest rate is equal to what they lose on the exchange rate.

The following example illustrates the argument. Suppose that an investor in the USA has $100 to invest for a year. She can put the money in a US bank and earn the dollar interest rate of 4 per cent, so that she has $104 after a year. Alternatively, she can exchange the dollars for $100 \times 0.714 = €71.4$ and put them in a European bank where they earn the double interest rate of 8 per cent. This gives $71.4 \times 1.08 = €77.112$ after a year. But selling these euros forward for dollars gives $77.112/0.741 = \$104$, the same as the dollar investment. It *has to be* the same, otherwise covered interest arbitrage would be a money machine.

The interest rate parity has two important practical applications. First, it offers an easy way to check whether the forward rate is at its equilibrium value or not. That is easily ascertained by comparing the ratio of forward to spot rate with the ratio of domestic to foreign interest rate. In the example we have used so far the numbers are:

$$1.038 = \frac{0.741}{0.714} = \frac{F_{€\$}}{S_{€\$}} = \frac{1+r_{€}}{1+r_{\$}} = \frac{1.08}{1.04} = 1.038$$

Second, the interest rate parity can be used to construct a synthetic forward when interest rates are quoted for a longer period ahead than currency forwards. In a multi-period notation the interest rate parity is:

$$\frac{F_{€\$}^{T}}{S_{€\$}^{T}} = \frac{\left(1+r_{€}^{T}\right)^{T}}{\left(1+r_{\$}^{T}\right)^{T}}$$

The interest rates are also time superscripted to allow different rates for different maturities. Although currency forwards may be available for up to ten years ahead, longer maturities can be required for e.g. international investment decisions.

---

6 The relation is named after the economist Irving Fisher; it should not be confused with the *international Fisher effect*, which is a different parity relation.

Exercises

1. Ola Norman thinks Norway is ripe for a futures market in typical Norwegian commodities and he collected the information in the table below. The spot prices, storage costs and convenience yields are in Norwegian kroner per kilogram. Storage costs have to be paid at the end of each period of three months. The convenience yield can also be assumed to occur at the end of each period of three months. Standard futures contracts are for 100 kilograms of the commodity. The risk-free interest rate is 4 per cent per year and fixed.

Commodity	Spot price	Storage costs	Convenience yield
Reindeer legs	50	5	1
Dried cod	100	2	10
Brown cheese	250	10	0
Cloudberry jam	500	15	20

(a) Calculate the price of a standard three-month futures contract for each commodity.
(b) Calculate the net convenience yield for each commodity.
(c) Explain why the net convenience yield can positive or negative.
(d) A trader has bought a batch of coffee in Brazil that will be harvested and delivered in three months' time. The coffee has to be paid for on delivery with 10,000 kilograms of dried cod (it is believed that only cod that is bartered against coffee will produce good bacalhau). How can the trader hedge the price risk of dried cod?

2. Blaufoss Automotive Company produces aluminium parts for the automobile industry. The company plans to increase production next quarter, but it fears the price of aluminium will go up. What can the company do to hedge the price risk of its main raw material, aluminium?

3. Use the prices in the table below (a shortened version of the table in the main text) to calculate the three months net convenience yield of aluminium. Assume a yearly interest rate of 6 per cent.

	Aluminium	Copper	Lead
Cash buyer	2241	6945	2365
Cash seller	2241.5	6946	2368
3-month buyer	2279	6994.5	2390
3-month seller	2279.5	6995.5	2395
15-month buyer	2378	7050	2445
15-month seller	2383	7060	2450

4. You are a citizen of Euroland and planning a holiday in the Scandinavian countries Denmark, Sweden and Norway. To hedge exchange rate risk you want to buy forward contracts on the local currencies and you have collected the following data:

Currency	Symbol	Spot rate $S_{\text{€}...}$	12-month interest rate
Swedish krona	SEK	0.0980	1.03%
Norwegian krone	NOK	0.1223	3.00%
Danish krone	DKK	0.1343	1.54%

The 12-month interest rate in Euroland is 1.2 per cent.
(a) Calculate the one-year forward exchange rates for these currencies.
(b) What other ways are there to hedge currency risk?

5. The main text demonstrates that a long forward is equivalent to a long call option that must be exercised. Construct a portfolio of ordinary options (that are exercised only when they end in-the-money) that replicates the payoff of a long forward on a non-dividend-paying stock. Use the portfolio to derive the forward price.

6. The main text describes a covered interest arbitrage to profit from a forward euro/dollar exchange rate that is too high. Elaborate a covered interest arbitrage strategy that will profit from a forward euro/dollar exchange rate that is too low, say $F_{\text{€\$}} = .72$. Demonstrate that the forward rate is too low using the interest rate parity. Assume $S_{\text{€\$}} = .714$, $r_{\text{€}} = 8$ per cent, and $r_{\$} = 4$ per cent.

7. BP (British Pencils Ltd.) has concluded an important deal with a Canadian customer and has shipped a large batch of its products to Vancouver. The deal stipulates that the customer has to pay CAD 200,000 in three months' time. The spot exchange rate is $S_{C\$£} = 1.6191$ (i.e. it takes 1.6191 Canadian dollars to buy 1 British pound). The British interest rate is 4 per cent per year, the Canadian interest rate is 8 per cent per year.
(a) If BP wants to avoid currency risk using the money market (i.e. by placing or borrowing money in bank accounts), what transactions are required?
(b) What is the three-month forward rate for the British pound?
(c) What transactions are required if BP wants to hedge the currency risk of the deal using forwards?
(d) Suppose BP uses one of the two hedging strategies above, and suppose also that after one month the spot rate becomes $S_{C\$£} = 1.75$, i.e. the Canadian dollar loses value relative to the pound. What additional actions are required from BP to keep the currency risk hedged?

Agency problems and governance

The models that we have discussed so far are based on market equilibrium or the absence of arbitrage opportunities. In such models, market participants reach consensus about arbitrage-free or market clearing equilibrium prices, which ensure that each participant gets their fair share. For example, in the CAPM all securities are held at their equilibrium market prices. Similarly, in the trade-off theory's optimal capital structure both equity and debt get their fair share of the firm's revenue, viz. the market price of the risk they bear. The first cracks in this equilibrium approach appeared in the pecking order theory, where managers with inside information can increase the wealth of the existing shareholders by issuing new debt or equity at too high a price. The cracks widened when we modelled equity as a call option on the firm's assets. We saw that equity holders can benefit at the expense of debtholders by choosing risky projects rather than safe ones. Such conflicts of interest are much more general. They are studied in agency theory, which looks at the firm as a team of different parties that realize their own interests by cooperating in the firm. That cooperation is governed by a set of contracts that specify how inputs are joined and outputs are distributed. The design of contracts that share risk and return in an optimal way is an important topic in agency theory. This chapter discusses some headlines of agency theory and its influence on the way firms are managed.

12.1 Agency theory

Agency theory has its roots in corporate governance theories that go back to the 1930s, but its application in finance is usually associated with Jensen and Meckling's (1976) pioneering paper. Agency theory is very general – it applies in principle to all situations that involve cooperation. It has a long tradition in political science and labour market economics. We have met several elements of agency theory before; we now summarize them in an agency-theoretic perspective.

12.1.1 Agency relations and contracts
What is an agency relation?

An *agency relation* exists when one person, *the principal*, hires another person, *the agent*, to perform certain tasks or services. The nature of the relation implies that the agent is likely to have different interests and incentives than the principal. The agent will want to maximize the reward for their effort or, if the reward is given, to minimize the effort. The principal will want to minimize the costs of hiring an agent or to maximize the output they receive. Consequently, the principal cannot take for granted that the agent will act in the principal's best interest. The contract, in which the agency relation is formalized, aims to overcome this conflict of interests by specifying, among other things, the agent's inputs and the distribution of the outputs. However, the contract will not fully resolve the conflict for two reasons:

1. Contracts cannot be complete; it is impossible to specify every eventuality in advance. Hence, the principal has to delegate some decision-making power to the agent which can be used to the agent's advantage.
2. The agent's inputs and/or outputs will not be fully observable for the principal. Effort is hard to measure and output is likely to be co-determined by external factors.

As a result, *agency costs* have to be incurred to prevent agents from looking after their own interests rather than the principal's. In a corporate context, the three main components of agency costs[1] are the costs of contracting, the costs of monitoring and the residual loss: the reduction in value of the firm's securities because of unresolved agency problems. We will look at these costs in more detail later.

The formal wording used here may suggest that agency relations are special cases, but they are, in fact, extremely common. Suppose, for example, that you take your car to the dealer's repair shop for periodic service. Then you are the principal that hires the repair shop to perform the service. Since you want the service done with minimal costs, while the repair shop wants to maximize its value, the potential conflict of interest is obvious. To limit its agency problems, the dealer probably has a standard service contract (somewhere in the small print of its standard terms of delivery) that specifies what periodic service entails. It is costly to let lawyers frame such a contract, these contracting costs are an agency cost. But even in the simple case of car service, it would be extremely difficult to make a complete contract. It is almost impossible to specify beforehand exactly what work needs to be done, which parts need to be replaced and by what. Hence, the service agreement involves the delegation of some decision-making power. Within certain limits, the dealer will replace small parts that are worn out, such as light bulbs and brake blocks, even if that is not included in the standard service schedule. Delegation of decision-making power is an efficient way to avoid excessively detailed contracts, but it leaves a (rich) potential for conflict.

As regards monitoring, you will not be able to observe how much time it takes the mechanic to service your car. Even if you could it would be very difficult to ascertain whether the job could be done in less time, or more thoroughly in the observed time. To avoid potential agency problems many car dealers charge a fixed, standard number of repair shop hours for periodic service. If the standard time is fairly set on the average, this will divide the risk equally between you and the dealer. If your car can be serviced in less than the standard time, you pay too much. The extra charge is an agency cost, induced by the fact that car owners, as principals, will not take for granted that the repair shop, as agent, performs the service according to the principal's best interests.

The conflicts of interest are less conspicuous in other common agency relations. If you hire an estate agent to sell your house, the agent's fee is probably a small percentage of the selling price, say 2 per cent. This fee structure appears to align the interests of the principal and agent: both want the highest possible selling price. The conflict lies in the

---

1 Jensen and Meckling (1976) use partly different cost categories.

agent's effort, particularly the marginal effort. You as a principal may be interested in an additional sales effort, e.g. organizing one more open house weekend, to try to find a buyer who is willing to pay €5,000 or €10,000 more than the best offer so far. But the agent's additional fee will be only 2 per cent of that, €100 or €200, too little to justify weekend working hours. The missed price increase is an agency cost.

The firm as nexus of agency relations

The power of agency theory is that it applies to a wide variety of business connections. The firm's relations with its customers, suppliers, employees, investors and authorities can all be described and analysed as agency relations. From an agency-theoretic perspective, the firm is not a single entity but a coalition of different parties or a 'set of contracts' between the various stakeholders in the firm (Fama, 1980). Each stakeholder acts according to their own interests, but the interests are best served by cooperating in the firm. The agency view of the firm can be depicted as in Figure 12.1, which shows the firm as a web of different agency relations or, as Jensen and Meckling (1976) put it, a 'nexus of contracts'.

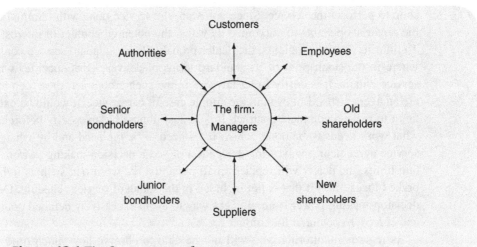

Figure 12.1 The firm as nexus of contracts

We have met some of these agency relations and their associated costs before under a different name, viz. the indirect costs of bankruptcy. For example, in the discussion of optimal capital structure we saw that firms selling durable products, that require future maintenance and service, have an incentive to use low debt ratios and, thus, have low default probabilities. Their products sharply decrease in value if the customer, as a principal, becomes uncertain whether the firm, as an agent, will be able to provide the necessary future service. If that occurs, sales will diminish or even stop.[2] To increase their reliability

---

2 A dramatic illustration of this was provided by the Swedish car manufacturer Saab, whose sales dropped by almost 75 per cent in October 2009 when the takeover negotiations with its troubled parent company General Motors appeared to fail.

as future service agents, firms selling durables will use relatively little debt. The reduced tax advantage is an agency cost of selling durables.

A similar agency relation exists between the firm and its suppliers and employees. Here, too, the firm must take certain actions, and refrain from other actions, in order to remain credible as a principal or agent. Employees will demand higher wages from a risky firm than from a safe one, other things being equal. Suppliers may adjust their terms of trade if they consider the risk, that the firm will default its obligations, too high. The extra charge is an agency cost of outside suppliers. If the firm reduces its riskiness with hedging, the hedging costs can also be considered agency costs. Needless to say that the authorities cannot expect all firms to voluntarily comply with all rules. Large government bodies see to it that taxes and duties are collected, that environmental and safety rules are enforced, and that economic activities are organised in a fair and competitive way, etc. The costs of these government institutions are agency costs.

Last but not least, there are many potential agency conflicts between the firm and its security holders and between different categories of security holders. Most firms have complex financial structures, and it would be very difficult to increase or decrease one capital category without an effect on any of the other categories. The same can be said of changes in investment policy, which inevitably will affect different security holders in different ways.

Optimal contracts

A key problem in agency theory is the design of optimal contracts. This is not an easy task because agency contracts have to both maximize some uncertain outcome and distribute it optimally over two parties with conflicting interests. To illustrate the problem we formulate it here in a somewhat simplified form and in terms of a common financial agency problem, say an investor/principal who hires a manager/agent to invest his money. The agent's task is to design the investment strategy, and the resulting investment outcome is a positive function of her effort: more effort gives a better outcome. The investment outcome is also a function of external, uncontrollable events such as positive or negative market developments. This has the important implication that the outcome is partly random and, hence, cannot be used to measure the agent's effort. The investment outcome is divided between the agent (her fee) and the principal (the rest). The problem is complicated by the fact that it is costly for the agent to exert effort, e.g. because the effort could be profitably used elsewhere. This gives a conflict of interest, because it makes the agent's wealth a negative function of her effort. As a result, the agent will require a certain minimum expected fee for her effort in order to accept the contract. The structure of this agency problem is depicted in Figure 12.2. In this setting, a contract is optimal if it induces the agent to exert the effort that maximizes the principal's wealth,[3] subject to the constraint that the agent's minimal requirements are satisfied so that she can accept the contract. Such a contract (if it can be found) is called a *first best contract* in agency theory.

3 Formal agency models are formulated mathematically and in terms of utility.

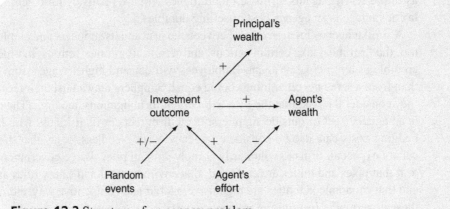

Figure 12.2 Structure of an agency problem

The first best optimization problem has been studied extensively in the literature.[4] A general conclusion of the studies is that first best contracts are possible only under one of two, rather unrealistic, conditions. The first is that the agent's effort is fully observable by the principal. This gives the principal the opportunity to make the fee dependent on the agent's effort and not on the uncertain outcome of the investment. By making the fee very low (or even negative) unless the agent exerts the optimal effort, the agent is 'forced' to choose the optimal solution. The second condition is that the agent is indifferent to risk. If that is the case then the optimal contract allocates all risk to the agent, which means that the principal gets a fixed return on his investment. The agent will then maximize the value of her fee, which consists of the uncertain investment outcome minus the fixed amount for the principal. This gives the agent the proper incentive, so the contract is 'self-enforcing'.

In most practical situations, first best contracts are impossible because agents are risk averse and their efforts cannot, or not completely, be observed by principals. Risk averse agents will not accept all risk of the investment. This would mean that they guarantee the principal's wealth, even if the investment gives a negative return. Similarly, if the principal cannot observe the agent's effort, it is impossible for him to write a 'forcing' contract in which the agent's fee depends only on her effort. The fee cannot be a fixed amount either, because that would give the agent no incentive to exert effort. So the fee has to depend on the observable outcome of the investment. However, an outcome-dependent fee does not give the agent the incentive to exert the optimal effort from the principal's point of view, as Figure 12.2 shows. Through the investment outcome, the principal's wealth strictly increases with the agent's effort. But the agent's wealth not only increases with her effort through the outcome, it also decreases as a direct function of the effort. So from the agent's point of view the optimal effort is smaller than from the principal's point of view. If the contract does not 'force' the agent, she will exert the effort that maximizes her wealth, not the principal's. We saw an illustration of that in the real estate

---

4 Often-cited papers on optimal contracting are Holmstrom (1979) and Shavell (1979). A more accessible introduction is provided by Barnea *et al.* (1985). Bolton and Dewatripont (2005) is a modern textbook.

example above, where an extra sales effort may be worthwhile for the principal but not for the agent.[5] This conflict of interest is inherent in virtually all agency relations. As a result, first best *contracts* are impossible, only *second best contracts* can be written. The difference in value between first and second best contracts is an agency cost, the residual loss of unresolved agency conflicts. It can be shown (see e.g. Shavell, 1979) that the attainable second best contracts always involve some risk sharing between agent and principal, so an outcome-dependent fee structure. It is also clear that second best contracts give the principal an incentive to incur various monitoring costs.

From this perspective we now look at the agency relations between the firm and its main categories of investors, the holders of debt and equity.

12.1.2 Firm–debtholder agency relations
Agency problems of debt

Stockholders hire managers to run the firm in their (i.e. the stockholders') best interests, which do not always coincide with the debtholders' interests. The firm can implement several investment and financial policies that benefit the stockholders at the debtholders' expense. We have already seen that the value of the firm's outstanding debt can be reduced by asset substitution, the replacement of safe assets by risky ones. The argument is illustrated graphically in Figures 10.1 and 10.2. Another investment policy that is detrimental to the debtholders is underinvestment, which we met in the previous chapter. Stated simply, underinvestment can occur if the firm has been performing poorly over some time, so that the market value of its assets has become smaller than its outstanding debt obligations. Under these circumstances managers can rationally reject positive NPV projects that require an equity investment. The value of these projects will primarily, or even exclusively, go to the debtholders, not to the stockholders.

A simple numerical example illustrates the argument. Suppose a firm has outstanding debt obligations with a face value of 150, which are due at the end of the period. The firm expects a cash flow of 75 at the end of the period, so that it is likely to go bankrupt. However, a new and extremely profitable investment opportunity presents itself. It requires an equity investment of 40 now and will pay off 60 at the end of the period, a certain return of 50 per cent. Managers acting in the shareholders' best interests will reject the project. Debt has priority over equity in the distribution of the firm's cash flows, so the entire payoff of the project will go to the debtholders. That is why good projects can be turned down! The example may seem extreme, but it is not unrealistic. Firms in financial distress can often continue their operations for some time, and generate cash flow, if only some vital machine is replaced or some important supplier is paid off, etc. The money for that has to come from the owners, who then face the situation described in the example.

The firm's financial policies can also harm its debtholders. If the firm increases its debt ratio by issuing new debt, the risk of the existing debt will increase. This will reduce the value of the existing debt, unless the 'old' debtholders are compensated for the increased risk of their loans. The 'new' debtholders will correctly assess the risk of their claims and demand proper compensation in the form of a higher interest rate or seniority (higher

---

5 Of course, the sales effort in the example is observable for the principal and could be written into the contract. However, the example illustrates the general principle that the agent's marginal trade-off differs from the principal's.

priority in case of financial distress). Issuing senior debt reduces the existing debt to junior debt with a lower priority and a correspondingly lower value. If that happens without compensation, the junior debtholders are expropriated, i.e. a part of the value of their claims is transferred to other security holders (the equity holders in this case). Stockholders can also reduce the value of debt by paying themselves dividends, so that less money is available to meet the debt obligations. In the extreme, they could sell the firm's assets and distribute the proceeds as dividends, leaving the debtholders with an empty firm. The agency problems of debt are summarized in Table 12.1, together with the associated agency costs.

Table 12.1 *Agency problems and costs of debt*

Agency problems of	Agency costs of
(1) Investment policy:	(1) Contracting:
– asset substitution	– covenants restricting:
– underinvestment	o borrowing
(2) Financial policy:	o (dis-)investment
– increase debt ratio	o dividends
– reduce seniority	– secured debt
– pay dividends	(2) Monitoring:
	– financial reports
	– ratings, credit checks
	– meetings with banks
	(3) Residual loss:
	– low debt limit – tax advantage
	– flexibility – short maturity

Agency costs of debt

Debtholders anticipate the agency problems described above and will incur costs to prevent or mitigate them. Table 12.1 summarizes the agency costs of debt in the three categories distinguished earlier. Debt contracts can include a variety of legal clauses (called covenants) that intend to prevent expropriation. They can prohibit the borrowing firm from issuing additional (senior) debt and from selling certain assets or using them as collateral for other loans. It is also common to restrict dividends payments before the debt obligations are met. Asset substitution can be prevented by securing debt with specific assets, so that they cannot be sold without paying off the debt first. Securing debt also gives its holders a priority claim on the proceeds if the assets have to be sold in a financial distress situation.

As Stulz and Johnson (1985) point out, secured debt can also be used to mitigate the underinvestment problem. If a positive NPV project can be financed by issuing more secured debt than is required for the project, the stockholders can pay themselves a dividend, while the remaining project value goes to the 'old' debtholders. In the numerical example above, the firm could raise 45 in secured debt, take on the project for 40 and pay a dividend of 5. The 'old' debtholders get the difference between the project's payoff of 60 and what is required to pay off the secured debtholders. Thus, secured debt enables the firm to undertake projects that would be turned down if they had to be financed with only equity or debt of equal seniority as the existing debt.

Another way to resolve agency conflicts is to include flexibility in financial contracts. This allows security holders to adjust their investments, depending on developments in the firm's risk and profitability or in external factors such as the interest rate. For example, corporate bonds can, in any combination, be putable (meaning that bondholders have the right to sell them back to the issuing firm before maturity), callable (meaning that the issuing firm has the right to redeem them before maturity) and convertible into shares.

Protective and other clauses make debt contracts complex and costly to write; these contracting costs are an agency cost of debt. However, clauses have value only if they are enforced. So debtholders have to incur monitoring costs to verify whether the firm observes them. To facilitate monitoring, debtholders will demand regular financial reports. It is costly for firms to provide proper and timely information to its investors. As a service to investors, firms can also hire rating agencies to assess the quality of a firm's outstanding bonds. Figure 10.3 shows an example of the information provided by rating agencies. Prospective lenders and suppliers can buy credit checks from specialized agencies that collect information on the creditworthiness of firms and persons. Large debtholders, such as banks, may insist on frequent meetings with their borrowers. Banks may also require that all the borrowing firm's payments and receipts go through the bank's accounts, so that cash flows can be monitored. In sum, monitoring costs can be substantial. Of course, debtholders take the expected monitoring costs into account when the conditions of a loan are determined, so stockholders have a strong incentive to use debt contracts with low monitoring costs. Secured debt plays a role here, too, as it is easily monitored.

As with all contracts, debt contracts cannot be complete and monitoring will not be perfect, so some agency problems will remain unresolved. Debtholders anticipate this and will apply a safety margin in their lending. For instance, banks tend to have (very) conservative lending policies, i.e. low debt limits relative to the value of the asset for which the loan is obtained. This reduces, among other things, the risk incentive of the firm's equity holders. Banks also prefer short-maturity loans, that give them the opportunity to frequently renegotiate and adjust the terms of the loan. These lending policies may force firms to use sub-optimal debt levels that give lower firm values: the residual loss of unresolved agency problems.

12.1.3 Management–stockholders agency relations
Agency problems of equity

The separation of ownership and management in most modern companies gives rise to the classic agency relation between stockholders and management. The stockholders, as principals, face the common agency problems regarding the agent's effort and fee. But the problems are aggravated by the difference in financial background between both parties. Stockholders can be (and should be) widely diversified, while managers are likely to be completely dependent on the firm for their incomes. This makes managers much more sensitive to the firm's unsystematic risk and this sensitivity can manifest itself in different ways. Among other things, it can give managers an incentive to choose 'safe' investment strategies that aim at growth and diversification. These 'overinvestment' strategies maximize the firm's (and the manager's) long-term survival rather than its market value. This incentive is reinforced by size-related remuneration: on average, managers of large companies earn more than their colleagues in smaller ones.

Shleifer and Vishny (1989) describe how managers can make it costly for shareholders to replace them by choosing investments that fit their managerial expertise. This strategy is called *entrenchment* and managers can use it to reduce the probability of being sacked and to extract higher wages and larger perquisites (or perks) from shareholders.[6] As an example, Shleifer and Vishny argue that managers of a railroad will prefer to commit the company's free cash flow to upgrading the railroad, even if paying it out as dividends would be the value-maximizing strategy. By upgrading, managers become more firmly entrenched; distributing dividends reduces the value of the manager-specific assets under their control. To avoid entrenchment, firms can apply costly organisational strategies such as job-rotation schemes. They have the disadvantage of stimulating short-termism: managers have no incentive to make investments that pay off after their expected time on the job. Remuneration systems based on short-term performance measures, such as last year's profits or stock prices, reinforce short-termism.

The exposure to the firm's unsystematic risk can also induce managers to implement financial policies that steer the firm towards safety rather than value maximization. Suboptimal, low debt ratios reduce default probability at the expense of value. The same effect is obtained by retaining earnings and maintaining large cash buffers instead of paying out dividends.

The structure of managerial compensation is probably the most contentious problem of the stockholder–manager agency relation. It is very difficult, if not impossible, to measure managerial effort, so that effort-based contracts are impossible. Performance-based compensation has disadvantages as well. It gives managers an incentive to increase the risk of the firm's operations. Moreover, it is inefficient when the firm's performance is heavily dependent on market factors beyond the managers' control. For example, the good performance of oil companies in times of very high oil prices is mainly attributable to market conditions and only in a minor degree to managerial efforts. In practice, it is difficult to design remuneration schemes that sufficiently align the interests of owners and managers, and each solution seems to create its own problems and costs. Some of these are discussed below. An additional complication is that an important part of managerial compensation is consumed in the form of perquisites, such as luxurious offices, company cars and jets. Jensen and Meckling (1976) argue that managers have a preference for perk consumption, since they enjoy all the benefits while the costs are mainly borne by outside stockholders. Table 12.2 summarizes the agency problems of equity.

Agency costs of equity

Stockholders use a variety of costly procedures to ensure that managers act in their best interests or, more generally, that they do not enrich themselves at the firm's expense. The procedures are formalized in the firm's corporate governance system, which assigns tasks, responsibilities and incentives to the firm's managers, shareholders and board of directors.

---

6 The term entrenchment is also used in a wider sense that includes all strategies aimed at securing managers' jobs.

Table 12.2 *Agency problems and costs of equity*

Agency problems of	Agency costs of
(1) Investment policy:	(1) Contracting
– safe investments	– corporate governance system
– entrenchment	– performance-related incentives
– short-termism	(2) Monitoring
(2) Financial policy:	– audited financial reports
– safe debt ratio	– stockholders' meetings
– retaining profits/cash	– board of directors
– managerial compensation	(3) Residual loss
o remuneration structure	– low price outside equity
o risk incentive	– low value – high/low risk
o perquisite consumption	– capital market intervention

Corporate governance systems can be elaborate and they are obviously costly. They are discussed later in this chapter.

An element of corporate governance is the remuneration of managers, which is determined by the board of directors.[7] Over the past two decades, performance-related incentive schemes have become an important part of managers' compensation. Examples are bonuses and stock-option plans, in which managers are paid with options on the firm's stocks. By setting the options' exercise price above the present stock price and the time to maturity equal to the duration of the manager's contract, the plans intend to align the interests of managers and stockholders. Many of these incentive schemes have become very lucrative for managers, and correspondingly costly for the involved firms.

Like debtholders, stockholders will demand regular financial reports: monitoring by outside investors and other stakeholders is primarily based on information provided by the firm. Hence, managers have extensive reporting obligations to their security holders, including auditor approved annual (often also quarterly) financial reports. Stockholders exercise their control over the firm directly in the annual stockholders' meeting, and indirectly through the board of directors. The tasks of the board of directors are to oversee management's policies and to ensure that the interests of different stakeholders in the firm are properly taken into account. Important decisions such as mergers and acquisitions require the approval of the board of directors and sometimes also of the shareholders' meeting.

As with debt, the various monitoring, control and compensation procedures will be imperfect and, hence, they will not completely resolve the agency conflicts between managers and stockholders. The residual loss can take various forms. In the extreme case, stockholders can lose their entire investment in a bankruptcy. An almost classic example is Enron, where monitoring by external auditors failed spectacularly.[8] Other

---

7 Increasingly, the approval of shareholders is also required.

8 Enron was a leading energy company in the USA. It went bankrupt in 2001 after it became known that large losses and debt obligations were not included in the financial reports, but hidden in special-purpose entities. Enron's bankruptcy, the largest corporate failure at the time, also caused the demise of its auditor, Arthur Andersen, one of the world's 'big five' auditing and accountancy companies.

examples are the many banks that went under during the 2008 credit crunch. With hindsight, excessive risk taking in response to performance-related remuneration schemes is generally regarded as a major contribution to these bank failures. A more moderate form of residual loss occurs when stockholders anticipate problems such as excessive managerial perk consumption and reduce the price they are willing to pay for the firm's equity. Similarly, stockholders will recognize entrenchment and safe, sub-optimal investment strategies and adjust their prices accordingly. Safe investment strategies, particularly keeping large quantities of cash and marketable securities, may also provoke capital market intervention. This means that other investors will buy a controlling part of the firm's stock, distribute the cash to themselves and then re-sell the stocks on the capital market. A variation on this theme is splitting up a diversified conglomerate and selling the parts as independent companies. The threat of capital market intervention can have an important disciplining effect on managers.

Faced with agency problems that are difficult to resolve, stockholders may prefer general measures, comparable to the safety margins used by lenders. For example, they may demand a high dividend payout ratio, so that little cash is left under the managers' control. Another possibility is maintaining a (too) high debt ratio. The obligation to service a large amount of debt forces the firm to generate enough cash, which leaves little room for entrenchment and safe but sub-optimal investments. In this way, debt can be used to discipline management.

12.1.4 Insights from agency theory
Theoretical insights

Agency theory emphasizes some aspects of corporate behaviour that are underexposed in the models we saw in earlier chapters. One important insight is that firms decide differently from individual persons because firms are not single entities but coalitions of different stakeholders. Decisions made by firms reflect the dynamic market equilibrium of the various stakeholders' interests, or the 'balance of power' within the coalition. In some circumstances the stockholders' interests prevail, in others the debtholders' or the employees'. For example, in many models the firm's goal is to maximize its market value. In a full-information equilibrium, this goal ensures that all parties get their fair share, i.e. the market price for their inputs. But if corporate control procedures are lax, managers can overinvest or consume excessive perks at the expense of firm value. In financial distress, the stockholders may refuse to supply additional capital, leading to underinvestment and lower firm values. Banks and other debtholders may use large safety margins in their lending decisions, resulting in below-optimal debt ratios and firm values. Agency theory highlights the deviations from full information equilibrium in which one of the stakeholders has the upper hand.

Agency theory is also a major factor in the explanation of the complexity of financial contracts. Theoretical models are mainly concerned with pricing and they use only a few categories of simple financial contracts, such as debt and equity. In practice, a wide variety of financial contracts is used and they often involve complex legal constructions. Chapter 5 sketches some of the diversity in securities. Agency problems are arguably the single most important cause of the observed complexity in financial contracting.

12.1 Agency theory

Jensen and Meckling (1976) demonstrate that agency costs can bring about an optimal capital structure that is independent of the trade-off between expected bankruptcy costs and tax advantages. Tables 12.1 and 12.2 summarize three categories of agency costs that are associated with the use debt and equity. If these costs increase more than proportionally with the share of the respective capital category in total assets, their sum can have a minimum between the extreme values of 0 per cent and 100 per cent debt. The argument is schematically illustrated in Figure 12.3. From left to right, the proportion of debt in total assets (D/TA) on the x-axis increases, as do the residual loss (R_d), monitoring (M_d) and contracting (C_d) costs of debt. The cost categories are stacked on top of each other. They reach their maxima at the right-hand side of the graph, where D/TA is 1, so 100 per cent debt financing. From right to left, the proportion of equity increases, together with the agency costs of equity, that are subscripted e. They reach their maxima at the left-hand side of the graph, that represents all-equity financing. The sum of all-agency costs reaches a minimum somewhere in between, so an interior optimal capital structure and not a corner solution.

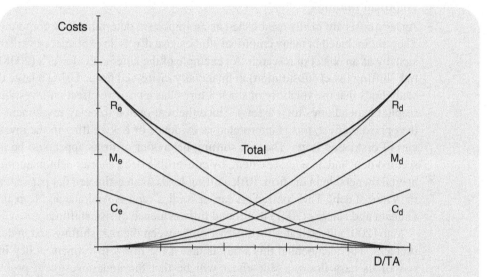

Figure 12.3 Agency costs as a function of capital structure, C = contracting costs, M = monitoring costs, R = residual loss, d = debt, e = equity, TA = total assets

As Jensen and Meckling (1976) point out, the conclusion of an interior optimal capital structure depends on the relative sizes and shapes of the agency cost functions. In Figure 12.3 agency costs have an interior minimum because they are of similar size and they increase more than proportionally with their capital category, i.e. they have increasing marginal agency costs. This is not an unrealistic assumption. Banks, for instance, will incur very little monitoring and other costs for firms that borrow a modest percentage of their total investment, and use a disproportionate amount of effort on firms with very high debt ratios that are in, or approaching, financial distress. This corresponds with the pattern in Figure 12.3. However, marginal agency costs are not necessarily increasing. If they are constant, agency costs will plot as straight lines and have no interior minimum.

Because it emphasizes deviations from equilibrium, agency theory is sometimes criticized for modelling opportunistic behaviour or representing a cynical view of the world. In essence, agency theory does nothing else than applying economic principles of value maximization to study contracts under conditions of risk, asymmetric information and conflicting interests. This facilitates the analysis of contractual mechanisms as e.g. managerial stock option plans and their impact on the way firms are managed. This is no more cynical than the condition max[exercise, expire] in option pricing. However, the discussion is often in terms of simple examples that can easily convey an impression of opportunistic behaviour. In practice, many long-term effects play a role in agency relations. For example, the decision to expropriate existing debtholders by issuing new senior debt should take account of the firm's reputation and its options to issue securities in the future. This makes the decision more complex and expropriation less likely, but not impossible.

Empirical findings

Agency costs are firmly established as an important determinant of corporate behaviour. They are included in many empirical studies, usually as an explanatory variable but occasionally as an object of research. An example of the latter is Eisdorfer's (2008) analysis of risk shifting (asset substitution) in financially distressed firms. Using a large data set, this study finds that the volatility of stock returns has a positive effect on investment intensity (capital expenditures/total assets). Since the real option to delay investment would have the opposite effect, this is interpreted as evidence of risk shifting in the investment policies of distressed firms. The risk shifting behaviour of firms appears to be mitigated by secured debt and, to a lesser extent, by convertible debt, shorter debt maturities and managerial ownership in the firm. Risk shifting leads to an estimated 6.4 per cent reduction in the value of debt. This contradicts earlier studies such as Andrade and Kaplan (1998) and Graham and Harvey (2001) that found little evidence of risk shifting.

Mao (2003) investigates the interaction between the risk-shifting and underinvestment problem. The idea behind this study is that if the firm's investment policy increases the risk of its cash flows, a side-effect will be that the underinvestment problem will be reduced. The higher risk will make projects more attractive to limited liability equity holders. Her empirical tests show that this is indeed the case: risk shifting by equity holders mitigates the underinvestment problem if the volatility of project cash flows increases with the size of the investments. An important implication of this study is that the total agency costs of debt may not be monotonically increasing, as is assumed in Figure 12.3.

Berger *et al.* (1997) examine the relation between entrenchment and leverage. They measure entrenchment with corporate governance variables such as the CEO's length of tenure (more entrenched), managerial compensation that has low sensitivity to performance (more entrenched) and the strength of monitoring by the board of directors or major stockholders (less entrenched). Their results are consistent with the prediction from agency theory that entrenched CEOs pursue less levered capital structures. They also analyse the changes in leverage after large changes in the companies' governance structures. For example, they find that book value leverage increases by an average of about 13 per cent of assets when firms are targets of unsuccessful tender offers (outside offer to take over the firm). Leverage rises by about 9 per cent of total assets when a company's CEO is 'forced' to resign from their job. These events are consistent with decreases in managerial entrenchment and the increases in leverage are in line with the predictions from agency theory.

Masulis *et al.* (2009) study agency problems in dual-class companies. Recall from Chapter 5 that these companies have two classes of stocks, one with enhanced and one with reduced voting rights. Usually, the company's founders and top managers own the stocks with increased voting rights, while the general public can only buy stock with reduced voting rights. Obviously, this ownership structure aggravates the agency problems between managers and outside stockholders. The insiders with enhanced voting rights have a greater ability to ensure their private benefits and continued employment, while they bear a smaller proportion of the financial consequences. The evidence presented by Masulis *et al.* is consistent with this view. As the proportion of insider voting rights increases, outside stockholders attach less value to the firm's cash holdings, CEOs receive greater compensation and managers become more entrenched because of acquisitions and large capital expenditures. These findings are in line with the predictions from agency theory and they demonstrate that firm value can decrease with insider excess control rights.

Many studies seek to disentangle the complex agency relations that surround the firm's decisions to hold cash reserves or pay out dividends. As we have seen, entrenched managers may reduce firm value by retaining earnings and keeping large cash buffers rather than paying out dividends. However, this relation is complicated by several factors. Differences in the financial environment can deter or stimulate entrenchment and firms can have different economic reasons for holding cash. The main relations are schematically depicted in Figure 12.4.

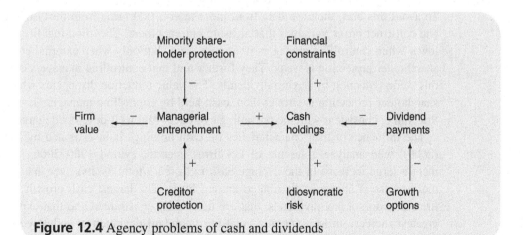

Figure 12.4 Agency problems of cash and dividends

La Porta *et al.* (2000) study dividends in an international context and they use differences in legal protection of minority shareholders across countries to analyse payout policy. Agency theory suggests that better legal rights enable outside shareholders to abate entrenchment and to extract dividend payments from corporate insiders.[9] La Porta *et al.* use a composite measure of legal shareholder protection in thirty-three countries and their results consistently support the entrenchment hypothesis. Firms in countries with better protection of minority shareholders pay higher dividends. They also find that, in countries with better protection, fast-growing firms pay lower dividends than slowly growing firms. Apparently, well-protected shareholders are willing to postpone dividends when investment opportunities are good. This effect is not found for poorly protected shareholders. La Porta *et al.* conclude that agency theory is highly relevant to an understanding of dividend policies around the world.

Brockman and Unlu (2009) investigate the counterpart of shareholder protection, viz. the legal protection of creditor rights. They argue that creditors will demand, and obtain, additional control rights as a substitute for weak legal protection. More specifically, they will demand a more restrictive payout policy so that the effect is comparable to managerial entrenchment. In their empirical analyses involving fifty-two countries, Brockman and Unlu show that creditor rights vary considerably, also across countries that have similar shareholder rights. But their main result is economically and statistically significant evidence that both the probability and the amount of dividend payouts are lower in countries with poor creditor rights. In this study, the agency costs of debt appear to determine dividend policies to a greater extent than the agency costs of equity.

The relation between firm value and cash holdings is investigated by Kalcheva and Lins (2007). As Figure 12.4 shows, agency theory predicts that entrenchment and large cash holdings will be associated with lower firm values. Shareholders will rationally include the expected value reduction of overinvestment and other agency costs in the price they are willing to pay for the firm's shares. However, this relation is not always found in empirical research and Kalcheva and Lins argue that this may be caused by sample selection bias. Most empirical research refers to well-developed, western capital markets where shareholders are well protected, so that expected agency costs are low. To avoid this bias, they use data from more than 5,000 firms from thirty-one countries and construct proxy variables that measure entrenchment. They find that firm values are lower when controlling managers hold more cash, but only when external country-level shareholder protection is weak. They further find that controlling managers can mitigate this value reduction by paying dividends. The value reduction disappears when external shareholder protection is strong: then, cash held by controlling managers is unrelated to firm value, consistent with the prevailing evidence from well-developed markets.

The influence of firm characteristics on cash holdings is investigated by Bates *et al.* (2009), who analyze a sample of US firms over the period 1980–2006. They document a large increase in the average cash ratio (cash/total assets) over that period, but the increase is unevenly distributed among firms. The largest cash growth is found in firms that do not pay dividends, that are financially constrained and that experience the greatest increase in idiosyncratic volatility (standard deviation of industry cash ratio). The analysis of Bates *et al.* (2009) attributes most of the cash increase to changing firm

---

9 An alternative hypothesis is that firms in unprotective legal environments voluntarily pay dividends to establish good reputations that enable future equity issues.

characteristics. Firms hold more cash because their inventories have fallen, their idiosyncratic risk has increased, their capital expenditures have fallen, and their research and development expenditures have increased. Agency costs play a minor role, according to their analysis. They find no evidence that cash ratios grow more for firms with more entrenched management or that the value of cash falls during the period they investigated. This is in line with most of the evidence for the US market.

12.2   Ownership and governance

The discussion of how business activities can best be managed goes back to classic economists such as Adam Smith and Alfred Marshall, but most modern summaries begin with the seminal work of Berle and Means (1932). Their book, which was controversial even before publication, started a debate that still goes on today.[10] More recently, the obvious failure of corporate governance in the mega scandals of the early 2000s, such as Enron, gave a fresh impetus to the discussion. Good governance can be of great value to companies. For example, research by Dittmar and Mahrt-Smith (2007) shows that $1.00 of cash in a poorly governed firm is valued at only $0.42–0.88. Good governance approximately doubles this value. We shall briefly introduce the two main systems of corporate governance and then focus on the relation between governance and performance.

12.2.1   Bank and market-centred governance

We saw earlier that a firm's corporate governance system assigns tasks, responsibilities and incentives to the firm's managers, shareholders and board of directors. This determines how a firm is directed and controlled. Corporate governance systems also have more general purposes, such as providing accountability, fairness, and transparency in the firm's relationships with all of its stakeholders. Corporate governance systems are tailor made for individual firms, but they are usually discussed in terms of two stylized governance models, the Anglo-American and German system.[11] As the names suggest, the Anglo-American system is prevalent in the United States and the United Kingdom, while variants of the German system are common in continental Europe and Japan. Both systems are deeply rooted in countries' legal systems and social conventions, which have very long traditions.

The Anglo-American system

The Anglo-American governance system relies primarily on market forces, combined with an extensive legal protection of investors, particularly shareholders. It is also called a *market-centred* or *outsider* system of governance. Because management is very autonomous in the system, companies that have adopted it are known as *managed corporations*. The Anglo-American system is modelled around a well-developed and active

---

10 A General Motors executive tried to prevent its publication because he objected to the work's critical implications about big business (McCraw, 1990).

11 The Organisation for Economic Cooperation and Development (OECD) publishes principles of corporate governance (latest revision 2004): www.oecd.org/daf/corporateaffairs/principles/text

capital market, that is the main provider of capital for firms. Ownership is widely spread and fragmented, corresponding to well-diversified shareholders. This means that no individual shareholder is large enough to monitor and influence the firm's management: the costs of an active role outweigh the individual benefits. Hence, shareholders delegate management to specialists with managerial skills and monitoring and control to the board of directors. This results in a clear separation of ownership, management and control. Management runs the firm. It is controlled by the board of directors, whose tasks include reviewing corporate strategy, monitoring corporate performance, overseeing major capital expenditures and selecting, compensating, monitoring and, when necessary, replacing key executives. The shareholders' formal role is limited to voting in annual or extraordinary general shareholders meetings, but this role is strongly protected by law. The legal framework enables shareholders, also with small holdings, to buy or sell shares easily, to participate in the appointment of directors independently of management's approval, and to sue directors if they fail their duties (Shleifer and Vishny, 1997). Additionally, the reliance on market forces allows shareholders to exercise indirect influence through the capital market, which provides them with a cheap and easy exit possibility. They can 'vote with their feet' by selling their shares in a company they consider to be poorly managed. This will depress firm value and if the board of directors does not take action, it will invite a correction through capital market interventions such as hostile takeovers.

Management has a high degree of autonomy in the Anglo-American governance system. This enables it to react quickly to market developments by re-allocating assets, including human capital. Flexibility and effectiveness are generally regarded as the main advantages of the market-centred governance system. A major drawback of the system is that it may lead to short-termism. Managers and directors that can easily be replaced and shareholders that can easily sell their investments in times of trouble do not stimulate a long-term perspective. Table 12.3 summarizes the characteristics of both governance systems.

Table 12.3 *Corporate governance systems*

	Anglo-American	German
Ownership	Fragmented	Concentrated
Control/management	Separated	Participation
Main financing source	Capital market	Banks
Correction	Capital market intervention	Shareholder initiated
Advantage	Flexibility	Long-term focus
Disadvantage	Short-termism	Inflexibility

The German system

The German system of governance relies less on legal protection and market forces and more on the influence of large investors, particularly banks. Hence the names *bank-centred* or *insider* system of governance. Because large owners participate in management decisions, companies that have adopted the German system are called *governed corporations*. This governance system is modelled around active, long-term shareholders, that do not adjust their portfolios in response to short-term stock-price movements. It is also based on concentrated ownership: only large investors can afford to play an active role in the firm's management and control. Large investors are typically represented in the board of directors, and this position enables them to prevent managerial entrenchment and force management to pay dividends rather than retaining earnings. It also enables them to effectuate important decisions such as mergers and the replacement of managers. The reliance on market forces is much less: hostile takeovers, for example, were virtually unknown in Germany for most of the post-war period. Concentrated and committed ownership allows a firm to pursue long-term goals such as technological leadership and long-term survival, regardless of short-term movements in stock prices. This long-term focus is often mentioned as a major advantage of the German governance system, together with the avoidance of disruptive capital market interventions. The reverse side of the medal is that active participation of major shareholders reduces managerial autonomy and, hence, flexibility in resource allocation. It also leaves very little room for participation by small shareholders, whose position is less protected than in the Anglo-American system.

Banks play an important role in the German governance system. They provide equity as well as debt, so they are shareholders as well as creditors. The direct shareholdings by German banks typically represent only a minority interest in any firm's share capital.[12] For example, Franks and Mayer (2001) report that only 5.8 per cent of the firms in their sample had a bank as a dominant shareholder, with more than 25 per cent of the shares. However, two characteristics of the German governance system strongly increase the influence of banks. The first is the German system of proxy rules (in German: *Depotstimmerecht*). Under this system, investors can deposit their shares in a bank, and the bank can vote on their behalf in the general shareholders' meeting. Investors can instruct the bank how to vote, but they usually give no instructions and let the bank vote as it deems best. This can dramatically increase banks' voting rights. For example, Becht and Boehmer (2003) report on a case in which two banks exercised more than 40 per cent of the attending votes in a general shareholders' meeting, without owning any shares themselves.

The second characteristic that enhances bank influence is the profusion of cross holdings and ownership pyramids. An *ownership pyramid* occurs when a controlling shareholder owns a company through one or more other companies that he does not totally own. For example, company A can have controlling interests in B and C, that together have a controlling interest in D. Many real-life examples of cross holdings and ownership pyramids can be found in La Porta *et al.* (1999). Voting rights in ownership pyramids easily accumulate in banks if they hold stakes in several companies in a pyramid. More generally, ownership pyramids result in an extraordinary concentration of voting power in German corporations. Becht and Boehmer (2003) document that, in their sample, 82 per cent of all officially listed companies have a large blockholder, controlling more than 25 per cent of the voting rights. (25 per cent of the votes are sufficient to block statute changes, which require a supermajority of 75 per cent.) Only a very small minority of 1.6 per cent of German companies have no blockholders at all.

---

12 Direct shareholdings are also called *cash flow rights*, as opposed to *voting rights*, which can be enhanced in several ways.

Finally, it should be noted that recent changes in the legal environment have moved the German governance system in the direction of the Anglo-American system, with more flexibility and widespread ownership. For example, the tax on capital gains from the sale of shareholdings was abolished in 2002 to increase the flexibility of capital allocation. This removed an important barrier for banks to sell shareholdings.

12.2.2 Governance and performance

The existence of two alternative systems of corporate governance begs the question of which system is superior under what combination of circumstances. That debate was started by the criticism of the Anglo-American system by Berle and Means (1932) more than eighty years ago and it has since spawned an enormous amount of literature. We shall briefly summarize some theoretical and empirical highlights of the discussion.

Theoretical argument

Berle and Means' original criticism is a straightforward application of agency theory 'avant la lettre'. They argue that ownership in a modern corporation is so widely dispersed that it is impossible for shareholders to effectively exercise control. Without controlling ownership, decisions about the diffused corporation devolve to management. Left to themselves, managers will use the firm's assets to pursue their own interests rather than to maximize shareholders' wealth. If the argument is correct, it implies that firm performance will be inversely related to the diffuseness of ownership, which would make the German governance system superior.

However, modern agency theory suggests that other agency relations should be taken into account as well. The large blockholdings in the German system may mitigate the owner-manager agency conflict, but they also create a 'secondary' agency relation between large and small shareholders. Blockholders have the possibility, as well as an incentive, to expropriate minority shareholders by endowing themselves with a disproportionately large share of the firm's revenues. Their ability to do so is particularly large if their voting rights are increased by pyramid constructions (Shleifer and Vishny, 1997). This is obviously harmful to minority shareholders. The same argument applies to other stakeholders such as creditors and even to employees who made large firm-specific investments in expertise. The resulting agency costs will reduce the value of the firm and compensate for the reduction in agency costs of owner–manager relation. Similarly, the costs of the owner–manager relation in the Anglo-American system can be abated by rewarding managers in relation to their performance, e.g. by making them shareholders or by paying them in bonuses or stock options. As we have seen, these solutions also create their own 'secondary' problems. Managerial ownership increases management's exposure to the firm's unsystematic risk, which increases management's incentives to entrench themselves, to consume perquisites and to implement risk-averse policies. Meanwhile, bonuses and stock options give managers an incentive to take excessive risks. The costs of these sub-optimal strategies will (partly) nullify the reduction in agency costs of the owner–manager relation. Since the relative sizes of the primary and secondary effects in both systems are impossible to anticipate, these arguments leave the ownership structure–performance relation as an essentially empirical question.

Authors such as Demsetz and Lehn (1985) and Himmelberg *et al.* (1999) take the discussion one step further and argue against any *a priori* relation between ownership and performance. In their view, ownership structure, whether concentrated or diffuse, is the result of transactions that are made to reflect the value-maximizing interests of the investors involved. If holding shares in large blocks would depress their value, the shares would be worth more to small investors and blockholders would sell their shares to them. If blockholdings would create additional value, the situation is reversed and small investors would sell their shares to blockholders. These transactions are very likely to reflect the characteristics of the firm and its environment. Certain combinations of characteristics lend themselves better to widely dispersed ownership, while other combinations favour concentrated ownership. For example, firms operating in a highly volatile environment with respect to input prices, output prices, technology, etc. will require a high level of managerial discretion. The payoff to the owners of strict control will be correspondingly high. Since strict control is costly, and since dispersed ownership cannot afford to incur these costs, volatile environments lead to concentrated ownership structures. Conversely, firms in stable environments are easier to monitor and are therefore better suited to widely dispersed ownership. Himmelberg *et al.* (1999) tie ownership structure to the type of assets in a firm. Intangible assets such as growth opportunities are subject to more managerial discretion and are therefore more difficult to monitor than tangible assets. Hence, they lend themselves less to widespread, diffuse ownership. If ownership structures are chosen to maximize firm value in the given combination of characteristics, then two important consequences occur. First, no systematic relation between ownership structure and firm performance can be expected. Second, ownership structure is an endogenous variable and this should be reflected in the procedure to estimate its effect on performance.

Empirical evidence

The theoretical arguments in the previous subsection are reflected in the increasing sophistication of the empirical studies of the ownership structure–performance relation. The definition of ownership structure gradually shifted from statistical measures of ownership concentration to the size of specific blockholdings by management, families, banks or other companies. A parallel development has been the introduction of increasingly complex relations between ownership structure and performance. For example, Demsetz and Villalonga (2001) summarize several studies that suggest a curvilinear relation between ownership concentration and performance. Low levels of concentrated ownership increase firm value, but after a certain point the costs of concentrated ownership outweigh the benefits, giving a lower firm value. Gugler *et al.* (2008) explicitly model this phenomenon by using separate variables to measure the benefits and disadvantages of insider ownership and they find optimal values for most of their samples. Further, following Demsetz and Lehn's (1985) suggestion, recent contributions such as Himmelberg *et al.* (1999), Anderson and Reeb (2003) and Maury (2006) present evidence that ownership structure and performance are jointly determined by characteristics of the firm and its environment. The endogenous nature of ownership is reflected in many recent empirical studies.

The empirical literature on the ownership–performance relation is vast. Table 12.4 summarizes some often cited contributions by the aspects of ownership they analyse

Table 12.4 *Ownership effect of performance, literature overview*

Ownership characteristic	Exogenous (Yes/No)	Concentrated	Managerial	State	Bank	Other corporate	Family	Country
Demsetz and Lehn (1985)	N	0						USA
Craswell et al. (1997)	Y		0				0	Australia
Xu and Wang (1999)	Y			–		+		China
Himmelberg et al. (1999)	N		0					USA
Bianco and Casavola (1999)	Y	–						Italy
Lehmann and Weigand (2000)	N				+	0/–	–	Germany
Thomsen and Pedersen (2000)	N			–	+	–	–	Europe
Demsetz and Villalonga (2001)	N		0					USA
Pedersen and Thomsen (2003)	N			–		+	0	Europe
Singh and Davidson (2003)	Y		+					USA
Anderson and Reeb (2003)	N						+	USA
Randøy and Goel (2003)	Y						+ founder – others	Norway
Villalonga and Amit (2006)	Y						+ founders – others	USA
Maury (2006)	N						+	Europe
Gugler et al. (2008)	Y		+/–					World

+= positive effect, – = negative effect, 0 = no significant effect, blank space = effect not investigated.

(ownership concentration, managerial ownership or various blockholders as families, state or other companies). Taken as a whole, the results of the studies in Table 12.4 illustrate the conflicting nature of the empirical findings. Positive and negative relations are found, as well as the absence of a relation between ownership structure and performance. The studies seem to agree on the negative effect of state ownership on performance, and the positive effect of bank ownership. Table 12.4 also indicates that the positive effect of family ownership seems to be confined to the founding member of the family. This may help explain the mixed results of the other analyses of family ownership where no distinction between founders and others is made.

The studies reviewed here refer to different countries, time periods, industries and size classes, which makes it difficult to formulate general conclusions. Collectively, however, the studies do not provide support for the superiority of either the German or the Anglo-American governance system. Rather, ownership structure and performance appear to be jointly determined in response to the characteristics of the firm and its environment.

Exercises

1. Suppose investors recognize that a firm's management is firmly entrenched. How will the stock price react to an announcement that:
   (a) the firm will take over another firm?
   (b) the firm plans a large divestiture, e.g. the sale of a subsidiary company?
   (c) the firm will skip dividends and invest the money in an upgrade of the existing operations?
   (d) the firm's CEO is forced out by the board of directors?
   (e) one or more investment groups have acquired a large block (>5 per cent) of the firm's shares?
   (f) a family member of the CEO is appointed to board of directors?

2. An often used fee structure for hedge fund managers is the (more or less standard) '2 and 20' rule: an annual management fee of 2 per cent of the funds under management, and a 20 per cent incentive fee of the returns that exceed some benchmark. Comment on this fee structure from an agency-theoretic point of view.

3. Consider a firm with a current market value of 50. At the end of each of the next two periods this value can either increase by 20 per cent or decrease by 10 per cent. The firm has debt outstanding in the form of a single zero-coupon bond with a face value of 40, to be paid at the end of the second period. The period risk-free interest rate is 10 per cent.
   (a) Calculate the value of the firm's debt and equity.
   The firm now considers changing its financial policy and increasing its debt ratio by issuing a new zero-coupon bond with a face value of 20 to be paid at the end of the second period. The bond has the same priority as the existing bond. The proceeds of the bond issue will be used to pay a dividend to shareholders.
   (b) Should the firm go ahead with this plan or not? Use calculations to support your answer. Show where the benefits, if any, for the shareholders come from.

After the bond has been issued, the firm comes across a safe and lucrative project. Instead of using the proceeds to pay a dividend, the firm could also use them to invest in the project that gives a payoff of 21 at the end of the second period in all states of the world.

(c) Should the firm go ahead with this project or not? Use calculations to support your answer. Show where the benefits, if any, for the shareholders come from.

Look again at the firm in question 1 (i.e. without the new issue or project). The firm has the opportunity to reallocate its resources with a new investment strategy, that has the same value now, i.e. 50, but that is more risky. With the new strategy, the value can either increase by 40 per cent or decrease by 25 per cent.

(d) Should the firm go ahead with this plan or not? Use calculations to support your answer. Show where the benefits, if any, for the shareholders come from.

4. SaBa is a Swedish car producer that got into financial difficulties after its parent company, Specific Motors, almost went bankrupt. SaBa's sales plummeted and the value of the company with it and now the company is worth just €40 million. That value develops over time like a binomial process with an up factor of 1.25 and a down factor of 0.8 per period. However, by the end of the period SaBa has to pay €60 million to various creditors, so it is technically insolvent. SaBa's chief engineer worked frantically to save the company and came up with a very lucrative rationalization project that will boost the company's end-of-period value by €7.5 million. The project requires an investment of only €1 million now. Since SaBa's bank and other creditors refuse to supply additional money, the €1 million is to be supplied by the shareholders. The risk-free interest rate is 7 per cent.

(a) Why do sales of a car manufacturer plummet when its parent company gets into financial difficulties? Answer from an agency-theoretic perspective.

(b) Should the shareholders go ahead with the chief engineer's plan? Use calculations to support your answer and make additional assumptions if necessary.

(c) Which agency problem is highlighted in question (b)?

(d) What type of security could be used to make this investment attractive to both creditors and shareholders? No calculations are required.

SaBa's chief financial officer came up with a plan to sell the entire production to an emerging economy in the Far East. That leaves the present value of the company unaltered at €40 million, but the end-of-period values become either 74 or 21.6. In addition, the plan requires an immediate investment of €1 million in retooling.

(e) Should the shareholders go ahead with the chief financial officer's plan? Use calculations to support your answer and make additional assumptions if necessary.

(f) Which agency problem is highlighted in question (e)?

5. Recall the discussion of economic depreciation in Chapter 2. We saw that, in the accounting representation of projects, book depreciation is stable while profit and book return can go wildly up and down. In the financial representation, economic depreciation goes strongly up and down while return on investment is constant and equal to the opportunity cost of capital. Table 12.5 summarizes the most relevant data from the example in Chapter 2.

Table 12.5 *Two representations of a project*

year	1	2	3
Accounting representation:			
Book depreciation	−65	−65	−65
Net profit	17.5	84	21
Book return on investment	.085	.560	.210
Financial representation:			
Economic depreciation	−21.1	−87.8	−96.8
Net profit	51.4	46.2	24.2
Return on investment	0.25	0.25	0.25

(a) Explain from an agency-theoretic perspective which representation would be preferred by managers whose compensation is (partly) dependent on the realized return in each year.

(b) What effect would accelerated book depreciation (more depreciation in early years, less in later years) have on the answer under (a)?

Solutions to exercises

Chapter 2

1. The time value of money and the risk premium, that together constitute discount rates, strongly reduce values over time. With a discount rate of 10 per cent, €1,000 to be received ten years from now has a present value of $1000/1.1^{10} = 385.54$, if the amount is to be received after twenty years the present value is $1000/1.1^{20} = 148.64$ and after thirty years $1000/1.1^{30} = 57.31$. The benefits have to be very large indeed to justify projects on such a timescale from an economic point of view. This effect also works for negative benefits. The demolition costs of a nuclear power plant can be enormous, but since they are incurred after the plant's lifetime of thirty years or more, their present value is small. The effect is illustrated in Figure S2.1. The economic viability of visionary projects can be enhanced by lowering interest rates and lowering risk premia, for example by guaranteeing a high, fixed price for green electricity for twenty or thirty years. With a 5 per cent discount rate, the present values are $1000/1.05^{10} = 613.91$, $1000/1.05^{20} = 376.89$ and $1000/1.05^{30} = 231.38$.

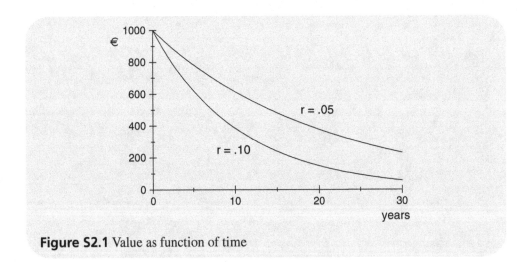

Figure S2.1 Value as function of time

2. To make amounts in different periods comparable, we have to discount or compound them to the same point in time. Here, discounting to the present is the easier way. Note that the annuity and perpetuity begin now, not at the end of the period.

(a) 300000 AED

(b) $425000/1.1^4 = 290281$

(c) using formula (2.2) we get:

$$PV = A\frac{1 - \left(\frac{1}{1+r}\right)^n}{1 - \frac{1}{1+r}} \Rightarrow 65000\frac{1 - \left(\frac{1}{1+.1}\right)^6}{1 - \frac{1}{1+.1}} = 311400$$

(d) $30000 + 30000/.1 = 330000$

So the perpetuity in (d) is the most valuable alternative. If the interest rate is 12.5 per cent, the amount now has the highest value:

(a) 300000 AED

(b) $425000/1.125^4 = 265325$

(c)

$$65000\frac{1 - \left(\frac{1}{1+.125}\right)^6}{1 - \frac{1}{1+.125}} = 296440$$

(d) $30000 + 30000/.125 = 270000$

3. The present value formula is:

$$PV = A\frac{1 - \left(\frac{1}{1+r}\right)^n}{1 - \frac{1}{1+r}}$$

and the future value is the compounded present value: $FV = PV(1 + r)^{n-1}$. Substituting:

$$FV = A\frac{1 - \left(\frac{1}{1+r}\right)^n}{1 - \frac{1}{1+r}} \times (1 + r)^{n-1}$$

Since $(1 + r)^{n-1} = (1 + r)^n/(1 + r)$ and $\left(\frac{1}{1+r}\right)^n = 1/(1 + r)^n$ we can write

$$FV = A\frac{1 - \frac{1}{(1+r)^n}}{1 - \frac{1}{1+r}} \times \frac{(1 + r)^n}{(1 + r)}$$

$$FV = A\frac{(1 + r)^n - \frac{(1+r)^n}{(1+r)^n}}{(1 + r) - \frac{1+r}{1+r}} = A\frac{(1 + r)^n - 1}{r}$$

4. Generally, book values are the same as market values when they are first entered in the bookkeeping. But while market values change continuously under the influence of new information, book values stay the same. So the differences increase with time: for short-lived items (current assets and liabilities) the differences are small, for long-lived items the differences can be large.

5. (a) The project should be accepted if it has a positive NPV. To calculate NPV we first have to calculate the proper cash flows and then discount them to the present. The calculations are shown in Table S2.1.

Table S2.1 *NPV calculations*

Year	0	1	2	3	4
Income		300	400	450	350
Production cost		−150	−175	−200	−150
Operating costs		−50	−75	−65	−60
Operating income		100	150	185	140
Depreciation		−87.5	−87.5	−87.5	−87.5
Income before tax		12.5	62.5	97.5	52.5
Tax @ 28%		−3.5	−17.5	−27.3	−14.7
Income after tax		9	45	70.2	37.8
Income after tax		9	45	70.2	37.8
Depreciation		87.5	87.5	87.5	87.5
Change in working capital	−20	−15	−15	−10	60
Investment	−350				
Cash flow	−370.0	81.5	117.5	147.7	185.3
PV of cash flows	408.7				
NPV	38.7				
IRR	14%				

The present value of the cash flows is calculated as

$$\frac{81.5}{1.1} + \frac{117.5}{1.1^2} + \frac{147.7}{1.1^3} + \frac{185.3}{1.1^4} = 408.73$$

(b) The internal rate of return is calculated by solving

$$-370 + \frac{81.5}{r} + \frac{117.5}{r^2} + \frac{147.7}{r^3} + \frac{185.3}{r^4} = 0$$

for r, which gives $r = 1.1415$ and $r = -0.73482$, corresponding to discount rates of 14 per cent and −173 per cent

6. For $U(W) = \ln(W)$ the first derivative is

$$U'(W) = \frac{\partial U(W)}{\partial W} = \frac{1}{W}$$

and the second is found with the quotient rule:

$$U''(W) = \frac{\partial^2 U(W)}{\partial W^2} = \frac{\frac{\partial 1}{\partial W} \times W - 1 \times \frac{\partial W}{\partial W}}{W^2} = \frac{-1}{W^2}$$

so that

$$ARA(W) = -\frac{U''(W)}{U'(W)} = -\frac{\frac{-1}{W^2}}{\frac{1}{W}} = \frac{1}{W} \qquad RRA(W) = -W\frac{U''(W)}{U'(W)} = 1$$

We see that ARA decrease with W and that RRA is constant; these are generally considered desirable properties for utility functions. They imply that the risk of losing

$1 million means fewer to Bill Gates than it does to you and me, but that losing 10 per cent of W means the same, no matter how large or small W is.

7. To answer the question we calculate the Arrow-Pratt coefficients of absolute risk aversion: $U'_A = 3 - .04W$ and $U''_A = -.04$; similarly $U'_B = 2 - .02W$ and $U''_B = -.02$. The coefficients are: $ARA_A = \frac{.04}{3-.04W}$ and $ARA_B = \frac{.02}{2-.02W}$. Multiplying the latter by $\frac{2}{2}$ makes is easy to see that $\frac{.04}{3-.04W} > \frac{.04}{4-.04W}$. Multiplication by W to find the RRA leaves the inequality unaltered, so person A is more risk averse than B. The utility curves are plotted in Figure S2.2; we see that the line representing the first function is more curved, while the second is flatter.

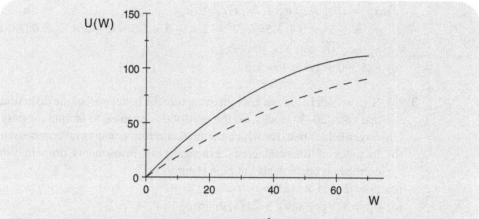

Figure S2.2 The utility functions $3W - .02W^2$ (solid) and $2W - .01W^2$ (dashed)

8. The budget line becomes more steeply downward sloping. If the opportunity cost of capital is higher, fewer projects are taken into production.

9. The optimum is reached with the following steps:

- At t_0, borrow the maximum against the t_1 budget; this gives a total t_0 budget of 19.
- Of this 19, invest 19–B01 in productive assets, this leaves B01–0 in t_0.
- Of this available budget in t_0, lend B01–B02, this leaves B02 for consumption, the optimal amount in t_0.
- The productive investments pay off B11–0 in t_1; the B01–B02 lent in t_0 has a t_1 value of B12–B11. Total budget in t_1 is thus $(B11 - 0) + (B12 - B11) = B12$, the optimal amount.

Chapter 3

1. (a) Yes, if the index fund is a good proxy for the market as a whole, then combinations of this fund and risk-free investing lie on the CML.

(b) $.5 \times .05 + .5 \times .15 = 0.1$ or 10 per cent

(c) $\sigma_p^2 = x_1^2 \sigma_1^2 + x_2^2 \sigma_2^2 + 2x_1 x_2 \rho_{1,2} \sigma_1 \sigma_2$

$\sigma_p^2 = .5^2 \times 0 + .5^2 \times .2^2 + 2 \times .5 \times .5 \times 0 \times 0 \times .2 = 0.01 \Rightarrow$

$\sigma_p = \sqrt{.01} = 0.1$ or 10 per cent

(d) $.5 \times 0 + .5 \times 1 = 0.5$

2. (a) By borrowing an amount equal to 50 per cent of his money and investing this together with his own money.

(b) Yes, if the index fund is a good proxy for the market as a whole, then combinations of this fund and risk-free investing lie on the CML.

(c) $-.5 \times .05 + 1.5 \times .15 = 0.2$

(d) $\sigma_p^2 = x_1^2 \sigma_1^2 + x_2^2 \sigma_2^2 + 2x_1 x_2 \rho_{1,2} \sigma_1 \sigma_2$

$\sigma_p^2 = -.5^2 \times 0 + 1.5^2 \times .2^2 + 2 \times -.5 \times 1.5 \times 0 \times 0 \times .2 = 0.09 \Rightarrow$

$\sigma_p = \sqrt{.09} = 0.3$ or 30 per cent

(e) $-.5 \times 0 + 1.5 \times 1 = 1.5$

3. (a) No, two stocks are not enough to capture the better part of the diversification effect, that takes 20–30 stocks. So the portfolio is exposed to unique (or unsystematic, or diversifiable) risk, for which the market return contains no compensation.

(b) In times of financial crises practically all investments drop in value, so their correlation coefficients are high (approach 1).

(c) $.5 \times .2 + .5 \times .125 = 0.1625$

(d) $\sigma_p^2 = x_1^2 \sigma_1^2 + x_2^2 \sigma_2^2 + 2x_1 x_2 \rho_{1,2} \sigma_1 \sigma_2$

$\sigma_p^2 = .5^2 \times .4^2 + .5^2 \times .25^2 + 2 \times .5 \times .5 \times 0 \times .4 \times .2 = .055625 \Rightarrow$

$\sigma_p = \sqrt{.055625} = 0.235\,85$ or 23.5 per cent

4. (a) $r = .05 + 2.1(.15 - .05) = 0.26$

(b)

	Market value	β	r
ZX Co before	4.25	2.1	.26
new investment	4.25	0	.05
ZX Co after	8.5	1.05	.155

(c) It doesn't matter where the money comes from, only where it goes to. A risk-free investment is just as valuable to the riskiest company on the stock exchange as it is to the safest company.

5. (a) Without short selling, the maximum return portfolio places the entire investment in the stock with the highest return, so 100 per cent in Amazon.

(b) We can divide the difference between the maximum return portfolio, with 0.125 return, and the minimum variance portfolio, with 0.092 return, in steps of, e.g. 0.005 and minimize portfolio variance for each step. Connecting the dots gives an approximation of the efficient frontier.

(c) The contribution of each stock to portfolio variance is the sum of its row (or column) entries in the variance-covariance matrix. The cells are calculated as $x_i x_j \sigma_i \sigma_j \rho_{i,j}$. The weights are given and the standard deviations and correlations are in the table in the exercise. So the contribution of Cisco is $(.02 \times .02 \times .363 \times .363 \times 1) + (.02 \times .36 \times .363 \times .34 \times .34) + (.02 \times .62 \times .363 \times .25 \times .43) = 0.00083872$. Similarly, for Amazon: $(.36 \times .36 \times .34 \times .34 \times 1) + (.36 \times .02 \times .34 \times .363 \times .34) + (.36 \times .62 \times .34 \times .25 \times .58) = 0.026288$ and Apple: $(.62 \times .62 \times .25 \times .25 \times 1) + (.62 \times .02 \times .25 \times .363 \times .43) + (.62 \times .36 \times .25 \times .34 \times .58) = 0.035513$. We can check this by recalculating portfolio variance: $0.00083872 + 0.026288 + 0.035513 = 0.06264$ and standard deviation: $0.06264^{.5} = 0.25$

To calculate β's we have to retrace the steps we took to derive them until we reach the data we calculated above. Recall that $\beta_i = cov_{i,p}/\sigma_p^2$ and that we obtained this by using the 'additive' property of covariance: $contr_i = weight_i \times cov_{i,p}$ and the relative contribution is $contr_i$ divided by portfolio variance $rel.contr_i = (weight_i \times cov_{i,p})/\sigma_p^2 = weight_i \times (cov_{i,p}/\sigma_p^2) = weight_i \times \beta_i$. So $weight_i \times \beta_i = contr_i/\sigma_p^2$. We just calculated portfolio variance and the stocks' contributions. Filling in the numbers we get for Cisco:
$.02 \times \beta = 0.00083872/0.06264 \Rightarrow \beta = 0.669$, for Amazon:
$.36 \times \beta = 0.026288/0.06264 \Rightarrow \beta = 1.166$ and for Apple:
$.62 \times \beta = 0.035513/0.06264 \Rightarrow \beta = 0.914$. We can check this with the additivity property of β's, $\sum x_i \beta_i = 1$: $.02 \times 0.669 + .36 \times 1.166 + .62 \times .914 = 1$.

6. The following analyses are based on 53 weekly closing prices from 22 October 2010 to 14 October 2011; the estimates and statistics can be produced with Excel or with any statistical package.

(a) The following descriptive statistics, which can easily be calculated from the data in a spreadsheet, are needed later:

	Mean $\bar{r}_i$	St. dev. $\widehat{\sigma}_i$
YHOO	0.105%	5.651%
MSFT	0.236%	3.081%
NDX	0.280%	3.017%

The characteristic line is obtained by a time series regression of the returns of a stock on the returns of the market (approximated by the index). For each stock, we estimate the coefficients of $r_{it} = \widehat{\alpha}_i + \widehat{\beta}_i r_{mt} + \widehat{\varepsilon}_{it}$ where r_{it} are the returns of stock i in period t, r_{mt} are the returns of the index in period t, $\widehat{\alpha}_i$ and $\widehat{\beta}_i$ are coefficients to be estimated and ε_{it} is the error term. The results are:

	$\widehat{\alpha}$	$t(\widehat{\alpha})$	$\widehat{\beta}$	$t(\widehat{\beta})$	R^2
YHOO	−0.133	−0.187	0.851	3.571	0.19
MSFT	0.023	0.077	0.763	7.872	0.55

(b) The average risk-free rate per week, $\bar{r}_f$, is approximately $5.2/52 = 0.1$ per cent. The Sharpe ratio is $(\bar{r}_i - \bar{r}_f)/\hat{\sigma}_i$, so for:

YHOO $(0.105 - 0.1)/5.651 = 0.00088$

MSFT $(0.236 - 0.1)/3.081 = 0.04414$

(c) The Treynor ratio is $(\bar{r}_i - \bar{r}_f)/\hat{\beta}_i$, so for:

YHOO $(0.105 - 0.1)/0.851 = 0.00588$

MSFT $(0.236 - 0.1)/0.763 = 0.17824$

(d) Jensen's alpha is $\bar{r}_i - (\bar{r}_f + \hat{\beta}_i(\bar{r}_m - \bar{r}_f))$ so for:

YHOO $0.105 - (0.1 + 0.851(0.28 - 0.1)) = -0.14818$

MSFT $0.236 - (0.1 + 0.763(0.28 - 0.1)) = -0.00134$

7. (a) Given the sensitivities of .75 and .7 we can calculate the portfolio return: $.075 + .75 \times .06 + .7 \times .03 = 0.141$ Together with the sensitivities we now have three equations for the three unknown portfolio weights:

$$.141 = x_1 \times .18 + x_2 \times .15 + x_3 \times .12$$
$$.75 = x_1 \times 1.5 + x_2 \times .5 + x_3 \times .6$$
$$.7 = x_1 \times .5 + x_2 \times 1.5 + x_3 \times .3$$

The solution to this system is: $x_1 = 0.2$, $x_2 = 0.3$, $x_3 = 0.5$.

(b) The pure factor portfolios are found in the same way, because we know their sensitivities and returns:

$$.135 = x_1 \times .18 + x_2 \times .15 + x_3 \times .12$$
$$1 = x_1 \times 1.5 + x_2 \times .5 + x_3 \times .6$$
$$0 = x_1 \times .5 + x_2 \times 1.5 + x_3 \times .3$$

Solution is: $[x_1 = 0.41,\ x_2 = -0.32,\ x_3 = 0.91]$

$$.105 = x_1 \times .18 + x_2 \times .15 + x_3 \times .12$$
$$0 = x_1 \times 1.5 + x_2 \times .5 + x_3 \times .6$$
$$1 = x_1 \times .5 + x_2 \times 1.5 + x_3 \times .3$$

Solution is: $[x_1 = -0.590\,91, x_2 = 0.681\,82, x_3 = 0.909\,09]$

(c) Return: $1/3 \times .18 + 1/3 \times .15 + 1/3 \times .12 = 0.15$, $b_1 = 1/3 \times 1.5 + 1/3 \times .5 + 1/3 \times .6 = 0.867$, $b_2 = 1/3 \times .5 + 1/3 \times 1.5 + 1/3 \times .3 = 0.767$. The return can be checked with the risk-return plane: $.075 + .867 \times .06 + .767 \times .03 = 0.15$

Chapter 4

1. Goldman's decision is an effort to 'time' the market, which assumes the ability to predict when valuations will go up again. In efficient markets prices cannot be predicted, the possibility that valuations will go up again is already included in today's price.

2. No, over short time intervals (e.g. days) the expected return is so small that it can be ignored in autocorrelation calculations. 20 per cent return per year over 250 trading days means less than 0.1 per cent per day, very small compared to daily price changes. The fair game model does not require returns (price changes) to have zero expectation, but the *excess returns*, or deviations from the expected returns. Similarly, the EMH does not require stock prices to be martingales but the *properly discounted* stock prices. The stock prices themselves are expected to increase with required rate of return on the stock.

3. No, the good news can have reached the market gradually in other forms, e.g. news that large contracts were concluded, personnel were recruited, new plants were being build, etc. The reflection of this news in the stock price does not contradict the EMH.

4. No, the market can have expected a larger increase in earnings based on the news that became available earlier.

5. No, the EMH does not say that excess returns are impossible, it says that excess returns cannot be systematically earned by using the available information set. In view of the very large number of investors, it is to be expected that a few will be lucky a number of times in a row. Similarly, a few people will be very unlucky and lose large amounts on the stock market.

6. That the NPV is zero. On efficient markets securities are priced such that they earn their expected return, which makes their NPV zero.

7. (a) That they do not exist.
(b) No. There is no mention of risk, so the extra return relative to the index could be a premium for extra risk, relative to the index. Even if the 3 per cent were truly excess returns, they could have been due to chance.

8. (a) No, it is to be expected that news reaches the stock market before it materializes in earnings (see question 3). It would contradict the EMH if it were the other way around (that earnings predict next quarter's stock returns).
(b) No, you have tried 1,000 different filter rules. Using a 5 per cent confidence interval with a two-sided test you would expect to find ± 25 rules with a significantly positive return and the same number with a significantly negative return, based on pure chance. If you re-run the analysis on a different period you will probably find about the same number of significant results but in different stock-rule combinations.
(c) Yes, the stocks of smaller, infrequently traded companies usually have higher transaction costs, e.g. a larger bid-ask spread.
(d) Predictability contradicts the EMH but in this case it is obvious that the relation you found is spurious. Re-testing on a different dataset and/or period will almost certainly not reproduce similar results. However, the same conclusion

would apply if your computer happened to find two variables that look plausible on first sight.

9. If the ranking is over a short period (six months to one year is typical), the benchmark index would be somewhere in the middle. Since excess returns are random, about equal proportions of the funds will over- and underperform the index. As the period becomes longer, the index would move higher up on the ranking. Excess performance is not persistent so that good and bad years alternate. In the (very) long run few, if any, funds will outperform the index, so that the index will be (almost) on top.

10. Investors will sell and short sell the stock when prices are predictably high and buy when they are low. This will drive the prices down at the top of the cycle and up at the bottom of the cycle, and they will keep on buying and selling until the cycle has disappeared.

11. Unknowledgeable investors are indeed protected in an efficient market, but only to a certain degree. Buying and selling at market prices will be fair, i.e. there is no mispricing that other, knowledgeable investors can profit from. But if you offer to sell below market prices (e.g. by making a typing error) other investors will quickly profit from your mistake. Efficient markets offer no protection against excessive trading and no reward for the unsystematic risk of poorly diversified portfolios.

12. No, even if many investors do not follow the information on a stock and even less trade, the price can still reflect available information. Market efficiency requires that trades take place and at prices that reflect all available information; the number of investors involved is irrelevant.

13. No, investors can disagree and prices will reflect some average of opinions. However, market efficiency requires that no (groups of) investors are consistently better at evaluating the impact on prices than others. Investors can earn excess returns, but not consistently.

14. (a) Dividend (omission) announcements are public information other than prices and volumes: Szewczyk *et al.* test semi-strong market efficiency. Their results do not contradict the EMH: caar are stable before the event, there is a sharp decline on the event date and again hardly any change in caar after the event date. This is shown in the data but it becomes more clear if we plot caar over time. Figure S4.1 shows an efficient market response to new information. The usual statistical assumptions apply.

(b) No! In order to say something about strong form market efficiency it has to be tested. For example, by taking a sample of insiders, analyze their investments, look at the excess returns, etc. It is not possible to draw conclusions about strong form efficiency from a test of semi-strong efficiency.

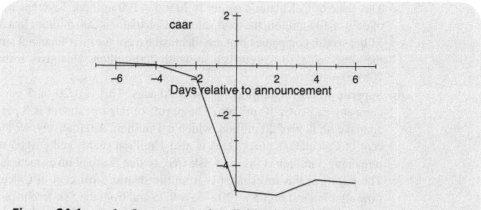

Figure S4.1 caar for firms announcing dividend omissions

Chapter 5

1. (a) Increase.
   (b) Increase.
   (c) Increase.
   (d) Decrease.
   (e) No effect if priority share has same rights as common shares plus priority.
   (f) Decrease.

2. (a) Decrease, income bonds only receive coupon (i.e. interest) payments if the issuing company has enough earnings to make the payment.
   (b) Decrease.
   (c) Increase.
   (d) Increase.
   (e) Increase.

3. No, if you are the only lender, the loan is already secured with all of the company's assets. If the interest is not paid, you can ask for the company to be declared bankrupt which may lead to the sale of the company's assets to repay the loan. Securing a loan is only meaningful if there are also unsecured loans.

4. The advantages are that the companies whose capital was tied up in internal capital categories get access to capital that can be invested in other projects and that investors get access to new securities. The pooling of internally held capital of many companies also gives an insurance and diversification effect. The dangers are that the internal control and risk-management procedures, that applied to the internal capital categories, no longer apply to external capital and have to be replaced by new, probably costly, procedures.

5. (a) The value of Calculator's equity is $20 \times 5 = 100$ million. Together with the value of debt of 100 million, the total value of Calculator is 200 million. In a Modigliani–Miller world, companies that are identical except for their financial structure have the same value, so Abacus is also worth 200 million. This gives a share price of $200/20 = 10$.

(b) Suppose we buy 1 million shares of Abacus. This is 1/20 or 5 per cent of the company and costs 10 million. The payoff of this investment is 5 per cent of the annual cash flow of 20 million, which is 1 million. Alternatively, we can buy 5 per cent of Calculator's stock. This is also 1 million shares and costs 5 million. The remaining 5 million is invested risk-free, so that the total investment is 10 million. The payoff of this investment is from the shares: 5 per cent of Calculator's cash flow after interest or $.05 \times (20 - 5) = 0.75$ and from the risk-free investment 5 per cent over 5 million which is 0.25. Total payoff is $0.75 + 0.25 = 1$.

(c) Suppose we buy 1 million shares of Calculator. This is 1/20 or 5 per cent of the company and costs 5 million. The payoff of this investment is 5 per cent of the company's cash flow after interest or $.05 \times (20 - 5) = 0.75$. Alternatively, we can buy 5 per cent of Abacus's stock. This is also 1 million shares and costs 10 million. The difference of 5 million is borrowed risk free, so that the total investment is 5 million. The payoff of this investment is from the shares: 5 per cent of Abacus's cash flow of 20 i.e. $.05 \times 20 = 1$ and we have to pay 5 per cent interest over the risk-free borrowing of 5 million which is -0.25. Total payoff is $1 - 0.25 = 0.75$.

(d) The return on Abacus' shares is $20/200 = .1$ or 10 per cent. Since Abacus is unlevered, this is also the return on assets for both companies. Modigliani–Miller proposition 2 gives a required return on Calculator's shares of:

$$r_e = r_a + \frac{D}{E}(r_a - r_d) = .1 + \frac{100}{100}(.1 - .05) = 0.15$$

We can check this result with the market value of Calculator's equity, which is 100 million. The cash flow for the equity holders is $20 - 5 = 15$. Solving $(15/r) = 100$ for r gives $r = .15$.

6. (a) The CAPM gives the return on ZX Co's equity before refinancing: $r_e = r_f + \beta_e(r_m - r_f) = .04 + 1.2(.06) = 0.112$. The WACC is then: $.2 \times .04 + .8 \times .112 = 0.0976$.

(b) First, we calculate β_a before refinancing: $\beta_a = D/V \times \beta_d + E/V \times \beta_e = .2 \times 0 + .8 \times 1.2 = 0.96$. With this asset β we can calculate the equity β after refinancing: $\beta_a = D/V \times \beta_d + E/V \times \beta_e \Rightarrow 0.96 = .6 \times 0 + .4 \times \beta_e \Rightarrow \beta_e = 2.4$. The CAPM gives $r_e = .04 + 2.4 \times .06 = 0.184$. The WACC remains: $.6 \times .04 + .4 \times .184 = 0.0976$.

Alternatively, we could have used MM proposition 2 to calculate $r_e : r_e = r_a + D/E(r_a - r_f) = .0976 + .6/.4(.0976 - .04) = 0.184$. In the absence of taxes, the WACC equals r_a. We can check this with CAPM and $\beta_a : r_a = .04 + .96 \times .06 = 0.0976$.

7. (a) First, we use MM proposition 2 and the data of the mining industry on average to calculate r_a, the return on assets:

$$r_e = r_a + (1 - \tau)(r_a - r_d)\frac{D}{E}$$

$$.114 = r_a + (1 - .3)(r_a - .07)\frac{.4}{.6} \quad \Rightarrow r_a = .1$$

Alternatively, we can use the formula for r_a under the MM assumptions:

$$r_a = r_d(1 - \tau)\frac{D}{V - \tau D} + r_e\frac{E}{V - \tau D}$$

The amounts D, E and V are not known, but we only need the proportions, which are known:

$$r_a = 0.07(1 - 0.3)\frac{0.4}{1 - 0.3 \times 0.4} + 0.114\frac{0.6}{1 - 0.3 \times 0.4} = 0.1$$

With this r_a we can calculate the required return on AG Goldmünzen & Verschuldung's equity investment in the planned mine:

$$r_e = r_a + (1 - \tau)(r_a - r_d)\frac{D}{E}$$

$$r_e = .1 + ((1 - .3)(.1 - .07)\frac{.8}{.2} = .184 \text{ or } 18.4 \text{ per cent}$$

8. (a) TechCon's value before refinancing is calculated as follows: over its EBIT of 100 it pays 20 in taxes. The net earnings have a value of $80/.1 = 800$. Refinancing with 50 per cent debt means issuing 400 debt, with a yearly interest bill of $.04 \times 400 = 16$. The division of the earnings (cash flow) then becomes:

EBIT	100.0
interest	−16.0
EBIT	84.0
taxes	−16.8
net earnings	67.2

To calculate the value of these earnings we need the cost of equity after refinancing, which can be calculated with MM proposition 2

$$r_e = r_a + (1 - \tau)(r_a - r_d)\frac{D}{E}$$

This calls for E, but since the cash flows are perpetuities we can use the balance sheet identity $V_a + tD = E + D$

$$r_e = r_a + (1 - \tau)(r_a - r_d)\frac{D}{V_a + \tau D - D}$$

$$r_e = .1 + (1 - .2)(.1 - .04)\frac{400}{800 + .2 \times 400 - 400} = 0.14$$

this gives an equity value of $67.2/.14 = 480$. The total company value is $480 + 400 = 880$. The change in company value is thus $880 - 800 = 80$.

A shorter calculation uses MM proposition 1: $V_l = V_u + \tau D$. The change in value is τD or $.2 \times 400 = 80$.

9. (a) The clientele effect says that investors select their portfolios in such a way that the dividend payments they receive are enough to cover their needs for cash. This does not create value for (non-)dividend paying stocks if there are enough dividend-paying and non-dividend-paying stocks to choose from. A change in dividend policy forces investors to make costly adjustments to their portfolios so that they prefer companies with stable, i.e. sticky, dividend policies.

(b) Firms with very high earnings in some periods and very low earnings in other periods can only maintain a stable (sticky) payout ratio if it is low.

(c) To the extent that the volatility is market synchronous (i.e. that it represents systematic risk) it reduces the value of the earnings. This may lead to the erroneous conclusion that a low payout ratio gives a low value.

(d) If earnings fall sharply because of a strike but dividends remain stable, the payout ratio will rise.

(e) A fall in earnings will be reflected in the stock price but the percentage decrease will be less than the percentage decrease in earnings, since an occasional strike will not affect the long-term earnings potential. This means that the price-earnings ratio will go up. An erroneous conclusion would be that an increase in the pay-out ratio leads to an increase in the price–earnings ratio, i.e. that investors would be willing to pay more for earnings that are paid in dividends than for earnings that are retained in the company. As a numerical example, consider a firm with perpetual earnings of 20; the firm pays 10 in dividends, so the payout ratio is 0.5. Its return on equity is 10 per cent so the value of the earnings is $20/0.1 = 200$, which gives a price/earnings ratio of $200/20 = 10$. This year the firm is hit by a strike, and its earnings are halved. Dividends are sticky and remain 10, so that the payout ratio becomes 1. The strike is a one-time event, so the firm's value becomes:

$$\frac{10 + 200}{1.1} = 190.9$$

The price/earnings ratio becomes: $190.9/10 = 19$. The erroneous conclusion would be: if the payout ratio goes up, the P/E goes up.

10. (a) Before the dividend payment, MacroHard holds assets worth $1,250 million, including the $250 to be paid as dividends. Its debt is worth $550 million, so its equity has a value of $1250 - 550 = 700$ million or $700/2.5 = 280$ per share. After the dividends are paid the firm holds assets worth $1,000 million, debt is still worth $550 million, so equity is $1000 - 550 = 450$ million or $450/2.5 = 180$ per share. The change in stock price is thus $100, exactly equal to the amount of dividend per share: $250/2.5$.

(b) The dividend payment reduces the value of the assets that MacroHard holds from $1,250 to $1,000 million. Equity is reduced from $700 to $450 million; this changes the debt-equity ratio from 550/700 to 550/450.

(c) If MacroHard wants to pay dividends without changing investment and financial policy it has to issue shares to pay for the dividends. After the dividends are paid the price per share is $180. So the firm has to issue $250/180 = 1.3889$ million shares. This leaves the values on the balance sheet unaltered but the firm now has $2.5 + 1.3889 = 3.8889$ million shares @ 180 instead of 2.5 million @ 280.

(d) If MacroHard uses the $250 million to buy back shares it has to buy $250/280 = 0.89286$ million shares. The total value of the firm will become $1,000 of which $550 is debt and $450 equity. The number of outstanding shares becomes $2.5 - 0.89286 = 1.6071$ million; the share price remains $450/1.6071 = 280$.

11. (a) Internally generated funds as retained earnings slip the control of the market because management does not have to ask the market to provide them, they are already under management's control. This increases the risk that these funds will be used on projects that increase management's wealth rather than shareholders'. Paying out all earnings eliminates this risk.

(b) Since there are no capital gains we can use Gordon's growth model to calculate the present value of the growing dividend stream:

$$P_0 = \frac{A}{r - g} = \frac{2.5}{.165 - .04} = 20$$

Chapter 6

1. (a) No! If the proportion of debt doubles the interest rate will not remain the same, nor will the required return on equity.

2. (a) With continuous rebalancing taxes drop from equation and $r_a = r_e \frac{E}{V} + r_d \frac{D}{V}$ so for the four firms:

$$.16 \times .4 + .052 \times .6 = 0.0952$$

$$.145 \times .5 + .049 \times .5 = 0.097$$

$$.136 \times .5 + .046 \times .5 = 0.091$$

$$.124 \times .6 + .043 \times .4 = 0.0916$$

The average of the four rates is $(.0952 + .097 + .091 + .0916)/4 = 0.0937$ or 9.4 per cent.

3. (a) Calculations are shown in the table below:

year	Loan at year end	Interest $r_d D$	tax saving $\tau r_d D$	PV(tax saving)
1	400,000	40,000	12,000	$12{,}000/1.1 = 10{,}909$
2	300,000	30,000	9,000	$9{,}000/1.1^2 = 7{,}438$
3	200,000	20,000	6,000	$6{,}000/1.1^3 = 4{,}508$
4	100,000	10,000	3,000	$3{,}000/1.1^4 = 2{,}049$
sum				24,904

(b) No, the point is not that the tax savings are stable, but that they are predetermined, i.e. their size does not depend on uncertain future developments. The tax settlement is already known, not uncertain.

4. (a) To find r_e we use the CAPM: $r_e = r_f + \beta_e(r_m - r_f) = .07 + 1.5 \times (.13 - .07) = 0.16$. We find β_d by running the CAPM in reverse: $.08 = .07 + \beta_d \times (.13 - .07) \Rightarrow \beta_d = 0.167$. r_a can be found in different ways:
we can use the formula for r_a under the MM assumptions:

$$r_a = r_d(1 - \tau)\frac{D}{V - \tau D} + r_e \frac{E}{V - \tau D}$$

$$r_a = .08(1 - .3)\frac{.5}{1 - .3 \times .5} + .16\frac{.5}{1 - .3 \times .5} = .127$$

we can also run MM proposition 2 in reverse:

$$r_e = r_a + (r_a - r_d)(1 - \tau)\frac{D}{E}$$

$$.16 = r_a + (r_a - .08)(1 - .3)\frac{.5}{.5} \Rightarrow r_a = .127$$

Similarly, β_a can be found with the formula equivalent to that for r_a

$$\beta_a = \beta_d(1 - \tau)\frac{D}{V - \tau D} + \beta_e \frac{E}{V - \tau D}$$

$$\beta_a = .167(1 - .3)\frac{.5}{1 - .3 \times .5} + 1.5\frac{.5}{1 - .3 \times .5} = .95$$

or by running the CAPM in reverse: $r_a = r_f + \beta_a(r_m - r_f) \Rightarrow .127 = .07 + \beta \times (.13 - .07) \Rightarrow \beta = 0.95$
The WACC can be found with the formula:

$$WACC = r_e\frac{E}{V} + r_d(1 - \tau)\frac{D}{V}$$

$$WACC = .16 \times .5 + .08 \times (1 - .3) \times .5 = .108$$

or by using the Modigliani–Miller formula:

$$WACC = r_a(1 - \tau L)$$

$$WACC = .127(1 - .3 \times .5) = .108$$

(b) If debt is rebalanced, the CAPM relations and r_e and r_d stay the same, so $r_e = r_f + \beta_e(r_m - r_f) = .07 + 1.5 \times (.13 - .07) = 0.16$ and β_d is: $.08 = .07 + \beta_d \times (.13 - .07) \Rightarrow \beta_d = 0.167$. With rebalancing, taxes drop from the equation and r_a is:

$$r_a = r_e \frac{E}{V} + r_d \frac{D}{V}$$

$$r_a = .16 \times .5 + .08 \times .5 = .12$$

r_a can also be found by running MM proposition 2 (without tax) in reverse:

$$r_e = r_a + (r_a - r_d)\frac{D}{E}$$

$$.16 = r_a + (r_a - .08)\frac{.5}{.5} \Rightarrow r_a = .12$$

β_a can be calculated in similar ways: $\beta_a = \beta_e \frac{E}{V} + \beta_d \frac{D}{V} = 1.5 \times .5 + .167 \times .5 = 0.8335$. Equivalently, β_a can be found by running MM proposition 2 (without tax) or the CAPM, both in reverse.

The WACC can be found with the formula:

$$WACC = r_e \frac{E}{V} + r_d(1 - \tau)\frac{D}{V}$$

$$WACC = .16 \times .5 + .08 \times (1 - .3) \times .5 = .108$$

or by using the Miles–Ezzell formula:

$$WACC = r_a - \frac{D}{V}r_d\tau\left(\frac{1 + r_a}{1 + r_d}\right)$$

$$WACC = .12 - .5 \times .08 \times .3 \times \frac{1.12}{1.08} = .108$$

(c) Rebalancing makes the tax savings more uncertain and, hence, less valuable. Notice that a change in financial policy from predetermined to rebalanced debt does not cause a change in r_a, i.e. you cannot change r_a by changing financial policy. We observe r_e, r_d and financial policy in the market and the given r_e and r_d correspond to a lower r_a in case of rebalancing than in case of predetermined debt, i.e. they are not the same assets (question (a) and (b) refer to different 'cases').

5. (a) To calculate APV we start with the base case, the value of the project as if it were all equity financed. The OCC is given as 12.5 per cent so the NPV of the cash flows is: $-1000 + \frac{333}{1.125} + \frac{333}{1.125^2} + \frac{333}{1.125^3} + \frac{333}{1.125^4} = 0.88$. The project has two side-effects, issue costs and tax shields.

To raise 500, the company will have to issue $\frac{100}{95} \times 500 = 526.32$ so the issue costs are $526.32 - 500 = 26.32$

The amount of debt will be available throughout the project's life so the yearly interest payments are $.08 \times 500 = 40$. This gives a tax advantage of $.3 \times 40 = 12$. Since debt is predetermined, the discount rate for the tax advantage is the cost of debt. The PV is $\frac{12}{1.08} + \frac{12}{1.08^2} + \frac{12}{1.08^3} + \frac{12}{1.08^4} = 39.75$.

The project's APV is $0.88 - 26.32 + 39.75 = 14.31 > 0$, E-razor should go ahead with the project.

(b) APV is the preferred method in this case because it involves issue costs that cannot be included in the discount rate. Moreover, because debt is predetermined and fixed, the D/E ratio will be different in each of the project's four years and, hence, the cost of equity, r_e, and the WACC will be different too.

6. Korkla should accept the project if it has a positive NPV; to calculate NPV we need the cash flow and investment (both given) and the proper discount rate. The discount rate is determined by the characteristics of the project; the background data on Korkla are irrelevant. The business risk and the corresponding opportunity cost of capital can be calculated from Checkers' data, since this is the only company active in the NO-WITS industry. We proceed as follows:

(a) First we calculate the return on assets, or the opportunity cost of capital (OCC), r_a, for Checkers. For this we need the return on equity, r_e, which we can find with the CAPM: $r_e = r_f + \beta_e(r_m - r_f) = .06 + 1.4 \times .08 = .172$

Return on assets can be found in three ways:

   i. By using the formula for r_e in reverse:
   $r_e = r_a + (r_a - r_d)D/E$
   $.172 = r_a + (r_a - .09).5/.5 \Rightarrow r_a = .131$

   ii. Alternatively, using unlevering:
   $r_a = .5 \times .09 + .5 \times .172 = .131$.

   iii. Finally, it is also possible to calculate β_d from the CAPM: $.09 = .06 + \beta_d \times .08 \Rightarrow \beta_d = .375$ and then use the β version of the formula to find β_a:
   $\beta_e = \beta_a + (\beta_a - \beta_d)D/E \Rightarrow 1.4 = \beta_a + (\beta_a - .375).5/.5 \Rightarrow \beta_a = .8875$.
   The CAPM then gives: $r_a = .06 + .8875 \times .08 = .131$

(b) Given the opportunity costs of capital in the NO-WITS industry and the financing characteristics for Korkla's project ($D/E = .25/.75$, $r_d = 8$ per cent) we can calculate the project's WACC in two ways:

   i. Calculate r_e for the project: $r_e = r_a + (r_a - r_d)D/E = .131 + (.131 - .08).25/75 = .148$, which gives a project WACC of: $(.75 \times .148) + (.25 \times (1 - .4) \times .08) = .123$

   ii. Alternatively, we could have used Miles–Ezzell's formula: $r' = r_a - \tau r_d L \left(\frac{1+r_a}{1+r_d} \right) = .131 - .4 \times .08 \times \frac{.25}{1} \times \frac{1.131}{1.08} = .123$

(c) With this WACC the value of the cash flow becomes: $100/.123 = 813$ so that NPV $= 813 - 750 = 63 > 0$, $\Rightarrow$ Korkla should accept the project.

(d) APV can also be used. We proceed as follows:

   i. Discount the cash flow at the OCC: $100/.131 = 763.359$

   ii. The tax advantage is $\tau r_d D = .4 \times .08 \times (.25 \times 750) = 6$

   iii. Discounting this at the OCC gives $6/.131 = 45.80$

iv. Multiply by $(1 + r_a)/(1 + r_d) = 1.131/1.08 = 1.0472 \times 45.80 = 47.96$

v. APV is then: $763.359 + 47.96 - 750 = 61.32 > 0$, so Korkla should accept the project.

Chapter 7

1. It may be helpful to calculate the options' payoffs on different points in the interval:

Share price (S)	0	50	75	100	125	150
short put (X = 75)	−75	−25	0	0	0	0
long put (X = 100)	100	50	25	0	0	0
long call (X = 75)	0	0	0	25	50	75
short call (X = 100)	0	0	0	0	−25	−50
Total position (O)	+25	+25	+25	+25	+25	+25

The positions are plotted in Figure S7.1. The plotted functions are $\min[0, x - 75]$, $\max[0, 100 - x]$, $\max[0, x - 75]$, $\min[0, 100 - x]$ and their sum.

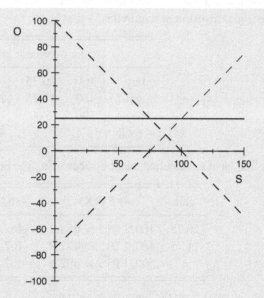

Figure S7.1 Payoff diagram for an option position

2. No, puts and calls do not cancel out, but buying a put is cancelled out by selling a put. Similarly, a short call is cancelled out by a long call. Also, the prices of otherwise identical at-the-money puts and calls are not the same, as is easily verified with the put–call parity: share + long put = long call + PV(X) or long put − long call = PV(X) − share. If the put and call have the same value, the share price has to be equal to the present value of the exercise price (so not the exercise price).

3. (a) A butterfly with calls consists of one long call with exercise price x_1, two short calls with exercise price x_2 and one long call with exercise price x_3.

(b) The same position with puts consists of one long put with exercise price x_3, two short puts with exercise price x_2 and one long put with exercise price x_1. The positions are depicted in Figure S7.2 below.

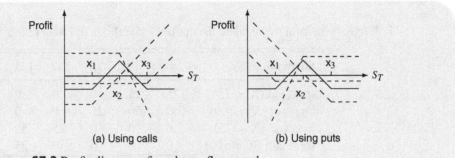

(a) Using calls   (b) Using puts

Figure S7.2 Profit diagrams for a butterfly spread

4. A butterfly spread involves buying one call with a low exercise price, selling two calls with a higher exercise price and buying one call with an even higher exercise price.

(a) The initial investment required is:

	strike	price	amount
buy 1	460	20.75	−20.75
sell 2	480	11.75	23.50
buy 1	500	6.00	−6
total			−3.25

(b) We first have to calculate the put prices using the put–call parity:

call	+PV(X)	−share	=price put
20.75	460/1.015 = 453.2	−462.50	= 11.45
11.75	480/1.015 = 472.9	−462.50	= 22.15
6	500/1.015 = 492.6	−462.50	= 36.10

Then we can set up the butterfly with puts:

	strike	price	amount
buy 1	500	36.10	−36.10
sell 2	480	22.15	44.30
buy 1	460	11.45	−11.45
total			−3.25

which gives the same initial investment.

(c) These prices are different because traded options are (almost) always American options and by using the put–call parity we calculated prices of European options. European puts trade at a lower price range than American puts because the right of early exercise is valuable (as well as frequently used).

5. (a) The bull spread is constructed by selling one put with exercise price x_2 and buying one put with exercise price x_1. In the bear spread the positions are reversed, i.e. a put with exercise price x_1 is sold and a put with exercise price x_2 is bought. The positions are depicted in Figure S7.3.

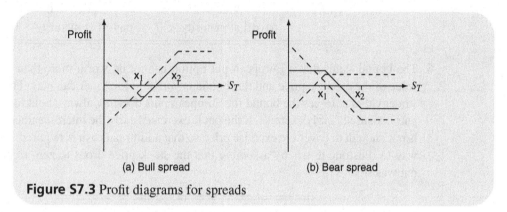

(a) Bull spread   (b) Bear spread

Figure S7.3 Profit diagrams for spreads

(b) The initial balances of option premiums (initial investments) are reversed compared with the same positions constructed with calls. The price of a put increases with the exercise price (call prices decrease). In a bull spread constructed with puts, the more expensive put with a high exercise price is sold and the cheaper one is bought so that the initial balance is positive (negative investment). On the other hand, the payoff at maturity is either zero or negative. In a bear spread constructed with puts the more expensive option is bought so that the initial balance is negative (initial investment required). However, the payoff at maturity is either zero or positive. The payoffs at maturity are depicted in Figure S7.4. The differences are summarized in the table below.

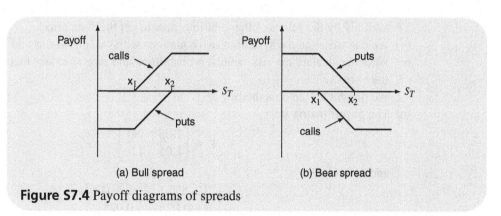

(a) Bull spread   (b) Bear spread

Figure S7.4 Payoff diagrams of spreads

	Bull	**Bear**
Calls decrease with X	buy low X (costs more) sell high X (costs less)	sell low X (costs more) buy high X (costs less)
	price < 0 payoff at maturity > 0	price > 0 payoff at maturity < 0
Puts increase with X	buy low X (costs less) sell high X (costs more)	sell low X (costs less) buy high X (costs more)
	price > 0 payoff at maturity < 0	price < 0 payoff at maturity > 0

6. The bound states that a European put option cannot be worth more than the present value of the exercise price and this bound is *not* valid for American puts. The arbitrage strategy that enforces the bound for European puts does not always hold for American puts because of early exercise. If the put is exercised early the interest earned on PV(X) is not enough to cover the exercise price so that additional cash is required. The easiest way to illustrate this is by assuming that the stock price drops to zero right after the put was sold:

	Now	At exercise $S_T = 0 < X$
Sell put	$+O_p^A$	$-X$
Lend $PV(X)$	$-PV(X)$	$PV(X)$
Total position	> 0	$PV(X) - X < 0$

7. State prices can be calculated in three ways (which all boil down to the same thing, of course):
   (a) We can construct the payoff matrix for the securities in this market, take its inverse to get the weights of the portfolios that produce the state securities and then multiply by the values of the securities now to get the state prices.
   (b) We can write out the system of two equations with two unknowns and solve it.
   (c) We can calculate the risk-neutral probabilities and then discount them to get the state prices.
   We present all three methods.
   (a) The payoff matrix is:

$$\Psi = \begin{bmatrix} 1.05 & 80 \\ 1.05 & 120 \end{bmatrix}$$

   and its inverse

$$\Psi^{-1} = \begin{bmatrix} 2.8571 & -1.9048 \\ -0.025 & 0.025 \end{bmatrix}$$

The prices of the securities now are:

$$v = \begin{bmatrix} 1 & 100 \end{bmatrix}$$

so that the state prices are:

$$v\Psi^{-1} = \begin{bmatrix} 0.357\,14 & 0.595\,24 \end{bmatrix}$$

The option's payoffs are

$$O = \begin{bmatrix} 0 \\ 20 \end{bmatrix}$$

multiplying these by the state prices gives the option price:

$$v\Psi^{-1}O = 11.905$$

(b) The system of two equations with two unknowns is:

$$1 = \psi_1 \times 1.05 + \psi_2 \times 1.05$$
$$100 = \psi_1 \times 80 + \psi_2 \times 120$$

and its solution is:

$$[\psi_1 = 0.357\,14, \ \psi_2 = 0.595\,24]$$

so that the option price becomes

$$0.357\,14 \times 0 + 0.595\,24 \times 20 = 11.905$$

(c) State prices are discounted risk-neutral probabilities:

$$p = \frac{r-d}{u-d} = \frac{1.05 - .8}{1.2 - .8} = 0.625/1.05 = 0.595\,24$$

$$1 - p = 1 - 0.625 = 0.375/1.05 = 0.35714$$

and the calculation proceeds as under (b).

8. (a) We calculate the values as the expected payoffs discounted at the risk-adjusted rate of return; since both states are equally likely:

$$A = \frac{0.5 \times 6 + 0.5 \times 12}{1.08} = 8.33$$

$$B = \frac{0.5 \times 4 + 0.5 \times 14}{1.12} = 8.04$$

(b) We can calculate state price by making portfolios of A and B that pay off 1 in only one state and 0 in the other. For the first state this means solving the equations:

$$6 \times a + 4 \times b = 1$$
$$12 \times a + 14 \times b = 0$$

for the weights a and b. The solution is: $a = \frac{7}{18}$, $b = -\frac{1}{3}$. This gives a state price of $\frac{7}{18} \times 8.33 - \frac{1}{3} \times 8.04 = 0.559$. For the second state price we solve the equations (re-using the symbols a and b):

$$6 \times a + 4 \times b = 0$$

$$12 \times a + 14 \times b = 1$$

The solution is: $a = -\frac{1}{9}$, $b = \frac{1}{6}$, so the second state price is $-\frac{1}{9} \times 8.33 + \frac{1}{6} \times 8.04 = 0.414$. We can also use matrix algebra:

$$\begin{bmatrix} 8.33 & 8.04 \end{bmatrix} \begin{bmatrix} 6 & 4 \\ 12 & 14 \end{bmatrix}^{-1} = \begin{bmatrix} 0.559 & 0.414 \end{bmatrix}$$

To calculate the risk-free interest rate we have to make a portfolio of A and B that pays off the same in both states. This means solving the equations:

$$6 \times a + 4 \times b = 1$$

$$12 \times a + 14 \times b = 1$$

which gives $a = \frac{5}{18}$, $b = -\frac{1}{6}$. The present value of this portfolio is $\frac{5}{18} \times 8.33 - \frac{1}{6} \times 8.04 = 0.9739$. We can check this with the sum of the state prices, which has to be the same: $0.559 + 0.414 = 0.973$. The risk-free interest rate is $1/0.9739 = 1.027$.

(c) The values of the securities A and B are re-calculated as follows:

i. using state prices:
A $= 6 \times 0.559 + 12 \times 0.414 = 8.32$
B $= 4 \times 0.559 + 14 \times 0.414 = 8.03$

ii. to use the risk-neutral valuation formula we first have to calculate the risk-neutral probabilities. These are defined as the state prices $\times (1 + r_f)$ so $p_1 = 0.559 \times 1.027 = 0.574$ and $p_2 = 0.414 \times 1.027 = 0.426$. The risk-neutral valuation formula then gives:

$$A = \frac{0.574 \times 6 + 0.426 \times 12}{1.027} = 8.33$$

$$B = \frac{0.574 \times 4 + 0.426 \times 14}{1.027} = 8.04$$

(d) At maturity the options pay off the maximum of zero and the difference between the security price and the exercise price: $\max[0, S - X]$, so:

	A	B
*State*1	max[0, 6 − 10] = 0	max[0, 4 − 10] = 0
*State*2	max[0, 12 − 10] = 2	max[0, 14 − 10] = 4

The state price for the second state is 0.414, so the options prices are $2 \times 0.414 = 0.828$ and $4 \times 0.414 = 1.656$.

We can also use the risk-neutral valuation formula and the risk-neutral probabilities we calculated above (which is, of course, basically the same thing):

$$\text{Option on } A = \frac{0.574 \times 0 + 0.426 \times 2}{1.027} = 0.830$$

$$\text{Option on } B = \frac{0.574 \times 0 + 0.426 \times 4}{1.027} = 1.659$$

9. (a) Since $u \neq r \neq d$ the stock and risk-free debt are linearly independent, so there are as many independent securities as there are states of the world, which means that the market is complete. Since $d < r < u$ there are no arbitrage opportunities on this market.

(b) We first calculate the value tree for the stock without and with dividends:

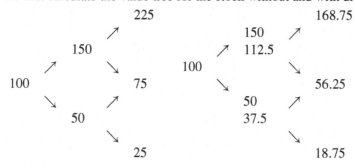

The parameters of the binomial process are: $u = 1.5$, $d = 0.5$, $r = 1.25$, $p = (r - d)/(u - d) = 0.75$

i. European call, no dividends:
$O_{uu} = \max[0, 225 - 110] = 115$
$O_{ud} = \max[0, 75 - 110] = 0$
$O_{dd} = \max[0, 25 - 110] = 0$
$O_u = (.75 \times 115) + (.25 \times 0)/1.25 = 69$
$O_d = (.75 \times 0) + (.25 \times 0)/1.25 = 0$
$O = (.75 \times 69) + (.25 \times 0)/1.25 = 41.4$

ii. European call, 25 per cent dividends:
$O_{uu} = \max[0, 168.75 - 110] = 58.75$
$O_{ud} = \max[0, 56.25 - 110] = 0$
$O_{dd} = \max[0, 18.75 - 110] = 0$
$O_u = (.75 \times 58.75) + (.25 \times 0)/1.25 = 35.25$
$O_d = (.75 \times 0) + (.25 \times 0)/1.25 = 0$
$O = (.75 \times 35.25) + (.25 \times 0)/1.25 = 21.15$

iii. American call on a non-dividend-paying stock is the same as a European call

iv. American call, 25 per cent dividend:
$O_{uu} = \max[0, 168.75 - 110] = 58.75$
$O_{ud} = \max[0, 56.25 - 110] = 0$
$O_{dd} = \max[0, 18.75 - 110] = 0$
$O_u - alive = (.75 \times 58.75) + (.25 \times 0)/1.25 = 35.25$
$O_u - dead = \max[0, 150 - 110] = 40$

$O_u = \max[alive, dead] = 40$

$O_d = 0$ both dead and alive

$O - alive = (.75 \times 40) + (.25 \times 0)/1.25 = 24$

$O - dead = \max[0, 100 - 110] = 0$

$O = \max[alive, dead] = 24$

v. European put, no dividends:

$O_{uu} = \max[0, 110 - 225] = 0$

$O_{ud} = \max[0, 110 - 75] = 35$

$O_{dd} = \max[0, 110 - 25] = 85$

$O_u = (.75 \times 0) + (.25 \times 35)/1.25 = 7$

$O_d = (.75 \times 35) + (.25 \times 85)/1.25 = 38$

$O = (.75 \times 7) + (.25 \times 38)/1.25 = 11.80$

vi. European put, 25 per cent dividends:

$O_{uu} = \max[0, 110 - 168.75] = 0$

$O_{ud} = \max[0, 110 - 56.25] = 53.75$

$O_{dd} = \max[0, 110 - 18.75] = 91.25$

$O_u = (.75 \times 0) + (.25 \times 53.75)/1.25 = 10.75$

$O_d = (.75 \times 53.75) + (.25 \times 91.25)/1.25 = 50.50$

$O = (.75 \times 10.75) + (.25 \times 50.50)/1.25 = 16.55$

10. Next period the stock price is either $50 \times 1.3 = 65$ or $50 \times .75 = 37.5$. The value trees for the options are:

$$\max[0, 65 - 45] = 20 \qquad\qquad \max[0, 45 - 65] = 0$$

$$O_c \qquad\qquad\qquad O_p$$

$$\max[0, 37.5 - 45] = 0 \qquad\qquad \max[0, 45 - 37.5] = 7.5$$

(a) For a call option, the option Δ and D are:

$$\Delta = \frac{O_u - O_d}{(u - d) \times S} = \frac{20 - 0}{(1.3 - 0.75) \times 50} = 0.727\,27$$

$$D = \frac{u \times O_d - d \times O_u}{(u - d) \times r} = \frac{1.3 \times 0 - 0.75 \times 20}{(1.3 - 0.75) \times 1.08} = -25.253$$

The price of the call is $O_c = S \times \Delta + D = 50 \times 0.72727 - 25.253 = 11.111$

(b) For a put option, the option Δ and D are:

$$\Delta = \frac{O_u - O_d}{(u - d) \times S} = \frac{0 - 7.5}{(1.3 - 0.75) \times 50} = -0.272\,73$$

$$D = \frac{u \times O_d - d \times O_u}{(u - d) \times r} = \frac{1.3 \times 7.5 - 0.75 \times 0}{(1.3 - 0.75) \times 1.08} = 16.414$$

The price of the put $O_P = S \times \Delta + D = 50 \times -0.27273 + 16.414 = 2.777\,5$

Chapter 8

1. As was pointed out by Fama, if *stock returns* are iid, then *stock prices* will not follow a random walk since price changes will depend on the price level.

2. Stability over time means that past returns are the best information to assess the distributional properties of the returns. However, they *cannot* be used to predict future returns because they contain no information on the *sequence* of future returns.

3. Volatility increases the probability of large price changes, both price increases and price decreases. For stockholders these price movements will tend to cancel out. But option-holders have an exposure to only one of these price movements: call holders to price increases and put holders to price decreases. For option-holders it doesn't matter how far out of the money the option ends, the option is worthless if it ends out of the money. So options profit from the upward potential of price movements but have a limited exposure to the downside risk, hence their values increase with volatility. This is illustrated in Figure S8.1 with the truncated normal distribution we used in the derivation of the Black and Scholes formula. The truncated distribution with the higher standard deviation has a higher expectation than the one with a lower standard deviation (14.5 versus 11.8).

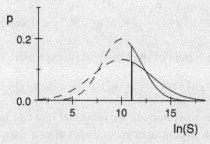

Figure S8.1 Lognormally distributed stock prices ($ln(S) \sim N(10, 2$ and $3)$, dashed), and their left truncations at $ln(S) = 11$ (solid)

4. Holders of a long call have a claim on the upward potential of stock, but they don't pay for it until maturity, if at all (the option may also expire out of the money). The possibility to delay payment is more valuable the higher the interest rate is (the holder can earn interest over the exercise price). Holders of a long put can sell the stock at the fixed exercise price in the future. The value of a future payment decreases with the interest rate.

5. The put–call parity states: $put = call + PV(X) - S$. If the stock price increases with 1, the call increases (by definition) with $\Delta_c \times 1 = \Delta_c$. The $PV(X)$ is unaffected by changes in the stock price. So the right-hand side of the equation changes with $\Delta_c \times 1 + 0 - 1 = \Delta_c - 1$. This must be the delta of the put: $\Delta_p = \Delta_c - 1$.

6. Economically, holding an extremely far in the money call option is equivalent to holding a share that is not yet paid for, i.e. $S - PV(X)$. Differences in volatility (practically) do not matter any more as the options are (almost) certain to be exercised anyway. The options in Figure 8.2 are paid for on the same date, so their PV(X) are the same and, consequently, they have a common value as a function of the stock price. The options in Figure 8.3 are not paid for on the same date, so their PV(X) are different and they do not have a common value as a function of the stock price.

   Technically, as the stock price S gets larger and larger, both the option delta $N(d_1)$ and the probability of exercise $N(d_2)$ approach 1. The Black and Scholes price then approaches $O_{c,0} = S_0 - Xe^{-rT}$. This price is independent of σ, but not of T, hence options with different volatilities converge to a common value, but options with different maturities do not.

7. We use the Black and Scholes option pricing formula:
   $O_{c,0} = S_0 \times N(d_1) - X \times e^{-rT} \times N(d_2)$ with
   $d_1 = \frac{\ln(S_0/X) + (r + \frac{1}{2}\sigma^2) \times T}{\sigma\sqrt{T}}$ and $d_2 = d_1 - \sigma\sqrt{T}$
   The input data are: $S = 240$, $X = 250$, $\sigma = 25$ per cent, $r = 6$ per cent.
   $d_1 = \frac{\ln(240/250) + (0.06 + 0.5 \times 0.25^2) \times 1}{0.25 \times \sqrt{1}} = 0.201\,71$
   $N(d_1) \rightarrow \text{NormalDist}(0.20171) = 0.579\,93$
   $d_2 = 0.20171 - 0.25 \times \sqrt{1} = -0.048\,29$
   $N(d_2) \rightarrow \text{NormalDist}(-0.04829) = 0.480\,74$
   $O_{c,0} = 240 \times 0.57993 - 250 \times e^{-0.06 \times 1} \times 0.48074 = 25.997$

8. (a) The parameters of the binomial process are:

   $$u = 1.075 \qquad d = .93 \qquad r = 1.025 \qquad p = \frac{1.025 - .93}{1.075 - .93} = .655$$

   With these parameters the binomial tree can be constructed as in Lattice S1. Note that the tree no longer recombines after a fixed amount of dividend payments. The option values are obtained by calculating their values at maturity, taking their risk-neutral expectation and discounting this back in time with the risk-neutral rate. This gives the values of the option alive, and since this is an American option the values alive have to be compared with the values dead, i.e. if exercised. Lattice S2 gives the results, the calculations are below.

   The options only ends in the money in the upper node at $t = 2$. Its value at expiration in that node is

   $$104.8 - 102.5 = 2.3$$

   This gives a $t = 1$ value alive of:

   $$(.655 \times 2.3)/1.025 = 1.47$$

   The value dead is $107.5 - 102.5 = 5$ so the option should be exercised which gives a $t = 0$ value of

   $$(.655 \times 5)/1.025 = 3.2$$

$$
\begin{array}{ccc}
& 107.5 & 104.8 \\
\nearrow \quad \downarrow & \nearrow & \\
97.5 & & \\
100 & & \searrow \\
& & 90.7 \\
\searrow & & \\
93 & & 89.2 \\
\downarrow & \nearrow & \\
83 & & \\
& \searrow & \\
& & 77.2 \\
t = 0 \qquad t = 1 \qquad t = 2
\end{array}
$$

Lattice S1 Value NSG stock

$$O_{uu} = 2.3$$

$$O_u = \max[(1.47), \max[0, (107.5 - 102.5)]] = 5$$
$$\underset{alive}{} \qquad \underset{dead}{}$$

3.2

$$O_{ud} = 0$$
$$O_{du} = 0$$

$$O_d = \max[(0), \max[0, (93 - 102.5)]] = 0$$
$$\underset{alive}{} \qquad \underset{dead}{}$$

$$O_{dd} = 0$$

$$t = 0 \qquad\qquad t = 1 \qquad\qquad t = 2$$

Lattice S2 Value call option on NSG stock

(b) To construct the hedge portfolio we first calculate Δ and D:

$$\Delta = \frac{O_u - O_d}{S_u - S_d} = \frac{5 - 0}{107.5 - 93} = .345$$

$$D = \frac{u O_d - d O_u}{(u - d)r} = \frac{1.075 \times 0 - .93 \times 5}{(1.075 - .93)1.025} = -31.287$$

As always, the hedging portfolio for a call is a levered long position in the stock. We sell the option at 3.2 and we buy the hedge portfolio to cover the obligations from the call. The fraction of the stock costs: $.345 \times 100 = 34.5$. We borrow 31.287 and the difference of $34.5 - 31.287 = 3.2$ is covered by the received premium from selling the call. If at $t = 1$:

i. The stock price is 107.5: the option will be exercised and we have to sell the stock at the exercise price of 102.5. We have .345 stock in the hedge portfolio, so we have to buy $1 - .345 = .665$ stock, which costs $.665 \times 107.5 = 70.41$. Hence, we receive $102.5 - 70.41 = 32.09$. This is exactly enough to pay off the debt, which now amounts to $1.025 \times 31.287 = 32.07$. We have a perfect hedge.

ii. The stock price is 93: the option is worthless. The debt amounts to the same 32.07, which is exactly covered by the fraction of the share: $.345 \times 93 = 32.09$. Again, we have a perfect hedge.

(c) The call option delta increases with the stock price, all other things equal. As the stock price increases, the option becomes more likely to be exercised and becomes more like a stock that has not yet been paid for. Ultimately, when the option is so far in the money that it is certain to be exercised the call option delta becomes 1. Conversely, when the stock price falls and the call is farther and farther out of the money, it becomes less and less likely to be exercised. Ultimately, when the option is so far out of the money that it is certain not to be exercised the call option delta becomes 0. The call has lost its value, no matter what happens to the stock price. This is the case in the lower node at $t = 1$ in Lattice 2: the option cannot get in the money from this node and is worthless and no longer sensitive to stock price changes.

9. (a) We use the put–call parity to construct a synthetic put and check for any mispricing:

$$long\ put = long\ call + PV(X) - share\ price$$

First we calculate the PV(X) using the corresponding IBOR rate and period:

NHY nov.5: $620e^{-.02235 \times 2/12} = 617.69$

NHY nov.5: $680e^{-.02235 \times 2/12} = 677.47$

NHY feb.6: $620e^{-.02337 \times 5/12} = 613.99$

NHY feb.6: $680e^{-.02337 \times 5/12} = 673.41$

ORK jan.6: $240e^{-.02313 \times 4/12} = 238.16$

NSG dec.5: $100e^{-.0229 \times 3/12} = 99.429$

We construct a synthetic put by buying a call, depositing PV(X) at a bank and selling the share. So we use the ask price for the call and the bid price for the share.

Synthetic and market option prices

Ticker	T	X	call ask	PV(X)	share bid	syn. put	put option bid	put option ask
NHY	nov.5	620	70.00	617.69	677.00	10.69	9.25	10.00
NHY	,,	680	30.25	677.47	677.00	30.72	29.00	31.25
NHY	feb.6	620	83.75	613.99	677.00	20.74	19.00	20.75
NHY	,,	680	47.00	673.41	677.00	43.41	41.50	44.25
ORK	jan.6	240	26.75	238.16	259.00	5.91	5.00	5.50
NSG	dec.5	100	11.00	99.429	108.75	1.68	2.85	3.35

The rows for NHY nov.5-620, ORK jan.6 and NSG dec.5 in the table show that the prices of the synthetic puts for these options lie outside the bid-ask spread on the market. But the first two are not arbitrage opportunities: you can buy a synthetic put NHY nov.5-620 at 10.69 or an ordinary put at 10, but you cannot sell at 10.69, only at 9.25. The same applies to ORK jan.6. They are outside the bid-ask spread, but on the wrong side from an arbitrage point of view. The NSG option is outside the bid-ask spread on the other side and that offers an arbitrage opportunity: we can buy the synthetic put at 1.68 and sell the ordinary put at 2.85. This gives an arbitrage profit of 1.17. If we manage to close a million of these contracts we have become millionaires overnight.

Such arbitrage opportunities are in practice not open to investors who get their information from a newspaper and on closer examination it appears that we made a typing error in Table 2: the bid-ask prices for NSG are 106.75 and 107.5. With the proper stock price, the price of the synthetic put becomes:

call + PV(X) − share = 11 + 99.429 − 106.75 = 3.679

The price of the synthetic put now lies outside the bid-ask spread on the other side and the arbitrage opportunity has disappeared. We can make sure by checking the relation the other way around by constructing a synthetic short put. Then we write a call, borrow PV(X) and buy the share. That costs: −10 + (−99.429) + 107.5 = −1.929 i.e. brings in 1.929. Note that we use the bid price for the call and the ask price for the share. If we sell the put in the market we get 2.85, so the synthetic price is on the wrong side of the bid-ask spread from an arbitrage point of view.

(b) Differences between implied and observed prices can occur because we apply the put–call parity, which is only valid for European options on non-dividend-paying stocks, to traded American options on stocks that may pay dividends. Further, price differences can occur because of non-synchronous trading. The prices in newspapers are generally closing prices, but we do not know when the last trade of the day took place. If the last option trade was at 13.00 hours and the last stock trade at 15.00 hours, the option trade could be based on a different stock price than the one we read in the newspaper.

Chapter 9

1. (a) If both the input market (smelters) and the output market (bulk aluminium) are characterized by perfect competition (large numbers of buyers and sellers, none of which can individually influence prices), Norsk Hydro has no lower exercise price nor a higher underlying value than its competition so that there is no source of real option value.

(b) City centre building plots are very valuable and by developing the plot, *the option to develop* is given up. If one development is chosen (say, offices), alternative developments (say, a hotel) are given up and the latter may prove to be very valuable in the near future. The option to develop may be more valuable than any particular development today.

(c) By assembling locally, HP introduced the flexibility to adapt to variations in local demand, e.g. to increase the number of French printers and decrease the German number. If demand is volatile, flexible production (although by itself more expensive) can be more profitable than other methods to match supply and demand (e.g. maintaining large buffer stocks).

2. Real call options are often exercised before maturity because the sources of option value tend to be eroded over time. This is plain to see in a patent that has a limited

lifetime and has to be used (= exercised) before it expires if its value is to be realized. The value of patents and other real options is further eroded over time because competitors will develop close substitutes. Also, if the option is shared in some degree, the game-theoretic anticipation of competitors' actions generally leads to an earlier exercise.

3. (a) The value of the gas reserve is $4 \times 100 \times 0.08 = \$32$ million. The cash flows from gas production occur on four future points in time, but both the expected return on gas and the time value of money are included in the binomial process. Feel free to check this using either the risk-neutral probabilities and risk-free rate or the real probabilities and the risk-adjusted rate.

(b) If the field is developed immediately, its NPV is $32 - 30 = \$2$ million. The concession gives State Drilling the flexibility to wait and see for one year. After one year, the investment amount is $30 \times 1.07 = 32.1$. The gas price is either $0.08 \times 1.25 = 0.1$ or $0.08 \times 0.8 = 0.064$, so the value of the gas reserve is either $4 \times 100 \times 0.1 = 40$ or $4 \times 100 \times 0.064 = 25.6$. Of course, the field will not be developed if the gas price becomes \$0.064, so the opportunity to develop the field in one year is $\max[0, 40 - 32.1] = 7.9$ in the up state and $\max[0, 25.6 - 32.1] = 0$ in the down state. The risk-neutral probability that the up state occurs is $(r - d)/(u - d) = (1.07 - 0.8)/(1.25 - 0.8). = 0.6$. So the value of the opportunity to develop the field is $(0.6 \times 7.9)/1.07 = 4.4299$. This is higher than the value if developed immediately, so development should be postponed and the value of the opportunity to develop the field is the option value, \$4.43 million.

4. (a) We can calculate the value of the inflexible project with the real probabilities and the risk-adjusted discount rate. The project will generate either €20 or €10 million per year, starting two years from now at $t = 2$. The $t = 1$ value of this perpetual cash flow is either $20/0.1 = 200$ or $10/0.1 = 100$.

$$Value = 20/0.1 = 200 \quad cfl = 20$$

$$\nearrow$$

$$125$$

$$\searrow$$

$$Value = 10/0.1 = 100 \quad cfl = 10$$

$$I = -120$$

$$t_0 \qquad\qquad t_1 \qquad\qquad t = 2, \infty$$

the real probabilities are 0.375 and 0.625 so the $t = 0$ value is

$$\frac{0.375 \times 200 + 0.625 \times 100}{1.1} = 125$$

and the NPV is $125 - 120 = €5$ million.

(b) With the flexible project, Smalldale can decide one year from now whether to build the centre or not, when the football association's decision is known. Of course, he will only invest if the project is profitable and abandon the project if it is not profitable.

$$Value = \max[(200 - 120), 0] = 80 \quad cfl = 20$$

$$\nearrow$$

23.81

$$\searrow$$

$$Value = \max[(100 - 120), 0] = 0 \quad cfl = 10$$

$$I = -12 \qquad I = -120$$

$$t_0 \qquad\qquad\qquad t_1 \qquad\qquad\qquad t = 2, \infty$$

To value the flexible project, we use the risk-neutral probabilities and the risk-free interest rate. Given the value of the inflexible project of 125, the up factor is $200/125 = 1.6$ and the down factor is $125/100 = 0.8$, so that $p = (1.05 - 0.8)/(1.6 - 0.8) = 0.3125$ and $1 - p = 0.6875$. The $t = 0$ value is

$$\frac{0.3125 \times 80 + 0.6875 \times 0}{1.05} = 23.81$$

The NPV is thus $23.81 - 12 = 11.81$. So postponement is profitable, the project value increases with $11.81 - 5 = 6.81$.

(c) The risk-adjusted discount rate can be calculated from the replicating portfolio. The ingredients of this portfolio are calculated with Δ and D:

$$\Delta = \frac{O_u - O_d}{S_u - S_d} = \frac{80 - 0}{200 - 100} = 0.8$$

and

$$D = \frac{u O_d - d O_u}{(u - d)r} = \frac{1.6 \times 0 - 0.8 \times 80}{(1.6 - 0.8) \times 1.05} = -76.19$$

So the replicating portfolio consists of $0.8 \times 125 = 100$ in the inflexible project and a loan of 76.19. The weighted average return of this portfolio is

$$\frac{100}{100 - 76.19} \times 0.10 + \frac{-76.19}{100 - 76.19} \times 0.05 = 0.26$$

A shorter calculation is solving:

$$\frac{0.375 \times 80 + 0.625 \times 0}{r} = 23.81$$

for r, which gives the same risk-adjusted rate of 26 per cent.

5. (a) The Wallenberg group held a long position in the shares of Aker Holding plus a long position in in-the-money European put options and a short position in out-of-the-money European call options on these shares, both with a time to maturity of four years. It is a 'share plus protective put' position, plus a short call position. The combined result is that the Wallenberg group is guaranteed to earn at least 10 per cent over four years, but cannot earn more than 40 per cent.

(b) The Wallenberg group held 10 per cent of 16 billion, or 1.6 billion, and had the right to sell it for $1.6 \times 1.1 = 1.76$ billion. The inputs for the calculation of the option's value are: $S_0 = 1.6$, $X = 1.76$, $\sigma = 0.2$, $T = 4$ and $r = 0.05$. The Black and Scholes formula then gives:

$$O_{p,0} = Xe^{-rT} N(-d_2) - S_0 N(-d_1)$$

with

$$d_1 = \frac{\ln(S_0/X) + (r + \frac{1}{2}\sigma^2) \times T}{\sigma\sqrt{T}} \quad \text{and } d_2 = d_1 - \sigma\sqrt{T}$$

$$d_1 = \frac{\ln(1.6/1.76) + (0.05 + 0.5 \times 0.2^2) \times 4}{0.2 \times \sqrt{4}} = 0.46172$$

$$N(-d_1) \rightarrow \text{NormalDist}(-0.46172) = 0.32214$$

$$d_2 = 0.46172 - 0.2 \times \sqrt{4} = 0.06172$$

$$N(-d_2) \rightarrow \text{NormalDist}(-0.06172) = 0.47539$$

$$O_{p,0} = 1.76 \times e^{-0.05 \times 4} \times 0.47539 - 1.6 \times 0.32214 = 0.1696$$

or 169.6 million Norwegian kroner.

(c) The call option position is valued along similar lines. The exercise price is $1.6 \times 1.4 = 2.24$ so that the inputs for the calculation of the option's value are: $S_0 = 1.6$, $X = 2.24$, $\sigma = 0.2$, $T = 4$ and $r = 0.05$. The Black and Scholes formula then gives:

$$O_{c,0} = S_0 N(d_1) - X e^{-rT} N(d_2)$$

with

$$d_1 = \frac{\ln(S_0/X) + (r + \frac{1}{2}\sigma^2) \times T}{\sigma\sqrt{T}} \quad \text{and } d_2 = d_1 - \sigma\sqrt{T}$$

$$d_1 = \frac{\ln(1.6/2.24) + (0.05 + 0.5 \times 0.2^2) \times 4}{0.2 \times \sqrt{4}} = -0.14118$$

$$N(d_1) \rightarrow \text{NormalDist}(-0.141\,18) = 0.44386$$

$$d_2 = -0.14118 - 0.2 \times \sqrt{4} = -0.54118$$

$$N(d_2) \rightarrow \text{NormalDist}(-0.54118) = 0.29419$$

$$O_{c,0} = 1.6 \times 0.44386 - 2.24 \times e^{-0.05 \times 4} \times 0.29419 = 0.17064$$

or 170.64 million Norwegian kroner.

(d) The inputs for the calculation of the option's value on 1 January 2011 are: $S_0 = 1.25$, $X = 1.76$, $\sigma = 0.2$, $T = 0.5$ and $r = 0.05$. The Black and Scholes formula then gives:

$$O_{p,0} = X e^{-rT} N(-d_2) - S_0 N(-d_1)$$

with

$$d_1 = \frac{\ln(S_0/X) + (r + \frac{1}{2}\sigma^2) \times T}{\sigma\sqrt{T}} \text{ and } d_2 = d_1 - \sigma\sqrt{T}$$

$$d_1 = \frac{\ln(1.25/1.76) + (0.05 + 0.5 \times 0.2^2) \times 0.5}{0.2 \times \sqrt{0.5}} = -2.172$$

$N(-d_1) \rightarrow \text{NormalDist}(2.172) = 0.98507$

$$d_2 = -2.172 - 0.2 \times \sqrt{0.5} = -2.3134$$

$N(-d_2) \rightarrow \text{NormalDist}(2.3134) = 0.98965$

$$O_{p,0} = 1.76 \times e^{-0.05 \times 0.5} \times 0.98965 - 1.25 \times 0.98507 = 0.46744$$

or nearly half a billion Norwegian kroner.

6. (a) The value of the project without flexibility can be calculated with the risk-neutral probabilities. Since $u = 1.667$, $d = 0.667$ and $r = 1.1$ so

$$p = \frac{1.1 - 0.667}{1.667 - 0.667}. = 0.433 \text{ and } 1 - p = 0.567$$

The pay-offs without flexibility are $(1\frac{2}{3} \times 75) - 67 = 58$ and $(\frac{2}{3} \times 75) - 67 = -17$, so the present value is:

$$\frac{0.433 \times 58 + 0.567 \times -17}{1.1} = 14.07$$

and the NPV is $14.07 - 10 = 4.07$

(b) If the production decision is made at t_1, the pay-offs are $\max[0, 125 - 67] = 58$ and $\max[0, 50 - 67] = 0$, but they will be available one period later so their present value is:

$$\frac{0.433 \times 58 + 0.567 \times 0}{1.1^2} = 20.76$$

and the NPV is $20.76 - 10 = 10.76$. The price dynamics and investments are shown in the lattice below.

$$
\begin{array}{ccccc}
& & 125 & \rightarrow & 125 - 67 = 58 \\
& \nearrow & & & \\
75 & & & & \\
& \searrow & & & \\
& & 50 & \rightarrow & 50 - 67 = -17 \\
I = -10 & & & & I = -67 \\
t = 0 & & t = 1 & & t = 2
\end{array}
$$

7. (a) We start by calculating the binomial parameters and the value tree for the cash flows from the fish farm: $u = 1.25$ and $d = 0.8$ and $r = 1.07$ so that $p = (1.07 - 0.8)/(1.25 - 0.8) = 0.6$. We treat the annual licence fee in the same way as dividends, i.e. as a value stream out of the project. The value tree then becomes:

$$15 - 0.5 = 14.5$$

$$12.5 - 0.5 = 12$$

$$9.6 - 0.5 = 9.1$$

$$10$$

$$9.4 - 0.5 = 8.9$$

$$8 - 0.5 = 7.5$$

$$6 - 0.5 = 5.5$$

$I = -8$	$I = -8.56$	$I = -9.16$
$t = 0$	$t = 1$	$t = 2$

The investment amount increases to $1.07 \times 8 = 8.56$ at $t = 1$ and to $1.07^2 \times 8 = 9.16$ at $t = 2$. To calculate option values, we start at the end of the tree, at $t = 2$:

$$\max[0, 14.5 - 9.16] = 5.34$$

$$\max[(\max[0, 12 - 8.56]), 2.99] = 3.44$$

$$\max[0, 9.1 - 9.16] = 0.0$$

$$10$$

$$\max[0, 8.9 - 9.16] = 0.0$$

$$max[\max[0, 7.5 - 8.56], 0] = 0$$

$$\max[0, 5.5 - 9.16] = 0.0$$

$I = -8$	$I = -8.56$	$I = -9.16$
$t = 0$	$t = 1$	$t = 2$

The option value alive in the upper node of $t = 1$ is:

$$\frac{(0.6 \times 5.34) + (0.4 \times 0)}{1.07} = 2.99$$

and the value dead is $\max[0, 12 - 8.56] = 3.44$, so the option should be exercised in this node. In the lower node of $t = 1$ the option has no value dead or alive. This gives an option value alive at $t = 0$ of:

$$\frac{(0.6 \times 3.44) + (0.4 \times 0)}{1.07} = 1.93$$

while the option value dead is $\max[0, 10 - 8] = 2$, so the licence has a value of €2 million and should be exercised immediately.

(b) Without the licence fee the value tree becomes:

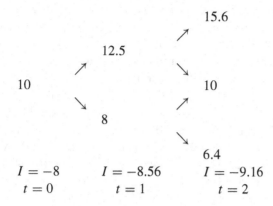

$$I = -8 \qquad I = -8.56 \qquad I = -9.16$$
$$t = 0 \qquad\quad t = 1 \qquad\qquad t = 2$$

Again, we start at t = 2:

max[0, 15.6 − 9.16] = 6.44

12.5

10   max[0, 10 − 9.16] = 0.84

8

max[0, 6.4 − 9.16] = 0.0

$$I = -8 \qquad I = -8.56 \qquad I = -9.16$$
$$t = 0 \qquad\quad t = 1 \qquad\qquad t = 2$$

The option value alive in the upper node of t = 1 is:

$$\frac{(0.6 \times 6.44) + (0.4 \times 0.84)}{1.07} = 3.93$$

and the value dead is max[0, 12.5−8.56] = 3.94, so the option should be exercised in this node. In the lower node of t = 1 the option value alive is

$$\frac{(0.6 \times 0.84) + (0.4 \times 0)}{1.07} = 0.47$$

This gives an option value alive at t = 0 of:

$$\frac{(0.6 \times 3.94) + (0.4 \times 0.47)}{1.07} = 2.39$$

The value dead remains max[0, 10 − 8] = 2. So without the fee the licence has a value of €2.39 million and should be exercised later, at t = 1.

8. (a) The options available to Smart Inc. are the option to expand production in one period and the option to abandon for second-hand value. Since both options can be exercised at different times they are an American call (the option to expand) and an American put (the option to abandon).

(b) The 'stand alone' value of each option can be calculated with the procedure for American options, i.e. by testing the exercise condition in each relevant node. We begin by constructing the value tree for the production process. Given the binomial price process, the current price of 1,000 will either increase to 1,500 or decrease to 500 per ton. The production will decrease to $0.8 \times 16{,}000 = 12{,}800$ tons. This gives values of the year 1 production of $1{,}500 \times 12{,}800 = 19.2$ million and $500 \times 12{,}800 = 6.4$ million. Their perpetual values for the process are $19.2/0.2 = 96$ and $6.4/0.2 = 32$. At $t = 2$ the prices are either $1.5 \times 1{,}500 = 2{,}250$, or $0.5 \times 1{,}500 = 1.5 \times 500 = 750$, or $0.5 \times 500 = 250$. The production further decreases to $0.8 \times 12{,}800 = 10{,}240$. This gives values of the year 2 production of $10{,}240 \times 2{,}250 = 23.04$, or $10{,}240 \times 750 = 7.68$ or $10{,}240 \times 250 = 2.56$. Their perpetual values are $23.04/0.2 = 115.2$, and $7.68/0.2 = 38.4$ and $2.56/0.2 = 12.8$. The value tree for the production process thus becomes:

$$23.04/0.2 = 115.2$$

$$19.2/0.2 = 96$$

$$16/0.2 = 80 \qquad\qquad 7.68/0.2 = 38.4$$

$$6.4/0.2 = 32$$

$$2.56/0.2 = 12.8$$

$$t = 0 \qquad\qquad t = 1 \qquad\qquad t = 2$$

The parameters of the binomial process are $u = 1.5$, $d = 0.5$, $r = 1.1$ so that $p = (1.1 - .5)/(1.5 - .5) = 0.6$. To value the option to abandon we start at the end of the tree. If the option is exercised, the payoff is the second-hand value of 50. The exercise price (= what is given up) is the value of the production process. So the value of the option to abandon is max[0, second-hand value – production value]. The optimal decision at the end nodes is not to abandon in the upper node and abandon in the two lower nodes.

$$\max[0,\ 50 - 115.2] = 0$$

$$\max[\underbrace{0}_{dead},\ \underbrace{4.22}_{alive}]$$

$$9.52 \qquad\qquad \max[0,\ 50 - 38.4] = 11.6$$

$$\max[\underbrace{18}_{dead},\ \underbrace{19.86}_{alive}]$$

$$\max[0,\ 50 - 12.8] = 37.2$$

$$t = 0 \qquad\qquad t = 1 \qquad\qquad t = 2$$

Discounting the expected values to t_1 values with the risk-free rate gives the values of the option alive:

$$\frac{.6 \times 0 + .4 \times 11.6}{1.1} = 4.22 \text{ and } \frac{.6 \times 11.6 + .4 \times 37.2}{1.1} = 19.86$$

The t_1 values dead are $\max[0, 50 - 96] = 0$ and $\max[0, 50 - 32] = 18$, so it is not optimal to exercise the option at t_1. This gives a t_0 value of

$$\frac{.6 \times 4.22 + .4 \times 19.86}{1.1} = 9.52$$

which is larger than the value dead: $\max[0, 50 - 80] = 0$

The option to expand is evaluated along similar lines. The option's payoff is the value of the year's production and the exercise price is the €5 million investment in repairs and spare parts. We start at the end nodes:

$$\max[0, 23.04 - 5] = 18.04$$

$$\max[\underbrace{14.2}_{dead}, \underbrace{10.82}_{alive}]$$

$$\max[\underbrace{11}_{dead}, \underbrace{8.28}_{alive}]$$

$$\max[0, 7.68 - 5] = 2.68$$

$$\max[\underbrace{1.4}_{dead}, \underbrace{1.46}_{alive}]$$

$$\max[0, 2.56 - 5] = 0$$

$$t = 0 \qquad t = 1 \qquad t = 2$$

So the option is exercised in the two upper nodes of $t = 2$ and not exercised in the lower node. Discounting the expected values to t_1 values with the risk-free rate gives the values of the option alive:

$$\frac{.6 \times 18.04 + .4 \times 2.68}{1.1} = 10.82 \text{ and } \frac{.6 \times 2.68 + .4 \times 0}{1.1} = 1.46$$

The t_1 values dead are $\max[0, 19.2 - 5] = 14.2$ and $\max[0, 6.4 - 5] = 1.4$ so it is optimal to exercise the option in the upper node of t_1. This gives a t_0 value alive of

$$\frac{.6 \times 14.2 + .4 \times 1.46}{1.1} = 8.28$$

The value dead is $\max[0, 16 - 5] = 11$ so the option should be exercised at $t = 0$.

(c) The two options can interact: abandoning the project can eliminate the value of the option to expand in the same or later nodes. Also, doubling the production in a node can reduce the value of the option to abandon in that node. However, because production can only be expanded in one period, the option to expand does not affect subsequent periods; this reduces the possible interaction. Moreover, both options are of opposite type (expansion is a call, abandonment is a put) so that they have value under opposite circumstances. This makes their interaction area small, but since they have overlapping exercise prices there is interaction. Interaction can be incorporated in the valuation procedure by including, in all relevant nodes, the condition that we choose to exercise the option with the highest value and adjust the value for the lost other option. In the middle node of $t = 2$, the option to abandon has a value of 11.6 and the option to expand has a value of 2.68. The latter value is given up when the option to abandon is exercised, so the underlying value of the option to abandon increases with 2.68. But even with the higher underlying value, the option to abandon is still more valuable than the option to expand, so production is abandoned. The payoff of the option to abandon becomes $50 - (38.4 + 2.68) = 8.92$ and the value of the option to expand becomes 0. In the upper and lower nodes of $t = 2$ there is no interaction and the values remain as before.

Discounting the expected values of the options back one period we get the $t = 1$ values alive. For the option to abandon these are

$$\frac{.6 \times 0 + .4 \times 8.92}{1.1} = 3.24 \text{ and } \frac{.6 \times 8.92 + .4 \times 37.2}{1.1} = 18.39$$

and for the option to expand the $t = 1$ values alive are:

$$\frac{.6 \times 18.04 + .4 \times 0}{1.1} = 9.84 \text{ and } \frac{.6 \times 0 + .4 \times 0}{1.1} = 0$$

The values dead remain as in the lattices above. The calculations are summarized in the lattices below. We see that in the upper node of $t = 1$, the option to expand should be exercised. This does not affect the value of the option to abandon, because it only has value alive. In the lower node of $t = 1$ the option to expand should also be exercised: it has a value of 1.4 dead and 0 alive. This value would be lost if the option to abandon would be exercised. However, the latter option is already worth more alive (18.39) than dead (18) and the higher value of the underlying will further reduce the value dead.

Discounting the expected values to present we get a value of

$$\frac{.6 \times 3.24 + .4 \times 18.39}{1.1} = 8.46$$

for the option to abandon and a value of

$$\frac{.6 \times 14.2 + .4 \times 1.4}{1.1} = 8.26$$

for the option to expand. The latter is lower than the value dead of 11, so the option to expand should be exercised at $t = 0$. The combined option value is $8.46 + 11 = 19.46$, a bit lower than the sum of the stand-alone values, $9.75 + 11 = 20.75$

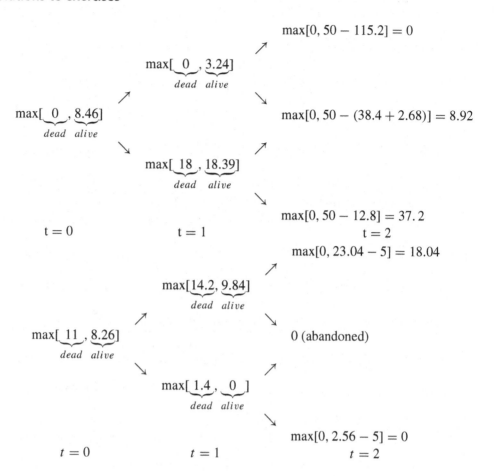

$\max[0, 50 - 115.2] = 0$

$\max[\underbrace{0}_{dead}, \underbrace{3.24}_{alive}]$

$\max[0, 50 - (38.4 + 2.68)] = 8.92$

$\max[\underbrace{0}_{dead}, \underbrace{8.46}_{alive}]$

$\max[\underbrace{18}_{dead}, \underbrace{18.39}_{alive}]$

t = 0   t = 1

$\max[0, 50 - 12.8] = 37.2$
t = 2

$\max[0, 23.04 - 5] = 18.04$

$\max[\underbrace{14.2}_{dead}, \underbrace{9.84}_{alive}]$

$\max[\underbrace{11}_{dead}, \underbrace{8.26}_{alive}]$

0 (abandoned)

$\max[\underbrace{1.4}_{dead}, \underbrace{0}_{alive}]$

$\max[0, 2.56 - 5] = 0$

t = 0   t = 1   t = 2

Chapter 10

1. We can construct the same payoffs using a combination of *safe* debt and put options. The payoff diagram is given in Figure S10.1. The equity-holder's position is equivalent to owning the project in combination with a risk-free loan and a long put that is written by the debtholder. If the project value is less than the face value of debt, the equity-holder can supplement the project value with the payoff from the put option and always repay the debt. Hence, debt is safe (default free). The debtholder's position is of course the opposite, i.e. equivalent to owning safe debt in combination with a short put option.

2. (a) We use the Black and Scholes formula to calculate the value of equity as a call option on NettIT's assets: $S_0 = 65$, $X = 50$, $\sigma = 0.3$, $T = 1$ and $r = 0.07$. The formula then gives:

$$O_{c,0} = S_0 N(d_1) - Xe^{-rT} \times N(d_2)$$

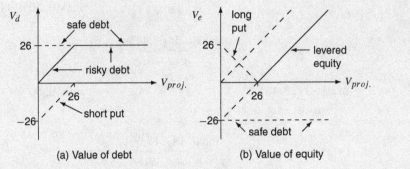

Figure S10.1 Corporate securities as put option combinations

with

$$d_1 = \frac{\ln(S_0/X) + (r + \frac{1}{2}\sigma^2) \times T}{\sigma\sqrt{T}} \quad \text{and } d_2 = d_1 - \sigma\sqrt{T}$$

$$d_1 = \frac{\ln(65/50) + (0.07 + 0.5 \times 0.3^2) \times 1}{0.3 \times \sqrt{1}} = 1.2579$$

$N(d_1) \rightarrow \text{NormalDist}(1.2579) = 0.89579$

$$d_2 = 1.2579 - 0.3 \times \sqrt{1} = 0.9579$$

$N(d_2) \rightarrow \text{NormalDist}(0.9579) = 0.83094$

$$O_{c,0} = 65 \times 0.89579 - 50 \times e^{-0.07} \times 0.83094 = 19.49$$

(b) When equity is valued as a put, its value is equal to the value of the underlying assets, minus the value of the loan as if it were risk free plus the value of a long put on the assets. The value of the assets is given as 65. The value of the loan if it were risk free is $50 \times e^{-0.07} = 46.62$, and the value of the put can be calculated with the formula

$$O_{p,0} = Xe^{-rT}N(-d_2) - S_0 N(-d_1)$$

$N(-d_1) = 1 - N(d_1) = 1 - 0.89579 = 0.10421$
$N(-d_2) = 1 - N(d_2) = 1 - 0.83094 = 0.16906$

$$O_{p,0} = 50 \times e^{-0.07} \times 0.16906 - 65 \times 0.10421 = 1.11$$

Using the put–call parity gives the same result:

$$O_{p,0} = O_{c,0} + Xe^{-rT} - S_0 = 19.49 + 50 \times e^{-0.07} - 65 = 1.11$$

So the value of equity valued as a put is $65 - 46.62 + 1.11 = 19.49$, the same value that we found under (a).

(c) The value of the loan is the value of the assets minus equity so $65 - 19.49 = 45.51$.

(d) The interest rate on the loan is found by solving $45.51 = 50 \times e^{-r}$ for r, which gives $-r = \ln(45.51/50) = -0.094$ or $r = 9.4$ per cent.

(e) The risk-neutral probability that the loan will be defaulted is the risk-neutral probability that the call option on the assets will not be exercised by the equity-holders, i.e. $N(-d_2) = 1 - N(d_2) = 0.16906$ or 16.9 per cent.

(f) The total value of the company will drop with €1 million from €65 to €64 million.

(g) We calculate the value of NettIT's equity as a call option on the firm's assets: $S_0 = 64$, $X = 50$, $\sigma = 0.5$, $T = 1$ and $r = 0.07$. The formula then gives:

$$O_{c,0} = S_0 N(d_1) - Xe^{-rT} \times N(d_2)$$

with

$$d_1 = \frac{\ln(S_0/X) + (r + \frac{1}{2}\sigma^2) \times T}{\sigma\sqrt{T}} \text{ and } d_2 = d_1 - \sigma\sqrt{T}$$

$$d_1 = \frac{\ln(64/50) + (0.07 + 0.5 \times 0.5^2) \times 1}{0.5 \times \sqrt{1}} = 0.88372$$

$$N(d_1) \rightarrow \text{NormalDist}(0.88372) = 0.81158$$

$$d_2 = 0.88372 - 0.5 \times \sqrt{1} = 0.38372$$

$$N(d_2) \rightarrow \text{NormalDist}(0.38372) = 0.64941$$

$$O_{c,0} = 64 \times 0.81158 - 50 \times e^{-0.07} \times 0.64941 = 21.67$$

so equity increases in value with $21.67 - 19.49 = 2.18$ or €2.18 million.

(h) The value of NettIT's debt will drop to $64 - 21.67 = 42.33$ or a decrease with $45.51 - 43.33 = 2.18$, the same as the value increase of equity.

(i) The risk-neutral probability that the loan will be defaulted is the risk-neutral probability that the call option on the assets will not be exercised by the equity-holders, i.e. $N(-d_2) = 1 - N(d_2) = 1 - 0.64941 = 0.35059$ or 35.1 per cent.

3. To calculate the default probability we use the logistic function:

$$p_i = \frac{1}{1 + e^{-(NM \times 0.35 + INC \times -0.3 + DFST \times -0.8)}}$$

in which p_i is the probability of default and the variables are defined as in the question.

(a) For the first client the inputs are $NM = 5$, $INC = 2.5$ and $DFST = 0$, which gives a default probability of

$$p_i = \frac{1}{1 + e^{-(5 \times 0.35 + 2.5 \times -0.3 + 0 \times -0.8)}} = 0.731$$

a. For the second client the inputs are $NM = 1$, $INC = 6.0$ and $DFST = 1$, which gives a default probability of

$$p_i = \frac{1}{1 + e^{-(1 \times 0.35 + 6 \times -0.3 + 1 \times -0.8)}} = 0.095$$

4. The parameters of the binomial process are: $u = 1.4 \quad d = .71 \quad r = 1.08$, so that $p = \frac{1.08 - .71}{1.4 - 71} = .536$ and $1 - p = .464$. The value tree for the project is:

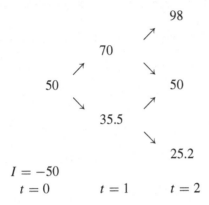

$$98$$
$$70$$
$$50 \qquad 50$$
$$35.5$$
$$25.2$$

$I = -50$
$t = 0 \qquad t = 1 \qquad t = 2$

The project's NPV is zero.

(a) A one year's delay gives Ottan the option to develop the plan if the value of its cash flows goes up, and to abandon it if the value goes down. The tree representing the equity value of this option is:

$$E^+ = \max[(70 - 54), 0] = 16$$

E_0

$$E^- = \max[(35.5 - 54), 0] = 0$$

$t_0 \qquad\qquad t_1$

Note that investment amount has increased with 1.08 to 54. The value of this option is:

$$E_0 = \frac{p \times E^+ + (1 - p) \times E^-}{r} = \frac{.536 \times 16 + .464 \times 0}{1.08} = 7.94$$

(b) Developing the plan in stages only has value if there is flexibility to decide about the stages, i.e. if the project can be continued or abandoned after a stage. If the construction stage has to be developed regardless of which state occurs at t = 1, then staged development has no additional value.

(c) Staged development gives Ottan the option to develop the second stage of the plan if the value of its cash flows goes up, and to abandon the plan if the value goes down. The tree representing the equity value of this option is:

$$E^+ = \max[(70 - 37.8), 0] = 32.2$$

E_0

$$E^- = \max[(35.5 - 37.8), 0] = 0$$

$I = -15$

$t_0 \qquad\qquad t_1$

Note that investment amount of the second stage has increased with 1.08 to 37.8. The value of this option is:

$$E_0 = \frac{p \times E^+ + (1-p) \times E^-}{r} = \frac{.536 \times 32.2 + .464 \times 0}{1.08} = 15.98$$

Together with the investment amount for the first stage, €15, this gives a total project value of €0.98 million.

(d) The value of the project after two years is only large enough to pay back the loan if the second phase of the project is developed. BB can anticipate that Ottan will not develop the second phase if the value of the cash flows goes down: Ottan will abandon the project and default the loan.

(e) The payoff to BB can be represented as follows:

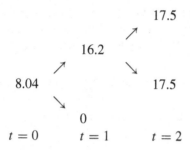

If the second phase is developed at t = 1, the loan will certainly be paid back at t = 2. The t = 1 value of this pay back is 17.5/1.08 = 16.2. The value now is:

$$\frac{.536 \times 16.2 + .464 \times 0}{1.08} = 8.04$$

So €8.04 million is what BB is willing to loan now in return for Ottan's promise to pay back €17.5 million in two years' time.

(f) To calculate the interest rate on the loan we have to use the real probabilities: $(.6 \times 17.5)/r^2 = 8.04$, which gives r = 1.1428.

(g) The value of the deal for Ottan is calculated by solving the value tree from the end backwards:

$$98 - 17.5 = 80.5$$

$$16.12 = \max[0, -37.8 + 53.92]$$

8

$$50 - 17.5 = 32.5$$

$$0 = \max[0, -37.8 + 19.44]$$

$$25.2 - 17.5 = 7.7$$

t = 0   t = 1   t = 2

The payoff for Ottan at $t = 2$ is the project value minus the amount due to the bank, i.e. 17.5. This gives $t = 1$ values of

$((.536 \times 80.5) + (.464 \times 32.5))/1.08 = 53.915$ and

$((.536 \times 32.5) + (.464 \times 7.7))/1.08 = 19.438$

At $t=1$ Ottan has the flexibility to invest his part of the project (37.8) or to abandon it. He will only invest in the upper node, where the project value is larger than his investment. The $t=0$ value of the project for Ottan is thus: $((.536 \times 16.115) + (.464 \times 0))/1.08 = 8$. By using the bank's money to finance the first, very risky phase, Ottan can use his own money for the very profitable second phase if the value goes up, and walk away without spending any money if the value goes down.

(h) The value of the payments to Savings Bank1 is the same as the value to BB: 8.04. Since Savings Bank1 provided 15, the NPV $= 8.04 - 15 = -6.96$. The loss results from the failure to anticipate that Ottan will not develop the second phase if the value of the cash flows goes down. The total project value is $8 - 6.96 = 1.04$, i.e. $\pm$ the same value as the flexible project.

5. (a) The value of Conglomerate's shares can be calculated as a call option on the firm's assets. The exercise price is the sum of the face values of the two loans, i.e. 80. $S_0 = 100$, $X = 80$, $\sigma = 0.25$, $T = 2$ and $r = 0.08$. The formula then gives:

$$O_{c,0} = S_0 N(d_1) - X e^{-rT} \times N(d_2)$$

with

$$d_1 = \frac{\ln(S_0/X) + (r + \frac{1}{2}\sigma^2) \times T}{\sigma \sqrt{T}} \quad \text{and} \quad d_2 = d_1 - \sigma\sqrt{T}$$

$$d_1 = \frac{\ln(100/80) + (0.08 + 0.5 \times 0.25^2) \times 2}{0.25 \times \sqrt{2}} = 1.2605$$

$N(d_1) \rightarrow \text{NormalDist}(1.2605) = 0.89626$

$$d_2 = 1.2605 - 0.25 \times \sqrt{2} = 0.90695$$

$N(d_2) \rightarrow \text{NormalDist}(0.90695) = 0.81778$

$$O_{c,0} = 100 \times 0.89626 - 80 \times e^{-0.08 \times 2} \times 0.81778 = 33.88$$

After the split-up, each of the new companies will have assets with a market value of £50 million; since there were no economies of scale or scope, no value is lost by the split-up. Each company still has a zero coupon loan with a face value of £40 million and a time to maturity of two years. Before the split-up Conglomerate was a portfolio of two companies and the portfolio variance is:

$$\sigma_p^2 = x_1^2\sigma_1^2 + x_2^2\sigma_2^2 + 2x_1 x_2 \rho_{1,2}\sigma_1\sigma_2 = 0.25^2$$

We know that the companies have about the same value and the same volatility, so $x_1 = x_2 = 0.5$ and $\sigma_1 = \sigma_2$. We also know that the companies' returns are uncorrelated, so $\rho_{1,2} = 0$. Solving the reduced equation:

$$(0.5)^2(\sigma)^2 + (0.5)^2(\sigma)^2 = 0.25^2$$

for σ we find that $\sigma = 0.354$. With this we can calculate the equity values of both companies: $S_0 = 50$, $X = 40$, $\sigma = 0.354$, $T = 2$ and $r = 0.08$, which gives:

$$O_{c,0} = S_0 N(d_1) - Xe^{-rT} \times N(d_2)$$

with

$$d_1 = \frac{\ln(S_0/X) + (r + \frac{1}{2}\sigma^2) \times T}{\sigma\sqrt{T}} \quad \text{and } d_2 = d_1 - \sigma\sqrt{T}$$

$$d_1 = \frac{\ln(50/40) + (0.08 + 0.5 \times 0.354^2) \times 2}{0.354 \times \sqrt{2}} = 1.0156$$

$$N(d_1) \rightarrow \text{NormalDist}(1.0156) = 0.84509$$

$$d_2 = 1.0156 - 0.354 \times \sqrt{2} = 0.51497$$

$$N(d_2) \rightarrow \text{NormalDist}(0.51497) = 0.69671$$

$$O_{c,0} = 50 \times 0.84509 - 40 \times e^{-0.08 \times 2} \times 0.69671 = 18.51$$

The combined share value after the split-up is $2 \times 18.51 = 37.02$, so the benefit to the corporate raider is $37.02 - 33.88 = 3.14$, or £3.14 million.

Chapter 11

1. (a) First we calculate the present values of the storage costs and the convenience yields:

    $5/1.04^{0.25} = 4.95$ and $1/1.04^{0.25} = 0.99$
    $2/1.04^{0.25} = 1.98$ and $10/1.04^{0.25} = 9.90$
    $10/1.04^{0.25} = 9.90$ and $0/1.04^{0.25} = 0$
    $15/1.04^{0.25} = 14.85$ and $20/1.04^{0.25} = 19.81$

    The futures prices are then found with the cost-of-carry relation:
    $F = [S_0 + PV(sc) - PV(cy)](1 + r_f)^T$
    $(50 + 4.95 - 0.99)(1.04)^{0.25} = 54.492 \times 100 = 5{,}449.20$
    $(100 + 1.98 - 9.90)(1.04)^{0.25} = 92.987 \times 100 = 9{,}298.70$
    $(250 + 9.90 - 0)(1.04)^{0.25} = 262.46 \times 100 = 26{,}246$
    $(500 + 14.95 - 19.81)(1.04)^{0.25} = 500.02 \times 100 = 50{,}002.$

    (b) $ncy = PV(cy) - PV(sc)$, so for:
    reindeer legs: $0.99 - 4.95 = -3.96$
    dried cod: $9.90 - 1.98 = 7.92$
    brown cheese: $0 - 9.90 = -9.90$
    cloudberry jam: $19.81 - 14.85 = 4.96.$

(c) The benefit of having the real commodity, rather than futures, is not very large when the commodity is readily available in the market and storage costs are high. By contrast, it is large when the commodity is in short supply and storage costs are low. The net convenience yield is typically positive for commodities that can be stored very cheaply and that are important in production processes, such as metals. The net convenience yield of agricultural commodities depends on the season. It is low or negative in the fall when crops are harvested. Then, supply is plentiful and storage facilities are full. In the summer, last year's harvest is largely used up and storage facilities are almost empty. Then, net convenience yield is likely to be positive.

(d) The trader can buy 100 futures contracts in dried cod: he has a short position of 10,000 kilograms so he can hedge the price risk with a long position in futures.

2. Blaufoss can buy aluminium future contracts, e.g. on LME. This will lock in the price of its future aluminium purchases. It can also buy aluminium now, at the spot price, and store it.

3. Using the cost-of-carry relation with ncy we get: $2{,}279 = [2{,}241 - ncy](1 + 0.06)^{.25}$ so $ncy = -5.042$ or $-5.042/2{,}214 = -0.2$ per cent.

4. (a) We can calculate the forward rate with the interest rate parity:
$$\frac{F_{€...}}{S_{€...}} = \frac{1+r_€}{1+r_{...}} \Rightarrow F_{€...} = \left(\frac{1+r_€}{1+r_{...}}\right) \times S_{€...}$$

$$F_{€SEK} = \left(\frac{1.0120}{1.0103}\right) \times 0.0980 = 0.0982$$

$$F_{€NOK} = \left(\frac{1.0120}{1.0300}\right) \times 0.1223 = 0.1202$$

$$F_{€DKK} = \left(\frac{1.0120}{1.0154}\right) \times 0.1343 = 0.1339$$

(b) Instead of buying forwards you can (in theory) open a bank account in each country, buy the present value of your local expenses on the spot exchange market and deposit the foreign currency on the accounts. Alternatively, you can go on holiday in Finland and avoid exchange issues all together.

5. The holder of a long forward is certain to end up with the stock at maturity against payment of the forward price F. This can be replicated by buying a European call option and writing a European put option, both with an exercise price equal to the forward price F, as the following table shows:

	Payoff at maturity	
	$S_T > F$	$S_T \leq F$
Long call	$S_T - F$	0
Short put	0	$-(F - S_T)$
Total portfolio	$S_T - F$	$S_T - F$

An expression for the forward price F can be found with the put–call parity: *share* + *put* = *call* + *pv(F)*. Rewriting we get: *share* − *pv(F)* = *call* − *put*. The right-hand side is the option combination that replicates the forward (long call + short put). This combination must have the same present value as the forward, i.e. zero. We can then write the left-hand side as *share* − *pv(F)* = *share* − $F/(1 + r_f)^T$ = 0, which gives $F = share \times (1 + r_f)^T$, the forward price we found earlier.

6. The interest rate parity gives:

$$1.008 = \frac{.72}{.714} = \frac{F_{€\$}}{S_{€\$}} = \frac{1 + r_€}{1 + r_\$} = \frac{1.08}{1.04} = 1.038$$

the left-hand side is lower than the right-hand side. A covered interest arbitrage involves the following steps:

(a) Borrow an amount in dollars, say $100,000.
(b) Exchange the $100,000 for dollars at the spot rate; this gives 100,000 × .714 = €71,400.
(c) Deposit these euros in a European account to earn the euro interest rate; this gives 71,400 × 1.08 = €77,112 after one year.
(d) Sell these €77,112 forward for dollars; this gives 77,112/.72 = $107,100 after one year.
(e) Use these dollars to pay back the loan and interest of 1.04 × 100,000 = $104,000.
(f) The difference of 107,100 − 104,000 = $3,100 is arbitrage profit.
(g) Repeat the above steps until the arbitrage opportunity has disappeared.

To take out the arbitrage profit today, take up a loan of 107,000/1.04 = $102,981 and continue as under (b). This gives an instantaneous arbitrage profit $2,981(= 3,100/1.04).

7. (a) BP has to borrow the present value of CAD 200,000, which is 200,000/1.08^0.25 = 196,190, and exchange these in the spot market to receive: 196,190/1.6191 = 121,172 British pounds. After three months the payment by the customer is used to pay back the loan with interest: 196,190 × 1.08^0.25 = 200,000.

(b) The three months forward rate can be found with the interest rate parity:

$$\frac{F_{C\$£}}{S_{C\$£}} = \frac{1 + r_{C\$}}{1 + r_£} \quad or \quad F_{C\$£} = \frac{1 + r_{C\$}}{1 + r_£} S_{C\$£}$$

Filling in the numbers gives

$$F_{C\$£} = \frac{1.08^{0.25}}{1.04^{0.25}} 1.6191 = 1.6344$$

(c) To hedge the currency risk with forwards, BP will have to sell CAD 200,000 forward against the forward price of $F_{C\$£}$ = 1.6344. The company will then receive 200,000/1.6344 = £122,369 in three months' time, which have a present value of 122,369/1.04^0.25 = £121,175.

(d) No actions are required, the currency risk is already hedged.

Chapter 12

1. (a) The stock price will fall.
(b) The stock price will rise.
(c) The stock price will fall.
(d) The stock price will rise.
(e) The stock price will rise.
(f) The stock price will fall.

2. This fee structure gives the managers a strong risk incentive: they participate in high returns but do not have to share in the losses.

3. (a) Since the value development of the firm is obviously binomial, we can begin by setting up a value tree for the firm:

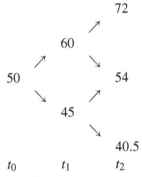

From the tree we can see that the value of the firm is always large enough to pay back the loan. The loan is therefore risk-free and has a present value of $40/1.1^2 = 33$. The firm's equity value is $50 - 33 = 17$. This value can also be found by using the binomial pricing formula on the values for equity, which are $(72 - 40)$, $54 - 40)$ and $(40.5 - 40)$. The binomial parameters are:
$u = 1.2 \quad d = 0.9 \quad r = 1.1$ so that $p = (1.1 - 0.9)/1.2 - 0.9 = .67$
This gives:
$(.67 \times 32 + .33 \times 14)/1.1 = 23.69$
$(.67 \times 14 + .33 \times 0.5)/1.1 = 8.68$ and
$(.67 \times 23.69 + .33 \times 8.68)/1.1 = 17$

(b) Because the new debt has the same priority as the old debt, they can be considered together for valuation purposes. This gives zero coupon bonds with a face value of 60. (Splitting the values at maturity in a 2/6 part for the new bondholders and a 4/6 part for old ones and discounting risk neutrally back gives the same results.) The bonds, both the old and the new, are no longer risk free. In the two lower nodes the bonds' face value is larger than the value of the firm. Consequently, the firm will default the loan in those nodes and transfer the value of the firm to the bondholders. This makes the bond values at maturity 60, 54 and 40.5, giving discounted values of:
$(.67 \times 60 + .33 \times 54)/1.1 = 52.73$

$(.67 \times 54 + .33 \times 40.5)/1.1 = 45$ and

$(.67 \times 52.73 + .33 \times 45)/1.1 = 45.59$

20/60 of this value is the new bond, or 15.20, and 40/60 is the old bond, or 30.39. This gives an equity value of $50 - 45.59 = 4.41$. This can be confirmed by calculating the equity values at maturity and discounting back:

$(.67 \times 12 + .33 \times 0)/1.1 = 7.27$

$(.67 \times 0 + .33 \times 0)/1.1 = 0$ and

$(.67 \times 7.27 + .33 \times 0)/1.1 = 4.41$

The total value for the equity-holders is 4.41 in shares and 15.20 in dividends, or 19.61. This is an increase of 2.61, so the firm should go ahead with the plan. The benefits for the shareholders come from the old bondholders: their value decreases with $33 - 30.39 = 2.61$. They are expropriated by the new issue, that increases their risk without giving any compensation.

(c) The proceeds of the bond issue are 15.20 and the value of the project is $21/1.1^2 = 17.35$. So the project is profitable and increases the value of the firm. To see whether it also increases the value of equity we have to calculate the values of debt and equity. Because of the new project, debt becomes riskless again and has a value of $60/1, 1^2 = 49.59$. One third of this, or 16.53, is for the new bondholders; their value increases with $16.53 - 15.20 = 1.33$. Note that the new bondholders got a fair deal to begin with: they paid the fair value of 15.20 for their bond, based on the firm value after dividends have been paid. Two thirds of the 49.59 debt value, or 33.06, is for the old bondholders: their value increases with $33.06 - 30.39 = 2.67$. We see that the new project makes debt safer and more valuable: the total increase in debt value is $1.33 + 2.67 = 4$. This is more than the increase in firm value of $17.35 - 15.20 = 2.15$. The difference is a reduction in shareholder wealth: the total firm value with the project is $50 + 17.35 = 67.35$, and with a debt value of 49.59, this leaves 17.76 for the shareholders. The same value can be found by discounting the after-debt values at maturity risk neutrally back to t_0. This gives a change in shareholder wealth of $17.76 - 19.61 = -1.85$. So the firm should not go ahead with the project; the 'benefits' to the shareholders of -1.85 come from an increase in bond values larger than the increase in firm value.

(d) The new investment strategy gives rise to a new value tree and new binomial parameters:

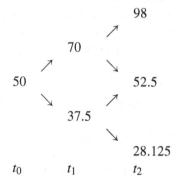

The new binomial parameters are:

$u = 1.4$ $d = 0.75$ $r = 1.1$ so that $p = (1.1 - 0.75)/1.4 - 0.75 = .54$.

With the new investment strategy, debt is no longer riskless. In the lower node at t_2 the face value of debt is larger than the value of the firm, the firm will default the loan and transfer the firm to the debtholders. So the value trees for debt and equity become:

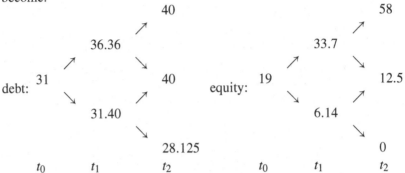

debt:

equity:

The new investment strategy increases equity value with $19 - 17 = 2$, and it decreases debt value with $33 - 31 = 2$. The benefits for the shareholders come from a decrease in debt value. Debt becomes riskier without any compensation for the debtholders; they are expropriated by the shareholders.

4. (a) Cars need maintenance and repair (spare parts) during their entire life, so customers not only buy a product, but also a stream of future services. When the customer, as a principal, cannot rely on the agent (i.e. the manufacturer) to supply the future services, the product will lose much of its value and sales will plummet.

(b) The plan is very profitable: €1 million investment now and a certain payoff of €7.5 at the end of the period, an NPV of $-1 + 7.5/1.07 = 6$. The end of period values become $1.25 \times 40 = 50 + 7.5 = 57.5$ in the up state and $0.8 \times 40 = 32 + 7.5 = 39.5$ in the down state. However, the entire value increase goes to the creditors, the share holders get nothing. The shareholders value is $\max[0, 57.5 - 60] = 0$ and $\max[0, 39.5 - 60] = 0$. So the shareholders should not go ahead with the chief engineer's plan.

(c) The underinvestment problem.

(d) If the investment is in assets that can be used to secure debt, then secured debt could be used. For example, by issuing more secured debt than is necessary to finance the plan, say 1.5 million, shareholders can be paid a dividend of 0.5 million, while the existing creditors get what remains of the value increase after the secured debtholders have been paid.

(e) The CFO's plan is not profitable, it has an NPV of -1, the immediate investment of €1 million in re-tooling without a value increase. But the high value in the up state allows the creditor to be paid in full with some value left for the shareholders. The shareholders value is $\max[0, 74 - 60] = 14$ and $\max[0, 21.1 - 60] = 0$. The risk-neutral probabilities are $(1.07 - 0.54)/(1.85 - 0.54) = 0.40$ for the up state and 0.6 for the down state, so the equity value increases from zero to $(0.4 \times 14)/1.07 = 5.23 - 1 = 4.23$. The shareholders should go ahead with the chief financial officer's plan. Notice that the creditors are worse off with the plan: their value drops from 40 to $((0.4 \times 60) + (0.6 \times 21.6))/1.07 = 34.54$.

(f) The asset substitution or risk incentive problem.

5. (a) Managers whose compensation depends on the yearly realized return would prefer the accounting representation. In this representation year two stands out as an exceptionally good year with a book return far above the opportunity cost of capital. This makes these managers eligible for a bonus in that year, and a rebuke (but probably no fine) in the other two years. In the financial representation all years are equally well and the return is never a reason for a bonus. In more general terms, asymmetric result-dependent compensation structures create option-like payoff structures with the associated preference for volatility.

(b) If depreciation is moved from year three to year one, the return in year three will increase and may reach the 'high water mark' for a bonus. This will, of course, increase the preference for the accounting representation.

Glossary

abnormal return	difference between realized return and the expected return according to the market model
accounts payable	amounts owed by a company to its suppliers and other creditors
accounts receivable	amounts owed to a company by its customers
adjusted present value	valuation method that adjusts a project's present value with the separately calculated values of all side-effects
agency costs	costs associated with an agency relation
agency problems	conflicts of interest arising from agency relations
agency relation	relation between one person, the principal, who hires another person, the agent, to perform certain tasks or services
American option	option that can be exercised at any time before it expires
annuity	series of equal payments
arbitrage	strategy to profit from mispricing in markets
ask price	price at which a dealer is willing to sell a security
assets	possessions
asset substitution	replacement of safe assets by risky ones
at the money option	option's exercise price is equal to price of the underlying
basis risk	risk that the prices of the two sides of a hedge develop differently
bear-, bearish	investor sentiment, fearful of falling prices
beta	measure of systematic risk: the contribution of a stock to the variance of a well diversified portfolio; also: a stock's sensitivity for changes in portfolio returns

bid–ask spread	difference between bid and ask price
bid price	price at which a dealer is willing to buy a security
binomial process	discrete stochastic process in which each step can have only two possible values
book value	value according to accounting system
bull-, bullish	investor sentiment, hopeful of rising prices
business risk	risk of the cash flows generated by the firm's assets
callable bond	bond that the issuing firm has the right to redeem before maturity
call option	option to buy something on a future date at a predetermined price
capital budget	budget for capital expenditures, i.e. a list of investment opportunities that a firm plans to undertake
capital budgeting	process of selecting investment opportunities for the capital budget
capital structure	combination of capital categories used
certainty equivalent	certain alternative with same value or utility as a risky alternative
clearing house	service institute of an exchange providing settlement, payment and insurance services
collateral	asset pledged by a borrower to protect the interests of the lender
commercial banks	banks that offer a wide range of services to the public and business community, including taking deposits
commercial paper	short-term loan issued by a company
compounding	moving money forward in time, adjusting for interest
compound interest	interest on interest
conglomerate merger	merger between two unrelated companies
convertible bond	bond that can be exchanged for a (pre-specified number of) shares
coupon bond	bond periodically paying interest
covered call	option position created by writing a call and buying the stock as cover

credit risk	risk that a financial contract loses value because the counter-party defaults (default risk), or because the risk of future default increases
current assets	assets that are converted into cash within a short period (one year)
current liabilities	obligations to be paid within a short period (one year)
depreciation	periodic book value reduction of long-lived asset
discounting	moving future money backwards in time, adjusting for interest
diversifiable risk	the idiosyncratic (or unique or unsystematic) risk of individual investments that disappears from a portfolio through diversification
diversification	reducing risks by spreading investments
dividend rate	payout ratio
efficient frontier	line connecting all efficient portfolios
efficient market	market that fully reflects available information
efficient portfolio	portfolio with maximal expected return given risk, or minimal risk given expected return
equity	capital supplied by owners
European option	option that can be exercised at maturity only, when it expires
event study	research technique to measure the effect of events on firm value
exchange rate	the price of one currency in terms of another
exercise price	predetermined price in option contract, at which the underlying may be bought or sold
face value	nominal value of a security as stated (printed on it) by the issuer; for bonds, it is generally the amount paid to the holder at maturity, also known as 'par value' or principal amount
financial asset	*see* security
financial engineering	the process of constructing new securities from other, existing securities

financial risk	risk caused by other claims on the cash flow with a higher priority
financial structure	*see* capital structure
fixed assets	assets that are converted into cash over a longer period (>1 year)
forward contract/price	contract to buy or sell something on a future date at a price determined today, the forward price
future contract	standardized forward contract
future price	price determined in a future contract
gearing	*see* leverage
hedge fund	investment fund exempted from most regulations because it is open only to a limited number or qualified investors; it can have more risky investment strategies than mutual funds
hedging	offsetting the price risk of one asset by taking an opposite position in another asset
implied volatility	volatility calculated from an option's market price
index fund	mutual fund that tries to replicate or track an index
initial public offering	first time public stock offering (*see* seasoned offering)
intangible assets	investments in non-physical assets, e.g. patents
in the money option	price of the underlying is such that immediate exercise of an option would be profitable
investment banks	banks that do not take deposits but specialize in aiding companies with large transactions such as issues and mergers
investment frontier	line connecting all investment opportunities
investment grade	ratings of BBB or higher, or Baa or higher, depending on the agency
junior debt	debt with a lower priority
junk bond	bond with a high interest rate and high default risk
leverage	use of debt as a lever to increase expected return on equity
levered firm/project	firm/project partly financed with debt

liquidity	measures how much value is lost if an asset is bought or sold; liquid assets lose very little value in a transaction
long position	positive net ownership position in an asset (more bought than sold), that profits from a price increase
margin	amount of money to be deposited as collateral for a risky position
marketability	measures how easy it is to buy or sell an asset
market capitalization	total value of a fim's outstanding shares (number × price per share)
market model	linear model that relates a stock's return to the return of the market as a whole
market price of risk	risk premium (over the risk-free rate) per unit of standard deviation
marking to market	settlement on a daily basis (not only at maturity) of futures contracts
maturity	period for which a financial contract is valid
mean reversion	process in which observed values have a tendency to return to their long-term mean values
mean variance efficient	*see* efficient portfolio
merchant banks	European banks with roughly the same specialization as US investment banks
moneyness	degree in which an option is in-, at- or out-of-the money
mutual fund	investment fund open to the public and, hence, regulated
Nasdaq	(obsolete) acronym for National Association of Securities Dealers Automated Quotation system; now Nasdaq, electronic US stock exchange
net present value	present value of cash inflows minus present value of cash outflows
net working capital	current assets–current liabilities
option	financial contract giving the holder the right, but not the obligation, to buy or sell something on a future date at a predetermined price

option premium	price of an option
out of the money option	price of the underlying is such that immediate exercise of an option would be unprofitable
payoff diagram	graph of option's payoff at maturity, ignoring the premium, as a function of the value of the underlying
payout ratio	fraction of profits paid out as dividends
perfect competition	competition by many buyers and sellers, all too small to individually influence prices, and all information is simultaneously and costlessly available to all investors
perfect markets	market without taxes, transaction and information costs, and limitations on shortselling and borrowing and lending
perpetuity	infinite series of payments
plain vanilla	simplest variant of a security
position diagram	payoff diagram
profit diagram	graph of option's payoff at maturity, including the premium, as a function of the value of the underlying
proxy variable	variable that is used to approximate another variable, e.g. personal costs to approximate number of employees
pure discount bond	*see* zero-coupon bond
pure play	stand-alone company engaged in a single activity, not a mix of activities
putable bond	bond that the holders have the right to sell back to the issuing firm before maturity
put option	option to sell something on a future date at a predetermined price
real asset	physical asset such as buildings and machinery, as opposed to financial assets
real option	option with real asset as underlying value
rebalanced debt	debt amounts adjusted to a constant proportion of (project) value
retained earnings	profits made in the past and not paid out as dividends but retained within the firm

risk incentive	higher value of risky investment than safe ones for some investors or managers
seasoned offering	public stock offering by an already listed company (*see* initial public offering)
security	financial contract of debt or of ownership
senior debt	debt with a higher priority
short position	negative net ownership position in an asset (more sold than bought), that profits from a price decrease
short selling	selling something that you do not own
single index model	simplified model of asset returns with only one common factor
spin-off	corporate restructuring in which a part of a company's assets is transferred to a new company, whose shares a distributed or sold to the parent company's shareholders, not exchanged for shares in the parent company
split-off	corporate restructuring in which a part of a company's assets is transferred to a new company; the parent company's shareholders obtain shares in the new company in exchange for a portion of their shares in the parent company
spot contract	contract for immediate delivery and payment
spot price	price for immediate delivery and payment
state price	price of a state security
state security	security that pays off 1 in a particular state of the world, 0 in all other states
sticky dividends	dividends that remain stable over time
stock index	price index of a group of stocks, chosen to represent (sections of) a market
strike price	*see* exercise price
swap	financial contracts to exchange one set of obligations against another, e.g. payments in one currency against payments in another currency

synthetic security	combination of securities that exactly replicates another security, e.g. a synthetic option can be created by the option's hedging portfolio and a synthetic forward by a cash-and-carry strategy
tender offer	outside offer to buy a firm's stock in order to take over the firm
time value of money	risk-free interest rate
treasury bill	short-term loan issued by a government
unlever	remove the effect of leverage, calculate as if all equity financed
warrant	call option written by a firm on its own shares
write an option	create and sell an option
zero-coupon bond	bond that pays interest at maturity only

References

Adam, T.R. and C.S. Fernando, 2006, 'Hedging, speculation, and shareholder value', *Journal of Financial Economics*, *81* (2), 283–309.

Aitchison, J. and J.A.C. Brown, 1969, *The Lognormal Distribution*, Cambridge University Press.

Akerlof, G.A., 1970, 'The market for "lemons": quality uncertainty and the market mechanism', *The Quarterly Journal of Economics*, *84* (3), 488–500.

Alderson, M.J. and B.L. Betker, 1995, 'Liquidation costs and capital structure', *Journal of Financial Economics*, *39* (1), 45–69.

Allayannis, G. and J.P. Weston, 2001, 'The use of foreign currency derivatives and firm market value', *The Review of Financial Studies*, *14* (1), 243–276.

Allen, F. and R. Karjalainen, 1999, 'Using genetic algorithms to find technical trading rules', *Journal of Financial Economics*, *51* (2), 245–271.

Altman, E.I., 1984, 'A further empirical investigation of the bankruptcy cost question', *The Journal of Finance*, *39* (4), 1067–1089.

Anderson, R.C. and D.M. Reeb, 2003, 'Founding-family ownership and firm performance: evidence from the SP 500', *The Journal of Finance*, *LVIII* (3), 1301–1328.

Andrade, G. and S.N. Kaplan, 1998, 'How costly is financial (not economic) distress? Evidence from highly leveraged transactions that became distressed', *The Journal of Finance*, *53* (5), 1443–1493.

Aparicio, F.M. and J. Estrada, 2001, 'Empirical distributions of stock returns: European securities markets, 1990–95', *The European Journal of Finance*, *7* (1), 1–21.

Ball, R. and P. Brown, 1968, 'An empirical evaluation of accounting income numbers', *Journal of Accounting Research*, *6* (2), 159–178.

_____ and S.P. Kothari, 1989, 'Nonstationary expected returns: implications for tests of market efficiency and serial correlation in returns', *Journal of Financial Economics*, *25* (1), 51–74.

Barnea, A., R.A. Haugen and L.W. Senbet, 1985, *Agency Problems and Financial Contracting*, Englewood Cliffs, NJ: Prentice Hall, Inc.

Bartholdy, J., D. Olson and P. Peare, 2007, 'Conducting event studies on a small stock exchange', *The European Journal of Finance*, *13* (3), 227–252.

Bates, T.W., K.M. Kahle and R.M. Stulz, 2009, 'Why do U.S. firms hold so much more cash than they used to?' *The Journal of Finance*, *64* (5), 1985–2021.

Battalio, R.H. and R.R. Mendenhall, 2005, 'Earnings expectations, investor trade size, and anomalous returns around earnings announcements', *Journal of Financial Economics*, *77* (2), 289–319.

Baz, J. and G. Chacko, 2004, *Financial Derivatives: Pricing, Applications, and Mathematics*, Cambridge University Press.

Becht, M. and E. Boehmer, 2003, 'Voting control in German corporations', *International Review of Law and Economics*, *23* (1), 1–29.

Benmelech, E. and N.K. Bergman, 2009, 'Collateral pricing', *Journal of Financial Economics*, *91* (3), 339–360.

Berger, P.G., E. Ofek and D.L. Yermack, 1997, 'Managerial entrenchment and capital structure decisions', *The Journal of Finance*, *52* (4), 1411–1438.

Berle, A. and G. Means, 1932, *The Modern Corporation and Private Property*, New York: Macmillan.

Bhootra, A., 2011, 'Are momentum profits driven by the cross-sectional dispersion in expected stock returns?' *Journal of Financial Markets*, *14* (3), 494–513.

Bianco, M. and P. Casavola, 1999, 'Italian corporate governance: effects on financial structure and firm performance', *European Economic Review*, *43* (4–6), 1057–1069.

Björk, T., 2004, *Arbitrage Theory in Continuous Time*, 2nd edn., Oxford University Press.

Black, F., 1972, 'Capital market equilibrium with restricted borrowing', *The Journal of Business*, *45* (3), 444–455.

_____ and M. Scholes, 1973, 'The pricing of options and corporate liabilities', *Journal of Political Economy*, *81* (3), 637–654.

Blume, M.E., 1974, 'Unbiased estimators of long-run expected rates of return', *Journal of the American Statistical Association*, *69* (347), 634–638.

Boehme, R.D. and B.R. Danielsen, 2007, 'Stock-split post-announcement returns: underreaction or market friction?' *The Financial Review*, *42* (4), 485–506.

Bollen, N.P.B. and J.A. Busse, 2005, 'Short-term persistence in mutual fund performance', *The Review of Financial Studies*, *18* (2), 569–597.

Bolton, P. and M. Dewatripont, 2005, *Contract Theory*, Cambridge, MA: MIT Press.

Bradley, M., G.A. Jarrell and E. Han Kim, 1984, 'On the existence of an optimal capital structure: theory and evidence', *The Journal of Finance*, *39* (3), 857–878.

Brav, A., C. Geczy and P.A. Gompers, 2000, 'Is the abnormal return following equity issuances anomalous?' *Journal of Financial Economics*, *56* (2), 209–249.

Brennan, M.J. and E.S. Schwartz, 2001, 'A new approach to evaluating natural resource investments', in E.S. Schwartz and L. Trigeorgis, eds., *Real Options and Investment under Uncertainty*, Cambridge, MA: The MIT Press, pp. 135–151.

Bris, A., I. Welch and N. Zhu, 2006, 'The costs of bankruptcy: Chapter 7 liquidation versus Chapter 11 reorganization', *The Journal of Finance*, *61* (3), 1253–1303.

Brock, W., J. Lakonishok and B. LeBaron, 1992, 'Simple technical trading rules and the stochastic properties of stock returns', *The Journal of Finance*, *47* (5), 1731–1764.

Brockman, P. and E. Unlu, 2009, 'Dividend policy, creditor rights, and the agency costs of debt', *Journal of Financial Economics*, *92* (2), 276–299.

_____ and H.J. Turtle, 2003, 'A barrier option framework for corporate security valuation', *Journal of Financial Economics*, *67* (3), 511–529.

Brounen, D., A. de Jong and K. Koedijk, 2004, 'Corporate finance in Europe: confronting theory with practice', *Financial Management*, *33* (4), 71–101.

Brown, S.J. and W.N. Goetzmann, 1995, 'Performance persistence', *The Journal of Finance*, *50* (2), 679–698.

Bulkley, G. and V. Nawosah, 2009, 'Can the cross-sectional variation in expected stock returns explain momentum?' *Journal of Financial and Quantitative Analysis*, *44* (4), 777–794.

Byun, J. and M.S. Rozeff, 2003, 'Long-run performance after stock splits: 1927 to 1996', *The Journal of Finance*, *58* (3), 1063–1085.

Campbell, J.Y., M. Lettau, B.G. Malkiel and Y. Xu, 2001, 'Have individual stocks become more volatile? An empirical exploration of idiosyncratic risk', *The Journal of Finance*, *56* (1), 1–43.

_____, S.J. Grossman and J. Wang, 1993, 'Trading volume and serial correlation in stock returns', *The Quarterly Journal of Economics*, *108* (4), 905–939.

_____, A.W. Lo and A.C. MacKinley, 1997, *The Econometrics of Financial Markets*, Princeton University Press.

Cantor, R., 2004, 'An introduction to recent research on credit ratings', *Journal of Banking & Finance*, *28* (11), 2565–2573.

Carhart, M.M., 1997, 'On persistence in mutual fund performance', *The Journal of Finance*, *52* (1), 57–82.

Carter, D.A., D.A. Rogers and B.J. Simkins, 2006, 'Does hedging affect firm value? Evidence from the US airline industry', *Financial Management*, *35* (1), 53–86.

Cerný, A., 2004, *Mathematical Techniques in Finance*, Princeton, NJ: Princeton University Press.

Chan, K., A. Hameed and W. Tong, 2000, 'Profitability of momentum strategies in the international equity markets', *The Journal of Financial and Quantitative Analysis*, *35* (2), 153–172.

Chen, N.-F., R. Roll and S.A. Ross, 1986, 'Economic Forces and the Stock Market', *The Journal of Business*, *59* (3), 383–403.

Chirinko, R.S. and A.R. Singha, 2000, 'Testing static tradeoff against pecking order models of capital structure: a critical comment', *Journal of Financial Economics*, *58* (3), 417–425.

Chopra, N., J. Lakonishok and J.R. Ritter, 1992, 'Measuring abnormal performance: do stocks overreact?' *Journal of Financial Economics*, *31* (2), 235–268.

Chordia, T. and L. Shivakumar, 2005, 'Inflation illusion and post-earnings-announcement drift', *Journal of Accounting Research*, *43* (4), 521–556.

_____, 2002, 'Momentum, business cycle, and time-varying expected returns', *The Journal of Finance*, *57* (2), 985–1019.

Connolly, R. and C. Stivers, 2003, 'Momentum and reversals in equity-index returns during periods of abnormal turnover and return dispersion', *The Journal of Finance*, *58* (4), 1521–1555.

Conrad, J. and M.N. Gultekin, 1997, 'Profitability of short-term contrarian strategies: implications for market efficiency', *Journal of Business and Economic Statistics*, *15* (3), 379–386.

Cooper, I., 1996, 'Arithmetic versus geometric mean estimators: setting discount rates for capital budgetting', *European Financial Management*, *2* (2), 157–167.

Cooper, M., 1999, 'Filter rules based on price and volume in individual security overreaction', *The Review of Financial Studies*, *12* (4), 901–935.

Copeland, T.E. and V. Antikarov, 2001, *Real Options: A Practitioner's Guide*, New York: TEXERE.

Corrado, C.J. and S.-H. Lee, 1992, 'Filter rule tests of the economic significance of serial dependencies in daily stock returns', *Journal of Financial Research*, *15* (4), 369–387.

Cossin, D. and H. Pirotte, 2001, *Advanced Credit Risk Analysis*, Chichester: John Wiley and Sons, Ltd.

Cox, J.C. and S.A. Ross, 1976, 'The valuation of options for alternative stochastic processes', *Journal of Financial Economics*, *3* (1/2), 145–166.

_____, _____, and M. Rubinstein, 1979, 'Option pricing: a simplified approach', *Journal of Financial Economics*, *7* (3), 229–263.

Craswell, A.T., S.L. Taylor and R.A. Saywell, 1997, 'Ownership structure and corporate performance: Australian evidence', *Pacific-Basin Finance Journal*, *5* (3), 301–323.

Cuthbertson, K., D. Nitzsche and N. O'Sullivan, 2008, 'UK mutual fund performance: Skill or luck?' *Journal of Empirical Finance*, *15* (4), 613–634.

Cutler, D.M. and L.H. Summers, 1988, 'The costs of conflict resolution and financial distress: evidence from the Texaco–Pennzoil litigation', *The RAND Journal of Economics*, *19* (2), 157–172.

de Bondt, W.F.M. and R.H. Thaler, 1987, 'Further evidence on investor overreaction and stock market seasonality', *The Journal of Finance*, *42* (3), 557–581.

_____ and R. Thaler, 1985, 'Does the stock market overreact?' *The Journal of Finance*, *40* (3), 793–805.

Demsetz, H. and B. Villalonga, 2001, 'Ownership structure and corporate performance', *Journal of Corporate Finance*, *7* (3), 209–233.

_____ and K. Lehn, 1985, 'The structure of corporate ownership: causes and consequences', *The Journal of Political Economy*, *93* (6), 1155–1177.

Dittmar, A. and J. Mahrt-Smith, 2007, 'Corporate governance and the value of cash holdings', *Journal of Financial Economics*, *83* (3), 599–634.

Dixit, A.K. and R.S. Pindyck, 1994, *Investment under Uncertainty*, Princeton University Press.

Droms, W.G. and D.A. Walker, 2001, 'Persistence of mutual fund operating characteristics: returns, turnover rates, and expense ratios', *Applied Financial Economics*, *11* (4), 457–466.

Durnev, A., R. Morck, B. Yeung and P. Zarowin, 2003, 'Does greater firm-specific return variation mean more or less informed stock pricing?' *Journal of Accounting Research*, *41* (5), 797–836.

Eckbo, B.E. and D.C. Smith, 1998, 'The conditional performance of insider trades', *The Journal of Finance*, *53* (2), 467–498.

_____, R.W. Masulis and Ø. Norli, 2000, 'Seasoned public offerings: resolution of the "new issues puzzle"', *Journal of Financial Economics*, *56* (2), 251–291.

Ederington, L. and W. Guan, 2002, 'Why are those options smiling?' *Journal of Derivatives*, *10* (2), 9–34.

Eisdorfer, A., 2008, 'Empirical evidence of risk shifting in financially distressed firms', *The Journal of Finance*, *63* (2), 609–637.

Elton, E.J., M.J. Gruber and C.R. Blake, 1996, 'The persistence of risk-adjusted mutual fund performance', *The Journal of Business*, *69* (2), 133–157.

_____, M.J. Gruber, S.J. Brown and W.N. Goetzmann, 2007, *Modern Portfolio Theory and Investment Analysis*, 7th edn., New York: J. Wiley and Sons.

Fama, E.F., 1970, 'Efficient capital markets: a review of theory and empirical work', *The Journal of Finance*, *25* (2), 383–417.

_____, 1980, 'Agency problems and the theory of the firm', *The Journal of Political Economy*, *88* (2), 288–307.

_____, 1991, 'Efficient capital markets: II', *The Journal of Finance*, *46* (5), 1575–1617.

_____, 1998, 'Market efficiency, long-term returns, and behavioral finance', *Journal of Financial Economics*, *49* (3), 283–306.

_____ and M.E. Blume, 1966, 'Filter rules and stock-market trading', *The Journal of Business*, *39* (1), 226–241.

_____, L. Fisher, M.C. Jensen and R. Roll, 1969, 'The adjustment of stock prices to new information', *International Economic Review*, *10* (1), 1–21.

_____ and K.R. French, 1992, 'The cross-section of expected stock returns', *The Journal of Finance*, *47* (2), 427–465.

_____ and _____, 1993, 'Common risk factors in the returns on stocks and bonds', *Journal of Financial Economics*, *33* (1), 3–56.

_____ and _____, 1996, 'Multifactor explanations of asset pricing anomalies', *The Journal of Finance*, *51* (1), 55–84.

_____ and _____, 2001, 'Disappearing dividends: changing firm characteristics or lower propensity to pay?' *Journal of Financial Economics*, *60* (1), 3–43.

_____ and _____, 2002, 'Testing trade-off and pecking order predictions about dividends and debt', *The Review of Financial Studies*, *15* (1), 1–33.

_____ and _____, 2008, 'Dissecting anomalies', *The Journal of Finance*, *63* (4), 1653–1678.

_____ and J.D. MacBeth, 1973, 'Risk, return, and equilibrium: empirical tests', *The Journal of Political Economy*, *81* (3), 607–636.

Farmen, T.E.S. and N. Van der Wijst, 2005, 'A cautionary note on the pricing of ethics', *The Journal of Investing*, *14* (3), 53–56.

Fatemi, A. and R. Bildik, 2012, 'Yes, dividends are disappearing: worldwide evidence', *Journal of Banking and Finance*, *36* (3).

Fischer, E.O., R. Heinkel and J. Zechner, 1989, 'Dynamic capital structure choice: theory and tests', *The Journal of Finance*, *44* (1), 19–40.

Fisher, I., 1974, *The Theory of Interest*, reprint edn., Clifton, NJ: A.M. Kelley, 1930.

Flannery, M.J. and K.P. Rangan, 2006, 'Partial adjustment toward target capital structures', *Journal of Financial Economics*, *79* (3), 469–506.

Frank, M.Z. and V.K. Goyal, 2003, 'Testing the pecking order theory of capital structure', *Journal of Financial Economics*, *67* (2), 217–248.

Franks, J. and C. Mayer, 2001, 'Ownership and control of German corporations', *The Review of Financial Studies*, *14* (4), 943–977.

Galai, D. and R.W. Masulis, 1976, 'The option pricing model and the risk factor of stock', *Journal of Financial Economics*, *3* (1–2), 53–81.

Gatev, E., W.N. Goetzman and K.G. Rouwenhorst, 2006, 'Pairs trading: performance of a relative-value arbitrage rule', *The Review of Financial Studies*, *19* (3), 797–827.

Givoly, D. and D. Palmon, 1985, 'Insider trading and the exploitation of inside information: some empirical evidence', *The Journal of Business*, *58* (1), 69–87.

Graham, J.R., 2000, 'How big are the tax benefits of debt?' *The Journal of Finance*, *55* (5), 1901–1941.

_____ and C.R. Harvey, 2001, 'The theory and practice of corporate finance: evidence from the field', *Journal of Financial Economics*, *60* (2–3), 187–243.

_____ and A. Kumar, 2006, 'Do dividend clienteles exist? Evidence on dividend preferences of retail investors', *The Journal of Finance*, *61* (3), 1305–1336.

_____ and D.A. Rogers, 2002, 'Do firms hedge in response to tax incentives?' *The Journal of Finance*, *57* (2), 815–839.

Granger, C.W.J., 1972, 'Empirical studies of capital markets: a survey', in G.P. Szegö and K. Shell, eds., *Mathematical Methods in Investment and Finance*, Amsterdam: North-Holland Publishing Co., pp. 469–519.

Grimmeth, G.R. and D.R. Stirzaker, 2001, *Probability and Random Processes*, 3rd edn., New York: Oxford University Press.

Grinblatt, M. and S. Titman, 1992, 'The persistence of mutual fund performance', *The Journal of Finance*, *47* (5), 1977–1984.

Groenendijk, A. and J. Spronk, 2000, 'Portfolio performance through the eyes of monkeys', in M.C. Bonilla and S.R. Trinidad, eds., *Financial Modelling*, Heidelberg: Physica Verlag, pp. 203–213.

Grossman, S.J. and J.E. Stiglitz, 1980, 'On the impossibility of informationally efficient markets', *The American Economic Review*, *70* (3), 393–408.

Guay, W. and S.P. Kothari, 2003, 'How much do firms hedge with derivatives?' *Journal of Financial Economics*, *70* (3), 423–461.

Gugler, K., D.C. Mueller and B. Burcin Yurtoglu, 2008, 'Insider ownership, ownership concentration and investment performance: an international comparison', *Journal of Corporate Finance*, *14* (5), 688–705.

Harford, J., S. Klasa and N. Walcott, 2009, 'Do firms have leverage targets? Evidence from acquisitions', *Journal of Financial Economics*, *93* (1), 1–14.

Harman, H.H., *Modern Factor Analysis*, 2nd edn., The University of Chicago Press, 1967.

Harris, M. and A. Raviv, 1991, 'The theory of capital structure', *The Journal of Finance*, *46* (1), 297–355.

Harrison, J.M. and D.M. Kreps, 1979, 'Martingales and Multiperiod Securities Markets', *Journal of Economic Theory*, *20* (3), 381–408.

Haug, E.G., 2007, *The Complete Guide to Option Pricing Formulas*, New York: McGraw-Hill.

Haugen, R.A., 1990, *Modern Investment Theory*, 2nd edn., Englewood Cliffs, NJ: Prentice Hall.

Helwege, J. and N. Liang, 1996, 'Is there a pecking order? Evidence from a panel of IPO firms', *Journal of Financial Economics*, *40* (3), 429–458.

Hendricks, D., J. Patel and R. Zeckhauser, 1993, 'Hot hands in mutual funds: short-run persistence of relative performance, 1974–1988', *The Journal of Finance*, *48* (1), 93–130.

Higgins, R.C. and L.D. Schall, 1975, 'Corporate bankruptcy and conglomerate merger', *The Journal of Finance*, *30* (1), 93–113.

Hillegeist, S.A., E.K. Keating, D.P. Cram and K.G. Lundstedt, 2004, 'Assessing the probability of bankruptcy', *Review of Accounting Studies*, *9* (1), 5–34.

Himmelberg, C.P., R.G. Hubbard and D. Palia, 1999, 'Understanding the determinants of managerial ownership and the link between ownership and performance', *Journal of Financial Economics*, *53* (3), 353–384.

Hol, S. and N. Van der Wijst, 2008, 'The financial structure of nonlisted firms', *Applied Financial Economics*, *18* (7), 559–568.

Holmstrom, B., 1979, 'Moral hazard and observability', *The Bell Journal of Economics*, *10* (1), 74–91.

Hovakimian, A., T. Opler and S. Titman, 2001, 'The debt–equity choice', *The Journal of Financial and Quantitative Analysis*, *36* (1), 1–24.

Ikenberry, D.L. and S. Ramnath, 2002, 'Underreaction to self-selected news events: the case of stock splits', *The Review of Financial Studies*, *15* (2), 489–526.

Inselbag, I. and H. Kaufold, 1997, 'Two DCF approaches for valuing companies under alternative financing strategies (and how to choose between them)', *Journal of Applied Corporate Finance*, *10* (1), 114–122.

Jacquier, E., A. Kane and A.J. Marcus, 2003, 'Geometric or arithmetic mean: a reconsideration', *Financial Analysts Journal*, *59* (6), 46–53.

Jegadeesh, N., 1990, 'Evidence of predictable behavior of security returns', *The Journal of Finance*, *45* (3), 881–898.

_____ and S. Titman, 1993, 'Returns to buying winners and selling losers: implications for stock market efficiency', *The Journal of Finance*, *48* (1), 65–91.

_____ and _____, 1995, 'Overreaction, delayed reaction, and contrarian profits', *The Review of Financial Studies*, *8* (4), 973–993.

Jeng, L.A., A. Metrick and R. Zeckhauser, 2003, 'Estimating the returns to insider trading: a performance-evaluation perspective', *The Review of Economics and Statistics*, *85* (2), 453–471.

Jensen, M.C., 1968, 'The performance of mutual funds in the period 1945–1964', *The Journal of Finance*, *23* (2), 389–416.

_____ and W.H. Meckling, 1976, 'Theory of the firm: managerial behavior, agency costs and ownership structure', *Journal of Financial Economics*, *3* (4), 305–360.

Jong, A. De, L. Rosenthal and M.A. Van Dijk, 2009, 'The risk and return of arbitrage in dual-listed companies', *Review of Finance*, *13* (3), 495–520.

Kahle, K.M., 2002, 'When a buyback isn't a buyback: open market repurchases and employee options', *Journal of Financial Economics*, *63* (2), 235–261.

Kalcheva, I. and K.V. Lins, 2007, 'International evidence on cash holdings and expected managerial agency problems', *The Review of Financial Studies*, *20* (4), 1087–1112.

Kallianpur, G. and R.L. Karandikar, 2000, *Introduction to Option Pricing Theory*, Boston, MA: Birkhäuser.

Ke, B., S. Huddart and K. Petroni, 2003, 'What insiders know about future earnings and how they use it: evidence from insider trades', *Journal of Accounting and Economics*, *35* (3), 315–346.

Kemsley, D. and D. Nissim, 2002, 'Valuation of the debt tax shield', *The Journal of Finance*, *57* (5), 2045–2073.

Keown, A.J. and J.M. Pinkerton, 1981, 'Merger announcements and insider trading activity: an empirical investigation', *The Journal of Finance*, *36* (4), 855–869.

Kidwell, D.S., D.W. Blackwell, D.A. Whidbee and R.L. Peterson, 2008, *Financial Institutions, Markets, and Money*, 10th edn., Hoboken, NJ: J. Wiley.

Kim, E. Han, 1978, 'A mean-variance theory of optimal capital structure and corporate debt capacity', *The Journal of Finance*, *33* (1), 45–63.

_____ and J.J. McConnell, 1977, 'Corporate mergers and the co-insurance of corporate debt', *The Journal of Finance*, *32* (2), 349–365.

Kohn, M.G., 2004, *Financial Institutions and Markets*, 2nd edn., Oxford University Press.

Kosowski, R., A. Timmermann, R. Wermers and H. White, 2006, 'Can mutual fund "stars" really pick stocks? New evidence from a bootstrap analysis', *The Journal of Finance*, *61* (6), 2551–2595.

Kothari, S.P. and J.B. Warner, 2007, 'Econometrics of event studies', in B.E. Eckbo, ed., *Handbook of Corporate Finance: Empirical Corporate Finance*, Vol. 1, Amsterdam: Elsevier, Chapter 1, pp. 3–36.

La Porta, R., F. Lopez de Silanes and A. Shleifer, 1999, 'Corporate ownership around the world', *The Journal of Finance*, *54* (2), 471–517.

_____, F. Lopez de Silanes, A. Shleifer and R.W. Vishny, 2000, 'Agency problems and dividend policies around the world', *The Journal of Finance*, *55* (1), 1–33.

Leary, M.T. and M.R. Roberts, 2005, 'Do firms rebalance their capital structures?' *The Journal of Finance*, *60* (6), 2575–2619.

Lee, C.M.C. and B. Swaminathan, 2000, 'Price momentum and trading volume', *The Journal of Finance*, *55* (5), 2017–2069.

Lee, U., 1992, 'Do stock prices follow random walk? Some international evidence', *International Review of Economics and Finance*, *1* (4), 315–327.

Lehmann, B.N., 1990, 'Fads, martingales and market efficiency', *The Quarterly Journal of Economics*, *105* (1), 1–28.

Lehmann, E. and J. Weigand, 2000, 'Does the governed corporation perform better? Governance structures and corporate performance in Germany', *European Finance Review*, *4* (2), 157–195.

Leland, H.E., 1998, 'Agency costs, risk management and capital structure', *The Journal of Finance*, *53* (4), 1213–1243.

Lesmond, D.A., M.J. Schill and C. Zhou, 2004, 'The illusory nature of momentum profits', *Journal of Financial Economics*, *71* (2), 349–380.

Levy, H., *The Capital Asset Pricing Model in the 21st Century*, Cambridge University Press, 2012.

_____ and M. Sarnat, 1970, 'Diversification, portfolio analysis and the uneasy case for conglomerate mergers', *The Journal of Finance*, *25* (4), 795–802.

Lewellen, W.G., 1971, 'A pure financial rationale for the conglomerate merger', *The Journal of Finance*, *26* (2), 521–537.

Liu, P., S.D. Smith and A.A. Syed, 1990, 'Stock price reactions to The Wall Street Journal's securities recommendations', *The Journal of Financial and Quantitative Analysis*, *25* (3), 399–410.

Liu, Y., S.H. Szewczyk and Z. Zantout, 2008, 'Underreaction to dividend reductions and omissions?' *The Journal of Finance*, *63* (2), 987–1020.

Lo, A.W. and A. Craig MacKinlay, 1988, 'Stock market prices do not follow random walks: evidence from a simple specification test', *The Review of Financial Studies*, *1* (1), 41–66.

_____, H. Mamaysky and J. Wang, 2000, 'Foundations of technical analysis: computational algorithms, statistical inference, and empirical implementation', *The Journal of Finance*, *55* (4), 1705–1765.

Loughran, T. and A.M. Vijh, 1997, 'Do long-term shareholders benefit from corporate acquisitions?' *The Journal of Finance*, *52* (5), 1765–1790.

MacKie-Mason, J.K., 1990, 'Do taxes affect corporate financing decisions?' *The Journal of Finance*, *45* (5), 1471–1493.

MacKinlay, A.C., 1997, 'Event studies in economics and finance', *Journal of Economic Literature*, *35* (1), 13–39.

MacMinn, R.D., 2005, *The Fisher Model and Financial Markets*, Singapore: World Scientific Publishing Co.

Malkiel, B.G., 1995, 'Returns from investing in equity mutual funds 1971 to 1991', *The Journal of Finance*, *50* (2), 549–572.

_____, 2003, 'The Efficient Market Hypothesis and its critics', *The Journal of Economic Perspectives*, *17* (1), 59–82.

Mao, C.X., 2003, 'Interaction of debt agency problems and optimal capital structure: theory and evidence', *The Journal of Financial and Quantitative Analysis*, *38* (2), 399–423.

Marin, J.M. and J.P. Olivier, 2008, 'The dog that did not bark: insider trading and crashes', *The Journal of Finance*, *63* (5), 2429–2476.

Markowitz, H., 1952, 'Portfolio selection', *The Journal of Finance*, *7* (1), 77–91.

Masulis, R.W., 1980, 'The effects of capital structure change on security prices: a study of exchange offers', *Journal of Financial Economics*, *8* (2), 139–178.

_____, C. Wang and F. Xie, 2009, 'Agency problems at dual-class companies', *The Journal of Finance*, *64* (4), 1697–1727.

Maury, B., 2006, 'Family ownership and firm performance: empirical evidence from western European corporations', *Journal of Corporate Finance*, *12* (2), 321–341.

McCraw, T.K., 1990, 'Review: Berle and Means', *Reviews in American History*, *18* (4), 578–596.

Mendenhall, R.R., 2004, 'Arbitrage risk and post-earnings-announcement drift', *The Journal of Business*, *77* (4), 875–894.

Merton, R., 1974, 'On the pricing of corporate debt: the risk structure of interest rates', *Journal of Finance*, *29* (2), 449–470.

_____, 'Theory of rational option pricing', *The Bell Journal of Economics and Management Science*, Spring 1973, *4* (1), 141–183.

Meulbroek, L.K., 1992, 'An empirical analysis of illegal insider trading', *The Journal of Finance*, *47* (5), 1661–1699.

Miles, J.A. and J.R. Ezzell, 1980, 'The weighted average cost of capital, perfect capital markets, and project life: a clarification', *The Journal of Financial and Quantitative Analysis*, *15* (3), 719–730.

Miller, M.H., 1977, 'Debt and Taxes', *The Journal of Finance*, *32* (2), 261–275.

_____ and F. Modigliani, 1961, 'Dividend policy, growth, and the valuation of shares', *The Journal of Business*, *34* (4), 411–433.

_____ and C.W. Upton, 2002, 'Strategies for capital market structure and regulation', in M.H. Miller and B.D. Grundy, eds., *Selected Works of Merton H. Miller: A Celebration of Markets*, University of Chicago Press, Chapter 23, pp. 575–609.

Mishkin, F.S. and S.G. Eakins, 2009, *Financial Markets and Institutions*, 6th edn., Boston, MA: Pearson Prentice Hall.

Mitchell, M.L. and E. Stafford, 2000, 'Managerial decisions and long-term stock price performance', *The Journal of Business*, *73* (3), 287–329.

Modigliani, F. and M.H. Miller, 1958, 'The cost of capital, corporation finance and the theory of investment', *The American Economic Review*, *48* (3), 261–297.

_____ and _____, 1963, 'Corporate income taxes and the cost of capital: a correction', *The American Economic Review*, *53* (3), 433–443.

Morck, R., B. Yeung and W. Yu, 2000, 'The information content of stock markets: why do emerging markets have synchronous stock price movements?' *Journal of Financial Economics*, *58* (1–2), 215–260.

Myers, S.C., 1974, 'Interactions of corporate financing and investment decisions – implications for capital budgeting', *The Journal of Finance*, *29* (1), 1–25.

_____ and N.S. Majluf, 1984, 'Corporate financing and investment decisions when firms have information that investors do not have', *Journal of Financial Economics*, *13* (2), 187–221.

Narayan, P.K. and R. Smyth, 2005, 'Are OECD stock prices characterized by a random walk? Evidence from sequential trend break and panel data models', *Applied Financial Economics*, *15* (8), 547–556.

Nielsen, L.T., 1999, *Pricing and Hedging of Derivative Securities*, New York: Oxford University Press.

Pedersen, T. and S. Thomsen, 2003, 'Ownership structure and value of the largest European firms: the importance of owner identity', *Journal of Management and Governance*, *7* (1), 27–55.

Peterson, P.P., 1989, 'Event studies: a review of issues and methodology', *Quarterly Journal of Business and Economics*, *28* (3), 36–66.

Pontiff, J. and A. Woodgate, 2008, 'Share issuance and cross-sectional returns', *The Journal of Finance*, *63* (2), 921–945.

Poterba, J.M. and L.H. Summers, 1988, 'Mean reversion in stock prices: evidence and implications', *Journal of Financial Economics*, *22* (1), 27–59.

Pring, M.J., 2002, *Technical Analysis Explained: The Successful Investor's Guide to Spotting Investment Trends and Turning Points*, 4th edn., New York: McGraw-Hill.

Rahman, S. Mahfuzur, S.C. Turner and E.F. Costa, 2001, 'Cross-hedging cottonseed meal', *Journal of Agribusiness*, *19* (2), 163–171.

Rajan, R.G. and L. Zingales, 1995, 'What do we know about capital structure? Some evidence from international data', *The Journal of Finance*, *50* (5), 1421–1460.

Randøy, T. and S. Goel, 2003, 'Ownership structure, founder leadership, and performance in Norwegian SMEs: implications for financing entrepreneurial opportunities', *Journal of Business Venturing*, *18* (5), 619–637.

Ready, M.J., 2002, 'Profits from technical trading rules', *Financial Management*, *31* (3), 43–61.

Reinganum, M.R., 1981, 'Misspecification of capital asset pricing: empirical anomalies based on earnings' yields and market values', *Journal of Financial Economics*, *9* (1), 19–46.

Reinhardt, U.E., 1973, 'Break-even analysis for Lockheed's Tri Star: an application of financial theory', *The Journal of Finance*, *28* (4), 821–838.

Rendleman, R.J., C.P. Jones and H.A. Latané, 1982, 'Empirical anomalies based on unexpected earnings and the importance of risk adjustments', *Journal of Financial Economics*, *10* (3), 269–287.

Roll, R., 1977, 'A critique of the Asset Pricing Theory's tests: Part 1: on past and potential testability of the theory', *Journal of Financial Economics*, *4* (2), 129–176.

_____, 1986, 'The hubris hypothesis of corporate takeovers', *The Journal of Business*, *59* (2), 197–216.

_____ and S.A. Ross, 1980, 'An empirical investigation of the Arbitrage Pricing Theory', *The Journal of Finance*, *35* (5), 1073–1103.

Ross, S.A., 1976, 'The arbitrage theory of capital asset pricing', *Journal of Economic Theory*, *13* (3), 341–360.

Rouwenhorst, K.G., 1998, 'International momentum strategies', *The Journal of Finance*, *53* (1), 267–284.

Rubinstein, M.E., 1973, 'A mean-variance synthesis of corporate financial theory', *The Journal of Finance*, *28* (1), 167–181.

Samuelson, P.A., 1965, 'Proof that properly anticipated prices fluctuate randomly', *Industrial Management Review*, *6* (2), 41–49.

Saunders, A. and M. Millon Cornett, 2011, *Financial Markets and Institutions: An Introduction to the Risk Management Approach*, 5th edn., Boston, MA: McGraw-Hill/Irwin, 2011.

Schwert, G.W., 2003, 'Anomalies and market efficiency', in G.M. Constantinides, M. Harris and R.M. Stulz, eds., *Handbook of the Economics of Finance*, Amsterdam: Elsevier, Chapter 15, pp. 939–974.

Scott, J.H. Jr., 1976, 'A theory of optimal capital structure', *The Bell Journal of Economics*, *7* (1), 33–54.

Seyhun, H.N., 1986, 'Insiders' profits, costs of trading, and market efficiency', *Journal of Financial Economics*, *16* (2), 189–212.

Sharpe, W.F., 1964, 'Capital asset prices: a theory of market equilibrium under conditions of risk', *The Journal of Finance*, *19* (3), 425–442.

_____, 1966, 'Mutual fund performance', *The Journal of Business*, *39* (1), 119–138.

Shavell, S., 1979, 'Risk sharing and incentives in the principal and agent relationship', *The Bell Journal of Economics*, *10* (1), 55–73.

Shleifer, A. and R.W. Vishny, 1989, 'Management entrenchment: the case of manager-specific investments', *Journal of Financial Economics*, *25* (1), 123–139.

_____ and _____, 1997, 'A survey of corporate governance', *The Journal of Finance*, *52* (2), 737–783.

Shyam-Sunder, L. and S.C. Myers, 1999, 'Testing static tradeoff against pecking order models of capital structure', *Journal of Financial Economics*, *51* (2), 219–244.

Siegel, S., 1956, *Nonparametric statistics for the behavioral sciences*, Tokyo: McGraw-Hill Kogakusha.

Singh, M. and W.N. Davidson, 2003, 'Agency costs, ownership structure and corporate governance mechanisms', *Journal of Banking and Finance*, *27* (5), 793–816.

Smit, H.T.J. and L. Trigeorgis, 2004, *Strategic Investment: Real Options and Games*, Princeton University Press.

Smith, C.W., 1976, 'Option pricing: a review', *Journal of Financial Economics*, Jan–March *3* (1–2), 3–51.

Stulz, R.M. and H. Johnson, 1985, 'An analysis of secured debt', *Journal of Financial Economics*, *14* (4), 501–521.

Sundaresan, S.M., 2000, 'Continuous-time methods in finance: a review and an assessment', *The Journal of Finance*, *55* (4), 1569–1622.

Supanvanij, J. and J. Strauss, 2006, 'The effects of management compensation on firm hedging: does SFAS 133 matter?' *Journal of Multinational Financial Management*, *16* (5), 475–493.

Sweeney, R.J., 1988, 'Some new filter rule tests: methods and results', *The Journal of Financial and Quantitative Analysis*, *23* (3), 285–300.

Syed, A.A., P. Liu and S.D. Smith, 1989, 'The exploitation of inside information at The Wall Street Journal: a test of strong form efficiency', *The Financial Review*, *24* (4), 567–579.

Szakmary, A., W.N. Davidson and T.V. Schwarz, 1999, 'Filter tests in Nasdaq stocks', *The Financial Review*, *34* (1), 45–70.

Thomsen, S. and T. Pedersen, 2000, 'Ownership structure and economic performance in the largest European companies', *Strategic Management Journal*, *21* (6), 689–705.

Titman, S., 1984, 'The effect of capital structure on a firm's liquidation decision', *Journal of Financial Economics*, *13* (1), 137–151.

Travlos, N.G., 1987, 'Corporate takeover bids, methods of payment, and bidding firms' stock returns', *The Journal of Finance*, *42* (4), 943–963.

Treynor, J.L. and R. Ferguson, 1985, 'In defense of technical analysis', *The Journal of Finance*, *40* (3), 757–773.

Trigeorgis, L. and S.P. Mason, 2001, 'Valuing managerial flexibility', in E.S. Schwartz and L. Trigeorgis, eds., *Real Options and Investment under Uncertainty*, Cambridge, MA: The MIT Press, pp. 47–60.

Tsay, R.S., *Analysis of Financial Time Series*, 2nd edn., Hoboken, NJ: John Wiley and Sons, 2005.

Van der Wijst, D., 1989, *Financial Structure in Small Business: Theory, Tests and Applications*, Berlin: Springer-Verlag, 1989.

Villalonga, B. and R. Amit, 2006, 'How do family ownership, control and management affect firm value?' *Journal of Financial Economics*, *80* (2), 385–417.

Von Eije, H. and W.L. Megginson, 2008, 'Dividends and share repurchases in the European Union', *Journal of Financial Economics*, *89* (2), 347–374.

von Neumann, J. and O. Morgenstern, 1944, *Theory of Games and Economic Behavior*, 60th-anniversary edn., Princeton University Press.

Wang, J., 1994, 'A model of competitive stock trading volume', *The Journal of Political Economy*, *102* (1), 127–168.

Warner, J.B., 1977, 'Bankruptcy costs: some evidence', *The Journal of Finance*, *32* (2), 337–347.

Welch, I., 2004, 'Capital structure and stock returns', *The Journal of Political Economy*, *112* (1), 106–131.

Wermers, R., 2000, 'Mutual fund performance: an empirical decomposition into stock-picking talent, style, transactions costs, and expenses', *The Journal of Finance*, *55* (4), 1655–1695.

Westgaard, S. and N. Van der Wijst, 2001, 'Default probabilities in a corporate bank portfolio: a logistic model approach', *European Journal of Operational Research*, December *135* (2), 338–349.

White, H., 2000, 'A reality check for data snooping', *Econometrica*, *68* (5), 1097–1126.

Wilmott, P., S. Howison and J. Dewynne, 1995, *The Mathematics of Financial Derivatives*, Cambridge University Press.

Winkler, R.L., G.M. Roodman and R.R. Britney, 1972, 'The determination of partial moments', *Management Science*, *19* (3), 290–296.

Xu, X. and Y. Wang, 1999, 'Ownership structure and corporate governance in Chinese stock companies', *China Economic Review*, *10* (1), 75–98.

Zarowin, P., 1990, 'Size, seasonality and stock market overreaction', *The Journal of Financial and Quantitative Analysis*, *25* (1), 113–125.

Index

Printed in the United States
By Bookmasters